North American X-15

North American X-15

Including the X-1, X-2 and Skyrocket

David Baker

Crécy
www.crecy.co.uk

Crécy Publishing Ltd

Crécy
www.crecy.co.uk

First published 2022 by Crécy Publishing Ltd.

Layout: Martin Preston

A CIP record of this book is available from the British Library.

ISBN 9781910809969

Printed in Bulgaria by Multiprint

Crécy Publishing Limited
1a Ringway Trading Estate, Shadowmoss Road, Manchester
M22 5LH

www.crecy.co.uk

Front cover: X-15A-2 pictured in August 1967 outside the hangar at Edwards AFB in the distinctive white finish that followed the application of an ablative coating to the airframe to increase its thermal resistance. *NASA*

Half title page: NASA research pilot William H. Dana poses in front of the X-15, in which he made 16 flights, reaching a personal peak altitude of 93,543m (306,900ft) and a top speed of Mach 5.53 (6,270kph/3,897mph). *NASA*

Title page: An X-15 pictured in flight as it skirts the very fringes of outer space. *USAF*

Back cover main picture: The first X-15 shortly after roll-out and in pristine condition, showing the aerodynamic data nose probe with pitot tube. *NASA*

Back cover insets (top to bottom): The first person to exceed Mach 4, 5 and 6, on 17 July 1962, USAF test pilot Robert M. White also became the first to fly wings into space. (*NASA*) A sectional view of the X-15 showing major systems and general layout of the aircraft. *NASA*

Contents

Preface

On speaking before a gathering of test pilots, technicians, engineers and programme managers at the Astronaut Wings Presentation at NASA's Dryden Flight Research Center in 2005, Neil Armstrong defined the true nature of the pioneering work at Edwards and its shared NASA facilities.

Remarking on the unique nature of the place, he reminded his audience that research is usually regarded as an exercise in ferreting out available but inaccessible information, unknown facts (which exist but are hidden somewhere) and investigations into areas about which the researcher is unfamiliar.

At Dryden, he said, research is about going out into unknown territory and discovering things that do exist in the physical world but about which nobody, anywhere, knows anything about or has already discovered in an environment which is uncharted and unexplored; that, he said, is the true nature of the word 'research' at Dryden and Edwards Air Force Base.

Introduction

Designed when the development of airframe and engine technology coupled with research into the thermal properties of hypersonic flight converged with the will to take the next big step in aeronautical engineering, the X-15 was unique. Challenged by limited technical and mathematical knowledge of the flight regime in which it would operate, it was a bold push against the aerothermal challenges it addressed.

It was a success on several separate levels, not least of which was the man-machine interface essential to future piloted flight at high speed and extreme altitudes, to space exploration in and around Earth and to the development of new and exotic materials, lubricants, sealants and propellants. But in achieving these successes it stimulated development of new and innovative devices.

The X-15 pioneered several key systems: the throttleable rocket motor, new thermal protection materials, the first full-pressure suit capable of supporting a pilot in space, a full telemetry suite for delivering data from multiple sensors and a digital flight management and control system operated through fly-by-wire. It developed these new technologies and operating capabilities and pushed them to new heights, lifting piloted flight from Mach 3 to an almost routine Mach 6, carrying men beyond the limits of the atmosphere and providing the first controllable vehicle capable of changing its flight path in space; both Russian and American spacecraft were incapable of that before 1965, achieved on NASA's first piloted flights with the Gemini spacecraft.

Along the way, the X-15 provided a more detailed knowledge of the supersonic and hypersonic flight regime, demonstrating that hypersonic air flow is turbulent and not laminar, that heating rates and thermal effects are less than those predicted, and that skin friction at hypersonic speeds is less than expected. It also provided information vital for the safe engineering design and acoustic response the Mercury spacecraft would encounter during ascent into orbit.

For a while it appeared to observers at the time as a general precursor to space travel, anticipating winged vehicles routinely plying between the surface of the Earth and space. It served as a test-bed for key technologies and it provided vast data sets crucial to understanding the aerothermal environment, critical for the next generation of aerospace vehicles – in fact, the X-15 played no small part in combining 'aero' and 'space' in the mind-set of the day, setting in place a new age of flying machines outperforming limits generally accepted only a few decades earlier.

Above all, however, the X-15 was a manned research tool designed to explore unknown regions of the hypersonic environment. As such it was the last of its kind. Future research on hypersonic flight would be conducted on unmanned air vehicles, in wind tunnels and through computer modelling, simulations and artificial intelligence. Not to mention high-velocity rocket tests with models and aero-body shapes launched by rockets.

When engineers defined the requirement which ultimately resulted in the X-15, it did not seek a performance goal in terms of a certain speed or altitude, specified as essential to its value as a research tool for hypersonic flight. Instead, the requirement was dictated by the need to stimulate research into areas which could not be defined by calculation alone, or by extrapolation from known parameters. Indeed, it could be said that its ambitious goals were a product of not having been ambitious enough in the development of existing research rocket-powered aircraft during the end months of the Second World War.

Contradictory to their nomenclature, precursor X-series aircraft were not 'experimental' types but research tools for investigation of the transonic and supersonic flight regimes and, increasingly, of different flight environments, flight control systems or aeronautical design options. Glamourised by the press and a public clamouring for ever-faster, ever-higher flight achievements in the wake of a global war just ended, these aircraft were acclaimed as super-machines; the men who flew them were lionised as super-heroes and not as the highly skilled and competent pilots they were.

Within the esoteric world of advanced aeronautical research and the scientific investigation of flight at the extremities of the known flight regime, X-craft pilots were valued

Above: A fine shot of X-15A-2 on the flight line for extended flight performance targeting Mach 7 with the assistance of additional propellant from the jettisonable fuel tanks. *NASA*

for their ability to add additional sensory awareness to the handling qualities of their aircraft and the flight characteristics they encountered. Situations that, but for the presence of a pilot would, all too frequently, have incurred a catastrophic loss of control. It was the ability of a human to correct for unanticipated occurrences that added value to the research.

For all aforesaid reasons, the X-15 was a unique vehicle. But it was a product of its age and only possible because of the time in which it was approved and developed. Such a programme could never occur in the 21st century environment of risk-avoidance, the unacceptability of failure and the ultra-conservative approach now taken to advanced technological projects. Today, the programme which nurtured the X-15 could not get a funded start – the risks would be considered too great and the very real possibility of a failure resulting in loss of life, too great for the cautious and over-conservative mind-set of the present age where certainty is the goal.

The X-15 programme existed because of the freedom then enjoyed by specialist teams in specialised industries, due in part to the 'hands-off' approach taken by the political decision-makers. Dispensing funds and persuasively subservient to the exotic world of advanced technology, their innate ignorance of mathematical and scientific principles kept politicians at arm's length from the interventions and micro-management by committee which has become so prevalent in the decades since the last X-15 was retired. Having delivered the 'arsenal of democracy' waging war against Nazi Germany and Imperial Japan, in the 1950s the engineering industries operated on a level of trust that they could deliver on promises made.

It is then, to be seen as fortuitous that the programme came along when it did, quickly delivering a research vehicle, still under development when it began flying and still incomplete until the flight test programme was well underway. It emerged when the US aircraft and missile industry was in buoyant expansion, with unprecedented growth in manufacturing units, sales and profits. All the contenders bidding for the job of building the X-15 were industry leaders with significant experience in aircraft design and manufacturing, although two had never built a rocket research aircraft before. In 1955, when the X-15 was placed under contract, the industry employed 750,000 people (second only to the automobile industry) and had a sales volume that year of \$8.4 billion (\$87billion in 2022 money).

But when North American Aviation Inc was selected to build three airframes for the National Advisory Committee for Aeronautics (NACA) it was not at all certain that the X-15 would be a success. Neither was it ever expected to bring a fortune to North American, which was already thriving on the mass production of subsonic F-86 and supersonic F-100 fighters; even before the X-15 flew it would be building the Mach 3 bomber, the XB-70. The X-15 would, nevertheless, be the first of three high-publicity projects in successive decades to bring kudos to this company: the hypersonic X-15 of the 1950s, the Moon-orbiting Apollo spacecraft of the 1960s and the reusable Space Shuttle Orbiter programme of the 1970s. Each of which brought great publicity value and investment to the company.

Seen alone, the X-15 was a worthy addition to the growing inventory of aeronautical research and flight evaluation tools. In context, it became a stimulus for expanding research and development of new aerospace engineering concepts. This gained impetus and public excitement after President Eisenhower announced on 29 July 1955 that the United States would launch an artificial Earth satellite during the International Geophysical Year of 1957-58. This, only a year after the go-ahead to develop the Atlas Intercontinental Ballistic Missile (ICBM) and an expanding demand for rocket motors built by Rocketdyne, an outgrowth of the company's Missile and Control Equipment Operations Propulsion Center.

Public enthusiasm for 'faster-higher-further' was raised to new levels through well publicised flights with German V2 rockets assembled and launched at White Sands Missile Range and Cape Canaveral. Photographs of Earth taken by cameras propelled to near-Earth space and the development of ballistic missiles such as Redstone, Jupiter and Thor raised expectations. While the X-15 was essentially a pure research tool for aerodynamic and aero-thermal data-harnessing, in the public mind it was one part of a brave new world in which piloted shuttlecraft would ply back and forth between the surface of the Earth and space.

A pioneer in the test and development of rocket motors, the appropriately named Reaction Motors Inc, grew in the mid-1950s on the expanding portfolio of work funded by demands from the X-series projects and soon for the X-15 as well. In 1955, the company moved in to a new joint Navy-RMI facility in northern New Jersey, significantly expanding the available work and manufacturing area and that became critical to the development of motors for both declared and classified work for the military.

Key to the inception and development of the X-15, the NACA celebrated its 40th anniversary with the contract to build the hypersonic aircraft – although the work package would not be officially signed with North American until later in 1956. But it focused attention on its future direction and the priority taken by this body regarding aeronautical research. In addition to the vigorous work programme in place on a wide variety of aeronautical challenges, active research into supersonic flight had become an increasing commitment. This period also saw the NACA expand its support work for the Air Force by actively managing programmes supporting ballistic missile research, warhead design and development of re-entry bodies.

In its annual report on the US aeronautical industry, the representative body for aircraft manufacturers summed up the situation eloquently:

'The gap between initial achievement of supersonic performance by a prototype or experimental airplane and day-to-day accomplishment of such performance under the rigors of service operation and maneuver can be very great. In the area of supersonic flight, in addition to problems arising from the demands for faster flight over longer ranges, it has become

Above: An X-15 mounted on the starboard wing pylon of its B-52 carrier-plane. *USAF*

obvious that more, much more, must be known about the laws of nature to enable more efficient, more satisfactory flight at faster than sound velocities.'

And in this year that the NACA determined to tackle the challenges of hypersonic flight, the review stressed the pressing urgency of such research:

'Already, much valuable information on hypersonic flight has been accumulated, but it is clear that vastly more knowledge will be required for designing successful missiles to attain these performance goals. Among the many difficulties of hypersonic flight, the aerodynamic heating problem appears to be the most troublesome at the present time although progress is being made.

'Temperatures high enough to melt or even vaporize most metals quickly develop in the skin of a hypersonic aircraft. Even at only half the speeds anticipated, or about 7,000 mph, sustained flight could produce temperatures of to 8,000degF. Very high rates of heat transfer exist at such elevated temperatures. This means that heat will flow rapidly into the aircraft's skin and structure.

'Accurate information on the heat effects on structure is essential for safe and efficient design, because it is presently doubted if cooling will take care of all the heat generated. Studies are being made to learn how heat flows through the skin and supporting structure of an aircraft. Mathematical procedures are used to analyze the flow of heat, and an electric analog computer has been built to help obtain rapid solutions.'

To these needs the NACA brought a range of tools, foremost of which in the mid-1950s was the X-15. That aircraft, and the rocket motors it employed, could never have been built had it not followed on the catalogue of data from several experimental research aircraft that preceded it by more than a decade. For that reason, this story unfolds out of the achievements of the Bell X-1, the Douglas D-558-2 Skyrocket and the Bell X-2.

David Baker, East Sussex 2022

About This Book

Many books have been written about the X-15 and its predecessors, and generally, these fall into three categories: a mixed history involving the when, why and how of its generic evolution; a semi-technical history of its design and evolution; and a detailed, semi-biographical discourse on the flights, the flyers and the motivational forces that drove them all ever upward, ever faster.

I chose to provide an engineering description of all the important types involved in this evolution, to explore the reasons why certain decisions were made and how they impact the story, and to do that for one reason. I discovered that it was difficult to find this level of inclusivity in a single volume and so I decided to write that in the hope that others would find this approach has filled a gap.

But I also wanted to include in this narrative story the industrial, governmental and pseudo-political ramifications of seminal events across the period between 1944 and the end of the 1960s. Because of this, I have separated the content into three sections:

SECTION 1	**Precursors – X-1 series, Skystreak, Skyrocket, X-2**
SECTION 2	**North American X-15 – Evolution and Engineering**
SECTION 3	**Test and Operational Flight Results**

Each defines a unique stage in the story of the X-15, from the search for solutions and challenges in aeronautical design and engineering concepts to the exploration of supersonic and hypersonic flight regimes. Accordingly, readers may wish to select certain parts of the book out of a particular interest in different aspects of this story. The progression from one to the other has been written as a seamless narrative with the recommendation that the reader start at the beginning.

I have also included commentary on the manufacturing base from which the X-15 emerged, incorporating potted histories of relevant companies and organisations, including the rocket engine builders who provided propulsion for all the aircraft included in the book, as well as those manufacturers supporting failed bids.

I begin with the challenge of compressibility at high subsonic speeds, and move along to the search for transonic and then supersonic test beds with the X-1 series, the Skystreak, the Skyrocket and the X-2, culminating in the hypersonic research platform – the X-15.

In selecting the manner in which abbreviations and acronyms are expressed I have retained the convention at the time they were first defined. For instance, the XLR-99 rocket motor is now referred to as the XLR99. But after it entered production for the X-15 it was also identified in some government documents as the YLR-99 (or YLR99). I have chosen to retain its original form to avoid confusion and to fall in line with the convention used by historians when compiling the history of the parent company, Reaction Motors Incorporated.

Above: Taken in July 1962, this image pays tribute to the team who kept the X-15s flying across nine years of successful operation, with the loss of only one pilot in 199 launches. *NASA*

Acknowledgements

The list of those who provided material from which the content of this book has been compiled is long and there is insufficient space here to mention everyone but a lifetime of research and analysis could never be accomplished without a very considerable number of people who have helped along the way. The list includes people who were at the NACA, NASA, the Navy and the Air Force and across industry, as well as professional historians and analysts, all of whom made a major contribution and for which I extend my eternal gratitude.

In no particular order, many years ago Robert C. Seamans provided great encouragement for this project and opened several doors which would otherwise have remained closed. As Deputy Administrator at NASA and then Secretary of the US Air Force, he had unique experience and his work as co-chairman of the Astronautics Coordinating Board provided special insight to the not infrequently challenging relationship between the civilian and uniformed sections of the US government. That played large in the story found in this book, especially with regard to the way the X-15 fitted within the strategic plan leading directly from the X-1 to Dyna-Soar.

Again, as I have with other titles, I would like to acknowledge the generous time and assistance provided by the late Jim Beggs, former NASA Administrator and industry executive who opened doors for me and encouraged a strong adherence to an unbiased approach in objective analysis. This is an endemic, cultural approach supported by many others from whom I had help and assistance, especially from NASA Headquarters. There, unwavering support over many years came from Lee Saegesser, Dr. Roger Launius, Dr. Bill Barry and, at the Armstrong Flight Research Center, Michael Gorn together with a generation of archivists and custodians of documents and records across the United States.

Industry sources provided prime materials and allowed publication of some previously unpublished quotes. In particular, David B. Alter and Sue Cometa of North American Aviation and Rockwell International respectively, opened filing cabinets and document archives to great effect. Research across industry was vital to ensuring an inclusive picture embracing many peripheral projects frequently ignored in telling the story of the search for hypersonic flight.

McDonnell Douglas helped with detailed information on proposals from Douglas and the assistance of Donald R. Stiess provided much that has been put into this book, especially on the failed contenders for the X-15 contract. Personnel at Bell and Republic were equally forthcoming, companies whose time in the field of high-speed aviation is now long gone. Before it disappeared in 1965, considerable interest was expressed by several personnel in seeing a dedicated book on Republic's history of high-speed concepts including that for the X-15 and some elements of that can be found here.

To fully integrate the story of the technical development of concepts throughout the period from 1945 to 1968 into the political shifts which played such an important role in how the projects evolved, I would like to acknowledge the help of several people including staffers at the US Office of Management and Budget (OMB). I also valued the help from Charles F. Ducander, Executive Secretary of the US House of Representatives Committee on Science and Astronautics, and George G. Feldman, Chief Counsel and Director, US Senate Select Committee on Aeronautics and Space Exploration together with James J. Gehrig, Senate Committee on Aeronautical and Space Sciences. I also received considerable help from Barbara Luxembourg from the Congressional Research Service.

Context and relevance are enablers in any technological story and the history of the X-planes and their operations has been followed by many who have provided able assistance stretching back many decades. Inspirational work by historians Jay Miller and Dr. Richard P. Hallion set this precedence early in their own work and their contributions together with those of Tony Landis, Henry Matthews, Dennis Jenkins and Michelle Evans have all contributed to a stacked learning curve, a legendary group to which this author pays tribute.

Of the above, who have each inspired the preparation and production of this history, very special thanks goes to Dennis Jenkins, aerospace engineer with hands-on experience across many projects and who has produced so much work over many years that all of us benefit from.

The production of any book of this size and extent requires a competent team and thanks go to Ann Page for proofing a chaotic text and to Martin Preston for taking all this material and making it into a proper book. Appreciation for giving me the chance to get this published goes to managing editor Charlotte Stear and especially to Jeremy Pratt, MD of Crecy Publishing Ltd for making the entire project possible. None of the above are in any way responsible for errors, omissions or incorrect information, shortcomings which, if they are there, are entirely my responsibility. *DB*

Section 1

Precursors – X-1 Series, Skystreak, Skyrocket, X-2

Chapter One

The Search for Speed

The early days of experimental X-series rocket-powered flight were conducted when the compressible effect of air on an object at high speed in the atmosphere was already a well-known phenomenon. Close to the speed of sound, shock waves form which have a significant effect on lift and drag, on the whole body of the aircraft and on any moveable control surface. The impact of this drastically affects lift and drag. In fact, it was directly because of this that the early test flights in the late 1940s specifically addressed the problems caused by compressibility.

At speeds up to approximately 322kph (200mph), the effect does not exist – at least, to any meaningful degree. Faster, and the effect is measurable until it becomes problematic very close to the speed of sound. And that became the underlying reason for development of a unique set of aircraft built to study the transonic and supersonic regime. For several centuries, mathematicians, engineers and physicists had wrestled the problem and seeking a simple phrase to encapsulate the challenge, the inappropriate term 'sound barrier' was born, misrepresentation by a journalist interviewing the British aerodynamicist W. F. Hilton in 1935.

Indicating on a sketch how the drag rises sharply at the transonic 'like a barrier', the reference stuck and has been misapplied ever since. Hilton never saw it as a physical barrier, defining it instead in scientific terms as a phenomenon to be understood. The speed of sound is not a unit of measurement, neither is it a constant, rather a value denoting the characteristics of a fluid flow and its compressibility, an indication of density. In this way, the speed of sound, which varies with temperature and altitude, should never be regarded as an indication of the speed of an object.

Above: The Moravian physicist Ernst Mach (1838-1916) stepped away from the philosophy of logical positivism which had taken up so much of his time and took the differential equations of Navier and Stokes to define the speed of sound and to give his name to the free stream airflow around a solid object. *Author's collection*

The term used to define the speed of sound has its etymology with the proposer – Ernst Mach (1838-1916), a Moravian physicist more universally remembered for his work on logical positivism. Mach went a step beyond the differential equations used in subsonic flight, defined by Claude-Louis Navier and George Gabriel Stokes, and took those probabilities and stated that while the free stream air flow around an object is below the speed of sound, the flow locally may exceed that – the speed of sound being defined as Mach 1.

It is for this reason that the calculated velocity in a measured atmospheric condition states it to be subsonic while local flow is transonic. It is here, and in this definition, that the various values of Mach number are best understood. And while the measured values for Mach numbers are modelled on a linearised prediction, there is no fixed value, the number depending on altitude. This is because the density and pressure effects cancel each other out and Mach number is governed purely by the temperature. Today, the speed of sound (Mach 1) is calculated to be 331.3m/sec (1,087ft/sec) or 1,193km/hr (741mph) at a temperature of 0°C (32°F), or 343m/sec (1,125ft/sec) or 1,235km/hr (767mph) at an ambient temperature of 20°C (68°F).

The subsonic regime has a Mach number below 0.8 (980kph or 609mph) and represents a state where no laminar or turbulent flow exceeds the speed of sound and therefore the critical Mach number is the lowest free stream flow across the surface of the moving body. Transonic speeds are represented by Mach 0.8-1.2 (980-1,470kph or 530-794mph) and here the critical Mach number (the lowest free stream value) is below Mach 1.3, with some laminar flow in the subsonic regime, which means that some surfaces are experiencing subsonic speeds while others are experiencing supersonic flow.

Fully supersonic flight is defined as a state in which all the flow over and across the surface of a body in motion is greater than the speed of sound, lifting the free stream air flow above Mach 1. It is generally regarded as starting at Mach 1.3 and extending up to Mach 5. Significant differences in air flow across the surface are observed in this region, dictating a unique set of engineering and design solutions involving shape and materials. The speed range extends from 1,470kph (913mph) to 6,126kph (3,806mph). And, as the velocity increases heating effects begin to rise significantly.

Hypersonic speeds are generally regarded as being between Mach 5 and Mach 25, where unique design challenges virtually dictate the shape of the free-flying body. Speeds in the hypersonic regime are generally regarded as 6,126kph (3,806mph) to 30,626kph (16,537mph). In this region, there is no upstream flow of air and the energy excites the chemical bonds which hold together the molecular oxygen and nitrogen of the atmosphere.

At Mach numbers above about 10, shapes and configurations must take account of the chemical reactions and external skin corrosion caused by free-atomic oxygen in exceptionally high speed flow. Interference effects come to dominate, where thermal effects and the temperature of protuberances such as wings and tail surfaces put constraints on the choice of materials. Aero-thermal heating becomes so great that active cooling and heat-sink materials dominate, or ablative materials for expendable vehicles. These are the defined categories accepted today.

In 1877, Ernst Mach demonstrated that shock waves form around a supersonic body. Using what he described as 'shadowgraphy', Mach showed visible proof of shock waves forming at both the bow and the trailing-edge of a moving bullet. The shadowgraph (or shadowgram) works on the principle that while the shock waves cannot be seen by the human eye or other conventional optical devices, the flow patterns created in air by those shock waves create shadows which, when cast upon a reflecting surface, allow a photograph to be taken of them.

The technical nuances of high-speed flight languished in the imagination of curious and inquisitive inventors and experimenters, driven by popular and specialised literature to speculate on just how far humans could push engineering principles toward ever higher and faster machines. Problems of compressibility and supersonic flight were already being seen as a limiting factor toward the end of the First World War. The problem arose not with the airframe but with the propellers. Aerodynamic research into propeller design exposed a challenge with higher rotational velocities for higher straight-line speed, seeming to limit the speed of the aircraft powered by existing engines.

The ideal propeller was large and experienced rotational velocities which carried the tips toward the transonic regime, threatening to upset the operating stability of the blades. All this, or course, before variable pitch and geared propeller shafts became standard. The challenge of propeller tip compressibility was considered by several scientists working with the Advisory Committee for Aeronautics (ACA), an organisation set up

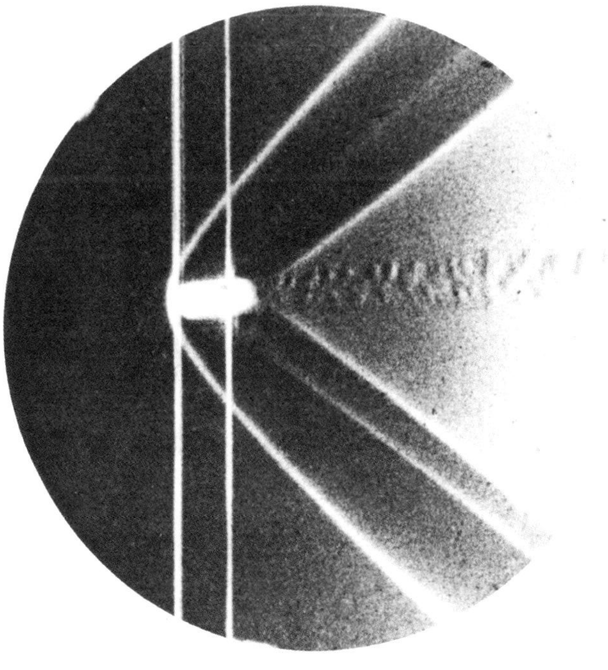

Right: Ernst Mach took this shadowgraph in 1887 to show the shockwave that formed at the nose of a brass bullet fired at supersonic velocity. *Author's collection*

by the British government on 30 April 1909 to carry out scientific research on the physics of flight and the development of aircraft, primarily for military purposes.

Quite quickly, in the United States research shifted to the National Advisory Committee for Aeronautics (NACA), a government body established on 3 March 1915 for research into the scientific principles of aeronautics and with a mandate to disseminate fundamental and advanced research to the expanding aircraft industry. The two organisations, on separate continents, were set up to carry out advanced research into flight and flying on different but complementary paths: the Americans on practical research and test, the British on advanced theoretical calculation and experimentation.

The British had taken a lead in defining in mathematical terms the characteristics of a lifting aerofoil when, in the 1880s, Osborne Reynolds gave his name to the Reynolds number, an abstract and dimensionless value applied to the ratio of inertial forces to viscous forces. His work defined the bulk (averaged) behaviour of motion between laminar and turbulent flow and, when integrated with Navier-Stokes equations, provided a basis for complex calculations essential for designing aerofoil sections and the flow of air across a solid body.

Wind tunnels had been the 'holy grail' for aerodynamicists since the first opened in Greenwich, England, in 1871. It was built for the Aeronautical Society of Great Britain, which had been formed in 1866, among whose founding members was the Duke of Argyll. Powered by a steam-driven fan blowing air through a box 45.7cm (18in) square and 3.6m (12ft) in length, the tunnel was designed and built by Francis Wenham, whose contribution to aeronautical science was international and did much to stimulate pressure in the United States for technical studies managed by government agencies, this in turn driving the Army toward experimental work as well as tests through the NACA's facilities.

Wenham postulated that by changing the coefficient of lift on one side of the flying machine to the other, the aeroplane would turn in direction by an amount directly proportional to the incidence of the deflected surface. It was this that became the basis of wing warping as well as the use of separate surfaces, or ailerons, for manoeuvring the aeroplane in flight.

An important contribution made by the NACA in the immediate post-war years was the inauguration in 1923 of the

Below: The first meeting of the National Advisory Committee for Aeronautics (NACA) on 23 April 1915. Seated from left: Dr. William Durand, Stanford University; Dr. S.W. Stratton, Director, Bureau of Standards; Brig. Gen. George P. Scriven, Chief Signal Officer; Dr. C.F. Marvin, Chief, United States Weather Bureau; and Dr. Michael I. Pupin, Columbia University. Standing: Holden C. Richardson, Naval Instructor; Dr. John F. Hayford, Northwestern University; Capt. Mark L. Bristol, Director of Naval Aeronautics; Lt. Col. Samuel Reber, Signal Corps. Also present were Dr. Joseph S. Ames, Johns Hopkins University and the Hon. B. R. Newton, Asst. Secretary of the Treasury. *NACA*

Langley Variable-Density (wind) Tunnel (VDT), preceded by Wind Tunnel No. 1, a closed-circuit type modelled on the British tunnel installed by the National Physical Laboratory. However, there was concern over the level of inexperience in the US and caution prevailed in making, and operating, a scale model first before proceeding with the full-scale tunnel. The No. 1 tunnel had a 1.5m (5ft) cross-section which quickly proved ineffective when using only very small scale models of real aeroplane designs.

It was here that the empirical approach broke down and forced introduction of a better tunnel. And it was all based on the elastic Reynolds number. Based on mathematical calculations, and as they relate to wind tunnels, Reynolds found that a measured flow parameter would be the same at whatever scale was being observed. He stated this in equation pVd / μ, where p is the density, V is the velocity, d is the diameter of the tunnel and μ is the viscosity of the air.

Because the small volume of the No. 1 tunnel could only accommodate models around 1/20th the size of the real aircraft, the measurements were out by a factor of 20 and therefore of only very limited value. In reality, if any one of the parameters (density, velocity, tunnel diameter or viscosity) had been adjustable it would have significantly improved the relationship of the model's measured values to the full-scale aircraft but the limitations of the No. 1 made that impossible and forced the decision to build the VDT.

Pressure for the VDT and the intensely theoretical work it both sponsored and inspired, left a lot of Langley engineers adrift from the value of the tests. Only the most highly tutored mathematicians and physicists could begin to fully absorb the value of the work it produced and this split the group in two: those who fully understood the results and those who did not. Nevertheless, it was from this work – too copious and comprehensive to give it justice here - that, through the VDT in

Above: The Langley Memorial Aeronautical Laboratory, named after the American aeronautical pioneer and experimenter Samuel Pierpont Langley, was the core centre for NACA's expanding science programme. Inspired by Wind Tunnel No. 1, the Variable-Density Tunnel (VDT) pictured (top) was inaugurated in 1923 and gave the Langley facility the first analytical tool designed to convert theoretical calculations into measured values. *NACA*

the late 1920s, NACA redefined the nomenclature for its test subjects into a format which became familiar across the world of aeronautical engineering and across all continents.

Scales of classification

Hitherto, the NACA had attached a numerical sequence to specific shapes of aerofoil it designed and recommended for the burgeoning aircraft industry, but the revised system adopted a nomenclature akin to that used by the metallurgical industry in identifying the chemical composition of steels and alloys. Under this system, the distribution of additives and chemical constituents instantly identifies the qualities and the responsive properties of the metal according to the allocated code. The NACA thought that a similar system would be good for aerofoil types, in which a specific shape would receive a NACA number. The four-digit suffix applied initially to the NACA identity would indicate: the maximum camber of the aerofoil; that value as a percentage of the chord; the measured point of the maximum camber as a percentage of the chord from the leading edge; and the thickness as a percentage of the chord.

Above: Pearl Young at the Langley Flight Instrumentation Facility, in 1922 – the first female professional at the NACA and only the second female physicist in US government service. Initially, she gained a reputation for her technical writing when almost none of her male peers commanded that skill. *NACA*

For instance, a NACA-3516 profile would indicate a 3 per cent camber (number 3) at 0.5 of the chord (5), with a thickness of 16 per cent (16) of the length of the chord. In the case of a purely symmetrical profile, the first two integers would be zeroes. This eventually grew to five digits which imposed a separate thickness value with the mean camber line and altered the preceding four-digit sequence. The first digit would now, when multiplied by 3/2 express the design lift coefficient in tenths. The next two digits when divided by 2 yielded the position of the maximum camber in tenths of the chord. The last two digits retained the same value as the four-digit series.

Increasing sophistication and refinement raised the system to six parameters, with the additions representing changes in the leading-edge radius of the location of maximum thickness with a dash as suffix and two additional numbers, in for instance NACA-35162-66. Over time these sequences would be modified into 6-series, 7-series and 8-series categories, each adding better detail on laminar flow characteristics and associated parameters, including independent values for upper and lower surface flow patterns. Each series represents an evolving series of aerofoil sections. By pulling a particular NACA aerofoil number off the shelf, a design team could instantly know the type of wing it would be choosing and have a proven type of aerofoil for a specific type of aircraft.

As use of the VDT increased, the drawbacks became ap-

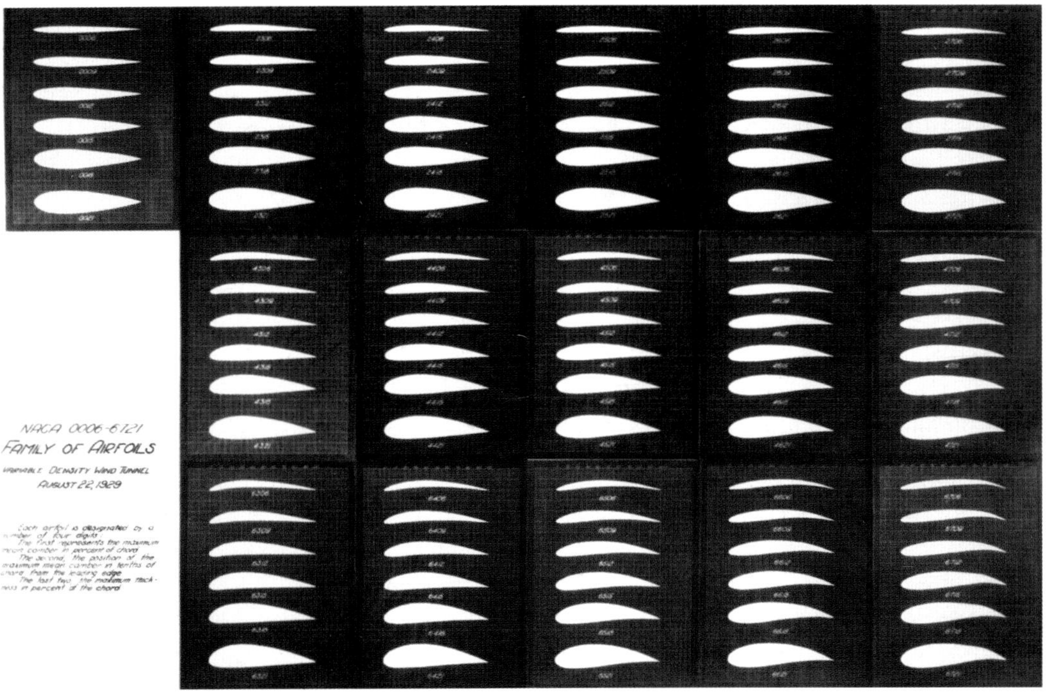

Left: Aerofoils were developed from work in the VDT to provide US manufacturers and design teams with a catalogue of selectable profiles for different applications, the familiar NACA-series. *NACA*

Above: A US Navy Vought O3U-1 positioned for test at the Langley Full Scale Tunnel (FST), which was developed after shortcomings to the VDT required an improved design. *NACA*

parent. Due to its design the attempt to produce a steady air flow was compromised; the turbulence caused by eddies and cross-currents significantly affected the measurements and fluctuations while the motor driving the tunnel made it doubly difficult to gain a consistent air speed. Thus was born the Langley Full-Scale Tunnel (FST), available from 1931 at a cost of $1million.

The physical dimensions of the FST were impressive. With a total length of 132.3m (434ft) by 67.7m (222ft) and a height of 29.6m (97ft), the building it contained loomed large on the facility. The design type was a double-return tunnel in which air speeds of 190kph (118mph) were possible. Much of the design influence came from Wilbur Wright (heavily involved with the Committee) and translated into a test environment engineered by the NACA's Smith J. DeFrance. The airflow was created by two wooden propellers, each 9.1m (30ft) wide and 17.1m (56ft) in length, driven by 2,984kw (4,000hp) electric motors. The throat where the aircraft were tested had a width of 18.3m (60ft) and a height of 9.1m (30ft).

During the 1930s, eminent aero-physicists and engineers argued for a wider range of test facilities in order to focus attention on areas where there was still a need for better data. The behaviour of air across lifting surfaces dominated much of the debate regarding future flight and high-speed capabilities, together with studies on the nuances of the boundary layer, of the areas where turbulent air attached and then detached from the aerofoil and on the entire spectrum of debate about laminar flow. When American scientists working with the NACA visited Britain and continental Europe they discovered considerable resources being applied to fundamental issues of aerodynamics and the behaviour of air flow on high-speed aircraft there too.

Great progress had been made with refining the design of the propeller, with a thinner cross-section and a more slender profile, fabricated from steel, driven through reduction gears and with variable pitch for dealing with different modes of flight. As aircraft speeds increased with the development of the reciprocating engine, the challenges faced by high subsonic speeds began to filter across to the research work being conducted in England where Hubert C. Townend solved the problem of high drag incurred by cowlings for radial engines while working at the National Physical Laboratory. The so-called Townend Ring brought great improvements in the performance of aircraft by significantly reducing drag.

In the United States the NACA developed an equivalent drag-reducing cowl. Great credit for this resides with the Propeller Research Tunnel (PRT). It was built in 1927 for research into the limitations both of propeller and cowling design and into the integrated air flow which reduced the theoretical performance of existing aircraft. The PRT was powered by two 746kw (1,000hp) engines from diesel submarines, driving a 8.2m (27ft) diameter, eight-bladed fan producing a stream of air at 177kph (110mph).

By the early 1930s a low-key discussion on transonic issues with high-speed aircraft was one part of a growing awareness that supersonic flight may be the next great challenge for aeronautics. Very little experimentation was underway in the United States, while in Britain and Germany there was a more resolute awareness of the need to develop test facilities for a better understanding of the problems involved. And yet again, it came down to the balance between theoretical analysis and practical testing, beginning with scale models in wind tunnels and progressing to flight tests.

As candidates for propulsion, only the concept of a reaction engine – so defined because such an engine would achieve forward motion as the consequence of an action – would achieve high speed without the use of a propeller while adding the advantage of an aerodynamically 'clean' airframe.

Reaction engines fall into two categories: the jet engine combusting a fuel in the presence of an oxidiser breathed in through an intake, or a rocket engine carrying its own oxidiser in addition to fuel, avoiding the need for an intake to spoil the clean lines of a sleek airframe. The simplest form of reaction propulsion was the rocket, arguably the oldest form of propulsion, and available long before the jet engine became an effective contender for manned aircraft. The story of both is pertinent to the search for a controllable aircraft for transonic, supersonic and hypersonic flight regimes.

By the mid-1930s, across continental Europe there was a concerted effort to develop reaction engines for very high speed flight and, in Britain, Frank Whittle was conducting an almost single-handed drive to procure government support for research on the jet engine. Recruits to the RAF frequently held debate and discussion over the future of military aviation, no less so than in the halls of residence at RAF College Cranwell.

Situated in the rolling rural landscape of the county of Lincolnshire, the College was filled with aspirational youngsters each wanting to be a fighter pilot. Progress in aircraft engineering and technology was a favourite topic of discussion. Few could envisage the challenges of the transonic region but there was a universal agreement that new and radical modes of propulsion would soon be perfected for tremendous increases in performance and capability. First, they thought, would come the jet engine rapidly followed by rocket propulsion for manned flight.

In magazines and at the cinema, public discussion within aviation circles in Britain and Europe was rife with portents

Below: NACA chief of aerodynamics Elton W. Miller gives scale to the exit cone at the Propeller Research Tunnel (PRT) in 1927, confronted by a Sperry M-1 Messenger. *NACA*

Right: European aircraft manufacturers were quick to exploit the development of drag-reducing cowls for radial engines. This Junkers Ju-52 in the Deutsches Museum, Munich, displays the NACA cowl on the wing-mounted engines with a British Townend ring on the nose engine. *Author's collection*

Below right: Indicative of the new generation of fast biplane fighters of the late 1930s, a North American Aviation P-51B is tested in the Full Scale Tunnel. Such aircraft would soon encounter compressibility. *NACA*

of a new age in which flights into space might become possible. The default assumption was enshrined: if people were ever going to leave the atmosphere and fly through space, it would be on rocket-powered aircraft with wings for a safe recovery on land. Professional engineers rarely considered these aspects when developing the jet engine, merely the greater efficiency and broader performance made possible. But even this would soon demonstrate performance which would open the door to transonic research. In the US, that required a strong and trustworthy relationship between industry, the research facilities of the NACA and the military.

In a later decade, the relationship with the military services would greatly influence the way the NACA could operate. Langley Field had been the home of the NACA Langley Memorial Aeronautical Laboratory but it was primarily a US Army base. It was the only NACA facility until the Ames Aeronautical Laboratory at Moffett Field, California, was authorised in late 1939. The very nature of the NACA's independence made it more difficult to get the cooperation of the Army in providing support and the provision of full-size aircraft for wind tunnels and flight research. This spasmodic relationship tipped the NACA increasingly toward the military for funding as the development of combat types grew rapidly during the 1930s.

The NACA found it valuable to foster interpersonal contacts, to name individuals to deal with Langley Field and other facilities for military aviation. In particular, the Navy appointed Lt. Comdr. Walter S. Diehl as liaison between the Committee and the Bureau of Aeronautics (BuAer), in charge of naval aviation in Washington DC. This forged a strong relationship which informed BuAer of programmes already underway at the NACA, about what it wanted for the future and what it aspired to in long-term projects. These bonds became increasingly important during the Second World War and helped form a strong working relationship during and after.

Below: With war clouds gathering across Europe, in 1939 the NACA got permission for its second research facility, the Ames Aeronautical Laboratory, Moffett Field, California, on the opposite side of the continental US to its existing Langley facility. *NACA*

Above: Staff at the newly opened Ames facility pose for a formal record of its establishment. Few in number at the time, women were already making a significant inroad to what had previously been considered an exclusively male domain. *NACA*

In 1939, as Europe descended into conflict the US Army established lines of communication which transcended an otherwise frosty relationship, by the establishment of a liaison office at Langley under Maj. Carl Greene and a civilian aeronautical engineer Jean Roché. Greene represented the engineering sector of the Air Service Technical Command and this prompted the NACA to set up its own liaison office at Wright Field, renamed from McCook Field, for a reciprocal exchange. There is no doubt that had this shift not taken place the impact that the NACA had on the future Army Air Forces would have had a very different outcome.

The continued liaison affected the NACA to a greater degree than anything else in its history, changing the ethos of Langley so that the independence of the Committee began to unravel as it became a servant of necessity rather than expediency; that is to say, it could no longer conduct areas of theoretical research pursued by scientists and aeronautical engineers divorced from the advancing state of aeronautics between the wars. Rather, to be directed by the changing requirements in military requirements. This provided the broad spectrum of demand-research which underpinned the wide base of capability and the extended facilities, available by the time America went to war in 1941.

Wartime expansion

Between 1939 and the attack on Pearl Harbor triggering America's entry into the war on 7 December 1941, the Army, the Navy and the NACA began a rapid transformation with new facilities and an increased set of research and test programmes. A lot of which came as a great surprise to congressional representatives and senators who had never heard of the NACA until this crisis alerted the relevant political caucuses to action. It was an exercise with benefits to each side. The NACA quickly learned how to fight its corner in the political maelstrom of the Washington legislature and Congress acquired a more fitting brief on national capabilities, assets and requirements to meet expanding national challenges.

The NACA had already responded to a growing demand for technical test facilities with the 2.4m (8ft) High-Speed Tunnel (HST) at Langley operational from March 1936 and a new facility for high-speed propeller research authorised largely because of the danger that the United States was falling behind. With pressure from concerns regarding the vulnerability of a single NACA laboratory complex, and the need to site a second facility on the West Coast, the special examining committee recommended Moffett Field in California.

A naval airship station and more recently an Army Air Corps training base, it had existing facilities and was suitably positioned for power supplies, which had been a consistent problem at Langley. Lewis went to Congress to endorse the request for funds, fought a good argument for the new facility and received approval on 9 August 1939. The following year the Moffett Field facility was named the Ames Aeronautical Laboratory after the recently retired chairman of the Committee, Joseph A. Ames.

The escalating political tensions in Europe and the urgent

need to set up a facility dedicated to propulsion resulted in Congress authorising a new Aircraft Engine Research Laboratory (AERL) on 26 June 1940. Until now, the NACA had focused on airframe and not engine development. The chosen site at Cleveland, Ohio was close to the municipal airport. The ground-breaking ceremony was held on 23 January 1941 and work began to build the new laboratory on the 80ha (199.7acre) site. It was to focus its attention on the development of new engines, fuels, lubricants, seals and high- or low-temperature hoses, pipes, electrical wiring and instrumentation.

Above: In an urgent desire to catch up with developments into aero-engine technology across Europe and the UK, the NACA opened the Aircraft Engine Research Laboratory (AERL) in 1941. Located in Cleveland, Ohio, it would be renamed the Flight Propulsion Research Laboratory in 1947, the Lewis Flight Research Laboratory the following year, the NASA Lewis Research Center in 1958 and the John H. Glenn Research Center in 1990. *NACA*

In America there was high interest in jet propulsion within the industry which would play an important part in the development of supersonic aircraft. But the pace was less than it might have been due to a high priority on the production of propeller-driven combat aircraft for the Army Air Forces and because of the vacuum in government-funded research into aircraft propulsion. There was some enthusiasm in the NACA for research into the transonic regime, however, but this was not as finely focused as that in Europe, where considerable progress had already been made.

Whittle is generally regarded in Britain as the inventor of the jet engine, and, in March 1936 founded Power Jets Ltd more than five years after he had taken out a patent for the design of a propulsion system marrying the gas turbine with the more generalised concept of the jet engine. In France and Italy there was growing interest in high-speed flight, where the development of the jet engine acquired a new status. The pioneering work of Frank Whittle was paralleled by a different type of jet engine designed by Pabst von Ohain in Germany. Both men could effectively lay claim to being the 'father' of the jet engine. Whittle ran his first test engine on 12 April 1937, five months before Ohain followed with his own axial-flow design.

Heinkel developed the world's first jet aircraft, the He 178, and took it into the air for the first time on 27 August 1939, piloted by Flugkapitan Erich Warsitz, three days after a modest hop down the runway. The second jet aircraft to make it into the air was the CC.2 designed by Secondo Campini and the Caproni company in Italy, that event taking place exactly one year after the flight of the He 178. The third jet aircraft to take to the air was the Whittle-engine powered Gloster E.28/39, on 15 May 1941. These events were seminal to a change of attitude in the United States, facilitated too by the new NACA engine research laboratory at Cleveland, Ohio.

Below: By the time the Ames facility was up and running the NACA already had its High Speed Tunnel at Langley in a concerted effort to catch up with major aeronautical developments in Europe and the UK. *NACA*

Working closely with the Navy, Langley, Ames and the aircraft engine facility at Cleveland expanded their activities from which came the Navy's new Office of Research and Inventions (ORI), pioneering a bold new era of electronics with the NACA to integrate systems into naval aircraft. To a greater extent than the Army, the Navy willingly sharing information of mutual benefit with the NACA. For its part, the Army never really trusted the NACA and refused to pass along information that could have helped the entire US aircraft industry push faster toward a viable jet engine programme, as well as high-speed research into the transonic.

The NACA tested almost every aircraft that saw combat and the enhanced efficiency and performance of engines with increasing output, sponsoring work to address transonic flight and the compressibility effect. While aircraft performance under normal flight conditions was formally in the subsonic, high-speed dives could readily push it into the transonic region, inducing buffeting, flutter, shifts in trim and in extreme cases into uncontrollable attitude excursions resulting in a crash and loss of life.

The NACA had for some time been keen to study the transonic and the Navy had done much to push it toward that. But war-work brought prescient demands and there was little scope for following speculative research initiatives. In 1943, however, the NACA gained recharged enthusiasm when it learned for the first time that, since April 1941 the Army had been keeping secret its knowledge about British developments with jet engines. It was appalled, and not a little shocked, to learn that the Army Air Forces had kept jet propulsion, the development of Britain's Gloster Meteor, and its own accelerated work on jet engine development, a secret.

NACA founder-member Prof. William F. Durand came out of retirement to chair a Special Committee on Jet Propulsion but it was not forthcoming to the Army about this. At an early meeting held on 22 April 1941 it was posited that a new series of laminar-flow aerofoils could equip an experimental aircraft capable of transonic, if not supersonic flight. The idea of a purpose-built experimental aircraft built, owned and operated by the NACA was unlikely, however. After several decades in which it had been unable to acquire the full-size aircraft it needed to deliver valid experimental results from piloted flight in the atmosphere, the idea that it should design and build an experimental aircraft was a radical departure from the way it had conducted business before.

This work evolved through 1942 but the services failed to support the idea and by early 1943 it was dead. Headquarters informed Langley on 23 March to stop work on a dedicated research aircraft. And for good reason. Unknown to the NACA the Army had just asked Lockheed to build a prototype jet fighter, based on the results of its own work merged with the Whittle research, and to power it with an Allison engine based on that British design. But this was not the project the NACA wanted to align itself with. The XP-80, as it was known, would be subsonic and have a top speed just below the transonic region. The NACA wanted a research tool for the transonic and into the supersonic.

By this date, considerable progress had been made by the Army Air Forces with a range of jet projects already underway. It had, since late 1942 been flying the XP-59A Airacomet, the first US designed and built jet aircraft. On 28 August 1941, the Army Air Force had asked Lawrence Bell, then President of Bell Aircraft, to meet with Gen. Arnold and discuss the possibility of his company building a jet fighter powered by the General Electric A-1 centrifugal jet engine. Also leaning heavily on the Whittle engine from Britain, the A-1 provided a fast solution to Arnold's demand for a jet fighter as quickly as possible. On 30 September, Bell signed the contract for his Model 27, the XP-59A, and began design work with a clean slate. To mask its identity it had the same model number as Bell's concept for a swept-wing fighter with tricycle undercarriage, with the A suffix added to confuse wartime spies – and the opposition!

Right: A radial engine under test at the AERL where so much development work was undertaken to the advantage of industry and aero-engine design and manufacturing companies. *NACA*

As an interesting side note, believing the predominately male workforce would soon be called up, Bell became a pioneer in employing women in aircraft manufacture by hiring them in large numbers for assembly and electrical work. Bell was used by the government when it conducted a survey into how well women integrated with traditionally male jobs, finding them to possess innate skills in precision and meticulous work such as assembling wiring looms, making far fewer mistakes than males doing the same job.

Neither was Bell lacking in technical and engineering

Below: The draughtsman's shop at the AERL as arranged in 1942, the first full year of operation as America girded itself for war. *NACA*

AERL

innovation. Conventional methods of production involved straight-line structural assembly with elements feeding in as subassemblies. Bell introduced a different concept, incorporating drag-line conveyor lines built into the floor with wheeled dollies down the line as the different operations built up the aircraft. This saved manpower, reduced costs and energy in the manufacturing process and made it easier for quality control checks. Bell also pioneered flush riveting which was low-cost and suitable for mass production, introducing a new machine capable of turning out 400,000 rivets a day with rejects falling by 80 per cent.

In other innovations, a pantograph router traced a template on one table and accurately cut complex parts out of aluminium alloy sheets on another. And the Farnham Spar Cap Milling Machine developed by Bell engineers cut the time required to mill wing spar cap extrusions required for the previous technique by 95 per cent. Bell was able to develop, and export to other manufacturers, labour or time-saving improvements to production operations or assembly methods. Lawrence Bell used savvy techniques developed in previous activities, including a time with the Martin Company, and as a machine tool salesman where he had learned how to do things more efficiently.

First jets

The contract to build the XP-59A came at an opportune time, building a highly specialised project with conventional design and engineering practices. While the incorporation of two GE jet engines was a revolutionary step forward, almost every other aspect of the Model 27 was conventional. Which explains

Above: The Lockheed YP-80 jet fighter undergoes tests in the altitude tunnel at the AERL. *NACA*

why the Army did not want the NACA involved. It needed a very basic aircraft with benign handling qualities but great performance and, potentially, value as a production fighter. It did not want a design compromised by research, experimentation and test equipment. The Army Air Forces saw the Airacomet as a very conventional fighter but with jet engines.

The YP-59As were to have been fitted with the GE I-16 engine delivering a thrust of 7,339N (1,650lb) but I-A engines, eventually designated J31, had to be installed due to development problems. The first two YP-59As arrived at Muroc Dry Lake in June 1943 with the first flight on 18 August. Its performance fell far short of the P-51B Mustang, then coming into service. The second YP-59A took to the air on 15 September 1943 and the third was sent to Britain in exchange for the first Gloster Meteor F.1, which flew at Muroc on 15 April 1944. The YP-59A was flown at Farnborough in Eng-

Below: The first truly successful US jet fighter, the P-80 Shooting Star, represented here by an F-80A-1-LO upgraded to an F-80C-11-LO bearing the Lockheed buzz letters PN with the individual aircraft's suffix number. *USAF*

Above: This YP-59A Airacomet (42-108778) displays its clean lines with jet engine intakes nestled underneath the wing and blended in to the sides of the fuselage. *USAF*

Above: The Bell XP-83 was designed as a twin-engine escort fighter but suffered from poor engine performance and never entered series production. *USAAF*

land between 5 November 1943 and April 1944 but only eleven times due to persistent engine failure.

The Airacomet was held distant from the NACA for two years after its inception and there was logic to the AAF wanting to keep this work away from the scientists. The AAF wanted to move swiftly to an operational jet fighter but raised expectations too high for the engine technology in existence at the time. But in April 1944 the AAF wanted wind tunnel tests on two pre-production prototype aircraft. The performance of the aircraft was brought into question when the tests showed it to have excellent aerodynamic qualities but poor characteristics for high-speed manoeuvring. The involvement of the NACA at this late stage in the aircraft's development prevented a scientific approach to overall design and engine integration.

Of interest to the NACA was the very different wing design to that of other jets, the Meteor from Britain and the Me 262 from Germany. Mounted in the shoulder position, the Airacomet's straight wing had a thickness ratio of 14 per cent. This was much more than the Meteor's wing, with 12 per cent at the root and 10.4 per cent at the tip. The Me 262's wing had a thickness ratio of 11 per cent at the engine nacelle and 9 per cent at the tip. Despite possessing a thrust/weight ratio some 30 per cent greater than that of the German fighter, the Airacomet was about 209kph (130mph) slower, accounted for to some extent by the 65 per cent greater wing area of the Bell fighter and less than half the wing loading of the Me 262.

The NACA could have assisted wind tunnel tests on scale models but the Army's attitude prevented that. Greater success came with the Lockheed P-80, incorporating information from the NACA. Lockheed had a history of scientifically engineered designs and was well prepared for an elegant solution to the challenge. Clarence 'Kelly' Johnson designed the airframe around the engine rather than build an experimental aircraft with jet propulsion bolted on, as had been the Bell approach. It had been the sluggish performance of the Airacomet that pushed the AAF to seek a more rigorous approach when, on 17 May 1943, its Engineering Division led by Brig. Gen. Franklin O. Carroll brokered discussions between Lockheed and the Air Technical Service Command for the solution which became the P-80.

Below: A German Messerschmitt Me 262A *Schwalbe* at the National Museum of the US Air Force displaying its highly developed fuselage and clean wing with sectionalised Junkers Jumo 004 engine. *Clemence Vasters*

The NACA was still not aware of any work on jet aircraft other than design studies and the Committee was not made privy to the fast pace of development. The level of secrecy was so complete that the two sections of General Electric working on the engine were unaware of each other's existence. When interviewed many years later, several of those who worked on the Bell and Lockheed projects said that they believed the level of security was about that of the Manhattan Project for the first atomic bombs. Surprisingly, the 'civilian' NACA failed to acquire security clearance for the jet programme, creating resentment and difficulty among the few who knew something was going on.

While working alongside the armed services on several important military projects, only the Navy had that 'special relationship', despite the fact that lower levels of contact worked closely together. Even as late as June 1943 the brittle relationship with the senior AAF leadership left the NACA disadvantaged with their own plans for a dedicated research aircraft which the AAF had been actively discouraging. NACA chairman Jerome Hunsaker expressed the bitterness which all felt, admitting that 'The idea that they (the British) are supplying us (the United States) everything they have (about turbojet development) does not apply to NACA but may apply to the services'.

The NACA was driven by aerodynamics and had been late in developing a propulsion research facility which, when built, focused its attention on reciprocating engines to further the war effort. Once aware of progress already achieved in Germany and Britain, the NACA was swift to compensate for a decided lack of foresight. By the end of 1943 it was up to date and seized the initiative. Accepting the inevitable, the Army swore a picked NACA team to secrecy and disclosed a test cell for engine development at West Lynn, Massachusetts, where GE had successfully run their first I-A turbojet engine on 18 April 1942.

After the Japanese surrender in September 1945, NACA's Cleveland AERL facility began a transformation as deep and enduring as anything the Committee would face for the next 13 years, when it metamorphosed into NASA. Late in 1945 the facility began switching to a concentrated research effort across a broad spectrum of jet and rocket motor engineering and design. Jets, turbojets, ramjets and liquid propellant rockets took hold as priorities for new and capable propulsion systems grew.

In late 1943 Bell refined the design for a twin-jet escort fighter powered by the General Electric XJ33-GE-5 centrifugal flow turbojet with a rated thrust of 17,792N (4,000lb). The AAF ordered two prototypes of what it designated the XP-83-BE, a design headed by Robert J. Woods. The aircraft borrowed a lot from the Airacomet, being of all-metal, stressed-skin, semi-monocoque design with a straight wing at the mid-fuselage position. The two engines sat under each wing root and snugly to the sides of the fuselage, minimising asymmetric thrust in the event of a single engine failure. The high-set tail was well clear of the hot exhaust gases and the aircraft had a tricycle undercarriage.

The first prototype took to the air on 25 February 1944, piloted by Bell's test pilot Jack Woolams. It was seriously underpowered and suffered from the same failings that had dented confidence in jet propulsion – only engineers could see the potential while the operational staff felt it a poor successor to high-performance fighters powered by conventional reciprocating engines. Nevertheless, it kept Bell Aircraft in the forefront of technological development and that would augur well for it as the NACA and the Air Force tackled a looming challenge – compressibility.

Below: Chairman of the NACA, Jerome Hunsaker lamented the lack of shared information from the armed services regarding the large volume of information provided by the British. *Author's collection*

Chapter Two

Cracking Compressibility

The effect of compressibility at the transonic region was demonstrated on 4 November 1941, when Lockheed test pilot Ralph Virden was flying the first of 13 pre-production YP-38 Lightning, twin-boom heavy fighters (39-689). During a high-speed dive he encountered compressibility at Mach 0.675, forming a shock wave over the inboard wing sections between the cockpit and the two engine nacelles. The inboard wing stalled, cutting off the airstream over the horizontal tail and causing what appeared to be severe flutter. The oscillation broke the tail causing the nose to pitch down (known as Mach 'tuck') and the aircraft to increase the angle of dive from an altitude of 457m (1,500ft).

Compressibility had been predicted but without any data from wind tunnels the precise location of its origin on the airframe and specific strength of the shock waves were unknown. In an attempt to offset the effects, the tail had been raised higher and tabs installed which, in the case of the YP-38 crash, only served to amplify the effect. The aircraft crashed into the home of Jack Jensen, 1147 Elm Street, Glendale, California, killing the pilot. At the time this was not talked about and, with America pitched into the Second World War a month later, priorities were elsewhere. Nevertheless, future aircraft incorporated balances to partially offset the ef-

Above: An early casualty of compressibility, Ralph Burwell Virden seen here with a Boeing Model 40 mail-plane. *San Diego Air & Space Museum* fect. But, paradoxically, compressibility close to the transonic had been known, and encountered, for several years.

Responding to the crash, Johnson sent the problem to the NACA and a solution was proposed by creating an 'all-flying' tail in which the entire surface area with a trim tab could maintain flight control while transiting the lower regions of the transonic. Such a modification, demonstrated to be effective in models tested in the NACA wind tunnels, was too complex and time-consuming a design and manufacturing change to implement. With war raging in Europe and the Pacific and an urgent need for combat aircraft, the NACA came up with a simpler solution.

Langley had begun evaluating the problem in the 2.4m (8ft) High Speed Tunnel using 1/6th scale models of the P-38. By attaching a small wedge-shaped flap to the underside of the wings, which automatically deployed at the onset of compressibility, some of the lost lift could be gained back allowing full control to be restored. Some commonly held interpretations claimed that this helped slow the aircraft down but that was not so and failed to understand the real cause of the instability. Langley handed the tests over to its Ames facility where the same models were subject to verification in their 4.8m (16ft) High Speed Tunnel (HST), a facility already working to support development of the aircraft, and in the Full Scale Tunnel.

Above: The building at 1520 H St, NW, Washington, DC, was headquarters for NASA from 1958 to 1961. Built in 1820 by Richard Cutts, from 1837 until 1849 it was occupied by Dolly Madison, wife of President James Madison. In 1886 it was the home of the appropriately named Cosmos Club. *Author's Collection*

The Langley 2.4m HST was increasingly committed to research on high-speed aerofoil configurations as part of a concerted attempt to apply theory to experiment, defining appropriate shapes for high-speed wings. As part of this work, largely at the direction of the NACA's John Stack, theoretical calculations appeared to show that lift and the control moment could be improved through inverted and negative camber. Stack became increasingly involved in compressibility research and this, when applied to the P-38, appeared to run counter to the accepted principle, which was that positive camber increased lift by causing relatively lower pressure on the upper surface.

Below: The YP-38 Lightning in the Langley Full Scale Tunnel for aerodynamic tests on the control surfaces. Aircraft of this era were pushing toward the transonic and experiencing the effect of shock waves. *NACA*

Left: In support of the Compressibility Research Division at Langley, H. Julian Allen from NACA-Ames served on a panel set up by George Lewis to study the effects of transonic flight. *NACA*

The calculations ran counter to every instinct of an aerodynamic design engineer and it was largely dismissed as inapplicable to the search for supercritical performance, even sparking jokes about flying aircraft upside down as they approached the transonic! In reality, the aerodynamicists had very little data to go on but found in the search for a solution an incentive to expand their base of experimentation and test. Stack forged ahead, searching for a way in which an aircraft could pass through the transonic regime under full control.

Work started in July 1943 with the formation of the Compressibility Research Division (CRD) at Langley. This work was coordinated five months later when George Lewis put together a panel to bring together all elements within the NACA committed to high-speed research. They included Stack, H. Julian Allen from Ames, Abraham 'Abe' Silverstein from the AERL in Cleveland and Russell G. Robinson from NACA headquarters. John Stack argued the case for a special experimental aircraft but George Lewis was opposed to that. But Stack was the more powerful and unremitting personality, devoid of any political agenda and forthright in his determination to get his research aircraft approved. Stack began 'back of the envelope' calculations for a suitable design.

Initial outlines were compiled by Milton Davidson and Harold J. Turner, work which was completed by mid-1943, coincident with the formation of the CRD. John Stack began to break down AAF opposition and to recruit support from those in the military who had always felt there was a requirement for a research aircraft. Those included Ezra Kotcher, chief of aeronautical research programmes at the Air Materiel Command (AMC) and a graduate in mechanical engineering from the University of California. As early as 1939 he had tried to bend the official view in support of a transonic research aircraft.

A staunch advocate, the Navy's NACA liaison officer Capt. Walter Diehl applied pressure for such work to be approved. The day was not far off when naval combat aircraft would fly and fight across the transonic regime. On 15 March 1944 two meetings were held at Langley, one chaired by Diehl, the other by the AAF liaison, Col. Carl Greene from AMC. They were there to discuss a cooperative venture between the NACA, the Navy and the Army Air Forces using Stack's envelope calculations as a starting point. This was the formal beginning to the emergence of the X-series research projects.

The wind tunnels required to obtain essential design information did not exist. Preliminary work had included dropping models from a set height and measuring their responses. This drop-body work was soon terminated when it was found that there was no means of measuring the high-speed flow on such a body. Incentive to resume drop-body testing came from William S. Farren of the RAE in Britain. Farren was in Washington DC giving the annual Wright Brothers Lecture and explained that they had dropped weighted bodies from extreme height using advanced techniques with radar and electronic telemetering instruments, unknown to the Americans at the time.

On 25 March 1944 the NACA approved the use of this method, incorporating the British principles applied to American equipment. These tests were more successful, with instrumented sensors developed by Langley's Edmund C. Buckley, transmitting data on radio signals. It was from this data that the NACA got what it needed to determine drag and required power levels for a transonic research aircraft. It also cemented an enduring relationship between the NACA and

Right: Abraham 'Abe' Silverstein joined the transonic effects study panel from the Aircraft Engine Research Laboratory and would play a major role in experimental aircraft designed for transonic and supersonic research. *NACA*

Above: The British introduced the NACA to telemetered data collection using drop-models. The technique evolved with the use of F-82 Double Mustang fighters for carrying scale models of transonic research concepts. *Author's collection*

the RAE. These tests would be a permanent part of test programmes into the 1950s, other aircraft including the F-82 Double Mustang being employed for high altitude drops.

By this time numerous aircraft were known to have encountered the compressibility problem. The laminar-flow wing of the P-51D, for instance, was able to keep the shock waves under control and provide stability of flight in a dive to Mach 0.81, which pilot Charles Yeager achieved in a vertical dive, while test pilot Bob Hoover achieved Mach 0.805 in a P-47. These encounters, most of which ended in a crash and the death of the pilot, focused attention in the mind of Robert R. Gilruth at Langley, where he discovered that the flow fields around an aircraft diving close to the transonic were up to twenty times greater than those observed on models in wind tunnels.

*Below:*While diving a Republic P-47 like this one shown here, pilot Robert Hoover experienced the effect of compressibility at Mach 0.805. *USAF*

Gilruth had a creative flare for innovative thinking and he crafted a small model of the aerofoil and placed that perpendicular to the top of the wing of a P-51D at just at the right location where it would encounter the supersonic flow under constant velocity. On loan, the P-51D was flown by a NACA test pilot in a dive under controlled conditions in which the instruments were monitored on the ground by a group of specialists. They could immediately advise the pilot of danger if they observed a combination of readings that indicated an imminent loss of control.

As the aircraft dived almost vertically it reached Mach 0.81 but the airflow across the model's wing passed through the transonic region and up to a calculated Mach 1.4. A balance device in the aircraft's gun bay made measurements recorded on the model and transmitted from small sensors installed within the pylon supporting it on top of the main wing. Assisted by Melvin N. Gough, Gilruth calculated the forces

Above: The F-82 had been adapted to carry a radar unit on the bridging wing between the two fuselage sections and this mounting was used to lift drop-models. *USAF*

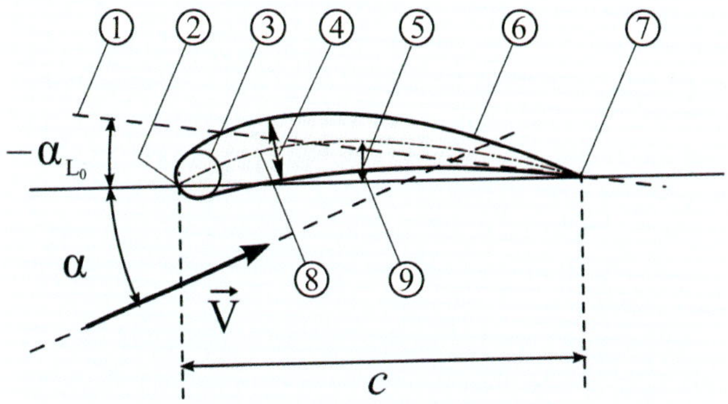

The identification and lexicon of terminology for an aerofoil as used variously throughout this book includes the following: 1, the line of zero lift; 2, the leading edge of the wing; 3, the circular nose section defined by radius; 4, the measurement point for maximum thickness of the wing; 5, the camber of the wing; 6, the upper surface of the wing; 7, the trailing edge; 8, the mean line of the wing camber; and 9, the lower surface of the wing. *Author's collection*

and flow angles of the airstream under different velocities. By measuring the flow above the wing he was able to demonstrate the changes to the supersonic flow as it moved away from the model.

But not everyone was pleased with this, other engineers believing passionately in obtaining data from wind tunnels. Work continued however with different thicknesses of wing models, assembling the most comprehensive information anywhere on transonic airflow and the challenges to developing a full-scale research aircraft. It was through these real-world tests that the NACA reached their conclusion that a thin wing was optimum for research into the transonic, ideally with a thickness ratio of 5 per cent, when most conventional aircraft had ratios of 12-15 per cent.

During the second half of 1944 the shift toward the enhanced use of models for aerodynamic data grew and by December the acting engineer responsible for all research at Langley (his title actually being Engineer-In-Charge) formed a dedicated team committed to using rocket-powered models fired high into the atmosphere. As the war began to draw to a close, a range of rocket and missile programmes emerged as potential post-war development programmes. With its interests in aerodynamics, Langley alloyed the work from Gilruth with that activity.

Below: Robert R. 'Bob' Gilruth would pioneer the use of rocket-borne models of high-speed aerofoil and fuselage shapes, eventually setting up the Pilotless Atmospheric Aircraft Division at Langley. Eventually, this would lead to design concepts for manned space vehicles. *NASA*

The use of small rockets to accelerate models to supersonic velocities would quickly be replaced by the arrival of the first generation of dedicated transonic and supersonic research aircraft. The missile work would bleed away into what would, in 1946, become the Pilotless Aircraft Research Division (PARD) under Gilruth as its team leader. At this time all missile work was referred to as 'pilotless aircraft'. Despite enormous activity in the field, the word 'rocket' still attracted negative connotations.

Setting parameters

Key to the future transonic, supersonic and hypersonic research aircraft was the ability to collect on-board data and transmit it to receiving stations on the ground. No suitable commercial equipment was available as a complete unit and the job of building a bespoke set for the drop tests was given to M. J. Stoller, the head of the Radio Control and Telemetering Section. Working with C. A. Taylor, A. Ruvin and H. H. Youngblood, Buckley integrated existing components on a breadboard assembly and built measurement capabilities by registering the linear movement of an iron core set within an inductance coil to modulate the frequency of a subcarrier oscillator.

The team already had oscillators operating in the 160kc range and were able to use these adapted for a four-channel set which used frequencies of 140kc, 150kc, 160kc and 170kc. To increase this to a six-channel system, 10kc and 180kc oscillators were added. The output of the FM oscillators modulated the amplitude of the main carrier, 118mc being selected simply because of their availability from commercial television sets and this became known as an FM/AM system. The initial four-channel system was completed by the autumn of 1944 and the first flight on a free-falling body occurred on 1 December. Due to a misunderstanding as to the precise release time for the instrumented test body, only the last ten seconds of the drop were recorded and only then when Ruvin saw the data beginning to flow and realised that the pilot had dropped it too early!

But it was a success and so began a protracted series of tests with this equipment and the instrumented test-drop bodies. This was a seminal turning point in directing the assembly of transonic data from extrapolated wind tunnel tests, where the choking effect of the narrow tunnels inhibited realistic data-gathering, on to physical bodies recording flow patterns and shock waves from real objects accelerated to high subsonic and transonic velocities.

While the NACA was developing effective ways to obtain actual, real-world data on high subsonic aerodynamics, on 30 June 1944 the Navy Bureau of Aeronautics (BuAer) requested assistance from the NACA on experimental ramjets, pulsejet engines and help with development of experimental vehicles. This was directly in support of the Navy's Gorgon programme, an air-to-air guided missile powered by a small turbojet engine which had been underway at the Naval Aircraft Factory (NAF) since receiving approval from the BuAer on 19 July 1943.

The AAF had not entirely disowned research into new forms of propulsion, the Army being particularly interested in rockets for jet-assisted-take-off (JATO) – avoiding the term 'rocket' which had received universal ridicule as something belonging to the fictional world of Buck Rogers comics. The Guggenheim Aeronautical Laboratory at the California Institute of Technology (GALCIT) had conducted extensive research and development into JATO packs for assisting large and heavily-laden aircraft to take off within a reasonable distance.

When thinking of high-speed flight research, attention generally focuses on the NACA and the Air Force. But the Navy had an early interest in new and unproven technology. It had sought assistance from the GALCIT group in 1939 when Lt. Cdr. Delmar S. Fahrney approached them about a potential anti-aircraft and anti-ship missile. Fahrney had become aware of the work of Frank J. Malina at the California

Below: Architect of the slotted-throat wind tunnel, John Stack was instrumental in developing aerodynamic theory to more effectively produce a solution, including the future Skystreak and Skyrocket. *NACA*

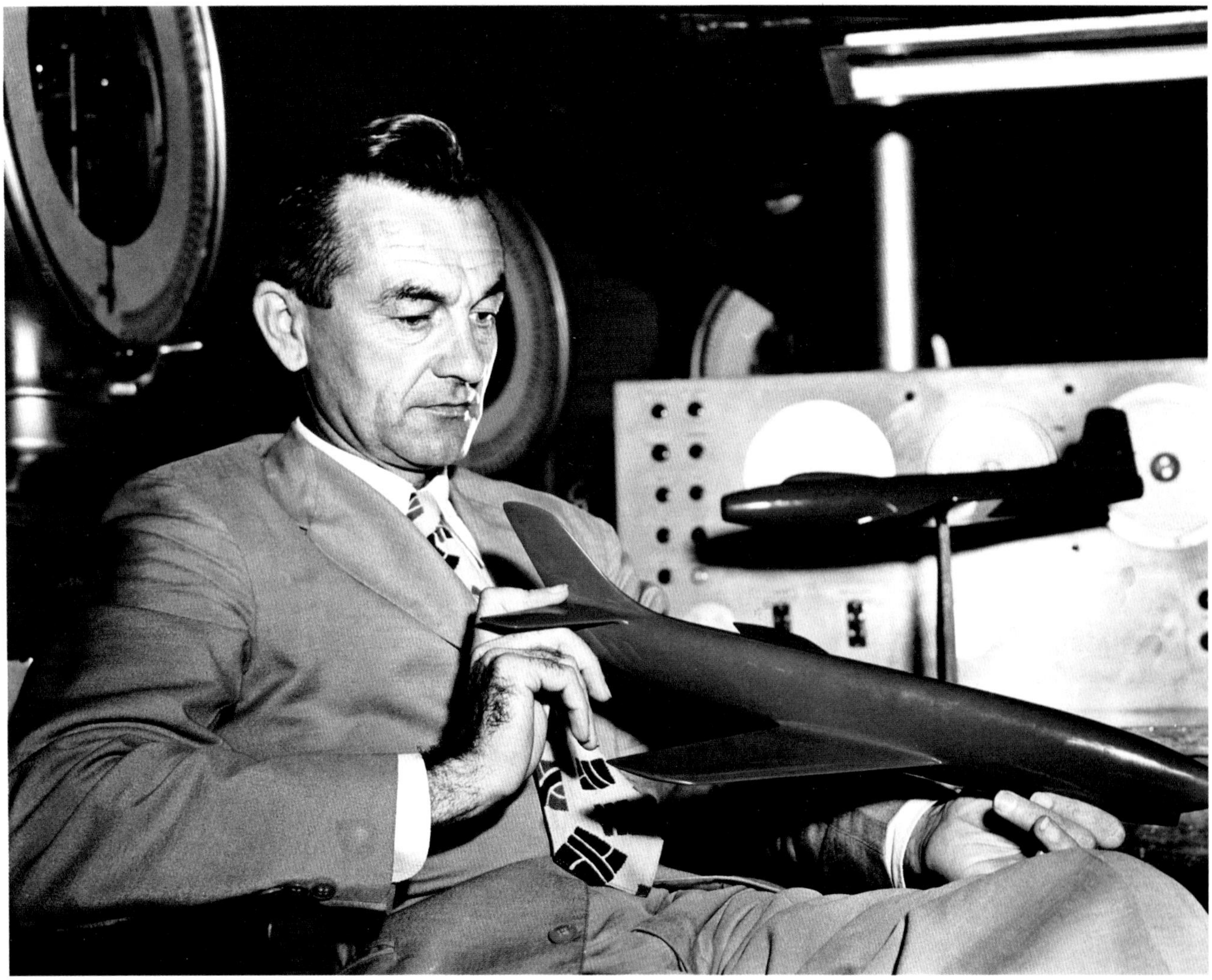

Institute of Technology and proposed an integration of jet or rocket propulsion, radio control with television guidance and a warhead capable of taking out airborne or surface targets.

Due to binding pressures and the official duties of his office, not until May 1943 could Fahrney team up with Ivan H. Driggs, a civilian scientist at BuAer, and develop a plan which he proposed to his superiors. Approval for development and a funded programme came two months later on 19 July, the date that the NAF became part of the Naval Air Material Center (NAMC), situated alongside the Philadelphia Naval Yard. The Gorgon programme evolved away from turbojet to rocket propulsion and epitomised the forward-thinking mindset of the Navy leadership.

By late 1944, the Navy had offered Gorgon to the NACA as a rocket-boosted carrier for instrumented aerofoils, which would provide the Navy with research data on high-speed flight. Twenty Gorgon III-C missiles were delivered to Langley for flight tests at a station on Wallops Island, Virginia. The solid propellant rocket motors fell into three classes: a GALCIT-developed composition of 75 per cent potassium or ammonium perchlorate and 25 per cent asphalt and oil, manufactured by Westinghouse; a composition of 45 per cent ammonium picrate and potassium nitrate with a resin binder, produced by Monsanto or the National Defense Research Committee (NDRC); and a double-base propellant consisting of nitroglycerine and nitrocellulose with an assortment of binders similar to British cordite, which had 9 per cent carbonite.

Reluctance by the AAF to involve itself with a dedicated transonic experimental research aircraft was not matched by its pressure for the NACA to help it design a new guided missile for countering the Kamikaze threat against naval task forces in the Pacific Ocean. It wanted an air-to-air weapon to knock down the approaching piloted suicide fighters and in early 1944 the Hughes Aircraft Company had been approached to build one. That proposal was submitted and Carl Babberger, a former NACA employee, visited Langley on 8 August to recruit the cooperation of Robert T. Jones in designing the control system. Due to its relative proximity to

Below: Under evaluation at the Naval Air Material Test Center, Pont Mugu, California, a Consolidated PB4Y-2 carries a CTYV-N-2 Gorgon missile. The nose of this aircraft came from a PB4Y-1. *Author's collection*

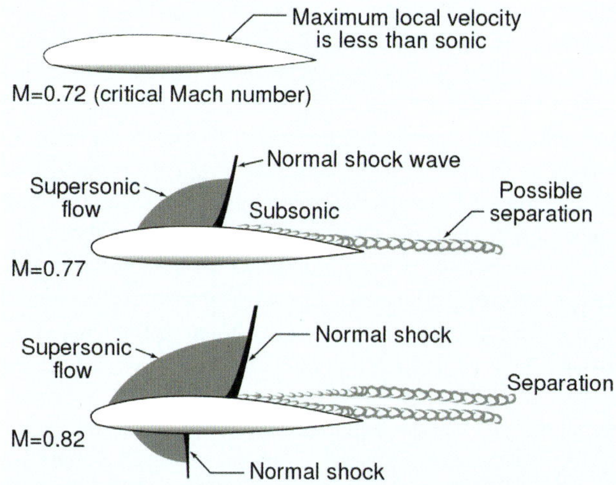

The critical Mach number is one where some part of the airframe experiences the speed of sound and forms a shock wave at the point where it collapses as it encounters subsonic flow. The shock wave grows in strength and moves progressively aft on the wing surface as the speed increases, eventually resulting in flow separation. *Federal Aviation Administration*

Hughes in California, the Ames facility had already begun wind tunnel testing of possible configurations.

By a circuitous, back-door route, the AAF found itself requesting the NACA to begin a research programme (MX-570) for free-flight trials of test models powered by rocket motors. The AAF Air Technical Service Command had approved Jones' proposal and designated the missile JB-3 Tiamat. In a complete reversal of its reluctance to get involved with the NACA in experimental designs, the AAF had unwittingly opened the door to working with the NACA on rocket-powered aerodynamic vehicles. And in a reversal of its less than willing cooperation on such projects, the request to the NACA for these test flights singled out Jones for permanent allocation to the effort, due to 'his untiring efforts and the inconveniences to which he has been subjected'.

As the war began to wind along to its final and furious conclusion, the approach date when the AAF would separate from the Army and become a force in its own right was matched by a wave of cooperation which overwhelmed the previous history of resistance to experimental research programmes. With a range of jet-powered combat aircraft on the horizon and the need to more fully understand the transonic regime, the AAFs were urgently in need of information about the transonic flight regime already encountered by a few, a large proportion of whom had died in the process.

The meeting between Army Air Force, Navy and NACA personnel on 15 March 1944 was the first occasion in which all significant parties came together to discuss a future plan for research aircraft and a scientific understanding of the transonic region. It would set the tone for the next two decades of research and scientific exploration of flight regimes from high subsonic to low hypersonic speeds. But while Maj. Gen. Oliver P. Echols, assistant chief of staff at AAF headquarters had opposed the decision to have the AAF build a transonic research aircraft, Ezra Kotcher consolidated the partnership with the NACA. From the outset it was clear that the NACA would have to make the final decisions regarding configuration, powerplant and test schedules.

The conservative engineers and scientists at the NACA were inherently opposed to the use of rocket motors for aircraft on the basis that there was little control over thrust and that they posed a serious risk to the pilot. They favoured turbojets, despite the lack of power believed to be ideal for transonic research and their unreliability – at least in 1944. The transition toward full support for a research aircraft occurred during a round of meetings on 13-14 December 1944 when Kotcher put his full weight behind a rocket-powered transonic research aircraft. It would be known as the XS-1 (Experimental Sonic-1), about which more later on in this chapter.

The NACA had proposed a turbojet-powered aircraft but now Kotcher felt this was too conservative and pushed the discussion toward an aircraft capable of Mach 1.2 – fully supersonic. The explanation for the change of mind was clear; the Army wanted to direct the requirement and set down the specification by themselves and without the NACA involved. It was the first indicator of a cultural split between the Army Air Forces and the NACA. Almost immediately, the AAF started negotiations with Bell for the XS-1. Stack was not content with this imposition and got in touch with the Navy to sound out their own plans.

Not content to follow the AAF's ideas, several months earlier Stack had sought out George Lewis and the Navy's Walter Diehl and sent his engineer Milton Davidson to Washington DC to sit down with the Bureau of Aeronautics and discuss a transonic research aircraft of their own, one powered by an air-breathing engine. Bureau engineer Abraham Hyatt suggested a combined Navy-NACA research programme which could satisfy both parties. But the Navy proposed a turbojet aircraft and made some minor changes to the configuration already drawn up by Stack.

Above: A progressive organisation pushing hard for research into transonic and supersonic flight, the US Naval Aircraft Factory in Philadelphia, Pennsylvania, had been at the forefront of shipboard aviation since 1918 and would provide welcome support to the NACA. *US Navy*

It would be a very different project to the XS-1 planned by the AAF. It would aim for a maximum speed up to but not exceeding the transonic and it would be closer to the design of a conventional aircraft, moving it closer in concept to an operational type than a purely experimental research aircraft. Moreover, it would take off and land under its own power; the XS-1 was already being seen as air-launched due to the short-duration burn of its rocket motor. But the inevitable conclusion to this energetic year was that, by the end of 1944, the NACA now found itself with not one but two experimental research aircraft programmes, neither of which was under its exclusive control.

Designed for test

In short order, the Navy decided upon a range of requirements to define what the aircraft should look like. It had to be a pure research tool unencumbered by military requirements but carrying a single pilot plus 227kg (500lb) of test instrumentation. It had to be able to take off from a runway under its own power and be capable of maximum speed on existing powerplants. No top speed was stipulated. Neither the Navy nor the NACA had defined the specifics of the requirement or a specification. The aircraft would be built by industry and that would require bids against a particular set of broad guidelines and requirements rather than definitive goals, yet to be written.

During these closing months of 1944, the NACA leaned most favourably toward the Navy project since it most closely resembled the type of aircraft they had wanted all along. They were not the only ones. One of those privy to the deliberations of late 1944 was L. Eugene Root, the chief aerody-

Left: Famous for having designed a wide range of Douglas aircraft for the Navy, Ed Heinemann played a seminal role in the development of both the Skystreak and Skyrocket research aircraft. *Author's collection*

namicist with Douglas Aircraft at its El Segundo, California, facility. On a visit to the Bureau of Aeronautics he obtained the general requirement and, on reporting this back to his company, the decision was made to put in a bid to build the aircraft. The preliminary proposal was put together by project engineer Robert Donovan, under the general supervision of Ed Heinemann and Leo Devlin.

Taking the Navy/NACA at their word, Douglas chose the most powerful engine then in development for the AAF, the General Electric TG-180 turbojet with an estimated thrust of 17,790N (4,000lb). Douglas was very well placed to get the job. There had been some preparatory work at the BuAer, when Milton Davidson had been seconded from Langley to Washington DC to work with the Navy's Ivan Driggs on drawing up a rough specification for a transonic research aircraft. Discussions got down to the detail – the Navy wanted side inlets for the engine, leaving the front of the fuselage free for armament, while Davidson and his colleagues at Langley favoured a nose inlet. Considerations such as this countered the ultimate edict not to compromise the design through considerations of weaponry.

Douglas had a reputation for possessing a highly competent and skilled engineering and design team, employing only the best and expecting perfection. It was that approach which provided the armed services with a satisfying range of aircraft such as the DC-3, A-20 Havoc, SBD Dauntless dive-bombers for the Navy and the A-26 for the Army Air Forces. Their reputation was high and they had produced more than 20,000 aircraft by the end of the war. But Heinemann was a key player in getting the design of the research aircraft shaped for the Navy/NACA requirement closer to the original purpose set out by John Stack. Nevertheless, it was still not a truly transonic test platform, requirements being more in the category of guidelines than elements of a specification.

Above: Achieving a compromise between different requirements and design preferences, the Douglas D-558-1 Skystreak was the Navy's bid to secure a strong presence in transonic research. *NACA*

The requirement was conservative and not at all indicative of the more aggressive approach taken by the Army Air Forces with the XS-1. The Navy was already looking to field an operational jet fighter of its own, despite initial trials with AAF fighters showing the drawbacks with early jet engines. On 5 September 1944, BuAer released its first fighter competition since 1940 and most of the requirements had been based on the performance of the German Me 262 and on the Me 163 rocket fighter. McDonnell made a bid with its Model 28 design powered by a single TG-180 and said by the company to be capable of 895kph (556mph) at sea level. The Navy would introduce this as the subsonic FH-1 Phantom, its

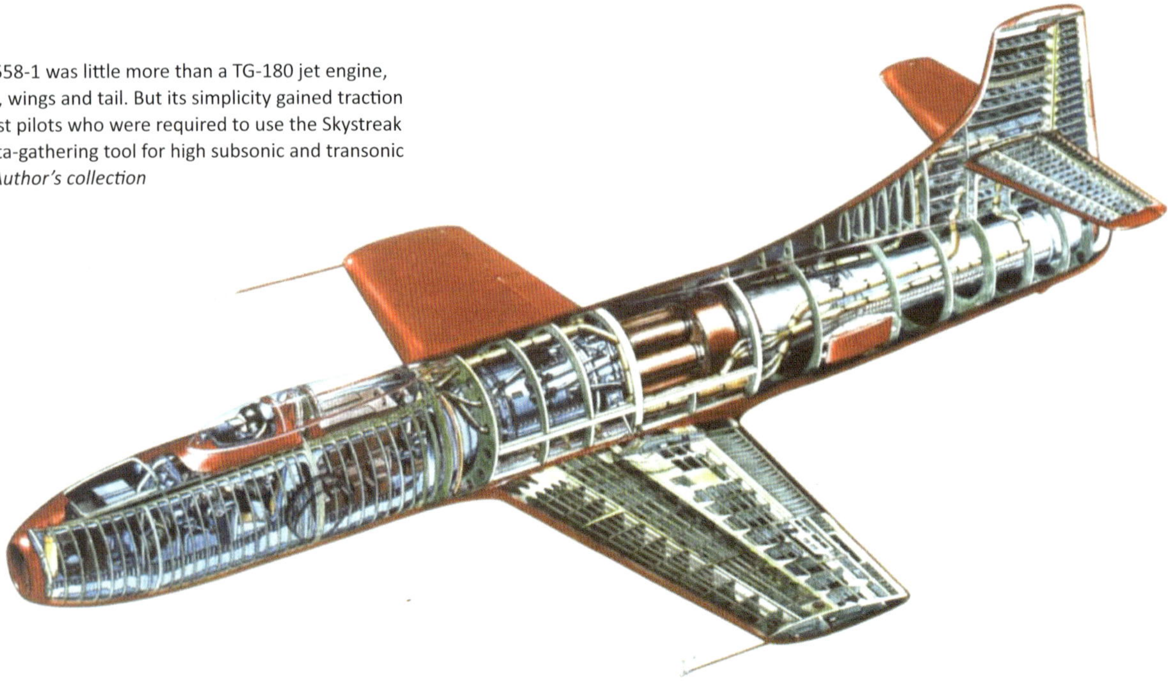

The D-558-1 was little more than a TG-180 jet engine, cockpit, wings and tail. But its simplicity gained traction with test pilots who were required to use the Skystreak as a data-gathering tool for high subsonic and transonic flight. *Author's collection*

first jet fighter, and go on to procure McDonnell's F2H Banshee while it pursued a separate strand of research into the transonic.

For the transonic research aircraft Douglas proposed three separate configurations for what was designated Model D-558 and it selected three separate wing shapes: a NACA 65-110 aerofoil with a 10 per cent thickness/chord (t/c) ratio as the default; a NACA 16-008 tapering from 8 per cent at the root to 6 per cent in NACA 16-006 at the tip; and a NACA 2417 aerofoil at the root, with a 17 per cent t/c ratio, tapering to a NACA 2413 at the tip with a 13 per cent ratio. This was a noted departure from convention in that most high-speed combat aircraft of the period had a thickness/chord ratio of 14-18 per cent. This was a method in which the drag of the wing, the fuselage and the tail would be measured separately and added together with little or no consideration for the drag of the entire aircraft.

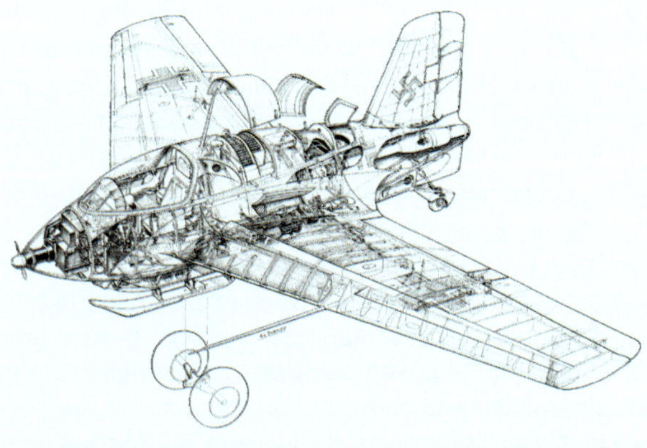

When the US Navy wrote the specification for a rocket-powered interceptor it leaned heavily on the German Me 163 for ideas but technical limitations soon replaced that with more practical solutions. *A. L. Bentley*

Initially, the Douglas proposal was for the Navy to order six aircraft, each employing a different wing and engine duct configuration, powered by a TG-180 for flight evaluation to Mach 0.89 and later with a Westinghouse 24C turbojet plus supplementary rocket propulsion for flights up to Mach 1. The engineering team calculated that for supersonic flight the entire external area would have to be completely redesigned, and all the determining criteria for shape would have to be reset. BuAer was determined to cede full design control to the NACA and for that Douglas shared Langley's concept and objectives for the type. The formal request from BuAer for development of the test aircraft was dated 19 December 1944.

Douglas completed its proposal in January 1945, with supporting drawings by company engineer Robert G. Smith, who was also a highly talented draughtsman and artist. The essential characteristics of the aircraft were defined simply: create the smallest possible aerodynamic structure around the existing TG-180 engine, with a bubble canopy protruding as little as possible above the fuselage line; set a straight wing low on the fuselage, with a span of 7.6m (25ft) and pronounced dihedral; set the horizontal stabiliser high on the tail and limit overall length to 10.7m (35ft).

The formal submission was delivered on 13 April 1945 in which Douglas suggested a three-phase programme: first, six aircraft would be built and flown, producing flight data to Mach 0.89; second, Westinghouse 24C turbojet engines and rocket motors would be installed to push the flight envelope to Mach 1; finally, based on results from the first six aircraft, Douglas would prepare the detailed engineering design and a full-scale mock-up for an aircraft capable of combat and operational service with the Navy. It said it could do this for just under $6.9million and deliver the first aircraft for flight within a year of go-ahead.

It took just thirteen days for the Bureau of Aeronautics to declare its approval and, on 26 April, to accept the broad outline, with reservations over the use of a rocket motor until further analysis had been conducted and it had seen flight results. Formal approval was provided on 9 May but, recognising that the AAF too had its experimental research aircraft under the XS-1 programme, BuAer maintained close contact with Wright Field so as not to duplicate work or potential research tasks. Within a few weeks, Douglas had a 25 per cent scale model under test. The NACA did, however, object to the third phase in which a proto-combat aircraft would be developed from this research, sticking rigidly to its desire for a purely scientific and engineering tool.

With the war in Europe over, a selection of aeronautical engineers and scientists were sent to that continent to examine the advanced work conducted by the Germans. From Douglas, Root and A. M. O. Smith were sent across as members of the Naval Technical Mission. What they found would have a significant effect on the D-558 programme. Their place was temporarily taken by Kermit E. Van Every, then assistant chief of aerodynamics at the Douglas El Segundo facility and now managing some serious concerns from the Navy, articulated by Capt. Walter Diehl.

Above: A key feature of the Skystreak design was that it had changeable wings with different NACA section profiles, six aircraft being placed under contract on 22 June 1945. *NACA*

The D558 Skystreak

The original proposal had shortcomings regarding its suitability for research work, Diehl pointing out that it did not have sufficient volume or weight capacity for test instrumentation. Nor did the Navy feel that Douglas had paid sufficient attention to the needs of the NACA and that, as the majority of information tasking the Navy to formulate the design came from them, Douglas should take guidance from the NACA as to the overall configuration. The years of close association between the Navy and the NACA had paid off. It was this two-pronged concern that had moved Douglas to the three-phase programme.

By March 1945 the general outline and capabilities of the D-558 had been completed and all considerations accommodated. The aircraft would have load factor of 18g (compared to 12-14g for a conventional aircraft), a gross weight of 3,400kg (7,500lb), an aspect ratio of 4.17 and a wing area of 13.935m^2 (150ft^2) supporting a maximum speed of 1,005kph (625mph) at sea-level and Mach 0.84 at 7,620m (25,000ft). Fuel would be in integral wing tanks. Wings and tail surfaces were to be removable for alternate planforms and both nose and side air inlets would be provided. For pilot safety, the entire forward nose section containing the cockpit would be detachable.

Very little reference information existed regarding escape from an aircraft at the transonic region. Heinemann suggested an escape pod. In the mid-1940s, however, the way to do that safely was difficult to envisage. Initially, it was thought that the separated capsule could be retarded by speed brakes, allowing the pilot to leave the capsule at a speed no greater than 563kph (350mph) but the complexity of building that in to the airframe proved risky. It would impose engineering challenges which would make the operation unsafe. Drag parachutes were looked at but nobody knew if it would be possible to produce such a retarding device for deployment at transonic speeds.

The problem with a separable capsule included the difficulty of designing controls passing across the mechanical divide which could operate normally but sever cleanly in the event of a jettisoning nose section. And to do that without compromising successful operation of the controls in normal flight and not becoming entangled at separation. The solution involved a novel design whereby quick-disconnect electrical lines were installed and push-pull controls attached to drums on opposing sides of the disconnect plane, with a tongue-and-groove attachment to inhibit any hang-ups.

The contract was awarded to Douglas on 22 June 1945 involving production of the six aircraft, the first three with BuAer numbers 37970, 37971 and 37972. Under the plan, the first four aircraft would have the default wing (NACA 65-110), the fifth would have the NACA 2417-13 wing and the sixth the NACA 16-008 wing. They would be called Skystreak. All would carry a redesigned horizontal tail which could be adjusted in pitch by the pilot, a feature which had been developed earlier as a candidate solution for the P-38E and which would also be employed, as an all-flying tail on the XS-1.

At the first mock-up inspection held 2-4 July, the NACA found fault with a wide range of design details but these were quickly rectified by Douglas. The major visual difference was that the side inlets, planned for all but the second aircraft with a nose intake, were dropped. This decision was commensurate with the realisation that jet-powered Navy fighters were already underway and that there would be no need to compromise the original purpose of the D-558. Apart from which, the Navy deferred to the NACA on all major aspects of the design.

There had been a formidable presence of NACA engineers at the mock-up inspection and there was further discussion regarding the possibility of fitting a swept-back wing to one of the Skystreaks. The aeronautical industry was awash with excitement over the German research on wing sweep and how it was part of the key to successful transonic flight. While in Germany, Root and Smith had been astonished at the advanced research conducted during and immediately prior to the war years, returning with data that appeared to verify the projections made by several NACA engineers, including Stack, that this was a possible solution to the compressibility problem.

During 14 August 1945, while detailed design on the D-558 was underway during the national V-J Day holiday, a team of Navy/NACA specialists visited Douglas for the second mock-up review to check on the changes requested the previous month at the first inspection. During this three-day activity they asked for a specification covering a second research aircraft with swept wings. Reports from the Naval Technical Mission trawling through the German research programmes were convinced that a straight-wing approach was limiting and would restrict research by adopting too much conventional theory in the design of high-speed aircraft.

Despite measured strides being taken with increased performance and reliability from jet engines, truly supersonic flight would require a more powerful propulsion system which, at the time, could only be provided by turbojet and/or rocket power. Douglas had already done some limited work on redefining the fuselage of the D-558 for swept wings but the volume of work required argued for a completely new configuration. There was just no way the original shape could accommodate a new wing and rocket power. The NACA had foreseen this need and the German research results verified that conclusion. The only logical way to test that idea was to convert the contract for the last three Skystreaks into a swept-wing version of the first three. The Navy liked the idea and a contract was eventually awarded, on 29 January 1946, for a new aircraft, substituting the last three Skystreaks for a new version, the D-558-2, re-designating the original model as the D-558-1.

The new, swept-wing model would have a Westinghouse J34-WE-40 as well as a Reaction Motors XLR-8-RM-5 rocket motor with four chambers, the same as that selected for the air-launched XS-1 but with a different designation. The D-558-2 would have two air intakes, one each side of the lower forward fuselage behind the cockpit area, which would itself consist of an escape capsule for pilot safety. Nobody had flown a swept-wing aircraft to the transonic zone and a completely redesigned fuselage gave the D-558-2 a distinctly different look to its predecessor.

At first, Douglas looked at the possibility of using the same fuselage shape as that for the straight-wing Skystreak and there were hopes that this might be possible after low speed wind tunnel tests produced positive results. On the engineering side, however, there was insufficient room for both turbojet and rocket engines plus the fuel required for each. The inspection of the new configuration took place on 18-19 March 1946 and revealed the results of a complete redesign by Heinemann's team and aerodynamicist Every. The fuselage was longer, fatter and had a cleaner, circular cross-section but retained the tricycle landing gear.

The purpose of changing the contract and adapting the programme to a two-phase approach shifted the axis of value away from high subsonic and transonic flight speeds into a combined transonic/supersonic research endeavour, primarily for the advantage of the NACA but with benefits for the Navy in keeping pace with the expansion of flight research in the Army. Politically, the timing was critical.

The Army was about to lose control of the Air Forces as it became an independent armed service under a new Department of Defense (DoD), which would see it compete for money during a post-war rundown in government funding for military infrastructure. None of this was of concern or even showed up on the desks of the engineers and scientists working the new programme. For the NACA, it was a vital component of its new relationship with the armed services and that would matter greatly over the coming decade.

Below: Powered by a Westinghouse J34-WE-40 with provision for a single RMI XLR-8 rocket motor, the D-558-2 Skyrocket introduced the new concept of swept wings to the transonic research programme. *NACA*

Chapter Three

Matching the Challenge

America was not alone in seeking a solution to the transonic challenge. In Britain during 1943 the Air Ministry issued specification E.24/43 for a jet-propelled research aircraft capable of exceeding Mach 1. The Royal Aircraft Establishment had already been conducting tests on high-speed flight using a modified Spitfire producing data that indicated various levels of drag, showing that thin wings were one part of the solution to effective transonic flight.

Seeking a contractor to build an experimental aircraft to probe the supersonic flight regime, the Ministry selected Miles, an independent aircraft design and manufacturing company. Already regarded as a talented and innovative outfit, Miles had the facilities and the capability for just such a challenge and there were additional advantages. The project received the highest level of Britain's security classification and that placed extra value on selection of a company which had little or no association with secret projects. There was, however, a transatlantic connection.

On several occasions in the history of US aviation from the time that country went to war in December 1941, the British were regarded as being ahead in the design and development of the jet engine, of technical devices supporting research and data-gathering and with theoretical research into high-speed flight. Due to the level of cooperation between allies pressed together in common interests, the NACA worked with various British institutions to share results and to exchange data. Progress with the jet engine in Britain led to a more general exchange of ideas in science and engineering. The level of cooperation and liaison between the two countries reached a peak in 1943-44 at the time when deeper consideration was being accorded to the challenges of high-subsonic and transonic flight.

The shared data regarding high-speed flight fell within the descriptive purview of the Most Secret category and it is clear that the Army Air Forces came to know of the British work through the NACA. To what degree this influenced their

Above: An artist's view of the second prototype Miles M.52 prepared by S. E. Porter, the technical illustrator for Miles Aircraft Ltd, in late 1945 or early 1946. Note the tiny cockpit. *Miles Aircraft Ltd via Tony Buttler*

Above: The Miles M.52 mock-up displaying the nose section and the annular air intake for the W.2/700 engine around which the fuselage was designed. *Peter Green via Tony Buttler*

decision to follow through is uncertain. Materials pertinent to further research on this in the United States has been either destroyed long ago or lost. Suffice to say that the critical meeting of 15 March 1944 was after a visit from the British to discuss some aspects of the Whittle engine and its production in the United States for early AAF fighter designs. The Air Ministry had insisted that the Americans fully share this information.

In Britain, the supersonic project was designated as the Miles M.52 and the unfortunate story of that fated concept and its cancellation in February 1946 has been well told elsewhere. The sudden and unexpected announcement by the Attlee government to stop work on the project was never completely explained. Politicians excused their decision on the basis that it was a waste of resources at a time when the nation was virtually bankrupt; civil servants doubted that routine supersonic flight would even be possible and government 'spinners' claimed it was inappropriate to subject pilots to such high risks. No post-war government was a friend of the British aviation industry.

Over time, few projects have created so much debate as to who benefited most from the quantity of material exchanged. The Americans certainly received a wide range of research results from the British. Over time, the most hotly contested aspect was the decision over the all-flying tail which was designed into the M.52 and incorporated into the Bell XS-1. As related earlier, that solution to wake turbulence and effective pitch control had already been proposed by the NACA as a solution to compressibility problems with the P-38E Lightning but it was not introduced due to a possible impact slowing production. Yet, beyond the specifics, both the quantity of information supplied by the British and the value it was to the Americans is indisputable.

During the period in which the Navy and the NACA were developing the Skystreak and Skyrocket research aircraft with Douglas, the Army Air Forces were fighting opposition over their preference for a rocket-powered equivalent. But why were there two NACA-supported research projects? The key is in the different objectives behind the respective decisions. The Army saw the XS-1 as a direct path to supersonic research aircraft and the Navy wanted a NACA-led research programme. And there was not a little concern on the part of the AAF that if the Navy was fully involved with the NACA, it just had to have a parallel research programme of its own.

The cultural ideology of the Army and the Navy is almost never mentioned in histories of these research programmes. Discussion of that has no further purpose here other than to explain a persistent competition for support and to acquire assets that directed each to possess, and retain, their independent resources. The AAF was moving toward full independence from the Army and laid claim to the need for scientific and engineering information to help it make appropriate decisions for future specifications involving high-speed combat aircraft. What had seemed inappropriate in wartime was now an essential investment in the anticipated peace to come.

What interested the Army and industry was the vastly superior power/weight ratio of the turbojet and rocket engines, that fact being driven home by Bell engineer Robert Wolff. It was he who first formulated the concept of an integrated AAF/Navy/NACA programme for a transonic research aircraft and in January 1944 the document titled Confidential Technical Instruction 1566 called for such a project. At Wright Field where much of the discussion was held, it was loosely designated as the 'Mach 0.999' study. This was the culmination of several months of study recommending rocket propulsion to take advantage of a greater performance margin, there being little concern over the risks involved. Of which there were a few, not least the general unreliability of such motors and the almost inevitable catastrophe should the rocket stop functioning just at the point of take-off.

It was for this reason, among several, that an air-launched approach was considered preferable, allowing the aircraft the option of gliding down to a safe landing after release from the carrier-plane. However, the incontestable necessity for an air-drop launch was the relatively short burn duration of a rocket motor, given that a small transonic research aircraft would not have the internal volume for a large quantity of rocket propellant and sustained operation of such a motor was impractical; the objective was to acquire data, not flight time. As it was, calculations in advance of the design of the XS-1 showed that about two-thirds of the aircraft weight would be fuel.

Nevertheless, the NACA persisted in pushing for a ramjet engine, a campaign sustained by Eastman Jacobs, Arthur Kantrowitz, Macon C. Ellis Jr, Clinton E. Brown and Coleman du Pont Donaldson. Throughout 1945 that effort was supported by an in-house NACA study culminating in December that year in an Advance Confidential Report where Brown and Ellis put their name to a supersonic project with such an engine for an aircraft capable of Mach 1.4 of up to five minutes in duration.

Towed to altitude or dropped by a carrier-plane, it would

Below: The Gloster E.28/39 greatly influenced support in America for jet powered aircraft and led directly to increased cooperation between the UK and the USA. *Via Tony Buttler*

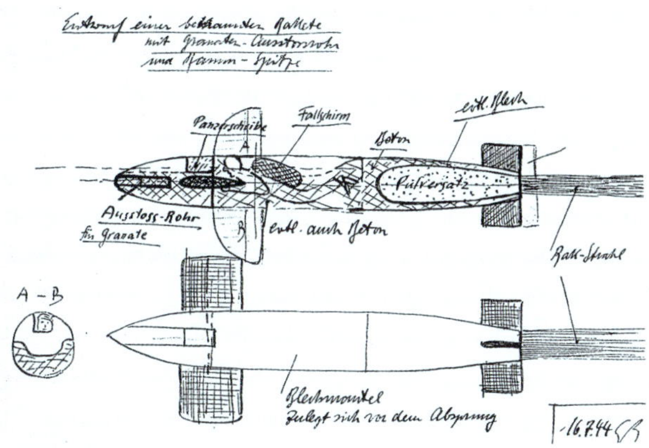

Retrieved from files covering rockets and jet propulsion, this speculative project was investigated at length in wartime Germany, including hybrid concepts which inspired the dual use of both types of engine in early Douglas transonic design studies. *Author's collection*

have employed rocket motors to push it to the transonic region where the ramjet would cut in and complete the run. With a length of 1,051cm (414in) and a wing span of 216cm (85in) it would have had a maximum weight of 1,134kg (2,500lb) and feature wings of 3-5 per cent t/c ratio, wedge-shaped aerofoil and raked wing tips. The idea never progressed and it disappeared, overwhelmed by success with the XS-1.

The design and development of the XS-1 pivoted around AAF control which, while incorporating technical recommendations from the NACA, was absolute. By mid-1944, Kotcher had the permission of his superior, Dr Theodore von Kármán, to find a contractor, now under the designation MX-524. That was not easy, the US 'arsenal of democracy' was in full swing and up to capacity, with all but a few companies incapable of taking this on. It would never be lucrative in the financial sense but some forward-thinking executives were open to unusual concepts. Others were fascinated by new challenges and that was how Bell came to build the aircraft for MX-524.

On 30 November 1944, Bell's design engineer Robert Woods happened by the office of Ezra Kotcher during a routine visit to Wright Field. In general conversation, Kotcher outlined the requirement and instantly got strong interest from Woods, who along with Lawrence Bell had been a founder of the company. Several days later he discussed the project with Robert Stanley, the chief engineer. They pulled together a team comprising Benson Hamlin, Paul Emmons, Stanley W. Smith and Roy Sandstrom. Each was an experienced aeronautical engineer and had been around the industry before joining Bell, bringing skills in stress analysis, materials, aerodynamics and flight testing.

This was to be a sole-source contract and during the next few weeks the NACA assisted the AAF with drawing up an initial specification, presented at a joint conference at Langley on 13-14 December. The general requirement for the test equipment stipulated that within the overall payload weight of 227kg (500lb) the instrumentation should weigh 168kg (370lb), the rest being in wiring and conduits for power and data collection. The equipment would be contained within a volume of 0.25m³ (9ft³) and comprise 60-cell manometers, control position and force recorders, an accelerometer and a Miller 12-element recording oscillography which would replace the manometers when used. This would also form the requirement for the D-558-1 Skystreak.

At meetings hosted by Kotcher on 20-21 December, the AAF met with Woods, Emmons and Hamlin and its own Dr. Vladimir Morkovin of the Air Technical Service Command at Wright Field. Still open was the question of an air-launched concept and the design load factor was, like the D-558, set at 18-g to accommodate uncertainties. But the requirement was a guess in the absence of firm data. Uncertainty also influenced the best known estimate of the environmental factors the aircraft would encounter. Various personnel went on a tour of relevant institutions to get some answers.

The California Institute of Technology was the first point of call for Emmons and Hamlin, where they met with Dr Clark B. Millikan before going on to the Aberdeen Proving Ground in Maryland. There were few satisfactory responses although none provided authoritative answers but, with a recommendation to visit the Ballistics Laboratory at Wright Field, Hamlin went there and Emmons went home. The only realistic advice from Wright Field was to recommend the design team copy the shape of the 0.5in bullet and scale it up to fit a man inside and the necessary propellants!

Nobody could satisfactorily explain precisely what happened to the shock waves of a supersonic bullet and the team were as confused at the end of the trip as they were at the beginning. To obtain some calibration on what they had been advised, the team obtained some Schlieren pictures showing what happened to the bullet as it decelerated on impact. But as the year came to an end there was no definitive decision as to precisely what shape they should decide upon for the MX-524, although it was becoming apparent that the bullet was a sensible starting point.

Finding an engine

Bringing together everything they had discovered, the team met on 15 January 1945 to collate information from the various visits and reach conclusions based on the interviews by Emmons and Hamlin. Concerned about stability and control issues, the desire on the part of the AAF to have a vehicle capable of true supersonic, and not merely transonic flight, and on the part of the NACA to possess a pure research tool, favoured the brave. The initial starting point in the design was to conduct their own research and arrive at their own conclusions, avoiding 'recommendations' from sources they knew were as ill-informed about the absolutes in aerodynamics and the mathematics of the transonic region as they were.

Not one aircraft had entered the design phase with so little information about the environment it was designed to operate in. The initial option was a hybrid mix of an I-16 jet engine for gaining altitude and speed, with an Aerojet rocket motor delivering a thrust of 26,688N (6,000lb) for supersonic flight and data gathering. The jet motor would be used by the pilot to return to base and land. But the additional fuel to get up to altitude and the reserve quantity for returning home would in-

Above: Work on liquid-propellant rocket motors took a back step during the Second World War as solid-propellant rockets were developed for assisted take-off, here depicted by a Grumman TBF Avenger torpedo bomber getting off the runway assisted by four small JATO packs. *US Navy*

crease the size and weight of the aircraft which, in turn, would call for a more powerful rocket motor and its own inflated propellant requirement – inflated, because it would have to haul a heavier aircraft carrying the inert jet and its fuel.

The second option was to use an all-rocket design with strap-on solid-propellant boosters to get off the ground. In this concept the same rocket motor would provide 6.5min of propulsive time for an aircraft weighting 9,525kg (21,000lb). With the JATO rockets the total weight would be 11,177kg (24,640lb) but those would be jettisoned after take-off. Calculations showed that with this configuration the aircraft would have a climb rate of at least 4,877m/sec (16,000ft/sec) and reach 10,668m (35,000ft) with a burn time of 2min 51sec remaining. But Bell did not favour an all-rocket design However, calculations for an all-turbojet aircraft proved that this would fall far short of the AAF's requirement and only cover transonic and not truly full supersonic flight. Bell decided there was no alternative and selected the all-rocket concept.

Bell asked the NACA and the Air Technical Services Command about the thickness-chord of the wing and the degree of thinness it should have. Ames laboratory favoured a 12 per cent t/c, while Langley (specifically Gilruth) wanted a thin wing. Langley had done research with rocket-propelled models and knew that a thick wing loses lift at the transonic. The decision came down to Floyd L. Thompson, then the assistant chief of research at Langley under whose remit the highly secret wing-flow tests had been conducted. The recommendation was for 5 per cent but, to hedge bets a compromise settled on two separate wing sets – one of 8 per cent and one of 10 per cent, a lot thinner than standard fighter plane wings. But there was doubt that Bell could fabricate wings of even those thicknesses and still retain the 18-g load factor.

Next was the decision over the type of rocket motor to adopt and the Aerojet Rotojet, with a thrust of 26,688N (6,000lb) was preferred. It would operate on a mixture of red fuming nitric acid (RFNA) and aniline, hypergolic propel-

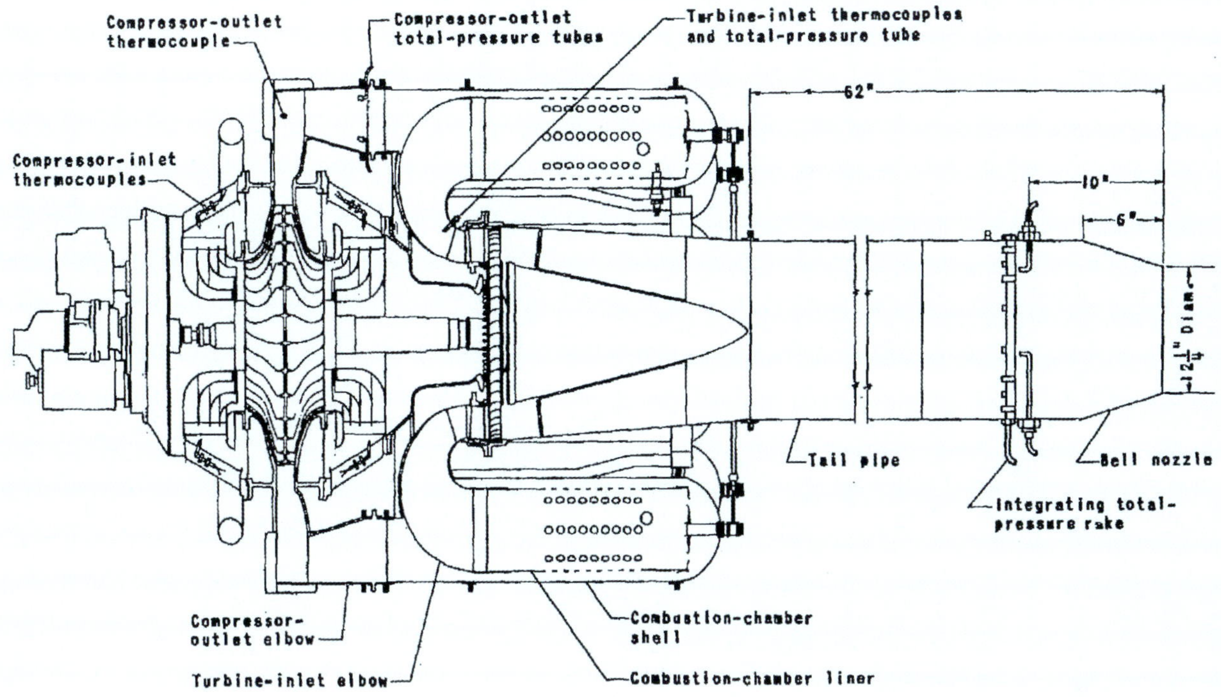

Above: Early consideration of propulsion for the XS-1 series included the General Electric I-16, a derivative of the Whittle W.2 engine, with an Aerojet liquid propellant rocket for high-speed flight. *NACA*

lants which would ignite on contact. In their basic ignorance of rocket propellants, seeking to understand the risk with these combinations, Bell engineers bought separate bottles of the two chemicals, bound them together, retired a safe distance and hurled them at the wall of the Buffalo gun butts. The consequent explosion impressed the engineers, convincing them that this was far too dangerous for a piloted aircraft.

The AAF did not have to look far to find a suitable alternative, originating from the design creativity of four rocket engineers: Lovell Lawrence Jr., H. Franklin Pierce, James H. Wyld and John Shesta. All had been early members of the American Rocket Society (ARS) and together they formed Reaction Motors Inc. (RMI) on 16 December 1941. Their respective affiliations gelled well. Wyld had worked on aerodynamics with John Stack at NACA's Langley Laboratory. The inferred association with 'motors' in the RMI title persuaded locals to turn up wanting help with getting their automobiles working, 'reaction' being interpreted as an outfit giving fast and efficient service!

The small company began to grow as war work intensified. As aircraft got bigger and heavier, adding supplementary rocket packs for take-off was far cheaper than adding more powerful engines to existing airframes. Initially RMI occupied an upper floor garage owned by John Shesta's brother-in-law, Hugo M. Reese at North Arlington, New Jersey. It had an area of 74m^2 (800ft^2) and from there they worked on JATO packs for Navy aircraft. Aspiring to better and more potent designs, they tested a device with a thrust of 4,448N (1,000lb) before moving the company to Pompton Lakes, where they developed and tested a still more powerful motor with a thrust of 15,123N (3,400lb).

In January 1943 RMI moved again, to Pompton Plains where they settled in to the spacious, 827m^2 (8,900ft^2) premises of a former electroplating facility, which some claimed had been used as a night club. This expanded area provided the opportunity to produce and test a motor with a thrust of 26,688N (6,000lb), an assembly of four grouped combustion chambers each delivering a thrust of 6,672N (1,500lb), appropriately naming it the 6000C4. How that came about is a classic example of creative thinking.

As well as regenerative-cooling, for some time Wyld had

Right: Bell would become a household name when associated with the XS-1 but it had already established a credible reputation for precision work with high priority on quality control. Here depicted at the Bell plant at Niagara Falls, NY, is the P-39 Airacobra assembly line. *Bell*

mused over the need for high thrust output. Instead of aiming for increasingly more powerful, single-chamber rocket motors as the Germans at Peenemünde had done with their A-4/V2, Wyld proposed achieving both higher thrust levels and controllable output by clustering several smaller rocket chambers, each of which could be ignited independently, stepping up thrust output at increments of 25 per cent. It was this that persuaded him to bring together separate chambers, an idea which he knew was practical. Two years later it would be the motor of choice for the XS-1.

The Navy was an enthusiast for rocket-assisted take-off and Comdr. C. Fink Fischer had defined the requirement for the 6000C4 and pressed for its use on Navy aircraft. No stranger to the rocket, in May 1942 Fischer had tested a Brewster F2A-3 Buffalo from Anacosta Naval Air Station powered for take-off by six British solid-propellant anti-aircraft rockets! But the energy released from solid rocket fuel was much less per mass than that obtained from liquid propellants and the latter were the only means by which rockets could power a conventional aircraft into the transonic. The price for liquid-propellant propulsion was that a much more complex motor was required for propellant storage and delivery to the combustion chamber.

The 6000C4 was largely the culmination of several innovative ideas developed and applied by Wyld, who had made a major contribution in the development of the regeneratively-cooled rocket motor. He recognised that a serious engineering challenge was posed by the extreme temperature of the combustion chamber walls and of the divergent (exhaust) cone from which the escaping gases were discharged after being accelerated in the convergent section of the combustion chamber. No material could be found which would survive very powerful, high-thrust rocket motors in which an oxidiser and a fuel were combined to produce heat in the combustion process.

Wyld calculated that alcohol was an ideal fuel due to its relatively low flame temperature, which reduced the cooling problem, and to the disassociation of combusted fuel and liquid oxygen. To get higher thrust output and to constrain rising temperatures in the combustion chamber and exit nozzle, regenerative cooling was the answer. In this, fuel is passed around the walls for cooling prior to mixing with the oxidiser in the combustion chamber. Shesta designed the initial motor with a thrust of 4,448N (1,000lb) and became the first practical exponent of this concept, opening the door to rocket motors of considerably greater thrust.

Wyld calculated that the 6000C4 would develop 8,948kW (12,000bhp) at the rated thrust level of 26,689N (6,000lb) which would power an aircraft the size of the XS-1 to a speed of 1,207kph (750mph) for a motor weight of 95kg (210lb). Aware that this thrust/output level was about as good as it could get, Wyld envisaged combustion chamber pressures increasing from the current 2,068kPa (300lb/in^2) to around 6,895kPa (1,000lb/in^2).

Recognising the limitations of the regenerative-cooling technique, Wyld correctly pointed out that the main problem with high chamber gas temperature was not the heat-rate, or the overall heat load in the propulsive cycle, but thermal spikes produced by inconsistencies in the ratio of fuel to oxidiser. His solution to this was a high level of quality control in machined valves and injectors at the combustion chamber head and in the on/off propellant delivery control valves. By achieving a very high standard of finish in the completed motor, combustion inconsistencies could be significantly reduced.

Clearly, throttleable motors with propellant delivery gradients were prone to imprecise mixture ratios at even small increments of settings applied by the operator (or by the pilot in an aircraft). This would easily result in thermal spikes due to changes in the mixture ratio – optimised for peak performance as well as efficient use of the thermal energy. By early 1945 some knowledge was being gleaned about the design of the rocket motor and control options for the German Me 163 Komet. It appeared that accidents were mostly attributable to variations caused by manual throttling by the pilot, although the control linkages operated a single valve downstream of the carefully balanced delivery of T-Stoff and C-Stoff. Nevertheless, it was a complexity Wyld considered to be a flaw in the design of the Walter rocket motor.

Calculations showed that the multi-chamber (or cluster) concept was a quick way to achieve far greater thrust levels, saving weight per unit-mass/thrust-unit output, albeit at the price of motor complexity and overall bulk. The vast array of unknown challenges inherent in early 1945 can be gauged from Wyld's extant view that only by clustering several separate rocket chambers could thrust levels above 889.6kN (200,000lb) be achieved. But this was where his crystal ball failed. Within 10 years, the F-1 rocket motor would be in

Right: A member of the American Rocket Society and a founding member of Reaction Motors Inc, James H. Wyld would be one of the team that provided the rocket motor for all the X-1 first and second generation series and the Skyrocket, as well as early flights of the X-15. *Author's collection*

Above: Known at RMI as the 6000C4 to define its thrust in pounds force and the number of combustion chambers, the compact XLR-11 would prove a good choice, helping lift the company to success, eventually putting its rocket motors on NASA's first Moon soft-lander, the Surveyor spacecraft. *Author's collection*

design by Rocketdyne with a chamber thrust of 6,672kN (1,500,000lb). Nevertheless, chamber-clustering would be the way Russian rocket engineers would create the motors for the world's first Intercontinental Ballistic Missile (ICBM) and the world's first satellite launcher. By harvesting in the foothills of the future, Wyld had nailed the problems, producing a highly practical, multi-chamber rocket motor devoid of throttle controls and capable of producing overall thrust levels at increments of 25 per cent but determined by the number of chambers lit. It was an elegant solution because it adopted proven technologies to solve an immediate need, rather than relying on more ambitious capabilities as yet unproven. We will return to the 6000C4 later.

Detailed design of the XS-1

Choosing a suitable rocket motor was only one of the challenges for Bell Aircraft. In advance of the decision which would be made by the Navy regarding the wing for the Douglas D-558, during the first quarter of 1945 the Air Technical Service Command stipulated the straight-wing configuration for the XS-1, despite mounting indications that a swept-wing configuration was preferable. Much has been made of the feedback from military intelligence regarding the advanced work carried out in German research facilities and wind tunnels but the core of information regarding swept-wing aerodynamics debated by US aircraft companies came from inside the United States. That work had been underway for several years, articulated by the NACA's Robert T. Jones but taken to the Army Air Force by Ezra Kotcher who introduced the research to Theodore von Kármán, then the head of the AAF's Scientific Advisory Group (SAG).

In late 1944 von Kármán introduced the concept to Dr. Hsue-shen Tsien before either of them knew about the German research work, obtained for the first time when they toured Germany several months later. In anticipation of importing the idea of a swept, thin wing into the transonic research aircraft, by February 1945 Jones had shared this US-based research with Jean A. Roché. But the AAF did not consider the work sufficiently well-defined by experimental verification testing to incorporate it into the XS-1. As we have seen, the Navy was not so conservative and went for the swept-wing design on the D-558-2 Skyrocket. Eventually, in pursuit of higher speeds, Bell would get to apply the swept wing to the ill-fated X-2.

The requirement for the XS-1 set down by the Army Air

Forces in late 1944 brought a shift in process and Bell would be called upon to apply unique and untested design criteria. All US aircraft manufacturers had pumped out an unprecedented array of designs and real aircraft around a document dated 1 July 1936 and titled *Handbook of Instructions for Airplane Designers*. In this single tome, the eighth edition, manufacturers were required to build aircraft to pre-set criteria concerning approved wing planforms, manufacturing and quality standards, stress levels, materials and regulations approved by the US government. These did not apply to the XS-1 and Bell was told to throw away that rule book and design it from a clean sheet for the requirement – an end goal rather than a process.

For Bell, this was approval for creative thinking and unique solutions. Working from the outside shape of the aircraft inward to the layout of equipment – what we would today call 'systems' – as said earlier, the overall outline had been defined as closely as possible by the shape of an 0.5in bullet. The thin wing, of which two optional thicknesses had been agreed, was set in the mid-fuselage plane. The horizontal tail had responsibility for restoring control of the aircraft should the wing stall or encounter compressibility. Some consideration had been given to a Vee tail but that was dropped for a more conventional arrangement. It was largely at the instigation of NACA-Langley that the horizontal tail was located about one-third up on the vertical fin. In this position it would not be directly set in the airstream flowing off the wing, or be influenced by any turbulence from that element. But there was an additional concern.

Considering that the tailplane may be the sole means of regaining, or maintaining, flight control through the transonic regime, several engineers recommended making the normally fixed portion of the horizontal stabiliser adjustable in pitch with respect to the fuselage. Thus, if the elevator was insufficient on its own to maintain control, it could be locked in the plane of the 'fixed' portion by the pilot, converting the whole tailplane itself into an 'all-flying' surface. NACA engineers believed that the tailplane could be key to maintaining control of the aircraft through the area of high compressibility but the belief holds firm that this design innovation was the sole reason why the XS-1 survived the transonic – which is not true.

Considering the external profile of the Bell design, great uncertainty surrounded the cockpit window. There was concern over the degree of influence a protruding cockpit canopy would have on the air flow and any resulting shock waves caused by the obstruction, however minimal. Emmons and Hamlin worked the problem and proposed the ideal aerodynamic solution: a flush, glazed forward section with the pilot situated immediately behind and able to see ahead. But only just! Test pilot Jack Woolams sat in a proportional mock-up and proclaimed it acceptable but modifications were applied to open up the glazed area to a wider view from inside the cockpit.

It was at this point, during the early weeks of 1945 that debate over the landing gear arose, polarising opposing interpretations of the aircraft's true purpose: was it purely a

Below: Theodore von Kármán (third from left) reviewed the work by the NACA's Robert T. Jones on the transonic concept. He is here seen during his days at JPL during the war. *Author's collection*

research platform for sensors and recording equipment or an aircraft designed as closely as possible to a future combat type which the Air Force had always been inclined to encourage? Bob Woods sought to bury within the overall design of the XS-1 the seeds of a potential interceptor, powered by rocket motor and controlled by a pilot. There was encouragement for such theoretical possibility from German projects such as the Me 163 and the Bachem Ba 349 *Natter*, the latter then unknown to Woods.

Developed during 1944 as the brain-child of Erich Bachem, the *Natter* adopted the same Walter 109-509A-2 sustainer motor as that used by the *Komet*. It would be launched vertically by solid propellant rockets to the altitude of intruders and use the sustainer motor to vector on to the bombers, where the pilot would fire a fusillade of rocket projectiles into the massed formations. The first launch occurred on 23 February 1945 and the use of rocket propulsion for rapid interception attracted attention from the AAF. That argued against moving the design of the XS-1 too far away from a military application. In which regard, there was opposition to an idea that the XS-1 should not have a conventional landing gear but use skids instead of wheels.

During a meeting at NACA-Langley, Woods pressed the case for landing wheels so that the XS-1 could take off from the ground but Hamlin disagreed and argued for skids. This debate occurred at the time a broader discussion was held over whether the aircraft should take off from the ground or be dropped by air from where it could achieve maximum value from the limited burn duration of its rocket motor. That decision was settled by the safety and performance advantage of an air-drop mode. But Woods vociferously argued for a ground-launch, pushing the case with Lawrence Bell and in so doing distancing himself from the corporate leadership.

Bell intervened to settle the issue, the XS-1 got a conventional landing gear, the air-drop mode promoted by Robert Stanley. Woods was moved to an administrative position leaving Stanley and Benson Hamlin in charge of the design office. Woods was sent on a fact-finding tour of German research installations and that moved him away from the critical path for impending design reviews. Lawrence Bell appreciated the potential inherent in the future for rocket-powered interceptors but would not have the XS-1 compromised for a potential and future production opportunity.

During the first half of 1945 many of the design details were settled, by empirical as well as calculated means. The baseline weight assumption had been for the XS-1 to have a loaded mass of 5,912kg (13,034lb) including 3,701kg (8,160lb) of propellant. Calculations indicated that it could achieve a maximum speed of 1,770kph (1,100mph) from a ground take-off or 2,574kph (1,600mph) from an air-drop launch and achieve a maximum altitude of 42,672m (140,000ft). The starting point for internal layout included two propellant tanks, the forward vessel containing LOX and the second vessel, aft of the wing, containing the alcohol fuel, both propellants fed by a single turbopump.

Even by spring 1945 the turbopump was clearly the pacing item with technical challenges proving difficult to resolve. This was dropped from the critical path in exchange for a simpler, pressurised system whereby nitrogen gas would be used to force propellants into the rocket motors. The turbopump would remain in development, to be adopted for the third of the three XS-1s which would also incorporate a higher propellant load.

Above: At the time decisions were made about the XS-1, Bell knew very little about the German Bachem Ba 349, a vertically-launched interceptor. There was an attempt by some to build in to the rocket-ship the same anti-air capability, an application dismissed by the Army Air Forces and the NACA. *Author's collection*

The decision to switch from the turbopump in favour of a pressurising gas system for the first two aircraft was taken on 3 May 1945 when the AAF was so informed. The switch irrevocably condemned the XS-1 to air-launch because of the need for heavy nitrogen storage tanks which increased the weight of the aircraft and reduced the overall performance.

Where the trigger decision for an air-launch had been predicated on the safety factor to prevent a disaster from an aborted ground-launch, it was now the only way to rescue some of the ambitious performance capability. The propellant weight was cut to 2,123kg (4,680lb) and the predicted burn time reduced from 4min 6sec to 2min 30sec, now with a predicted maximum speed of at least 1,448kph (900mph) and a maximum altitude of 26,747m (87,750ft).

Renewed challenges

Critical to the success of the XS-1 was a reliable carrier-plane. From a performance and suitability standpoint, the Boeing B-29A was the first choice, closely followed by the Douglas C-54 Skymaster. The Skymaster had been designed as a transcontinental airliner (the DC-4A) and took to the skies in 1938 but on the outbreak of war in December 1941 it was adapted for military transport duties and acquitted itself well in several theatres around the globe. Only 74 were built for

Above: A mock-up of the XS-1 at Bell's Niagara Falls assembly plant. *Bell*

airlines but the military took 1,084 for a variety of roles.

By contrast, the B-29A had been developed as a 'Hemisphere Defense Weapon' and would find exclusive wartime assignment to the 20th AF in the Far East. But it had only been operational for little more than eighteen months when the carrier-plane was being considered. As the only long-range bomber capable of taking the offensive to mainland Japan, it was a premium asset and the AAF had resisted its use, inferring that none could be spared for conversion to a carrier-plane. But it had superior performance to the C-54, both in speed and altitude, and had pressurised crew compartments which was an advantage for the prime role it could play.

With the end of the war coming much earlier than many believed it would – the surrender of Japan was unexpected – many B-29s became redundant and would soon be piling up on the scrap heap. The B-29 became the carrier of choice and that helped seal detailed planning for flight operations and decisions about the type of equipment necessary to support research flights. It also cleared the way for infrastructure at Muroc, the remote site where all flight tests would originate, necessary to get the bullet-shaped XS-1 hauled up into the much modified bomb bay. Meanwhile, the detailed design of the XS-1 picked up pace, faced now with the need to incorporate the nitrogen pressurisation system within an already crammed fuselage and wing assembly.

The fuselage was of semi-monocoque construction in 24ST aluminium, comprising a tapering cylinder with transverse frames and longitudinal stringers enclosed by a stressed skin and a total length of 9.42m (30.90ft). Forward of the wing, the spherical LOX tank had a capacity of 1,177lit (311USgall), or 1,324kg (2,920lb). It was fabricated from annealed stainless steel with a thickness of 4.745mm (0.187in) to avoid embrittlement at the -149°C (-300°F) temperature of the liquid oxygen and to retain integrity when pressurised to 2,412kPa (350lb/in^2). The fuel tank was located aft of the wing, fabricated from SAE4130 steel with a wall thickness of 3.175mm (0.125in). Both tanks had anti-slosh baffles to prevent instability from a shifting centre of gravity during manoeuvres.

While the turbopump would not be ready for the first two XS-1s, the pressurisation system had its own challenges and it too raised serious problems. To do its job the system had to have a pressure of 31,027kPa (4,500lb/in^2) and the nitrogen was stored in 12 vessels at various locations around the

Below: The overall configuration of the Bell XS-1 strongly resembled a winged bullet with a tailplane and that epitomised the general conclusion regarding the optimum way to successfully cross the transonic. Here, X-1-2 is parked for a photo-shoot on the dry lakebed at Muroc. *NACA*

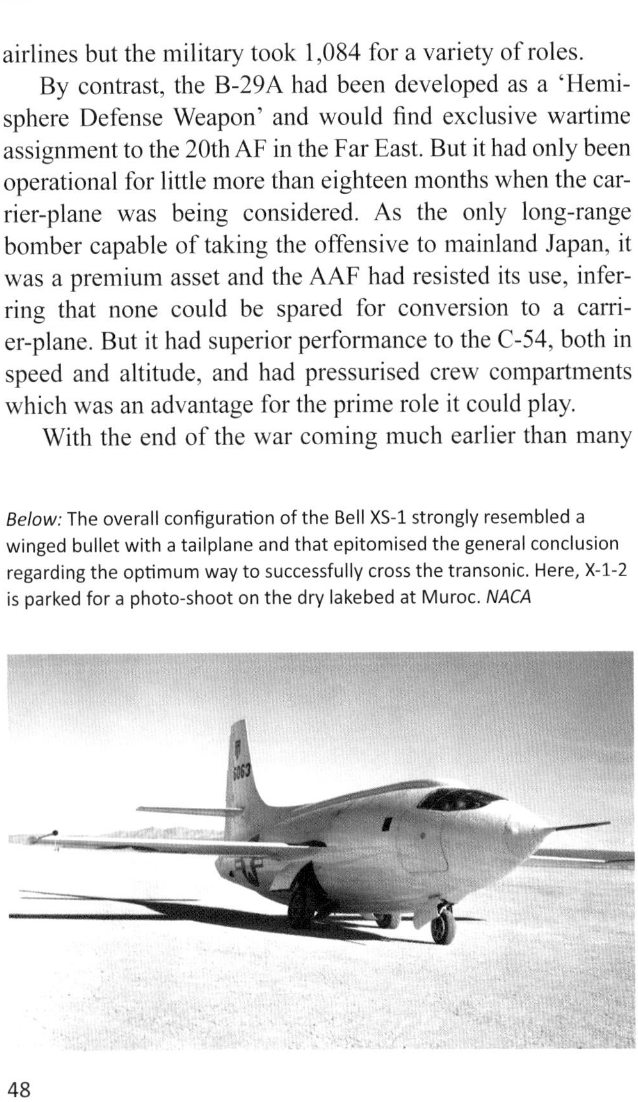

Right: A mock-up of the XS-1 under test at the NACA's Langley Memorial Laboratory. *NACA*

fuselage with a total capacity of 0.495m³ (17.5ft³) or 136.5kg (301lb). The nitrogen tanks were fabricated in varying thicknesses, between 0.65cm (0.25in) and 1.57cm (0.62in) depending on size and location. A single tank was located in the fuselage nose, seven were placed in a ring aft of the cockpit, two were directly behind and below the LOX tank and two were behind the fuel tank.

An interconnect system was installed with high-pressure, welded joints rather than detachable connectors to prevent leakage and three regulators controlled the pressure delivered to the propellant tanks. These could be operated by the pilot, reducing stored pressure to 10,342kPa (1,500lb/in²) for operating the landing gear and the wing flaps, and to 2,344kPa (340lb/in²) for pressurising the propellant tanks. Despite the additional weight, this complex system had an inherent advantage by replacing the need for hydraulic pumps or batteries for operation. Generally, nitrogen was not available at the pressure required, most being sold in containers at 13,790kPa (2,000lb/in²).

Bell's Lloyd Bevin was tasked with the challenge of developing a nitrogen evaporator which boiled it off as a high pressure gas from a 91.4cm (36in) sphere so that it could be carried by tube directly into the aircraft's tanks at the required pressure. Fabricating the boil-off tank brought its own challenges, which was fabricated from 7.62cm (3in) thick stainless steel tested to withstand a pressure of 62,055kPa (9,000lb/in²). The need for cleanliness and engineered seals was a prerequisite for safety. Oil contaminating the gas would cause an explosion when mixed with liquid oxygen. Seals were also a factor in the overall design of the cockpit, which would be pressurised to 20.68kPa (3lb/in²) above ambient pressure. Tests showed that the leak rate was only 6,895kPa/hr (1lb/in²/hr), quite sufficient for the brief flight.

Below: The NACA's Robert T. Jones tried to convince the Air Force to incorporate swept wings into the XS-1 but that was considered too radical a departure from the 'keep it simple' imperative. *NACA*

Development of the cockpit included a yoke-control rather than a conventional stick so that the pilot could maintain better control of the aircraft under heavy loads. The yoke and pedal controls were supplemented with a thrust selector, instrument switches, a control for the stabiliser and power shut-off, located on the yoke for ease of operation under high loads or buffeting. The conformal glazing consisted of a double pane with special treatment to prevent the build-up of condensation. The external face had laminated glass panes with internal panes of methyl metacrylate and a defrosting system.

Due to the climb time to the drop altitude, the pilot would rest in the carrier-plane and only enter the aircraft from an access-way in the bomb bay shortly before the drop. Using a ladder, he would climb into the cockpit via a hatch in the starboard side of the XS-1. Crew would then seal the cockpit with a panel locked in place from the outside and the cabin pressurised. The pilot had no ejection seat, the weight of such a device being too great, but he could release the side hatch and bale out, resorting to a conventional back-pack parachute to get back down on the ground.

One of the greatest unknowns was the wing itself. Nobody quite knew for sure precisely how the wing would behave, hence the argument over thickness which culminated in the decision to build two – one with an 8 per cent t/c ratio and another with a ratio of 10 per cent. The 8 per cent wing was frighteningly thin, given the +/- 18-g load factor. Several engineers failed to see how they could reconcile the two but with caution to the fore, the first and third aircraft had the thinner wing, the second aircraft the thicker wing.

The 8 per cent wing was shaped from an NACA 65-108 section while the thicker wing adopted the NACA 65-110 profile. The 8 per cent wing had a root thickness of 15.08cm (5.94in) with skin tapered from 1.27cm (0.5in) at the root to nearly 0.78cm (0.31in) at the tip, with a taper ratio of 2:1. The root chord was 188.5cm (74.2in) with the tip chord 94.2cm (37.1in). The incidence angle was +2.5deg at the root and 1.5deg at the tip, with no dihedral, a leading edge sweep of 5.46deg and an aspect ratio of 6.03.

The thicker 10 per cent wing had a root depth of 18.85cm (7.42in), both having a span of 8.53m (28ft). Difficult enough to fabricate and still achieve the required load factor, the NACA also had Bell cut 240 pressure orifices in the surface and install 12 strain gauges on the port wing providing data on the distribution of pressure and on air loads.

The control surfaces were conventional and included ailerons with a total surface area of 0.585m² (6.3ft²) and +/-12deg of travel. Each 0.483m² (5.2ft²) elevator had a movement of travel 15deg up and 10deg down. The wing flaps had a total area of 1.077m² (11.6ft²) and a deployed deflection of 60deg. The vertical tail had a surface area of 1.37m² (25.6ft²) and the rudder had an area of 0.48m² (5.2ft²) with a deflection angle of +/-15deg. Due to the small size of the XS-1, there was little need for boosted control. With a surface area of 2.45m² (26ft²) the horizontal stabiliser could be moved from +5deg to -10deg at 1deg/sec to effect trim changes by way of an electrically-driven screwjack. On its gear, the aircraft had a total height of 3.30m (10.85ft)

The landing gear was conventional too, with a tricycle layout and a single wheel on each leg set on a wheelbase of 255.78cm (100.7in) and a tread of 129.5cm (51in). The main wheel tyres were 60.96cm x 18.29cm (24in x 7.2in) and the nose wheel tyre was 40.64cm x 14.73cm x 21.59cm (16in x 5.8in x 8.5in) set on magnesium alloy wheels and rims. The nose leg had a hydraulic shimmy damper and could be moved 40deg either side of the centreline. The legs were nitrogen-actuated and deployed by gravity assist. The forward leg was not steerable but directional control on the ground was facilitated by differential braking on respective main legs. Gear deployment was speed-limited to 483kph (300mph).

Overall design was completed during the summer months of 1945 and a wooden mock-up was prepared which aided inspection of the interior equipment layout. The NACA and the Air Technical Service Command inspected the mock-up on 10 October and were generally pleased with the result, although a few minor tweaks were made. There was some discussion about the straight wing. A lot had happened since the decision for that had been made and several manufacturers had received word back from their inspection teams sent to Germany to get the latest information about research into swept wings and other technical innovations. This resulted in questions over the decision, which stimulated Bell to reopen internal discussion.

In conversation with teams at Wright Field, Bell's Robert Stanley learned about the excitement over swept wings and the rapid conversion in both the Air Force and industry about its potential value in transonic and supersonic flight. Benson Hamlin was set to work in a hurried analysis of designing a swept wing option for a future development of the XS-1. But the swept wing configuration brought more problems than could be met by merely adapting the existing fuselage. A completely new aircraft would be necessary, designed from a clean sheet, to which could be applied all the newly retrieved aerodynamic test data on this type of wing.

Stanley reported to Bell, who organised the company behind a push to convince the AAF that it should not only press ahead with flight tests but that it should immediately begin work on a new project, an X-2, designed for supersonic research. It was timely for both the Air Force and the NACA to carry out independent research on swept wings. Industry was already working on potential combat aircraft with swept wings and threatening to eclipse the activities of the government scientists and engineers. If not in research terms, certainly in performance. It would be some time before they could begin work on the X-2 but the die had been cast.

Below: The Boeing B-50 was introduced later in the programme to carry second-generation series aircraft, seen here jacked up to accept the second XS-1. *NACA*

Chapter Four

Mach One

The contract for the XS-1 was signed on 16 March 1945, requiring Bell to produce three aircraft bearing serials 46-062, -063 and -064. In a little over two years, under the reallocation of designations with the newly independent US Air Force, the 'S' for sonic would be dropped and hereafter we will refer to this aircraft as the X-1. With the design acceptance review approved there was now nothing standing in the way of building on the ethos adhered to by most manufacturers. That, when balancing further time-consuming and costly design debates with pressing need to get the product off the blueprints and into the sky, it was 'time to cut the c..p and cut metal'!

Each X-1 was hand crafted and, like all machines made by human hands, each was unique and possessing almost animal-like idiosyncratic characteristics during control and handling. The X-1 was unique also in the range of equipment installed and the assembly process brought several minor challenges which helped build a new learning curve at Bell. After a brief and broken Christmas, by a small but thoroughly preoccupied work team tempted away from their Yuletide festivities, X-1-1 was rolled out of the Bell assembly facility at Wheatfield, New York, on 27 December 1945. There were still several critical steps necessary to equip it for flight and it had yet to sport its bright orange paintwork and black serial number (46-062) that would define its presence. But it had a visual impact on even the most hardened Bell worker, as well as personnel from the NACA and the Air Force.

Several years into the programme, engineer J. van Lonkhuyzen defined the effort and the creative talent that had characterised the programme from its inception, placing into prose the emotions and drama of this seminal moment in aviation history: 'It required an unhesitating boldness to undertake a venture so few thought could succeed, an almost exu-

Above: The overall configuration of the XS-1 was dictated by the need to explore the transonic and to do that that it incorporated an optional set of three wings of different thickness-chord ratios and an all-flying tail which had been developed by the British at the same time. *NACA*

berant enthusiasm to carry across the many obstacles and unknowns, but most of all a completely unprejudiced imagination in departing so drastically from the known way.'

The flight test programme laid out by Bell preceded the handover to Army Air Force test pilots and set out to verify design expectations and clear the general handling and performance characteristics for research flights. But the Air Force made it plain that it was to be their pilots that would attempt the transonic and achieve Mach 1 in level flight for the first time.

On the cusp of independence, the Air Force was well aware of the value which would accrue from being the first armed service in the world to fly through the, misnamed 'sound barrier', although there was a determination to maintain secrecy on both the attempt and the achievement until released sometime after the event. Balancing this, there was to be a conservative approach in the research programme, managed in large part by the NACA's own attitude toward the acquisition of data – slow and incremental but remorseless nevertheless.

Above: The landing gear for the XS-1 afforded ground or air-launch capability, the decision to provide a tricycle undercarriage was made before the judgement on that was finalised. The only ground take-off under rocket power occurred on 5 January 1949. *NACA*

Uncertainties faced by Bell during the checkout phase included verification of the carriage and separation techniques involving the carrier-plane. Nobody knew for sure that the two would separate cleanly, or that the X-1 would not rise up and collide with the underside of the B-29. There was also an extended phase necessary for verifying the integrity of the RMI rocket motor, now designated the XLR-11-RM-3 for X-1-1 and X-1-2 and XLR-8-RM-5 for X-1-3. These activities would take place at Pinecastle Field, Orlando, Florida for initial evaluation of the aircraft's free-flight characteristics in glide drops from the carrier-plane. Initially, there had been uncertainty over where to conduct the flight trials. The NACA wanted Langley and cited its large military airfield there but the Air Force got its way and preparations were made to fly the aircraft from New York to Florida.

The carrier-plane for the X-1 was a B-29-96 (45-21800) assembled at Boeing's Wichita facility and assigned to support for the transonic project. The first X-1 was air-lifted to Pine-

Below: The bulbous fuselage was sufficiently large to accommodate propellant tanks for the XLR-11 rocket motor with a conduit spine running from the vertical stabiliser to the rear of the cockpit area. *NACA*

Right: Jack Russell, the XS-1 crew chief undertakes diagnostic checks on a four-chamber XLR engine of either -11 or -8 derivative. *NACA*

castle Field on 19 January 1946, the carrier-plane piloted by Harold Dow and Joseph Cannon with an additional three crewmembers on board. There, the NACA had put together a small group of personnel including engineers from the Langley Flight Research Division and also from the Instrument Division. They were under the leadership of Walter C. 'Walt' Williams, late of the Martin company before working on aircraft stability and control at Langley. Imported to conduct trials planning for the X-1, Williams would provide guidance on the evolving aircraft experimental programmes and on the emerging manned spacecraft concepts during the late 1950s.

The X-1 had been completed before the engine was ready and initial flight trials would focus on glide tests to determine the aerodynamic characteristics. Bell's chief test plot, Jack Woolams, would conduct those at Pinecastle. By March 1945 the decision had been made to move the powered flight trials to Muroc, the limitations of Pinecastle for these exotic activities being all too obvious. That, and the certainty over maintaining a degree of security over the programme, argued for a more remote and less publicly accessible location. But there were many tests to conduct before then and the first captive flight took place on 10 January with the X-1 shackled to the converted bomb bay and pressure distribution mapped by carefully positioned sensors to determine the air flow between the two.

Although the flight went well and sensor data indicated that any separation between the two aircraft would be clean and without risk of collision, technicians installed a special tube forward of the propellant tanks flanking both sides of the X-1's nose. Wooden pegs were fixed to the B-29 so that if any yawing motion occurred after release they would guide the nose back into the straight and narrow for a safe drop. The consequences of getting it wrong could easily result in the loss of both aircraft and all personnel.

The first air-drop took place on 25 January 1946 without drama but under limits. The inboard engines on the B-29 were feathered to avoid side-draughts and the flaps were deployed to the take-off position and speed held to a stately 241kph (150mph). The flanking pegs were painted in red to determine whether there was any sideslip during release – no paint marks were found on the steel post. With Jack Woolams at the controls, the X-1 fell away at an altitude of 8,230m (27,000ft) and with a slightly nose-up attitude. Excited and delighted at finding the X-1 compliant and a delight to fly, Woolams had to regather his attention for a landing that very nearly undershot the runway, displaying unusually prescient emotions for a test pilot!

It would be some time before the second X-1 (46-603) got the first rocket motor for powered trials and drop tests with the unpowered precursor (46-602) and until that time the drop

Below: With selectable thrust in 25 per cent increments of full power by optional switching of each chamber, the XR-11 rocket motor was selected for X-1-1 and X-1-2 and the XLR-8 motor for X-1-3. *NACA*

Below right: Encapsulated by a closeout panel shown here, the injector plates can be seen inside each combustion chamber. *NACA*

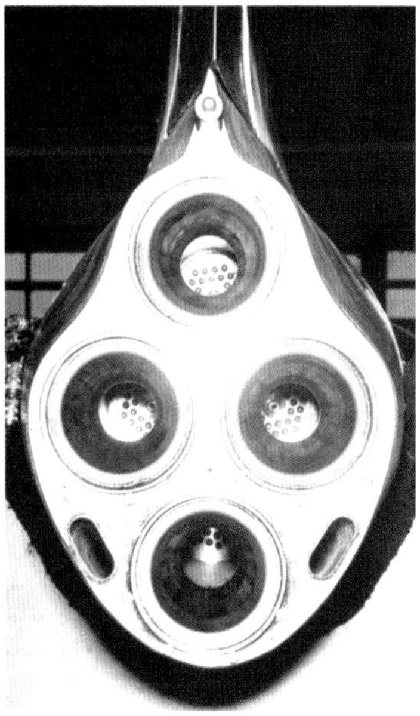

tests continued, the second and third occurring on 5 February. The fourth test brought mild drama when, on 8 February the main landing gear collapsed on landing damaging the port wing. On the fifth flight on 19 February the nose leg retracted back into its well pitching the aircraft forward and damaging the underside of the fuselage. After each incident the repairs quickly restored the aircraft and the trials continued. The last drop test occurred on 6 March bringing to a close the 10 glide flights from Pinecastle Field.

Tragedy struck the programme on 30 August. Woolams was killed when he crashed into Lake Ontario while flying at low level over the water in a P-39 Airacobra configured as an air racer and dubbed Cobra I. It was one of two which had been entered by Woolams in the 1946 Thompson Trophy. During the event itself, on 2 September fellow test pilot and friend of Woolams, Tex Johnston flew Cobra II and took the record in style. He gave over half the winnings to his friend's widow, around $10,000. Up until the time of his death, Woolams had been convinced that he would fly the X-1 through Mach 1 and lived his last year in anticipation of that.

The following day, Bell announced that Chalmers H. 'Slick' Goodlin would take his place as chief test pilot. After getting his wings on several light aircraft before his seventeenth birthday, Goodlin volunteered for the Royal Canadian Air Force, served as a fighter pilot flying Spitfires and left to join the US Navy in December 1942. Since December 1943 he had worked for Bell as a test pilot. Goodlin was one of the last 'seat of the pants' flyers with no engineering qualifications but a natural aviator with instincts that made him an outstanding test pilot. With steel nerves and a survivor's self-confidence,

Above: Hooked up to data cables, the second XS-1 undergoes a ground engine test at Muroc prior to flight. *NACA*

he had several near misses and displayed heroic approach to encroaching disaster, on one occasion staying with a flaming aircraft until a fellow crewmember got out, before abandoning his stricken plane.

To Goodlin fell the task of flying the X-1 through its powered trials, most of which were conducted on the second aircraft, 46-603, from mid-October 1946. Before that, several changes in personnel took place. Stanley Smith was moved from the X-1 to lead the design of the X-2, his replacement being Richard H. Frost who had the daunting task of getting the rocket motor accepted, installed in the X-1 and tested – on the ground and in the air. Also in September, Walt Williams was appointed project engineer on the X-1 and sent over to

Below: With side hatch removed and sunlight flooding the cockpit, X-1-2 poses alongside the carrier-plane at Muroc. *NACA*

Above: With all engines running on the B-29, X-1-2 is held in position with the port side sway-brace visible. Note the minimal ground clearance. *NACA*
Above right: Pre-flight preparations and servicing of fluids and propellants for the XS-1. *NACA*

Muroc to head up preparations for inducting the experimental rocket-ship.

Williams had an outstanding boss in Hartley A. Soulé, then chief of the Stability Research Division at Langley and ultimately in charge of Muroc flight operations. The significance of this shift is written in the long history of Muroc and its enduring role in the story of transonic, supersonic and hypersonic flight research, in addition to a long list of experimental types and arcane research projects brought to flight status and including the test flights of NASA's Space Shuttle. But, with an eye on the swept-wing X-2, Soulé had just received word of the tragic loss in Britain of a D.H.108, an experimental research aircraft with wings swept back at 45deg. Powered by a Goblin 3 jet engine, on 27 September the second aircraft was taken on a high-speed dive from 3,048m (10,000ft) by chief test pilot Geoffrey de Havilland. It broke up in mid-air at Mach 0.9, destroying the aircraft and killing the pilot.

For more pressing matters, Williams set off for Muroc Dry Lake, and with him four technicians specialising in instrumentation, radio and radar tracking, sensors and flight recorders, flight planning and communications between ground facilities and flight activity. They arrived on 30 September 1946 and by the end of the year their group would number 13. Both Langley and the Muroc group had the British disaster on their minds as they arrived at the dry, dusty and scorched facility from where they would conduct some of the most audacious high-speed flight activity yet attempted. In several ways, not always apparent, the facility was ideal, having been formed long ago from a small inland sea out of which had emerged a vast area of clay and silt capable of withstanding surface pressures of up to 1,723kPa (250lb/in^2) across an area of approximately 168.35km^2 (65mls^2).

The impending independence of the Air Force energised change on several fronts and at Muroc it resulted in the merging of the previously separate crew training and flight activity into the Muroc Army Air Field which came directly under the authority of the Air Materiel Command at Wright Field. The place had already seen foreign and domestic aircraft on specific test operations, from ex-Luftwaffe types such as the Heinkel He 162 jet-powered interceptor to remotely-controlled Boeing B-17s flown with crew from Hawaii. Any visitor to Muroc in 1946 could witness a unique collection of aircraft types from vanquished and victor alike.

For the transonic test programme, special facilities and equipment were necessary and the team from Langley got to work preparing for powered flights with the X-1 by first organising the construction of two large tanks. One with a capacity of 56,775lit (15,000USgall) for LOX and a second with a capacity of 12,490lit (3,300USgall) for liquid nitrogen. Existing fuel trucks were modified for mixing alcohol and water and hardstand facilities were built to support the mating of the X-1 with its carrier-plane. The X-1 would be attached to the underside of a converted bomb bay by way of a loading pit which would be straddled by the B-29, allowing the research aircraft to be placed underneath and lifted up into the belly of the carrier-plane. Changes would be made later in the programme to accommodate larger variants of the initial X-1 series by raising the B-29 up on jacks.

The initial drop tests had been conducted with X-1-1 fitted with the 10 per cent wing and 8 per cent tail and on its return to Buffalo it received the newly completed 8 per cent wing and 6 per cent tail which, due to manufacturing challenges had not been ready. In any event, Bell wanted to conduct flight tests with the thicker wing which posed fewer questions about its suitability. With wing configurations in place as originally intended, on 7 October X-1-2 was mated with the B-29 at Bell's Niagara Falls facility. Accompanied by a P-51D chase-plane which would be used during flight trials, and by a Douglas C-47 for transporting personnel, the B-29 left for Muroc, all three arriving within the next two days after overnight layovers.

Plans to conduct a single glide flight on 10 October were thwarted when Goodlin had to abort the attempt. After getting sealed inside the X-1, cabin pressure began to rise despite efforts to adjust the relief valve and then the emergency dump valve. With no option other than jettisoning the side hatch, with the internal pressure now at a differential of 62kPa (9lb/in^2)

above atmospheric pressure, the panel shot off and struck the side access ladder, bending it out of shape. The deformation had jammed the ladder against the X-1 and Goodlin had to remain with the aircraft as the B-29 returned to base.

Following an inspection, the malfunctioning oxygen valve was repaired and the ladder returned to its required shape. The first drop test with the second X-1 took place the following day, conducted during the afternoon hours with the X-1 descending to a landing – the first of its kind at Muroc – less than seven minutes after separation from the carrier-plane. Two more drop tests were conducted, the last on 17 October. Lessons were learned and applied and preparations were made for the first powered flight. Before that could take place some modifications were made to the P-51D chase-plane, changes were made to the filter for the water-alcohol mixing equipment and a manual control for the nitrogen pressurisation system was added to the X-1's cockpit.

Above: Several changes were made to the XS-1 instrument panel and each first-generation aircraft had a slightly different layout. *NACA*

A division of labour

Before the first powered flight could take place, a final drop-test was conducted on 2 December with 875kg (1,930lb) of water-alcohol as ballast, jettisoned in a further test of the dump valve so that it would not land heavy. Facilities at Muroc dedicated to the XS-1 slowly evolved, with additional aircraft assigned to cover powered flights. Recognising that the P-51D would be quickly outpaced by the high-speed XS-1, an Air Force Lockheed FP-80 was brought in to act as a photo-ship. The P-51D would still operate as chase-plane for the initial drop and ignition phase of the rocket motor but the FP-80 would maintain pace for at least the early part of the powered phase.

The first powered flight attempt got under way two days later with a special group of company executives flown in by Lawrence Bell to witness the event. It was not to be. On the climb to altitude a nitrogen delivery valve froze, preventing pressurisation of the LOX tank and Goodlin from jettisoning the propellant. The mated aircraft would have to return to Muroc Dry Lake but to further complicate the situation, the X-1's nose leg extended unexpectedly. Under normal conditions, with the gear retracted, less than 30.5cm (12in) separated the underside of the X-1 from the ground. On the final approach, Goodlin retracted the nose leg and it remained up, arguably saving the two aircraft from disaster.

The first powered flight was achieved during the late morning on Monday 9 December 1946. Dropped from its carrier-plane at 11:54hrs local time and an altitude of 8,230m (27,000ft), the second X-1 fell away with a loaded weight of 5,448kg (12,012lb), falling notably quicker with a full fuel load than when empty on previous glide drops. Just 10sec after release, Goodlin lit the first of the four rocket chambers followed by the second, putting the X-1 on 50 per cent of maximum thrust. Shutting down the second chamber, Goodlin maintained a consistent speed of 531kph (330mph) and climbed to 10,668m (35,000ft) where he re-lit the second chamber and increased speed to Mach 0.79.

Following the meticulously organised flight plan, shutting off both chambers Goodlin began a dive, noting a small snaking motion caused by lateral sloshing of the propellants. Levelling out at 4,570m (15,000ft) he lit all four chambers but a few seconds later pressure began to fall away in the LOX line and he cut power. At that instant a fire warning light came on and remained so all the way through the final descent and landing. A small fire had indeed occurred and a couple of wires were burned through but damage was easily

repaired. Piloting the P-51D, and citing the rapidity with which he had been left behind, Richard Frost pressed for a P-80 Shooting Star to replace his piston-powered chase-plane and promptly got his wish. In all essential aspects, the flight had been a total success.

Under the terms of its contract, Bell was required to perform 10 demonstration flights, followed by a further sequence to demonstrate structural integrity and engine reliability. Only after those would the Air Force and the NACA take over for transonic tests and experimental research flights. By early February 1947, Goodlin could begin the second phase, having demonstrated stability and control at speeds up to Mach 0.8, where he encountered very mild buffeting which the strain gauges showed to be minor. The X-1 had demonstrated 0.79g pull-ups between Mach 0.4 and 0.8 without any structural effect and the RM-11 engine was proving far more resilient than forecast – far exceeding the one-hour operating life predicted by the company.

After completing eleven powered flights, and one week after an aborted flight due to low engine pressure, the X-1-2 was returned to Bell's Buffalo plant on 28 February 1947. After a detailed inspection, it would receive a range of modifications and improvements. Meanwhile, at Buffalo X-1-1 had received its rocket motor and the 8 per cent wing and on 5 April it was delivered to Muroc where it would take over the flight trials. Goodlin made a single glide flight five days later and took it through its first powered flight on 11 April. On touching down the aircraft bounced back into the air and came down hard causing the nose leg to retract, damaging the underside of the fuselage as it slewed to a stop. It would be out of action for more than two weeks before returning to flight on 29 April, a period during which the opportunity was taken to install some instrumentation.

Seemingly mundane to the casual observer, it is hard to overestimate the work conducted during these several months of verification and qualification testing. The Muroc facility was evolving as it worked up toward a concentrated series of research flights, its personnel acquiring new skills and learning how to conduct a scientific transonic and supersonic test programme. All the achievements that would follow in the years ahead originated in these early flights with the X-1 and were as valuable for the future investment in high-speed flight as they were for the activities of the first transonic aircraft.

Those events unfolded progressively during the first half of 1947, with a succession of powered flights with X-1-1. It was joined by X-1-2 which arrived back at Muroc on 8 May and resumed powered flights exactly two weeks later. The first flight of that aircraft since its return had been flown by Bell test pilot Alvin Johnston to Mach 0.72 (783kph/487mph) on 22 May. By the end of the month Bell had completed all 20

Far left: Photographed during restoration at the National Air & Space Museum, Washington, DC, the seat pan and backrest for the X-1 pilot were of conventional design as was the standard harness both in design and manufacture.
Left: The port side and forward area of the X-1 cockpit showing the minimal instrument displays and limited view for the pilot. The black panel above the 'Instrument battery' sign displays nitrogen pressure levels and jettison switches. *Dwayne Day*

Above: Bell test pilot Alvin 'Tex' Johnston took the X-1-2 into the air on 22 May 1947 for the first time after modifications at Pinecastle. *Bell Aircraft*

contractor flights at the increasingly busy facility where ever greater numbers of exotic aircraft were arriving for test, including the XB-43, XB-46, the N9M, P-82, P-84 and the Navy's XFJ-2 and XF6U. With the X-1 about to be handed over to the Air Force and the NACA, the facility hosted a special press day on 5 June, shipping in a group of aviation writers aboard five C-54s to see for themselves the post-war age of jets, rocket-ships and sleek new prototypes.

After a series of displays and impressive jet-engine runs, and a powered drop from the B-29 by Goodlin in X-1-1, the general cacophony was joined by Bell firing up the rocket motor on X-1-2 – first one chamber, then the second which promptly exploded causing a fire to break out in the aft fuselage. Amid the din nobody noticed this, until Richard Frost realised what was going on, jumped out and ran back to find the paint blistering. He summoned the ground crew who quickly opened panels to allow fire crews to dowse the flames, the alcohol burning almost invisibly. X-1-2 was flown back to Buffalo for the entire aft fuselage to be replaced by that element, cannibalised from the third X-1. It would not make another flight from Muroc for four months. But the Bell flights were now complete, 37 drop tests achieved of which 21 were under rocket power. It was time to turn the X-1 over to the clients.

The flight research programme originated with the development of the aircraft and evolved over time but responsibility for the division of labour had not been finalised when the contract had been awarded to Bell. Consequently, with an end to the war and significant progress made toward an independent Air Force, the fine details were only emerging as the contrac-

Above: Chuck Yeager poses in the X-1 cockpit and displays the limited space available for the pilot. *NACA*

tor acceptance flights came to an end. The initial plan to have Bell carry out the research programme was cast aside and replaced with a separation of roles.

In February 1947, the NACA hosted a conference at headquarters where it could lay out the programme with the Air Materiel Command. It agreed to fund the flight crew, maintenance tasks and X-plane fuel for research flights while the AMC provided equivalent funds for the B-29 carrier-plane. To support research flights by Air Force and NACA test pilots, the NACA sent De Elroy Beeler from Langley to its Muroc unit, where Gerald M. Truszynski would be assigned as the instrumentation engineer. Joseph R. Vensel would be seconded from the Lewis Laboratory to take charge of flight operations at Muroc for the NACA. The AAF agreed that AMC's Flight Test Division at Wright Field would assume responsibility for the military contribution to the flight research programme.

A further conference at Wright Field was held on 30 June where the NACA and the AAFs worked out the way the two would cooperate on research. It was clear that the newly emerging US Air Force, officially and institutionally independent from 18 September, wanted to conduct the initial flights through Mach 1 and it was decided that the Flight Test Division would handle that. It asserted the intention to achieve that as soon as possible and in as few preliminary flights as necessary. The NACA agreed to conduct a slower and more measured evaluation of the flight environment up to and through the transonic region. Stability, control, flight loads and aerodynamic performance were key aspects of the NACA's anticipated programme of work and from this decision grew the separate flight-by-flight objectives and timeline.

The very separate tasks made it necessary to assign the X-1-1 to Air Force activities, with X-1-2 supporting NACA activities. Instrumentation for each would be unique to respective aircraft. The Air Force would want to measure precisely the speed of the aircraft, normal, longitudinal and transverse accelerations, elevator stick forces, measurements of the relative positions of all flight control surfaces and loads. For the NACA, X-1-2 would be instrumented to record all those parameters as well, plus angular velocity in pitch and roll, angle of sideslip, forces acting on ailerons, elevators and rudder and calibrated measurement of the sensors and recorders. Both aircraft would have a 6-channel telemetry installation to transmit to ground receivers, speed, altitude and acceleration with respect to the ground. Far less dramatic than the flights required to compile this information, these elements of the programme fundamentally underpinned the way future X-series aircraft would integrate with a network of sensors and recorders of increasing capability.

The Air Force had yet to appoint pilots to fly the X-1-1 and a selection process was overdue. In charge of that was Col. Albert Boyd, then chief of the AMC's Flight Test Division. Himself a seasoned pilot, on 19 June Boyd claimed back the world speed record for the United States for the first time since 1923 when he flew the XP-80R (44-85200) over a 3km (1.864mls) course at an average speed of 1,003.811kph (623.738mph), over Muroc Dry Lake. It was the first world air speed record verified by the FAI to exceed 1,000kph (621.4mph) but that only lasted two months before the Navy seized it back with the Douglas Skystreak.

Before this event, in early June, Boyd turned to Maj. Kenneth Chilstrom, chief of the Fighter Test Section, to choose

Right: Photographed in 1961 after promotion to full colonel, Maj. Kenneth Chilstrom USAF had been tasked in June 1947 with selecting from a group of volunteers the pilots who would fly the X-1. *USAF*

pilots for the X-1. Chilstrom called a meeting of all the pilots at Wright Field, briefly informed them of the requirement and asked for volunteers. Very few people knew about the 'Sonic' project and for some the news was a surprise. Among them was Capt. Charles E. 'Chuck' Yeager, then 24 years old and already a veteran 'ace' of the Second World War with numerous decorations. Boyd already knew of this pilot and liked his can-do, no-nonsense style, assigned as a flight instructor at Perrin Field before secondment to Wright Field and the Fighter Test Section.

Yeager had joined up at the age of 18 years, and eighteen months later graduated with wings before flying P-39s, one of which disintegrated after a fire from which Yeager escaped by parachute, cracking a vertebra on landing. Shipped to England in January 1944, after achieving his first 'kill', he was shot down in a P-51 Mustang, escaped capture and got back to the UK while nursing a wounded colleague with the help of the French underground. Back in the air after D-Day on 6 June, Yeager raised his score to eleven German fighters before the end of the war, five of which he claimed in a single day.

Yeager expressed his interest, and when Boyd asked him to name two other pilots, recommended 1st. Lt. Robert A. Hoover and Capt. Jack Ridley. Already a serving aviator when America entered the war in December 1941, Hoover requested combat duty and flew Spitfires with 52nd Fighter Group but was shot down and spent the rest of his war as a prisoner of the German in Stalag Luft I. After liberation, he went straight to the Flight Test Division. Ridley was a graduate of the University of Oklahoma and obtained a master's degree in aeronautical engineering at Caltech in July 1946 from where he went to test pilot training. Boyd agreed with Yeager's choice and received confirmation of these appointments from his superior, Lt. Gen. Benjamin W. Chidlaw, deputy commander of Air Materiel Command.

Boyd pulled the three men together and told them that Yeager would be the project pilot with Hoover as his reserve and Ridley as the flight test engineer. Maj. Robert L. Cardenas would pilot the B-19 carrier-plane with Lt. Edward L. Swindell his flight engineer. Almost immediately, the three Air Force X-1 pilots were sent to Buffalo for familiarisation and training with the aircraft at the Bell factory. While there, they observed repairs to the damaged X-1-2 together with new plumbing and conduits in the aft fuselage area connecting propellants and nitrogen lines before a test firing of the rocket motor. Together with the repaired X-1-2, the Air Force team arrived back at Muroc on 27 July.

Support at Muroc had switched from the small contractor team to the Air Force with the completion of acceptance trials at the end of May but Bell was contracted to maintain a small familiarisation 'school' on site to give the AMC team guidance on operations and handling. There was still much for the Air Force to know about the project and as the focus switched from development and qualification trials, more still to learn about how to operate the aircraft on the ground and in flight, not least integration with the carrier-plane. For several weeks, ground personnel and flight support crew worked up toward the first Air Force flight and in early August the NACA put its own pilots in at Muroc for the scientific flights scheduled to follow after the priority speed flights.

Yeager's first flight in the X-1-1 occurred on 6 August, a glide down from 5,486m (18,000ft) during which he was able to delight in the aircraft's excellent handling qualities, performing three slow rolls on the way down! Two more glide flights followed, on the last of which he mockingly conducted simulated unpowered dog-fights with Hoover in the P-80 chase-plane. Yeager named the orange-coloured X-1-1 'Glamorous Glennis' in honour of his wife and with it so embellished he made his first powered flight in the type on 29 August.

Falling away from the B-29 at an altitude of 6,400m (21,000ft) and a speed of 410kph (255mph), he lit three rocket chambers separately in sequence and conducted a slow roll inadvertently experiencing negative g, causing LOX starvation and one chamber to shut down. Restoring level flight he relit the third chamber, shut it down and lit up the fourth. When he shut that down he went into a dive and logged Mach 0.85, higher than the Mach 0.8 limit required by the flight plan. This overshot brought a mild rebuke from Boyd, who asked Yeager to 'approach higher speeds progressively'.

Another powered flight followed on 4 September with a third four days later and a fourth on 10 September where he attained Mach 0.91. This was the area of greatest concern and the engineers debated the next steps which they cautioned should be taken progressively – but they were not test pilots and Yeager was convinced that the push through Mach 1 was a breeze; everything he had seen in the aircraft so far led him to believe that it was perfectly formed for this event. But some minor changes were necessary, such as a faster-responding horizontal stabiliser, and during the hiatus in flying he flew to Wright Field for checking out a pressure suit he would have to use for high altitude flights then being planned.

Through the transonic

Boyd was right behind Yeager in his confidence to press on. Already, the Air Force was chided by some industry giants for being too cautious over the transonic challenge. Much had been learned about this region from German research reports, from manufacturers pressing ahead with theoretical designs of transonic combat aircraft and from the various experiments which research establishments had been carrying out. Some of this knowledge came about as a result of great progress in wind tunnel development and new capabilities for such research, a lot of it prompted by the universal challenge it posed. While the Air Force and the NACA were creeping toward Mach 1, designers were already ahead of the X-programme in their assumptions of impending capabilities.

During this period the NACA had been readying its own flight test programme and on 25 September, back at Muroc, Yeager checked out the repaired X-1-2 and made its powered acceptance flight. Returning to the Air Force's X-1-1, Yeager carried out a powered flight in that aircraft on 3 October and another five days later for an airspeed calibration, reaching Mach 0.925. One more flight was planned before the attempt on Mach 1 and that occurred on 10 October.

It was an unusually flawed performance which, nevertheless, nudged the X-1 closer to the speed of sound than it had ever been before – it may even have exceeded that speed on this day. It began when Cardenas dropped the X-1 and Yeager lit the four chambers before shutting them down in sequence, Yeager entered a fast stall and then relit two chambers, soaring to 12,192m (40,000ft) where he registered Mach 0.94. Starved of fuel, the chambers were shut down and Yeager pushed the nose forward but, descending fast, the windscreen frosted over turning it opaque. Flying chase, Hoover and Frost talked Yeager down to a perfect landing. On the ground, calibration of the Machmeter and reconstruction of the flight path revealed a true speed of Mach 0.997, or 1,058.7kph (658mph), had been achieved at an indicated altitude of 11,278m (37,000ft).

It truth, it had been a close run thing. As he approached the transonic, Yeager lost all pitch control and could not raise or lower the nose, only regaining control by allowing the speed to bleed away. Tasked with interpreting the data and deciphering that for Yeager, Ridley believed that a shock wave had developed at the elevator hinge line, rendering it ineffective. He recommended that the only way to retain control was to lock the elevator in the plane of the stabiliser and use the complete surface for pitch control. Designed as a trim for the elevator, the pilot-adjustable horizontal stabiliser would allow Yeager to safely transit Mach 1 and maintain full control of the X-1. Yeager placed more faith in Ridley than in any other person in the team and he agreed to that procedure.

The team was now ready, no more preparatory tests were necessary and the flight plan was laid down for an attempt at Mach 1 on Tuesday, 14 October. To date, there had been 49 drop tests of the two X-1s, 30 with the first aircraft and 19 with the second, of which a total of 33 had been under rocket power. But in the lifestyle of the times and the hectic raciness of youthful test pilots, the weekend before the flight Yeager, his wife and a group of fellow revellers had lit up the desert from the raucous bar-room of 'Pancho' Barnes' *Fly-Inn* hostelry. Taking a horse out for a desert ride under a clear sky, Yeager failed to see a gate. But the horse knew it was there and bolted, throwing Yeager to the ground and breaking two ribs on impact. Fearing a grounding for the upcoming attempt, Yeager sought advice from a civilian doctor in Rosamond who bound his ribcage tightly and sent him on his way.

Preparations for the 50th drop from the carrier-plane began in the early dawn and involved briefings and advice from the NACA test team at Muroc and with Walt Williams, who urged caution in the their ever-conservative approach to flight tests. Ridley was there along with the rest of the flight crew, the B-29 piloted as always by Bob Cardenas. Taking to the air shortly after 10:00hrs local time, the B -29 chugged its way to altitude with Hoover and Frost flying flank chase in their P-80s. Climbing through 1,524m (5,000ft) Yeager worked his way down into *Glamorous Glennis*, Ridley sealing him in for cockpit pressurisation. At 10:21hrs Yeager pressurised the propellant tanks and ensured that the fuel jettison valve worked. At 6,096m (20,000ft) and a speed of 402kph (250mph), the X-1 was released – it was just 10:26 and the chase planes were in place.

In a carefully planned sequence, Yeager first lit up chamber 4 and then chamber 2 before shutting down chamber 4 and igniting chamber 3. Then chamber 2 was shut down and chamber 1 fired up, leaving that and chamber 3 to power the aircraft as it began to climb. Cutting in chambers 2 and 4 again put the X-1 on full thrust as it climbed to altitude and acceler-

Left: Col. Albert Boyd, chief of the AMC Flight Test Division (left) with the NACA's Walter C. 'Walt' Williams who would play an instrumental role in activities at Muroc before moving to NASA's manned space flight programmes. *NACA*

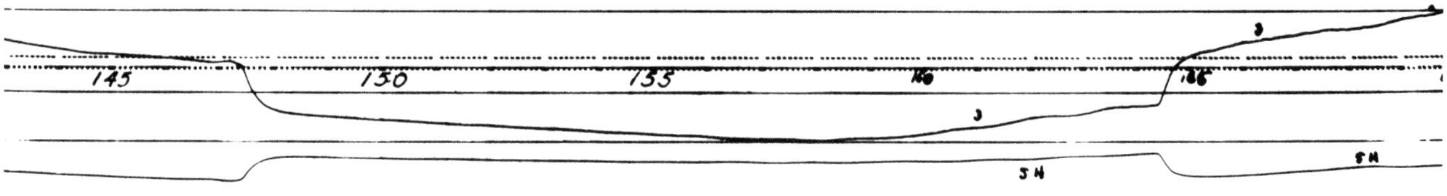

Above: The 'Mach jump' trace on the data recorder, proof that X-1-1 had successfully flown through the transonic. *NACA*

ated through to Mach 0.92. Here, the pilot carefully tested the controls, with rudder and the elevators losing effectiveness and the moveable horizontal stabiliser taking over pitch management. Reaching 10,668m (35,000ft), Yeager shut down two chambers and continued to climb before re-igniting them and levelling off at 12,192m (40,000ft).

The stabiliser was set at 2deg and Yeager accelerated through to Mach 0.99 at which point he noted that full control authority was regained and the aircraft benignly increased speed until the Mach meter registered 1.02, at which point it stopped momentarily before jumping to Mach 1.06 at an altitude of 13,106m (43,000ft). Yeager shut down the four rocket chambers with 30 per cent of propellants remaining and the X-1 gradually slowed back down through the transonic.

At an indicated Mach 0.98 there was a sharp bump akin to a sudden, momentary buffet and nothing else to mark the passage of flight toward the supersonic. To recover, Yeager continued to climb to 13,716m (45,000ft) before conducting a 1-g stall, silently gliding down toward the lakebed – so quiet in fact that he could hear the mechanical clock ticking on his instrument panel. A liberal coating of *Drene* hair shampoo applied before flight prevented the recurrence of the frosting experienced previously. Touching down at 10:40hrs, *Glamorous Glennis* rolled out across 4km (2.5mls) of desert floor before arresting completely the 257kph (150mph) landing speed.

Knowledge of the attempt at the speed of sound was restricted to those with a strong 'need to know' but that itself was highly limited and included only those at the facility directly supporting the flight. For instance, the 27-strong team from the NACA as well as Gerald Truszynski and his SCR-584 tracking radar, in addition to the Air Force crew attending to the mechanics and the aircraft crews directly involved. Word passed quickly through senior ranks within the military establishment but the public was not informed and there was no press conference or any of the public-relations paraphernalia that would attach itself to later flights. Neither was it mentioned in Muroc's official semi-annual report. For the Air Force, this was a military operation and as such it would be contained within the *cordon sanitaire* of high-level security.

Apart from which, there was a lot going on at Muroc, with more conventional aircraft and fighter prototypes such as the XP-86 (45-59597) which had arrived there on 10 September impressing ground crew with its 35deg swept-back wing. Test pilot George Welch would claim later that he had actually been the first man to fly through Mach 1 and there is little doubt that he may have been correct, as initial flight trials began with the XP-86 two weeks before Yeager's transonic passage. But that would have been in a dive, a capability officially recognised as being achieved by this aircraft during a shallow dive on 26 April 1948, when it became the first supersonic combat aircraft in the world. Production aircraft would be limited to Mach 0.95.

Exactly one week after Yeager's Mach-busting flight, it was the NACA's turn. It had been agreed that the Air Force would have priority with the facilities and equipment necessary to support flight activity with X-1-1 as it pushed forward with achieving Mach 1. The second X-1 had been at Muroc since the end of July and apart from Yeager's checkout flight in that aircraft on 25 September, the NACA had been waiting

Above: Personnel supporting the first test flight from Muroc pose for a group photo on 30 September 1946, with the B-29 carrier-plane straddling the pit in which the X-1 can be seen in a pitched-up attitude prior to mating. *Above right:* Yeager (left) and Capt. James T. Fitzgerald (right) with XS-1. Maj. Gustav E. Lundquist (centre) conducted the pressure distribution surveys and stability and control issues anticipated around Mach 1. Fitzgerald was a member of the test team and replaced Herbert H. Hoover while the latter was grounded for three months after an incident with a Republic F-84 when he broke both legs. *USAF*

for clearance to begin their more measured engineering and data-acquisition flights.

During August, the two NACA pilots assigned to fly the X-1 had arrived at Muroc to begin familiarisation and bedding-in activities. On secondment from the Lewis Flight Propulsion Laboratory, Howard C. Lilly was ex-Navy and had taken part in several air race competitions. But he had no experience with high subsonic speed and lacked knowledge of the X-1. Herbert H. Hoover had been with the NACA for seven years as a test pilot, pioneering the study of thunderstorms and their effect on aircraft by deliberately flying through them to gather data. It would fall to Hoover to brief Lilly on compressibility and to fit a P-51 with a Mach meter to give him experience with the buffeting and control issues as he approached the transonic.

Herbert Hoover made his first flight in X-1-2 on 21 October, the first NACA flight in the new, two-pronged approach to research with the type. Delighted with its handling qualities during this glide drop, Hoover came in hard and collapsed the nose leg on landing, putting the No. 2 aircraft temporarily out of action. Delayed by repairs to the aircraft and winter rains, on 16 December Hoover returned for a powered flight reaching Mach 0.84, the first rocket-powered aircraft flight performed by a NACA pilot. Hoover made three more flights before Lilly got his first opportunity with the No. 2 aircraft on 9 January 1948, followed by a second just six days later to Mach 0.76 while studying buffets and sideslips.

The Air Force lost no time in pushing ahead with its own research aimed at evaluating the X-1 at ever faster speeds. Yeager's next flight was on 27 October when he suffered an electrical failure and returned to land without having fired the rocket chambers. This was followed on each of the next two days by additional flights, on the first of which there was a failure of telemetry, still a new and evolving capability in manned aircraft. Additional flights were mounted on 31 October and on 3 and 4 November. Two days later, Yeager ran a full performance flight and achieved Mach 1.35 at 14,813m (48,000ft) taking the X-1 to uncharted regions.

Not before 10 March 1948 would the second X-1 give the NACA its first supersonic flight when Herbert Hoover took it to Mach 1.065. Lilly became the second civilian pilot to exceed the speed of sound by reaching Mach 1.1 on 31 March, five days after Yeager pushed the X-1-1 to Mach 1.45 (1,540kph/957mph) at 12,232m (40,130ft) in a dive. This was the highest speed recorded by any of the first generation of X-1 aircraft.

By this time the Air Force had intentionally leaked the secret of the first flight through Mach 1. Secretary of the Air Force Stuart Symington had decided a month after the historic flight that it would be necessary to allow industry in on the event so that it could benefit from the work underway. But the leak was staged as unofficial and came out to the public through the pages of the trade magazine *Aviation Week* in its issue dated 22 December. Unaware that the Air Force was behind the leak, Attorney General Tom C. Clark began an investigation at the Justice Department to seek ways it could prosecute the magazine for leaking national secrets but that was quickly outflanked when senior officials in the military met with civilian industrialists from the aviation industry to discuss the findings to date.

Meeting on 9 January 1948, the conferees heard about the flight operations and reviewed initial findings, drawing the conclusion that Mach 1 was a surmountable challenge met through adequate engineering information and appropriate design innovations. The expanding capabilities of jet combat aircraft, it was said, would soon allow fighters to fly and fight at supersonic speeds. Moreover, the value of the X-1 rested on the ease with which it could be transformed into a platform for research into thermal aspects of supersonic flight, on the development of weapon systems capable of being flown and fired by such aircraft and on the engineering challenges both in manufacturing and fabrication.

A key speaker at the seminar, Charles L. Hall from the AMC's Aircraft Projects Section informed his audience that in light of the relative ease with which the matter of compressi-

Right: Exhibition and aerobatics pilot 'Pancho' Barnes and her pilots of the Powder Puff Derby during the early 1930s performing stunt flying at Los Angeles, California. In the 1950s Barnes would open, and run, the often riotous *Fly-Inn* drinking den in the desert frequented by test pilots and flight crew alike. *Author's collection*

bility had been addressed, the Air Force was to procure additional and more capable X-1 series aircraft and that Bell was already working on those. From the outset, the third X-1 was to have carried the steam-driven turbopump instead of the nitrogen pressurisation system installed in the first two aircraft but this was proving problematic and difficult to design and integrate within the limited volume available. Nevertheless, additional X-1 aircraft would be designed to incorporate this as standard.

Under the plan outlined at the seminar, there were to be four more rocket-powered research aircraft based on the X-1, each bearing a suffix letter to indicate a particular design defined under MX-984, in a contract which would be signed with Bell Aircraft on 2 April 1948. Defined as X-1A, X-1B, X-1C and X-1D, each would be slightly different, with X-1B originally assigned the job of evaluating armament on a supersonic carrier. As existing combat aircraft became available for that work, that adaptation was cancelled. Nevertheless, the Air Force considered the X-1 series to be the workhorses for transonic and supersonic flight, anticipating research well beyond Mach 2. Not for a further five years would those flights begin, however.

Skystreak successes

While the Air Force had possession of the X-1 and a sustained and continuing supersonic research programme of its own, the Douglas Skyrocket was providing the NACA with vital aerodynamic data in its cooperative programme with the Navy. Although the greatest beneficiary was the NACA, now working closely with the Air Force and Bell to complement the other test regimes, the combined programmes began to build a consensus for a sustained programme of experimental projects. With the establishment of the National Defense Act of

Below: Flight support personnel for X-1-2 gather in front of the B-29 carrier-plane during October 1947. *Author's collection*

1947 that cooperation began to take on a realistic form; as related earlier, dedicated experimental aircraft had been denied to the NACA since it first conducted aerodynamic research. Equally important for the NACA, but arguably more so for the nation, it placed the newly independent US Air Force firmly in the centre of supersonic and hypersonic research.

The level of cooperation between the NACA and the two armed services was not reciprocated between the Air Force and the Navy, however. Each had a distinct line of dialogue and working relationship with the non-uniformed scientists and engineers of the NACA but not with each other. Paradoxically, as opined by John Stack, the X-1 was powered by a rocket motor developed with Navy funds and the D-558 was powered by an Air Force sponsored turbojet – at least until it too incorporated a rocket motor in the Skyrocket for added performance capability. Not until the development of the X-15 would the Air Force and the Navy work closely together on these research projects. As such, the experience of the NACA in working with the two uniformed services proved useful in the long term if not a little frustrating for immediate projects.

While plans were underway for converting three of the six D-558-1 Skystreak types on order into three D-558-2 Skyrockets, work pressed forward with the initial, turbojet-powered model. The fuselage was of semi-monocoque construction with aluminium alloy frames devoid of stringers or stiffeners and a magnesium skin of 0.254cm (1in) thickness. Wings and tail assemblies were fabricated from 75S aluminium alloy known for its high strength. Too ensure a high degree of smoothness on the exterior skin, Douglas fabricated a rigid assembly of firmly held jigs for accurately placing the panels in juxtaposition with each other. Thus, the structure was built up from the outside in.

The stabiliser could be set from an electric switch in the cockpit but the conventional controls were not power boosted and there were no aerodynamic balances or tabs on the ailerons or elevators. The Douglas team followed Bell's practice in providing their pilot with a control wheel for added leverage control under stresses and to counter surface flutter they added hydraulic dampers for the control surfaces. Although the NACA would provide the scientific instruments for research flights, Douglas came up with its own package for contractor flight trials. It also developed a sophisticated cooling system for the cockpit and the science instrumentation package, taking air from the engine.

Powered by a single Allison J35-A11 turbojet engine (the TG-180) delivering a thrust of 22,240N (5,000lb), the D-558-1 had a take-off weight of 4,584kg (10,105lb) and a maximum landing weight of 3,498kg (7,711lb). With a wing span of 7.62m (25ft) and a length of 10.88m (35.7ft), it had a height of 3.7m (12.14ft) and a wing area of 14m^2 (150.7ft^2). This was never going to be a supersonic aircraft and with the 65-110 aerofoil section the anticipated performance limit was about Mach 0.832 at sea level, a speed of 1,017kph (632mph).

There was some debate about speed brakes. The NACA did not like them but the test pilots did and complained loudly with such determination that, late in the construction phase, they were added to the outside of the aft fuselage. Capable of opening 60deg in three seconds at Mach 0.9, they each had deployment limiters so that they would not open fully should the loads be too high but, effectively they could slow the Skystreak by 80.45kph (50mph) in 15 seconds.

Above: It was never going to go supersonic but the Douglas D-558-1 Skystreak (top) was the first of its kind in providing the NACA with three practical research aircraft, flying between 14 April 1947 and 10 June 1953. The Allison J35-A11 turbojet engine which powered it was a production version of the TG-180 developed by General Electric. *Author's collection*

There was some uncertainty as to where the Skystreaks would conduct their flight research work. It had been assumed by some in the team that the Navy would use the Inyokern, California, facility where, nestled on the eastern slopes of the Sierra Nevada, compared to Muroc there was better accommodation for personnel and engineers but less support infrastructure for operating the aircraft. In early 1947 the Navy informed Douglas that they would have no call upon the aircraft until Douglas had completed evaluation flights to their satisfaction and the NACA went along with that.

Muroc won out to Inyokern and at the beginning of April 1947 the first tranche of the company test team arrived at the desert range, headed by Alden B. Carder and including test pilot Eugene F. 'Gene' May who had just been assigned as the project pilot. Personnel from the company's Experimental Flight Test Division were also sent across. May too was a veteran test pilot, having been with the company during the wartime years testing a wide range of aircraft. In time, the Navy's test pilot Comdr. Turner Caldwell would join as the project officer and would make the Navy's test flights together with Marine test pilot Lt. Col. Marion Carl. As with the Air Force's X-1, the NACA's Gerald Truszynski would provide the ground tracking equipment and set up the instrumentation for logging data from the flights.

Above: An evocative shot of the Skystreak in flight under wispy cloud out of Muroc over the Mojave Desert. *NACA*

The Skystreak was similarly equipped with the instrumentation installed in the X-1s, including a 12-channel oscillograph connected to the strain gauges, a 60-capsule monometer for measuring pressure and control forces, a 3-channel recording accelerometer, 4-channel telemetry circuit for airspeed, altitude, accelerations and the position of the control surfaces, a separate airspeed/altitude recorder, sideslip angle transmitter and a gunsight camera to photograph the instrument panel. Connected to all this instrumentation was a timer operating in 0.1-sec increments to get all the equipment operating on the same time base.

The phrase 'time base' as a separation of flight events would evolve from the NACA research aircraft across to test operations with rockets and missiles. It would be adopted when large rockets developed later by NASA were monitored in flight by separate sequences of events marked out as separate time bases. In that application, separate time bases would indicate a set of parameters aligned with the requirements of that specific phase of the flight. This was but one example of the numerous ways in which the evolving era of flight testing with telemetry and data processing would benefit from the combined work of government and industry.

All this would develop over the next decade with advanced equipment and increasingly more effective and reliable instrumentation, adding greatly to the value of the future X-series research projects and particularly to work carried out in support of the X-15 programme, without which the high performance capabilities of that aircraft would have been greatly reduced. As with the X-1 series, the instrumentation would frequently fail, requiring repeat flights to gather the same information, but this improved over time as technicians and engineers developed levels of reliability undreamed of in the late 1940s.

The first D-558-1 (BuAer 37970) arrived at Muroc on 10 April 1947 and was immediately admired for its highly polished, sleek appearance gleaming in a gloss coat of red paint with a silver tail cone. Test pilot Eugene F. May took it into the air for the first time on 14 April, the first of 101 flights with this type performed by the contractor before it was handed over to the NACA on 21 April 1949. They never used it, scavenging it for spares to operate the third Skystreak (BuAer 37972). Apart from two world record flights, the only notable achievement for this aircraft was on 29 September 1948 when Douglas test pilot May pushed it through Mach 1 during a 35deg dive on the final contractor flight for this particular aircraft. It was the only time a Skystreak reached the speed of sound.

Long before that, during October 1947 the Navy Bureau of Aeronautics had finalised its plan for the operational flight phase of the Skystreak programme and in a letter sent to both Douglas and the NACA dated 4 November, defined the role for each. Douglas would continue to fly the Skystreak and investigate its capabilities. The other two aircraft would go to the NACA for detailed science research. The Navy accepted responsibility for servicing and maintenance work conducted by Douglas and to furnish and pay for the engines, while the NACA would buy the fuel and oils from the Air Force. The

Navy also agreed to provide and fund all administrative support, leaving the NACA to coordinate research flights after the contractor handed over each aircraft.

The second aircraft (BuAer 37971) made 27 flights by a range of Navy and Marine Corps pilots before being handed to the NACA for their first flight on this aircraft on 25 November 1947. It made only 19 flights with them, the last on 3 May 1948 when it suffered a compressor break-up on take-off, severing control lines and killing its pilot, Howard C. Lilly. The third Skystreak made its debut in early 1948 before the NACA took it over with a flight on 22 April 1949 piloted by Robert A. 'Bob' Champine. The NACA flew 78 flights with this aircraft, the last on 10 June 1953 when test pilot Scott Crossfield flew it with tip tanks on a buffet test and an evaluation of low-speed stability and control techniques.

The value of the Skystreak rested on its ability to remain in the air for extended periods and while not as fast as the X-1 it was not limited to a few minutes of powered flight. In that respect, the two programmes were complimentary, with the Skystreak never getting the same adulation from the general public as the X-1 and its flights through the speed of sound and beyond. Nevertheless, 'plane-watchers' of this period enthused over the visually attractive and sleek appearance of the Skystreak, which was already seizing headlines before the public knew very much at all about the X-1 or its flight through Mach 1.

The first Skystreak seized the world air speed record back from the Air Force on 20 August 1947 when Navy pilot Cdr. Turner Caldwell averaged 1,030.8kph (640.663mph) on four passes of a 3km (4.8mls) course. Five days later, Marine test pilot Marion Carl flew the second Skystreak to a new record of 1,047.356kph (650.796mph), also at low level. But these were not merely record-breaking, propaganda flights. Over time, and as a result, the general operating standards for research aircraft improved, a lot of it based on lessons learned with these highly specialised aircraft, changes to design and flying routines which helped military aviation particularly and civilian aviation in general.

Below: Seen here with ground crew on the ramp with the Skystreak, Robert A. Champine joined the NACA as a test pilot in December 1947 and would play an important role in this and the X-1 programmes. *NACA*

The crash that killed Howard Lilly resulted in better protection for containing compressor blades during a malfunction, and for armouring the control cables to reduce the likelihood of damage. The red paint applied to the aircraft included the flight control surfaces but the sensitivity to changes in their weight and their dynamic characteristics was such that even changing the paint altered their response. This was discovered when the gloss red colour rendered the aircraft almost invisible at high altitude when viewed from the ground. To make them easier to identify in recording cameras, they were repainted which – with the control surfaces remaining red – marked a shift to all NACA research types receiving a white finish rather than the silver of the Air Force's X-series, or the red of the initial Skystreaks.

As with the X-1 series research aircraft, the NACA required the Skystreak's wings to be perforated for pressure distribution measurements and Douglas had to provide 400 orifices for these sensors. The challenge to manufacturing and assembly of the wing sections was significant and helped lower tolerances to new levels. During flight tests the stick force increased significantly, going from 22.24N (5lb) to 133.4N (30lb) between Mach 0.82 and Mach 0.87. At the lower value lateral stability dropped appreciably and above Mach 0.84 there was marked wing-drop. After much work on the issue, vortex generators fitted to the wings stabilised the flow of air and solved the problem. In no time, manufacturers across the country added vortex generators to existing and planned aircraft with notable effect.

Over time the research equipment and instrumentation changed and for many flights the D-8558-1 had 287kg (634lb) of equipment installed. For several years it was the only aircraft for which the NACA could obtain detailed information and useful data in and around the transonic region. This allowed the Air Force and the NACA to get on with the job of exploring supersonic flight with the X-1s. It had always been understood that the Air Force and the Navy, along with the direction of the NACA, would cover the range of test requirements set down toward the end of the Second World War. It could also be said that at a time of worsening political tensions between the United States and the Soviet Union, the need for faster and better combat aircraft was never as great as it was in the period served by the Skystreak.

Test pilots in general liked the Skystreak and research engineers, as well as aerodynamicists and design teams testified to the seminal role it played in establishing baselines for how aircraft operated in the transonic zone, each conducting highly important work without which the progress in both civilian aircraft and combat planes would have been impossible. In hindsight, it was the work conducted by these aircraft that helped push US aeronautical engineering to new heights, when compared with the sluggish progress and false starts in European aviation at the time.

Chapter Five

On to Mach 2

As noted, in the immediate aftermath of the Second World War American aviation companies sought new government projects and programmes to maintain their workloads and production lines and to invest in new products. But they were not without their own, and frequently energetic, search for the means to fly faster and higher in pursuit of advanced goals and new capabilities. Merely as one example, North American Aviation had pushed for swept wings on jet-powered combat aircraft, transforming the Navy's straight-wing Fury into the Air Force's F-86 Sabre. The research work already conducted by the Skystreak resulted in further interest in the NACA acquiring an early example of the F-86 for their own purposes and they managed to obtain on loan the fifth production F-86A (47-609). First flown in June 1948 it had been seconded to the manufacturer for tests.

The F-86A was eventually bailed to the NACA-Ames Laboratory on 10 April 1950. Registered as NACA-135, it would remain with them until 15 March 1956 for evaluating flying qualities and for research into stability and control. It was also equipped with sensors for measuring variable stability and as such played a major role in defining high subsonic responses which interleaved with similar work on the third Skystreak. While the intensive work to plumb the depth of the high subsonic and transonic regions was continuing at Muroc, advancing the speed envelope to true supersonic research was already underway with the next generation. With authorisation to develop the new swept-wing Skyrocket signed on 29 January 1946, and the decision to shift the last three Skystreaks over to the new and faster design, the Navy and the NACA set their sights on Mach 2.

Existing interest in swept-wing research for supersonic flight was sustained, if not accelerated by the Naval Technical Mission to Europe in May 1945, the month the war ended on that continent. Douglas had sent Eugene Root and A. M. O. Smith to Europe to gather details from the German research establishments. They brought back to the US a significant collection of material which produced microfilmed documents,

Above: Encouragement to study the advantages of swept-wing configurations for supersonic flight came from detailed examination by US aircraft manufacturers of the Messerschmitt Me 262, which paradoxically was not originally designed to have such wings. *USAF*

summaries, reports and photographic evidence of a very large research effort conducted by the Germans into swept-wing aircraft.

As set out, the Skyrocket airframe was to be built for three separate power configurations. The first aircraft would be equipped with a Westinghouse J34-40 turbojet with a thrust of 13,344N (3,000lb). This aircraft was designed to operate at speeds up to Mach 0.825. The second Skyrocket would be a rocket powered version using a motor almost identical to that installed in the X-1s and capable of flight to Mach 2. The third option would incorporate both a single, four-chamber rocket motor and a J34-40 turbojet and would cover the flight regime up to Mach 1.08.

All three were dimensionally identical, with a length of 9.41m (30.9ft), a wing span of 7.62m (25ft) and a height of 3.85m (12.66ft). The first, turbojet-powered Skyrocket configuration had take-off and landing weights of 4,659kg (10,572lb) and 3,589kg (7,914lb) respectively. The second, rocket-powered aircraft configuration had comparative design weights of 7,161kg (15,787lb) and 4,273kg (9,421lb) while the hybrid powered third Skyrocket option had a maximum take-off weight of 6,924kg (15,266lb) and a maximum landing weight of 4,309kg (9,500lb).

Below: With a sweep angle of 35deg, the wing for the Skyrocket afforded the same aspect ratio as the Skystreak but with 16.7 per cent greater area and a slightly increased thickness/chord ratio of 12 per cent. *NACA*

As Douglas developed the shape of the D-558-2 Skyrocket it came more to resemble that of the Bell X-1 series, particularly the later models, but there was no wing fillet as such. Led by Van Evry, the design team chose the NACA 65-series wing section for its better performance at low speed and good stall characteristics, tapered at the tip to a NACA 63-012 section (going from 10 per cent to a 12 per cent t/c ratio). The wing area was increased to 16.257m^2 (175ft^2), expanding the area by approximately 16.7 per cent compared to the D-558-1. The sweep angle was set at 35deg at the 30 per cent chord line, which promised good high and low speed handling. In addition, the Skyrocket would have wing fences and leading edge slats. With the same span as the D-558-1, the -2 had an aspect ratio of 3.57. Just as on the X-1, the horizontal stabiliser had a thinner section, the same 63-010 as the wing, and it had an increased critical Mach number by providing a sweep angle of 40deg.

The same design of escape capsule was used for the Skyrocket and the aircraft was built to a maximum load factor of 12-g at a weight of 5,103kg (11,250lb) and a total limit load of 7.3-g at 6,123kg (13,500lb). As with the Skystreak, with the turbojet engine the Skyrocket was expected to explore the transonic regime to a maximum Mach 1. A significant shift away from the Skystreak required Douglas to relocate the landing gear and the fuel to the fuselage, which required a greater diameter than that of the D-558-1 because the common structure to all versions was required to contain the

more voluminous propellant tankage for the rocket motor when it was carried.

Three options were available for the Skyrocket: turbojet only, rocket and turbojet or rocket only and the propulsion adopted for each aircraft would depend to a large extent on the availability of the rocket motor. For the conventional configuration of D-558-2, the turbojet was located in the lower fuselage below the wing interface with 984lit (260USgall) of gasoline in two tanks, rather than the kerosene used in the D-558-1 contained in a single tank. The exhaust canted downwards at an angle of 8deg.

The XLR-8-RM-6 rocket motor was powered by diluted ethyl-alcohol fuel and liquid oxygen (LOX) with a turbopump powered by the decomposition of hydrogen peroxide over a catalyst for driving the propellants into the chambers. For the rocket-only powered second Skyrocket, a 1,430lit (378USgall) fuel tank was located on top of the tail pipe in the aft fuselage and the spherical 1,305lit (345USgall) LOX tank was situated in the fuselage above the intake duct line. The hydrogen peroxide tank was placed forward of the LOX tank and had a capacity of 41.6lit (11USgall) with a 90 per cent purity. The pump was situated between the alcohol tank and the fuel tank for the turbojet.

The propellant delivery was effected through two pumps, one each for fuel and oxidiser respectively. Three spherical and four cylindrical helium tanks were installed for pressurising the fuel tank to 206.8kPa (30lb/in²), the LOX tank to 344.7kPa (50lb/in²) and the hydrogen peroxide tank to 2,758kPa (400lb/in²). Pressurised to 13,790kPa (200lb/in²) in the seven holding tanks, by choosing helium over nitrogen the design team saved 13.6kg (30lb) in weight.

The dual-powered D-558-2 with its hybrid propulsion system incorporated the same gasoline for its J34-40 turbojet engine and the XLR-8-RM-5 rocket motor as in the respective second and third aircraft. As reflected in the designation, the XLR-8 for the hybrid adaptation was slightly different to the all-rocket configuration. Fuel capacity for the rocket motor in this hybrid version was limited to 726lit (192USgall) while the LOX tank held 643lit (170USgall). Like modifications applied to the first aircraft, the third D-558-2 would be converted to an all-rocket, air-launched configuration.

Instrumentation was carried ahead of the LOX tank in the fuselage and consisted of the same equipment, sensors and transmission gear as that developed for Skystreak, using the

Douglas D-558-2 Skyrocket

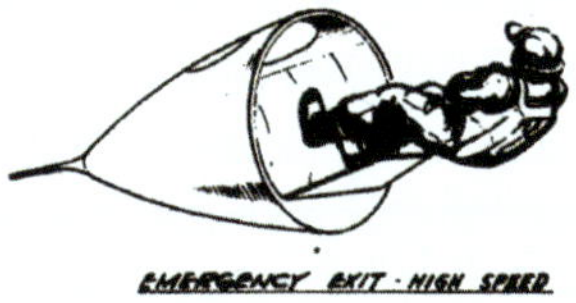

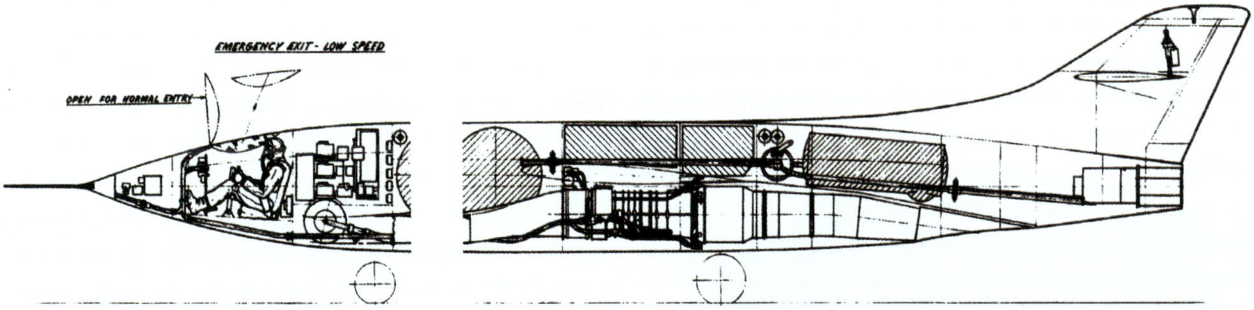

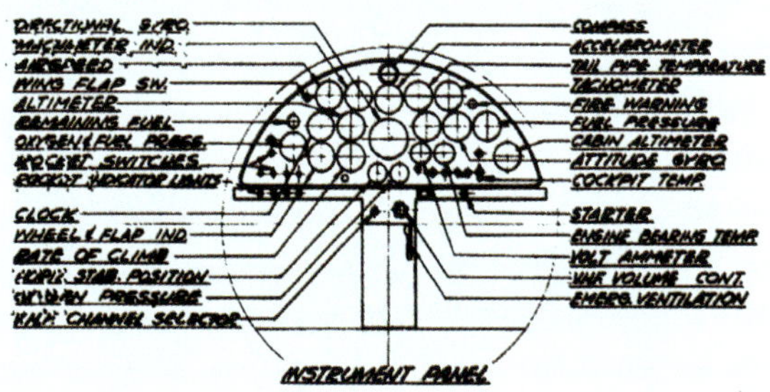

Above: An early design submission for the D-558-2 Skyrocket dated 18 March 1946 accommodating both jet engine and rocket motor. *Author's collection*

Above right: Initially, the Skyrocket had a conformal cockpit window but tests would show that this was unnecessary and, like the second-generation X-1 series, it was replaced with a more conventional, stepped window. *NACA*

INBOARD PROFILE

Left: Skystreak gets airborne on its Westinghouse J34 turbojet engine for an early development flight. *NACA*

same Miller oscillography as that designed for the D-558-1. The design team was able to equip the Skyrocket with 904 strain gauges in the wing, consisting of 226 channels of four gauges each for detailed mapping of stress points. In all, 6.4km (4mls) of gauge wiring and some 4.8km (3mls) of pressure tubing from wing and tail surface stations direct to the instrumentation compartment were installed in the Skyrocket. In addition, some 400 pressure orifices were cut into the wing and tail surfaces directly connected to the Miller oscillograph. These assisted with pressure distribution surveys.

The detailed design decisions and most of the engineering drawings for the D-558-2 were completed by October 1946 along with 80 per cent of tooling and 70 per cent of fabrication by the time the Skystreaks were close to completion. By this date the first two swept-back wings were being assembled and while there were similarities between the two types, few manufacturing differences were evident. Like the Skystreak, the Skyrocket was constructed of heavy-gauge magnesium sheet over an aluminium frame and no stringers. The wings and tail surfaces were in high-strength 75S aluminium alloy and of rib and stringer construction. The flight control surfaces were devoid of any aerodynamic balances and there were no tabs or power boost, although tungsten alloy counterweights were attached to the ailerons.

The evolution of flight operations with the Skystreak resulted in a rapid decision to go forward with this second-generation research project well ahead of Air Force plans for the X-1 series. As described in the previous chapter, not until the end of 1947 did the Air Force and the NACA agree to push forward with further development of the X-1. When these aircraft did arrive they were not as flexible in flight research capabilities or as effective in obtaining the data required.

The Skyrocket was three years ahead of the second-generation X-1 series in getting into the air and did much more flight research, conducting many more flights. Yet for all that, the Skyrocket is not as well remembered as the evocative Air Force flights under the X-1, invoking a sense of secrecy and mystery under the very nature of its designation.

Left: With various powerplant configurations, the control panel in the Skyrocket cockpit varied according to the propulsion and changed over time, this being a representative arrangement of dials and switches. *NACA*

A surfeit of research

The sleek, swept-wing D-558-2 Skyrocket appeared at Muroc on 10 December 1947, trucked in under a tarpaulin covering its glossy white finish. When unveiled it looked every inch a high performer. While attention to the Air Force X-1 had attracted interest, two months on from its flight through Mach 1 a very large number of people at the facility knew nothing of the record flight. It is entirely coincidental that within two weeks the Air Force would leak its historic achievement, awakening the world to the supersonic era. But the rumours were already muttering concerns, that while the Navy now had its own swept-wing contender – perhaps for Mach 2 – and industry was already testing a swept-wing fighter, the F-86, the Air Force had nothing to show in the realm of research aircraft incorporating wing planforms more suited to future combat aircraft design. But there were other high-speed X-planes in the mix, not least the X-2 which was being designed for Mach 3.

All that was in the future and in the late 1940s there were Skyrockets to fly. Flight tests with the first D-558-2 (BuAer 37973) were delayed a little as technicians waited for its Westinghouse engine. Those began with the first flight on 4 February 1948 piloted by test pilot John F. Martin who had been with Douglas since 1940. But underpowered with the turbojet, managers decided to attach JATO rocket packs to assist it into the air. Some changes were required as a result of early trials, including a modification to the vertical tail and a much modified cockpit and windscreen assembly. As delivered, it had the same glazed-over nose section as that of the X-1 series but a more conventional raised cockpit and a forward wind shield assembly was retrofitted. After a total of fifteen flights, Martin handed the aircraft over to the company test pilot Eugene F. May. Douglas would conduct a total of 122 contractor flights.

The second Skyrocket (BuAer 37974) was also completed for flight exclusively with the J34-WE-40 turbojet engine and the first flight occurred on 2 November 1948 with May at the controls. Delays in development of the rocket motor and its installation forced changes to the original schedule. The

Above: Pre-flight preparations for a ground launch of the Skyrocket with diagnostic equipment attached. *NACA*

NACA worked its plans into a mixed test programme, starting out with turbojet-powered operations until the rocket motor was ready and could be used for flight trials. A second flight took place on 7 November and it was turned over to the NACA on 1 December, marking the start of its flight research programme. There was trouble with the turbojet engine and the aircraft was grounded until 24 May 1949 when Robert Champine took it on its first flight for the NACA. But without its rocket motor the aircraft had limited value and stability with air loads tests limited it to Mach 0.85.

In the interim period it had been equipped with instrumentation and a second flight followed on 1 June 1949 when Champine experienced a sudden pitching moment, which unsettled the pilot, inducing him to land immediately. This phenomenon had been expected for aircraft with swept-back wings and it focused the NACA on exploring the reasons. Thus began a highly concentrated endeavour undertaken by pilots Champine and John Griffith and, with forewarning of when that might occur, provided the opportunity to fly right through the violent manoeuvre and explore recovery solutions. This extended period of investigation lasted for the remainder of the year and into January 1950, after a total of 21 NACA fights with this aircraft had been completed and flown by Champine and John H. Griffith. It was returned to Douglas, the first rocket engine for this aircraft now available for installation.

Throughout the development of the Skyrocket programme attention had been given to the possibility of an air-launched mode. Initially, the rocket motor had been intended as a supplementary form of propulsion, adding energy to an aircraft already in flight for high-speed runs. But in 1948 initial studies by Douglas had been shared with the Navy and the NACA where a suitably modified Skyrocket would adopt the flight profile of the X-1 series. If taken into the air by a carrier-plane it could be dropped for runs of up to a theoretical Mach 2. Due to uncertainties about handling the aircraft with both jet fuel and rocket propellant, on 21 October 1948 it was agreed to postpone that decision until flight experience with the turbojet-powered aircraft had provided basic handling and operational experience.

With flight trials clearing the way, a decision was taken to equip the third Skyrocket (BuAer 37975) with a rocket motor but calculations showed that on its own the additional propulsion would only increase the speed from Mach 0.82 at 6,096m (20,000ft) to Mach 0.99. With both powerplants, it was projected to reach Mach 1.08 at 12,192m (40,000ft). The first flight of the hybrid Skyrocket (BUAer 37975) took place under turbojet power alone on 8 January 1949 followed by the first rocket-powered flight on 25 February, both flown by Gene May. Four months later, on 24 June it exceeded Mach 1 successfully and uneventfully.

All the problems that had persuaded the Air Force and the NACA to air-launch the X-1 were revisited for the Skyrocket: laden with volatile rocket propellant a power failure at take-off could be catastrophic. The advantages of an air-launched mode became very clear and were decisive in adapting the programme for an air-launched, rocket-powered test series. It melded too into a fully integrated research plan involving the X-1 series where comparable performance from the Skyrocket could provide data between swept-wing and straight-wing aircraft at the same Mach numbers. The logic was indisputable. Douglas calculated that with an air-launch the Skyrocket could achieve at least Mach 1.46 and possibly Mach 1.6. It

Right: A Navy Boeing B-29 type designated P2B-1S (BuAer 84029) raised on jacks for fit checks on the hoist before heading out to the ramp for mating with the Skyrocket. *NACA*

would generate highly valuable data which would assist with detailed design of the X-2 which was to have an unusual bi-convex wing section.

The decision was endorsed by NACA director Hugh Dryden and Douglas received a supplementary order from the Bureau of Aeronautics on 25 November 1949 to modify the second aircraft (BuAer 37974) when it went back for installation of its rocket motor and to adapt that and the third aircraft for air-launch capability. With good results from the decision to use a B-29A for the X-1 series, another aircraft of that type was selected by the Navy as a carrier for the Skyrockets. Under its unique type badging system, it was acquired and given the Navy designation P2B-1S with BuAer number 84029.

That move also set in motion a supplementary programme to adapt facilities at Muroc for receiving the second carrier-plane while Douglas continued testing with the first aircraft, which on 25 October had begun its 'performance investigation' flights. The first Skyrocket would be handed over to the NACA on 31 August 1951 but in 1954 it was returned to Douglas for adaptation to an all-rocket, air-launch configuration. Back at Muroc on 15 November 1955 it was flown once on 17 September 1956 when John McKay took it on a familiarisation flight before the aircraft was retired, work with the other two Skyrockets being completed during the second half of the year.

William B. Bridgeman, the Douglas pilot assigned to fly the drop-tests with the second and third Skyrockets, was an ex-Navy pilot who had conducted wartime shipping strikes in PB4Y-1 Liberators right across the Pacific Ocean. Decorated for his achievements, Bridgeman joined Douglas at its El Segundo division in 1948 and became familiar with the Skyraider and the F3D Skyknight programmes. Joining the Skyrocket programme in 1949 he flew some of the contractor flights with the first aircraft.

The third aircraft had made 15 ground-launched flights piloted by May but in early September 1950, Bridgeman began captive airborne tests, verifying the fuel jettison system and restarting the turbojet at altitude. The first drop flight was conducted on 8 September at a speed of 362kph (225mph) from 7,574m (24,850ft). A planned sequence of tests on the way down had to be aborted when the airspeed system froze up but three more flights were conducted by the beginning of October, all with the turbojet only. Bridgeman made the first air-launched, rocket-powered drop with this aircraft on 17 November and pushed the aircraft through Mach 1 in a gentle dive.

One more flight was to be completed by Bridgeman before handing it over to the NACA, a combined turbojet/rocket flight to verify the operation of integrated propulsion. It began according to the flight plan when the Skyrocket dropped away from the B-29 at 9,144m (30,000ft) and after lighting up two rocket chambers he began a climb on both systems, pushing over at 12,192m (40,000ft). Igniting the other two chambers, negative-g starved the rocket motor of propellant and he shut it down. Bridgeman got some buffeting around Mach 0.92 which was not unusual at this point but realised that this was compressor stall, getting a flameout as he idled the throttle. Yeager was flying chase and as the Skyrocket's forward windshield fogged over he talked Bridgeman down. At 7,315m (24,000ft), Bridgeman successfully relit the J34 and got cockpit pressurisation to clear the windscreen.

The third Skyrocket was officially handed over to the NACA on 15 December 1950, when it received the NASA number 145. Scott Crossfield was assigned to this aircraft and made his flight in that aircraft seven days later. For the next six years he would share flights with Robert T. Jones, Stanley F. Butchart, Marion Carl, Joseph A. Walker, Frank K. Everest and John McKay. On 14 August 1951, Brig. Gen. Albert Boyd made the NACA's ninth flight on this third Skyrocket for familiarisation, reaching Mach 1.05. Some flights were made with shaped external stores for studies of stability and control and some were intentionally turbojet or rocket powered alone. The last of 66 flights with this aircraft was made by McKay on 28 August 1956.

Modifications to the second Skyrocket were comprehensive and after the turbojet flights ended in January 1950, the aircraft was given the most substantial rework into a rocket-only research aircraft. The Westinghouse J34 was removed together with the fuel tanks with fuel and LOX tanks

Left: August 1953 and the No. 3 rocket-powered Skyocket is mated to the P2B-1S for a test flight. *NACA*

Above: Dropping cleanly away from the US Navy P2B-1S, the Skyrocket begins another test flight from Muroc. *NACA*
Right: Seen here with the Douglas X-3, ex-Navy pilot William B. Bridgeman made a major contribution to the Skyrocket programme, including test flights with the second and third Skyrockets. *Author's collection*

installed and capacity increased as noted earlier in the description of the various propulsion configurations. The additional plumbing and circuitry was not as dense as the hybrid configuration and on a par with the first Skyrocket before its own modification.

Several other changes were necessary to transform the visual appearance of this aircraft, including removal of the exhaust pipe for the turbojet and blanks placed across the air intakes on either side of the fuselage. Engineering modifications had been completed by August 1950 after which Douglas fitted instrumentation and associated test equipment. In its new configuration, carried aboard the P2B-1S the Skyrocket was back at Muroc on 8 November by which date the third Skyrocket had made four launches to pioneer the new air-drop technique.

The attempt to join it in air-launched trials in December got off to a frustrating start when the carrier-plane laboured to altitude only to abort the attempt on three occasions. The first because of a communications problem with the Skyrocket and then because of bad weather. Conducted on 26 January 1951, the first drop was very nearly a disaster. On entering the cockpit prior to the drop, Bridgeman noticed a slow fall in propellant pressure and tried to call an abort within seconds of release, conducted by the carrier-plane pilot George Jansen. But Jansen had his finger on the 'talk' button as he counted Bridgeman down and failed to hear Bridgeman calling out to stop the release. At issue was the balance of weight in the two propellant tanks. With falling pressure it was unlikely the rocket motor would start and if, after falling away, the tanks jettisoned their contents disproportionately, the imbalance would send the Skyrocket out of control. Jansen pushed the release button and the Skyrocket dropped away from the carrier-plane at an

Left: Chatting with Williams (left) and Joe Vensel (right), Crossfield savours the moment, the only NACA pilot to break through a Mach-number for the first time. The others were taken by Air Force pilots. *NACA*

altitude of 9,754m (32,000ft).

Uncertain as to the motor's response under such low pressure, Bridgeman hit the start switch for the first chamber and was relieved to feel the positive punch of its thrust. Lighting up the other three chambers he accelerated up through 12,497m (41,000ft), descended slowly and levelled off at 2,709m (8,890ft), achieving Mach 1.28 before starting the descent. Again, there were some oscillations around Mach 0.9 and the Skyrocket started into a 'Dutch roll' from which Bridgeman was able to recover stable flight and land. To prevent a recurrence of the problem on future flights, a green light was installed in the P2B-1S to indicate continued readiness to release. Problems continued, however. Some involving an inability to jettison propellant after an aborted attempt, the mated aircraft having to land with the Skyrocket full of propellant.

As the contractor fights built up, Douglas got permission to conduct full performance runs and on 18 May 1951 Bridgeman achieved Mach 1.72 at an altitude of 16,764m (55,000ft), a speed of about 1,818kph (1,130mph). Technically, this was to have been the final contractor flight but Douglas was allowed to conduct several more attempts, on each achieving higher Mach numbers. On the penultimate performance flight, on 7 August Bridgeman achieved Mach 1.88 at 20,117m (66,000ft), approximately 2,027kph (1,260mph), the fastest speed recorded by that date of any aircraft. On the last of his seven flights eight days later, Bridgeman took the Skyrocket to a record altitude of 24,229m (79,494ft).

Mach 2

By the time Douglas handed over the second of the three Skyrockets on 31 August 1951, the NACA had three aircraft in the hangar at Muroc. The first Skyrocket was capable of only subsonic flights, usually verifying wind tunnel predictions and calibrating the measurements with those on the ground. The third Skyrocket had the hybrid propulsion and would be used for sustained research activities as recorded above. But the second Skyrocket had the potential for flying at twice the speed of sound.

NACA flights got under way with that aircraft on 28 September in a programme designed to probe the maximum performance potential and so construct a research programme limited only by its maximum performance. On his second flight Crossfield reached Mach 1.28. After the fourth such flight on 16 November, inclement weather set in for the usual rainy season and flights with the second aircraft did not resume until Crossfield again went into the air on 13 June 1952. Eight more flights followed with a wide range of test objectives and stability and control measurements, the last for the year on 23 October before, again, rain stopped play.

Flights with the second Skyrocket resumed on 26 March 1953 and followed a busy pattern, one in which Crossfield attained Mach 1.878 on 5 August. During the preceding weeks plans were laid for a pressure suit and physiology test flight be flown by Marion Carl, courtesy of a special Navy request. The first attempt had to be aborted but on 14 August he failed to achieve the target altitude of 24.384m (80,000ft) and failed again four days later. But on 21 August he finally broke through the target altitude, reaching 25,370m (83,235ft). Carl made a few more flights supporting medical research and tests with the high-altitude pressure suit before handing the Skyrocket back to Crossfield.

Some technical changes had been made to improve the performance of the aircraft and increase the thrust of the rocket motor by 6.5 per cent. This was achieved by extending the nozzles of the four combustion chambers, which also prevented the exhaust plume impinging on the rudder above Mach 1. The first flight with this modification occurred on 17 September 1953, when Crossfield achieved Mach 1.85 at 22,555m (74,000ft). More flights followed for stability and roll control and several in addition for lateral control tests. On 14 October 1953 he nudged the Skyrocket to Mach 1.96 – the fastest so far.

Much data had been obtained and a lot of information accumulated in the 30 NACA flights with the second Skyrocket. It had been more than six years since Yeager took the X-1 through the speed of sound and engineering discussions were held with aerodynamicists as to whether the aircraft could be pushed through Mach 2. For several years now, the rocket-plane had reduced these ambitious test flights to an almost routine exercise, all the planning, calculations and precise flight parameters honed to a slick operation far removed from the cluttered days of learning when all this was new, novel and unique.

Much debate surrounded the plans for a Mach 2 attempt and a precise set of information, together with a request for approval, was sent up to Hugh Dryden. Instrument records, oscillography data and reams of detailed flight charts defined the precise operating corridor for the all-rocket research aircraft. Approval was granted and the aircraft's project engineer, Herman O. Aukenbruck compiled a detailed flight plan for the attempt. The trajectory was simple, a well-defined parabolic arc in which Crossfield would fall away from the B-29, push up to an altitude of 21,945m (72,000ft), place the nose into a gentle dive and accelerate to Mach 2.

Right: Welcomed back by 'Walt' Williams, Scott Crossfield pictured after his successful flight to Mach 2 on 20 November 1953. *NACA*

More than a month after achieving Mach 1.96 and a further three interim flight evaluation runs, Crossfield was ready for the attempt on Mach 2. There had been competition from the Air Force with its second-generation X-1 series, about which more later, but the desire for the NACA to be the first through Mach 2 was palpable. It played no small part in the NACA's expanding competition with both the Air Force and the Navy as confidence in the organisation's skills and capabilities grew with each passing year. It underpinned an increasing resilience in providing baseline data for ever more advanced aircraft, although the irrevocable link with the Air Force and the Navy was both necessary and productive.

Considerable attention had been paid to preparing the Skyrocket for this attempt, the stainless steel propellant jettison pipes replaced with light aluminium tubes which would burn away when the rocket motors ignited, their function redundant. A small weight saving measure but one welcomed, nevertheless. The panel lines were smoothed with covering tape carefully applied and the entire exterior of the aircraft polished with several coats of wax. The propellant was prepared especially for this flight, the fuel being pre-chilled so that more could be added to the existing tank. And the oxidiser tank was to be pre-chilled with LOX five hours before the flight, with more added just before launch after cold-soaking the system, including its plumbing.

As preparations for flight got under way at an early hour on the morning of 20 November 1953, a launch panel operator working the hydrogen peroxide valves received an unexpected shower from a sudden spillage, covering him in a thin film of the toxic fluid. A quick-witted mechanic grabbed a hose and dowsed him down. His skin was bleached white for several days but a trip to the medical room saved him from any other consequence. Preparations continued and by mid-morning the B-29 pilot, Stan Butchart, was starting up the four clattering radial engines as they spat out smoke and dispersed it into the morning air.

Above: A wing chord extension on the outer panel of the Skyrocket for aerodynamic tests in 1953. *NACA*

Climbing ponderously to the drop altitude, Crossfield made his way down into the cockpit of the Skyrocket. An hour after taking off, they were at 9,753m (32,000ft). As the laden Skyrocket dropped away, Crossfield prepared the pressurisation valves and got the turbopumps up and running, pushing the propellants to the rocket motor. Igniting the chambers in sequence, he carefully maintained the precise flight trajectory, eliminating any lateral or transverse motion which could sap energy from the accelerating rocket ship. At the planned altitude he levelled off and began a shallow dive, passing through Mach 2 at 18,897m (62,000ft) finally reaching Mach 2.005, 2,077kph (1,291mph). On the way down he did aileron rolls at Mach 1.95 and reported superb performance from the controls.

This was the only time highly refined preparations like those around this special flight were made. The programme never again went for such a high speed run; there were other aircraft capable of conducting that but the first flight through Mach 2 made the Navy proud – that it had been accomplished by an aircraft they had been so instrumental in supporting – and gave the NACA a wetted appetite for a new and more sustainable attack on high-speed research.

But risks were there and while procedures and safety criteria continued to improve there was always the unexpected to test the unwary. Like all the research operations out of Muroc, the Skyrocket programme was not without its challenging drama. Such as the incident on 22 March 1956 when the second (all-rocket) aircraft was carried aloft under the P2B-1S. The generally unsung coordinator of all activity associated with getting the carrier-plane satisfactorily on to its planned flight path was the carrier-plane commander. It was he who would oversee the preliminary procedures for getting the pilot down into the Skyrocket and checking and managing all the countdown events to the drop. He was arguably the most important member of the team.

On this day, Stanley Butchart was in the left seat of the B-29 with NACA test pilot Neil Armstrong to his right.

Everything went according to plan as events counted down to the drop. Then Skyrocket pilot McKay called an abort when a series of malfunctions presented to him on his instruments. Almost immediately, the outer engine on the B-29's starboard wing ran away with itself and threatened to disintegrate. Proceeding according to contingency plans, Butchart dropped the Skyrocket which safely jettisoned its propellants and went back for a safe landing. But the drama was only just beginning.

Almost immediately after releasing McKay, the whirling propeller from the failed engine tore loose and cartwheeled across to the fuselage, slicing open the underside of the wing and the bomb bay where, just seconds before, the Skyrocket had been nestling – full of propellant. Potentially worse, the propeller blades had sliced right through the control cables on the starboard side and Butchart's control wheel was useless, flailing around with the pilot powerless to control the aircraft. Armstrong immediately took over from the right seat and brought the aircraft around to make an emergency landing back on the Muroc runway.

It took four months for the severely damaged B-29 to receive the repairs it needed to get the carrier-plane operational again and not until 24 August did it carry the Skyrocket back into the air when McKay conducted a vertical loads test run to Mach 1.1, the 68th NACA flight with the all-rocket aircraft. Only seven more flights remained for this venerable research platform, which conducted its last flight on 20 December 1956. Armstrong would go on to fly the X-15 between 1960 and 1962 and to play an important part in the operational flights, achieving Mach 5.74 and a maximum altitude of 63,246m (207,500ft).

As a passing footnote, exactly 10 years to the month after bringing the B-29 safely back to the ground on three engines, Neil Armstrong would once again bring a potentially uncontrollable vehicle back from potential disaster. As a NASA astronaut and commander of the Gemini VIII spacecraft in March 1966 he regained control of a tumbling capsule before returning to Earth in the first abort from a space mission in history.

As related earlier, as the Skyrocket programme began to wind down it focused increasingly on high subsonic and transonic research, the hybrid Skyrocket never having the performance of the second aircraft and its all-rocket propulsion. By 1954 the NACA was winding up flights investigating the pitch-up programme, underway for three years, and much data had been acquired as engineers modified the aircraft with wing slats and various wing fences and a leading edge extension. Much of the work fed back into wind tunnel investigations and there was a belief that an extension of wing chord at the 32 per cent position might solve the pitch-up problem but it never did.

The third, hybrid, Skyrocket did get some further modification in the form of external stores pylons added during 1954. On 27 April 1955 the first flight in a series investigating the effects of such additions in the high subsonic region began, most flown by McKay. Initially, 304cm (120in), 453.6kg (1,000lb) bomb shapes were used but these seemed to be too ineffective for a realistic test and larger, 567lit (150USgall) fuel tanks were attached. Crossfield had been pilot for most of the flights conducted by the third Skyrocket after it was handed over from Douglas on 15 December 1950. He left the NACA in September 1955 and went to North American to be the company test pilot for the X-15. McKay took over the pylons programme, completed on 8 December 1955, followed by two flights in February 1956 after which the hybrid Skyrocket was returned to a 'clean' configuration. Lakebed flooding and generally inclement weather kept the third Skyrocket grounded until its final flight, the 66th it flew for the NACA, was made on 28 August.

The second, rocket-powered Skyrocket was unsuitable for continuing the stores pylon research but there was one last role for the first Skyrocket with the turbojet engine and it was modified for an air-launch configuration and for flights with stores pylons. It was sent to Douglas in 1954 for that work to be carried out and the aircraft was back at Muroc on 15 November 1955. Various instrumentation issues kept it on the ground until 17 September 1956 when it was flown by McKay in a 'clean' configuration pending attachment of the pylons. They

Below: An F-86 chase-plane flies formation on the rocket-powered Skyrocket as it returns from a test run. First flown on 4 February 1948, the last Skyrocket flight landed on 20 December 1956. *NACA*

Chapter Six

The Air Force X-series Plus

Throughout the eleven years of flight activity with the six Skystreak and Skyrocket research aircraft, much had been learned about the transonic and supersonic flight regimes. Information and data which both supported and consolidated further work with existing wind tunnels. It also provided information for the design and development of new tunnels to carry out ground-based testing based on information from experimental flight operations. It is now time to look to the broader picture and review activity with the US Air Force X-1.

As related previously, very soon after Yeager exceeded Mach 1 in level flight, on 2 April 1948 the Air Force signed a contract for four more X-1 series research aircraft, designated X-1A, X-1B, X-1C and X-1D. The four aircraft were based on the original three X-1 aircraft with each assigned a very particular set of research parameters. The X-1C was to have been used for testing a new and exotic form of rocket propulsion specifically designed for supersonic flight, fitting it with an improved turbopump and changes to the design of the combustion chamber. In the rapidly evolving development programmes of the time, that requirement went away and the X-1C was never built.

But the other three aircraft would take up technology developed for the third X-1 (X-1-3) which had been put on hold pending development and qualification of the new turbopump using hydrogen peroxide, replacing the nitrogen pressurisation system installed in the first two X-1s. The three new X-1s, however, were structurally identical with common dimensions of the original X-1s but each was fitted with the wing carried by the X-1-1 and X-1-3 and displayed a span of 8.53m (28ft) with the NACA 65-108 aerofoil section.

Before operations could begin with the second generation X-1 aircraft, the X-1-3 gave promise of a much improved performance, although it would not arrive before 1951.

The Air Force would never get to be first through Mach 2,

Above: Seen here about to test fly an F-100D, Herbert Hoover made the first NACA flight through Mach 1 in X-1-2 on 10 March 1948. *NACA* as told earlier, that event being achieved by Scott Crossfield in the second Skyrocket on 20 November 1953, two years after the loss of the X-1-3 and its carrier-plane. But much had been going on with the first two X-1s as the Air Force and the NACA utilised these aircraft for their own research purposes.

Test pilot Herbert Hoover had flown the first supersonic flight for the NACA in the second X-1 on 10 March 1948 when he achieved Mach 1.065 or 1,131kph (703mph) at 12,192m (40,000ft). The very next day, Yeager took X-1-1 to a new record of Mach 1.25, 1,359kph (845mph), and on 26 March achieved Mach 1.45 at 15,240m (50,000ft), a speed of 1,540kph (957mph), the fastest ever flown by one of the original X-1 aircraft.

After an award ceremony in the Oval Office of the White House on 17 December 1948 recognising the first flight through Mach 1, the Air Force called a meeting with Richard Frost from Bell who had replaced Stanley Smith in detailed design of the X-1 when the latter moved to the X-2. It wanted to know whether a ground-launched rocket flight could be made with the X-1 and what would be required to make that possible. There was general enthusiasm for the idea and Yeager personally supported the proposition. Frost was tasked with coming up with a plan. This was a novel idea, as the aircraft had been designed for carrier-plane drops but with conventional landing gear for getting back on the runway, not for taking off from it.

New wheel assemblies of the same type would be fitted including tyres and brakes, the weight of the aircraft would be reduced by only filling tanks three-quarter full and a full weight-and-balance check would be made shortly before take-off. To minimise changes in the centre of gravity, the flight attempt would be made in the early morning when temperatures were stable and reduce LOX boil-off. Yeager would take off maintaining accelerations to less than 1-g to minimise the risk of a dreaded engine shut-down prior to rotation, and climb to altitude in a series of spirals.

The attempt took place on 5 January 1949 with Yeager in X-1-1 holding the brakes on until rocket ignition was shown to be stable as the four chambers were switched on in succession. The take-off roll was without event and the landing gear was retracted before the aircraft reached 402kph (250mph). Yeager kept the speed below Mach 0.85 to prevent any control instability. The powered flight phase lasted 1min 40sec, at which point the X-1 was at an altitude of 7,010m (23,000ft) and starting its descent toward a conventional landing. This was the only time an X-1 made a ground take-off but it demonstrated that it could be done.

Since achieving independence from the Army, the Air Force had had an eye on attracting film companies to proclaim its message, and the final air-drop of its X-1-1 took place on 12 May 1950 when Yeager conducted a powered flight to support the movie *Jet Pilot*. The NACA flew its last flight with the X-1-2 on 23 October 1951, bringing to a close a total of 157 drop-tests and one ground launch for the two first-generation X-1s.

As described earlier, completion of the third X-1 (46-064) had been deferred pending completion of its turbopump but in 1947 the Air Force ordered Bell to stop work on this aircraft, before rescinding that order a year later after finding the money to resume work on it. When engine delivery problems arose, the Air Force once again cancelled it but in a special deal worked up with the Cornell Aeronautical Laboratory, Bell was again asked to complete it and X-1-3 was delivered to the NACA at Edwards in April 1951 in anticipation of flight tests.

Identical in external configuration and wing to the first X-1 it was completely different on the inside, no longer fitted with the pressurisation tanks containing 136.5kg (301lb) of nitrogen. The turbopump was driven by superheated steam created

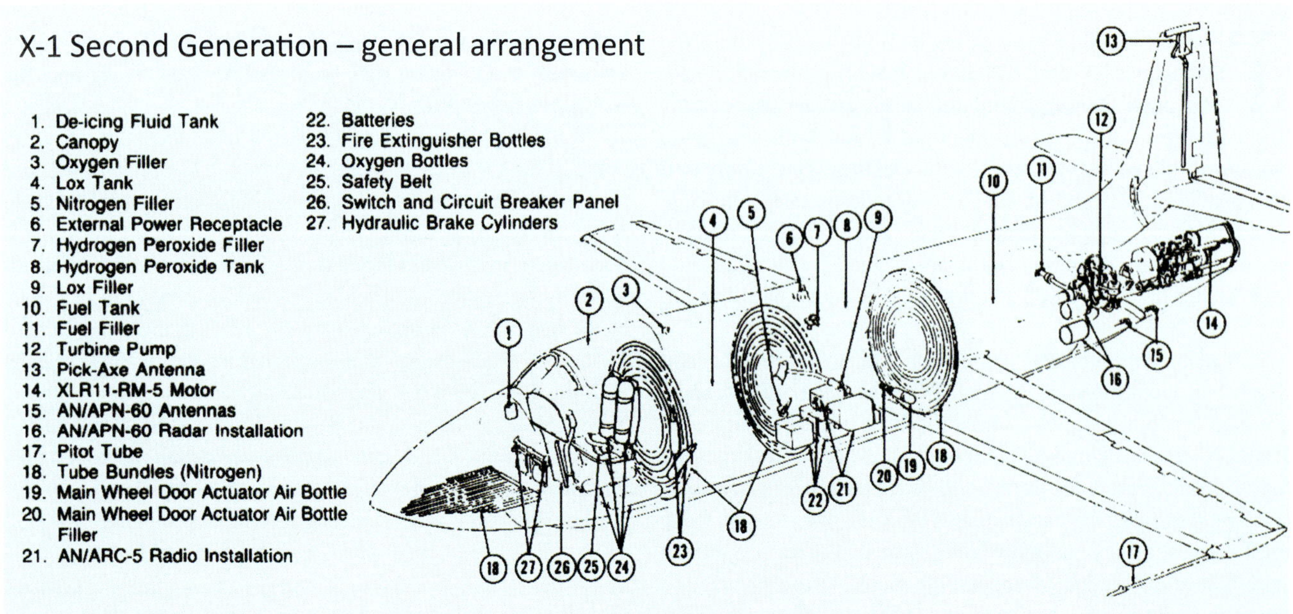

Below: The general configuration of the second-generation series comprising the X-1A, X-1B and X-1D had an extended fuselage and a stepped cockpit enclosure. The X-1C was never built and the X-1D was destroyed on 22 August 1951 in preparation for its second flight. *NACA*

Above left: Long in development, the turbopump fitted to X-1-3 allowed additional propellant in the space available after removal of the nitrogen pressurisation equipment. *NACA*

Above: Looking aft in the fuselage of X-1-3 with the hydrogen peroxide tank for the turbopump in view. The aircraft was destroyed on 9 November 1951. *NACA*

by the hydrogen peroxide passed over a manganese dioxide catalyst. The deletion of the nitrogen pressurisation system allowed an additional quantity of propellant, increasing to 1,654lit (437USgall) of fuel and 1,885lit (498USgal) of LOX and 117lit (31USgall) of hydrogen peroxide for the turbopump. This increased the launch weight to 6,691kg (14,751lb) and the landing weight to 3,105kg (6,847lb). Bell calculated that the third X-1 would now have a powered burn time of 4.1min and a theoretical maximum speed of Mach 2.44 at 21,336m (70,000ft), or 2,593kph (1,612mph).

As related earlier, all second-generation X-1s had the same wings and tail as the first-generation but with an extended fuselage for additional propellant and a more conventional cockpit including a stepped canopy like the Douglas Skystreak and Skyrocket; the ultra-conformal bullet shape of the forward fuselage on the first three X-1s was found to be unnecessary. The canopy allowed the pilot to access the cockpit more comfortably, from the top rather than via the side hatch fitted to the first three X-1s. There had always been concerns about the pilot's ability to extricate himself through the side hatch during an emergency and bale out directly into the slipstream of the wing's sharp leading edge. This change would prevent that and avoid a potential disaster for the pilot.

The length of the fuselage on all second-generation X-1s was 10.83m (35.55ft), some 1.41m (4.65ft) greater than the first three X-1s, limited at the front by the need to provide

Below: The first of the second-generation X-1s to conduct a lengthy programme of flight research, the X-1A (48-1384) displays a noticeably extended fuselage allowing additional propellant and extended burn duration. *NACA*

Left: Seen clearly in this view looking across the upper section of the fuselage, the X-1A exhibits the sharp dorsal spine blending into a semi-circular cross-section at the rear of the revised cockpit canopy. *NACA*

space for the carrier-plane's nose leg to retract and at the back to avoid the rear pressure bulkhead on the B-29. Nevertheless, the propellant tanks on the second-generation X-1s carried 2,157lit (570USgall) of diluted ethyl alcohol fuel and 1,892lit (500USgall) of liquid oxygen. In addition, 140lit (37USgall) of hydrogen peroxide was carried for the turbopump. Launch weight was 7,478kg (16,487lb) with a nominal landing weight of 3,296kg (7,266lb). Powered by a four-chamber XLR-11-RM-5 rocket motor, the second generation series had the theoretical potential for Mach 2.47 at 21,336m (70,000ft), or 2,630kph (1,635mph).

The first attempt with X-1-3 called for an initial glide flight on 20 July 1951 with Boyd piloting the B-29 and Bell test pilot Joseph A. Cannon in the X-1-3. Falling away, Cannon reported the heavier X-1 to be very light on the controls and he was able to fly a couple of stall checks before touching down on the lakebed. At which point the nose leg collapsed, damaging the aircraft and necessitating repairs which would keep it out of action for more than three months. But there was still time for the Air Force to check out the new aircraft and get an attempt on Mach 2, which it still hoped to achieve ahead of the Navy Skyrocket.

Assembled in no specific order, the X-1D (48-1386) was the first of the second generation to fly. Four days after the glide flight with the X-1-3, the X-1D was ready for its own drop test, this time with another carrier-plane, a converted B-50A-5-BO (46-006A). Piloted by Bell test pilot Jean 'Skip' Ziegler, the X-1D fell away and in a test of that aircraft's low-speed handling characteristics, touched down at the lake bed nine minutes later just before the nose leg collapsed. It was repaired and back a month later for a powered flight by Air Force test pilot Frank Everest.

On 22 August 1951, the B-50 took off and at an altitude of 2,134m (7,000ft), Everest worked his way into the X-1D's cockpit and began checks. The X-1D had a nitrogen system for pressurising the fuel tank regulators, the flaps and the landing gear extension. Noticing that the pressure had decayed from the ideal 33,096kPa (4,800lb/in²) to 10,342kPa (1,500lb/in²), Everest decided to return up into the carrier-plane and confer with co-pilot Jack Ridley and the Bell engineer Wendell Moore. They decided to abort the flight, jettison the propellant in the X-1D and return to Edwards with the X-1D intact.

Everest returned to the X-1D cockpit to pressurise the propellant tanks for jettisoning their content, beginning with the LOX tank. Pausing to check the valve, he opened it to bring the pressure in the oxidiser tank up to the required 317kPa (46lb/in²). At that instant a deep rumble, indicative of a muffled explosion, shook the X-1D, almost knocking Everest to

Estimated Flight Plan Chart

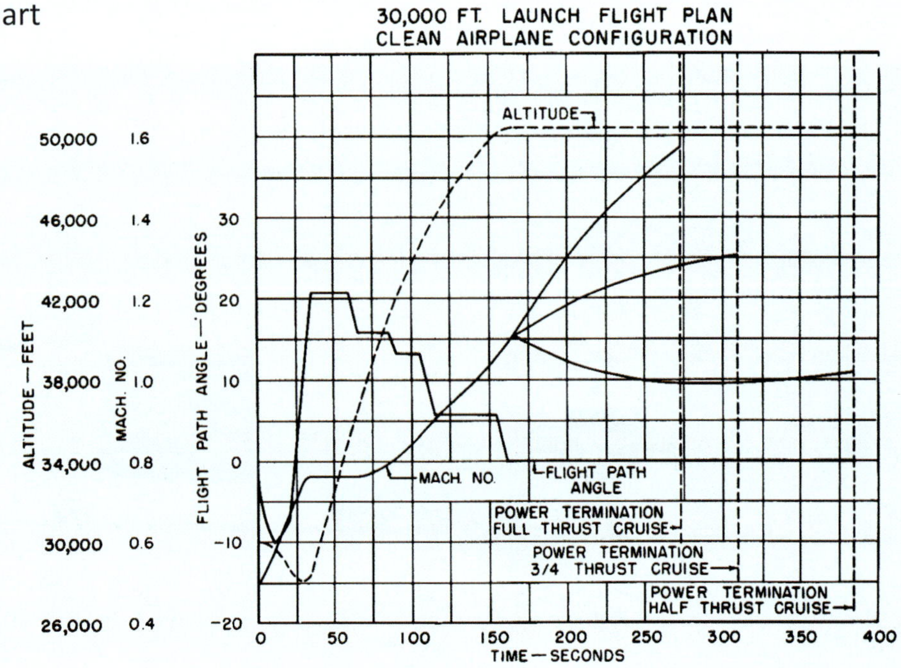

The anticipated performance envelope for the second-generation X-1 series, parameters which were to be greatly exceeded in reality. *NACA*

Above: Following the loss of X-1D (48-1386) on 22 August 1951 and X-1-3 on 9 November 1951, X-1A was in the air for a glide test on 14 February 1953 with Bell's Jean 'Skip' Ziegler at the controls. *NACA*

the floor. Flying chase in a T-33, Lt. Col. Gust Askounis called out 'Drop her, she's on fire' and Everest leapt up and out of the cockpit seeking refuge in the bomb bay. Flames could be seen from the top of the X-1D, licking up into the bay.

At that moment Ridley was a second away from pulling the jettison handle which, had he done so would have jammed the X-1D in place because the locking pins were still engaged. As Everest collided with Ridley, knocking him over, that action was aborted, the pins were removed and the flaming rocket-ship fell away. As the X-1D fell to utter destruction, the B-50 returned to base undamaged, its personnel safe. A full investigation failed to find the precise reason for the fire, save for the possibility that there had been a fuel leak and that an electrical spark from some unknown source had ignited the diluted alcohol, setting the interior of the aircraft ablaze.

Going for speed

The same carrier-plane was back in the air with the repaired X-1-3 on 9 November 1951, little more than 10 weeks after the loss of the X-1D. It was to be a captive check on the aircraft's jettison system. Part way through the in-flight jettison test, X-1-3 pilot Joseph Cannon lost nitrogen pressure and decided to abort the propellant jettison procedure. Back on the ground, the mated aircraft were towed to the loading area where nitrogen would be pumped in so that the propellants could be jettisoned. With Cannon in the X-1-3 cockpit and fire trucks around the rear end of the B-50, ground crew gave the all-clear for him to start pressurising the tanks for that event.

As pressure reached 289.6kPa (49lb/in^2) there was deep-rooted rumble inside the X-1 and Cannon jumped from the cockpit, being flattened to the ground by an explosion followed by a succession of further blasts that pinned him to the concrete. Seeing him helpless to get up against the pressure, Bell engineer William H. Means and project foreman Walter Myers ran back around and pulled him to safety followed by a rapid trip to the hospital where he recovered from wounds. The resulting fire and succession of explosions completely destroyed the X-1-3 and the B-50 carrier-plane.

Three aircraft destroyed and two lives very nearly lost in less than three months. It had been hoped that, with its more powerful engines providing a better performance than the B-29, the B-50 could have gradually taken over the functional work of carrier-plane duties but that hope was now ashes. Some attempt was made to replace it but funds, and willingness to oblige, prevented the Air Force coming up with a replacement. There was even an attempt to get special funds for a successor type but that was not found to be possible.

The disconcerting report from the investigation board found that the explosion was most likely caused by the use of 410 stainless steel, which had been used to fabricate the tubes for the on-board nitrogen storage system. That type of steel has a much reduced brittle value at low temperatures. The storage tubes were located alongside the LOX tank, which reduced the temperature in the surrounding volume. When the pilot began pressurising the tank it appears it shattered, a conclusion supported by pieces of the nitrogen tubes found 76m (250ft) away from the aircraft.

The next of the second-generation X-1 aircraft, the X-1A made its first flight on 14 February 1953 with Bell's Jean Ziegler at the controls for an unpowered familiarisation glide flight. This was followed by five more Bell flights piloted by Ziegler with several technical problems constraining objectives. As a result of the nitrogen tubes problem with the X-1-3 and a similar problem with the X-2, in June 1953 the X-1A was returned to Bell for removing the suspect equipment. It returned to Edwards on 16 October where Air Force technicians replaced the tubes removed by Bell with storage tanks as a safer option.

Yeager took it back into the air for its first post-renovation flight on 21 November 1953 – the project pilot Jean Ziegler had been killed in the X-2. On his second flight in the X-1A on 2 December, Yeager encountered unusually high stick forces with aileron control, which prompted a recommendation that a control wheel be installed for better authority. Six days later, Yeager pushed the X-1A to Mach 1.9 at 18,288m (60,000ft). On 12 December, the Air Force mounted an all-out speed run and had Crossfield's run to Mach 2.005 in the second Skyrocket just over three weeks previously as the target. It would be Yeager's last flight of the year.

There had been some concern about the stability of the X-1A at speeds approaching Mach 2.3 and Yeager was already aware of control issues on approaching Mach 2. Dropping from the B-29 at 9,296m (30,500ft), Yeager lit three rocket chambers and accelerated to 13,716m (45,000ft) where he lit up the fourth chamber and powered on up to 21,336m (70,000ft). Still climbing, Yeager levelled off at 23,165m (76,000ft) and traded altitude for speed as the X-1A accelerated through Mach 2 and kept on going, approaching the area where control instability had been forecast.

Ten seconds after levelling out the flight path, at Mach 2.3 the X-1A began a roll to the left but when Yeager corrected this it snapped quickly to the right in a violent motion that reversed the flip when he tried to straighten up. Realising that the aircraft was about to go completely out of control, Yeager cut the rocket motor with the aircraft now at Mach 2.44. More violent motions ensued, with Yeager being thrown around the cramped confines of the tiny cockpit, bruised and battered, the aircraft tumbling out of control as he fell through 10,363m (34,000ft) where the X-1A entered a subsonic spin and upside down.

Above: NACA test pilot Joe Walker strikes a 'bucking bronco' pose climbing into the cockpit of the X-1A. Walker made his first flight in the type on 23 February 1955. *NACA*

Below: Yeager manoeuvres down from the bomb bay access hatch to the X-1A cockpit. The aircraft was destroyed on 8 August 1955. *NACA*

In their F-86 chase planes, Jack Ridley and Maj. Arthur 'Kit' Murray tried to raise Yeager on the radio – to no avail. Now semiconscious, as he dropped through 8,839m (29,000ft), Yeager recovered the X-1A into the familiar motions of a conventional spin and by the time he was down to 7,620m (25,000ft) he managed to get X-1A back into level flight and bring it down to a safe landing. Radar verified that at 22,555m (74,000ft), Yeager had achieved a speed of 2,594kph (1,612mph)! Never again would the Air Force attempt to take an X-1 beyond Mach 2.3.

What Yeager had encountered was an inertia coupling phenomenon, reducing directional stability while virtually eliminating all roll-damping. This had been predicted five years earlier by NACA aerodynamicist William H. Phillips and this single flight made a major contribution to the design of future aircraft entering the zone above Mach 2. It required much larger control surfaces to counter the effect and would bring design changes to future combat types. A classic example of how a single flight can bring significant changes to an entire design philosophy.

The Air Force decided to abandon high-speed flights after Yeager's record breaking runs and to focus on high-altitude records instead. In this period there was a significant increase in defence spending. The armed services were seeing expansion of force levels through their annual budgets, largely as a result of the shock from the Berlin Airlift and the Korean War but also under the new resilience forced into a rearmament programme. All of that required new recruits; America was never again going to use conscript intakes for establishing force levels.

The Air Force had a proud new start and was forging ahead with exciting new combat aircraft with supersonic capabilities and the addiction to film promotion spawned a wide range of exciting films and TV programmes aimed at attracting young men. A master in the exploitation of print and electronic media, President Dwight D. Eisenhower – the first Republican president for more than 20 years – supported promotional information outlets, sometimes through the US Information Service (USIS) and sometimes by other means, to project the military lifestyle as an attractive and secure future for young American males.

Key to a lot of that was the propaganda value of the new jet age and the achievements of its rocket pilots. In many ways, this was a prescient foretaste of what would emerge just a few years later with the selection of America's first astronauts, the next goal to inspire American youth and reassure the wartime generation that the United States was on top of world crises. Moreover, it was the X-pilots and the achievements of the Douglas Skyrocket that nurtured the image of a steadfast and resolute nation, if in reality that was far from reality. America was engaged in a desperate arms race and the results of the experimental research aircraft were eagerly awaited by plane-makers across the country.

For now, there was much to be learned from the altitude flights and out of 14 attempts with the X-1A during the spring and summer months of 1954, only four were successful. On 26 August, Maj. Arthur Murray reached 27,566m (90,440ft), which was at the time an unofficial world record. After that, the X-1A was handed over to the NACA for its own research. Before that, Bell received it back for it to be fitted with an ejection seat, largely because of the flight in which Yeager had come perilously close to losing his life. There was a degree of nervousness about leaving the pilot vulnerable to the uncertainty of escaping a tumbling aircraft.

The X-1A was back at Edwards on 23 February 1955 and the first NACA flight with Joseph Walker at the controls took place on 20 July 1955. He reached Mach 1.45 at 13,716m (45,000ft), encountering a rippling, or 'buzz', effect at Mach 0.9, as had so many X-1s in that low transonic region. A second flight later in July failed to occur due to some minor technical problems but the next flight, on 8 August would again bring near disaster and the destruction of the X-1A.

Climbing toward the drop altitude, the B-29 hauled the X-1A aloft and at 2,438m (8,000ft), Walker clambered down into the cockpit and settled into the seat. At 9,449m (31,000ft) with checks complete and a minute to go to the drop, the LOX tank exploded and sent shards of material hurtling out, fracturing the canopy on the F-86 chase aircraft flown by Arthur Murray. This was a relatively minor explosion and afforded time for Walker to climb back up into the B-29 and start a debate over what to do. There were very few options but everyone wanted to try and get the aircraft back to where it could be repaired.

Compromised by the X-1A's landing gear having been deployed due to the shock of the explosion, and the visual indication that the aircraft had dropped slightly on its restraints, there was no possibility of landing with the X-1A on board. Discussion extended to visual descriptions from Neil Armstrong in a chase F-51 Mustang as the aircraft crew chief Richard Payne went down and noted that the gear deploy handle was still in 'up' position. When Payne tried to jettison the propellant, Armstrong reported that only a very small quantity was discharged, far too little to risk landing with it intact. And the explosive hydrogen peroxide was still on board.

There was no alternative to jettisoning the crippled X-1A and the B-29 pilot, Stan Butchart turned to the bombing range at Edwards and sent it earthward, the impact creating a tremendous explosion and starting minor fires, the carrier-plane returning to a safe landing. Thus did the third of six X-1 aircraft end up on the desert floor, in addition to the second X-2, which we will encounter in the next chapter. These losses demanded an incisive investigation to find whether a common cause could identify a single reason, indicated perhaps by the fact that they all involved explosions near the LOX tank.

The combined Air Force/NACA investigation began with

Below:The X-1B (48-1385) made 27 flights between September 1954 and January 1958. NACA

the meticulous assembly of the wreckage from the X-1A which was paired with the X-1B alongside for comparison. As the parts of the wrecked aircraft were assembled, the X-1B was also examined to determine whether there was any underlying cause that could be found in comparable systems. As inspection of the X-1B LOX tank access doors were being examined, traces of tricresyl phosphate were found. The source was traced to leather gaskets which had been treated with this substance and known as Ulmer leather. Investigation revealed the disturbing fact that the manufacturer of the product cautioned against its use near liquid oxygen, as even a moderate impact could cause an explosion. The NACA still had two X-1 aircraft available for research flights: the X-1B and a rework of the X-1-2 aircraft, which would be re-designated X-1E.

The comeback kid

The loss of the X-1-3 and the X-1D in 1951 denied the Air Force the two aircraft with which it had hoped to expand the flight envelope and advance the research to greater capabilities. Their availability would compensate for the X-1-1, retired to the Smithsonian Institution, and the X-1-2. Also this year, inspection of the high-pressure nitrogen spheres, and actual tests, revealed a weakness rendering them liable to explode after more than 700-800 fill/refill cycles. Three nitrogen vessels were scavenged from X-1-1 and used to replace suspect spheres in X-1-2. There was also a keen interest in applying a new, low-pressure turbopump. The only solution to advancing the research programme was to convert X-1-2 into a completely new aircraft with the capabilities expected of the X-1D.

After the last X-1-2 flight on 23 October 1951, the aircraft was stood down for a complete re-build incorporating upgraded systems and a completely new wing funded by the Air Force, who wanted to conduct high-speed tests with a new configuration. The NACA decided to fit the new low-pressure turbopump to replace its existing high-pressure nitrogen system for the propellant tanks. Bell also fitted a stepped-up canopy similar to those fitted to the second-generation X-1 series, together with an ejection seat, which had originally been fitted to the second Northrop X-4.

The new wing was specifically designed to incorporate lessons from the data gathered by the X-1A which would allow better handling qualities on high-speed flights and obtain important data relevant to new designs of military aircraft capable of flights up to Mach 3. More information was required to better understand the aerodynamic effects of aircraft operating routinely in these exotic realms. Accordingly, the NACA sought a wing which would allow the X-1E to achieve speeds in excess of Mach 2.5. With the loss of the X-1-3 and the X-1D, at that time only the X-1B and the X-1E remained to carry out high-speed research.

Rework of the second X-1 got underway in early 1952 when the NACA started design work on the new propellant delivery system, applying much useful information from the turbopump fitted to the Douglas D-558-2 Skyrocket as well as to the X-1-3 and the X-1D. But the real core change to the X-1E was its incredibly thin wing with a thickness/chord ratio of 4 per cent versus 8 per cent on the original airframe and an aspect ratio of 4:1. The re-profiled, super-thin wing was an evolution of that fitted to the X-3 Stiletto, with a root chord of 2.32m (7.62ft), a maximum thickness of 8.55cm (3.37in) at the root and a tip chord of 1.16m (3.81ft) on a modified NACA 64A-004 symmetrical aerofoil section.

Designed by project engineer Gordon Valentine, the wing was produced by the Stanley Aviation Corporation of Denver, Colorado, maximum torsional stiffness obtained through a multi-spar structure with tapered milled skins attached by bolts to solid ribs and spars. More than 200 orifices were provided in the wing for instrumentation measurement points, with 343 gauges built in to the wing surface for measuring structural loads and heating. The various sensor points were connected to the array of manometers by 457m (1,500ft) of aluminium tubing with a thickness of 3.96mm (0.156in).

Overall, the X-1E had a wing span of 6.946m (22.79ft), 1.59m (5.21ft) less than the original X-1-2. This was the most significant change to the X-1 series and the opportunity was taken to make several changes to the airframe as well, to improve ancillary systems and controls. Propulsion was provided by an LR-8-RM-5, a developed and improved version of the XLR-11 rocket motor originally built for the D-558-2. The X-1-2 had been completely transformed into the X-1E by mid-1955, officially designated as such in March the previous year.

The first attempt at launch on 3 December was aborted due to a loss in source pressure and the first drop test took place on 12 December, Joe Walker being the pilot on each attempt. This was followed three days later by the first powered flight, when

Left: The X-1B cockpit bore strong resemblance to that for the X-1A but minor changes were made according to equipment installation. *NACA*

Walker piloted it to Mach 0.85, 902kph (561mph). A series of evaluation flights followed in 1956, Walker taking it supersonic on 7 June, achieving Mach 1.55, 1,646kph (1,023mph), followed by incrementally faster flights, reaching Mach 2.0, 2,124kph (1,320mph) on 31 August. Flight runs continued but for the rest of the year a series of aborts and malfunctions prevented the schedule being met.

Returning on 15 May 1957 from the second flight that year, Walker's view through his faceplate distorted his vision and he landed hard, snapping off the nose leg and causing damage to the main landing gear and the skin of the fuselage. During the downtime for repairs, engineers replaced the cockpit pressurisation system from a nitrogen gas to air so that the pilot could raise his faceplate for better vision and still breathe. Not until 19 September was it back for a flight attempt, aborted by a problem with the engine. Three weeks later, on 8 October Yeager reached Mach 2.24, about 2,378kph (1,478mph), the highest speed logged by the X-1E.

Above: After a four-year hiatus the reworked X-1-2 emerged in 1955 as the X-1E, with a shorter span, a very thin wing and the cockpit and canopy design from the second-generation X-1 series. *NACA*

During the pause in flight tests due to the seasonal rains, a series of upgrades and performance enhancements were implemented. Proposed initially by NACA engineers Hubert M. Drake and Donald R. Bellman during the previous year, these were expected to fill the void in high-speed research left by the loss of the Mach 3 X-2 and by the enhanced X-1D. Just as the X-1E had itself emerged to cover the loss of the X-1-3 and the X-1D, so too would it now have to import enhanced capabilities so that it could conduct research into high temperatures around Mach 3, anticipated but not

Below: Subject here to a ground test, the X-1E had the more efficient XLR-8-RM-5 engine developed for the Skyrocket from the XLR-11.
Below right: The X-1E is lifted into the bomb bay of the carrier-plane for one of its 26 flights, of which the first 21 were flown by Joe Walker and the rest by John McKay. *NACA*

achieved with the ill-fated X-2.

Unique to this aircraft, ventral fins were added to the X-1E in an attempt to counter the persistent lack of proper directional stability reported by a number of X-craft over the years. It was, with these installed, that flights resumed once more with a flight on 14 May 1958. But on the next flight on 10 June, a landing accident that broke the nose leg paused operations for repairs which afforded the opportunity to plan a further upgrade, increasing the pressure in the engine combustion chambers from 1,723kPh (250lb/in^2) to 2,068kPa (300lb/in^2). Also, a more potent fuel was prepared. Known as Hydyne, it was comprised of 60 per cent unsymmetrical dimethyl hydrazine and 40 per cent diethylene triamine.

Walker made the next two flights on 10 and 17 September before McKay took over for the next four flights, the first on 19 September and the last on 28 October 1958. Between these dates, on 1 October, the National Advisory Committee for Aeronautics became the National Aeronautics and Space Administration (NASA), changing everything in response to Russia's launch of Sputnik 1 in October 1957. It was not immediately apparent but the urgency with which the US now pitched into the Space Age closed a chapter in aeronautical history and opened a new period of intensive research and development.

The last flight of the X-1E, its 26th, was conducted on 6 November before a planned replacement of the emergency egress system. During that work, X-ray scans of the fuel tank showed cracks which demanded a replacement. Given the investment already made and the uncertainty about the potential for this ageing airframe, which had made its first drop as the X-1-2 more than 12 years earlier, the decision was made to end the programme. The hypersonic X-15 was close to flight and there was no further reason to continue investment in a design which dated back to 1944.

After 27 flights between 24 September 1954 and 23 January 1958, the X-1B (48-1385) had already been retired. That aircraft had been checked out by more pilots than any other in the X-1 series: Lt. Col. Jack Ridley, Maj. Arthur Murray, Maj. Robert Stephens, Maj. Stuart Childs, Col. Horace Hanes, Capt. Richard Harer, Lt. Col. Frank Everest and the NACA's John McKay and Neil Armstrong. It was also flown by Brig. Gen. Stanley Holtoner, the highest ranking Air Force office to fly a research aircraft.

The NACA had assigned the X-1B to high-altitude research flights where control effectiveness in the upper atmosphere could be assessed and understood. The X-2 had already demonstrated the ineffectiveness of conventional control surfaces when it reached an altitude of 38,465m (126,200ft), finding the aircraft completely uncontrollable in attitude or directional flight until descending to denser layers in the atmosphere. Reaction control system thrusters were already being developed for the X-15 and more precise data on the threshold for shifting between the use of aero-surfaces and jet

Opposite: Displayed here on the configuration mock-up, the new cockpit windscreen and shroud transformed the appearance of the X-1E.

Left: The cockpit for the X-1E was considerably different to that in the X-1-2 and is shown here for left (above), middle (centre) and right panel (below) arrangements. *NACA*

Left: Returning from a flight on 18 June 1956, the X-1E nose wheel leg collapsed, causing minor damage. *NACA*

thrusters for attitude control was still to be determined and would come to depend on better data regarding the mass of the aircraft and its velocity.

The X-1B was also assigned to an aerothermal research programme designed to provide reference data for high-speed combat aircraft then on the drawing board. The Air Force was interested in knowing the heat rate as well as the total thermal load at different reference points in speed and air density (altitude). This programme was undertaken with the X-1B piloted by McKay in the second half of 1956 and it was completed following a run to Mach 1.94, a speed of 2,059kph (1,280mph) on 3 January 1957. McKay was also at the controls of the X-1B on 29 July when it flew with extended wing tips for hydrogen peroxide thruster control calibration. This was the first aircraft so equipped and the first flight with active thrusters took place on 29 July when a speed of Mach 1.55 was logged at 18,288m (60,000ft), although the thrusters were never actually used.

The concept of attitude control thrusters carried forward to the X-15 which would operate at altitudes unimaginable to the X-1 designers when they first drew up plans for a high-speed/high-altitude workhorse. There was still much to be explored with thruster operations and with the flight control systems designed to switch modes from aero-surfaces to reaction jets. That work switched to a NACA Lockheed F-104A which took up the work instead. There had been several expanded plans for the X-1B when it made its last flight in early 1958. A pre-flight inspection in May revealed cracks in the LOX tank. Welds closed the cracks but X-ray inspection showed flaws in the repair and it was decided to retire the aircraft from flight.

By the end of the year, the X-1E too had been retired. The days of the X-1 series was over. Six aircraft shared research time and commitments with six Skystreak and Skyrocket aircraft but several tasks remained unfulfilled. The X-1B had been set to have several modifications in support of armament tests, briefly alluded to earlier. These included a wide variety of gun configurations with various ventral and dorsal fins attached to the wings for yaw stability and directional stability. There were other, more exotic applications and the Air Force looked at a reconnaissance variant for carrying an RX-1, although very little reference to that is found in any surviving documents.

Below: The X-1E had two ventral fins under the tail section to help improve directional stability. To the 26 free flights it made between 12 December 1955 and 6 November 1958 should be added the 54 flights conducted in its original configuration as the X-1-2. *NACA*

Chapter Seven

Seeking a Mach 3 Ride

Over the 12 years of flight operations with the experimental research aircraft the facilities and the operational management of the programmes matured and became increasingly sophisticated. But the expansion of flight test activity had evolved in parallel with the design and operation of the aircraft and their derivatives. To support this, the 1950s brought tremendous change to NACA flight testing at Muroc, which in 1954 had been named the High Speed Flight Station (HSFS) and would be renamed the Flight Research Center in September 1959. The Air Force host facility had been named Edwards Air Force Base in early 1950 (see Appendix 2).

There was a degree of interchangeability on the research tasks defined for the Air Force and Navy programmes – the X-1 series and the D-558 respectively. That was experienced through the Skyrocket test programme, funded by the Navy and also operated by the NACA which provided science research of its own. But the objectives of both the Air Force and the Navy in developing and operating high performance combat aircraft forced a unified approach to common needs and data derived from Air Force flights was frequently of value to the Navy and vice versa. An example of this was the need for information on the heating effects of the atmosphere on materials used in aircraft skins and on the conductivity of increased temperatures through the fuselage and wing structure.

Pursuant to that, during the last year of Skyrocket testing, NACA engineers had been keen to use the all-rocket aircraft for measuring the way the structure of the aircraft dealt with heat produced by the kinetic energy of the airframe as it moved through the atmosphere. Materials capable of withstanding high temperatures were key to faster flight through the atmosphere and with an increasing bank of knowledge about the

Above: Impressing the taxpayer. On one of its periodic open-day events, a display of equipment and technology is laid out along the wing of an X-1 at Edwards Air Force Base. *NASA*

Above: In the 1950s, Muroc laid on a photo-shoot for key experimental aircraft. In the foreground is the Douglas D-558-1 Skystreak. In the centre are the supersonic Douglas D-558-2 Skyrocket (left) and the Bell X-5 with variable-sweep wings. At the back are the Northrop X-4 (left) for transonic research into tailless configurations and the delta-wing Convair XF-92A powered by a ramjet and three small rocket motors. *NACA*

supersonic environment, the ability of structures to withstand the rigours of high speed flight became a focus for work at Muroc and other NACA facilities.

In late 1955 some engineers worked up a plan for instrumenting the Skyrocket for testing the thermal equilibrium at high speed. They reluctantly concluded that this aircraft could not maintain those speeds for long enough to allow the temperature to stabilise so that reliable data could be obtained and it was abandoned. Other means of obtaining that information were at hand, the X-1B would get that role. By 1956 the initial tranche of high-speed/high-altitude research aircraft was winding down and only the last few second-generation X-1 series were still flying. The wider X-series had diversified into an ever-broader range of research aircraft, each designed specifically for changes in configuration or design concepts as requirements evolved.

As we will see, by this date the hypersonic X-15 programme was well underway but the Skyrocket too made its own contribution, test results forming the basis for finessing the design of that project as it had been in providing basic aerodynamic data supporting the X-2. But the X-2 was the final evolution of a second-generation approach to high-speed flight, aiming as it did for Mach 3+ to provide vital data for a range of highly speculative projects already conceived on the drawing boards of aircraft design and manufacturing teams. Nevertheless, as an advanced research aircraft of the time, it is an important adjunct to the evolution of high-speed/high-altitude types.

In October 1945, long before the first XS-1 had been built, Bell had been working on a swept-wing successor. The results from German research facilities was too empowering to ignore. However, they quickly discovered that a modified XS-1 would be neither practical nor productive and that a completely new design would be essential to achieving higher performance. Design work on the Bell Model 52 was placed in the hands of George Ray and a contract for development was signed by the Air Force on 14 December 1945 for what was then designated XS-2 (as aforementioned, the 'S' was deleted in 1947 for all in the X series). The primary objective was to achieve Mach 3.5 and altitudes up to 38,100m (125,000ft), with two aircraft, each exploring compressibility and heating respectively.

Bell had no prior experience with swept wings and relied heavily on the now well trawled-over German research results. They even considered a variable-geometry wing but decided against that, claiming that this would be too many steps into the dark. In fact they were dissuaded by the NACA, which already had a variable geometry test aircraft in the form of the X-5 and had already refrained from spreading too many research requirements across different projects.

The basic airframe was to be stressed to 8-g under manoeuvring but the project would be the first to try some new materials thought beneficial to future combat aircraft, these to include K-Monel which was applied to much of the fuselage assemblies. The wing had a biconvex NACA aerofoil section with an aspect ratio of 4.0, a taper ratio of 0.5, a 40deg sweep angle at the 25 per cent chord line and a dihedral of 3deg. The horizontal tailplane matched the wing sweep-back angle at 40deg and the elevator had a range of travel from 7deg up to 10deg down.

Most of the wing structure and control surfaces were fabricated from stainless steel. This, and the copper-nickel alloy for the fuselage assemblies was selected in an attempt to withstand the anticipated skin temperatures calculated to reach as high as 332degC (630degF) at speeds above Mach 3. The K-Monel materials for the X-2 proved difficult to work with and new techniques had to be devised to produce satisfactory results. New fabrication methods such as spot and fusion welding had to be developed, replacing traditional welding practices, considerably delaying the programme as manufacturing of the airframes slipped.

Another reason for the delays was attributable to the advanced concepts for systems and controls. Bell wanted the Bendix Corporation's fly-by-wire (FBW) electrical-driven power control system rather than the cables and linkages used in the X-1 series, as they were in all aircraft of the period. A specially developed test rig was ready by mid-1950 on which the stabiliser actuator was mounted with special power controls and that provided good results. But it took more than eighteen months for the aileron actuators to operate correctly with a new control stick and by early 1952 it had to be abandoned. In its place, conventional push-pull tubes were installed for ailerons and stabiliser and cable links for the rudder, these features built in to the second X-2 (46-675). The first aircraft (46-674) had an irreversible hydraulic system for the ailerons and all-flying tail supplemented with a mechanical cable system for the rudder.

The instrumentation compartment was situated immediately forward of the front LOX tank and this was specifically reserved for instrumentation provided by the NACA. Any change here would impact plans for the suite of experiment instrumentation. Bell changed from a nickel-cadmium battery, supplied by the Nickel Cadmium Battery Corporation, to two larger lead-acid batteries and a third sandwiched between as a back-up. The company's W. S. Swanson informed the NACA on 8 September 1948 and the instrumentation was rearranged around the larger boxes. The NACA came up with a mock-up to help Bell design around those elements. This interchange helped the NACA and the contractor develop the concept of 'interchangeable baskets' shaped to conform to different places where science instruments could be located, rather than stick rigidly to unchanging void into which instruments had to be made to fit.

Although several years away from its most fulfilling application in the X-15, it nevertheless introduced a new doctrinal approach to matching essential aircraft operating systems with the space they needed to operate properly. This fostered a flexible and sustainable research programme, where equipment would be designed to fit the volume available rather than the instrument section constraining the size and proportional dimensions of the technical equipment. In the X-2, this dialogue and the instrument-section mock-up provided to Bell allowed speedy interchange of the 30-channel telemetry equipment and the 30-channel oscillograph.

The extremely small cockpit was pressurised with air contained in a single cylinder just behind the pilot. In the normally seated position looking forward, the pilot had no view of any part of the aircraft other than the frame of the windshield. The pilot would wear a T-1 partial-pressure suit with a tight helmet and forced breathing at high altitude. Insulated from the hot

Below: An exterior view of the SCR-584 tracking radar van, utilised for tracking the X-2 in flight. *US Army*

Below right: Although in its infancy, considerable progress had been made in telemetering data but the equipment was primitive, a legacy of wartime expediency as evident from this SCR-584 operator console. *US Army*

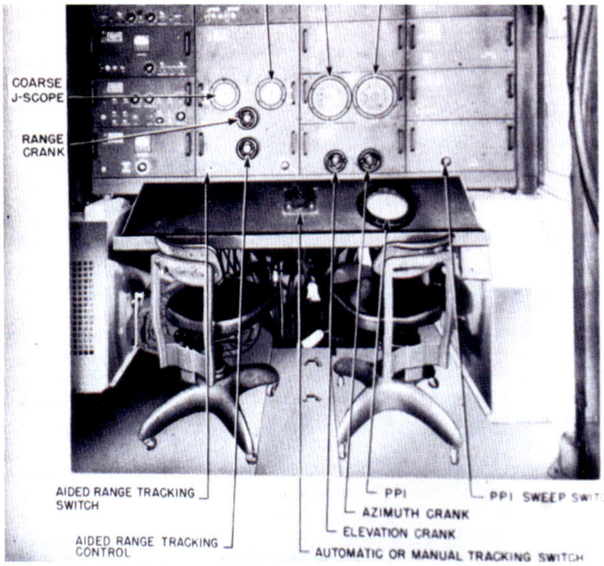

skin by layers of glass-fibre insulation, the cockpit was not heated and pilots had to wear long-johns as underwear, a bulky flying suit on top and two pairs of socks and flying gloves to counter the cold of higher altitudes and normal flight. Information presented to the pilot on control displays was provided by miniaturised Magnesyn instruments produced by the Eclipse-Pioneer Division of the Bendix Aviation Corporation.

Starting with a clean slate, the landing gear was highly unconventional in that it was a tandem system employing a nose wheel with castor, stowed immediately behind the pilot and in front of the instrumentation bay, and a ventral skid, 30.5cm (12in) wide, made from cast steel fused with Stellite. As a late addition, just before the first flight, small bumper skids were provided to prevent damage to the wingtips after landing. These were replaced with whisker skids attached to the centre of each wing to prevent damage and to assist with balance during roll-out on landing.

The selection of measuring instruments was made with the assistance of Hartley Soulé, then chief of the Stability Research Division at Langley, following a discussion at Bell on 6-7 January 1949. The selection would be key to how the NACA could gain value from the programme. The internal systems measured by the instrumentation would include altitude and airspeed, acceleration in longitudinal and transverse axes, angular velocity in roll, pitch and yaw, angular orientation of ailerons, elevator, moveable stabiliser, rudder and flaps, stick force for ailerons and elevator and angle of attack and angle of sideslip.

To obtain these measurements, data points were placed at various locations around the airframe and would operate also by a SCR 584 radar on the ground for trajectory and flight path tracking. The accelerometer was positioned 3.1m (10.25ft) forward of the centre of gravity and all the instrumentation was aligned with a central timer and connected with 1,219m (4,000ft) of wire protected by fluoroethane plastic on the inner conductors. When tests revealed that moisture seeping in to the Bakelite potting on the strain gauges produced high variations in signal and resistance, General Electric provided Formex insulating material instead.

Both the Air Force and the NACA were largely in the dark when wrestling the problem of pilot safety and the very real possibility that the occupant would have to escape an X-2 out of control and unable to land. Nobody quite knew how to provide an effective and reliable escape system. The practical limit for a conventional escape by bailing out and taking to a parachute was approximately 885kph (550mph). Several escape methods were examined including the new-fangled ejection seats, but these were extremely heavy and nobody had designed one for operation at such high speeds.

The solution chosen for both the Douglas D-558 and the X-2 was to completely separate the forward section of the fuselage containing the pilot so that it would eject forward from the rest of the aircraft. At a predetermined distance, a ribbon parachute would deploy to stabilise and decelerate the nose section to a vertical descent speed of approximately 193kph (120mph). At terminal velocity and below 3,048m (10,000ft), the pilot would separate from the nose section and land with a standard, 8.53m (25ft) personal parachute.

Right: The first Bell X-2 (46-674) poses with a representative selection of support personnel and equipment, dominated by the Boeing EB-50D-95-BO (48-96A) carrier-plane. Conceived in 1945, the X-2 had a protracted development phase and would not make its first unpowered drop flight until 27 June 1952. *NACA*

The separation of the nose section would be facilitated by four explosive pistons arranged at 90deg intervals around the circumference of the break line separating the front 2.83m (9.3ft) of the aircraft. This would begin a sequence starting with deployment of a 2.4m (8ft) ribbon parachute which would be attached to the centre of the cabin to slow it down to a level where the pilot could open the cockpit canopy and bail out. The ribbon parachute had been selected based on the highly successful sequence of tests carried out by the Germans for retarding the speed of fighters during high-velocity flutter trials. The system had a warning tone to indicate to the pilot when he was approaching the minimum altitude for taking to his personal parachute.

An extensive series of tests was carried out by the NACA to examine the various technical design features and to trial the concept. They began with rocket models in a sequence starting on 11 September 1947 using small models of the pilot's cockpit launched from Wallops Island. These provided some confidence that the concept was sound – in theory – but that it could only be a safe means of escape if sufficient energy was applied to separate the nose section from the rest of the X-2, and if any violent motions could be damped out by the sequence. One test was dedicated exclusively to testing an appropriate windshield shape.

Under the Army's Blossom III programme using German A-4/V2 rockets from White Sands, New Mexico, in August 1948 a launch was made carrying a full-scale X-2 nose section instrumented with linear and angular accelerometers to test the forces involved in ejection at high velocity. The nose section was ejected at an altitude of 45,720m (150,000ft) and a speed of 61m/sec (200ft/sec) 1min 41sec after launch, or 46sec after the engine shut down. The detonators worked perfectly and the 612kg (1,350lb) nose section ejected with a maximum forward acceleration of 15.84-g for a 0.1sec peak, deploying the reefed drag parachute as planned. Equipped with a separate 19.5m (64ft) recovery parachute, the nose section fell to earth but tangled lines prevented recovery.

While the sequence of events went exactly as intended, the test was virtually useless for verifying the integrity of the design for actual use on a simulated X-2 flight. The deployment altitude was too high to get useful simulation of dynamic loads at the likely altitude of use and the readings from the accelerometers were brought into doubt. After release of the ribbon parachute it rotated in the highly rarefied density of the upper atmosphere and could not provide an effective simulation of how it would behave lower down.

Nevertheless, the escape system was passed for installation in the two X-2s. Several NACA engineers were highly suspicious of the device and did not believe it would be effective, some arguing that it had too many single-point failure probabilities throughout the entire sequence to risk a pilot's life on its use. They were not alone in coming to that

U.S. AIR FORCE
6674
BELL X-2

conclusion. Air Force test pilot Frank Everest spoke candidly about the system when declaring that the accelerations were so high that he believed it could be a fatal mistake to use the jettison device and that he could not contemplate using it short of certain death otherwise.

Power development

Unlike the X-1 series and the Skyrocket, power for the X-2 would be provided by a single Curtiss-Wright XLR-25-CW-1/3 rocket motor with a variable thrust range of 11,120-66,720N (2,500-15,000lb). Difficulties with the development of this engine, relatively advanced for its time, severely hampered the programme, delayed delivery and compromised its operational debut. Selecting an appropriate engine was not an easy decision and at first Bell wanted to use a rocket motor of its own design. A certain amount of political wrangling was involved in the decision to choose the XLR-25 and the final agreement was much fought over.

The design of the XLR-25 involved two combustion chambers stacked one above the other in the aft fuselage, the lower one delivering a maximum thrust of 44,480N (10,000lb) and the upper one a maximum 22,240N (5,000lb). Regeneratively cooled and fed with propellants delivered by a turbopump, the engine operated on an ethyl-alcohol fuel and liquid oxygen. Propellant capacity included 5,760kg (12,700lb) with the turbopump delivering at a rate of 2,270lit (600USgall) per minute. The mixture ratio of oxidiser to fuel was 1.16:1. The maximum thrust of 66,720N (15,000lb) would have a maximum burn duration of 2min 55sec while the minimum thrust level of 11,120N (2,500lb) would operate for 10min 50sec for sustained speed runs. The maximum range with intermittent use of the rocket motor was 527.7kph (328mph).

The manufacturer announced the decision to build this engine for the X-2 on 6 April 1949. Curtiss-Wright had a long history of building aircraft and of extending out to the design and manufacture of engines, latterly rocket motors. The two companies Curtiss and Wright had merged in 1929 after 20 years of acrimonious battling over patents and design rights only truly resolved when the two got together. But the impact of cancelled orders at the end of the Second World War placed them in a dire position and the Aeroplane Division was sold to North American Aviation.

In one year alone, between 1945 and 1946, after-tax profits for Curtiss-Wright fell from $24.4million to $8.7millon while in a similar period Bell profits fell from just over $5million to $658,000. There was a universal acceptance of the need to spread work to prevent bankruptcies. It was partly for this reason that politics had a hand in the contract. The engine configuration proposed by Bell used the XLR-11 supplemented by solid propellant boosters but there were many flaws and drawbacks with that concept. Not only was such a hybrid mix likely to add weight to the overall configuration. It would also increase complexity and reduce reliability due to multiple locations for single-point failure.

The Curtiss-Wright Corporation based its engine business out of the Propeller Division at Wood-Ridge, Caldwell, New Jersey where it had a number of staff who had worked with

Below: Least publicised of all the NACA facilities, yet one which today plays a leading role in space and rocket launches, Wallops Island was the home of tests carried out by the Pilotless Aircraft Research Division (PARD) on 0.14 scale models of the X-2 for measuring aerodynamic characteristics of the swept-wing design. *NACA*

Above left: The Republic XF-91 Thunderceptor was to have been powered by the Curtiss-Wright XLR-27 for take-off and acceleration, supplementing a conventional jet engine as required. This engine sucked resources from the XLR-25 which resulted in delivery and test delays. *Author's collection*
Above right: The dual-chamber XLR-25 had a troublesome history, delayed in development by attention to the XLR-27 and suffering from test problems at a time when the manufacturer was getting out of the rocket engine business. *Author's collection*

Robert Goddard. A lot of that pioneer's ideas were imported to the XLR-25, including variable thrust and combustion chamber film cooling via tangential injection. But it was one thing to produce an elegant design, quite another to come up with a simplified and reliable, working motor with few flaws and foibles. Although struck by numerous minor technical difficulties, the Reaction Motors Incorporated XLR-11 had become what was, for its day, a highly reliable motor for the X-1 and Skyrocket aircraft. But it was insufficiently powerful for the X-2 and would require supplementary boosters.

The motor was not unique in having separate combustion chambers fed by a common propellant delivery system and it had the hallmarks of an innovative concept. The design of the combustion chamber provided a maximum pressure of 2,758kPa (400lb/in^2), the engine being throttled by controlling the propellant flow ratio, varying the pressure which incurred a drop of 517-586kPa (70-85lb/in^2) across the injector orifices. Despite a wide thrust capacity of 50-100 per cent, and an injector orifice pressure drop down to 386kPa (56lb/in^2), surprisingly tests failed to produce any vibrations or 'chugging' which might have been expected in a less flexible design.

The injector plate accommodated 300 LOX and 90 fuel orifices with up to 10 per cent of the fuel spread across the splash plate for cooling. Some 60 per cent of the fuel supply was used for film-cooling the combustion chamber, a high number for the time but one which contributed 1,950m/sec (6,400ft/sec) to the exhaust velocity, a figure which represented 87 per cent (or 60.96m/sec/m or 200ft/sec/ft) of the specific impulse. The engine was designed for cold starts at altitudes up to 21,336m (70,000ft), allowing shut-down and restart cycles during flight.

The single fuel tank occupied the centre section of the fuselage with the two LOX tanks immediately forward and aft, the rocket motor itself situated in the tail and aft of the rear LOX tank. All essential parameters including engine pressures, turbine performance, pump pressures, engine bay temperature, fuel temperature and line pressures were instrumented for constant monitoring. Thus was the X-2 the first in the series to benefit from progress made in telemetry, radio and communications from the earlier X-1 and Skystreak/Skyrocket series where this technology had evolved.

The turbine was started by compressed nitrogen fed from the carrier-plane with the aluminium turbine driven by the vapour generated by a mixture comprising approximately 45 per cent ethyl alcohol, 18 per cent carbon dioxide and 37 per cent water. This vapour was produced in a combustion pot to a temperature of 218-233°C (425-475°F). Using a mixture of 83 per cent alcohol-water and 17 per cent oxygen, the pot had a diameter of 10.16cm (4in) and a length of 20.32cm (8in) and drove the turbine to a speed of 12,000rpm. A tap-off from the low-temperature turbine exhaust was used to pressurise the main fuel tank to 139.9kPa (20lb/in^2). A heat exchanger at the combustion pot pressurised the main LOX tank.

The basic design of the engine was in the hands of the chief rocket engineer at Curtiss-Wright, C. W. Chillson, with G. T. Docktermann, R. E. Shain and A. J. Perle in the supporting team. Work progressed well, acceptance trials scheduled to begin in January 1950 ready for delivery of the first engine later that year. To evaluate the operability and performance of the engine, the department built a sophisticated electrical monitoring system. This was aimed at refining and simplifying the timing and control system for the motor, which the team felt had to be calibrated to very high tolerances for safe operation. A wide range of almost 50 operating combinations were simulated and monitored by this electronic system, satisfactorily passing around 2,600 separate cycles by 1 November 1949.

Given the parlous state of the immediate post-war aircraft engineering industry, any chance for a production contract was immediately sought as a priority. At the time, rocket motors were never as profitable as airframes and Curtiss-Wright was developing another motor, the XLR-27 under military project requirement MX-909. This engine was proposed for the hybrid propulsion of the Republic XF-91 Thunderceptor, where the manufacturer sought to employ a rocket motor for take-off and for periodic use during flight to aid in closing on a target or to improve power for combat.

The development of that motor was causing problems and

Republic would eventually opt for the XLR-11-RM-9. Although a credible aircraft, its hybrid complexity denied it a production contract. But Curtiss-Wright were pulled both by the XLR-27 and by the XLR-25. When Bell was struck by a striking workforce, Curtiss-Wright shifted priority to the XF-91 project and the troublesome XLR-27. Time lost while attending to the XLR-27 did little to help the XLR-25 schedule, which lost out further due to its own problems. The timetables for both the engine and the X-2 slipped inexorably to the right of the schedule charts.

While the electronic simulation had demonstrated excellent reliability and recovery levels from all kinds of potential malfunction, the physical tests with real engines were not going well. Curtiss-Wright was stretched due to cutbacks and post-war economies but they had three test cells for rocket engine development: one cell for the 44,480kPa (10,000lb) thrust motor, the second for the 22,240kPa (5,000lb) thrust motor and the third for a 17,792kPa (4,000lb) thrust JATO unit it had under development for potentially lucrative Air Force and Navy clients.

Back on development with the XLR-25, tests with the larger main rocket motor began in October 1949 but difficulties with starting were traced to a frozen main LOX valve. Then problems prevented full thrust operation of that engine, which displayed a run time of only 40 seconds at a thrust level of 31,136kPa (7,000lb). But there were other issues too.

Obtaining an accurate thrust measurement was proving elusive until Curtiss-Wright began development of a sophisticated device which itself had problems until Air Materiel Command told the company to derive thrust levels from mathematical calculations rather than dynamic measurements. The company resorted to fitting Fisher and Porter flow meters with photographs taken of the panel of gauges and dials to work out the actual value on slide rules and calibration graphs. One step forward, two steps back.

Left: The X-2 programme represented a broadening of applied research testing. Where the earlier research concepts had built on empirical tests and wind tunnel data, the NACA now applied the use of scale models launched on rockets. *NACA*

The X-2 carrier

The development of the Air Force's X-1 series had only marginally involved the NACA when it got under way in 1944. By 1946 the Air Force had grown to accommodate the NACA to a greater extent than it ever had before and, as we have seen, grew to harness a collaboration involving the same airframe in different aircraft aligned with the unique requirements of each body. The X-2 provided a better start for both the Air Force and the NACA, resulting in a shared responsibility and a more productive and coordinated programme of research and experimentation.

A special Stability and Control Subcommittee of the NACA met on 11 July 1946 and recommended that the organisation fly scale models of the X-2 on rockets. These would identify aerodynamic characteristics of the proposed design and provide answers to matters such as protuberances and intersections of the wing and the body of the aircraft, something which had not been done with the X-1. The NACA-Langley Pilotless Atmospheric Research Division (PARD) proposed to fly 0.14 scale models of the X-2 on standard D3 research rockets from Wallops Island, Virginia. The wings would be of steel and possess a 40deg sweepback and 10 per cent arc sections. The replicated fuselages would be of monocoque structure fabricated from magnesium and aluminium, containing instruments for measuring parameters during flight.

With a six-channel telemetry system, the X-2 rocket models would be propelled by a Deacon booster rocket to a maximum speed of Mach 1.36 with instruments for measuring longitudinal stability and control. The X-2 models would descend on a glide path across the Wallops Island test range. To induce instability and measure the consequential airflow, a deliberate diversional disturbance in the performance of the rocket motor simulated an erratic and disrupted flight path. Telemetry would record the angle of attack and the possible methods of recovery by pulsing the aircraft model's flight control surfaces.

The first successful flight with these models occurred on 12 May 1950 when PARD engineers measured instability induced by small tangential thruster rockets made to pulse and disturb the flight path. Two more flights had been completed by January 1952 and a fresh set of tests got underway on 2 December 1953, again using a single Deacon rocket. The model involved weighed 86kg (190lb) and achieved a maximum speed of Mach 1.18. These tests were extremely successful and the 12-channel telemetry system satisfactorily measured normal, longitudinal and transverse accelerations as well as roll, angle of attack, angle of sideslip, total aerodynamic

Above: Attachment straps and sway braces hang ready for assisting ground crew lift the X-2 into the adapted bomb bay of the B-50 carrier-plane. *NACA*

pressure and all rudder positions.

Several other tests were conducted directly by the Air Force quite early in the programme. While convinced that the X-2 should have swept-back wings, the Air Force tapped in to a programme Bell had underway with the US Navy on development of the D-558-2 Skyrocket. For that, two P-63C fighters had been used for comparative flight trials – one with the aircraft's conventional straight wing and the other with 35deg swept wings, designated L-39-1 and L-39-2 respectively. These two aircraft were flown by Alvin Johnston on 23 April and 29 May 1946, the initial results appearing to show that there was no difference in the general handling of the aircraft.

During the summer months of 1946, the Air Force paid for the L-39-2 to be fitted with an X-2 wing, with the same 40deg sweep, the bi-convex profile and sharp leading edge. Bell test pilot Jack Woolams took it into the air on 20 July at the start of an extended sequence of tests completed in December that year. The results were unambiguous: there was no inherent instability during low-speed handling, as a result of which Bell received the full X-2 programme contract on 3 July 1947. Intriguingly, when the NACA results were distributed, in May 1947 John D. Bitner and Hermann L. Meyer of the Martin Company dropped in at Langley to discuss the use of the X-2 planform for a proposed missile!

Below: Two modified P-63C fighters were re-designated L-39-1 and L-39-2, the latter carrying the 40deg sweep on the wing leading edge to replicate that carried by the X-2. Successful tests with this aircraft cleared the way for approval to proceed with the Mach 3 challenger. *Bell Aircraft*

Discussion regarding the test programme for the X-2 got under way between Bell's Richard Passman and Langley managers in early August 1949, by which date the company declared, somewhat over-confidently, that it would deliver the first X-2 complete with rocket motor on 1 November that year. As noted, the year saw several unexpected industrial and technical delays, in addition to the engine contractor choosing to switch priorities between the XLR-25 and the XLR-27. By mid-1950, while most of the primary elements and subassemblies had been completed there was much still to be done. On 6 June the Air Force arrived at Bell to see the work and examine a mock-up of the engine and its turbopump.

At the end of August 1950, the first aircraft was moved to a separate location at Bell's Wheatfield facility where work could continue toward completion, including the attachment of the wing outer panels to the centre-section. The aft fuselage and the LOX and fuel tank assemblies had been proof-tested and were being installed and work started on the pipes, conduits and tubing as the build-up progressed. After all the test

Above: A clear view of the X-2 with its protruding twin XLR-25 expansion chamber nozzles visible at the rear. *NACA*

instrumentation and wiring had been installed, the first aircraft was moved to the Structural Test Factory, there to receive detailed inspection and test of the completed airframe. The second aircraft was pacing some way behind but commensurate with the completion schedule of the first X-2.

The first aircraft (46-674) was not the first to be completed but it was the one assigned to pressure-survey testing, collecting together information from a wide range of transducers delivered to recording or transmitting devices. This was a tedious and meticulous task, as each assembly containing the transducers had to be tested, calibrated and the data system synchronised with the central timer during fabrication, embedded as they were within the structure.

Overall, the X-2 had a length of 11.53m (37.83ft), excluding the nose data probe, a wingspan of 9.84m (32.28ft) with a tail span of 3.91m (12.83ft) and an overall height of 3.58m (11.75ft). Both aircraft had a total wing area of 24.19m² (260.4ft²). Weights would change according to propellant loads and specific mission profiles but the specification rated the empty weight at 5,606kg (12,375lb) and the gross weight at 11,284kg (24,910lb).

Below left: The front end of the bomb bay with the boxy access enclosures – a far better method of pilot ingress to the cramped cockpit than that provided for the three X-1s. *NACA*

The second X-2 (46-675) was the first to be rolled out at Wheatfield, that aircraft appearing on 11 November 1950 without its rocket motor. The first X-2 was assigned the first XLR-25 and the schedule was contingent upon Curtiss-Wright delivering the engine to Bell, the second X-2 being used for initial captive and unpowered drop tests. Much of 1951 would be spent on an extended programme of ground tests with the X-2 strapped in a static test rig, a period during which the chosen carrier-plane was modified and made ready for flight operations.

The choices for a carrier-plane were limited. Very few aircraft had the lift capacity or the proportional configuration to allow conversion. This was a much heavier aircraft than the X-1 or D-558 series aircraft, although the length was less than that of the Douglas types and only a little more than the second-generation X-1 series. The candidates included the Convair B-36, which had itself been subject to consideration as a carrier-plane for escort fighters and reconnaissance aircraft.

Left: Another view of the refined adaptation and modifications to the carrier-plane for the X-2 and the access enclosure. *NACA*

The selection was based as much on cost, availability and reliability as well as on the technical and engineering requirements.

Traditionally used for the research flights, the B-29 had insufficient lift capability to carry the X-2 and the B-50 was the only logical choice. The aircraft available was an EB-50A-5-BO (46-11) from the same production batch as that used for the later X-1 series, destroyed on 9 November 1951. It was that event which prompted its replacement but specifically for the X-2. The choice of carrier-plane would indirectly control the operational capabilities of the X-2; a faster launch speed would result in added speed for the end of the X-2's powered flight, or a higher launch altitude would allow it to achieve greater altitude.

It was for these reasons that some thought was given later to converting a B-52 for carrier-plane duties, providing a cruising speed double that of the B-29/B-50 types, adding 402kph (250mph) to the airspeed at X-2 release. There was even some talk about using a proposed all-jet version of that aircraft with swept-back wings, the YB-60. But there was little Air Force interest in that aircraft anyway and the AMC would not issue a development contract before March 1951. But that was an uncertain long shot and still a paper study when the X-2 was rolled out. The B-52 had traction as a carrier for later and more advanced capabilities and it would of course be selected as the only aircraft capable of carrying the X-15, which would weigh more than twice as much as the X-2.

Several modifications were required to make the B-50A suitable for carrying the X-2, including cutting away a section of the bomb bay. Also, following the practice with the later X-1 series carried by the preceding B-50, installation of a box-structure which would cover the cockpit and its canopy so that the pilot could get into the aircraft before launch protected from the airstream. The X-2 would be held by two adapted bomb shackles connected to a lever in the cockpit for release to free flight. Stability during mated flight was provided by two sway braces connected to either side of the B-50's fuselage. A control panel was added for operating the interface between the two aircraft, a LOX top-off tank being fitted in the fuselage – 50 per cent of the liquid oxygen placed in the X-2's tanks before take-off would boil away by the time of the drop. A nitrogen tank was also installed to start the X-2's turbopump prior to the countdown for release.

Tragedy and transformation

Unlike preceding research aircraft, the X-2 could not be wheeled around on the ground due to its unique landing gear and ventral skid. Bell designed and built special dollies on which to mount the aircraft so that it could be manoeuvred underneath the carrier-plane. But instead of it being placed in a pit and the carrier-plane moved above it, the main landing gear on the B-50A had to be jacked up by separate 20 ton (18.1tonne) hydraulic jacks, pivoting it up on its nose wheel and creating a space into which the X-2 could be moved on its dolly. After lowering the aircraft back on to its main wheels, the X-2 would be raised up and shackled inside the converted bomb bay.

Bell test pilot 'Skip' Ziegler would fly the initial drop tests. Between July 1951 and early 1952, several captive flights were made with the mated aircraft to check out procedures, verify the newly installed equipment in the carrier-plane and evaluate the operation and handling of the various fluids passing between the two. Ballast compensated for the absent engine to maintain centre of gravity but the captive flights went well and preparations were made to fly the aircraft to Edwards. By this time, supersonic flight was becoming routine and a wide range of wind tunnels and test facilities to support this new development had begun operating across the United States. The next big step forward was needed urgently to maintain pace and to keep the research ahead of operational requirements with combat aircraft.

But problems with the XLR-25 persisted, especially with explosive ignition on the higher thrust combustion chamber. There was discussion about replacing that single chamber with two of the less powerful, 22,240N (5,000lb) thrust chambers but the redesign and engineering challenges would have delayed the programme by several years. Then, NACA engineers reviewing the programme proposed replacing the XLR-25 with two separate power units of the proven XLR-11 from the X-1 and Skyrocket programmes. There were delay challenges and other negative considerations with that, including the changes required regarding tankage and reduced performance of the X-2 as a result.

Worse still, in early 1952 news came that Curtiss-Wright

Right: On 6 June 1952, Col. J. S. Holtoner, commander of the Air Force Flight Test Center, gave his permission to commence glide tests with the second X-2, the first to be put under test operations. *USAF*

was getting out of the rocket engine business and that it was trying to fulfil its obligation to Bell, the Air Force and the NACA by putting together the contracted engines using spare parts. The original contract had been for two engines but two more had been added later. Much of this was due to the total transformation in the US aviation and ancillary industry during the second half of the 1940s. The industry would recover, adapt and expand again but this was a spectacularly dramatic period as companies folded, amalgamated, merged or simply went bust.

On 22 April 1952 the second X-2 was flown from Bell's Wheatfield facility to Edwards where it was received by the special team of personnel from Langley and the Air Force were waiting to begin drop tests. The first flight from there took place on 5 June with Ziegler at the controls. This went so well that the following day Col. R. L. Johnson, chief of the Weapon Systems Division at Wright Air Development Center wrote to Col. J. S. Holtoner, then commander of the Air Force Flight Test Center, that the X-2 was 'ready for glide flight testing'. As preparations began for the first drop test, a second captive flight took place on 15 June where several instruments failed in simulated data transmissions.

Ballasted but weighing only half as much as it would for a powered run, the X-2 made its first drop flight on 27 June 1952 seeking to gauge aerodynamic stability, low-speed handling and overall control and landing characteristics. Ziegler climbed down into the cockpit as the B-50A chugged uphill through 1,524m (5,000ft), sealed and locked in the cockpit before the aircraft reached 3,048m (10,000ft) as the support personnel had no oxygen masks. Ziegler noted the cramped confines of the cockpit when he observed that his helmet touched the canopy and his legs were bent to get his feet on the rudder pedals.

At a speed of 331kph (206mph) and an altitude of 9,449m (31,000ft), the X-2 dropped away and, reaching 359kph (223mph) Ziegler deployed the flaps, slowed to 338kph (210mph) and initiated a landing approach at 294kph (183mph). With flaps at 28deg, he started the final approach phase and touched down at 228kph (142mph) in light winds. But the unusual configuration of the landing gear caused the X-2 to experience very high pitching moments on contacting the ground, breaking the nose leg and slewing the aircraft to the left. That caused the wingtip to scrape along the lakebed, tipping it so that the starboard wingtip struck the surface hard, breaking off the bumper skid on that side. The X-2 came to a stop after a run of 307.8m (1,010ft).

Bell shipped parts to repair the X-2 but they were delayed and did not arrive at Edwards before August. A wider, central skid was fitted and two retractable whisker skids were added under each wing at the mid-span location. The second drop test was accomplished by Ziegler on 10 October and the changes proved fruitful, that landing going off perfectly. Bell was so confidant, and perhaps wanting to raise confidence in the whole programme, that it invited the Air Force to try out a drop test too. That occurred after Ziegler's flight the same day when Maj. Frank Everest dropped away from the carrier-plane at 9,144m (30,000ft) and completed a successful descent and touchdown.

As the New Year arrived, rocket motors were finally available for both X-2s and were available for installation. One engine was completely ready and installed in the first aircraft (46-675) with a planned sequence of captive flights, initially to check out the X-2 with 25 per cent propellant followed with progressively greater loads up to the maximum capacity of the aircraft's tanks. As previous checks and tests had shown, there was some danger involved, with caution being the driving factor in the schedule. Initially, these tests would be conducted by Bell flying out of Wheatfield with the carrier-plane placing itself over Lake Ontario for LOX top-off and propellant jettison tests.

Left: The B-50 had a series of vent and purge lines along with ancillary equipment supporting the X-2 and other research aircraft it was called upon to carry. *NACA*

The flight was conducted on 12 May 1953, with the B-50A at 9,144m (30,000ft) which was the height at which the X-2 would be dropped for powered flights. Piloted by William 'Bill' Leyshon and David Howe, there were six other crew on board the carrier-plane with Ziegler monitoring activities in the bomb bay for the LOX topping-off tests. These were successfully completed twice and next up was the nitrogen pressurisation process which would normally have supported pre-launch preparations. It was about 13:05hrs local time and the mated aircraft were flying straight and level at a speed of 322kph (200mph) in an overcast sky. Approximately 90 seconds after the start of the pressurisation activity, but with the value at its normal level, a terrific explosion tore through the X-2, hurling Ziegler out of the bomb bay. The detail is best described by the official report:

'As described by the chase pilot who was flying near the left wing of the B-50, a large ball of red flame originating below the B-50 engulfed all of the X-2 and part of the B-50. There was no sustained fire of any magnitude aboard the B-50. The ensuing blast rolled the chase plane violently into a left bank and the B-50 was seen to rise about 30.5m (100ft). The chase pilot described the X-2 as having disintegrated. The largest piece he saw leaving the B-50 was apparently the outer half of a wing panel which passed within 15m (50ft).

'As described by the crew, one or perhaps two explosions occurred in quick succession. The B-50 experienced violent positive and then negative accelerations and rose between 61m (200ft) and 198m (650ft). The bomb bay was first engulfed in a gray fog and then by small particles of burning debris for a short period after the explosion...A scanner, having a position in the rear compartment of the B-50, bailed out through the aft side door. The chase pilot saw a body leaving the B-50 at about this time but did not see any others.'

The crewmember who bailed out was Bell technician Frank Wolko and an immediate search for him, and Ziegler, across Lake Ontario was mounted by the US Air Force and the Royal Canadian Air Force but to avail. At the time the accident happened the aircraft were over the central portion of that water but their bodies were never recovered, Wolko's parachute apparently failing to open. Although damaged, the carrier-plane landed back at Edwards, news about Ziegler and Wolko having already coursed through the close-knit community, senior managers and Air Force officers quickly taking on the grim task of supporting the distraught families. The Air Force wanted to put the B-50A back in operation for the sole surviving X-2 but Bell disagreed and it was retired from use.

Bell had several modifications planned for the first X-2 (46-064), the second to be completed and in the grounding that awaited an official report on the disaster, used the time to make several improvements to that aircraft. A lot of which

Below: Ziegler's first glide flight in the X-2 ended when it slewed off the prescribed landing strip and broke the nose wheel leg. *NACA*

came as a result of an intensive investigation into the loss of the X-1D on 22 August 1951 and the third X-1 on 9 November 1951. In a conference held on 9 June 1953 at Wright-Patterson AFB, the Air Force concluded that the accident had probably been caused by a malfunction in an electrical circuit and that this had led to ignition of the oxygen mixture. It recommended modifications to prevent the need to top-off the LOX tank from the carrier-plane and that procedures be developed to prevent premature bail-out and loss of life.

Bell began their own investigation the morning after the accident and had not yet reached firm conclusions but it wanted to integrate the loss of the three aircraft and to seek out the possibility of a common cause. As discussed earlier, they found that the use of 410 steel in the nitrogen tube-bundles was the link between the three losses in less than two years and that it should be replaced. The report also pressed for further improvements, including wherever possible the elimination of mechanical joints in propellant lines and gaskets replaced with welded or brazed joints. It also suggested that fuel delivery lines should be re-routed through the ventral trunk of the fuselage and fume-tight bulkheads installed to prevent the clouding of gas and its accumulation in the bomb bay of the B-50, a potentially explosive hazard.

For flights with the remaining X-2, the Air Force moved the B-50 selected for launching the X-1A and X-1B to the X-2 programme, bringing in a JTB-29-96-BW (45-21800) for the two second-generation X-1s as replacement. Although it would be used before, it was permanently assigned to NACA Langley Field from 15 December 1954. Although Curtiss-Wright was exiting the rocket engine business it continued to support the XLR-25 programme and to work on potential upgrades in performance. Meanwhile, the stand-down for improvements to the sole surviving X-2 allowed the NACA to implement a series of changes which could increase its potential. But in the fullness of time it was not the X-2 which would be the beneficiary of these new technologies but an entirely new programme on the horizon – the X-15.

The potential changes and enablers included studies into the use of new and exotic materials to find solutions to aero-thermal problems with high-speed/high-altitude flight. It indicated that 302 steel, with 74 per cent iron, 8 per cent nickel and 18 per cent chromium, and Invar, comprised of 64 per cent iron and 36 per cent nickel, would have great benefits if used in a different type of construction. This would interlace Warren-trusses at right-angles to each other fabricated out of these materials. With this combination, it was believed that high heat loads and high heat rates peaking at high loads, could be endured under atmospheric heating without developing thermal stress levels. This, said the NACA and the Wright Air Development Center (WADC), would make hypersonic aircraft a possibility.

Below: Test pilot Jean Ziegler, shown here at the side of the Bell X-1A, would lose his life in the X-2 on 12 May 1953. *NASA*

Chapter Eight

Mach 3

The recent losses shook both the NACA and the Air Force and many changes would be made in successive programmes then getting under way. Renewed concern over the XLR-25 would bring a continuous re-evaluation of the practicality of using this engine at all in the X-2 and during 1954 and 1955 there were several team members who doubted that it would ever support a powered flight. As noted earlier, the X-series was going through a major transformation in the type of project embraced by this sequence and the Air Force began to get increasingly involved, both in selecting the type of research aircraft to procure and the kind of programmes it should carry out. This brought both delays and opportunity.

Some progress had been made with the XLR-25 and six had been delivered to Bell with testing underway on a seventh by 1 October 1953. But NACA engineers at Edwards were still looking at the possibility of replacing it and, despite earlier arguments regarding the difficulty of doing that, the determination to have a research aircraft capable of exploring the region around Mach 3.5 was very attractive, especially so given the increasing commitment toward a manned hypersonic project. The loss of the first X-2 delivered for flight and the increasing support for a reliable and sustainable programme did result in a reopening of the debate regarding the future of the X-2.

This determination spawned a special meeting of Langley's Research Aircraft Panel on 4-5 February 1954 to debate the future of the X-2 research programme and also to involve the Air Force Flight Test Center more closely in those decisions. On 9 March, the Wright Air Development Center told the FTC told that the remaining X-2 would be delivered to Edwards in July but that it would not make powered flight attempts before a protracted series of captive and glide drop tests had been completed. But still, the XLR-25 was the limiting element in the schedule.

Exuding confidence, Bell produced test figures in April which showed good results. But these were misleading, being a 'breadboard' duplication of the engine and the supporting contributory systems rather than being in a 1:1 scale duplication of the aircraft and its layout. It was one thing to lay out all the components, subsystems and systems and demonstrate sat-

Above: The loss of the first X-2 delivered (46-675) was a blow to the entire programme from which only a semblance of the planned research programme could be fulfilled by the second X-2 flown. *NACA* isfactory results. Quite another to package it all up tight and compact inside the aircraft for which it was designed to operate. But this is what a 'breadboard' layout is: an artificial, usually two-dimensional, arrangement of integrated elements of a system. When Bell tested the engine connected to the X-2's plumbing, pipes and conduits in a fully operational condition, it began to fail and to do so spectacularly.

By October 1954 the NACA had lost faith in the engine and the doubters expanded their ranks in questioning the validity of the powered test programme. To a certain extent, events were overtaking the qualification of the engine. The first captive flight with the carrier-plane had put the first X-2 (46-605) into the air over Wheatfield on 13 July 1954 and two days later it had been delivered to Edwards, complete with rocket motor. For the next two weeks it was fitted out with instrumentation to support the next level of captive and glide flights but there would be many delays, problems and changes to the schedule over the next year.

With so many variables involved in attempting to push the speed range from around Mach 2.4 to Mach 3.5 or more, at the recommendation of the NACA the Air Force invested in a special type of analogue computer known as the Goodyear Electronic Digital Analyzer (GEDA). The programme engineer for the X-2, Richard Day was assigned the task of working it up as an informational simulator which, when programmed with the characteristics of the X-2 and equations and motion data, could provide information from stick inputs, providing readouts on a cathode ray tube (CRT), a novel addition for the early 1950s. Day would use the GEDA to check out pilots and test them on a variety of contingencies that could arise in flight.

The GEDA was an early form of electronic simulator and the progress made in a wide range of fields directly applicable to the upcoming X-15 programme was significant between the loss of the second X-2 and the first flights with the first. There was a direct relevance here to the development of test rigs, pilot simulators and complex instrumentation, telemetry and recording capabilities which greatly benefited the hypersonic programme, a factor vital to explain the progress made with the X-15. All this activity stimulated ideas regarding further development of the aircraft, some engineers at the Ames facility suggesting a thinner wing and improved planform while others proposed additional rocket power for stretching the performance to Mach 4. But those aspirations would be locked into its successor. With the X-2 fully instrumented by 3 August, it was handed over for flight operations.

For those, there was the little matter of a pilot. Ziegler, the most experienced test pilot had lost his life in the tragic loss of the first X-2 carried into the air and there was no one to take his place. The Air Force supported the now Lt. Col. Frank Everest, who volunteered to step in and, after sending a letter to Bell dated 7 May 1954 suggesting that for the company flights they consider Everest as their pilot, it was agreed. Everest went to Wheatfield a few weeks later for familiarisation

Below: The Goodyear Electronic Digital Analyzer (GEDA) provided an early form of informational simulator which would prove useful for predicted conditions. It represented the first really useful attempt at testing certain flight processes.

Below right: Assigned the X-2's flight engineer at the High Speed Flight Station, Richard E. Day had been with the Dynamic Stability and Analysis Branch and is here seen working the GEDA on roll-coupling simulations using a hand-stick controller and a cathode ray tube. *NACA*

Left: Frank Everest was selected by the Air Force to replace Ziegler and he would conduct initial tests with the second X-2. *USAF*

with the X-2 and a briefing from their engineers on the capabilities and layout of the type. Preparations for the first flight included a cautionary approach to operations with the rocket motor, still proving troublesome and erratic in tests.

On 5 August the X-2 made two flights, the first a captive run to check out both aircraft at the operating speed and altitude and the second a glide test for Everest to familiarise himself with the aircraft in flight. Fitzhugh Fulton was the pilot for the B-50, personally selected by Everest and a pilot in whom he placed a lot of trust. Weighing half its normal drop weight, notwithstanding ballast, and released at 9,144m (30,000ft), Everest tested the longitudinal control and stability characteristics before ending his unpowered flight with a landing which brought similar results to that experienced by Ziegler. Powerless to control it after touchdown, Everest became a passenger as the aircraft slewed and scraped its way along the desert floor, gouging ruts with its wingtips and breaking the nose leg.

Back at Wheatfield for repairs on 20 August, the X-2 would remain there for almost four months. The landing problems were extensively explored and debated but largely in the dark because, as intended, the aircraft had not had its instrumentation on for that initial glide flight. There was no strain gauge data or telemetry readings to indicate loadings or accelerations which could have helped revise the landing system. During detailed inspection at Bell, the instrument gauges were found to be in poor condition, necessitating replacement, and double-shielded cable, found to be brittle, was replaced with a substitute material.

A meeting was held at the Wright Air Development Center on 8 December where the flight test programme was laid out. The Air Force would conduct tests with three captive flights followed by three glide flights and four powered flights up to a maximum Mach 0.9. The NACA would then take it over for transonic and supersonic research flights. The test schedule was verified and passed to the Air Research & Development Command on 5 January 1955 with a timeline calling for those activities to begin by the end of the month and to be concluded by 30 November that year. The X-2 was flown from Wheatfield to Edwards on 16 January, the first two captive flights taking place on 2 and 3 February and the third on 1 March during which the propellant handling and pressurisation systems were checked out.

The first drop test was made on 8 March with a test of the propellant dump sequence where it was discovered that it took 10 minutes to get the tanks completely empty. Later, this would be reduced to two minutes when larger jettison tubes of 7.6cm (3in) diameter were installed. Everest conducted a perfect flight after the drop and made a good landing, although the X-2 skidded on roll-out and damaged a wingtip. A repeat scheduled for 5 April was aborted in flight for a minor technical issue. The next day the drop took place as planned but again there was damage on landing as the X-2 swung violently and ended up sideways.

Everest made his criticism of the landing system clear to Bell and on 8 April the aircraft was returned to Wheatfield again for repairs. As usual, where failures are an orphan, nobody wanted to claim responsibility but extensive testing at Bell did show that the failure to obtain good roll-out characteristics came down to an early requirement from the Air Force that the X-2 be installed with a nose leg possessing fighter-standard shock absorbing capability. The simplest solution was to halve the distance of travel in the oleo leg by reducing the sink speed from 3.65m/sec (12ft/sec) to 1.83m/sec (6ft/sec), raising the down-pointing angle of the aircraft on the ground from -7deg to -3deg. The width of the main skid was increased to 50.8cm (20in) and the shape was re-contoured, which improved the roll-moment.

Firing up the X-2

The X-2 was back at Edwards on 21 July 1955 complete with repairs, modifications and a rocket motor. Three days later it was delivered to the NACA's Flight Test Station for instrumentation. Urging caution, the Air Force overrode Bell's plan for an immediate powered drop and insisted on an additional glide flight. An intensive sequence of ground runs with the XLR-25 was taking place in parallel with the anticipated flight trials and the programme was entering a key phase. Not all of those were satisfactory and the upcoming flight runs were considered part of the qualification programme for the engine itself, as well as the airframe and support infrastructure.

In the wider world of global events, 1955 was a seminal year in which the United States made the formal announcement that it would launch an artificial Earth-orbiting satellite in support of the International Geophysical Year of 1957-58. Until this time, sounding-rockets ('sounding' the upper atmosphere) and scientific instruments carried by balloons had been the only means by which scientists could probe heights where no manned aircraft had flown, gathering snapshots of the outer atmosphere in the several minutes they were exposed to the near-vacuum of space.

This event would have seismic repercussions, prompting the Russians to match the deed and creating a Space Race from late 1957 when they became the first country to launch a satellite, up-ending perceptions about future world leadership and launching a race for technological superiority in both space and weapons. In 1955 too, the contract for the hypersonic X-15 was issued to North American, opening a window on manned flights into space and speeds in excess of Mach 6. Notwithstanding the reality that this project was several years away from putting research aircraft into the sky, it had a significant impact on the decisions made about the existing inventory of second-generation X-1s, the Skyrocket and, not least the future of the X-2.

It was also the year in which the Air Force and the NACA received a stark reminder of the dangers lurking frequently unseen beneath the shiny polished skin of high-performance rocket-planes. On 8 August 1955 the X-1A was destroyed in an explosion which has been described previously, the replacement of Ulmer leather with Flexitallic and Teflon implemented universally across the inventory of NACA research aircraft. This event and the sustained problems with the rocket motor put further delay into the X-2, now ten years and $16million into a programme which had yet to achieve a single powered flight. Aware of the impact, Bell doubled efforts to solve recurring problems and spent company money on overtime and engineering solutions to issues not all of which were of its own making.

The first powered flight was scheduled for 25 October 1955 and preparations went well until shortly before the drop when Everest called an abort after a nitrogen leak developed and propellants were jettisoned. This time, the landing was perfect, with a straight-line roll-out bringing the X-2 to a graceful stop. After the cause of the leak had been found and fixed, another captive flight was mounted on 17 November to check out the propellant system and the repairs to the pressurisation system.

The following day, Everest attempted the first powered flight and after completing his check list of 127 items, dropped free from the B-50 at 9,235m (30,300ft), the heavy aircraft falling faster than previously due to the propellant load. Everest conducted several intermittent engine firings with the smaller, 22,240N (5,000lb) thrust chamber and took the X-2 through three separate bursts of power achieving Mach 0.95 before an automatic shutdown. A small fire had started in the engine but the auto-extinguisher had put it out. At that point, Everest noticed a 189lit (50USgall) disparity in the quantity levels in the two LOX tanks and used a manual propellant transfer system to restore the balance and the centre of gravity.

The chase pilot had moved in close and reported flutter on the stabiliser but the pilot never felt that, although some buffeting was noticed. The fire had been started when propellant dumped into the underside had been sucked back up into the engine bay. There was also considerable scorching of the aft fuselage and tail assembly which had to be repaired. The next powered flight was attempted on 10 December when the jettison pump failed and again the same day because of a problem with one of the engines on the B-50. Yet another attempt on 18 December had to be called off when the turbopump failed to start and the X-2 made yet another captive return to Edwards. Additional technical problems and adverse weather would keep the X-2 grounded for three months.

The litany of problems, technical troubles and a dysfunctional rocket motor broadcast a depressing sense of inevitability that the X-2 would not match the performance it had been built to achieve. In the first few months of 1956, a development plan was formulated in which the Air Force and the NACA would complete basic powered drop flights to check out the systems followed by a series of high-speed flights to see just how fast the X-2 could fly. After that, a series of high-altitude flights would be made to secure the limits of that capability. Only then could a series of scientific research flights be mounted by the NACA, already drawing up a programme of test runs with instruments aimed at supporting the existing programme and requirements feeding back from the X-15, now in full-scale development.

Delivery to the NACA was put back by these accumulating delays and on 21 February 1956 a letter from the Air Force explained that the airworthiness demonstration programme would not be completed until early April, citing the rocket motor as the primary cause. But there was great uncertainty as to funding beyond the year. In a modest sign of some limited success, the second powered flight took place on 24 March when Everest reached Mach 0.91 and an altitude of 13,716m (45,000ft), slower than expected due to the smaller of the two rocket motors failing to fire. The 44,480N (10,000lb) thrust motor did perform as expected, however. The reluctance of the other motor to fire prompted Curtiss-Wright to provide a new safety circuit, qualified in several bench runs.

Powered flights resumed on 24 March 1956 when Everest flew the X-2 to Mach 0.91 and an altitude of 13,716m (45,000ft) using the higher-thrust motor, the smaller one failing to ignite despite repeated attempts to reset the ignition sequence. Noting a quantity discrepancy of 946lit (250USgall), Everest also had to do a manual balancing of the LOX tanks to restore the centre of gravity. Again, a successful landing was achieved. Curtiss Wright made some adjustments to the start and safety circuit, which was deemed excessively sensitive, to

Left: On 18 November 1955, Everest took the sole surviving X-2 (46-674) on its first powered run although a small fire broke out in the engine bay due to fuel being sucked back in. *NACA*

Right: Yeager prepares for a high-altitude test flight with an NF-104A. *USAF*

ing extended operations into new and untested flight environments, was the need for adequate funding to prevent surges of stretched budgets and shoestring operations; the X-2 had been particularly badly affected by the continuous need for adequate funding.

It was felt that there was a need for a central coordinating project officer placed between the requirements of the programme and the men selected as test pilots. And it was felt that pilots should be given adequate familiarisation experience with the experimental aircraft so as to avoid pitching them directly into the detailed research flights. This was a transformational shift, placing a responsible individual between the sometimes over-excessive demands of the programme managers and the capabilities of the flight teams, including pilots. Gone were the days when a leatherneck would be thrown into a new aircraft and told to go test it; the log books of many test pilots from long before the Second World War would register several different kinds of aircraft tested in a single day. But those days were gone and not everyone recognised that.

As an example of this, it was pointed out that after Kincheloe's record-breaking altitude flight, the Air Force planned flights to 45,270m (150,000ft) without even talking to him about his own experience or what he felt he had discovered. This is a highly relevant aspect of the changes which were introduced by the focused analysis as to why five aircraft and three people had died in the programme to date. It would result in a general, and quite rapid, transformation of the test-pilot culture to more usefully acquire his engineering and operational experience and expertise. It raised the bar and featured strongly in Scott Crossfield's decision to go to North American and spend several years living, working and qualifying in flight, the hypersonic X-15. Many would fail to understand the reason why he left the NACA and went to play a significant role in its development. Rather than wait it out for chance at having his name attached to a particular speed or altitude record, he chose to play an integral part of the type's development and to hand to others a carefully prepared machine for high performance.

Below: The JF-104A took over from the X-1A for research into the use of thrusters for attitude control in the rarefied upper layers of the atmosphere. The technology was vital for the X-15, then in development, and for manned space vehicles. *NASA*

This approach would move higher up the scale of professionalism just two years and six months after the loss of Millburn Apt when NASA selected its first seven astronauts in April 1959 – test-pilot engineers who would take the role to another level in forcibly campaigning for greater participation in programme development, hardware design and fabrication and in writing the requirements for qualification flights and flight plans to fulfil those objectives. It inherited the lessons from the NACA research programmes by appointing an astronaut as head of the office managing those men and, by the 1980s, women too.

The X-1 series, both first and second generation, the Skystreak and the Skyrocket and the X-2 were essential elements in the building blocks defining the type of programme the Air Force, the Navy and the NACA – soon to be NASA – would shape. The success of the X-15 would be testimony to the achievements, the contribution and the legacy of those precursor test teams who had taken high-speed flight from subsonic to supersonic speeds. It would be the purpose of the X-15 to more than double the Mach number and take winged aircraft out of the atmosphere and into the hard vacuum of space. Which is why it is considered a vital step between the early days of testing and the more demanding engineering and human standards of later years.

Separated by type numbers and formal military designations, it is all too easy to think of these separate programmes and individual aircraft as detached from a linear progression, as though each was distinct and unconnected with those that came before or after. That interpretation is quite wrong. As seen through the evolving flow of high-speed and then high-altitude types, one programme learned from another, and each leaned on its precursor for experience and comparison. Which is why the story of the X-2 has been told last, even though other research aircraft flying long before the X-2, continued tests more than two years after its demise.

The first and second-generation X-1s and the Skystreak and Skyrocket had been defined by narrow requirements strapped to technology outclassed by the time the X-2 flew for the first time. But the requirements that specified the X-2 were set down before the first powered flight through Mach 1, while evolving progressively and setting down new technology sought by the Air Force and the NACA as a successor to the earlier types. The X-2 is a starting point for the X-15 and not an end in itself, or more appropriately, without the experience with the X-2 its successor might never have been built.

As a critique of the period 1944-1958, it has been said by many of those involved at the time that the latter phases of these research programmes were redundant to purpose. That their objectives could readily have been carried out by existing aircraft already in production, the Lockheed F-104 being a case in point. As noted NACA research scientist and engineer John Becker pointed out, when speaking of this phase and the aircraft it produced, 'Some had lagged so seriously in procurement that their designs had become obsolescent before they were flown. In a few cases tactical designs superior to the research aircraft were in hand before the research aircraft flew'.

In other asides relating to this period at NACA's Muroc and the Air Force's Edwards AFB, research engineer Gene Matranga noted that they 'could probably fly the X-1E two or three times a month, whereas Kelly Johnson was flying his F-104s two or three times a day into the same flight regimes, so it really didn't make sense for us to be applying those kinds of resources to [get] that kind of information'.

If the aircraft described here were deemed to be outdated and outclassed by the time the programmes wound up in 1958, it was because their very development had stimulated a surge in high-velocity and supersonic wind tunnels, from which bank of data industrial design teams and manufacturers were able to find the information they needed to fast-track new combat types fully capable of flying to the profiles demonstrated by the research types.

But the very fact that these new Century-series types were being produced, when they were, was a powerful motivating factor in planning the next step as a leap above and beyond what was known at the time about the supersonic/hypersonic zone and the edge of space. The origin of those concepts is cemented firmly in the first half of the 1950s and the very fact that such a major step forward appeared practical at that time demonstrates the level of development in ground facilities, tracking and telemetry, data handling, flight operations management and engineering knowledge for material and structures. By the time the X-15 was placed under contract, the definition of that programme was plausible through each of these evolved capabilities.

Left: The three NF-104A aircraft were modified from standard production models but with a supplementary rocket motor and attitude control thrusters for very high altitude flight and testing of attitude stabilisation systems. *NASA*

Section 2

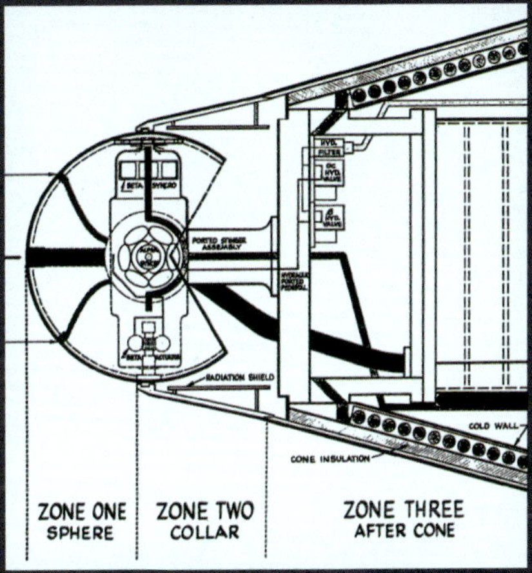

North American X-15 – Evolution and Engineering

Chapter Nine

The Origins of an Idea

It was clear from early research into high-speed aircraft that materials and structures would need to be developed to protect any aircraft moving into high supersonic speeds within the atmosphere. Friction with the air would raise temperatures to the limits of known materials and new design concepts would be required to make hypersonic flight possible. Driven by the need to develop re-entry bodies for ballistic missiles, much attention had been given to that problem, however. Research into that converged with similar activity which began much earlier in plans to develop a wind tunnel proposed in August 1945 by John Becker from the Compressibility Research Division at Langley Aeronautical Laboratory.

Where most tunnels at Langley and Ames could barely reach Mach 2, Becker wanted a tunnel capable of Mach 7 and this became possible when Arthur Kantrowitz and Coleman Donaldson proposed a configuration in which the wall contours of the tunnel would be shaped to form a secondary throat, reducing losses from shock waves in the diffuser. It was suggested that a 28 x 28cm (11 x 11in) test section be constructed as a demonstrator but there was resistance from those who believed such a tunnel was unnecessary. Becker finally got his way when wrapping it up into a research activity – Project 506!

It found a home in the former Propeller Research Tunnel at Langley and was effective once an electric heater had been installed to maintain the temperature at 454ºC (850ºF) to prevent liquefaction, where the gas would have been turned into a liquid. Charles McLennan was the chief engineer on the tunnel and attached a mechanical throat which significantly extended the run time from 50sec to 90sec. The first demonstration took place on 26 November 1947 and achieved a uniform flow of Mach 6.9. For three years it remained the sole example of its kind anywhere in the world.

Encouraged by the work at Langley, Alfred J. Eggers Jr. built a 25 x 35cm (10 x 14in) continuous flow tunnel at the NACA's Ames Aeronautical Laboratory in California. This was integrated with the compressors which had already been built for the existing facilities. One curious fact about the hypersonic tunnels was that they required a higher pressure to

Above: From late 1945, the NACA Langley's John Becker was an early advocate for better tunnels to progress research into Mach 7 flight, a baseline target for future development. He finally got his way when it was embraced by Project 506. *NACA*

Left: At the NASA Ames Aeronautical Laboratory, Alfred J. Eggers set up a continuous flow tunnel which was installed in conjunction with existing facilities. *NACA*

start than to run, although for Mach 7 flow they would operate at six atmospheres, or 607kPa (88lb/in^2), but require a pressure of 3,034kPa (440lb/in^2) to start them. In building this tunnel Eggers also came up with a less costly way of operating it.

By 1950, based on reports of the Mach 10 wind tunnel which the German rocket engineers had planned for their test facility at Peenemünde during the war, the Naval Ordnance Facility got their own hypersonic tunnel. But progress with testing hypersonic conditions was hampered by the sluggish improvements, which indicated a reluctance to invest in what was clearly an emerging and demanding requirement to support possible trans-atmospheric vehicles. Tweaks allowed modest improvement through the addition of more powerful heaters but this was seen as only a temporary fix. Nevertheless, some improvement was obtained when modifications to Langley's Gas Dynamics Laboratory allowed test runs of up to 15 minutes and removed the need for the continuously running mode.

Very little of this work was aimed at high-speed aircraft but at the various missile programmes and rocket projects which grew and expanded exponentially during the 1950s. From 1954 there was a large scale effort to develop and deploy intercontinental ballistic missiles and to find a way of developing survivable re-entry warheads carrying nuclear weapons. It was from this research that the knowledge which underpinned the coming X-15 programme converged with results from the tunnels. It is perhaps ironic that the aircraft designed to operate in high temperature regimes was made possible by research into ballistic missile warheads.

Much of that development came from breaking research conducted by H. Julian Allen and Alfred Eggers who proved conclusively that a spear-pointed nose shape was not the best way to dissipate thermal energy. Rather, a blunt-body shape which would produce a bow-shaped shock wave to spread out in front of the bluff body and carry away much of the thermal energy which would otherwise go by conduction into the material structure of the body itself – be that a warhead or manned aircraft. At hypersonic speeds the shock wave from this rounded shape would stand off and not attach directly to the surface, as it would to the pointed tip of the needle-shaped nose.

Containing most of the thermal energy, only heat radiated across the boundary later would raise the temperature in the structure itself while the shock wave would carry away most of the heat. But it was counter-intuitive and Allen and Eggers had to fight hard for it to become universally accepted – and applied. Which it quickly was when requirements urgently pressed for a solution to challenges building survivable warheads to be propelled on arching trajectories and speeds in excess of Mach 12 on re-entry. The operational viability of relatively lightweight, thermonuclear warheads as a credible deterrent depended more upon their survivability getting back down on to their targets than on getting them up off the ground in the first instance.

The convergence of Air Force interests and an expanding portfolio of new combat types did little to dampen enthusiasm for projecting forward to advanced aerospace concepts proposed for future deployment. There was perhaps a none-too-obvious but very real connection between requirements of supersonic and hypersonic combat aircraft and the technology underpinning the missile deterrent. Due in some small part to the onset of the Korean War, in the spring of

Right: Before the development of intercontinental ballistic missiles from the mid-1950s, long-range strike systems such as the North American Aviation Navaho found favour. It was boosted to flying speed by solid propellant rockets for sustained cruise utilising turbojet engines. *USAF*

Right: Austrian engineer Eugen Sänger had radical ideas about integrating rocket propulsion and glide vehicles accelerated to hypersonic velocities. After the war he lived in France and founded the *Fédération Astronautique* in 1949. *Author's collection*

1951 Convair Aircraft Corporation received a contract for studies into the relative merits of air-breathing cruise missiles versus ballistic rockets. Cruise weapons of that period were largely unmanned aircraft powered by jet engines boosted into the air by solid propellant rockets, or large, vertically launched missiles with turbojet engines for the long flight to their targets.

In this period, development of long-range ballistic missiles was increasingly seen as practical. It had been difficult for the concept to take hold and after the general distribution of the results in 1953 of the work by Allen and Eggers a fight began to apply the principle in real-world projects. When a breakthrough in the miniaturisation of thermonuclear weapons significantly lowered the weight of the rocket and, de facto, reduced the thrust required to achieve that function, the blunt-body concept was adopted and shown to work. Previously, there had been two big challenges to the logic of intercontinental ballistic missiles: the enormous weight of the nuclear warhead and the ability to keep it intact on re-entry to the target. Now, both obstacles had been resolved. Vehicles could now be built to survive the most intense thermal environment as they speared back through the atmosphere from space.

Stimulated by these possibilities, the Air Force supported theoretical studies into the possibility of a manned boost-glide bomber which it would name BoMi (Bomber-Missile). Based on discussions with Walter Dornberger, the German general in charge of work at the Peenemünde rocket site, the Air Force was keen to study in greater detail the scientific principles and engineering challenges of just such a concept merged with the brainchild of the Austrian Eugene Sänger and his antipodal-bomber. Very different to the V2 rockets managed by Dornberger, the boost-glide concept would use a rocket-sled to launch into the air and accelerate to an altitude above the atmosphere on a ballistic trajectory short of orbital velocity but sufficient to take it halfway around the world.

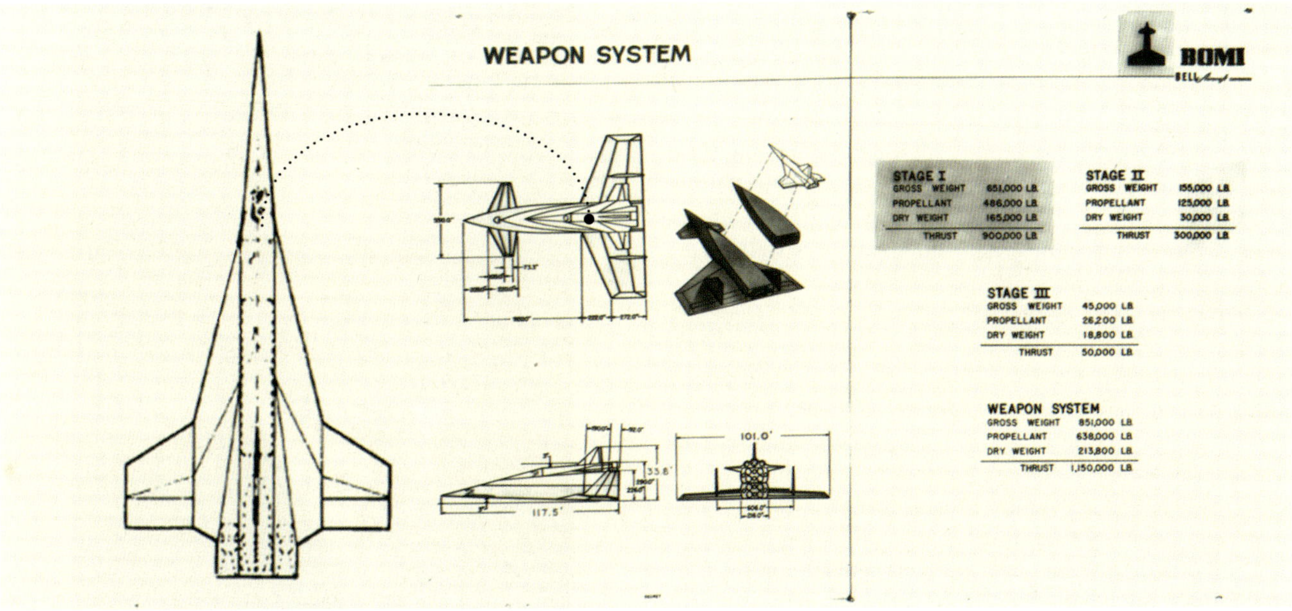

Above: With Walter Dornberger a consultant with Bell, the *Silbervogel* inspired concepts leading to the BoMi boost-glide design. *Bell Aircraft*

When Dornberger was employed by Bell Aircraft, these concepts were encouraged and in them several advocates saw the way forward to hypersonic air vehicles, merging the manned aircraft with the ballistic missile propelled by powerful rocket motors. These 'exo-atmospheric' capabilities required a great deal of preparatory research and technology development and that stimulated discussion within the Air Force and at the NACA for a suitable means of testing the operating environment. Bell was well placed to pitch into this area, as it had achieved success with its Shrike and Rascal missiles and was deeply involved with management of the X-1 and X-2.

The concept appealed to the Air Force too on grounds of invulnerability. Operating at speeds of at least Mach 4 and altitudes of 30,480m (100,000ft), such a vehicle would be largely immune to enemy radar and achieve impunity from attack for several decades to come. It was also attractive to Air Force chiefs such as Gen. Curtis LeMay, who had achieved fame and recognition in the air war against Japan and would, in time, come to be regarded as the man who shaped Strategic Air Command, managing the Air Force's land and air-based nuclear deterrent.

By this time there was a general acceptance that many air forces around the world were equipping with fast jets. Contemporaries of the X-1 series, the Skyrocket and the X-2 were a range of high-speed combat aircraft then entering service with several countries around the world. The F-100 Super Sabre had a top speed of Mach 1.26, the prototype MiG-19 had a Mach 1.35 capability, in Canada the Avro CF-105 interceptor was on the drawing board promising Mach 2.3 and Britain was developing the precursor to the Mach 2+ English Electric Lightning. The incremental approach to US air superiority was not working, mused the Air Force. It was too sluggish. What was needed was a capability to leap-frog over interim and intermediate technologies and it was in this context that the BoMi appeared as a plausible option for doing that.

It should be said, however, that there was no single-minded approach to future air power and its use in force projection. So recently independent from the Army, the Air Force was essentially a 'pilot's' service and 'things with wings' ruled supreme. The idea of wingless missiles, precursors to a 'push-button' age of armchair warriors, supplanting the stick-and-rudder leatherneck pilots flying close-engagement combat with winged adversaries, did not sit well with senior ranks so recently back from global war zones. With each service fighting for its own budget and an adherence to the philosophy of piloted aircraft, there was solid support for trans-atmospheric air vehicles with a human crew.

But support for unmanned missiles, particularly ICBMs, was highly polarised. And many of those blue-suits who did support ICBMs felt the Air Force should have them if only because it would prevent the Army and perhaps the Navy stripping the Air Force of a strategic strike role. Since the Korean War sank into a stalemate through armistice in 1953, President Eisenhower had purposefully sought to shift the main deterrent power of the United States from long-range bombers to nuclear weapons. Whoever got to control those would have pre-eminence in the Department of Defense; whosoever did not, would face an enduring support role for land and sea forces, a bomber force being redundant, and face long-term decline. This was why the Army fought so hard to get control of the long-range missiles and why the Air Force latched on to advanced, hypersonic strike platforms.

During the first half of the 1950s, there was much talk in the Air Force of it developing a trans-atmospheric capability and the work of Sänger, Dornberger and the initial BoMi studies endorsed that expectation of a linear progression, which was the root reason why the Air Force looked to the

Left: Sänger progressed the wartime concept of the boost-glide vehicle and named his design *Silbervogel* (silver bird). It lacked credibility on several counts but was embraced by a fascination in the USA with German research. *Author's collection*

Right: Within NACA there were advocates for a Mach 5-10 research programme to aid not only manned aircraft but also to provide data for unmanned missiles, chief among which was Maxwell Hunter. *NACA*

hypersonic research programme with some enthusiasm. It assuaged those who sought to retain manned, winged flight in all domains and it justified securing a strong grip on the national strategic nuclear deterrent with missiles as well.

To infinity and beyond

Within the general whirlpool of debate about hemispheric strike systems and hypersonic research aircraft, for its part the NACA was at the centre of a discussion which had its origins in a meeting of the Committee on Aerodynamics held on 4 October 1951. It was there that Robert Woods from Bell proposed a research aircraft capable of providing that 'leap-frog' into the hypersonic and received general approval for further discussion and definition of ideas. He supported that idea through a letter dated 8 January 1952, requesting that the NACA set up a special programme and presented as an attachment a concept worked up by Dornberger for a vehicle capable of 6,580kph (4,090mph) and to an altitude of 80.45-120km (50-75mls).

The proposal received interest but it was not the first time the Committee had listened to appeals for such a project. Several months before the October 1951 meeting, the noted NACA aerodynamicist Max Hunter pointed out that research in the area of Mach 5-10 would greatly assist not only manned aviation but also make a useful contribution to missiles operating in that region. The latter justification was not as convincing to the NACA at large as an association with hypersonic manned aircraft, although, as noted earlier, there were elements of the engineering fraternity at Langley who would provide a splinter-programme supporting rocket work – the Pilotless Aircraft Research Division (PARD) for instance.

Following Woods' letter, on 30 January 1952 at a further meeting of the Committee on Aerodynamics, the Bell representative again argued for a very high altitude research aircraft specifically to explore various mechanisms for attitude control in regions where aero-surfaces were ineffective and where thrusters were the only means of maintaining stability and attitude control. Woods went further, advocating a special group to explore all aspects of space flight and how it related to high-performance aircraft. But there were serious opponents who believed that the NACA could be easily dragged into the development of a particular type of aircraft of use to the military and that it should not become embroiled in distractions away from pure aeronautical research. Notably, Simon J. DeFrance from Langley voiced opposition to the ideas put forward by Woods.

The potential reorientation of the NACA from pure research into a proactive focus on what the 'customer' might require in terms of future performance and capability was a seminal moment in the history of the organisation and is all too frequently ignored by official histories of these two enabling government agencies. It would quickly set up the NACA for transitioning into NASA when the national and political mood was right for that. Pursuant to that broader analysis of what was required, as early as June 1951 the Subcommittee on Stability and Control heard from eleven missile manufacturers seeking to persuade the NACA to investigate aerodynamic problems of flight at Mach 4-10. They identified aircraft manufacturers already planning Mach 3 platforms and cited the requirement for their air-to-air rockets to operate at hypersonic speeds. Ground-to-air missiles too were being designed for operation in these regions.

The definition of a future research programme was discussed too at a meeting of the Committee on Aerodynamics held on 24 June 1952 where they heard about Allen's work on blunt-body re-entry dynamics, work which had direct relevance for missiles. At the meeting, the ideas put forward by Woods and Hunter were aired again and organised into a policy proposal embracing the NACA as an organisation, penned by Albert Lombard, an Air Force science adviser.

One resolution recommended that the NACA should expand investigations of flight through the upper atmosphere at altitudes of 19,312-80,467m (63,360-264,000ft) and at speeds of Mach 4-10. This was a performance band significantly greater than that capable of being achieved by the X-2, the most potent research aircraft then in detailed development, and was an incremental rather than a major leap forward. The second resolution defined a less intensive and more modest programme for altitude flights to 'infinity' and speeds from Mach 10 to orbital velocity. By implication, it directed the NACA to get involved in space flight, but through winged, piloted vehicles, which was the prevailing view at the time.

In ratifying the resolution on 14 July 1952 in its Washington DC headquarters, the Executive Committee of the NACA authorised the most audacious research programme

Right: Under pressure from some representatives at Bell for a research aircraft aimed at supporting development of a winged space vehicle, the director of Ames Simon DeFrance (seated) and his deputy Jack Parsons, (right) opposed that idea. *NACA*

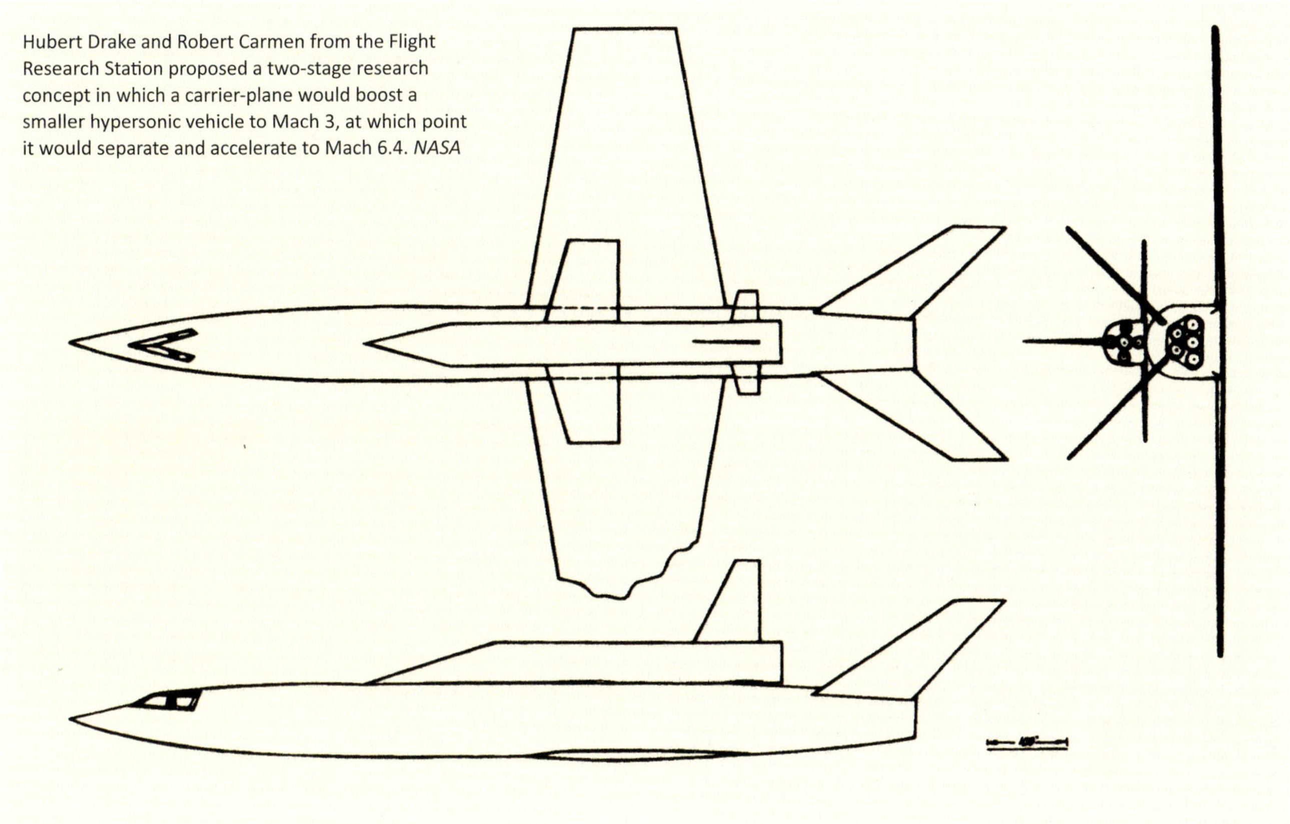

Hubert Drake and Robert Carmen from the Flight Research Station proposed a two-stage research concept in which a carrier-plane would boost a smaller hypersonic vehicle to Mach 3, at which point it would separate and accelerate to Mach 6.4. *NASA*

in its history and asked for recommendations for implementation from Langley, Ames and Lewis and for proposals on how to accomplish these goals. The most immediate response was for Langley to expand PARD, already making a significant contribution to existing aircraft research programmes, and its activities at Wallops Island. Thus, in a historical context, the NACA embraced the encroaching possibility of orbital flight long before it changed its name to NASA and expanded greatly into that sector, when winged flight into orbit was a possibility displaced by manned capsules launched by unmanned rockets.

The call for ideas resulted in a few unsolicited proposals defining a research aircraft fulfilling the first resolution and effectively serving as a successor to the X-2. From the High Speed Flight Research Station at Edwards, Hubert M. Drake and L. Robert Carmen proposed a parasitic, two-stage concept in a report dated 21 May 1952. It envisaged a large carrier lifting a smaller vehicle to a speed of Mach 3 on the power of rocket motors burning alcohol and liquid oxygen. At separation, the small craft would operate at speeds of up to Mach 6.4 and altitudes of up to 202km (125mls), their calculations showing that it could operate for one minute at Mach 5.3. Drake and Carmen believed it would be possible to develop this for flights up to Mach 10 and altitudes as high as 306km (190mls), remaining at Mach 8 for up to one minute and accommodating all anticipated research requirements.

The Drake-Carmen carrier-plane would have had a length of 25.9m (85ft) and a maximum fuselage width of 2.13m (7ft) and a low mounted wingspan of 19.3m (63.3ft) covering an area of 92.9m^2 (1,000ft^2) with a thickness ratio of 4 per cent. The slender fuselage would have an aft-mounted vee-tail and the total vehicle would weigh in at 12,200kg (26,900lb) or 44,906kg (99,000lb) fully loaded. In several respects the choice of design and wing thickness represented the existing view that thin wings were optimum for supersonic flight but this was not so and when it came to designing the control surface of the X-15 – and much later the Shuttle Orbiter – the Allen-Eggers work on thick bodies would show that wedge structures are optimum for the hypersonic flight regime, particularly for tail surfaces. There was little in the proposal to tackle the problem of materials withstanding the heat produced through friction with the atmosphere.

Langley's PARD engineer David Stone had another proposal to match the requirement, based on the existing X-2. Stone believed that the NACA could significantly improve the performance of this aircraft by attaching two Sergeant solid-propellant rockets which he calculated could push it to Mach 4.5 and altitudes of up to 91,440m (300,000ft, or 56mls) which would in effect be carrying it out of the atmosphere and into space. The concept did receive support, particularly from Henry J. E. Reid and John Stack, but it would require a special study to flesh out the requirements for any programme based on this concept. Attacking the requirement from a cost-saving position, Stone's idea was to maximise existing hardware rather than develop a completely new vehicle.

In several respects, the mandate for the new and more vigorous approach to demands for a hypersonic research aircraft brought unique challenges to the NACA as it struggled to define the particular needs of the various teams working options. The need for specialists in hypersonic flight was left largely unsatisfied when Floyd L. Thompson, associate director of Langley from September 1952, rejected specialists in thermodynamics or aerodynamicists working in hypersonic flight over creative engineers with new ways of thinking. Thus it was that engineers were selected for a three-man team to study requirements and report back, consisting of team leader Clinton E. Brown from the Compressibility Research Division, William J. O'Sullivan from PARD and Charles H. Zimmerman from the Stability and Control Division. Their purpose was to evaluate all options and report on a recommended series of programmes or projects that could be started in 1954, given adequate funds.

In its analysis, the team examined work already underway on ICBMs and warheads, looking at work on re-entry vehicles and hypersonic aerodynamics (although there were no specialists on that in the group) as well as evaluating the Drake-Carmen, piggy-back concept and that from Stone based on the X-2. Modifications to the Stone plan rejected the Sergeant solids in favour of a new and more powerful rocket motor with the potential for pushing the X-2 to Mach 3.7. But this was still deemed insufficient for the more universal requirement now agreed upon. Concerns were also expressed regarding the ability of the aircraft to survive the aerothermal environment at this speed and it was considered too reliant on an as-yet unproven performance. It would be four years before the X-2 became the first to achieve Mach 3 and only then under a tragic circumstance.

Below: In determining the optimum performance goal for future hypersonic research aircraft, the NACA and the Air Force used Schlieren photographs of Allen's blunt-body shapes to study shock waves at Mach 7 and define potential configurations. *NACA*

When the Brown group presented its findings on 23 June 1953 it was clear that none of its members had expertise in the theory of hypersonic flight, as the principle challenge for that envelope was judged to be aerodynamic heating. Moreover, it concluded that flight experience above Mach 4 would have to substitute for any ground-based work. The Brown team had rejected ground-based research on the basis that the facilities did not exist but this was a conclusion generated by the rejection of the newest, small hypersonic tunnels then available. They felt that the 'hot' environment of actual flight at hypersonic speeds would be so different to the 'cold' environment of the wind tunnel that there could be little correlation between the two and that only by flying in that environment could the data be gathered.

In effect, the conclusion reached required design teams to come up with an experimental aircraft which would fly into areas of the aerodynamic and aero-thermal environment without having been configured by a known set of parameters. But the Brown committee did acknowledge the need for more information about this region and proposed the use of PARD rocket tests to launch models for data-gathering, much as rockets had been used for testing models of the X-2. But in several ways this reopened the classic argument between 'fly' or 'wind-tunnel' approaches and the specialists in hypersonic theory argued strongly for the use of, for instance, the 15.4 x 35.5cm (10 x 15in) continuous-flow tunnel at Ames and the 28cm (11in) tunnel at Langley, for using these facilities to determine flow characteristics and the general aerodynamics of hypersonic flight.

Three months after the Brown report, Drake and Carmen broadened the range of their analyses and, diverging somewhat from their original concept of the previous year, put forward a five-phase plan for hypersonic research from the present capabilities up to and including orbital flight. Which was timely because there were new ideas emerging which included some very advanced ideas, including the BoMi concept.

By early 1952 the Air Force was ready to factor in a very much more ambitious development plan for an aerospace vehicle than it had admitted to just a year earlier. With conceptual proposals from Bell and Woods proclaiming the future, it fell to the Air Force to define the roles and missions for such a vehicle. The Air Force saw hypersonic flight, trans-atmospheric flight and reconnaissance and bombing missions as integral value-gains from such research. In April 1952, William E. Lamar, then the chief of the New Development Office, Bombardment Aircraft Branch of the Wright Air Development Center, focused on one of those objectives: 'We were looking for a way of getting (a bomber) from Omaha to Moscow...We began looking at high speed and began to realise that by going higher and faster, we could get the range we needed'.

Above left: Floyd Thompson rejected the notion of thermodynamicists or aerodynamicists determining the next steps in high-speed/high-altitude research and chose a group of engineers instead. *NACA*
Above right: From the Compressibility Research Division, Clinton E. Brown led an engineering team to evaluate all the available options for a new research aircraft which would be practical to develop from 1954. *NACA*

In 1952, US intelligence was aware of Soviet developments with intercontinental boost-glide vehicles, long range rockets and its aspirations for a space-based capability. Within the context of the Korean War, the push to outpace the Soviet Union and develop a superiority in these areas became an implicit part of a renewed US national defence strategy based on 'leapfrog' rather than 'incremental' steps toward those achievements. Pressure from Bell for the BoMi concept received new energy when the Air Force began to apportion time to proposals and presentations from leading aircraft manufacturers. R. J. Sandstrom, Bell's chief of engineering development, discussed with Lamar the possibility of extending the capabilities of the BoMi concept.

Lamar wanted to know if Bell could stretch the capabilities of a boost-glide system by using a third 'stage' to bring the air vehicle back by going around the world after hitting Moscow. He wanted to have it come back to land in the United States after a suppressed, sub-orbital trajectory around the Earth and short of going into orbit. Interest was high among those who believed in the future of rocketry and space travel for defence applications but most of the recipients at a presentation to Air Force headquarters were unconvinced. Abuse hurled at Dornberger, one of the proponents, sparked a cutting repost from the German in reference to what he considered to be their outmoded thinking: 'I wish we had shot down more of your bombers!'

Skirting the naysayers, Lamar convinced Col. Jules C. Maxwell, chief of the Bombardment Aircraft Branch at WADC that it was worthy of further investigation and he set up a feasibility study to take Dornberger's projections and determine their applicability, filling roles first as a reconnaissance system and then a bombing system. Specifically, to carry a 3,175kg (7,000lb) nuclear weapon with an operational date of 1962. Lamar worked closely with Forrest to examine what would be required to bring this to fruition and to use existing rocket and missile data to determine the necessary characteristics such a vehicle would have. Their self-imposed mandate was to examine how these technologies could mesh together and to defer the reason why it should be built, a decision it was felt best left to policy makers and politicians. Finally, Lamar and Forrest convinced Col. Donald H. Heaton, director of aeronautics and propulsion at the Air Research and Development Command (ARDC) to assign $250,000 to a limited study.

Optimising the design

A defining moment in the evolution of the X-15 came with the conclusion drawn in 1954 that boost-glide vehicles could only play a part in these advanced concepts after a concerted effort to more fully understand the hypersonic environment. In October 1953, the Aircraft Panel of the Air Force Scientific Advisory Board (SAB) had met to discuss future possibilities and the conclusion was that it was the right time for a combined USAF and NACA research aircraft to tackle those issues. At the meeting was Robert Gilruth from Langley, a vital player in this development and in the years ahead.

But there was caution in the assessment of what was required and nobody really believed that Dornberger's ambitious concept was practical without a great deal of research into aerothermal effects and high temperature structures supported by exotic materials. By the early part of 1954, reality had overwhelmed grandiose claims. In several ways, this was the right time to launch a new aircraft programme, the supersonic programmes from the NACA having already fleshed out most of the possibilities inherent in the X-1 series and the Skyrocket. With an accelerated commitment from the Pentagon for a new class of weapons, including ICBMs and plans for an all-jet bomber force, momentum for new research in the hypersonic regime was on the side of the proponents.

As noted earlier, after the Second World War cooperation between the US Air Force and the NACA grew into a productive and mutually beneficial relationship quite different to that which had prevailed before. Chair of the USAF-NACA panel, Hartley Soulé presided over a series of meetings at NACA headquarters on 4-5 February 1954 at which the Stone proposal to use an X-2 equipped with supplementary propulsion was discussed and rejected as providing too little advantage to justify development. The discussion then turned to possible development of a thin-wing Skyrocket but, as with the preceding proposal that was also considered too limited in scope and potential. From which emerged the suggestion that a completely new aircraft was required to obtain the data sought.

The panel consisted of Lawrence A. Clousing from Ames, Charles J. Donlan from Langley, William A. Fleming from Lewis and Walt Williams from the High Speed Flight Test Center. They unanimously agreed to forward a recommendation to NACA headquarters for a detailed specification and set of requirements from which a suitable aircraft could be designed. This would call for input from all three major NACA facilities and consign to each responsibility for expertise in their respective sectors. Flowing from this, on 15 March Gilruth wrote to Clark Millikan outlining priorities for research and development. In an all-sweeping embrace of essential research categories, Gilruth identified the need to study new materials, examine ways of cooling and insulating hot structures, studying the aerodynamics of hypersonic flight

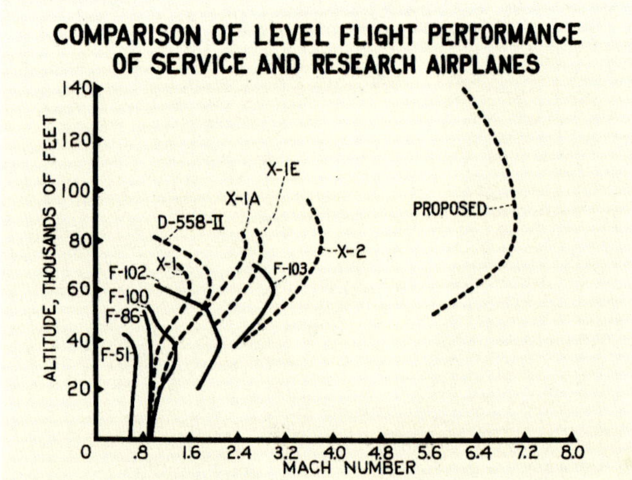

Examination of the flight corridors defined by production-line combat aircraft and experimental research aircraft identified the encroaching performance capability of service types (defined by the prefix 'F') compared with the Skyrocket and X-series. It illuminated the requirement for a significant leap forward to a hypersonic capability. *NASA*

and pressing for the development of a completely new manned aircraft capable of supporting this work.

The February meeting of the USAF-NACA panel and the Gilruth letter of March defined the starting point for the development of the X-15. Acting immediately, NACA headquarters put out to the field centres their own requirements for such an aircraft, expecting to find a consensus for design needs. Across all areas, high-temperature aerodynamics and structures were a key part of the baseline research requirements and the centres themselves responded by setting up ad hoc panels to provide those details. Each centre had a different range of priorities and sought to emphasise the advantage such an aircraft could bring to existing and planned research at that location.

While clearly Langley was going to play a central role, it wanted to continue with the research it had been conducting under Charles McLellan since opening the 27.9cm (11in) hypersonic tunnel in 1947. Becker, now chief of the Aero-Physics Division, was instrumental in bringing together much of the work already going in to studies on the interface between the shock waves and the boundary layer. In association with this, the centre also set up a programme to investigate the structures and materials which would be required for the new aircraft to survive in the hostile aerothermal environment. Langley also wanted to have the aircraft make flights out of the atmosphere lasting up to three minutes to explore the effects of weightlessness on the aircraft systems as well as the human body.

It was within the group selected to conduct the survey at Langley that Becker, the chair of the ad hoc group, deliberate-

Left: At ground level, engineers and mathematicians helped define the catalogue of requirements and not all were male. Born in 1921, Mary W. Jackson went to Hampton Institute in 1942 and joined the NACA in 1951 where two years later she accepted a position working with engineer Kazimierz Czarnecki at the Supersonic Pressure Tunnel. Her speciality was studying complex boundary layer effects at high supersonic speeds. *NACA*

Left: From Langley, Charles J. Donlan played a significant role in forging a special working relationship with the NACA and the Air Force, a seminal event in the transition from competition to cooperation. *NASA*

ly brought in people who had been working on hypersonics and these included Maxime A. Faget who focused on rocket propulsion from the Performance Aerodynamics Branch of PARD, Thomas A. Toll who specialised in controls and hailed from the Stability Research Division, Norris F. Dow from the Structures Research Division and James B. Whitten, a test pilot. The panel felt it was vital to have a pilot's input and to embed within the evolution of the design the ergonomic and systems layout which best supported the objectives of the aircraft and with whom rested conclusions gained through actual flight experience.

The Ames panel examined all possibilities and concluded that an air-breathing engine rather than a rocket motor would best fulfil requirements and provide a capability in the range of Mach 4-5. This was seen outside of the facility as a move too close to the potential development of a high-speed interceptor or spy-plane and not sufficiently attentive to the research requirements of the original objective. The High Speed Flight Station favoured a more conventional approach following in the pattern of the X-1 series or the D-558-2 Skyrocket but that was altogether too little an incremental step to satisfy requirements. The Lewis facility questioned the need for a manned aircraft at all and recommended a programme based on rocket-launched models and turned the argument for a manned aircraft upon itself by claiming that this would be just a development exercise for an Air Force project.

Universally, the great challenge now lay in finding a way to explore the high temperature environment and to building an aircraft which could survive structurally in that environment. For the first time, the primary research objective became the principal problem to solve in guiding the specification for a new high-speed/high-altitude research aircraft. Becker guided thinking at Langley and the group settled on a Mach 7 capability to keep the project within acceptable limits of the technology, although much would have to be 'invented' specifically for the programme. All agreed that pushing to the Mach 10 limit discussed by Hunter, Drake and Carmen was too big a step into unknown territory.

Overall, from wind tunnel studies and extrapolation of known data, it appeared almost impossible to survive re-entry from very high altitude at Mach 7. Along with Peter E. Korycinski from the Compressibility Research Division, Becker worked out the solution with the 27.9cm (11in) tunnel. They had run the numbers on a relatively shallow angle of attack on re-entry and found that both the heat rate and heat load were unacceptable and would significantly increase the maximum dynamic pressure (Max q) beyond the limit of 6,895kPa (1,000lb/in^2) set by the structural materials available.

The solution was to move the greater portion of aerodynamic deceleration higher up in the atmosphere, the greater percentage of the heat load, and therefore the heat rate, being dissipated before entering the denser regions. The only way to do that was to raise the angle of attack (α) so that the aircraft would re-enter pitched up higher than normal and simultaneously raise the drag coefficient which would lower its exposure to peak dynamic pressure. This was an elegant application of the blunt-body concept published by Allen and Eggers which had made possible the hyper-velocity re-entry of warheads for rockets and missiles. Tweaking the concept, Becker and Korycinski suggested the use of speed brakes to further decelerate the vehicle as it entered the outer regions of the atmosphere.

Improvements too were made in the proposed design of wing and tailplane leading edges, where traditional thinking had suggested the use of large radii to limit the thermal transfer rate. But here too, further study revealed the advantage of a relatively acute sweep on the leading edges, which would reduce drag while necessitating new materials which could survive the higher temperatures. Nevertheless, tunnel tests increased during 1954 with priority on analysis of the problem created by the higher α-angle now suggested for minimising high heat rates.

Nobody knew how to control an aerodynamic body with wings and a tailplane at these hypersonic speeds and all indications were that this could be a significant problem. Yeager had already flown the X-1A to Mach 2.5 where he encountered uncontrollable lateral oscillations and powered flights with the X-2 were still several months away; as related earlier, it would be a further 18 months before any high-speed runs were attempted with that aircraft. These issues were of great concern to the High Speed Flight Station at Edwards where they had been acutely aware of stability and control problems beyond Mach 2. This encouraged strong dialogue with Langley over possible solutions and placed the problem alongside inertial-coupling which had been experienced by the F-100 fighter-bomber.

All indications were that with higher Mach numbers, the problem would get increasingly worse and there was no way of knowing how to counteract the phenomenon, except through use of the Langley hypersonic tunnel. All indications

Right: Inconel, a complex alloy of chromium and nickel, attracted the attention of the NACA team as a material capable of withstanding the searing heat of Mach 3-plus speeds. Developed in the 1930s, one of its first applications had been in the W2 jet engine designed by British engineer Frank Whittle to power the Gloster E.28/39. *Ministry of Supply*

from that pointed to the need for an unacceptably large vertical stabiliser – but only if retaining the thin-section tails then adopted for supersonic aircraft. Completely confounding intuition, McLennan proposed a thick, wedge-shaped tail with a blunt trailing edge. Supported by tests in the 27.9cm (11in) tunnel it was a compelling solution, already having been proposed by McLennan in a previous paper which had remained buried as a research report.

The engineering application of this work to the X-15 was enhanced in a proposal from McLennan that the rudder be designed as a surface split vertically into two halves hinging out in opposing directions to serve as a speed-brake for reducing velocity on re-entry. It would combine a bluff trailing edge with a split-rudder for directional control and retain the wedge shape which would restore the lift-curve slope at these high Mach numbers. As it matured, the design of the X-15 would not adopt the split-rudder proposal but this solution would appear fifteen years later in the design of the Shuttle Orbiter, which used the split-rudder/air brake design as a fundamental aspect of its design.

Meanwhile, further studies and some additional tunnel tests pointed to an optimum design with a 10deg wedge angle supporting a high-drag re-entry with control over attitude excursions. Nobody suggested that by adopting such a tail, the X-1A would be able to achieve greater results, and better control of inertia-coupling, but it was a significant development for the X-15. By adopting this tail shape, the X-15 would perform better as a platform for evaluating a range of attitudes and to better support the primary role of the aircraft, which was to study stability, control and handling across a range of speeds and altitudes.

While all these considerations were evolving toward a defined specification, further analysis challenged the conventional practice of placing the horizontal tail high up on the vertical tail and out of the turbulent flow coming off the wings. That was already noted as a problem for aircraft attempting to recover from divergent manoeuvres and after tackling the issue Becker's team came up with a radical departure from the conventional approach: place the horizontal stabiliser directly in the plane of the wing and between the upper and lower high downwash regions. The only alternative had been an X-shaped tail which, placed in the high downwash regions directly below and above the wing, would have caused greater problems with consequent loss of longitudinal control.

Out of this extended evaluation came another solution to the total loss in directional stability at angles of attack in excess of 20deg. This had been directly explored by several research aircraft at supersonic velocities and the solution appeared to be quite radical – to add a second vertical tail in the ventral position. Wind tunnel tests showed that as the angle of attack increases a ventral tail would come under the direct influence of an increased high dynamic pressure from the compression face of the wing. As the dynamic pressure from the underside of the wing increases with the angle of attack, the ventral tail more than compensates for the loss of effectiveness on the dorsal, or upper tail.

Gathering consensus

While the overall design considerations regarding shape and form had been worked through, other specialists were examining structures and materials, for this was the area where engineers faced the biggest challenges. There were essentially two paths to follow. One in which the structure was fabricated from well known, tried and tested materials protected by insulation or a second approach in which special materials resistant to very high temperatures would be used. The insulation approach would compromise the ability of scientists to determine the thermal effects of the environment in which the aircraft was operating and a failure of insulation would inevitably result in a total loss of the vehicle.

But there were problems with orientating toward a hot structure as the anticipated equilibrium temperature of 1,093°C (2,000°F) was approximately 427°C (800°F) higher than the best available materials. But that was a problem for the insulated structure too. Solving the problem would leave unresolved whether the design should be for a cold or a hot structure. Bell had discussed the use of thermal insulation for high-temperature operating environments, suggesting the use of an intermediate layer of heat-soak material which would protect the conventional internal structure. This left completely unresolved, the underbody surface which, upon re-entry would be exposed to the higher temperatures.

Fortunately there was a material which appeared suitable, known as Inconel X, a product of the International Nickel Company which was incorporated in thermal tests by Norris Dow and his colleagues to see how it might be suitable as a hot-structure candidate. The material was relatively new but it proved sufficiently capable of handling the temperatures, showing that the thickness of the skin required to tolerate anticipated aerodynamic stress was about the same as that which was required to tolerate the thermal load. Significantly, studies showed that the high altitude flights would generate higher temperatures than would high-speed flights lower in the atmosphere. Which was logical, since the energy expended to reaching the outer atmosphere was greater than that needed to achieve a hypersonic run and that additional energy had to be dissipated through kinetic energy on re-entry.

But on detailed examination, the situation became more complex when simulated tests revealed wide differences between temperatures across the structure, particularly between the upper and lower surfaces during pitch-up. To avoid buckling due to uneven temperatures, shear members would be necessary, capable of accepting, rather than resisting, expansion and contraction with span-wise and chord-wise variables tolerant of differential heating. Care was required to calculate contraction and expansion at the stringer/frame joints and adjust the fixture accordingly. This flexure and movement engineered in to the structure allowed differential deformation without reducing the integrity of the material. Areas of potential concern were the leading edges of wing and tail, where differential heating would produce compression, so designers had to segment those areas to prevent any buckling.

Overall, the two highly distinct flight profiles – high-altitude or high-speed runs – exacerbated the design problem. An infinitely flexible application of rocket power and the use of attitude control thrusters were essential prerequisites for maintaining a broad set of research options, insofar as they translated into trajectories and power settings. Because of that, the method used to date with the X-1 series, the D-558-2, the Skyrocket and the X-2 left a lot to be desired. Various levels of power could only be provided in those aircraft by switching on additional combustion chambers, as with the XLR-11 and the XLR-25.

As part of the list of requirements was an engine with variable thrust through a single combustion chamber, allowing graduated increments of subtle throttle variation to ensure a smooth, linear flow of thrust output. By adopting a throttleable engine, a wide range of test objectives could be met without the step-surge in thrust coming from separate sets of combustion chambers. It was also decided to employ hydrogen peroxide thrusters for attitude control outside the atmosphere.

But in defining the requirements, the Becker team ran into opposition from those who still saw the hypersonic research aircraft as a stepping-stone to space flight rather than a tool for basic aerodynamic research. They defined the emerging specification and its search for a high-lift/low-lift-over-drag for re-entry as being distinctly different from the constant-alpha-angle/constant-altitude requirement for consistent but fast runs within the atmosphere. Finding a consensus and producing a vehicle which provided both capabilities, without compromise, was the challenge.

In working through the problems anticipated for a high-altitude/high-speed research aircraft, the Becker team had to fight some opposition to the radical new approach each member felt was correct. No new aircraft of this type had been defined, or a specification written, within the last decade and the advance in knowledge and the theoretical capabilities now possible were always going to be very different to those which had defined its predecessors. Traditionally, it had been Floyd Thompson's aim to import new thinking, challenging established old-hands reluctant to change the formula in defining the requirements. That had succeeded admirably and many of the design elements were to influence aircraft design in several ways over many years.

As the Langley team wrote up their specification they set a target of Mach 7, while recognising that in several respects the overall design was a compromise but they understood the urgency with which the programme had to move. Already, commercial plane-makers were designing aircraft for Mach 3 and the need to get far ahead of that with a research programme based on a flying test vehicle to flesh out the hypersonic environment was imperative for the next steps toward both manned combat aircraft and early BoMi-type space vehicles. In a 10-page set of requirements, of which six presented supporting information, they advised that such a programme could be flying within three years and that the aircraft developed from this should be as simple and adaptable as possible.

To make this happen, the NACA needed the support of the Air Force, and to start a discussion at a formal level, on 4 May 1954 Hugh Dryden wrote a formal letter to Lt. Gen. Donald L. Putt declaring interest in developing a new, hypersonic research aircraft and suggesting a meeting between them to discuss it. The response was highly favourable and it was endorsed in a meeting between USAF headquarters staffs, the Air Force Scientific Advisory Board and it was suggested that the Navy be invited along as well. The following month, on 11 May Dryden formally invited those bodies to a meeting at the NACA headquarters at the Dolly Madison House in Washington DC on 9 July.

At that gathering, Clark Millikan and Ezra Kotcher represented the Wright Air Development Center, with Hartley Soulé and Walt Williams making the formal presentation. Dryden reminded the group why the NACA believed that it was possible to build such an aircraft but subjectively asserted that the question as to whether it should be built was still open to discussion. He did, however, assert that the best mix to obtain the necessary information was to conduct both a ground-based and a separate in-flight programme to share information and compare data, as well as creating a fresh body of knowledge to better inform the development of future ground-based test facilities. The baseline recommendation was the Langley study, presented by Becker and John Duberg, the latter standing in for absentee Norris Dow.

Not altogether unexpectedly, although it was not known to the group until declared, the Navy explained that it had already commissioned a study from Douglas and that the proposed aircraft should have some slant toward military requirements, rather than being a pure research tool without addition applications. But this ran counter to the theme adopted by the NACA when it had discussed that leverage earlier, declaring that it was not the NACA's job to design the next-generation of military aircraft but that it was its purpose to provide tools for the armed services and their industry contractors investigating the high-speed/high-altitude environment. And that could not be achieved by flying the progenitor for new combat aircraft.

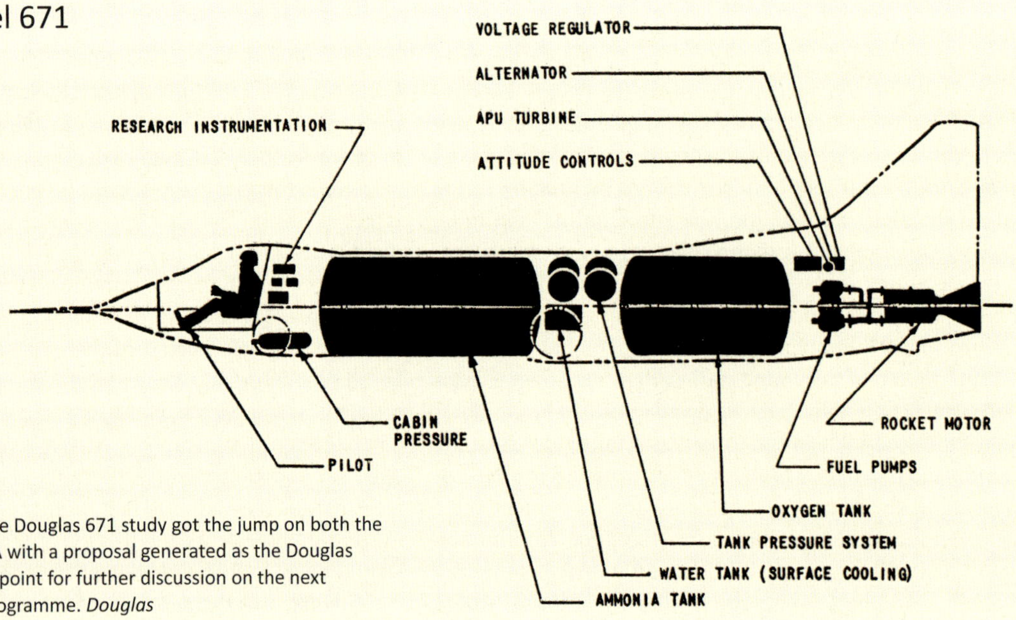

Funded by the Navy, the Douglas 671 study got the jump on both the Air Force and the NACA with a proposal generated as the Douglas D-558-3, a key starting point for further discussion on the next generation research programme. *Douglas*

Douglas Model 671

To place this in chronological context, the Douglas study was a natural continuation of the work it had already been conducting with the Navy since the wartime decision to build the straight-wing Skystreak, which had completed its last flight the previous year. Also in the previous several months, Scott Crossfield had flown the swept-wing Skyrocket through Mach 2 for the first time. This aircraft would continue to fly until the end of 1956.

But in June 1953, Douglas had generated its own study as a proposed D-558-3 with a projected speed of Mach 9, or 9,735kph (6,050mph) and a potential maximum altitude of 228.6km (142mls). Chief of the aerodynamics section of the El Segundo Division, Kermit Van Every conceived a vehicle with the thin, straight wing, a conventional fuselage and Skyrocket-type cockpit and canopy with a horizontal stabiliser high up on the vertical tail. Known as the Douglas Model 671, the Office of Naval Research (ONR) had funded the study, managed by Duane N. Morris out of Every's office. It was not a detailed design and was not developed as a specific configuration. But it did incorporate many of the preferred solutions favoured by the NACA Langley study under Becker.

The ONR was particularly supportive of the idea that a hypersonic aircraft could be used for very high-altitude research and that it could contribute greatly to future programmes for winged space vehicles, eventually maturing into orbital vehicles for reconnaissance or weapons delivery. In this it was singularly unique among the potential funding agencies for seeing this opportunity as a roadmap to the future, waxing almost lyrical in the introduction to its report:

'The project is partially a result of man's eternal desire to go higher, faster, or further than he did last year. Of far more importance, however, is the experience gained in the design of aircraft for high-speed, high-altitude flight, the collection of basic information on the upper atmosphere, and the evaluation of human tolerance and adaptation to the conditions of flight at extreme altitudes and speeds.

'The design of an airplane for such a purpose cannot be based on standard procedures, nor necessarily even on extrapolation of present research airplane designs. Most of the major problems are entirely new, such as carrying a pilot into regions of the atmosphere where the physiological dangers are completely unknown, and providing him with a safe return to Earth. The type of flight resembles those of hypersonic, long-range, guided missiles currently under study, with all of their complications plus the additional problems of carrying a man and landing in a proper manner.'

The Model 671 had a length of 12.57m (41.25ft) or 14.32m (47ft) with pitot boom attached, and a wing span of 5.48m (18ft) with an area of 7.52m² (81ft²). It had a gross weight of 10,069kg (22,200lb). The fuselage supported integral propellant tanks and incorporated dive brakes at the rear of the fuselage in common practice with most jet fighters of the day. The study emphasised the conventional layout and claimed that it could not find any advantage in an unconventional layout. It also asserted that for high-altitude flights the overall shape of the aircraft was 'relatively unimportant'.

Recognising that stability and control were required, the report claimed that the configuration had to 'create sufficient lift for the pullout and for landing' but that it did not see the reduction of drag as a critical problem and believed that it 'is to some extent extremely beneficial'. Confidently stating that the planform of the wing 'is unimportant from an aerodynamic standpoint at the higher supersonic Mach numbers', it believed it was possible to 'select the platform (design) based on weight and structure and landing conditions', which it said 'led to the choice of an essentially unswept wing of moderate taper and aspect ratio'.

The Douglas team admitted to concerns about the lack of knowledge regarding tailplanes and stabilisers and that their choice of a highly conventional layout was to ensure 'proper size for stability at the lower supersonic Mach numbers',

Right: The early 1950s saw a surprising synergy between the rising world of rockets and missiles and the evolving need for a hypersonic research aircraft. The Viking sounding rocket shown here stimulated development of rocket engine technology which would be looked to for power to push manned aircraft to performance levels beyond existing capabilities. *Martin Company*

cautioning that 'there is some question of their adequacy at very high supersonic speeds' and admitting that there was a need for more data. This was addressed directly by the Becker group at Langley in a more scientific manner, especially when designing vertical fins in dorsal and ventral positions to avoid wing wake disruption.

Somewhat surprisingly, Douglas proffered the view that 'a certain amount of instability with the proper automatic servo controls' may solve the issue. In fairness, nobody had at this early date had experienced the dramatic effects of inertia-coupling as would Yeager and X-2 pilots later in the decade. However, the report did say that it believed 'extremely large tail surfaces, approaching the wing area in size, are required to provide complete stability at the maximum Mach number of about 7'. They did appreciate that increasing the area of the vertical tail might cause problems with directional stability 'due to an unfavourable inclination in the principle axis of inertia and the large aerodynamic rolling moment due to sideslip'.

The company had some novel solutions to operating procedures, areas which had not been addressed by Langley's study. It suggested that the large vertical tail preferred for flight at high-Mach numbers could prove troublesome during landing and with handling on the ground, suggesting that it could be folded on the ground and jettisoned prior to landing. The Model 671 team also believed that an autopilot could be useful in helping to size down the control surfaces.

The study included discussion about an optimum carrier-plane, since it had selected an air-launch approach as essential for obtaining the flight performance required, avoiding equipment necessary for a conventional take-off and the waste of propellant achieving altitude when it could be used for the research profile. Douglas calculated that by dropping the aircraft at 12,192m (40,000ft), it could add an extra 60,960m (200,000ft) in altitude. But dropping it off at a still

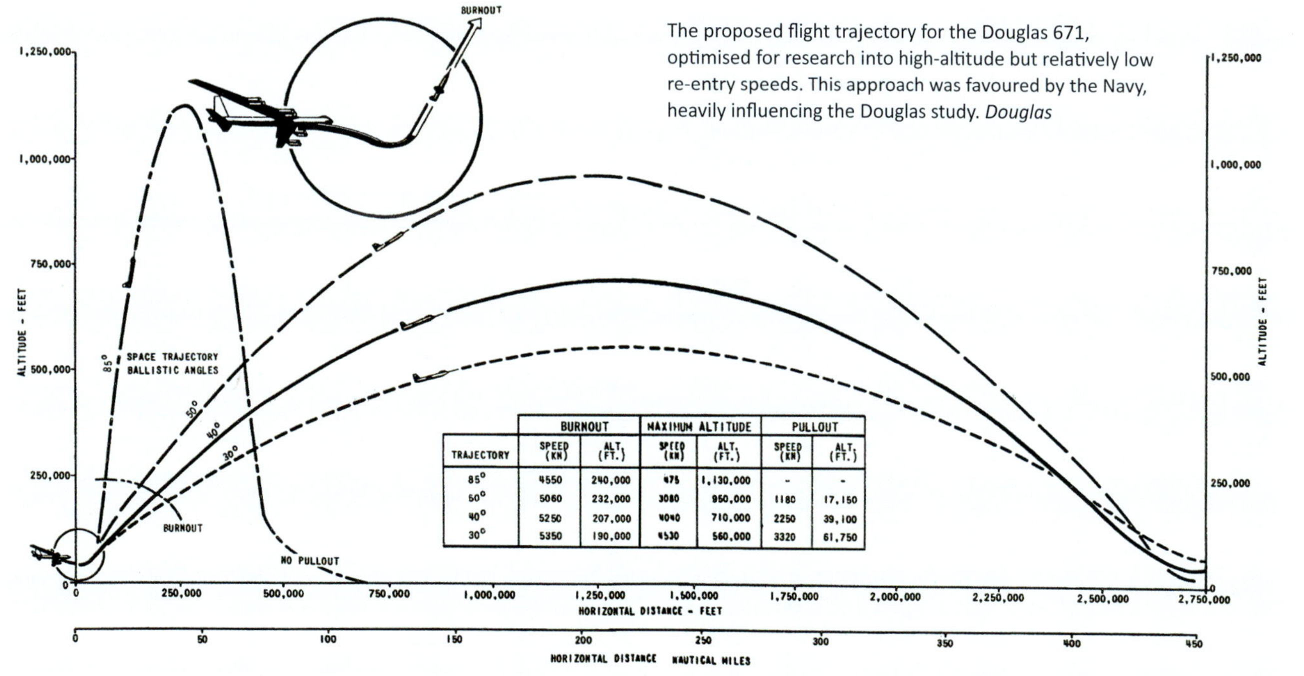

TRAJECTORY	BURNOUT SPEED (KN)	BURNOUT ALT. (FT.)	MAXIMUM ALTITUDE SPEED (KN)	MAXIMUM ALTITUDE ALT. (FT.)	PULLOUT SPEED (KN)	PULLOUT ALT. (FT.)
85°	4550	240,000	475	1,130,000	-	-
60°	5060	232,000	3080	950,000	1180	17,150
40°	5250	207,000	4040	710,000	2250	39,100
30°	5350	190,000	4530	560,000	3320	61,750

The proposed flight trajectory for the Douglas 671, optimised for research into high-altitude but relatively low re-entry speeds. This approach was favoured by the Navy, heavily influencing the Douglas study. *Douglas*

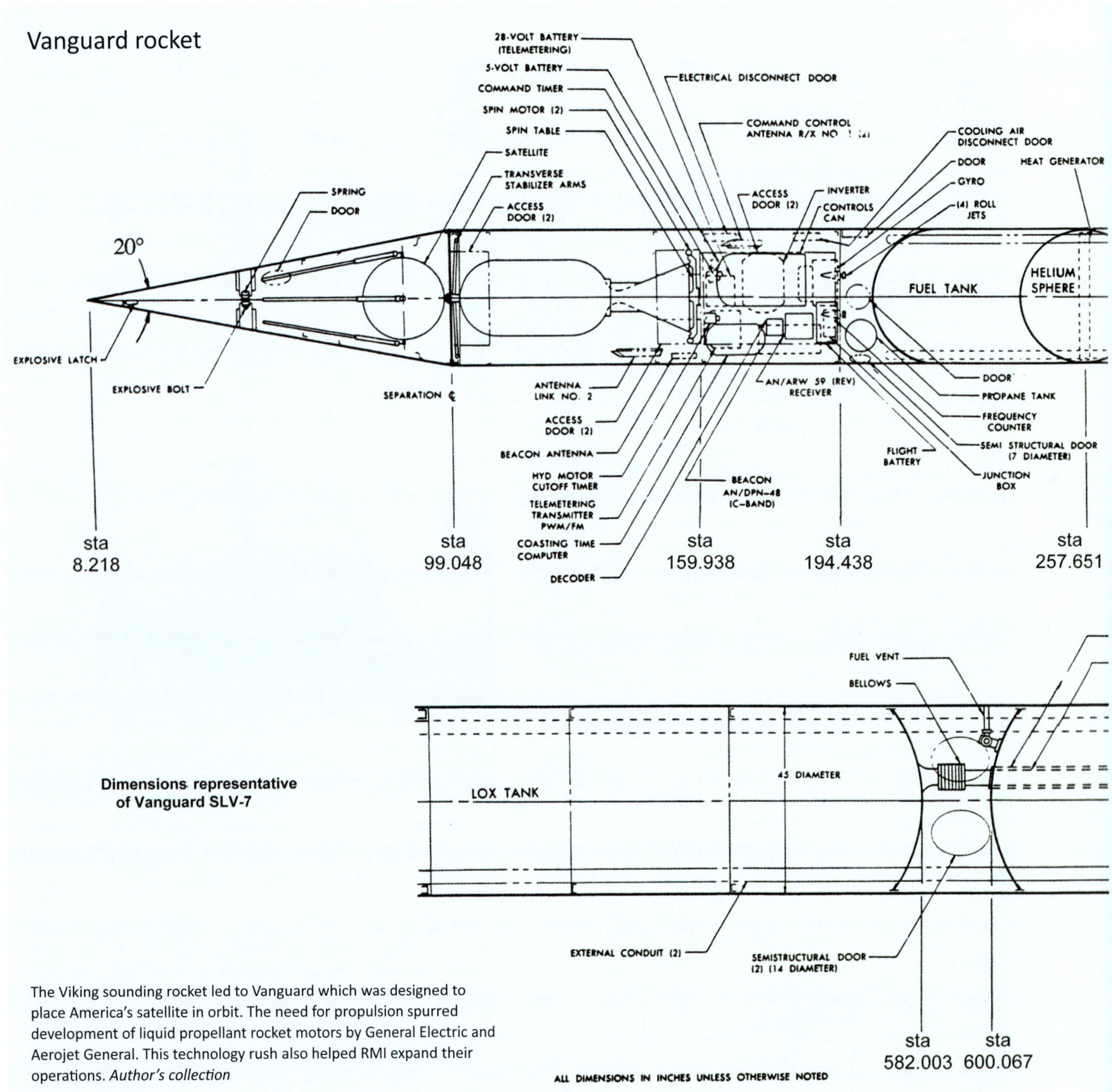

The Viking sounding rocket led to Vanguard which was designed to place America's satellite in orbit. The need for propulsion spurred development of liquid propellant rocket motors by General Electric and Aerojet General. This technology rush also helped RMI expand their operations. *Author's collection*

higher altitude would have little advantage since most of the gain came from the decreased density of the atmosphere and above that height there was little return. But the flight profile assumed a release speed of Mach 0.75 which, along with the postulated drop altitude, was above the capabilities of any aircraft other than the B-52.

When looking for a suitable rocket motor, Douglas believed it was necessary to provide a thrust of level 222,400N (50,000lb) with propellants delivering at a consumption rate of 90.7kg/sec (200lb/sec). The only candidate motor at this date was the XLR-30-RM-2 operating on liquid ammonia and LOX but there were concerns. This motor was in the development stage and was not 'man-rated' for use in piloted aircraft.

The RMI motor was a proposed upgrade to the XLR-10-RM-2 engine used in the Viking sounding rocket but in 1951 there was a secret plan to adapt this into a guided missile with a range of 241km (150mls) employing a guidance and control system. But the following year a new plan was formulated to convert the Viking into a missile with a range of 965km (600mls) by uprating the thrust with a new engine, the XLR-30-RM-2, or Super Viking. The original Viking engine, the XLR-10-RM-2, delivered a thrust of 88,960N (20,000lb) and an RTV-N-12a (Research Test Vehicle) for accommodating the LOX/ammonia propellants was designed for high-altitude or for greater payload.

The development was supposed to be completed in 1954

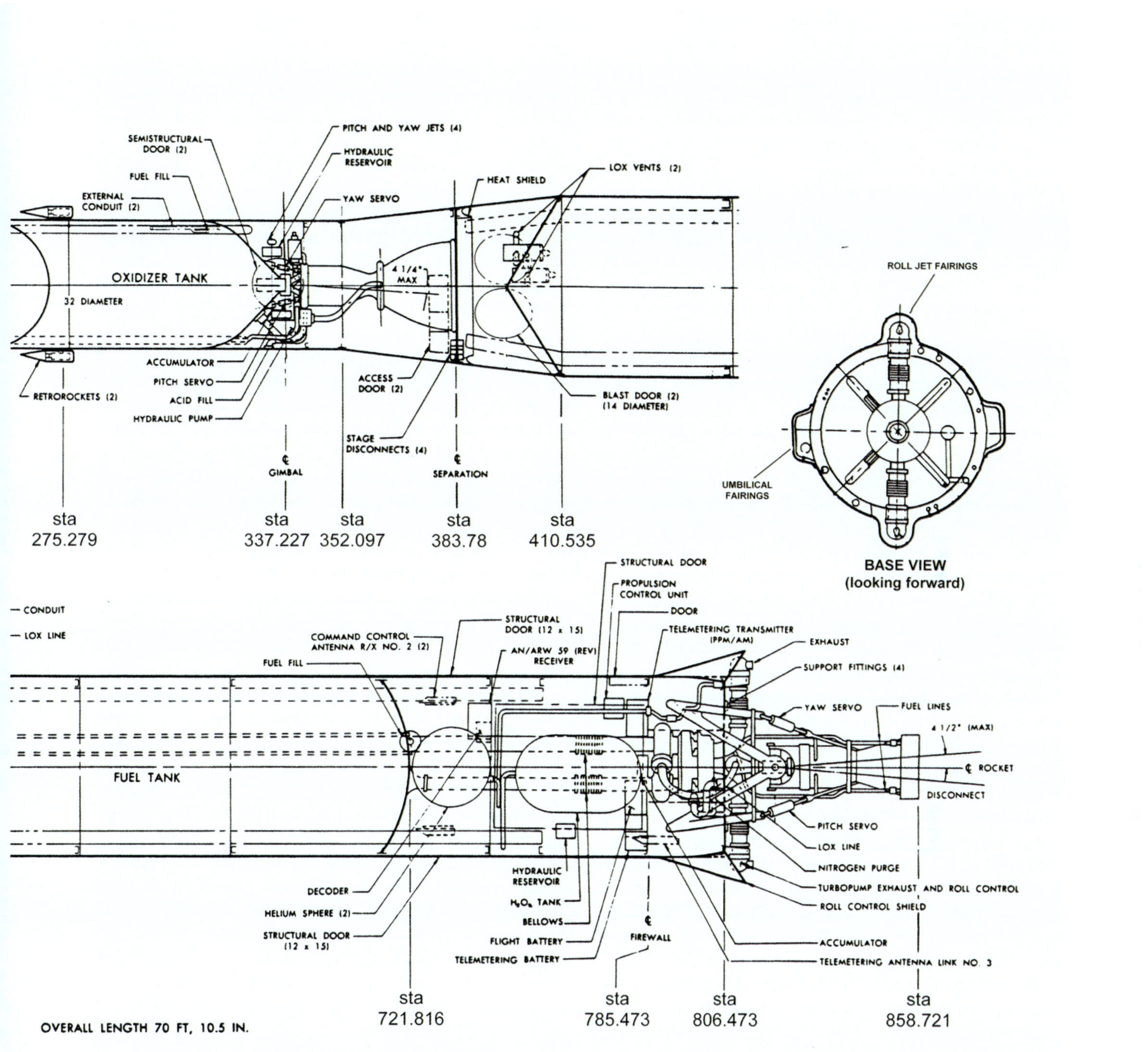

and turbopumps were built and thrust chambers fabricated but the cost began to grow and Reaction Motors could not afford to continue with it. Lacking a customer, by the end of 1953 work on the motor had stopped but the story does not end there, for it was on the technical work associated with the XLR-30-TM-2 that the XLR-99 would emerge as the propulsion system for the X-15. But in 1953, when Douglas worked up its ideas through the Model 671 concept, it appeared a possible contender. As for Viking as a ballistic missile, that fell foul to success with the Redstone missile developed by the von Braun team at Redstone Arsenal, Alabama.

Douglas liked the specification of this engine because it had high-density propellants which minimised the volume of the tanks and therefore had less of an impact on the overall size of the aircraft. Moreover, the motor had a relatively high specific impulse of 245sec and was therefore highly desirable for the energy it could produce for a given propellant mass. But the NACA was already looking at this and we will return to the story of its successor, the XLR-99 when discussing the motor for the X-15.

Douglas had spent considerable time on evaluating various aspects of the Model 671 and had broadened their analysis to take in several elements that the Becker group still had to consider. But the function of the NACA was to gather data from their wind tunnels, which Douglas did not have, and to define the aerodynamic and aerothermal aspects of a hypothetical design; Douglas was more attuned to preparing the outline of a complete programme. In doing so they considered engineering aspects of flight operations and specified two flight profiles: the high-altitude boundary was set at 344.4km (214mls) at a speed of 8,367kph (5,200mph) while the high-speed profile anticipated a maximum speed of 9,895kph (6,150mph) at an altitude of 57.9km (35.99mls).

Considerable attention was paid to just how these flight profiles would match existing ground facilities and what would be necessary for launch and flight paths and trajectories. Radar and communications would be key to maintaining contact and receiving data. The study documentation expressed concern about the range aspects and recognised that at these speeds and altitude profiles the aircraft would very quickly be out of contact and also very far from Edwards, if the present operating profiles were retained in terms of where and when the carrier-plane dropped it.

Because of the speeds and heights envisaged for reference flight profiles, the study believed it would be necessary to have the drop some considerable distance from the desired landing spot and turn toward that when releasing the aircraft. The Model 671 would land at 343kph (213mph) while possessing a stall speed of 285kph (177mph). It indicated that this might call for leading-edge devices to lower the stall speed by increasing the lift but it was uncertain whether, merely claiming that 'the high skill levels of the pilots that will be flying it' would allow for the high landing speed, would suffice. Much remained uncertain.

A singularly unresolved aspect was the guidance and attitude displays which Douglas initially proposed could be accommodated with flywheels and gyroscope, and jet thrusters for exo-atmospheric control. But the flywheel was rejected due to its complexity for a tri-axis system and the gyroscopes were judged to be too heavy for the aircraft. In any event, attitude control would be effected through the use of thrusters distributed at locations around the wings and the fuselage. Each thruster would have a thrust of 444.8N (100lb) operating at a rate of 0.45kg/sec (1lb/sec) from a 11.34kg (25lb) supply of hydrogen peroxide, turned to steam over a catalyst at 2,758kPa (400lb/in^2).

In a prescient foretaste of the debate which would occur for the X-15, the Model 671 team addressed the vexing question of how to provide accurate angle of attack and sideslip information during the extremes of flight profiles. The team was undecided about the ultimate solution but they did suggest a range of devices which might be of use, while minimising the necessity for highly accurate measurement 'for it is only to serve as a guide for pointing the nose into the wind at heights where a pilot might otherwise lose all sense of orientation'. Among potential solutions suggested was a weathervane-type device, a pitch and yaw indicator measuring relative Mach number or the pressure ratio on opposing sides of a symmetrical sphere, or a vane inside an instrument case indicating the direction of momentum from two jets of air brought by a pair of external tubes. They rejected these in favour of a modified Reichardt gauge, which they described thus:

'Air is picked up by the yawed total head tubes and carried into the two chambers. The chambers are separated by a pivoted flat plate which has a small clearance on all four sides so that it is completely free to pivot. When the pressure is higher [in one chamber than the other] the needle will move to the left to allow more air to flow through the porous or perforated plate… [and] equations show that the needle position will be a function only of the ratio of the pressure rises, independent of the dynamic pressure. The needle fluctuation is almost proportional to the pressure ratio. The vane system used can be very sensitive…since there is neither torque nor load on the vane, it should be satisfactory at very high indicated speeds.'

The ability of the pilot to escape in flight caused much analysis, the team rejecting a conventional bail-out, a chute through which the pilot could be ejected, or an ejection seat of the type fitted to combat aircraft, with the latter believed only effective in their purpose to a maximum of Mach 1 at sea level or a little higher at greater altitude. They turned to the type of escape capsule as that designed in to the X-2, estimated to add 68kg (150lb) to the weight of the aircraft. But that was almost certainly far too low a figure. Concerns for the pilot extended beyond the ability to escape. The team also looked into the amount of solar radiation to which the occupant would be exposed and found that it would be acceptable for the brief period spent at the edge of the atmosphere and beyond.

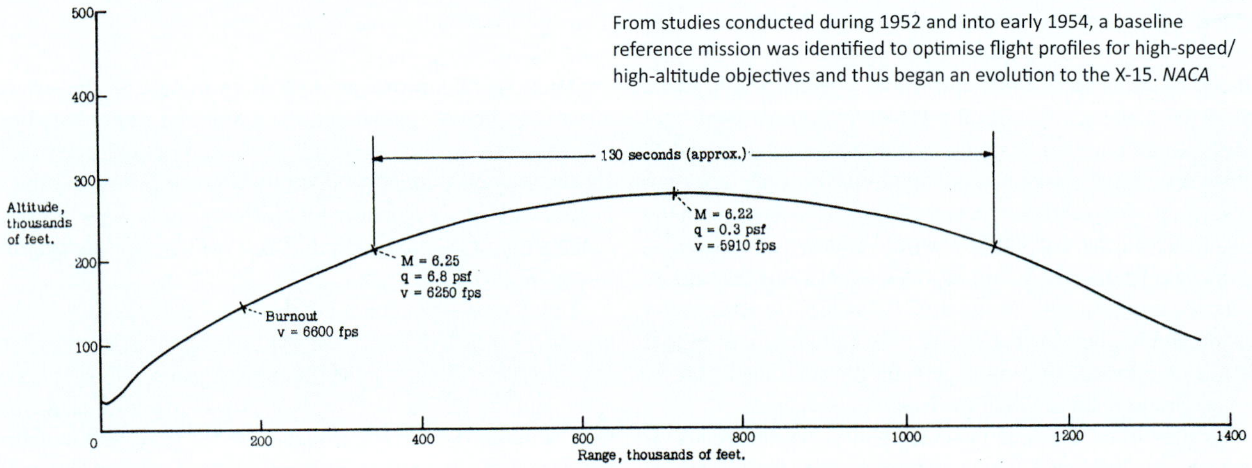

From studies conducted during 1952 and into early 1954, a baseline reference mission was identified to optimise flight profiles for high-speed/high-altitude objectives and thus began an evolution to the X-15. *NACA*

Chapter Ten

Choices and Options

Douglas and the NACA met with the ONR on 16 July 1954 when they learned that it would take $1.5million to conduct a detailed design study of the Douglas Model 671 which could be completed, they said, within a year. The ONR did not view it wise to embark upon a separate study to that which had already been completed by the NACA and, in the certain knowledge that a full specification would soon be raised for a formal bidding process, were not inclined to spend more money on this one concept. But, notable for its historical commitment to research projects with the NACA, they would become a strong partner in the new programme. Douglas too would seize the opportunity to put forward their own alternative design concepts.

As for the Air Force, they acknowledged the necessity for such a project and placed it with the Air Research and Development Command (ARDC). Exactly one week after the meeting at NACA headquarters on 9 July 1954, where principal organisations and their representatives had met to discuss the Langley concept and where the NACA learned about the Douglas study for the Navy, three representatives from the ARDC met with Becker. They received a detailed briefing on the Langley work and an invitation to bring together a larger group from each organisation to put more detail on the recommendations.

With approval from the Navy and the Air Force pending,

Above: Opposing the decision to build a hypersonic research aircraft, Lockheed's Clarence L. 'Kelly' Johnson dismissed the existing X-series and Skyrocket programmes as 'stunts', believing that industry, left alone to get on with the job, would achieve more than the NACA could. *Lockheed* on 21 July the NACA declared that it was proceeding with the high-altitude/high-speed project, come what may. The initial tranche of work anticipated the use of a 20.3cm (8in) model tested in the 27.9cm (11in) wind tunnel for evaluating various parameters up to Mach 6.86. But the approval from headquarters provided authorisation for the separate field centres to conduct their own research within their recognised fields. There was dissension on some aspects of the Langley proposal, including the use of Inconel X which Richard V. Rhode from headquarters considered too exotic a material to use in the structure. He proposed a material more representative of those which would be used by industry but Robert Gilruth defended the use of Inconel and retained it in the specification.

Over the next few months a flurry of activity from government and some industry representatives deepened the investigation of various technologies and design options. On 29 July Robert Woods and Krafft Ehricke met with the NACA to discuss the concept and to put Bell's thoughts across. On 9 August, personnel from the WADC's Powerplant Laboratory met with Langley engineers to discuss propulsion, which was shaping up to be a major issue, since much of the performance would be determined by the type of rocket motor selected. While there, they expressed their own views about a suggestion from Langley that the motor from the Hermes A-1 rocket was a potential candidate.

Hermes began as a research project in 1944 and it evolved to flight tests of a vehicle based on the V2 rocket tests conducted at White Sands Missile Range, New Mexico. By 1950 the Hermes A-1 had emerged as a potential ballistic missile but the outbreak of the Korean War accelerated development into the A-2, which would have been powered by a solid propellant rocket but this was never flown. The A-3 would have had a range of 241km (150mls) with a 454kg (1,000lb) warhead but only a few were ever flown and it was cancelled in December 1954, by which date the Redstone was in production for the Army.

The Hermes engine had no throttle capability and could be fired only twice. Neither limitation made it a reasonable candidate. But the idea was long in its demise, sales representative K. W. Mattison from the General Electric Company visiting Becker, Faget and Soulé on 6 December to promote its use, while admitting that, when asked what level of commitment for a developed variant would be forthcoming, he could not speak for the company. GE clearly had sights on exploiting the development of the rocket motor but was unwilling to support more research without having someone else pay for that.

Col. Victor R. Haugen from the WADC responded to the NACA concept on 13 August with strong support and a technical endorsement of the outline but it was emphasised that the right type of rocket motor was considered crucial to the success of the project. The WADC also provided an estimate of the costs involved, suggesting a total of $12.2million for initial studies, design, the fabrication of two aircraft and conversion of a suitable carrier-plane. Nobody expected it would be as low as that. Releasing a summary of work to date, and the consensus of conclusions from relevant bodies, at the end of August the NACA issued a very short paper asserting that two areas would generate the greatest challenges: preventing the destruction of the aircraft by aerodynamic heating of the structure and stability and control at high altitude.

Above: Developed during the second half of the 1940s, the Hermes rocket series began with the A-1 and a propulsion system which significantly improved the technology for increasingly more powerful motors for the advanced, hypersonic research platform. *US Army*

By the end of the month the Air Force, the NACA and the Navy had met with the Assistant Secretary of Research and Development where these two challenges were agreed, together with a single project to embrace and address the interests of all partners in the venture. But there would be no definitive selection of a concept until all interested parties had pooled their respective needs and requirements and those would be aired at a further meeting in October. At the same time it was recommended that the project would benefit from wide consultation with industry and that design teams should propose their specific conclusions through a competition from which a prime contractor could be selected.

On 13 September Maj. Gen. Floyd B. Wood, the deputy commander of the ARDC, sent a letter to Air Force headquarters endorsing the proposed project and recommending that it 'design, construct, and operate a new research aircraft similar to that suggested by NACA' and that it should do so without any further delay. He backed the NACA view that it should be for pure research without compromise for any specific military function and that it should not be tailored to any anticipated military need of the future. In a switch from tradition, the letter also suggested that the Air Force should have 'sole executive responsibility' for the programme and that design and manufacture of the aircraft would take three years and six months to complete. Research would be conducted by the

NACA after the Air Force had completed a series of airworthiness flight tests.

Verification of the outline management structure was granted on 4 October when Brig. Gen. Benjamin S. Kelsey, deputy director of research and development at Air Force headquarters confirmed that the project would be a joint endeavour between the Air Force, the Navy and the NACA, that it would get a priority classification for its budget, materials and resources and that a detailed study fund of $300,000 would be found from the current budget, then in fiscal year 1955 since 1 July 1954. Although the Air Force considered it to be their project, they acknowledged that the NACA would play a vital role in guiding the technical standards required and the basic specification of the aircraft.

But within the NACA there was still a level of disagreement over precisely what the research programme should be. And in a meeting on 4 October Lockheed's 'Kelly' Johnson refuted the claim that another manned research aircraft was needed, reiterating his earlier belief that none of the current projects had provided data which was meaningful for either the industry or the military requirements of the nation. Dismissing the X-1, Skyrocket and X-2 as 'little more than stunts', he did accept that they had provided valuable information about stability and control at high Mach numbers. Johnson was, however, a lone voice in voting against the hypersonic research project, advocating an unmanned vehicle which could double as a reconnaissance platform.

On 5 October the NACA Committee on Aerodynamics convened at the High Speed Flight Station to make a final decision regarding the configuration of the programme and with the intention of passing a resolution. During that day, various speakers testified about progress and technical developments in their own discrete fields, with Crossfield strongly supporting the need for a manned aircraft. Floyd Thompson verified that ground-based test facilities alone did not have the capability of obtaining the information required to understand the hypersonic environment. The resolution endorsing a manned research aircraft was passed this day and with it affirmation that its primary role was to study aerothermal conditions at high Mach numbers and stability and control at high speeds and high altitudes.

Procurement bids

With a unanimous decision defined through the 5 October resolution, the NACA was formally committed to the concept and the following day Air Force headquarters published its Technical Program Requirement to begin the process of acquiring and building a manned hypersonic research aircraft. The ARDC followed this on 26 October with its own requirement document. Between these dates, Soulé and Clotaire Wood met with the Navy Bureau of Aeronautics and received their specification requirements for feeding into the evaluation of what each party wanted from the programme. Surprisingly, they expressed an interest in having a second occupant in the aircraft rather than the usual suite of experiment instruments, a proposition also supported by some in the Douglas team behind the Model 671. That idea got nowhere but the Navy persisted and it was agreed that this should be left to the bidders to put up proposals as an option.

It was during this period in which the various parties expressed their needs and requirements that preferences began to emerge. The pressure for a second occupant reflected the Navy's interest in supporting the 'space' component of the programme and it was for this reason that they sought to include a second crewmember. This was so that the Navy could focus on the acquisition of physiological data and conduct tests which would support further decisions regarding flight beyond the outer fringe of the atmosphere. There was still very considerable concern about what the human body would be able to withstand, both physiologically and psychologically, and the Navy sought to import that research into the project.

It was generally agreed, however, that each contributory party should be free to express preferences for the direction and orientation of research as it pertained to the development of a concept, from which the industry requirements and guidelines list would be compiled. The NACA in particular was very concerned not to cast aside aspects they had not originated and in so doing limit the range of potential applications. For the first time, this high-speed/high-altitude research project was a true team effort and the broader diversity of requirements would be central to how the project was presented to industry bidders.

It had been thought advisable in the X-1, Skystreak and Skyrocket programmes to buy three separate aircraft but to date the hypersonic project had only considered two. This was largely on grounds of cost and the complexity of operating three aircraft in an operational flow where, conceivably only one carrier-plane would be available. At a meeting on

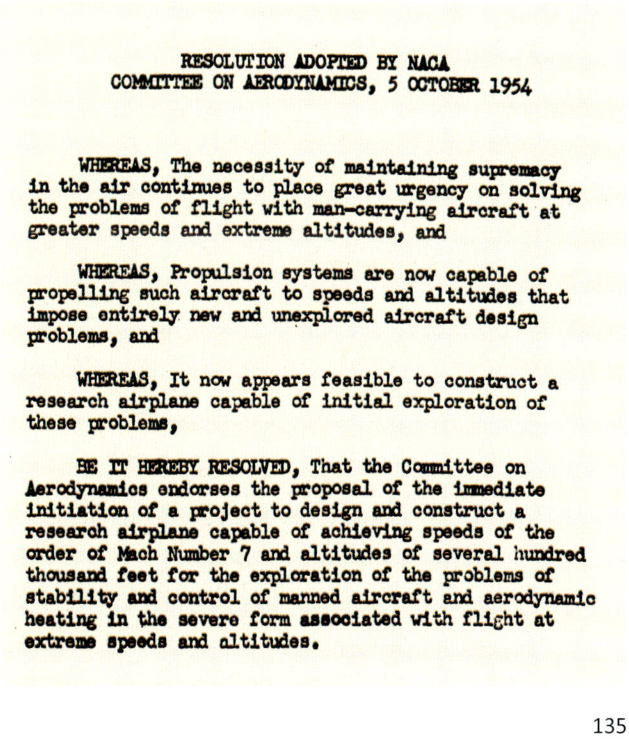

RESOLUTION ADOPTED BY NACA
COMMITTEE ON AERODYNAMICS, 5 OCTOBER 1954

WHEREAS, The necessity of maintaining supremacy in the air continues to place great urgency on solving the problems of flight with man-carrying aircraft at greater speeds and extreme altitudes, and

WHEREAS, Propulsion systems are now capable of propelling such aircraft to speeds and altitudes that impose entirely new and unexplored aircraft design problems, and

WHEREAS, It now appears feasible to construct a research airplane capable of initial exploration of these problems,

BE IT HEREBY RESOLVED, That the Committee on Aerodynamics endorses the proposal of the immediate initiation of a project to design and construct a research airplane capable of achieving speeds of the order of Mach Number 7 and altitudes of several hundred thousand feet for the exploration of the problems of stability and control of manned aircraft and aerodynamic heating in the severe form associated with flight at extreme speeds and altitudes.

Right: The formal agreement by the NACA's Committee on Aerodynamics dated 5 October 1954 put the seal of commitment on the hypersonic research project. *NACA*

22 October with the WADC, Soulé was asked by John B. Trenholm from the Fighter Aircraft Division whether it would be possible to fund three hypersonic aircraft but the matter was deferred. Nevertheless, this was the first occasion where that possibility was raised.

On this day too, a decision was made to split the programme into two: airframe and powerplant. The integrated specification for both was to be completed by 17 November. And yet another important decision was written up on this day when senior Air Force and Navy officers met with Dryden at NACA headquarters to formalise the structure of funding and management. As with earlier research programmes of this kind, the military would provide the money for development and fabrication from a commercial aircraft manufacturer and the NACA would fund the research when they took it over following contractor and customer acceptance flights. That would be the situation here, with the Air Force and the Navy agreeing to share the development costs.

For the Air Force, management would rest with the New Developments Office at the Fighter Aircraft Division at Wright Field and the NACA would manage flight results while the Navy would pay some of the costs, provide a test pilot and carry out some of the physiological research on human factors. Dissemination of results would flow through the Research Airplane Committee, out to the services and to industry as well as to technical and research organisations through the NACA's usual reporting conduits which included unclassified science results, open and widely available to all.

The formal agreement to proceed with the project was issued by Trevor Gardner, the Air Force Special Assistant for Research and Development, and sent to James H. Smith Jr., the Assistant Secretary of the Navy for Air, and Hugh Dryden, director of the NACA, in November. It was signed by Dryden on 23 December 1954. Nine days earlier, Becker, Dow and Soulé had briefed the Air Technical Advisory Panel at the Department of Defense, which formally approved it and committed funds for its development and fabrication, pending an industrial competition and the selection of a prime contractor.

Several companies had already expressed interest, particularly during the second half of the year when the programme came together and became a formal project. On 30 December 1954 the Air Force sent invitations to 12 plane-makers: Bell, Boeing, Chance-Vought, Convair, Douglas, Grumman, Lockheed, Martin, McDonnell, North American, Northrop and Republic. Accompanying the invitation was a chart showing an anticipated 2min 10 sec of research flight time after rocket motor burnout. They were informed that interested parties should submit their intentions by 10 January 1955 and that a bidders' conference would be held eight days later. And still, there was emphasis that it was an invitation for 'possible solutions' to the requirement and not a specific concept.

With hindsight it was a given; who would not want to have on their advertising billboards the claim to being the 'highest and the fastest' in the world? In reality it was far from self-evident that this was something a company, with shareholders, would want to get involved with. There was no guarantee of being the selected bidder and there were questions regarding the highly limited profits for a lot of work, where equivalent

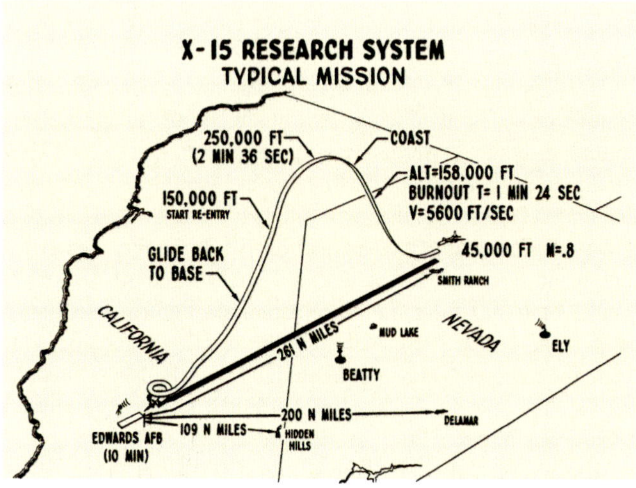

Above: For what would eventually become the X-15, the NACA provided industry with a generalised requirement built up through consultation with the Air Force and the Navy, the latter now playing a much more passive role than they had in earlier research projects. *NACA*

man-hours and development time could be more effectively spent bringing to revenue-earning production lines aircraft which would underpin corporate profits. Nevertheless, notwithstanding some powerful caveats, only Grumman, Lockheed and Martin failed to turn up for the bidders' conference on 18 January 1955.

Each attendee was told they could propose a prime and one alternate solution, that they need only provide an engineering study for a two-place configuration (to satisfy the Navy) and that it had to be capable of 7,240kph (4,500mph) and an altitude of around 76,200m (250,000ft, or 47.35mls). It would be required to carry up to 362kg (800lb) of instrumentation in 1.132m^3 (40ft^3), drawing on 2.25kW of electrical power for that equipment. There was a demanding requirement that flight tests were required to commence 2.5 years after the award of a contract. The only clear and obvious void in the requirement was selection of a suitable engine, which, as noted earlier, was causing serious concern. Interested parties were required to submit their bids by 9 May.

Of the nine companies attending the bidders' conference, Boeing, Chance-Vought, Grumman and McDonnell decided not to continue, leaving six to work up proposals. Of those, Bell and Douglas had a head start in that they were already working on high-speed/high-altitude projects and were familiar with the way the NACA ran its flight tests and conducted research. Convair, North American and Republic had no such experience but were already working on hypersonic projects involving rocket and missile contracts. Northrop was noted for its original thinking and innovative designs but had no experience in this field. Douglas had already completed their Model 671 study for the Navy and felt confident that they would be a strong contender.

In charge of technical consultation and essentially managing the engineering questions, the NACA employed an open-door approach, receiving bidders and their representatives for discussions over ideas and concepts. There was also a large volume of data from the wind tunnels that became available and this only became more accessible when Arthur W. Vogeley was appointed the project engineer on 10 January 1955. An aeronautical research scientist from the Langley Flight Research Division, Vogeley had a strong personality and worked to integrate the offices at Langley and another at Wright Field set up specifically for liaison.

Competing proposals

On 17 January 1955 the Air Force received NACA representatives to learn that it had designated the effort as Project 1226, System 477L. It would very soon be designated X-15 and the Air Force Fighter Aircraft Division, in which rested authority for the project, would assign 1st. Lt. Chester E. McCollough Jr. as the WADC project engineer, along with George A. Spangenberg in an equivalent position for the Navy. By early March the NACA had formally approved research authorisation to embrace work on Project 1226. As part of the process, both the Air Force and the NACA worked up protocols regarding the selection of an evaluation group to sift and filter the bids.

The NACA Evaluation Group was selected in March and comprised Hartley Soulé as the chairman, Arthur Vogeley as executive secretary, and John Becker from Langley, Harry J. Goett from Ames, John L. Sloop from Lewis and Walt Williams from the High Speed Flight Station. The various proposals would be evaluated by the Research Airplane Committee at Wright Field from 17 May but a reclassification of the work by the Air Force prevented some members of the engineering and research group from continuing to receive access. When the bidding deadline closed on 9 May 1955, Convair and Northrop had declined to submit a proposal, leaving Bell, Douglas, North American and Republic. These four companies sent in their technical data in several voluminous packages two days later with the expectation that answers to queries would be in by 22 June.

The criteria by which the bidders would be assessed were divided into several separate categories: technical and manufacturing; schedule and cost estimates; design approach of prime and alternate options; and applicability to research, science and engineering. All submissions were to be in by 13 June, nine days before responses to queries. The propulsion issues would be collated by the WADC, the Navy and the NACA and those would be submitted to the Research Airplane Committee on 12 July.

In parallel, the various NACA centres would contribute work supporting their respective interests in the programme, with aerodynamics covered by Langley and Ames, flight control covered by Ames, Langley and the HSFS, cockpit, crew provisions and the carrier-plane covered by HSFS, and engine and propulsion systems by Lewis and HSFS. This work would continue throughout the development phase of the programme.

The contractor bids were to be evaluated during a meeting at Wright Field on 25 July. Reviewing them in alphabetical order, the four proposals each had distinct and legacy heritage in the way they interpreted the requirement and how their design teams sought to satisfy the several different categories. And each leaned on their own build experience and type development over the preceding years.

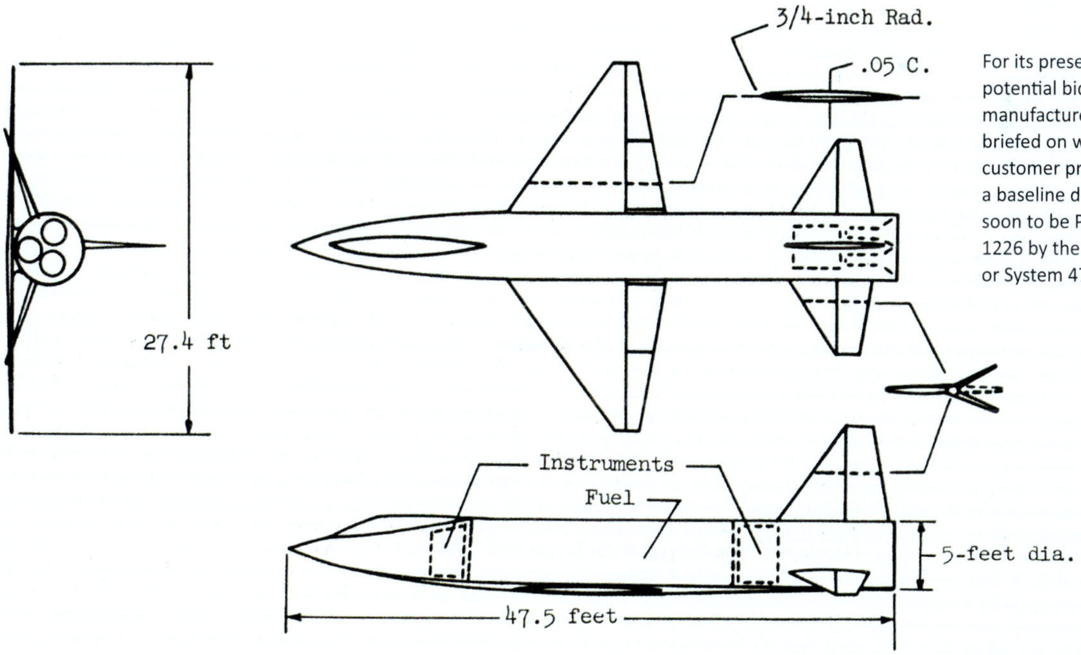

For its presentation to potential bidders, manufacturers were briefed on what the customer proposed as a baseline design, soon to be Project 1226 by the Air Force, or System 477L. *NACA*

$\frac{\text{Thrust}}{\text{Gross Weight}}$ (sea level), 1.8
$\frac{\text{Fuel Weight}}{\text{Gross Weight}}$, 0.6
Spec. Impulse (Alc.-Lox.), 223 sec.
$V_{max.}$ (B-50 Launch), 6800 ft/sec

Gross Weight 30,000 lb
Fuel " 18,000 lb
Wing Loading 48 PSF (empty)
Aspect Ratio 3.0
Thrust 54,000 lb (sea level)
(3 Hermes A3A Engines)

BELL MODEL D-171

With the possible exception of Douglas, no manufacturer had as much experience as Bell Aircraft in designing and developing high-speed aircraft. Luminaries such as Lawrence Bell, Walter Dornberger and Robert Woods consolidated work already underway on projects such as BoMi and future rocket motors developed in-house. The company also had experience with heat-resistant structure and materials capable of withstanding high stresses and extremes of temperature. Almost all of this converged on their Model D-171 which in some respects was a natural application of previous experience, in others a complete departure, in a configuration which bore more than passing resemblance to the X-2.

Bell divided the fuselage into separate sections: the forward section housed the pilot, the nose gear and a compartment for the research equipment as well as a pressurised area for hydraulic, electrical and environmental control equipment; the centre-section contained the wing carry-through structure, main landing gear skids, the hydrogen peroxide thruster supply and propellant pressurisation equipment, an aft oxidiser tank and a fuel tank; the aft fuselage section contained the rocket motor and the tail assembly, complete with dorsal and ventral vertical stabilisers. The forward fuselage supported a flush canopy, much like the X-1 series, for eliminating the possibility of shock wave attachment to a protruding canopy frame and windshield.

With its own engine design team, Bell selected its XLR-81 for the prime proposal with its alternate configuration, the Model D-171B, powered by the XLR-30. The XLR-81 had evolved in the Convair B-58 Hustler programme, a Mach 2.5 bomber with a separate rocket-boosted pod carrying a nuclear weapon for extended range in a pseudo stand-off capability. That engine had been developed from the GAM-63 Rascal missile which the Air Force had bought in limited numbers as a stand-off weapon for the B-47.

The engine operated on RFNA (Red Fuming Nitric Acid) and jet fuel and that dictated the larger fuel tank which pushed the oxidiser into two separate tanks straddling the wing carry-through.

Above: Like all four bids, Bell's design favoured a straight-wing configuration as research results showed a preference for a low aspect-ratio planform and a large vertical stabiliser. The D-171 incorporated a ventral stabilising fin with different optional engine configurations for the single-seat or two-seat concepts. *Bell Aircraft*

Fabricated from 615-T aluminium, the tanks were also inherited from the Rascal missile. Bell had looked at the possibility of attaching the wing to a single oxidiser tank but dismissed that size-reduction feature as a potential failure point when, for instance, pressurising it for engine operation.

To obtain the necessary thrust, three XLR-81 motors were arranged in a triangular configuration in the aft fuselage. Much as with the XLR-11, power levels would be achieved in a thrust-step increment, each chamber producing a maximum thrust of 64,496N (14,500lb). However, one of the three would be capable of operating at 35,584N (8,000lb), or 55 per cent, to reduce the shock-start and the acceleration level to a controllable magnitude. A single throttle lever in the cockpit would control the total thrust output, the lowest setting starting one chamber at the 55 per cent level before advancing the lever to bring that up to 100 per cent thrust, and progressively igniting the remaining two motors at 100 per cent for a total output of 193,488N (43,500lb). Bell dismissed thrust asymmetry as an issue, believing it would have little impact on the flight path.

Bell went to some considerable effort to balance the wing sweep at 37deg, to prevent control problems with pitch-up and roll-damping effects taking over at greater sweep angles. It also balanced shifts in the centre of pressure at subsonic and transonic speeds. The design team decided that the aspect ratio was not a critical issue and a balance was set between subsonic and landing control and stability issues, the wing area of 20.43m^2 (220ft^2) providing a moderately high landing speed of approximately 273kph (170mph).

Recognising that there was little or no precedent for attitude control outside the atmosphere, they calculated a level where the aerodynamic surfaces would no longer have authority over orientation of the aircraft. Bell set this at 0.4788kN/m² (10lb/ft²) which for certain specified flight profiles would be endured for up to 1min 55sec before the aircraft descended to a level exceeding the threshold pressure on the aero-surfaces. The consequences of re-entering the denser layers of the atmosphere without precise attitude control could be catastrophic and adequate control in and out of the atmosphere was vital.

To ensure that attitude control was maintained, the D-171 would carry eight hydrogen peroxide thrusters, two on each wing tip for up and down roll movements, two separate thrusters either side of the tail firing in opposing lateral directions for yaw control and two in the tail firing up and down for pitch control. Bell calculated that if they were in continuous use for 1min 55sec, which of course they never would be, the thrusters would consume 122kg (269lb) of propellant so the design team accommodated a tank containing 249.5kg (550lb) of hydrogen peroxide, thus ensuing 100 per cent redundancy.

In addressing control and stability issues, Bell added a ventral stabiliser, the presentation asserting that this would be especially beneficial due to the 'compressive flow field beneath the wing', a matter which had already been outlined by the NACA in the Langley configuration. With consideration of it potentially fouling structural elements of the carrier-plane, Bell rejected a retractable vertical tail but designed it to be jettisoned for the approach phase and ground clearance on landing. It also offered the option of parachute recovery, if the weight penalty was considered acceptable.

One of the most intractable issues was the arrangement of the landing gear which, in the case of specialised aircraft designed for research, invariably means a high landing speed with no propulsion and very little terminal energy management. This had already proved a tough challenge with the X-2 and the relatively high landing speed and greater mass of the D-171 increased the challenge by minimising the options. Some potential solutions involved only skids and a parachute for deceleration, others were more conventional in arrangement. But it did produce headaches for the design team. After considering a wide range of different configurations of landing gear, the proposed arrangement provided for a nose wheel and two main skids, the latter at the mid-fuselage position deployed from bays covered by doors.

The D-171 was heavy, weighing 15,485kg (34,140lb) fully fuelled with 9,796kg (21,600lb) of propellant and with a landing weight of 5,713kg (12,595lb). In considering a suitable carrier-plane, Bell began with the B-50 with which it was familiar in the second-generation X-1 series and the X-2. Equipped with the necessary support equipment, the B-50 fell short of the required lift capacity and was slow and incapable of reaching a suitable altitude for the drop. Bell turned to the B-36 as a solution which, with some examples having already been adapted to carry a fighter or reconnaissance aircraft in a converted recess on the underside of the fuselage, appeared suitable.

In using data from Convair on the precise dimensions of the FICON (Fighter Conveyor) project, Bell decided that the D-171 could take up three of the bomber's four bomb bays and still ensure an acceptable centre of gravity. The D-171 incorporated the structural attachment with the carrier-plane on the centreline of the fuselage and between the two oxidiser tanks. Bell assumed the same drop procedure as that which had been used for the X-1 and the X-2. The pilot would enter the D-171 as the carrier-plane ascended through 10,668m (35,000ft) prior to the drop, checking out the controls, pressurising the propellant tanks, falling away and lighting up the rocket motors.

The emerging debate about 'hot' or 'cold' structural materials

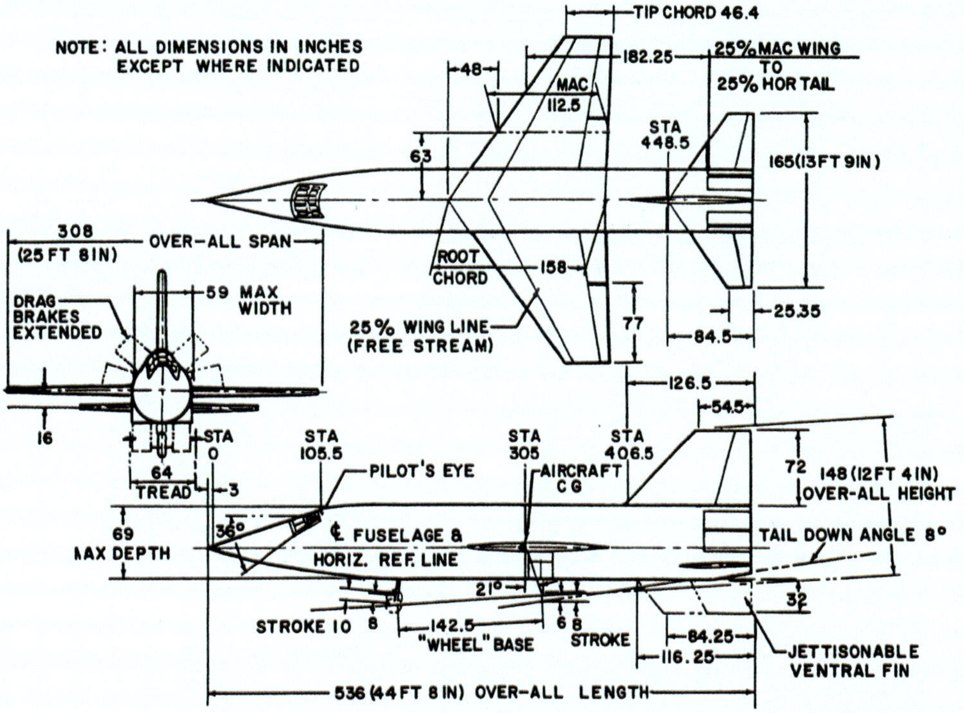

Right: The D-171A was Bell Aircraft's conservative proposal for the X-15 bid and incorporated more design features from its BoMi work than it did from the X-2. *Bell Aircraft*

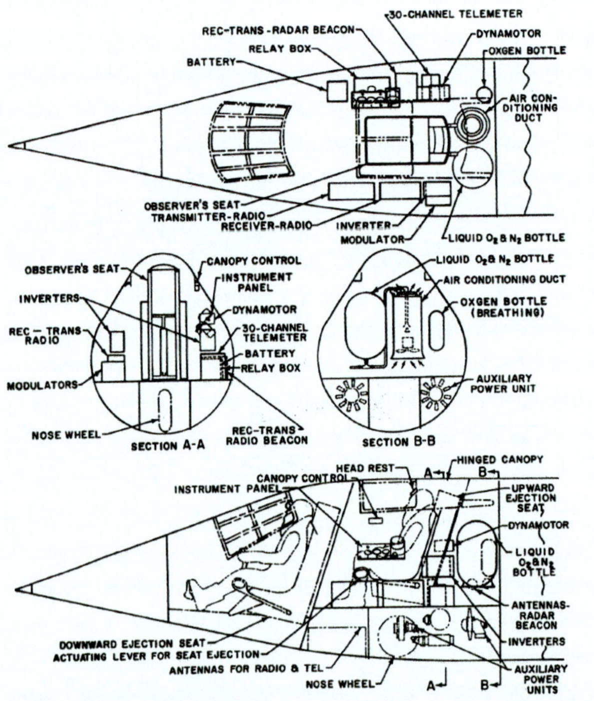

Above: Bidders were required to provide a two-seat optional alternative for their proposals. Bell's D-171B came with a preference for this configuration to suit Navy persuasions. The second crewmember was required to conduct science experiments. *Bell Aircraft*

was addressed by Bell in their proposal, where they presented a detailed discussion as to why they had chosen a 'cold' solution and the reason for believing that the NACA figures, based on Becker's work, were wrong. While accepting that Inconel X was arguably the optimum alloy for high-temperature applications, an airframe fabricated from this material would weight 180 per cent as much as a 'cold' structure made from 75S-T aluminium. In the belief that Inconel X would place impossible weight demands on the design, Bell opted for a concept, straight out of their BoMi studies, in which a double-wall structure used air as an insulator allowing heat transfer by radiation supporting conduction.

In this design, only the outer wall would be a series of Inconel X skin panels, each a mere 0.127mm (0.005in) thick, 10.16cm (4in) long and 20.32cm (8in) wide and welded to a corrugated sheet of Inconel X, each corrugation being 0.7937cm (0.3125in) deep and with the same spacing. Each panel would be held in place by an outside retaining strip, 3.17cm (1.25in) wide and 0.142cm (0.056in) thick. On the inner face, protruding dimples with a depth of 0.038cm (0.015in) would increase the space to the inner structure to 0.952cm (0.375in), sufficient for it to be serve as an insulator. A precisely aligned set of screws and floating anchor nuts would hold the retaining strip to the structure, ensuring the necessary air space was maintained between the two surfaces to minimise conduction. Fibrous insulation placed precisely between the retaining strips would stop boundary air leaking between the panels.

The outer panels would be free to expand in a direction parallel to the corrugations and by separating the skin into 10.16cm (4in) segments thermal expansion would be provided for. By also incorporating attachment pins fitted into slotted holes, the outer skin was free to move under thermal expansion or contraction without compromising the integrity of the structure. Moreover, the weight saved would, said Bell, provide a lighter overall structure than could be obtained using the 'hot' structure concept. But it did propose the use of Haynes 188 in locations where temperatures exceeded the limit of Inconel X.

Bell had done a considerable amount of research work on structures designed to retain their integrity in extremely high-temperature environments Derived primarily from its contractual work on the BoMi and RoBo (Rocket Bomber) concepts, Bell had one of the most knowledge-based data sets of any manufacturer of the mid-1950s. The D-171 proposal took full advantage of this and the double-wall structure would form the basis of several follow-on studies unrelated to any specific project. That would come back to provide much needed insight on the design and development of reusable shuttlecraft which would begin to attract interest in the mid-1960s.

For this work on the D-171 proposal, Bell claimed that their system could save up to 1,360kg (3,000lb) in weight over a 'hot' structure and that it would reduce development and fabrication time, due largely to the highly conventional aluminium structure it protected. Moreover, since the individual panels were easy to remove and replace, instrumentation and sensor points could be readily installed or removed as required for specific research purposes. But there were compromises. Calculating that the equilibrium temperature of the wing leading edge could reach 1,371°C (2,500°F), the D-171 would have a heat-sink structure of 0.1cm (0.04in) Inconel X with a chord of 16.5cm (6.5in). Here too, provision for linear expansion was made by allowing for span-wise movement.

Interestingly, the proposal discussed possible alternatives, raising uncertainty as to the thermal transfer coefficients and questioning whether metal alloys would be as efficient as ceramic materials. Bell noted that these were uncertain areas which could only be satisfactorily resolved when the data was in from high-speed flight runs. The development of materials and the design of both 'hot' and 'cold' structural design concepts was a motivating factor in selecting either for specific projects and the design proposals submitted by all contenders highlighted the areas lacking definition at this early stage.

Bell submitted an alternative configuration, the D-171A, a two-place design with essentially the same structural choices and a pressurised compartment for the second occupant. The weight remained the same because the instrumentation, removed for this configuration, and the second crewmember came out to be the same. Bell also provided a single-seat D-171B configuration which switched the XLR-81 for the XLR-30 rocket motor. Although it had the advantage in being a single-chamber motor, it had a minimum thrust capability of only 60,048N (13,500lb) and, because it used LOX as an oxidiser, would add a weight burden to the carrier-plane due to the necessary top-off tank in the B-36. However, only one oxidiser tank was necessary within the D-171B fuselage and that improved the propellant management for maintaining the centre of gravity.

Above: Magnesium HK31 was favoured by Douglas for a radical approach to thermal protection and the 684 incorporated a jettisonable nose section for crew escape. Systems tunnels ran the length of the fuselage, top and bottom, and a single ventral stabiliser was provided for the 684. *Douglas Aircraft*

DOUGLAS MODEL 684

With just over 10 years of experience in the high-altitude/high-speed research business, Douglas shadowed Bell but only by a margin. But they had a head start on the next generation requirement and the Navy had paid for them to do a study on the Model 671. But the Model 684 had to be different; instead of being conceived from an undefined start, this proposal had a specific set of requirements, guidelines and constraints. On 21-22 April 1955, Douglas conducted some limited wind tunnel studies of a 6.5 per cent model at its own facility at El Segundo, California, which consisted of a test cell 76.2cm (30in) by 114.3cm (45in). The results were of only moderate help but verified that the Model 684 was stable at subsonic speeds.

Douglas selected the XLR-30 rocket motor for a relatively small aircraft weighing only 11,476kg (25,300lb) fully loaded, which allowed Douglas to claim that it could achieve a speed of 7,300kph (4,537mph) at an altitude of 33,528m (110,000ft). The company also claimed that for a high-altitude flight the 684 could reach 114,300m (375,000ft) while remaining within the structural capabilities of the aircraft and the physiological abilities of the pilot. Douglas projected a landing weight of 4,740kg (10,450lb). Overall, the company adopted the research data from Charles McLennan and provided wedge-shaped horizontal and vertical tail sections and gave the fuselage a flared aft assembly for additional stability at high Mach speeds. The flight controls were power-boosted and the aircraft was fitted with an all-moving horizontal stabiliser. Located at the rear, two speed brakes were capable of decelerating the aircraft at 1.5-g and would automatically close at a pressure of 6,895kPa (1,000lb/in^2).

The forward section of the fuselage consisted of the pressurised instrument unit and the cockpit but here too Douglas said that the instruments could be replaced with a second occupant. The only other pressurised compartment was a small area in the aft fuselage for the gyroscopes, accelerometers and various assorted equipment. For the pilot to escape in an emergency the forward section of the fuselage would separate by explosive bolts and a propulsive solid propellant rocket would eject it away from the rest of the fuselage. A reefed parachute would stabilise the capsule and then pull out a metallic parachute at 4,572m (15,000ft) from which point it would descend to the ground. This followed the general concept employed by Bell with the X-2 but as time would show, that was a more hazardous method of escape. Douglas hoped that by bringing the capsule down safely with the pilot inside, the procedure would be less risky. But it proffered caution about the final design selection, adding a personal bail-out parachute as a last resort.

Unique among all four proposals, Douglas selected a tricycle landing gear with nose leg and main wheels, the former set well back behind the cockpit and the latter retracting up into wing wells. The ventral stabiliser would be retracted for take-off under the carrier-plane but deploy when the auxiliary power units started. It held a tail wheel, felt to be prudent given the high angle of attack on landing. The LOX tank was situated forward of the wing, with two ammonia fuel tanks to properly locate the centre of gravity. One tank was in the upper fuselage above the wing carry-through structure and the second was set behind the wing.

As with the Bell proposal, Douglas paid great attention to exo-atmospheric control and distributed 12 thrusters across the elements, suggesting redundant systems at six locations for up-and-down/left-and-right control in roll, pitch and yaw axes. Either system could maintain full control of the aircraft. The pitch and yaw jets each had a thrust of 222.4N (50lb) while the roll jets each had a thrust of 53.3N (12lb), with a total propellant supply more than six times the maximum amount of propellant deemed necessary for a single high-altitude flight. Common throughout all design proposals was the degree of uncertainty regarding attitude control outside the atmosphere and Douglas suggested special training aids would be necessary for the pilots involved.

Situated between the two main landing gear wheel wells were three hydrogen peroxide tanks, two for the exo-atmospheric attitude control thrusters and a 234.7lit (62USgall) tank for the turbopump, sealed with a vinyl lining and a vent line installed to prevent any mixing with spilled fuel. In addition, within the fuselage were two independent Walter Kidde ethylene-oxide auxiliary power units (APUs) for the hydraulic pump together with an AC/DC inverter, each one of which could provide sufficient power to operate these elements.

The structure of the wing was based on seven spars which were spaced through the fuselage with thick, tapered sheets stiffened by spars and chord-wise ribs. Douglas raised the thickness of the skin at the wing-fuselage juncture so as to allow a heat-sink effect to better accommodate the thermal load at high temperatures. The wing and tail leading edges as well as the canopy frame were fabricated from copper which extended sufficiently far back across the wing that it acted as a heat-dump, dissipating high temperatures back into the aft area of the structure where they were lower and could dissipate the thermal

Below: The Douglas 684 configuration incorporated many design characteristics of the D-558-2 Skyrocket and had similar features to those favoured by Bell. *Douglas Aircraft*

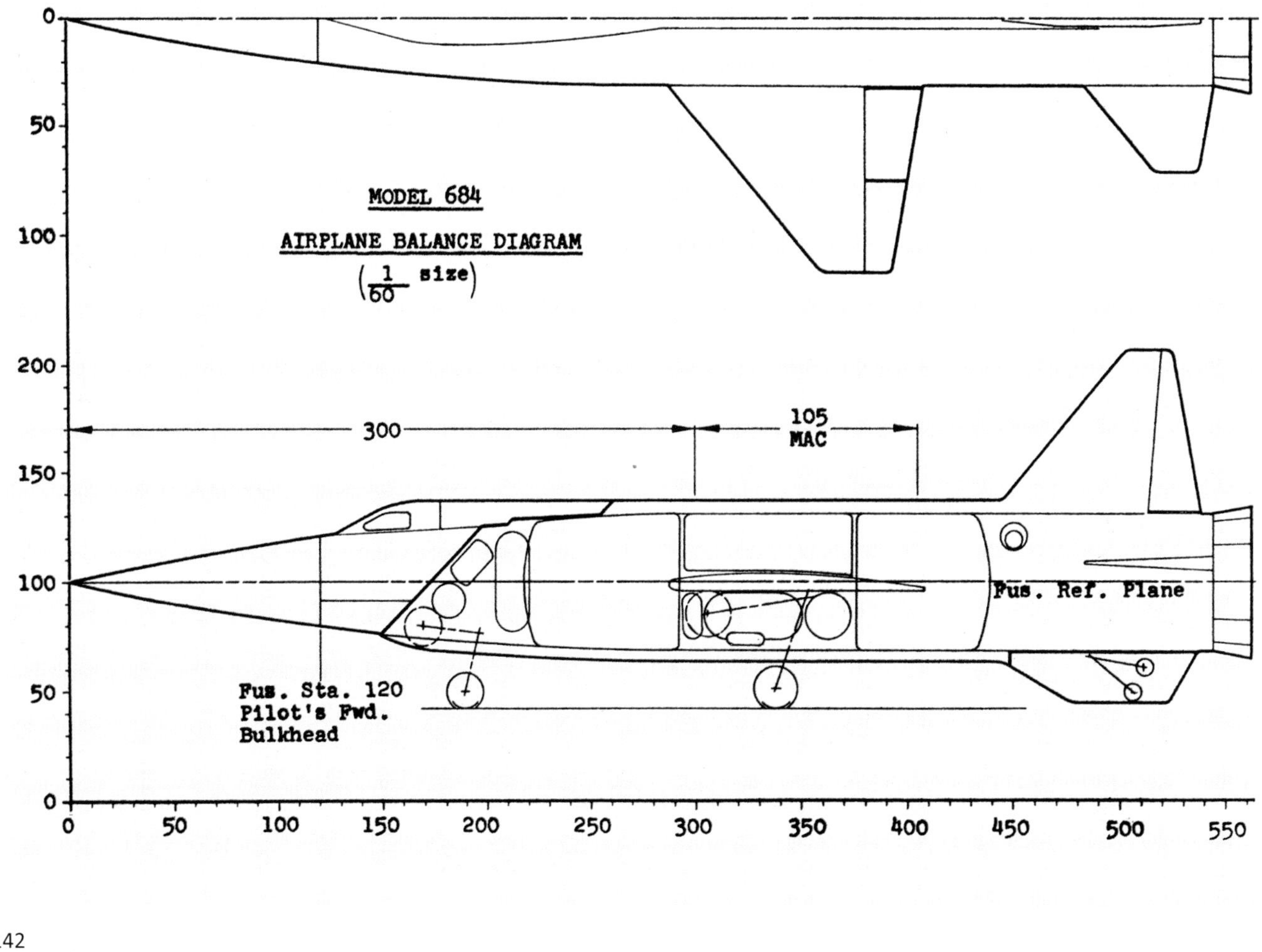

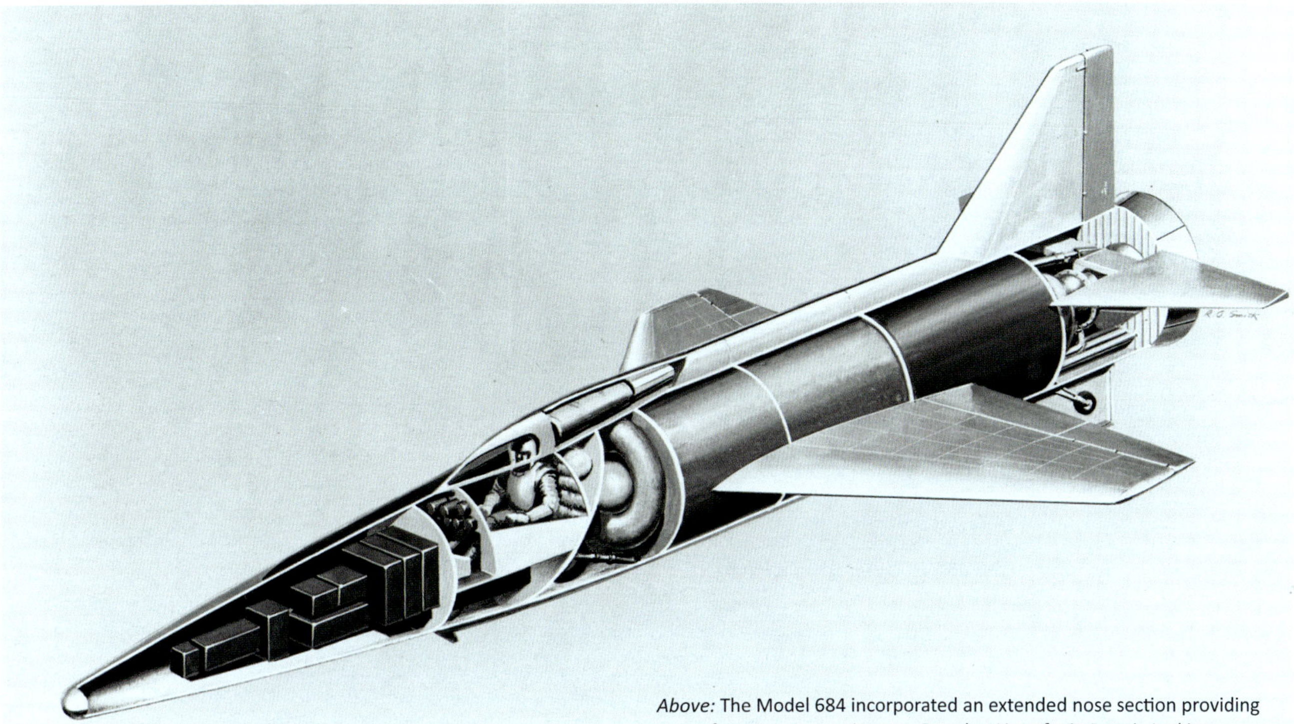

Above: The Model 684 incorporated an extended nose section providing space for science experiments. *Douglas Aircraft via Dennis Jenkins*

energy from the stagnation zones.

Douglas conducted several studies on materials which they could use for the windshield and canopy frame, discovering that the Teflon seal which they had selected outgassed measurable quantities of fluorine at the anticipated temperatures of 204-315°C (400-600°F). Douglas considered that this was acceptable since there would be a positive expulsion of the gas overboard from the interior which the pilot could not breathe in. The windshield comprised a 1.9cm (0.75in) thick pane of high temperatures glass with a 0.63cm (0.25in) gap between that and an inner panel of similar thickness to the gap. The exterior pane was not expected to receive temperatures above 260°C (500°F) and the inner pane would have a tint to block ultraviolet light and to resist radiated heat.

The design team for the Model 684 took a very different view regarding the materials from which it would be constructed, deciding on HK31 which is an alloy of magnesium also containing thorium and zirconium. They had examined Inconel X but focused their attention on solving the problem caused by thermal spikes the aircraft would experience on short-duration, high-speed runs rather than stabilised heat loads which would be encountered by sustained speeds in high-Mach regions. Because HK31 has twice the specific heat tolerance of Inconel it was chosen as the primary structural material, with the added advantage that it was much easier, and less costly, to work with. This reduced the thickness required for the same structural properties to be retained and it required less supporting structure.

Douglas engineers claimed that HK31 would cut 25 per cent of the weight of an airframe compared with a similar structure worked in Inconel. In choosing the magnesium material, Douglas kept with tradition since this had been the material they used for the Skystreak and Skyrocket, although the Model 671 had incorporated a C-110M titanium-alloy structure. Because it contained thorium, which is mildly radioactive, aircraft fabricated in part from this material are prohibited from display in museums on grounds of public health.

The proposal to use HK31 in the Model 684 highlighted the savings in weight, manufacturing complexity, time and manpower, citing it as being worked using conventional machine tools. They also emphasised the reduction in internal support structure by using this material, allowing greater volume for instrumentation and data-gathering equipment. To demonstrate this, Douglas showed skin panels 1.27cm (0.5in) thick, retained only at each of the four corners, compared with an Inconel skin that required panels of 0.25cm (0.1in) thickness supported right across the surface, to achieve the same aerodynamic and thermal loads.

One uncompromising aspect of the use of HK31 was the gauge of the material, ranging from 2.3cm (0.92in) on the under-surface near the nose to 0.63cm (0.25in) on the aft centreline, and on the upper surface from 0.89cm (0.38in) to 0.30cm (0.12in). The thickness of the material on the underside of the wing ranged from 1.62cm (0.64in) just behind the leading edge to 1.1cm (0.43in) about 1.2m (4ft) aft.

As noted above, copper was employed to transfer heat from the very hot leading wing and tail leading edges back into the cooler parts of the structural assembly.

Douglas assumed the carrier-plane would be the B-50 and worked to make the suspension and release fittings similar to those utilised for the Bell X-2. Only minimal work was required to carry the Model 684, including opening up additional area in the front and rear bomb bay housings. The company did not adopt the more progressive suggestion of using the B-52, as they had for the Model 671 study. This is perhaps surprising, given the availability of the all-jet carrier and its higher performance, providing an operating advantage for the Model 684 by releasing it at a much higher altitude and greater speed.

NORTH AMERICAN AVIATION ESO-7487

Above: The North American Aviation proposal was conventional, unsophisticated and impressive on several counts, including one of simplicity and compliant with the desire for it to be a research tool capable of carrying a wide range of experiments as needs arose. *NAA*

Of the four bidders, two had no experience of designing and building high-altitude/high-speed research aircraft and North American Aviation (NAA) was one of those. But its greatest asset of all contenders was its diversity and the breadth of capabilities across several divisions which, in 1955 would be strengthened and formalised. In terms of how it viewed the invitation to bid, and the proposal which it framed, it was unique in that it gave priority to how the NACA and the Air Force and the Navy had conducted previous research aircraft programmes. North American based its proposal on adhering to those practices rather than changing the status quo.

Under the guiding hand of Hugh Elkin at its Advanced Design Group, NAA departed from practice, avoiding the pursuit of performance requirements to propose a programme which 'determined that the specification performance can be obtained with very moderate structural temperatures; however, the airplane has been designed to tolerate much more severe heating in order to provide a practical temperature band within which exploration can be conducted'. NAA matched this with a strong determination to engage with the research scientists and engineers already working experimental research aircraft projects at Edwards and elsewhere. In this, they were very different to the other bidders.

Taking an approach which some may say would be at best a high-risk strategy, the company admitted that 'compromise in favor of extreme simplicity in order to assure a high degree of ruggedness and reliability' was an important factor in making the aircraft as adaptable as possible to an evolving set of needs, asserting too that 'detailed definition and solution of all problems which will be encountered in this program are believed impossible for a proposal of this scope; indeed, if this were possible, there would be little need for a research airplane'.

NAA designed the ESO-7487 for a nominal high-altitude flight to 76,200m (250,000ft) and a maximum speed of 7,240kph (4,500mph), asserting that limiting factors included 'time, safety, state of the art, and cost'. But it did allude to the programme objective which it interpreted as 'exploration of the flight spectrum which will be traversed by a future generation of military aircraft', something which was not altogether an objective for the NACA.

Like all other proposals, NAA put structural heating and appropriate materials at the centre of the design process, seeking to satisfy those before fitting other essential elements around them. It defined limits by asserting that at Mach 7 the temperature of the boundary layer would be about 1,926°C (3,499°F) and

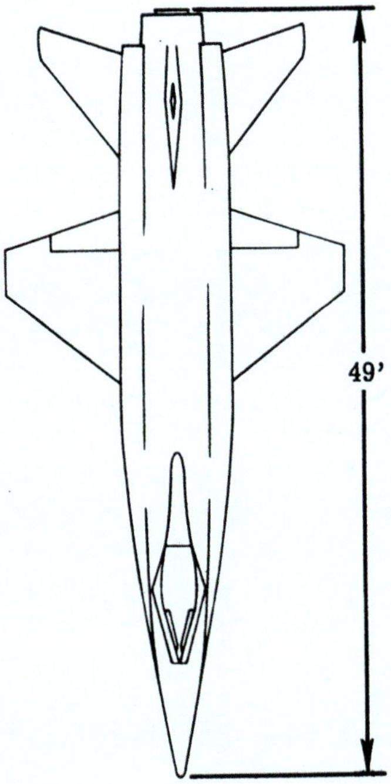

DESIGN BRIEF

PERFORMANCE

MAX. VELOCITY AT BURNOUT (DESIGN MISSION)	6800 FT. PER. SEC.
MAX. ALTITUDE DURING COAST (DESIGN MISSION)	250,000 FT.
TOTAL FLIGHT TIME (DESIGN MISSION)	20 MIN.
MAX. ATTAINABLE ALTITUDE	800,000 FT.
MAX. TIME OF "WEIGHTLESS" FLIGHT	6.5 MIN.

WEIGHT

EMPTY	9,959 LB.
USEFUL LOAD	17,763 LB.
(PROPELLANT ONLY)	(16,410 LB.)
GROSS	27,722 LB.

POWER PLANT

REACTION MOTORS INC.	XLR-30RM2
MAX. THRUST, 40,000 FT	57,000 LBS.

WING

AREA	200 SQ. FT
SWEEP	25 DEGREES
THICKNESS	5 PERCENT
ASPECT RATIO	2.5

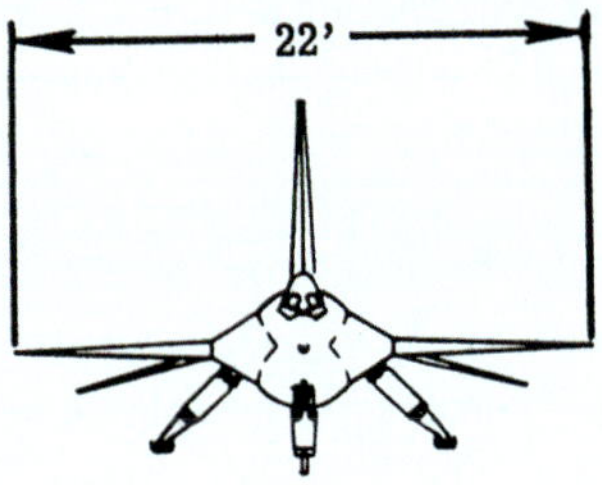

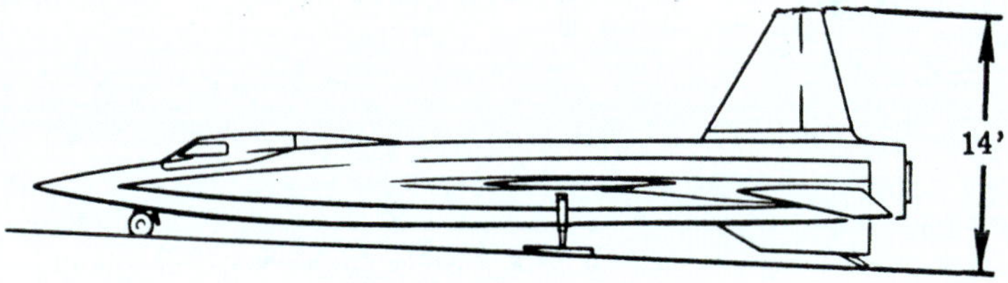

NORTH AMERICAN AVIATION, INC.
INTERNATIONAL AIRPORT • LOS ANGELES 45, CALIFORNIA

Above: A distinctive feature of the NAA proposal was the two side-fairings for conduits, plumbing, pipes and cables, leaving the interior clear for propellant tanks. It also incorporated a ventral stabiliser. *NAA*

that even the skin equilibrium temperature would exceed 649°C (1,200°F) 'even at altitudes above 30,480m (100,000ft)'. While accepting that this was almost at the upper limit of Inconel X, careful use of skin thickness and relatively brief duration of exposure would be acceptable, although the proposal admitted that the wing leading edges could exceed 760°C (1,400°F). With these parameters in mind, the proposal documentation expressed a deep understanding of the challenges:

'High temperatures will affect not only the static properties of structural materials, but also the allowable stresses under repeated loads. Loss in stiffness, or Young's modulus, is detrimental from the flutter standpoint. The unequal deflections, caused by dissimilar metals heated to the same temperatures or by unequal heating of a homogeneous structure, result in high order induced stresses built up between expanding and contracting portions of the structure.

'This effect is very important in considering the distortions set up by unequal heating between a hot skin, and cool inner structure, or between upper and lower skins on the wing during high-angle-of-attack flight. Widespread buckling of skins which are restrained by stringers or longerons, warping and curling of wing chord planes, large wing tip deflections, changes in wing camber, gross wing flutter, or localized panel flutter may be the symptoms of these thermal stresses.'

Adopting the hot-structure concept from the outset, Inconel X was selected for the external skin but with integral propellant tanks. In other respects, the overall configuration, shape and preferred materials closely followed the Becker concept from NACA-Langley. The wing, they said, would be fabricated as a complete semi-span unit for rigidity, fuselage ring frames carrying loads from the wing skins right across the fuselage itself. These frames would be fabricated from titanium alloy with web beads to reduce thermal loading. Span-wise shear beams in corrugated 24S-T aluminium with titanium-manganese alloy attachment points supported the Inconel X skins. Skin panels would vary in thickness from 0.152cm (0.060in) at the tips to 0.317cm (0.125in) at the juncture with the fuselage fairing. But some aspects of the design assumptions raised a few eyebrows:

'Wing and tail leading edges and the fuselage nose may experience temperatures approaching adiabatic stagnation maximums on the order of 2,649°C (4,800°F) during extreme test conditions. It is proposed to provide easily replaceable leading edges of laminated glass cloth which will be permitted to actually melt or burn locally during these extreme cases. The leading edges will be segmented for easy replacement. Tests indicate good dimensional stability, low thermal conductivity and stable decomposition for this type of material.'

Equally unconventional, the semi-ablative nature of the thermal protection for the aircraft was a calculation based on estimates from data on known thermal characteristics and properties of particular materials. But the uncertainty regarding the aero-thermal environment in which the aircraft was expected to operate left little margin for error. Nevertheless, the overall design approach was one which would satisfy most operational requirements across a wide range of flight profiles, as described in the proposal:

'The air-foil shape has a rounded leading edge and a conventional cross section for low drag, reduced leading edge temperatures, and good subsonic characteristics. The leading edge section with a chord of 8.89cm (3.5in) throughout, is made of laminated Fiberglass. The most severe flight profile will result in about 1.57cm (0.62in) of material being burned away, but since the leading edge is separated into 61cm (24in) lengths, the damaged sections may be cheaply and easily replaced.

'The Inconel X skin increases in thickness chordwise from the front spar to the leading edge to form a heat sink. The square wing tip allows the tip rib to be at the same temperature as the skins. The rib at the fuselage juncture is titanium-manganese alloy, while the mid-span and nose ribs are corrugated 24S-T with titanium-manganese attach angles.'

With integral propellant tanks in the fuselage, cables, conduits and propellant lines were placed in fuselage side fairings with Inconel X segments repeated every 50.8cm (20in) to accommodate thermal expansion and contraction. There had been some early concern regarding the thermal impact of these fairings but wind tunnel tests provided data for reshaping them in a manner which not only alleviated the problem but provided additional lift. During flight tests the panels were shown to be prone to flutter, which necessitated additional stiffeners.

NAA proposed that the tanks for LOX and anhydrous ammonia propellants be assembled from four separate sections consisting of top and bottom and paired beaded sides, the latter helping to reduce stress due to shielding from the side fairings. Access was provided by a single manhole in each tank. Those areas of the fuselage not part of the integral propellant tanks were supported in the semi-monocoque assembly by bulkheads at 63.5cm (25in)

Below: NAA identified the various flight regimes requiring different solutions for stability and attitude control, as defined here showing the various operating requirements with altitude and dynamic pressure. *NAA*

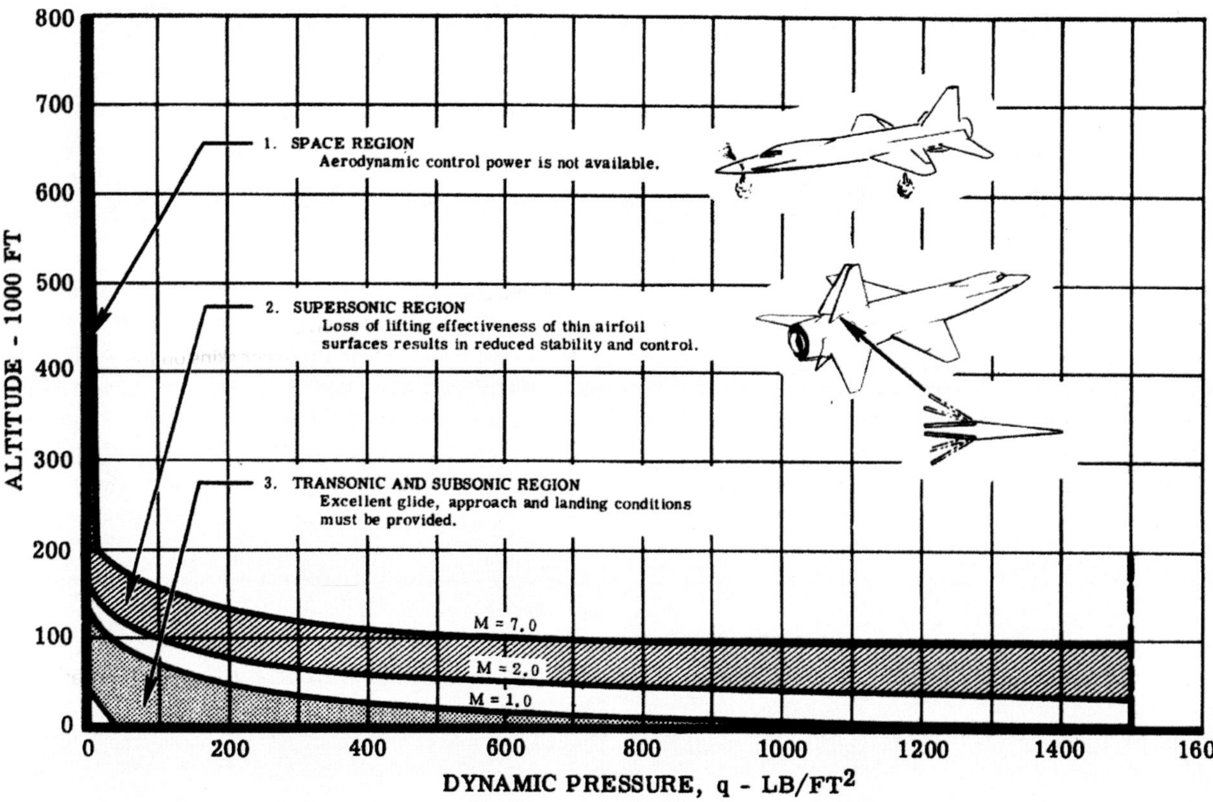

intervals, stiffened with radial beads which also reduced stress.

Again, when addressing the extreme forward section, the proposal alludes to an acceptance of ablation: 'The Inconel X nose cone forward of the cockpit is tapered in thickness from 0.15cm (0.06in) to 0.25cm (0.10in) at a point 20.3cm (8in) from the tip. A replaceable laminated glass cloth fairing forms the foremost nose tip, which at the temperatures attained during the most severe flight profile, will partially burn away at the surface, thus protecting the remainder of the nose.'

Aluminium alloy shells were used for pressurised areas of the fuselage with a canopy seal inflated by nitrogen to isolate the thermal path from the hot skins. The windshield comprised fused silica (Pyrex) outer panes with stretched acrylic inner panes, the latter also serving as a pressure seal. NAA chose cryogenic nitrogen to provide cooling, the vapourisation of which would serve as a heat sink for refrigeration with the gaseous nitrogen utilised for pressurisation of the cabin and the equipment compartments. In its proposal, NAA simplified the cockpit and provided a conventional ejection seat for the pilot, since it believed, probably correctly, that complex escape pods were hazardous and unlikely to provide the required safety margin. A separate 35.8lit (9.46USgall) oxygen supply was provided for the pilot independent of cockpit pressurisation.

NAA adopted the wedge-shape for the vertical stabilisers from the NACA studies, 10deg for the upper and 15deg for the lower, ventral stabiliser which was much smaller, but with the thickest part at the 50 per cent chord line. NAA themselves discovered that vertical stabilisers in both upper and lower positions reduced sudden trim changes in addition to greatly improving directional stability. The design team paid particular attention to aerodynamic attitude control. Incorporating variably-selectable, all-flying horizontal tail surfaces, they would be operated symmetrically for pitch control and in opposing elevation (up and down) for roll, eliminating the need for ailerons.

NAA chose RMI XLR-32-RM-2 thrusters for exo-atmospheric attitude control, with four 400N (90lb) thrust jets set at 90deg spacing around the nose and one 75.6N (19lb) thrust jet set into each wing tip. Unlike the other three proposals, NAA added a separate control stick in the cockpit for the thruster jets, fed from an 11.9lit (3.15USgall) supply of hydrogen peroxide, much less than the other bidders and considerably less than was estimated by the NACA as necessary. North American estimated that only about five major attitude changes would be required on each high-altitude flight.

The engine of choice was the RMI XLR-30 but the proposal left the decision on that to the customer, claiming that any of the alternative options were equally suitable. In addition to the main integral ammonia tank a second, non-integral, supplementary tank was provided. In total, the NAA proposal quoted a LOX load of 3,434lit (907.5USgall) and a fuel load of 4,693lit (1,240USgall). Helium was chosen for propellant pressurisation stored at 20,685kPa (3,000lb/in^2) and at a temperature of -184°C (-300°F) in a tank located inside the LOX tank. But there was sufficient helium for only three engine starts.

Two redundant RMI X50AP-1 gas generators were fitted for the auxiliary power units (APUs) with either bank providing sufficient power for the electrical and hydraulic requirements. Two bladder-tanks were built in to the airframe for the reaction control thrusters and for the APU, the latter budgeted for 68 per cent usage of the total supply. The APUs powered the flight controls, speed brakes and landing flaps. Furnished by the APUs, electrical power was provided by two, 30v, 100-ampere generators. The electrical system was a regulated 24-28vdc system and a secondary 115v, 750-ampere system with three-phase inverter.

North American had some experience with obtaining air data from high speed projectiles, implicitly the Navaho programme, and presumed to lean on this for the X-15 but it was only thinly referred to in the formal proposal. The only usual information obtained from Navaho would provide dynamic pressures in angle-of-attack and sideslip together with air-stream temperatures. Vital for flight operations, they were incidental for the initial proposal.

Landing aircraft of this type had proved problematical with the X-2 and NAA selected a two-wheel nose leg and two strut-mounted skids, one either side of the aft fuselage, and a small tail bumper at the base of the ventral stabiliser. The gear would be deployed through release of the uplocks and gravity assisted by bungee spring. The system was simplified by not requiring a retraction device and the skids were felt optimum to keep stowage volume to a minimum. NAA estimated a rollout distance of 2,438m (8,000ft) without the need for a braking parachute.

NAA gave design priority to simplification of the systems layout, emphasising the ease with which mechanics could access internal equipment via removable panels on the side fairings, a significant advantage over dorsal tunnels. The layout allowed removal of all the engine equipment and support elements via a set of access panels and the hydraulic components were grouped together in the aft fuselage. All the research equipment and instrumentation would be housed in a single compartment with a wide access door.

Stipulated by the Navy and incorporated in the requirements document, a two-seat version was presented with the occupant and ejection seat taking up the area dedicated to research equipment in the single-seat aircraft. A single, clamshell canopy hood covered both cockpit positions with the observer having side windows and limited information displays for 'flight and research data'. The company presentation emphasised that the two-seat version would retain all the published performance data applicable to the single-seater.

North American opted for the Convair B-36 when selecting a carrier-plane; the B-50 was incapable of lifting it to the required altitude and the B-52 was not considered on grounds that it had not been adapted for such a role. To get the X-15 attached to the B-36 the carrier-plane would be jacked up on its main landing gear, tipping it on its nose leg at an acute angle sufficient to allow the X-15 to be moved in underneath and engaged on shackles. Once secured, the hydraulic jacks would lower the main landing gear on the B-36 back to the ground. The pilot would enter the cockpit of the X-15 at altitude via a protected enclosure, removed prior to release.

REPUBLIC AVIATION CORPORATION AP-76

Above: The Republic contender was unique among all bids by having no forward-looking windows for the pilot, the conventional windscreen replaced by a periscope device for landing. Like North American, Republic did not propose an ejectable pilot capsule. The wedge-shaped tail surfaces included split air brakes and also like NAA, the structure was primarily constructed from Inconel X. *Republic Aviation*

Founded by Alexander Seversky, the company began in the 1930s as the Seversky Aircraft Corporation of Farmingdale, New York, with Alexander Kartveli its chief designer. In 1934 it was awarded a contract for 35 basic trainers and the following year it produced a privately-funded experimental fighter, the SEV-2XP, which in 1936 was bought by the Army as the P-35. This led to the XP-41 and in 1939 the P-43 and a major production contract with the government.

By this time Alexander Seversky had left the company, which was renamed Republic Aviation in October 1939, most famous during the ensuing war years for the P-47 Thunderbolt. Before the war was over, Republic had sold its straight-wing jet fighter, the F-84 Thunderjet, to the Air Force and followed that with the successful swept-wing F-84F Thunderstreak, ordered during the upsurge in spending after the Korean War broke out in 1950. This was quickly followed by the F105 Thunderchief fighter-bomber for which the first contracts had been placed in 1954.

Although the company had no direct experience with high-altitude/high-speed research aircraft, it had worked up some high performance rocket and jet powered design concepts, beginning with the XF-91 in 1946. This had a dual-propulsion system using a jet engine for cruise and a rocket motor for high-speed intercept but difficulties due to nascent technology saw it overtaken by other, simpler designs. In 1949, Republic received a development contract for the XF-103 with a Mach 3 capability on both turbojet and ramjet propulsion. This too proved too big a step and other, more conventional types stepped in.

By this date materials research for the XF-103 was giving the company some knowledge regarding the thermal environment in which the X-15 would be called upon to operate and that gave Republic some confidence to submit its proposal. However, arguably its most valuable asset was Kartveli who had already established for himself a worldwide reputation with innovative design. However, for the X-15 proposal, Republic offered the heaviest of all contenders and, on performance, only slightly exceeding the speed requirement but falling 15 per cent short of the desired altitude.

In its proposal, Republic quoted a launch weight of 17,735kg (39,099lb) carrying 362kg (800lb) of research instruments and a landing weight of 6,713kg (14,800lb). A dominant design feature was the cockpit, with the pilot being completely submerged in the nose section with three glass panels either side from the time of launch until an altitude of 7,620m (25,000ft) was achieved during the glide back down. At this altitude and Mach 0.7, the pilot would raise the upper part of the compartment by 1deg at its leading edge and expose a mirror which would provide forward visibility

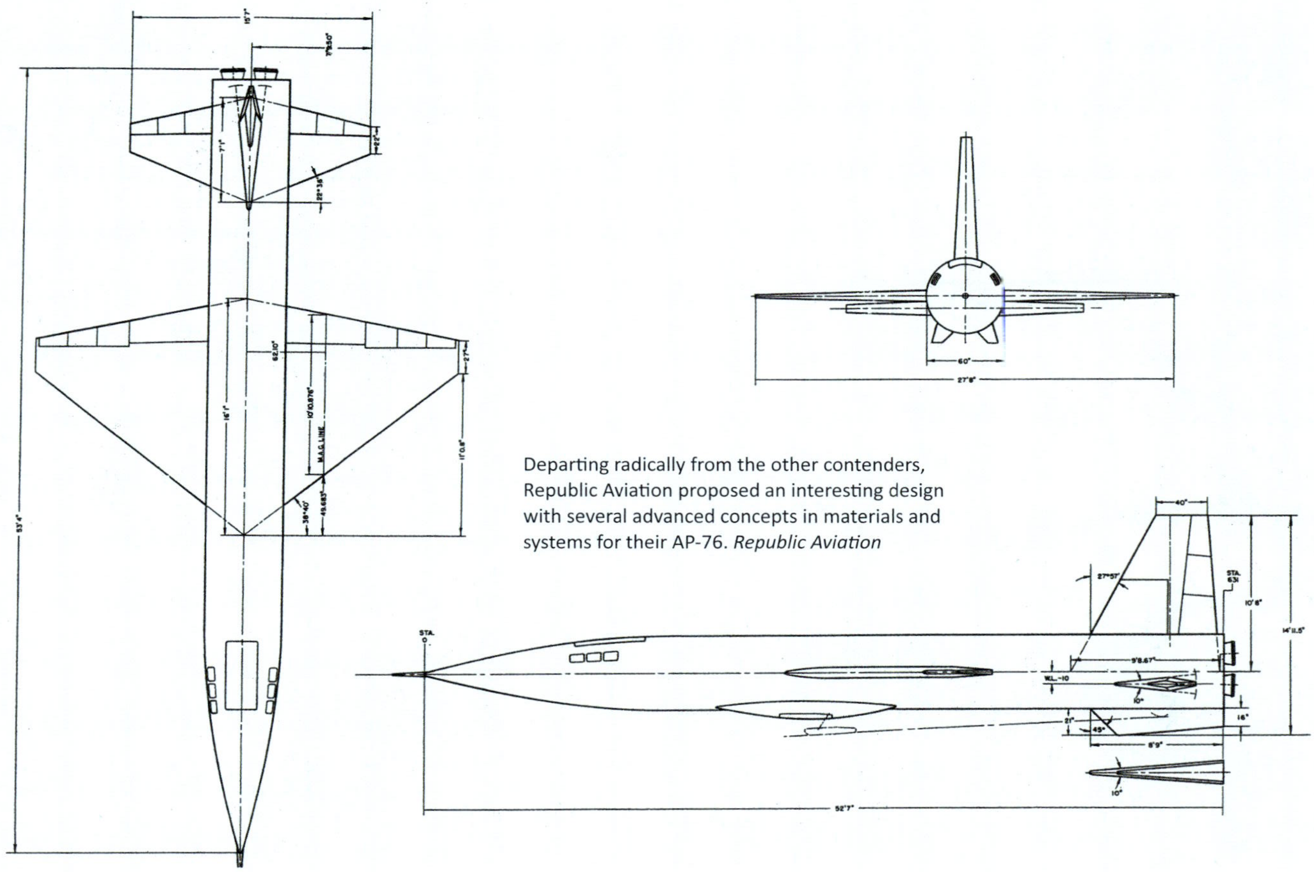

Departing radically from the other contenders, Republic Aviation proposed an interesting design with several advanced concepts in materials and systems for their AP-76. *Republic Aviation*

for terminal descent and landing. This system was considered best for protecting the cockpit from thermal effects of high-speed flight and radiation to which the pilot would be exposed at high-altitude.

With regard to the general design layout as presented in the summary section to the proposal brochure:

'The air foil section has a conventional leading edge with flat upper and lower surfaces between the 20 per cent and 80 per cent chord lines and a blunt trailing edge equal to 2 per cent of the chord. The horizontal and vertical tail surfaces are of conventional size made possible by the use of double wedge type sections with rounded leading edges. The included angles of these sections are 10 and 12 degrees respectively.

'The horizontal surfaces consist of a fin and rudder above the fuselage and a jettisonable ventral fin below. The rudder design is based upon data obtained from wind tunnel tests on the Republic XF-103 interceptor and, by combining the upper half of the vertical tail with its entire trailing edge, is effective through the sub, trans and supersonic regimes.'

The front 28 per cent of the fuselage took the form of an ogive with the aft section a cylinder with a diameter of 152.4cm (60in) and of semi-monocoque construction to 'shield the pilot and the equipment from very high temperatures (649°C/1,200°F)' encountered during certain flight conditions. Republic chose titanium for the primary structural element, which consisted of longitudinal Z-stringers disposed with 10deg separation. The structural skin was attached to the inner leg of the stringers with the frames and formers on the interior attachments. Republic believed it could use titanium due to a 'mildly corrugated' Inconel X of 0.50cm (0.20in) thickness insulating it from thermal conductivity with 1.27cm (0.5in) blocks of Marinite from Johns Manville, or some other such suitable mater al.

It was proposed that the Inconel outer skin be manufactured in separate sections with longitudinal dimensions of about 61cm (24in), running from the top to the bottom centrelines where the splices were located extending over three frames. Thermal expansion and contraction would be accommodated by elongation of the hole to which the sheets would be attached to the 'valley' of the corrugations. The holes would be sized to allow fore and aft

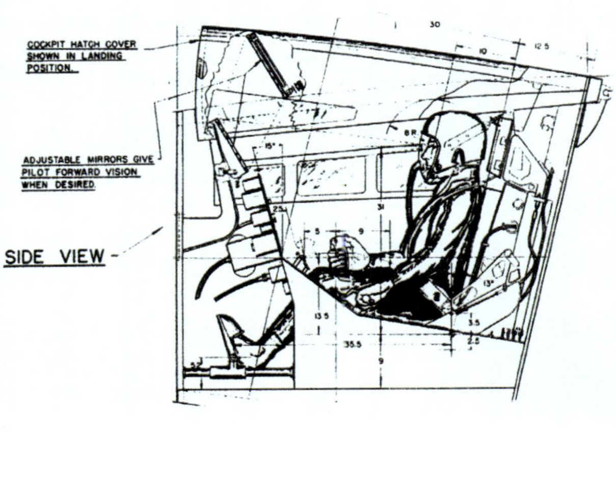

Right: Raised for the landing position, the cockpit hood on the Republic design provided a forward view by way of adjustable, reflecting mirrors. *Republic Aviation*

movement according to the ratio of thermal expansion and contraction and small bolts would be used in those locations. Republic chose very shallow corrugations, with a depth of 0.2cm (0.08in), with formers and frames in titanium. The end domes of the oxidiser tank were formed from aluminium alloy made possible by the thermal cooling effect of the oxidiser as well as the nitrogen gas used for pressurisation.

Republic chose four Bell XLR-81-BA-1 rockets each producing a thrust of 64,496N (14,500lb) at 12,192m (40,000ft) for a total thrust of 257,094N (57,800lb). These motors would run on JPX fuel, a solution of JP4 with hydrazine, and RFNA (Red Fuming Nitric Acid) as oxidiser, the hypergolic combination providing a specific impulse of 257sec. Two oxidiser tanks were to be situated in the space in front of and behind the wing carry-through box and have a total capacity of 5,412lit (1,430USgall), with the fuel tank containing 2,672lit (706USgall) of JPX aft of the second RFNA tank. JPX consisted of 40 per cent unsymmetrical dimethyl hydrazine and 60 per cent JP-4, a jet fuel.

Two hydrogen peroxide tanks for the APUs and the attitude control thrusters were placed above and below the carry-through box. There were six attitude control jets, each with a thrust of 400N (90lb), four at the rear of the fuselage and one in each wing tip. In the area above the wing and between the two nitric acid tanks, a 0.15m^3 (5.3ft^3) nitrogen tank operating at 20,685kPa (3,000lb/in^2) was situated for purging the rocket engines and pressurising the propellant tanks. An extra, small nitrogen tank was placed next to the lower hydrogen peroxide tank. Nitrogen would be used to pressurise the hydrogen peroxide tank to 2,758kPa (400lb/in^2).

Two redundant APUs were provided, each 18.65kW (25hp) driving a single hydraulic pump and one alternator. They would be started just before the AP-76 dropped from the carrier-plane and would allow nitrogen to flow to the expulsion bladder in the hydrogen peroxide tank, moving it to the throttle valve, started by activating fire switches and allowing it to open and the peroxide to decompose through a silver catalyst into the gas generator. The expanding gas would drive the turbine wheel on which a gear would wind up the alternator and the hydraulic pumps. A governor would control the speed of the pumps by throttling the amount of peroxide required.

Republic spent much time on developing the structural design of the AP-76 by incorporating several lessons learned during the detailed design of the XF-103. In some respects, in this they held an advantage over the other proposers. The shear loads were taken by heavy frames fore and aft of the wing carry-through and the connection of the wing to the fuselage consisted of a heavy pin on each of the four corners of that box. The fuselage received vertical and horizontal tail loads through three frames near the aft end of the fuselage, to which were also attached a tubular steel engine mount for the four rocket motors. The fuel and the oxidiser were incompatible at high temperatures and required aluminium liners with heating by radiation inhibited by an insulating blanket between the Inconel outer and the titanium inner skins.

Apart from the overall design approach, Republic took a lot of science and engineering for the AP-76 wing from the XF-103 and set up a sharply tapering trapezoidal planform. The wing had a root chord of 4.90m (16.08ft) and a tip chord of 68.5cm (27in), a leading edge sweep of 38.66deg and an aspect ratio of 3.0. The thickness of the wing was 5 per cent, increasing linearly to 7.5deg at the tip, thus providing sufficient thickness in the outer wing section for the chosen structural design. In cross-section, the lower and upper surfaces were parallel straight lines between 20 per cent and 80 per cent of the chord, with the leading edge having a radius of 0.85 per cent of the chord, blending into the upper and lower surfaces at the 20 per cent chord line.

The area of maximum wing depth was between 20 per cent and

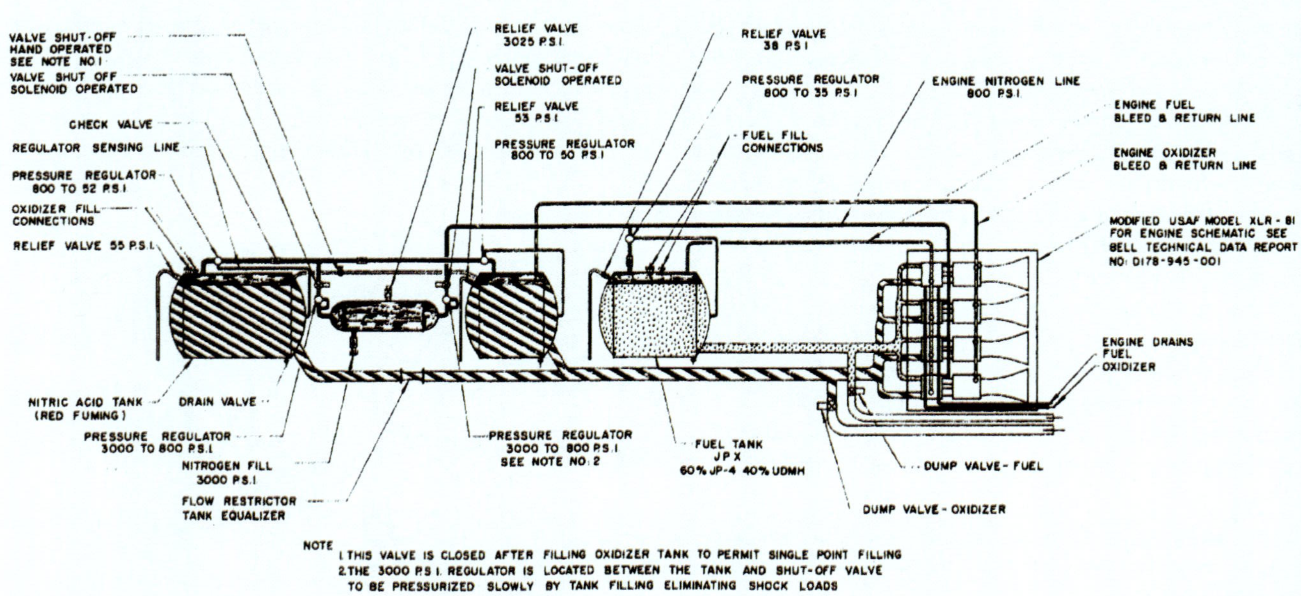

Below: A schematic of the Republic propulsion and propellant delivery system based on employment of the XLR-81 rocket motor. *Republic Aviation*

71.5 per cent of the chord and it was here that the designers located the multi-cell structural box carrying the primary wing loads. It was to this box that the leading and trailing edges were attached at its front and rear spars while flaps were supported by two masts cantilevered from the rear. The ailerons were supported by a set of fittings at the rear of the box. Because the wings were essentially a single structure from tip to tip, it could be supported at three points, two for each wing with a piano hinge providing a shear fitting. Throughout their work on this proposal, Republic had sought a simple and efficient structure, relatively easy to fabricate and engineered to take high loads.

The company took great pains to describe its features in the proposal documents and to explain how it selected the assembly and structure, using the multi-cell box as the primary load-bearing elements of the wing. Intermediate spars were spaced equally at a constant 13.97cm (5.5in) running parallel to the rear spar, of which there were 15 at the root section, decreasing in number outboard as they intersected the front spar, four remaining at the tip. Stabilised by this multi-spar approach, the primary bending strength was located in the skins, in the stabilising spars attached to the skin and in the spar webs with the whole assembly devoid of cut-outs.

As were the other proposers, Republic was right to emphasise the high-temperature environment for which the structure was optimised, the design allowing for deformation to minimise stress. All the spar webs were corrugated to allow for differential span-wise expansion in the wing skins caused by the variations in temperature with the cooler, inner structure. An advantage of having many spars allowed ribs to be light and used primarily for supporting flaps and ailerons, only one being required to accept shear loads from the spars and redirect them to the fuselage reaction points. Inconel X was selected as the preliminary structure, the only exception being local castings.

Design ingenuity was also found in the tail surfaces and speed brakes. The horizontal stabiliser was all-flying, trapezoidal in plan and with a root chord of 216.6cm (85.3in), a tip chord of 55.9cm (22in) and a semi-span of 2.37m (7.79ft). Wedge-shaped with an included angle of 10deg, split air brakes made up the area aft of the 65 per cent line, each half extended to make a 50deg angle with the plane of symmetry. The trailing 30 per cent of the vertical tail would serve as a split brake, as would the trailing 35 per cent of the horizontal stabiliser, actuated hydraulically by a

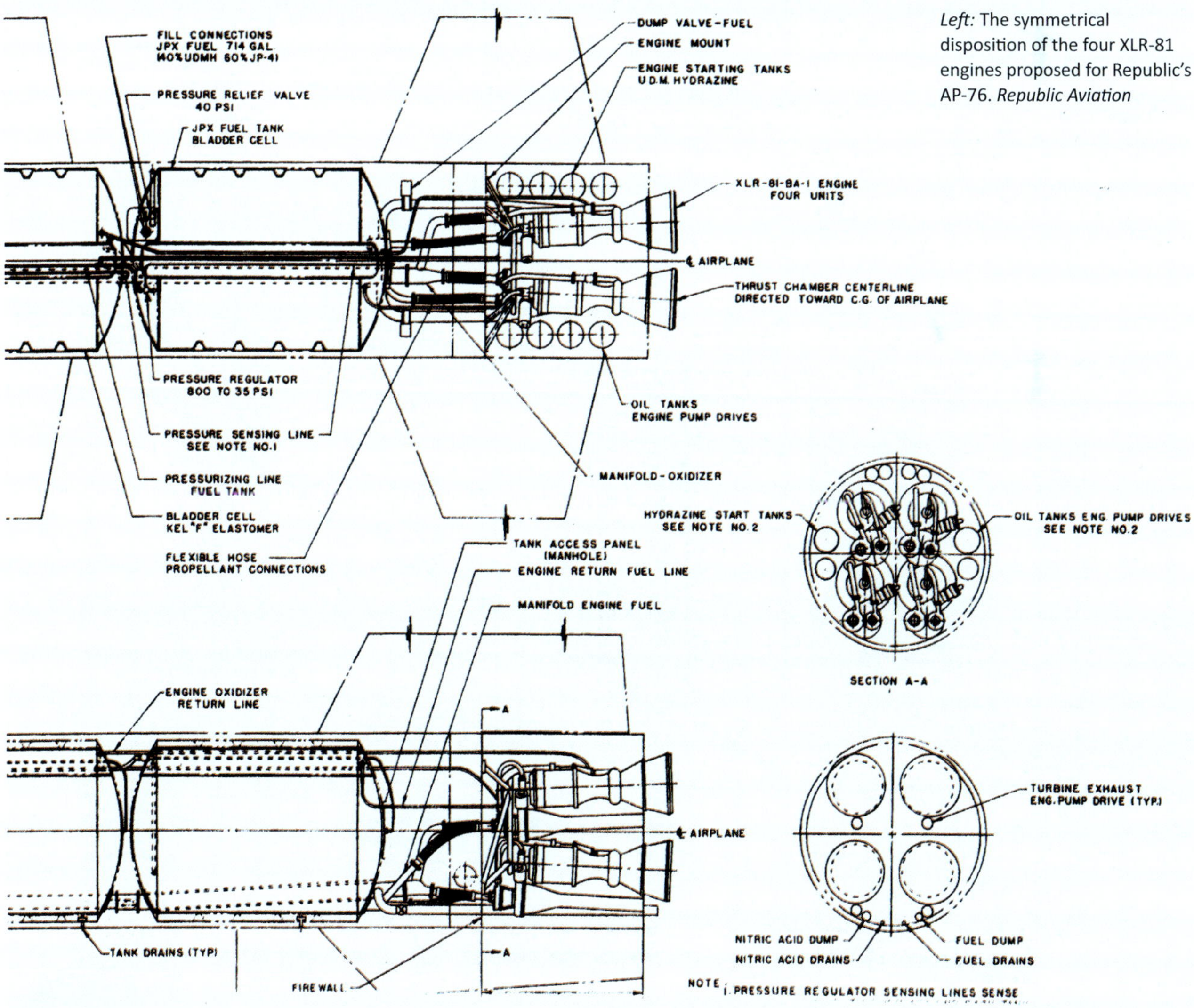

Left: The symmetrical disposition of the four XLR-81 engines proposed for Republic's AP-76. *Republic Aviation*

switch in the cockpit.

The wedge-shaped, trapezoidal vertical tail had a root chord of 254cm (100in), a tip chord of 101.6cm (40in) and a span of 2.48m (8.16ft) with an included angle of 12deg. It was constructed from three beams attached to parallel mating frames in the fuselage, the cover skins completing the fin torque box but not connected to the fuselage. The extreme leading edge consisted of sections of titanium carbide for accommodating local high temperatures, attached by shouldered bolts in slotted holes for thermal movement. The rudder consisted of a two-spar box beam with the rear spar supporting the split dive brakes. As with the wings, Inconel X was used throughout except for the extreme leading edges but the air brakes were in three sections to allow for thermal distortions.

Like North American, Republic studied pilot safety and possible means of escape at hypersonic speeds and concluded that a capsule was unlikely to provide safe release from a doomed aircraft. They also found it difficult to reduce the speed of any capsule to a safe recovery speed during descent. Any potential solution was far too heavy. It was surprising that Republic chose to reject this method, since it had done considerable work on an escape capsule for the XF-103. Consequentially, an upward-firing ejection seat was selected but this was unlikely to permit safe escape above supersonic speeds and the only sure way to survive would be to ride the AP-76 back down from maximum speed and only fire the ejection seat well below hypersonic velocities.

Republic selected the B-36H as the carrier-plane and identified only minor modifications required to carry the AP-76 to its drop altitude of 12,192m (40,000ft) and a speed of 648kph (403mph), citing the optimum location for that as 870km (541mls) from Edwards. After the drop, the pilot would ignite the four rocket chambers and climb at 20deg for a powered duration of 1min 45sec, reaching an altitude of 42.672m (140,000ft) and continuing in unpowered flight to a peak altitude of 67,056m (220,000ft), the maximum achievable with the AP-76.

At an altitude of 30,480m (100,000ft) the pilot would arm the thrusters and use the conventional controls to 'steer' the aircraft as it ascended and then entered a ballistic descent trajectory. Republic estimated that aerodynamic control would be restored at

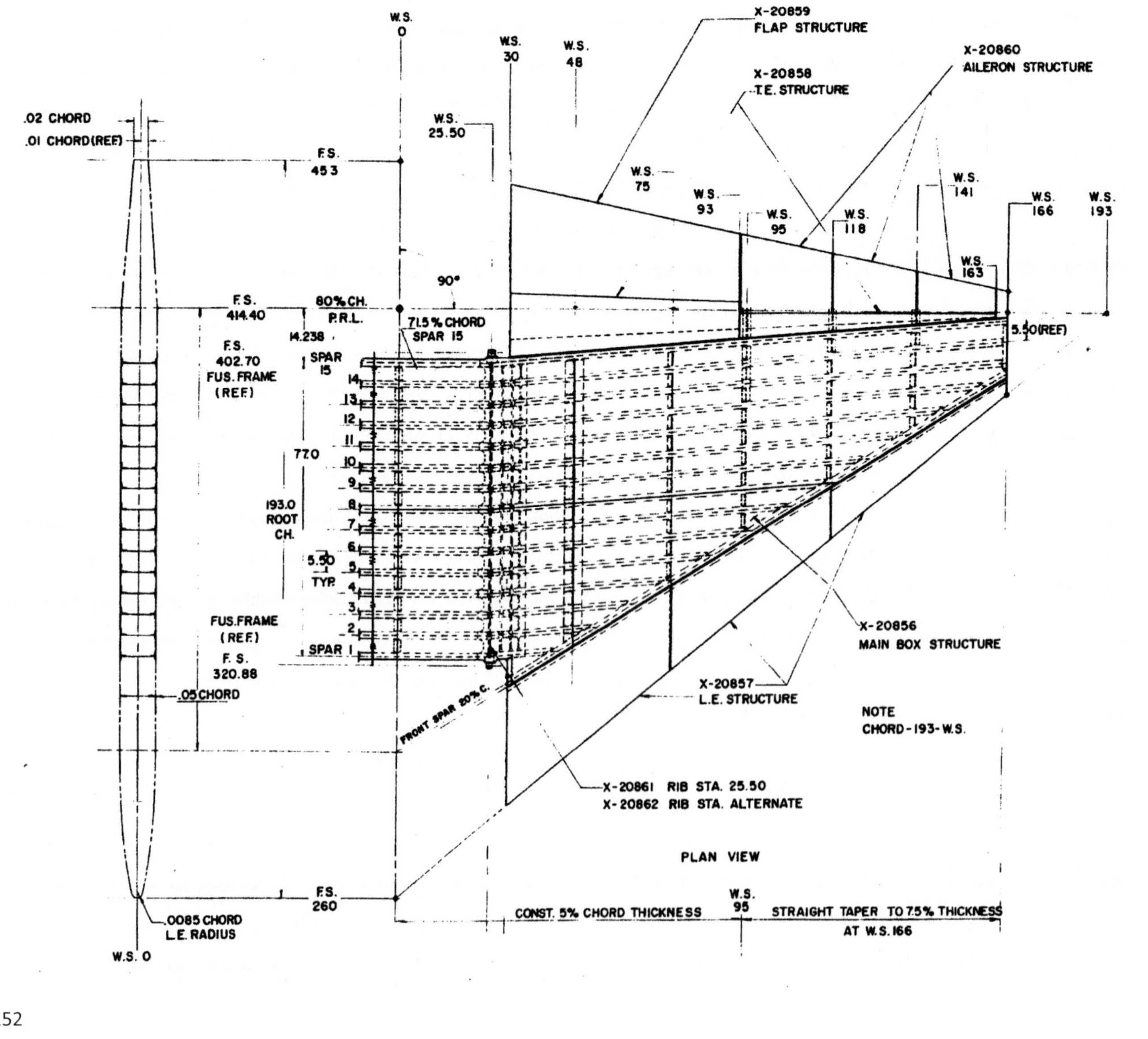

Below: The wing took a lot from work already done on the proposed Mach 3 XF-103, with a sharply tapering trapezoidal planform, comparatively simple and relatively easy to fabricate. *Republic Aviation*

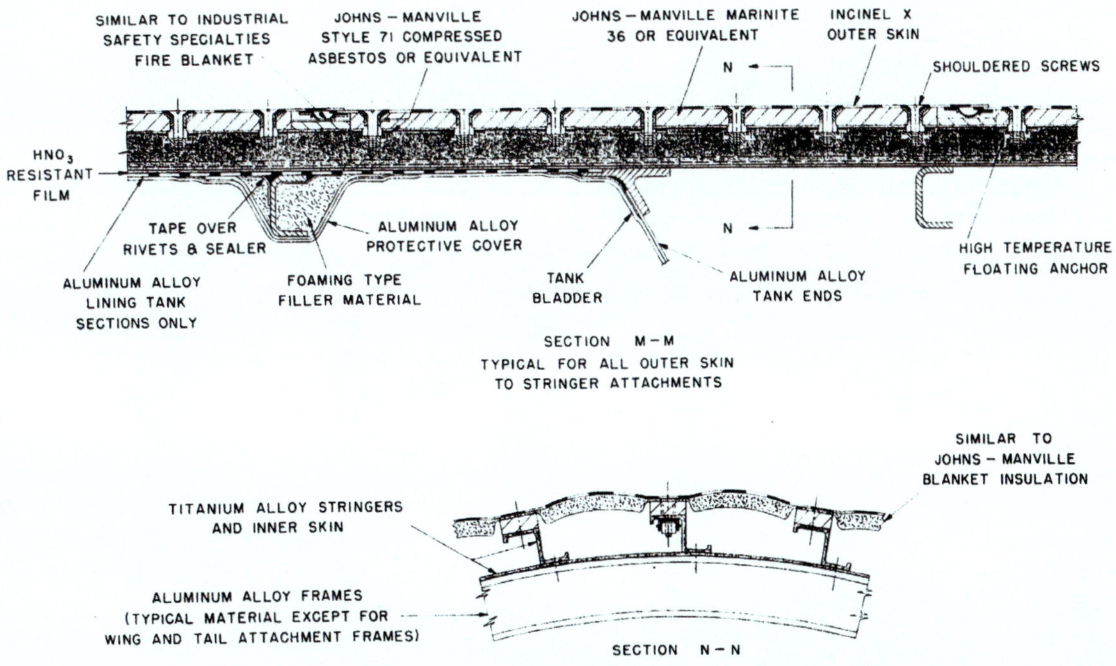

Above: Republic's proposal brochure took great strides in briefing the customer on the multi-cell box structures which were defined as primary load-bearing elements accommodating thermal expansion and contraction. *Republic Aviation*

a height of about 45,720m (150,000ft) from where the pilot would begin a series of manoeuvres, maintaining a 6deg angle of attack. At 7,620m (25,000ft) and Mach 0.7, the pilot would jettison the ventral fin and raise the hatch to obtain a forward view by the reflected image on to a screen directly in front of him at the top of the instrument panel.

The landing gear consisted of two main skids and a single tail skid, the former attached to the side of the fuselage ahead of the centre of gravity. They would extend by 47cm (18.5in) and the tail skid would deploy prior to touchdown but the descent rate was limited to 1.8m/sec (6ft/sec), well below the specified tolerance for combat aircraft but higher than that achieved by pilots ever likely to fly the AP-76.

As required, Republic also offered a two-seat version and in this they achieved a far superior layout and better provision for instruments than any of the other contenders. By adding a 73.6cm (29in) plug into the fuselage constant section in front of the forward propellant tank, they were able to accommodate a second crewmember in a full-size cockpit while also retaining capacity for 249.4kg (550lb) of instruments, unlike the others who deleted completely the experiment compartment when adding a second crewmember.

The single-seat version had one experiment compartment in front of the pilot and a smaller, 113.4kg (250lb) compartment aft of the pilot. In the two-seat version the larger compartment was retained. The empty weight of the two-seat version was 172.4kg (380lb) heavier, and the drop weight 276.7kg (610lb) heavier, which translated into a slight reduction in top speed.

In some respects the Republic proposal was several steps back, while in others it offered a credible approach bearing the hallmark of considerable research work already conducted on high-performance airframes – principally the XF-103. In its design approach it misread the NACA's priorities and misinterpreted the lesser demand for high-altitude flight, compromising the design around high speed while paying significant attention to the aerothermal problems attached to hypersonic flight. There were many aspects in the XF-103 concept which revealed intensive analysis on engineering highly stressed structures and exotic materials, imported to the AP-76 but not applied elsewhere.

Right: The hinged cockpit canopy afforded access to the AP-76 from the carrier-plane and provided a forward view via mirrors when raised during the approach phase. *Republic Aviation*

Chapter Eleven

Development of the X-15

Submissions were received from Bell, Douglas, North American and Republic on 9 May 1955 and two days later copies of the proposal documents were distributed to the Wright Air Development Center, to the NACA and to the Navy. An X-15 Project Office was set up to coordinate responses and all technical appraisals were to be submitted by 22 June. Analysis of the four proposals kept the Air Force, the Navy and the NACA busy from the day they arrived on 9 May until late July, conducting separate and independent evaluations at the Wright Air Development Center (WADC) and relevant NACA groups.

Comprising NACA director Hugh L. Dryden, Brig. Gen. Benjamin Kelsey and Adm. R. S. Hatcher, on 17 May the Research Airplane Committee met with WADC personnel to hear the four bidding contractors with larger NACA and Navy groups observing. Hartley Soulé was chairman of the NACA evaluation group, which sent its initial response to the laboratories with a request for comments by 13 June. Langley would look at aerodynamics, structures and the flight control system, the latter being also addressed by Ames and the High Speed Flight Station, while the Lewis Laboratory and the HSFS would look at propulsion and the HSFS alone would evaluate crew systems.

The initial evaluations had been delivered to Soulé on 6 June and Langley's recommendations were considered crucial, as they had been at the core of Project 1226 long before it had a designation. They placed North American ahead of Douglas followed by Bell and Republic. Langley's John Becker liked the hot-structure approach from NAA which was felt to outclass the use of magnesium in the Douglas proposal. But in its appraisal dated 3 June, Ames recommended the reverse order, selecting Douglas as their first choice over

Above: A mock-up cleared for inspection showing the general configuration of the X-15 as presented by North American Aviation at an industry review. *NAA*

NAA followed by Bell and Republic. It too, however, questioned the use of magnesium and the hot-structure preference because it preferred to evaluate design approaches likely to be adopted by future, operational aircraft.

This was the major difference between Ames and Langley, the latter wanting to have the X-15 as a survivable platform for research results, without recourse to any future direction in overall aircraft design. But Ames worried too about the flammability of magnesium and proposed that, if it won the contract, Douglas should build two aircraft in HK31 and a third with a higher-temperature wing but insulated in a manner likely to be appropriate for future applications in other projects. Langley also contested the need to change the wing sweep angle to 53deg, as proposed by Ames, to reduce by 21 per cent heat transfer to the leading edge, noting that the existing design was well capable of accepting the higher heat load.

Soulé received the results from the HSFS on 10 June and they too set the proposals in the order preferred by Ames, citing the Douglas approach as preferable for research, for the flight control system and for propulsion, cockpit, handling and carrier-plane compatibility and for supplementary support. It did, however, see very little difference in all aspects between Douglas and North American. Surprisingly, for all the attention paid by Republic to finding out the operating, handling and flight requirements, the HSFS rated them last. But from both Langley and Ames and now the HSFS, there was a distinct danger in selecting a specific design rather than a contractor capable of handling the entire programme.

Also on 10 June, Ames submitted its final recommendation which displayed a change from its initial ranking the previous week. Some consideration had been given over to Langley's arguments for North American and Ames followed them by reversing their initial choice, still placing Republic last. Some of the argument had been won on financial grounds, as there was simply no money for the third aircraft carrying a different wing structure. But there was also a convincing argument that the NAA concept was superior on grounds of research capabilities. Persuasive argument had diminished the case for a proto-futures aircraft over one for basic hypersonic and high-altitude research, the NACA wanting a durable, rugged, survivable platform.

In its final recommendation delivered to NACA headquarters on 14 June, Langley stuck with its original selection but leaned somewhat toward the magnesium wing from Douglas, despite suspecting that local hotspots could potentially result in deformations. It was attracted, however, to the possibility of intriguing engineering nuances such as that posed by the possibility of a different wing, much as it had supported wings of different thickness ratio for both first and second generation X-1s. Advocates of a 'fixed' design structure did point out that the alternative wing in that programme had been designed for an optimum research aircraft rather than applying wing changes as part of any future application. Langley liked Inconel and that did much to

Below: The X-15 required a highly integrated network of government agencies and industry partners as well as a wide range of people in small units drawn from a base of highly experienced specialists in science, engineering, operational planning and flying. At the head of it all was the Research Airplane Committee represented through the NACA/NASA, the Air Force and the Navy. *NACA*

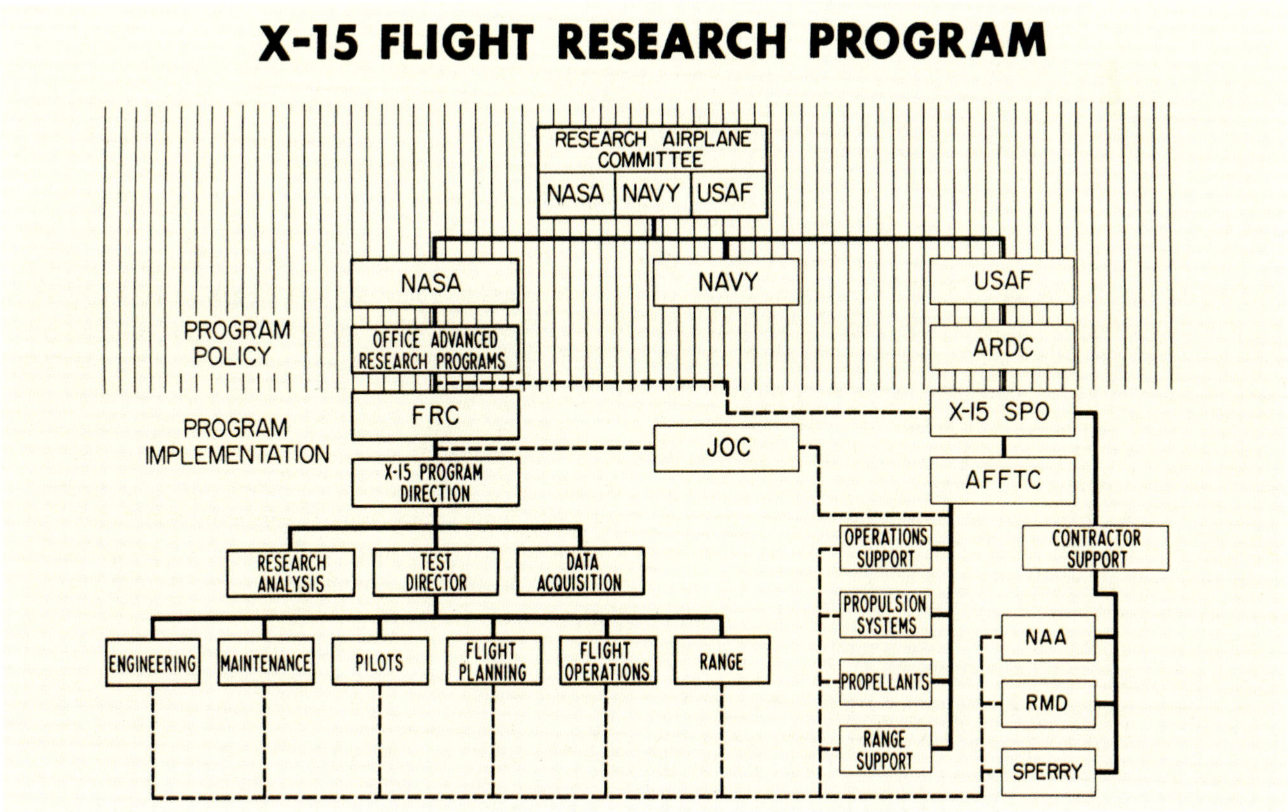

Above: The contenders for the X-15 contract included submissions from (top left rotating clockwise) North American Aviation ESO-7487, Republic Aviation AP-76, Douglas Aircraft Model 684 and Bell Aircraft D171. At the centre is a representative model of the second-generation X-1 series. *NACA*

back the requirement for a safe and survivable vehicle.

In the first half of July 1955 the evaluation list was sent to the WADC, with a separate design approach and utility ratings for each category of airframe, flight controls, propulsion, crew provisions, handling (including launch operations) and miscellaneous factors. From these marks were obtained an average weighting as a final rating out of a total 100 applied to each proposal. The NACA's average rating put North American on equal level with Douglas at 79 points for design approach, followed by Bell on 73 and Republic on 58. For utility rating, Douglas scored 73 followed by Bell on 72, NAA on 71 and Republic on 68.

Soulé backed Langley in selecting North American in the recommendation sent to the various laboratories but during the first two weeks in July the WADC Project Office was given the reports and, not surprisingly given its association with the company on Skystreak and Skyrocket, the Project 1226 chief engineer at the Navy's Bureau of Aeronautics expressed his preference for the Douglas design. The formidable George Spangenberg headed the Navy's examination of the proposal and would evaluate the relative merits of each. Interestingly, the Navy fleshed out some trends which, if implemented, the programme would benefit from. Not least, a deferral on an engine decision until the airframe contractor had been selected, so as to prevent a mismatch between optimisation of each.

The Navy decided its position on 15 July, which summed several concerns from specialist groups looking at the proposals system by system. For instance, the electronics group from the Bureau of Aeronautics judged the electrical system on the Bell proposal as unsatisfactory and rated the North American proposal last for its equipment and subsystems. The BuAer judged Douglas and Republic the best for potential flying qualities and felt that North American had incorrectly attributed laminar flow to much of their configuration, with the consequence that they had underestimated the heating levels. In its final recommendation, the Navy rated Doug-

Above right: In its proposal, North American Aviation defined the speed and altitude flight profiles set against trajectories selected for high or optimal temperature regimes.
Below right: NAA displayed the reasoning behind its engineering and materials choice through projections of skin temperatures versus time and the critical area of the structure against limits to flight profiles. *NAA*

DESIGN MISSIONS

. . . altitude and speed vs. time

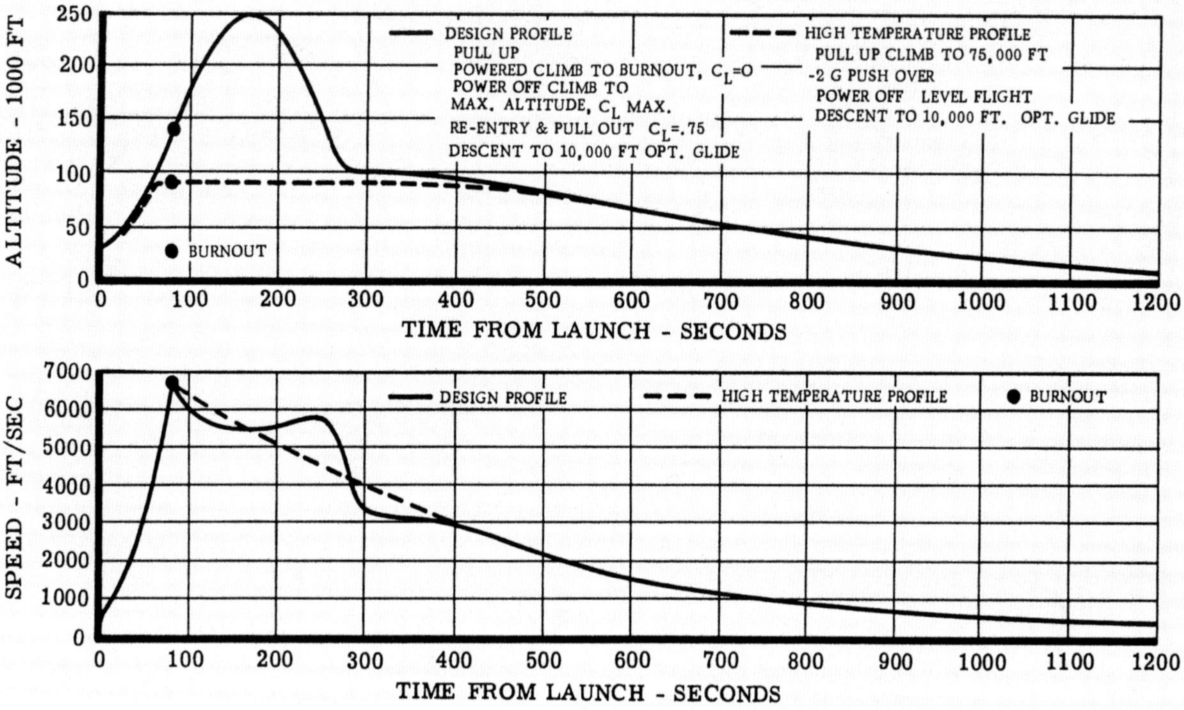

DESIGN MISSIONS

. . . temperature vs. time

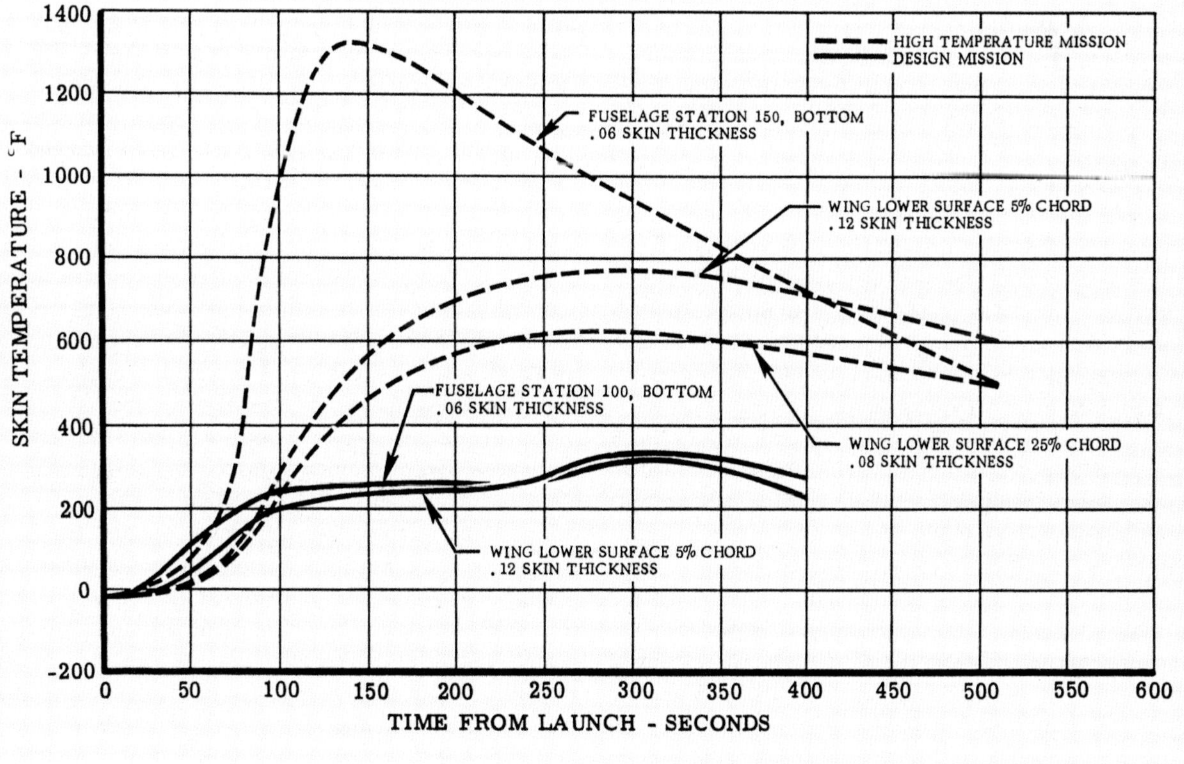

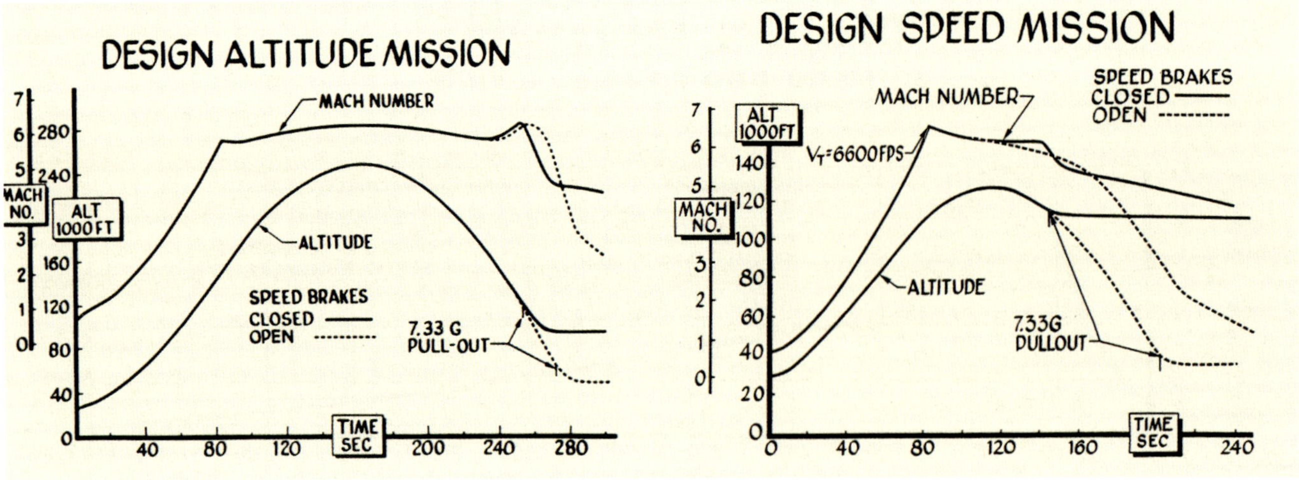

Above: NAA identified the way the speed brakes would play a crucial part in shaping the flight profiles for both altitude and speed runs, the former engaging with re-entry tests and the latter with tolerances in the aero-structures. *NAA*

las first, followed by North American, Republic and Bell.

On 26-28 July the Air Force, the Navy and the NACA gathered at Wright Field for a final determination, only the Navy expressing a preference for Douglas over NAA. Spangenberg expressed the view that by summing averages the points would not reflect outstanding performance in one category and good in others while companies scoring lower levels across the board could obtain a higher score overall. He also challenged the design imperatives driving the proposals, expressing preference for a hot-skin structure to better determine higher temperature data. Over these three days, the broader picture of corporate and industry capacity was reviewed, with a view to determining the suitability of each contender to take on the X-15.

In a seemingly unconnected but highly relevant issue, two weeks previously on 13 July, a joint ARDC-AMC Source Selection Board had noted six contractors capable of meeting the requirement for a high-flying Mach 3 bomber defined through a general requirement as WS-110A/L. This would mature into the B-70 programme intended as a successor to the Boeing B-52. Of these, only Boeing and North American Aviation would submit proposals but the nature of this potentially lucrative work was conceivably disruptive to the requirements of the X-15, which was far less profitable and would incur greater cost in terms of potential profit/per-resource unit, both human and industrial.

NAA also had the YF-107 programme underway, a Mach 2+ fighter development from the F-100. Companies had to bid on the basis of potential corporate value (usually profit) from one contract versus another. Time, resources and investment in the X-15 would never yield the returns of a large-scale production contract. And although further down the points list, but working with the same econometric, Republic had expanded its activity with the XF-103 and was stretched with production of existing types, as noted above. These aspects, plus the capacity of the industrial groups to support an added work package was at least a peripheral consideration in the evaluation.

On the final day of the conference at Wright Field, the recommendation of the group placed North American as the first choice, followed by Douglas and then Bell with Republic a distant fourth. Some had wanted to go with Douglas but for an Inconel skin rather than the magnesium in the formal company proposal. In the end the Navy too fell in line and supported that selection order. It was primarily an Air Force/NACA programme and there would be time during the forthcoming development stage for subtle changes, time to tweak and adjust requirements and design aspects. This was, after all, a contractor selection and not the final decision on a definitive design.

Decisions and woes

On 1 August the WADC began five days of deliberations over their own conclusions, together with a set of evaluations which covered five distinct areas of the separate proposals: performance, technical details, suitability for research and the potential for development and cost estimates. The first two were concerned with the viability of the design proposal, the last three with its applicability to the task required by the customer.

On performance, while each of the four submissions were capable of meeting the requirements of the programme, North American was ranked top, followed by equal sharing of Bell and Douglas, followed by Republic. On technical design, while the view was expressed that none of the submitted designs was capable of safely accommodating requirements, North American came top with Douglas, Bell and Republic following.

For research suitability, North American was considered 'acceptable' with the others 'unacceptable' for reasons associated with insulation and the doubtful value of Douglas' magnesium structure. Development potential for the work task focused on the overall competence, manpower levels, resources and work commitments of the company and of the time scale offered. While North American and Douglas appeared capable of delivering within the requested 30 months, Republic's time scale was considered unrealistic and Bell only offered 40 months.

Costs were expected to be a little over $12million on the

original assessment but none of the bids came anywhere close: Bell quoted $36.3million, Douglas $36.4million, Republic $47million and North American $56.1million. Very few had expected the cost projection to be anywhere close to the in-house valuation and over time even the highest contractor estimate was woefully short of the final budget, although the last accounting included far more than had been expected from the original estimate – which is frequently the case with aerospace projects, where the customer adds and extends needs, wants and requirements.

Together with a group of senior officers, Brig. Gen. Howell M. Estes, chief of the Weapons Systems Division, received the results of the evaluation on 9 August at the hands of Capt. McCollough. Two days later, McCollough gave similar presentations to Gen. John W. Sessums, commander of WADC, and Gen. Marvin C. Demler, commander of ARDC, and to the NACA's Hartley Soulé. The following day, NACA headquarters hosted a final briefing with the Air Force and the Navy where several leading figures from the field centres and BuAer were in attendance.

Immediately after this 12 August meeting, the NACA Research Airplane Committee met and gave their approval, accepting the recommendation which was to be passed across to the Assistant Secretary for Research at the Department of Defense. But they had a couple of requests of their own: that the original cost estimate be adjusted to take account of the received figures; and, believing that the original schedule of 30 months was too restrictive, that this be extended by up to 18 months.

With the decision all but cemented, on 23 August North American's representative in Dayton informed the WADC project office that they wished to withdraw their proposal, citing the 30-month delivery requirement which, with the increased contract work they had on hand and were working toward, they could not fulfil. With intense company interest in the emerging B-70 programme, NAA managers feared that the number of skilled engineers required for the X-15 would imbalance the allocation of human resources. NAA was aware that the B-70 represented a major earner and would far outrank the relatively small X-15 programme.

It took only a few days for the WADC to contact North American to ask them to reconsider and after McCollough informed Soulé a debate was sparked over how best to recover. The NACA was generally opposed to giving the work to

Below: The success of the X-15 programme would rest on the shoulders of three men: Paul Bickle (left) who in August 1959 replaced Walt Williams (right) as the director of NASA facilities at Edwards Air Force Base and Hugh Dryden (centre), director of the NACA from 1947 to 1958 and deputy administrator of NASA from 1958 to 1965. *NASA*

Near right: Key to the development of the company that produced it and to the X-15 itself, NAA's Harrison A. 'Stormy' Storms gained a creditable reputation for his design work on the P-51 Mustang, the F-86 Sabre and the F-100 Super Sabre. Eventually rising to president of North American Aviation Space and Information Systems Division in 1960, he died in 1992 at the age of 76. *NAA*

Centre right: Chief engineer under Harrison Storms, Charles H. 'Charlie' Felz managed the emerging X-15 programme and played a seminal role in adapting it to the needs and requirements of the NACA, the Air Force and the Navy. *NAA*

Far right: A key influence over the NAA team was the experience of Theodore von Kármán, under whose tutelage both Storms and Feltz had learned the vicissitudes of their trade at the California Institute of Technology. *Author's collection*

Douglas, an action preferred by the AMC in the event that NAA did pull out, citing the amount of work they considered the D-684 would need to get it to meet requirements. North American backed up its withdrawal with a formal letter to the Air Force dated 30 August but it only reached the NACA after Hugh Dryden had decided to press on with the procurement process! After receiving the withdrawal letter, on 7 September, speaking on behalf of the Research Airplane Committee, Soulé pressed Dryden to give the work to Douglas but was left in no doubt that if NAA were out of the competition he would start the competition again rather than give it to runner-up Douglas.

Bizarrely, the Air Force sailed along with its procurement procedures and on 14 September submitted the NAA proposal to the Defense Air Technical Advisory Panel for its approval. In heated discussion regarding costs, a decision was made to lower the amount the Air Force would carve out of its budget and it also took a second look at the 30-month completion clause in the pending agreement. The cut in funding was an implicit part of formal DoD approval for the X-15 on 21 September, together with verification that they wanted to sign a contract with NAA. Well aware of their favoured position in the ranking, senior managers at North American, including Raymond Rice, vice-president and chief engineer, struggled to find a way to reconsider their decision. On the formal approval at the Department of Defense, the company notified the Air Force that it would accept the project if they could have an eight-month extension of the delivery date. That approval came in a formal letter dated 30 September.

Satisfying a set of user requirements is only the first part of a successful project. Readers familiar with aerospace industry proposals, submissions and contracts which pass muster on technical grounds, will be aware that three imperatives underpin a successful bid: the ability of the bidder to carry out the work; the human and industrial resources required to complete the project; the money the contractor will have to spend to complete the job and the amount the customer can pay for the finished product. Defence project estimates are an implicit part of the government department receiving the necessary funds from the Pentagon, equally important for the DoD to receive political approval for its decisions.

In the case of the X-15, costs loomed large from the outset and at a meeting on 5 October at Wright Field the projected total cost of \$30million, with annual expenditure of \$10million, was reassessed in the light of disclosures from the several proposals. The revised figure of \$56.1million, with first-year funding of almost \$26million, was examined and a series of cuts made to bring that down. These included deleting the planned static-test model and cutting back on modifications to the carrier-plane, at this time assumed to be the B-36H. These changes brought the cost estimate down to a little over \$50million with peak-year funding of \$16.6million. The budget awarded 77.4 per cent to the airframe, 19.8per cent to the propulsion unit and 2.8 per cent to the flight test range at Edwards, upgraded to support the X-15.

Still unsatisfactory, it was not these figures the AMC used at a meeting with the DoD on 11 October but a value revised down to around \$45.3million together with a peak-year funding of under \$15million. Using this as a working baseline for further discussions, the formal processes for definitive contract award rolled along. On 7 November 1955 the Directorate of Procurement and Production signed off on a letter which the AMC approved eight days later for dispatch to North American authorising a \$2.9million contract which was signed and returned on 5 December. At this date, the apportioned amounts for airframe, engine and test range were 83.2 per cent, 13.7 per cent and 3.1 per cent respectively.

The X-15 programme would eventually absorb more than two million man-hours and 4,000 hours of tests in 15 different wind tunnels and it would reveal unimagined problems to which solutions were found only as the programme evolved. It was essential that the NACA and the Air Force kept close contact with the development of the programme and for that a series of conferences would be held to monitor progress and air problems. Long before that, however, immediately after the decision to give NAA the job of building the X-15, engineers from Ames and the HSFS raised concerns on several

aspects of the design, which differed some way from the Becker/Langley concept on which they had all been sold.

Expressed in a communication to Soulé in October 1955 were concerns about NAA's decision to add augmentation systems for better control of longitudinal damping, about the leading edge of the wing, the nose and the ventral stabiliser. Ames wanted further work to be conducted on the overall shape of the fuselage and the position of the horizontal stabiliser. And again, as expressed before, they worried about NAA's estimate of heat transfer. For their part, the HSFS wanted to change the basic load factors, challenging the wing leading edge, the endo-atmospheric and exo-atmospheric flight control systems, propellant procedures and the crew provisions including landing gear. Also reiterating their preference, the HSFS pushed for an interim XLR-8 engine for early powered flights.

All these issues called for a series of meetings to thrash out issues relating to the configuration. The first of these was held at Wright Field on 24-25 October where NAA, RMI, the Air Force and the NACA examined all these issues plus the differential-deflection of the horizontal stabiliser for roll control, a feature of the proposal to eliminate the need for ailerons and elevons. NAA agreed to carry out further wind tunnel studies on the side-tunnels for ancillary equipment but defended their 'rolling-tail' concept by demonstrating that it proved highly effective and would not cause control problems.

Further meetings were held at NAA's Inglewood facility beginning on 27-28 October where questions were raised regarding vortices from the side tunnels adversely affecting the horizontal tail and this was agreed as a necessary investigation using appropriate wind tunnels. That resulted in a discussion involving NACA engineers and NAA aerodynamicists about the necessary support from such facilities. North American requested use of the X-15 1/15th scale model in the Unitary Tunnel at Ames for tests at Mach 0.7-3.5 and tests with a 1/50th scale model in the 25.4 x 35.5cm (10 x 14in) tunnel for Mach 3.0-6.3. But this raised issues and Becker's team suggested a two-phase programme using several tunnels at Langley as well.

There was a rational argument for leaning on facilities at Ames – there was much less distance between NAA and that location – but the core facilities for NACA wind tunnels were at Langley. It was agreed that their full range of facilities would be utilised and these included the 2.43m (8ft) transonic tunnel, the 1.2 x 1.2m (4 x 4ft) unitary tunnel, the 27.9cm (11in) hypersonic tunnel, the 1.2 x 1.2m (4 x 4ft) Supersonic Pressure Tunnel, the Mach 4 jet facility and Langley's 25.4 x 35.5cm (10 x 14in) hypersonic tunnel. North American wanted quick results from the 1/50th scale model tests to equip the 1/15th scale model with modifications.

Decisions and solutions

During the closing months of 1955 considerable discussion took place regarding the engine. That will be dealt with later, although it should be said that the commitment to the XLR-30 was substantial, with different views regarding alternative propellants. There was increasing evidence that the airframe would be ready for flight long before the definitive engine and HSFS's push for interim use of the XLR-8 began to gain traction. This was supported by RMI, who saw pressure offloaded to some extent from the inevitable exposure they would have should the X-15 be sitting about for an extended period without an engine! And in any event, the initial drop-tests would

Above: The general configuration of the X-15 would change very little from the initial proposal, with the trapezoidal wing and the anhedral horizontal stabilisers. *NAA*

not require that additional power during the crucial contractor flights for aerodynamic handling.

Much of the responsibility for bringing the X-15 to the customer would depend to a large extent on the contractor, the personnel in charge of the programme, the engineers responsible for it and the integration between the supply-side and the user community at Edwards who would implement it. NAA's Harrison A. Storms was head of the division working the X-15 and in charge of all its other engineering projects, so management of the programme would be handled by Charles H. 'Charlie' Feltz. Both men had mighty reputations and were highly respected for their work. Storms had studied under Theodore von Karman at the California Institute of Technology and after joining NAA became chief engineer for the prestigious Los Angeles Division. Feltz joined the company before the war and had worked on every major NAA project from the P-51 to the F-86 and would manage the design team, along with the personnel working the project.

Key to all the pilot-related decisions was test pilot A. Scott Crossfield, who had already left the NACA to join North American specifically to work on engineering the ergonomics and pilot-related design and development including flight control systems. While 'Chuck' Yeager had been a pilot's pilot, 'Scotty' was the pilot-engineer genius who could apply an intuitive scientific and technical understanding to what the aeroplane was doing. He would prove vital as the aircraft was developed. Also on board were project engineers Roland L. Benner, George Owl, Raun Robinson, Robert Field, John Gibb and Laurence P. Greene, the chief aerodynamicist.

An enabling factor was integrating personnel between the various industrial and government elements involved. The first step was for NAA and the NACA to get to know each other on a day-to-day basis, working through decisions and the multitude of changes involved in finessing a preliminary design. For the NACA side Hartley Soulé was responsible for managing the requirements of the user and Harrison Storms for moving the aircraft through its various developmental stages, both agreeing that neither should get in the way of the other! And that was how it was and why it was a successful working relationship.

Critical meetings in decisions regarding the overall configuration occurred in November. The first, held 14-15 November at NAA's Inglewood facility provided an opportune moment to discuss several outstanding issues, including the design limit for dynamic pressure. This was a fundamental feature of the design goals. The experimental scientists at NACA wanted a design capability all the way up to 119.7kPa (2,500lb/ft^2) while NAA had originally set the limit at

Right: Unique to the ESO-7487 proposal, two side-tunnels gave the NAA design a distinctive appearance and this overhead view shows those well, together with the air data probe installed for development flights. *NAA*

71.82kPa (1,500lb/ft²). NAA calculated achieving the higher value would add 45kg (100lb) to the overall weight of the aircraft. Also, increasing the load factor from 5.25-g to 7.33-g would require a further 61kg (135lb). There was already some slight weight growth but there was unanimous agreement to achieve those levels and that it was worth the weight penalty in each case.

Many decisions were still pending regarding the materials which would be used in the aircraft. Debates would ensue during this first year of activity about the type of tail to build in to the X-15 and the nature of dorsal and ventral stabilisers. For this initial meeting at Inglewood, however, attention focused on options for leading-edge materials, where there was a great deal of uncertainty regarding the various options considered. These included metallic, copper, fibreglass, plastic and titanium carbide materials but one desirable advantage was NAA's proposal to incorporate detachable leading edge sections at the cost of complexity and a slight weight penalty. There was also a preference for 0.5cm (0.20in) titanium alloy instead of 24S-T aluminium for structural members on the internal wing and stabiliser assemblies.

The increase in dynamic pressure for the structure challenged NAA's initial decision not to pressurise the propellant tanks. The increase in the dynamic pressure argued that this was essential, or pay substantial penalties in additional structural weight to withstand the added stress. But Inconel X would be used for the speed brakes and the additional brake hinges made necessary by the increased dynamic pressure.

With an aircraft of this size and power, issues which had been tolerable on smaller, less powerful X-series aircraft became critical for the X-15. Any small misalignment of the engine thrust line would have disastrous effects at the speeds and altitudes envisaged, aerodynamic trim no longer able to compensate. It was calculated that a 2.54cm (1in) misalignment of the engine longitudinal axis would be unacceptable and NAA agreed to provide unusually stringent checks on engine alignment. This also triggered a redesign of the vertical tail for better aerodynamic control.

All these minor changes and 'tweaks' added weight, a further 56.7kg (125lb) being added when the Air Force insisted on a Stability Augmentation System (SAS) for pitch and yaw motion. Several factors surrounded discussion regarding the capabilities of the SAS and it would persist throughout the development phase. It was also found desirable to incorporate redundant ballistic recovery systems and to provide three times the amount of hydrogen peroxide than that in the original proposal. It was agreed to provide separate supplies for the reaction controls jets and the APUs, adding a further 53kg (117lb).

Decisions about centre stick versus side controller were also thrashed out, it being decided that the centre stick would be connected to the side controller for operating the aerodynamic surfaces while a separate side stick on the left side of the console and above the throttle would be specifically for operating the attitude control jets. The X-15 pioneered the use of a side-stick control system, albeit one with mechanical linkages and not the fly-by-wire (FBW) employed in most combat aircraft from the 1970s. Nevertheless, this was the first aircraft designed for flight in high altitudes where the low level of atmospheric pressure was incapable of controlling the attitude of the aircraft. X-15 flight research would add valuable data to the design of those later devices.

One issue raised some contention. The Air Force needed some convincing that the standard ejection seat was preferable to an encapsulated system, to which they had been committed on the XB-58A Hustler and which they would adhere to for the upcoming XB-70A Valkyrie. There were also discussions about the temperature regime for the X-15 and these were modified upward after wind tunnel test results were in from the Unitary Plan tunnel at Langley and from the Arnold Engineering Development Test Center in Tennessee. Temperature predictions for the interior structure was, however, found to be less than anticipated.

The Navy had been playing a passive role in the decisions regarding proposals and configurations and had not attended the Inglewood meeting on 14-15 November. However, on the second day and before the group broke up, Douglas gave a presentation in which it pushed HK31 as their preferred material and attempted to overturn the decision favouring Inconel X. While positing some useful data and securing an attentive audience, it did nothing to change the decision.

That meeting was followed over the following two days with a gathering of personnel from the HSFS and Langley to decide on the instrumentation and the method of obtaining and saving data. The HSFS pushed for recording all the data on board while Langley argued for a high-speed telemetry link but that was too expensive to develop with available funds. It was agreed that wing pressure distribution measurements would not be required but that strain gauges should be fitted to the main wing spars, at least for the first few flights.

It had been suggested that NAA would install the equipment provided by the NACA. That fitted well with the divisions of responsibility set out by Storms and Soulé and it was so agreed the following day when a further meeting was held at HSFS. Early flights would use an air-data probe rather than a ball-nose device which will be described later, the latter in development for the advanced performance and research flights.

Significant decisions still had to be made and throughout November 1955 various team structures and a subcontractor base were being compiled at North American. The NACA was also doing materials tests and it released a paper during the month which cast some doubt on the tensile strength of Inconel X as published by the International Nickel Company. This prompted NACA headquarters to press Langley for further tests to determine if there were any flaws in milling procedures or the way the tests had been conducted. To the relief of many, the negative results were found to be flawed but it did emphasise the need for care in producing and applying the material.

Before the end of the year the definitive wind tunnel programme was worked out, whereby Langley would carry out flutter tests on the speed brakes using the 1/15th scale model, while PARD would conduct similar analysis on the wing planform. This was necessary because NAA wanted flutter data on a large model at Mach 5 and that could not be provided by any available wind tunnel. It was also proposed that NAA build two 1/50th scale models, one each for Ames and Langley, but there was no money for those until funds were found. One of those would be tested in the Langley 27.9cm (11in) hypersonic and 22.9cm (9in) blowdown tunnels.

It would be on results from the Unitary Plan tunnel at Langley that one of the most disruptive changes to the structural design of the X-15 came about, due in part to uncertainties about the aero-thermal environment in which the aircraft would operate. In its initial proposal, NAA had assumed laminar flow for most of the flight profile and built its expectations of design surface temperatures on that. Results from the Langley tunnel and a facility at the Arnold Engineering Development Center showed that the heat transfer coefficients were a lot higher than calculations alone had predicted.

The changes required to make the X-15 capable of accepting the higher temperatures added 907kg (2,000lb) and threatened to lower the flight goal to Mach 6. Ironically, flight results would show that in fact the temperatures on the primary structural elements were lower by several hundred degrees than the original calculations from North American. Such was the justification for having an aircraft such as the X-15; not for the first time would theoretical calculations, model tests in wind tunnels and extrapolated data from other programmes prove inadequate to the task of finding definitive results from in-flight measurements.

A raft of changes were effected during the early months of 1956, the most significant of which was the admission by the Air Force that they had no suitable stable platform for the X-15. It had been assumed from previous presentations that they had. The NACA's Arthur Vogeley had reported during the November meeting at Inglewood that the Air Force had such an all-attitude inertial system, produced by Bendix with a weight of 12.7kg (28lb).

It helped little that the Eclipse-Power division of Bendix stepped in during a meeting in May 1966 and promised to produce the required device in 24 months, with a unit weighing 29.5kg (65lb). As explained later, within three months they were no longer involved and the X-15 Project Office opened discussions with the Sperry Gyroscope Company.

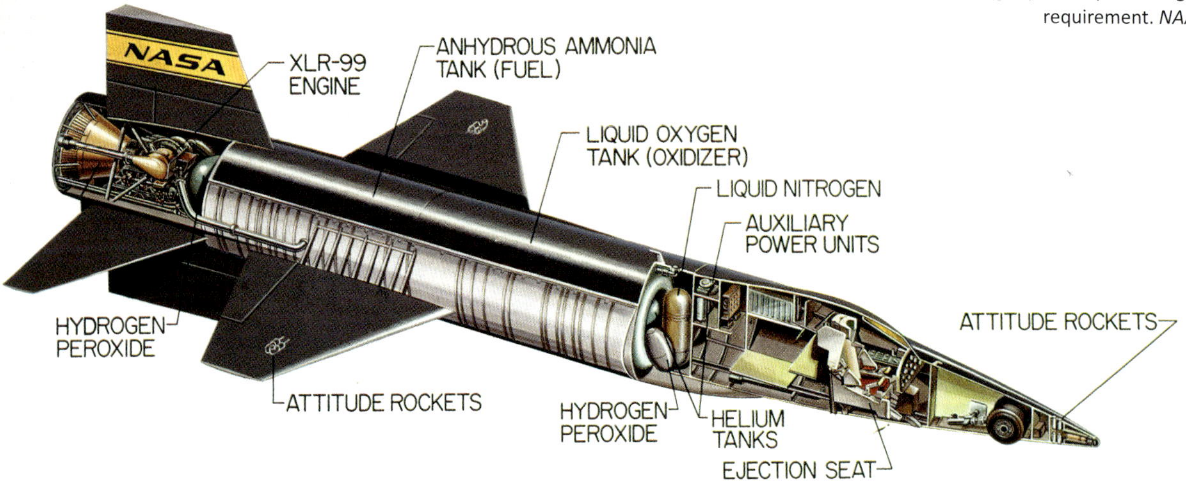

The operational layout of systems and subsystems provided an elegant and practical solution to challenges posed by the design requirement. *NAA*

Three-view drawing showing the general configuration differences between the air data probe and the ball nose. *NAA*

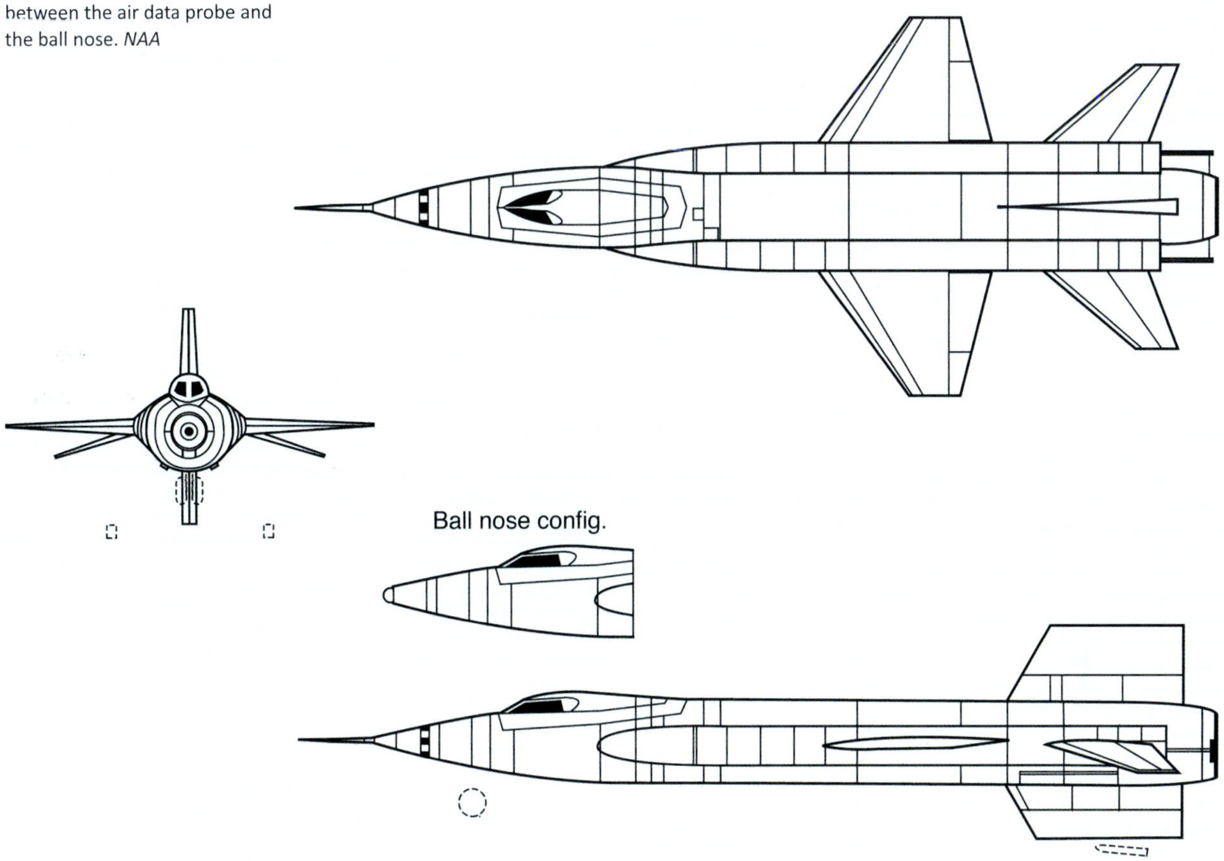

Other changes during these early months of the year included a decision to revise the operating procedure for the speed brakes so that they opened progressively at the higher dynamic pressure of 119.7kPa (2,500lb/ft²). But there was again a concerted effort by the Air Force to replace the proposed ejection seat with an escape capsule. During a meeting on 2-3 May, the recent WADC directive mandating all new aircraft to have escape capsules was discussed, the Air Force justifying the change, in part, on the basis that it would provide research data on the operation of such capsules, implicit within which was the obvious expectation that it would be used!

There was fierce opposition to this, not only on grounds of added complexity and design delay but also due to arguments articulated by Scott Crossfield, who had no faith at all in capsules. He firmly supported the use of an ejection seat, citing it as a thoroughly safe and effective means of escape. The Air Force maintained their ground, but only as far as to require North American to provide written justification for why they would not use a capsule system but without pressing for a requirement to replace the ejection seat.

Contracts and conferences

The definitive contract would encompass three aircraft, a high-speed and a low-speed wind tunnel model, a free-spin model and one full-size mock-up. It had already been decided to order three flight vehicles because experience with the X-series showed that it was possible to carry out a meaningful research programme with two but a third aircraft provided a quicker response to evolving requirements. Embedded within the X-15 programme from the outset was a deep need to provide a research tool which could fly an expanded research effort based on knowledge gained during initial flight activity, rather than having to develop another air vehicle for further research work. There was also the prudent hedge against the loss of a single aircraft bringing the entire programme to a halt, as had already happened with the X-1 series.

All these aspects folded in to the final production go-ahead on 11 June 1956, followed four days later by the allocation of serial numbers: 56-6670 (MSN 240-1), X-15-1; 56-6671 (MSN 240-2), X-15-2; and 56-6672 (MSN 240-3), X-15-3. On this day too, the Contract Reporting and Bailment Branch verified the contract and the production details in writing.

The first industry/government conference on the progress of the programme was held at Langley on 25-26 October 1956, hosting 313 representatives from across government, industry and academia but notably without Air Force participation in any of the presentations despite their personnel making up 10 per cent of the attendees. The NACA presented the majority of the papers followed by North American and then RMI, each addressing various aspects of the programme on a 'reporting' basis to inform of developments and progress. And there was some good news as well as the unexpected.

In wind tunnel tests from low subsonic to Mach 6.9, the fuselage side-tunnels were found to generate almost half of the total lift at higher Mach numbers. But they were also found to induce longitudinal instability and they were to be shortened as a result. But there were issues too with the configuration of the landing gear. In the proposal, two skids were located on opposing sides of the fuselage under the forward section of the wing and stowed in the side tunnels. Anticipating a high angle-of-attack on touchdown, NAA had positioned a tail wheel to protect the aft fuselage but this was found not to work and the skids were relocated further back to a position below the leading edge of the horizontal stabilisers. But that built in an enduring problem with forward rotation of the aircraft at nose-down, causing at least one bad accident.

Further analysis of heat loads dictated that a solid bar of Inconel X replace the proposed fibreglass on the wing leading edge due to its better strength and creep where temperatures of around 649°C (1,200°F) would be experienced. This would serve as a heat sink but it too came at a price. No longer would the leading edge sections be easily removed, as boasted in the proposal. The highest heat load would occur on re-entry but critical loads would be encountered during the initial power-on phase. And this brought an additional issue.

Calculations of thrust/mass ratios indicated a 5-g acceleration and to help the pilot an armrest would be provided with the stick-control handle. The improved method of flight control would now have a central stick for aerodynamic controls working through a SAS operating as a damper. A separate right-hand stick controller would be provided for aerodynamic and augmentation control but the left-hand stick would be retained for ballistic control during the high-altitude, unpowered phase. Counter-intuitively for pilots of conventional aircraft, it was noted that a motion to roll to the right would continue until an equal force in the opposite direction brought that motion to a stop.

In other papers, it was noted that simulator work displayed discouraging indications of uncontrollability without damping and that even with some damping it was only marginally controllable across certain manoeuvres. But free-flying models had vindicated NAA's decision to go with a roll-tail on the horizontal stabilisers, despite some aerodynamicists and engineers previously having questioned the stability of such a system. But overall, flight safety was deemed good and separate analysis of potential accidents showed that only 2 per cent would occur at high speed or high altitude. The flight control information fed to the safety analysis, further endorsing the pro-ejection seat lobby.

In summary, the conference had shown how experimental the X-15 programme was proving to be, with uncertainties about design details, further work being required to understand the material selected for its structure and how best to support the pilot with augmentation systems and rate damping. Much had still to be learned about the use of Inconel X, a new material about which there was little information regarding the best methods to use in its application. Overall, the

Below: The decision over whether to employ an ejection seat or an escape pod was fiercely contested, the latter being much preferred by the Air Force. This pushed Convair to develop the pod system for the B-58 Hustler, as shown here with a mock-up under test on a rocket sled, a concept recommended by the Air Force for the X-15. *Convair*

Above: North American Aviation had one of the largest business development programmes of the post-war period and would diversify from aircraft into electronics, rockets, missiles and spacecraft. Here a group of NAA test pilots pose for a formal shot in 1957, probably at the Downey, California, headquarters. *NAA*

conference papers helped industry come to terms with a completely new era in aircraft engineering with a complex set of requirements to satisfy.

Over the preceding year several design changes had already resulted from intensive definition of systems and subsystems, as well as with the overall shape of the aircraft and specific detail on the radius of leading and trailing edges of the wing and the tailplanes. As increasing amounts of data and analysis narrowed the anticipated heating loads, the diameter of the fuselage was increased by approximately 6 per cent. The horizontal stabilisers were moved back 13.7cm (5.4in) and the wing was moved forward 9.1cm (3.6in) with the centre of gravity moved forward 25.4cm (10in) to improve longitudinal stability.

Of significant, visual difference, the vertical stabiliser was increased in area by 50 per cent, revised to 6.96m^2 (75ft^2), the double-wedge dorsal and ventral fins being replaced by a single wedge shape of 10deg included angle, with the distribution adjusted 55/45 in surface area for the upper and lower elements respectively. Both were modified to incorporate rudders, rather than the dorsal stabiliser only, and both operated symmetrically to the point where the ventral stabiliser was jettisoned prior to landing.

The full-scale development mock-up was subject to a formal inspection on 12-13 December 1956. This time, of the 49 people in attendance, 34 were from the Air Force. Which was to be expected. Mock-up inspections were formal occasions for the Air Force and of the Air Force contingent, 22 were from the WADC. The Air Force committee was headed by Maj. E. C. Freeman from the ARDC and a single member was present from the Navy along with one representative from the NACA. There was little doubt that this was an Air Force project and it assigned Capt. Iven Kincheloe to the event, selected by the Air Force as their first X-15 pilot. Only three months previously he had flown the Bell X-2 to a height of 38,465m (126,200ft).

The scrutiny produced requests for 84 changes to the aircraft, of which 34 were either rejected or deferred until later scrutiny but these were minor issues related to preferences by the scrutineers rather than issues with the basic design of the aircraft. One sticking point was the absence of interchangeable wing leading edges, which Ames had wanted and which they considered to be a key feature enhancing the value of the NAA design. This issue failed to raise serious comment until the mock-up inspection and although there were valid grounds for restoring that capability the added weight and the increased complexity, given the shift to an Inconel X block, failed to get it restored.

In the 21 months between the first and the second industry conference, considerable development of the airframe and engine took place and North American was nearing completion of the first airframe when the second report to industry took place in Los Angeles on 28-29 July 1958. This was the presentation and review of Configuration 3, Configuration 1 being the proposal and Configuration 2 the product of the first industry review in July 1956. For the two-day event, 443 attendees with emphasis on engineering and technology development heard papers and discussed progress to what was a fluid programme developing on a very steep learning curve.

The conference heard 28 papers from North American,

the NACA, the WADC, the Air Force Flight Test Center, RMI and the Naval Aviation Medical Acceleration Laboratory. The intention of this conference was to convey a broad progress report on the X-15 project and to inform industry and service organisations about the pace and development in bringing the aircraft almost to completion in the preceding period since the Configuration 2 submission.

Checks and balances

Summarising the changes which had taken place since the first industry conference, NAA described the shorter side fairings to increase longitudinal stability, changes to the relative locations of the horizontal stabiliser and the wings, the increase in the area of the vertical stabiliser and significant improvements to the damper system. An all-moving directional control capability was added to the outer span of the dorsal and ventral stabilisers, the latter so as to ensure directional control at high angles of attack. To evade compounded flutter problems the speed brakes were moved to the fixed parts of the vertical stabilisers and reduced in surface area. There was also discussion about the load limits, now set at +4.0/-2.0- at fully loaded weight and +7.33/-3.0-g at 30 per cent propellant remaining. To avoid challenging weight limits, it was agreed that only one pull-up at 7.33-g would be acceptable per re-entry.

During the preceding year a lot of discussion had surrounded the instrumentation and the NACA had asked the Air Force to double the weight of equipment carried for research. That sparked a broad weight-saving programme which focused improvements to the propellant plumbing system and to the design of the nose gear. Feltz introduced the innovative idea of holding the strut under compression when stowed which simplified the overall design and saved significant weight.

Changes necessary to accommodate the additional loads the X-15 was now required to accept added 347kg (765lb) to the overall weight due to strengthened structural elements in the fuselage, wing and tailplane. Of this, 83.4kg (184lb) was in the empty weight and 263.5kg (581lb) was in the useful load the aircraft could carry. When assembly began, the additional empty weight had been reduced to 27.6kg (61lb) while the useful load had increased by 88.9kg (196lb), with research instrumentation increasing by 236.7kg (522lb). A significant number of improvements and weight-saving

Above: North American emerged from the Second World War with two jet projects at the forefront of development: the B-45C Tornado (A), the first US jet bomber to enter service, and (B) and the swept-wing YF-93 escort fighter, which took to the air in 1950 as a greatly reworked F-86 Sabre. The requirement was later dropped, but two YF-93s were delivered to the NACA and employed as chase aircraft until 1956. Further expansion of NAA technology applications came with the F-107A (C), a tactical fighter-bomber rework of the F-100 Super Sabre. First flown in 1956 it represented a new approach, with variable-area inlet duct, an all-flying vertical stabiliser and a recessed bomb bay. During the X-15 procurement process, NAA was also developing the A-5 Vigilante (D), which took to the air in 1958 as a Mach 2 nuclear-capable bomber of which 167 were built for the US Navy. *NAA*

measures had made this possible.

Significantly, the number of intermediate spars in the wings had increased from seven to 15 which, together with a reduction in the skin gauge and the decision to replace the titanium-carbide/nickel leading edge with Inconel X, saved 4.9kg (11lb) in weight. However, applying the same switch in materials for the leading edge of the tail bought a weight deficit of 7.7kg (17lb). By chemically milling pockets in the outer skin, reducing skin gauge, incorporating Z-stiffeners and switching aluminium for Inconel X in sections of the intermediate propellant tank bulkheads a net weight reduction of 39.4kg (87lb) was achieved. A further weight saving of 5.4kg (12lb) was obtained by replacing four speed-brake actuators with two connected by a common linkage.

Conferees heard that the weight of the engine had grown by 134kg (296lb) and the decision to fit an engine purge system added a further 30.4kg (67lb), the latter incorporating a weight saving of 13.1kg (29lb) in plumbing for the LOX system to produce a net increase of 17.2kg (38lb). Reported too was a 1.8kg (4lb) growth in the weight of the APU and by this date the weight of the fixed equipment such as ejection seat, instruments, nitrogen pressurisation system and the air conditioning system had grown by 4kg (9lb). Most of the decrease in the latter two systems had been offset by a significant increase in the first three, notably the ejection seat which had an increase of 34.4kg (76lb).

A major part in monitoring progress in any new aircraft is the net mass increase or decrease in both empty and loaded weights. It was particularly acute with the X-15 and as the development programme progressed, changes to what is referred to as the 'useful load' were effected. Monopropellant for the turbopump was reduced by 88.9kg (196lb), the quantity of allocated propellants trapped in the engine grew by 31.7kg (70lb), the quantity of helium for propellant tank pressurisation grew by 5.9kg (13lb) while the nitrogen allocated to pressurisation of the cockpit increased by 37.2kg (82lb).

The original specification cited a design target of 4,713kg (10,390lb) for the empty weight, raised to 4,796kg (10,974lb),

Below: While working the X-15 contract, pressing activity on a future Mach 3 bomber was getting underway at Boeing in a study with RAND to follow its MX-2145 concept study. North American entered the resulting competition in 1955 and would get the contract to build the XB-70A, shown here at Edwards. Two were built but the intense effort put in by NAA threatened to floor the X-15 contract. *NASA*

against which the Configuration 3 design came out at 4,824kg (10,635lb). The original target for the loaded weight was 13,839kg (30,510lb), revised up to 14,186kg (31,275lb), with NAA delivering a weight of 14,362kg (31,662lb). Equipped for the high-speed profile, 167.8kg (370lb) of equipment specifically related to high-altitude flights could be removed, bringing the gross weight for that requirement down to within 7.7kg (17lb) of the updated specification, an increase of 0.05 per cent on the baseline target.

A major point of discussion was the delay in developing the XLR-99, the primary propulsion system for the X-15, which represented one of the greatest achievements of Reaction Motors Incorporated and which, as noted earlier, evolved out of the XLR-30 from the Viking programme. At the time of the second industry conference in July 1958, the first engine firing at Edwards was still a year and more away. The first powered flight with this engine would not take place until November 1960. Conferees heard that two XLR-11-RM-5 engines would provide power for the initial flights, as had already been decided.

But from an engineering perspective, the basic challenges faced by design engineers were the high heat loads to be encountered on high-speed flights, and on re-entry from high-altitude runs out of the sensible atmosphere. Those aspects of the programme will be dealt with in the next chapter, where discussion of the engineering and systems layout can be found.

Above: Decisions over a carrier-plane focused on two prime candidates, including the Convair B-36 which had already debuted a parasitic role for the RF-84K Thunderflash – proposed and tested as a means of conveying a reconnaissance aircraft to enemy airspace. *Convair*

Right: A schematic showing how the rear of the aircraft could be raised to accommodate an X-15 semi-recessed within the aircraft's capacious bomb bay. *Convair*

Carrier-plane options

Three of the four proposals to build the X-15 opted for the Convair B-36 as the carrier-plane. That preference was maintained by the Air Force and the NACA until early 1957 when the Joint Operations Committee began to examine alternative options. They were worried that the B-36 would not achieve required levels of stability in flight for the drop and, with the performance of the X-15 beginning to degrade slightly due to weight increases and other factors, a faster drop speed would buy back some of the loss. Also, with the aircraft due to be phased out of service as a strategic bomber, the availability of spares and maintenance issues could slow flight operations. And there were additional pros and cons.

The cavernous interior of the B-36 provided plenty of space for the associated support equipment and for the propellant top-off tanks during the long climb to its drop altitude. The proposed flight plan would have the B-36 release the X-15 at any altitude anywhere between 9,144m (30,000ft)

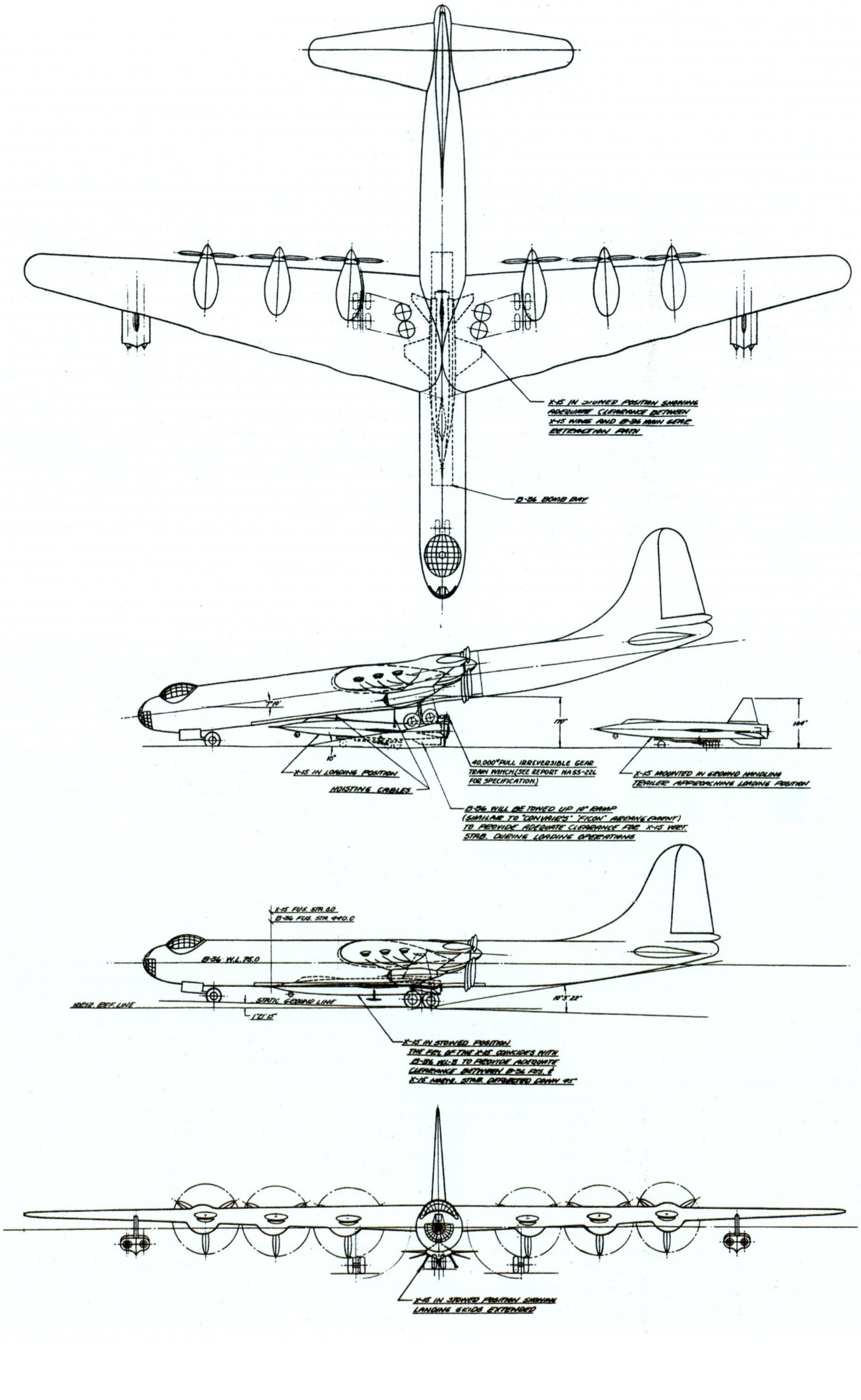
X-15 IN STOWED POSITION SHOWING ADEQUATE CLEARANCE BETWEEN X-15 WINGS AND B-36 MAIN GEAR RETRACTION PATH
B-36 BOMB BAY
7°10'
170"
164"
10°
X-15 IN LOADING POSITION
HOISTING CABLES
40,000# PULL IRREVERSIBLE GEAR TRAIN WINCH (SEE REPORT NA55-226 FOR SPECIFICATION.)
X-15 MOUNTED IN GROUND HANDLING TRAILER APPROACHING LOADING POSITION
B-36 WILL BE TOWED UP 10° RAMP (SIMILAR TO "CONVAIR'S" "FICON" ARRANGEMENT) TO PROVIDE ADEQUATE CLEARANCE FOR X-15 VERT. STAB. DURING LOADING OPERATIONS
X-15 FUS. STA. 0.0
B-36 FUS. STA. 440.0
B-36 W.L. 75.0
HORIZ. REF. LINE
STATIC GROUND LINE
10°5'22"
X-15 IN STOWED POSITION
X-15 IN STOWED POSITION SHOWING LANDING SKIDS EXTENDED

and 15,240m (50,000ft). Several different methods of loading the X-15 into the carrier-plane were considered, although no one liked the pit method adopted for the earlier X-series research aircraft. The sheer size of the new rocket plane and the possible accumulation of toxic and potentially explosive fumes made that method unwise. One method only briefly considered was to remove the dorsal stabiliser section, move the X-15 under the B-36, lift the aircraft into the bay and re-attach the fin. Repeated removal and reattachment brought its own threat of weakened structural interface and that too was quickly rejected.

The only plausible solution was to reverse the B-36 up two sloping ramps with an inclination of 10deg, aligned with the track of the main landing gear so that the aft end was raised sufficiently high off the ground to allow the X-15 to be moved beneath the fuselage and then winched into position. This scheme was incorporated into the Project 1226 brochure and at that time the X-15 had a vertical stabiliser tip height of 4.17m (13.7ft) above ground level with the aircraft standing on its landing gear.

While the B-36 had all the technical requirements to carry the X-15 it did require the removal of bulkhead No 7 so as to open up the combined voids of bomb bays 2 and 3, together with additional stiffening members for maintaining structural integrity. With this modification the X-15 could be accommodated in bomb bays 1, 2 and 3. A special compartment would be installed in the forward section of bay No 1 to provide a means by which the X-15 pilot could access his cockpit in flight. The X-15 would be restrained inside the bomb bays by means of a forward fixture behind the cockpit and by two shackle points, one on each wing spar, all three of which would be severed by explosive bolts to release the rocket plane. Special provision was also made for engineering access to the X-15 in flight and during the cruise to altitude, a luxury not afforded to the earlier X-series.

Although the B-36 was more than capable of lifting the X-15 to drop altitude and had more generous and better comfort conditions than the aircraft used to launch previous rocket planes, there were some aspects which were not ideal. Conceived in the early 1940s and brought into service with Strategic Air Command in June 1948, it remained operational with SAC until 1958, when it was withdrawn as its successor, the B-52, became the sole intercontinental strategic bomber.

Below: A close-up of the B-36 being loaded with an RF-84, though this weighed much less than the X-15 and was considerably smaller. Consideration of the B-36 as an X-15 carrier-plane hinged on availability, maintainability and durability, none of which were considered sufficiently robust to warrant its selection, particularly at a time when the bomber variant was coming to the end of its service life. *USAF*

Powered by six reciprocating engines and four turbojets this 'six-turning/four-burning' behemoth was a hybrid blending the old technology of World War Two – with piston engines and high-explosive bombs – with the jet age and nuclear weapons.

It had an exceptionally high aspect ratio wing for an aircraft of this type, which gave the B-36 (informally named Peacekeeper) an operating ceiling greater than 16,764m (50,000ft) but with a cruising speed of only 362kph (225mph) and a maximum speed of 706kph (439mph). Complex to operate, expensive to maintain and not noted for its reliability or serviceability, the B-36 had its days rooted firmly in the time when America thought it would have to fight Germany from the continental United States to liberate Nazi occupied Europe and the United Kingdom.

Yet the B-36 had a track record for carrying aircraft. In 1953 it successfully demonstrated that it could carry a Republic RF-84F, semi-submerged within the bomb bay and attached to a trapeze which would be lowered to allow the aircraft to detach and conduct free-flying reconnaissance missions before returning for retrieval and safe carriage back to base. The extraordinary range of the B-36 prompted plans to use it as a 'flying airfield', transporting short-range, high-speed reconnaissance fighters to carry out low level photography over enemy territory. In all, 12 B-36 aircraft were modified for this role along with 25 RF-84F Thunderflash fighters.

Tests were also conducted with similar Thunderflash aircraft operating as escort fighters, attached wingtip-to-wingtip with the B-36 which would be released in hostile skies to protect the bombers from enemy attack. This programme was known as the Fighter-Conveyor (FICON) programme but it pressed the concept too far. When trials with two converted EF-84B aircraft formed up on a modified B-29 and brought the three-plane assembly crashing down on 24 April 1953 that application was placed in serious doubt. However, some tests were successfully completed with two RF-84Fs attached to the wing tips of a B-36 before the project was abandoned.

But there were practical reasons for raising concerns about the B-36 as an X-15 carrier-plane. In addition to the suspicion that it would be unstable with the rocket plane attached, and with little or no performance excess, there would be no margin or potential to compensate for any overweight condition as the X-15 went from blueprint to metal. Managers knew only too well from their experience with the B-29 and B-50 carrier-planes used with the early X-series and the Skyrocket that as aircraft went out of service, parts were increasingly hard to come by and maintenance became a problem.

So it was that by early 1957 the Joint Operations Committee began looking for a more suitable alternative and three candidates were short-listed: the Convair B-58 Hustler, the Boeing KC-135 Stratotanker and the Boeing B-52 Superfortress.

The B-58 was an interesting, if not exciting, proposition. Designed as the B-36 was entering service with SAC, this Mach 3 four-jet high altitude delta-wing bomber made its first flight in November 1956. It had the unusual arrangement of carrying its bomb load in a pod beneath the area-rule fuselage which incorporated fuel for the outbound flight and which could be jettisoned along with the nuclear bomb. A later adaptation provided a double-pod arrangement in a single conformal structure whereby the lower pod containing fuel would be jettisoned first, exposing either reconnaissance sensors or a weapon. The prodigious fuel consumption dictated this design concept but it was certainly unique in post-war bombers.

If utilised as a carrier-plane both the wing span and the tail assembly on the X-15 would conflict with the B-58's main landing gear retraction cycle and, if moved forward to avoid this interference, the nose leg on the B-58 would have to be moved forward. Bizarrely, B-58 advocates even suggested that a lengthened nose leg for the X-15 could serve as a forward gear for the mated assembly, leaving the carrier-plane's nose leg retracted until the X-15 had been released. Moreover, the inboard engines would have had to be moved further out, and the X-15 vertical stabiliser would have to fold until the rocket plane was dropped, because there was no place for it on the underside of the carrier-plane.

To get a pilot's view on its suitability, Neil Armstrong went to Convair to examine the concept and quickly found it to be full of problems. A really serious concern was the weight of the X-15 compared to that which the aircraft had been designed to operate with. The B-58 pod weighed 13,600kg (30,000lb) at take-off and only 7,250kg (16,000lb) when jettisoned, the difference being fuel it contained which was consumed prior to release – a novel form of 'staging'! The B-58 had not been cleared for heavier separation weights. An entirely separate set of development tests would be required to clear the heavier X-15 for effective separation from the B-58 at supersonic speeds. This was clearly adding to the complexity and cost of the application and the B-58 was eliminated as a carrier-plane contender.

The four-jet KC-135 Stratotanker was a vaguely preferable contender over the B-58, if only for its availability and performance. It was developed from the Boeing 707 commercial airliner, which integrated technical and engineering lessons from the B-47 and B-52 bomber projects. Adapted as a cargo-tanker for the US Air Force, the KC-135 made its first flight in August 1956 and entered military service less than a year later. As a low-wing aircraft with a relatively short undercarriage, it was not suitable for carrying the X-15 under the fuselage and there was no ability for an under-wing option. It was quickly rejected. Which left the B-52 as the only viable candidate after the B-36.

The B-52 carrier-plane

The B-52 had been designed between 1945 and 1948, when Boeing received a contract to build prototypes. Initially conceived to carry four turboprop engines, it matured into an eight-jet, swept-wing, long range bomber and made its first flight in October 1952. Three years later it entered service with Strategic Air Command and became the mainstay of the nuclear strike force, eventually becoming one leg of the nuclear triad which also embraced land-based and submarine-launched ballistic missiles. In 1957 it was available, in full scale production and had a ready-made supply line to parts and spares.

As a high-wing aircraft it made possible the carriage of the X-15 on a pylon placed inboard of the inner pair of Pratt

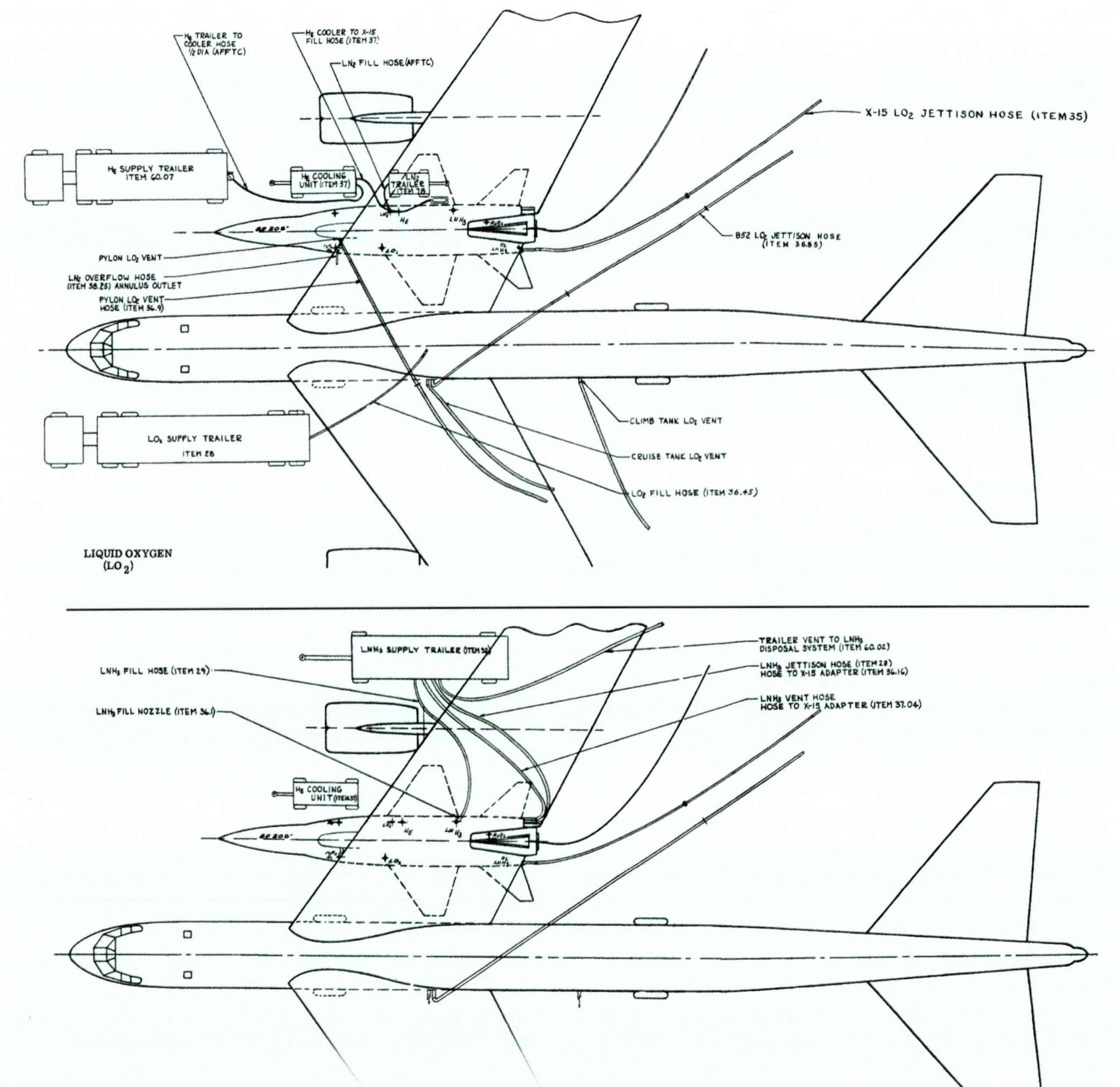

Above: Propellant and fluid delivery lines and conduits are plotted on this plan view of the B-52 and an X-15, now suitably identified as being carried under the starboard wing. *NACA*

& Whitney J57 turbojet engines, a position which had never been possible with other aircraft. It was a location already under analysis for a pylon carrying air-to-surface missiles and in May 1957 further investigations began into its suitability for the X-15. From the outset, the sheer performance of the B-52 was in its favour. With a cruise speed of more than 804kph (500mph) – more than twice that of the B-36 – and a maximum speed of 965kph (600mph), it would spend less time getting to the drop zone and achieving the necessary altitude and it would add a considerable amount to the launch speed of the X-15, especially when compared with the B-36.

The only carriage position for the X-15 was the underside of an inboard wing section as there was no space beneath the aircraft to mount it semi-submerged within the bomb bays. But the unique tandem arrangement of the aircraft's main landing gear meant that this potential obstacle was well away from underslung appendages, which also made the B-52 suitable for carrying cruise missiles and stand-off weapons for which studies were already well underway. The B-52 had four main landing gear legs, each with two wheels. A single set of legs were attached each side of the fuselage, forward and aft of the bomb bays, each leg rotating around and up into bays inside the fuselage. Outrigger stabilisers were located at each wing tip to keep the aircraft's wings level on the ground. It was an ideal configuration for a role as carrier-plane.

Several modifications would be required, not least the trailing edge cut-out required to provide space for the X-15 vertical stabiliser. The wing pylon suspension point would be located at a position 18 per cent out on the semi-span of the starboard wing. Other modifications would be required to

Above left: The X-15 would be carried snug inside the shoe-shaped pylon at a hard point already designed into the B-52 for carrying the Hound Dog cruise weapon.
Above right: A cut-out on the trailing edge flap of the B-52's wing was necessary to accommodate the X-15's fixed vertical stabiliser. *NASA*

install two liquid oxygen tanks of 3,795lit (1,000USgall) and 1,897.5lit (500USgall) in place of the forward fuel tank and to allow installation of fluid and gas lines. The mid-body fuel tank was also taken out to accommodate 15 nitrogen and nine helium storage cylinders, as was the No. 3 right wing fuel tank for installation of pylon fittings and support structures to front and rear spars.

The inboard flaps were disconnected and bolted closed to facilitate the inboard cut-out for the X-15's vertical stabiliser. The pylon itself carried hydraulic and pneumatic lines for release of the X-15. The forward fuselage fuel cell was removed to provide space for access to a variety of fluid and pressure lines in the wing as well as additional equipment for a liquid nitrogen supply line for cooling the stable platform in the X-15. Breathing oxygen supplied to the B-52 crew was tapped off for use by the X-15 pilot prior to release.

It is all too easy to under-emphasise the number of changes required at an engineering level and all too difficult to over-emphasise the amount of work required to equip the B-52 as the X-15 carrier-plane. Several assumptions were made initially that were changed after further calculation or test and these are reflected in the catalogue of work packages during the conversion of each aircraft. Initially, a pressurised observer station had been planned for the bomb bay but largely as a legacy from previous experience with the B-29 and B-50 carrier-planes for X-1, X-2 and Skyrocket. When that was finally deleted, the space originally planned for that station became the location for the LOX top-off tank.

Two TV cameras were installed in special streamlined fairings on the right side of the fuselage, with the rear camera and zoom lens pointing forward and a fixed-length forward camera to show the forward fuselage of the X-15. The launch operator had monitors to control selection of images and floodlights and 16mm motion film cameras were also installed. The B-52 flight deck was modified to include a launch panel to the lower left of the main instrument display, which was also required to contain an emergency jettison handle. The launch operator console was on the right on the upper rear flight deck, replacing the bomber's electronic countermeasures station.

Considerable debate surrounded the inevitable consequence of hanging the X-15 out on a pylon – the pilot would have to ingress the cockpit before flight and remain there until the aircraft was back on the ground. This had never been necessary on previous rocket plane programmes and NAA gave particular attention to the physical stresses of being in the X-15 for the 1.5 hours it would take to climb out and reach altitude before the drop. Scott Crossfield addressed the ergonomic issue from the outset and provision was made to use the ejection seat at any point it was occupied by the pilot from the ground up – the forward section of the X-15 fuselage being well forward of the leading edge of the wing on the B-52. This also answered concerns about pilot safety in the event of a fire or some other emergency after he entered the cockpit.

There had been debate too about where to hang the wing pylon and the initial recommendation was to the port side of the fuselage. A number of tests were conducted on that assumption. Then, for some not entirely understood reason, it was changed to the starboard wing position on the basis, it was said, that this would ease servicing of the X-15. There is some justification for that based on the preferred disposition of ground servicing vehicles. No further tests were required to validate the concept and so the decision was made to hang the rocket plane under the right wing.

The dorsal stabiliser on the X-15 would protrude into a slot cut out of the wing trailing edge of the B-52. There was a 61cm (24in) gap between the two and any significant roll moment on the X-15 as it separated could result in contact. During flight tests with the mated configuration there was indeed a tendency for the X-15 to roll to the right. This was because of the proximity of the rocket plane's starboard wing to the leading edge of the B-52 wing due to its sweep angle. This asymmetry in the relative position of the X-15's lifting surfaces sent airflow from the B-52 downward rather than over the rocket plane's starboard wing, causing the roll.

Calculations showed that the X-15 could roll up to 20deg as it dropped the 0.76m (2.5ft) to clear the wing and for this reason the X-15 flight controls were in neutral allowing the automatic dampers to null the roll dispersion. Films of the X-15 dropping away from the carrier-plane show this characteristic tendency for it to drop its right wing immediately after separation. The optimised range of settings to achieve that safely was evaluated by Scott Crossfield on his early flight tests and a recommended set were handed to future pilots.

When the NACA discussed availability of B-52s with the Air Force they were offered two prototypes, the XB-52 (49-230) and the YB-52 (49-231), but this posed certain problems for HSFS. The two prototypes were non-standard aircraft and had certain differences to the initial production aircraft, the B-52A. The tandem cockpit arrangement on the two prototypes, reminiscent of the B-47, was replaced by the more conventional side-by-side seating of all future variants. Some systems too were changed and the extensive flight evaluation upon which the NACA relied for air vehicle performance data had been more meticulously conducted on the production version. Moreover, underwing pylon studies for missile carriage had not been conducted on the prototypes.

Worried about spares and maintenance on a seriously non-standard design of which only two had been built, the Air Force acquiesced and at meetings on 18-19 June 1957 formal approval was given to use the B-52 as the X-15 carrier-plane. Two months later the Air Force agreed to release two early production models, a B-52A-1-BO (52-003), given over to the programme in October, and an RB-52B-10-BO (52-008) assigned to the NACA in May 1958. These two aircraft had been used by the Air Force for defensive fire control tests and were flown to North American for conversion. The B-52A arrived at Palmdale Plant 42 on 29 November 1957 for modifications and delivery to Edwards, completed on 14 November 1958, from whence it was known as the NB-52A and named *The High and Mighty*. The RB-52B was flown to NAA on 5 January 1959 and, as NB-52B, to Edwards where it arrived on 8 June 1959, briefly named *The Challenger*.

Tests to qualify the pylon which would be used to carry the X-15 were added to the existing trials on the pylon being designed to carry the Hound Dog missile. The X-15 mock-up was used to conduct vibration analyses. These included tests on a special steel frame which was attached to the interior of the wing to provide a rigid attachment. Results were used to carry out flutter tests on a scale model in a low-speed wind tunnel. The results confirmed that excessive flutter would not be encountered at the operating speed of the mated configuration.

Concern was also expressed that the jet efflux from the two inboard engines on the starboard wing (nos 5 and 6) could impinge on the tail area of the X-15 and that acoustic loads could seriously affect the rocket plane's fatigue life. Initially at least, throttle settings on those two engines were restricted to no more than 50 per cent of rated power. But this was a compromise which was not ideal for the operating requirements of the carrier-plane. NAA engineers raised the fatigue life hours in the X-15 by increasing the rivet diameter in the vertical stabilisers and by the use of dimple-skin construction over countersunk rivets. Changes were also made to the horizontal stabiliser but these were introduced after flight trials began as retrofit on the three X-15s.

A range of flight conditions were tested once trials began with the full scale X-15. Stabiliser settings on the B-52 were optimised only after different trim angles had been tested. Fuel was added to the starboard wing to simulate a fully loaded X-15 and a trim angle of 2deg nose up was required to get the aircraft to unstick at the predicted take-off roll of 3,200m (10,500ft). Normally, a fully loaded B-52 would rotate with zero degrees trim. Landings too were made by letting down on the rear paired legs rather than on all four and lowering the nose on to the forward legs, a practice which brought a noticeable jolt!

Below: The definitive general arrangement and the selection of a suitable carrier-plane moved the X-15 programme into top gear during 1955 as the manufacturing and flight planning teams set to work. *NACA*

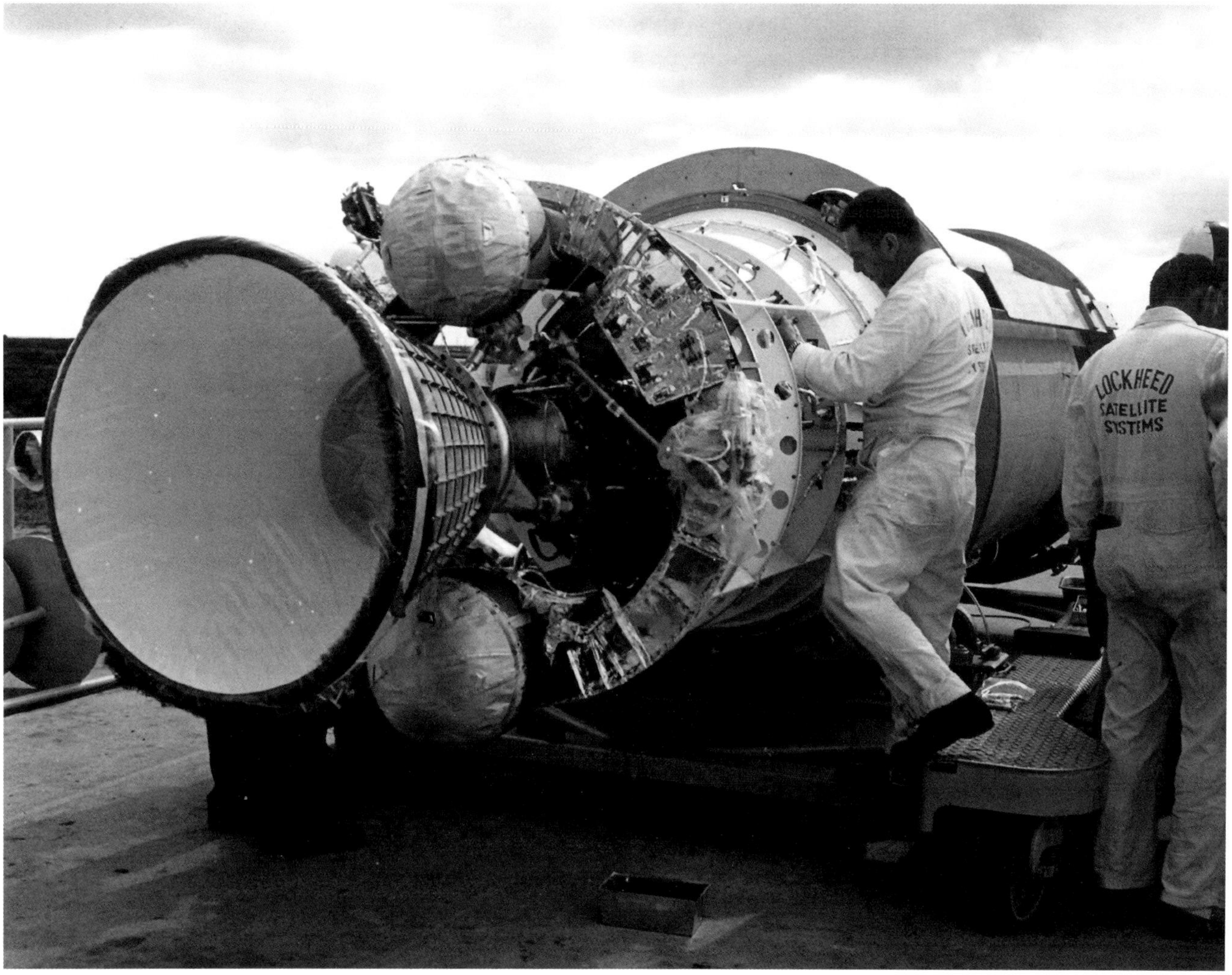

Chapter Twelve

X-15 Propulsion

When consideration had first been given to the requirements for a hypersonic research aircraft the choice of rocket motor had been problematical. High thrust engines simply did not exist, yet the power required to push an X-plane to speeds in excess of Mach 5 required a sea-level thrust of at least 222.4kN (50,000lb). Also, it had to be possible to vary the thrust output of the rocket to adjust the power-to-weight ratio as propellant was consumed. Most important, it had to be man-rated for operation where a human was carried throughout the propulsive stage.

Initially, this was a largely undefined level of reliability demanding extraordinarily high standards of quality control and test to prevent a catastrophic disaster and loss of life. In the mid-1950s, risk mitigation in rocket motor engineering was compounded by a high level of failure in rocket motors large and small. Levels hard to fully appreciate today, where performance and reliability are well defined, predictable and largely understood. Erratic performance, combustion instability and the lack of instrumented monitoring standards led to high failure rates, compounding the difficulty in selecting a single source for reliable performance.

For the initial experimental, rocket-powered aircraft described in Section 1, the problem of thrust had been solved by using the RMI 6000C4 (XLR-11), a cluster of four separate combustion chambers each delivering a fixed thrust of 6,670N (1,500lb), selectively ignited to cumulatively provide integral steps in total power output. Initially, as described earlier, the

Above: Developed for the B-58 Hustler weapons pod, the Bell Aerosystems XLR-81 was an unlikely contender for powering the X-15. With a fixed thrust, three would have been needed for the required power output. With a design thrust of 66.7kN (15,000lb), it was used by the Agena rocket stage as shown here but for the X-15 it would have been significantly de-rated to increase reliability. *USAF*

Left: A more promising contender, the RMI's XLR-10-RM2 emerged from the Viking rocket programme, with a thrust of 92.5kN (20,800lb) it was the largest rocket motor of its time and had the first application of a gimbal to vector thrust. *Author's collection*

NACA's Langley laboratory had proposed the use of three General Electric Hermes A-3A motors, each delivering a thrust of approximately 80kN (18,000lb) clustered so as to provide the necessary thrust.

The Hermes A-3A was a proposed US Army tactical ballistic missile of which seven were launched between March 1953 and January 1954, only two of which were successful. Hermes was cancelled in 1954 and the requirement was handed to Wernher von Braun who produced the Redstone missile. With lacklustre performance and a comparatively unsatisfactory, stepped method of adjusting thrust, the Hermes motor was rejected. The search for a suitable engine to power the X-15 began in 1954 when the Air Force, the Navy and the NACA short-listed four candidate rocket motors.

These included the Aerojet XLR-73, the Bell XLR-81, the North American NA-5400, and the RMI XLR-10. None of these produced the desired thrust alone, three of the four would need clustering and one held promise of future development which got everyone's attention. The XLR-73-AJ-1 had a single combustion chamber producing a thrust of 44.48kN (10,000lb) on a mixture of jet fuel and white fuming nitric acid (WFNA) propellants. Aerojet claimed that by fitting a different expansion skirt, or nozzle, the motor could be uprated to produce a thrust of 52.26kN (11,750lb). It could, they said, be shut down and re-ignited with an electrical system and it could be throttled between 50 per cent and 100 per cent of maximum thrust. To achieve the required thrust, the X-15 would have to incorporate at least four of these motors.

The XLR-81-BA-1 had been developed as part of the B-58 Hustler programme and was to have been used in the weapons pod to propel it some distance from the release point and allow the Hustler to turn around, which was highly desirable for its survival since it was delivering a nuclear weapon. Operating on a mixture of jet fuel and red fuming nitric acid (RFNA), it had a fixed thrust of 51.15kN (11,500lb) at sea level and 66.7kN (15,000lb) at an altitude of 21,336m (70,000ft). The downside to this engine was that it was not restartable and that it too would require a cluster of at least four motors to produce the required amount of thrust. Within a few years this motor would be developed into the propulsion system for the Agena rocket stage and into a series of evolving, and increasingly powerful upper stages which would be used in the space programme for several decades.

The NA-5400 had nothing going for it and its inclusion by the Power Plant Laboratory as a potential candidate for the X-15 is surprising since it was little more than an assembly of experimental parts leading toward a motor which would, theoretically, have produced a thrust of 24kN (5,400lb), which defined its designation. It operated on a propellant mixture of jet fuel and hydrogen peroxide and employed a catalyst to effect the hypergolic reaction. Like the XLR-73, it could be restarted electrically but it had a fixed thrust and employed a turbopump driven by decomposed hydrogen peroxide, one sufficiently powerful however to service three chambers.

The most interesting of all the candidates recommended by the Power Plant Laboratory was the RMI XLR-10, not because it held great promise but because it formed the basis for a projected version, the XLR-30. The XLR-10 operated on a mix of liquid oxygen and alcohol to produce a thrust of 92.5kN (20,800lb) and it had a reliable record with the Viking sounding rocket, propelling packages of science instruments to great altitude and outside the Earth's atmosphere since 1949. It was adopted for the Vanguard satellite launcher which, in 1956, was still in the development stage, anticipating the launch of the world's first artificial satellite as the US contribution to the International Geophysical Year.

Although the XLR-10 was not restartable, neither was the more powerful 'Super Viking' motor which RMI designated Viking II and which the Pentagon knew as the XLR-30. The Viking rocket and the Vanguard satellite launcher had a substantial input from the US Navy and in 1950 the Navy Bureau of Aeronautics reported to the Secretary of Defense that they were working on a modified Viking with greater performance capability which would require a thrust of 222.4kN (50,000lb), informing them that this work had started a year earlier. But the same pronouncement also identified a much smaller engine, the XLR-22, with a thrust of 22.24kN (5,000lb) powered by liquid oxygen and ammonia and incorporating regenerative cooling whereby thin tubes appropriately shaped would form the structure of the combustion chamber and the expansion skirt.

RMI had been the pioneer in regenerative cooling, the company's Edward A. Neu Jr. originating this concept in 1947. Identified by RMI as the XLR-22-RM-2 Bleed Turbine Turbo Rocket, it was designed as propulsion for short-range missiles or as supplementary power for a jet-powered combat aircraft. This so-called 'spaghetti' arrangement of cooling tubes dispensed with a separate cooling jacket and saved weight while significantly increasing performance and design efficiency. It was 50 per cent lighter than an equivalent motor designed for the same purpose and the concept quickly caught on, becoming the standard for most rocket motors by the mid-1960s. Various methods for shaping and fixing the tubes were

Right: The XLR-10 evolved into the XLR-30-RM-2, the pressure for development of which had been at the urging of the Navy for a rocket motor to power a submarine launched ballistic missile. *RMI*

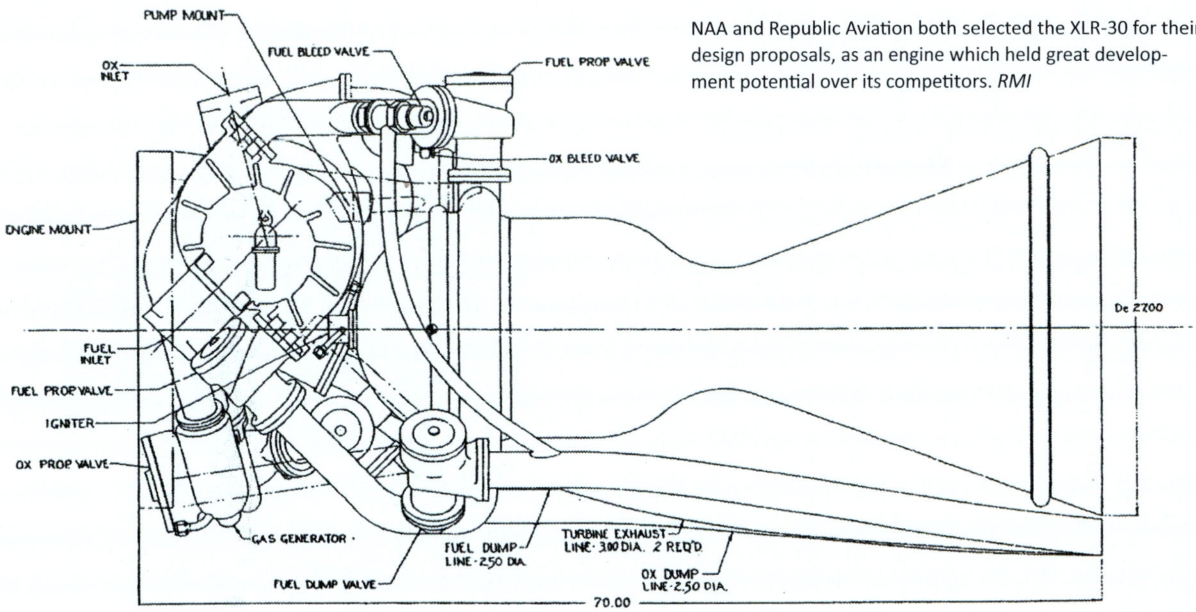

NAA and Republic Aviation both selected the XLR-30 for their design proposals, as an engine which held great development potential over its competitors. *RMI*

tested, the preferred way being to braze the separate tubes together in the forming process. Because of its efficiency overall, this technology was incorporated into the XLR-30, which some came to regard as an enlarged development of the XLR-22.

The other merging of technology applications was the switch from LOX/alcohol of the XLR-10 to a LOX/ammonia combination which was, just conceivably, first proposed by Austrian chemist Dr. Paul F. Winternitz, who, after he arrived to work for RMI, prepared a range of exotic chemical cocktails as propellant combinations including boranes, which eventually found their way as additives into more conventional rocket propellants. This was a time of expanding research in new formula for efficient combinations of oxidiser and fuel for liquid propellant rocket motors. The growth in applications showed no sign of diminishing as ballistic missiles and motors, from which the space launch industry grew, expanded in capability and performance.

RMI applied several innovative technologies to the new XLR-10 derivative, including the bleed turbine design in which gases were diverted from the main combustion chamber and diluted with fuel to reduce the temperature for driving the turbine. Added to the higher efficiency of the LOX/ammonia propellant combination and the regenerative cooling, the bleed turbine presaged a new generation of RMI motors which were industry leaders in their day. So much interest surrounded the Super Viking motor that the Naval Research Laboratory and the Naval Air Rocket Test Station became involved and began testing the new designs while supporting the work of the design team by starting their own parallel test programme, defined under Project PP207.

By April 1951 the Navy was satisfied that the job of designing an effective rocket motor with a thrust of 222.4kN (50,000lb) was complete and the XLR-30 emerged with a length of 136cm (53.6in), an external diameter of 74cm (29in) with a chamber diameter of 37cm (14.7in) and a weight of 109.7kg (242lb). Parallel work on the new technologies continued apace on the XLR-22 and its bleed system and on 15 February 1952 the Navy Bureau of Aeronautics announced its formal clearance by designating the XLR-10 derivative as the XLR-30-RM-2.

Despite its promise, the developed version of the XLR-10 for an advanced Viking rocket languished on the shelf and the host which it would have propelled never materialised. Instead, the XLR-30 was submitted to the Navy as a propulsion system for a submarine-launched ballistic missile. The Navy

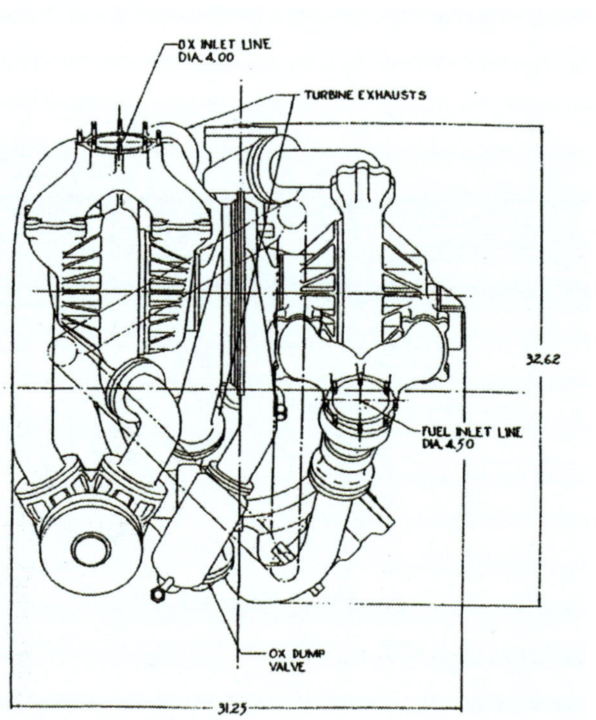

Right: The compact turbopump was designed for the XLR-30 to support a throttle range for the manned X-15 and the projected lower thrust level of 30% was set for safety. *RMI*

had researched the possibility of firing a medium-size rocket from the gently wallowing deck of a ship at sea when it flew Viking rocket No 4 from the deck of the USS *Norton Sound* on 11 May 1950, and the Navy was also interested in carrying ballistic missiles aboard submarines, conducting analyses on a variety of ways this could be achieved. Notwithstanding the destructive effect of the exhaust efflux, rocket motors bring unique hazards to ships at sea, particularly submarines where contained environments are not sympathetic to toxic gases. The ammonia fuel for the XLR-30 was a problem and in February 1953 the Navy Bureau of Aeronautics issued a memorandum drawing attention to a report identifying those concerns. The motor appears again in reports dated June 1954 where the XLR-30 is still in consideration for a 'medium range ballistic missile', although reports that the motor was in 'full scale development' may have been a slight exaggeration.

For all its interest in ballistic missiles fired from surface vessels, and its interest in submarine-launched rockets, development of its own ballistic missile would not receive official sanction from the Pentagon before September 1955 when Secretary of Defense Charles Wilson decreed that the Navy would cooperate with the Army in development of the SM-78 Jupiter. Capable of being launched from land or the deck of a ship, the Navy was unhappy about the prospect of carrying missiles powered by liquid propellants on ships. With the substantial reduction in the size of nuclear weapons, and the development of nuclear-powered propulsion, the Navy began studies of a solid propellant missile which could be carried in submarines.

Named Jupiter S, this matured into the Polaris programme and in December 1956 the Navy pulled out of the cooperative venture with the Army and transferred its interest in the Jupiter missile to the Air Force. Jupiter would emerge as a land-based missile with a range of 2,844km (1,767mls) powered by a Rocketdyne S-3 engine, ending US Navy involvement with liquid propellant rockets for its ballistic missiles. Polaris was an outstanding success with a fast track development which had the first nuclear powered submarine on station on 15 November 1960, when the USS *George Washington* went on patrol.

XLR-30 development

The Air Force and the NACA had agreed that the airframe and engine contracts would be awarded separately but that the engine preferences of the airframe bidders would be honoured. Unless technical difficulties along the way prevented that and some alternative was necessary. As noted earlier, when the four bids came in they were split evenly between the Bell XLR-81 and the RMI XLR-30. Bell (naturally) and Republic Aviation chose the XLR-81 while Douglas Aircraft and NAA chose the XLR-30. The NA-5400 and the Aerojet XLR-73 were rejected.

Bell emphasised that they were taking a cautionary approach and their proposal was to integrate three substantially modified XLR-81 chambers, each of which was capable of delivering a thrust of 35.58kN (8,000lb) for the rated 64.5kN (14,500lb). These were different thrust ratings to the standard XLR-81 as designed but de-rating was suggested to improve safety, considering that it was for a manned aircraft and not an unmanned projectile. Thrust levels offered for the cluster of three Bell motors were 35.58kN (8,000lb), 64.5kN (14,500lb), and 193.5kN (43,500lb), the latter by maximum thrust on all three motors. The motors would be grouped together within the rear fuselage and operated separately, albeit with less thrust than the original specification had implied would be necessary. Nevertheless, Bell calculated that they could deliver the fastest aircraft of all four contenders for the airframe contract.

Bell did some work with their engine division to determine the optimum propellant combination, from the standpoint of engine performance and that of the airframe contractor. They suggested a change in propellant combinations from RFNA and jet fuel to a mixture known as JP-X, diluting the latter to 40 per cent unsymmetrical dimethyl hydrazine (UDMH) and 60 per cent jet fuel. The RFNA remained as the oxidiser which can be stored at room temperature and therefore does not rely on cryogenic liquid oxygen.

Among other reasons, the use of a storable propellant combination also persuaded Republic Aviation to select the XLR-81 but this proposal adopted four motors of this type, raising the maximum thrust level to 258kN (58,000lb) while retaining the intermediate thrust output provided by the three-motor configuration of the Bell airframe proposal. Bell had a clear interest in having their engine selected for the X-15 and were quick to point out that it eliminated the need for a LOX topping off system in the carrier plane. They also pointed out that because the propellants were hypergolic,

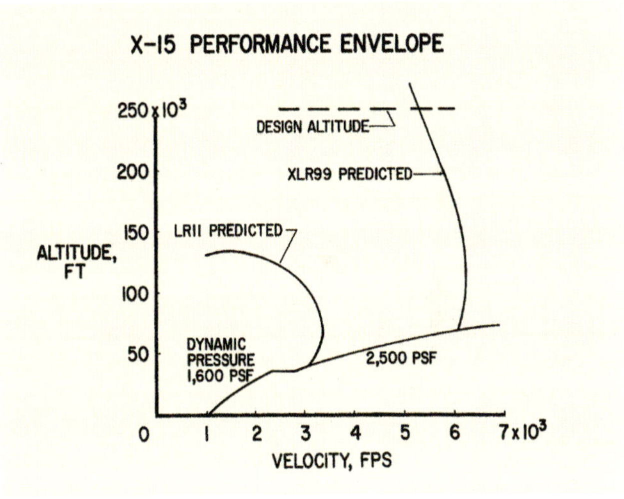

Above: Concerned at the development time required to transition from the XLR-30 to the derivative engine, the throttleable XLR-99, it was decided to adapt the XLR-11 so that two could be 'stacked' in the aft fuselage for early development flights without holding up flight tests. A simple frame allowed the dual motors to be installed within the aft fuselage of the X-15. *Right:* Interim flight activity with the XLR-11 would be strictly limited, with full potential only realised when the XLR-99 became available for flight operations. *NACA*

igniting on contact, the elimination of an ignition system reduced the number of components and increased reliability.

The two airframe bidders which selected the XLR-30 had the advantage that they would require only one engine and this showed up in the weight estimates from the contenders, both Douglas and NAA proposals being 19-35 per cent lighter in drop weight and 9-31 per cent lower than the other two in landing weight. Both Bell and Reaction Motors Incorporated were sparse in their presentation materials supporting the bids. RMI were able to show that development of their XLR-30 engine was far along and that it was already in an advanced stage of refinement, evidence from the US Navy tests substantiating that.

But RMI impressed with the news that if their motor was selected they were able to offer a throttleable engine and that this would not be a step-thrust system but one which could be variously adjusted like a jet engine, with thrust ranging from 60kN (13,500lb) to 222.4kN (50,000lb). Moreover, they claimed they could build the engine to perform at least five successive restarts. Both proposed rocket motors would require modification and changes to the technical operability of their designs and both had to be man-rated, raising the requirement for safety and reliability as well as the obvious desire for maximum performance.

In reality, the XLR-30 was far from ready for the role for which it was proposed and would not be applicable in its existing form, it being useful only as a temporary reference motor in the submissions. This was recognised by the NACA/Air Force teams and continuing discussions over the projected performance of the XLR-30 changed the throttle band from a lower limit of 27 per cent to 30 per cent in order to place less stringent demands on the design. But there was concern about the position the government customers would take over engine selection and that was a clarification sought by all four bidders.

This confusion was worked through at a meeting held at NACA headquarters in Washington DC on 27 June 1955 and the decision was reached that the government would only override the engine selected by the winning airframe bidder if either of the two contenders was clearly so inferior or outstandingly superior that it warranted intervention. Otherwise,

Above: From left, the XLR-11 utilised for the X-1 series, the slightly improved version for the X-15 and the definitive XLR-99. *RMI*

the NACA said that the engine chosen by the winning airframe bidder would be their affair. It could be said, however, that since airframe and engine were a bid package it would have been implausible to imagine that the Research Airplane Committee would not include the engine in their appraisal and that it would be retained by the winning bidder.

The NACA reported its findings on the three plausible engine contenders, finding that none of them were at a stage of development commensurate with the 30-month build period then required for the X-15. There was a growing concern at the mismatch between the development times for the airframe and its engine. When Walter Williams proposed that an interim engine, the XLR-11, be considered for early flight tests that provided room for manoeuvre and took pressure off RMI to develop the XLR-30 into the derivative engine. During a series of meetings at Wright Field on 6-7 July it was agreed that since none of the engines were at a sufficient state of readiness to unequivocally decide on their relative merits, it was agreed that it would be left to the airframe contractor to decide. But since none of the bidders selected it, the XLR-73 would be removed from the list of contenders.

Following selection of North American Aviation to build the X-15, on 26 October 1955 the Air Force notified RMI that it had been selected to develop the XLR-30. Later in the year, after some discussion about which organisation should be responsible for the work, the Air Force usurped the Navy and got the job with an announcement to that effect on 3 January 1956. There had been concerns that the Navy had underestimated the required development time and that it was not fully aware of the technical challenges, which were strongly identified by the Air Force. It was also thought that development of both airframe and engine should be vested in a single agency.

RMI presented its technical proposal to the Power Plant Laboratory on 24 January with a statement that it could deliver the engine in 30 months. On 21 February 1956 it gave the derivative engine the designation XLR-99-RM-1. The initial cost estimate for the development programme and the supply of rocket motors was $10.478million with a requirement to deliver within 24 months. The final contract for the engine was signed on 7 September 1956, initially embracing one engine, a single mock-up and all the associated tools and maintenance equipment for what the Air Force designated as Project 3116, a separate technical development to Project 1226 – the X-15 airframe. By this time the estimated cost of XLR-99 development had already increased to $10.77million.

XLR-99

The single-chamber engine was required to deliver a maximum thrust of 222.4kN (50,000lb) at sea level and 257.32kN (57,850lb) at 30,480m (100,000ft), be throttleable between 30 per cent and 100 per cent of rated thrust and to have a maximum burn duration of 90 seconds at full power. The dry weight was specified at 280kg (618lb) and a wet weight of 339kg (748lb). It had to fit within a space in the rear fuselage 182cm (71.7in) in length and 109.7cm (43.2in) in diameter and it was to be capable of up to six restarts within a single flight. Internally at RMI, the motor was assigned the company designation TR-139, aptly known as Pioneer. But at the second industry conference in 1958, reportedly the XLR-99 programme was a year behind schedule.

RMI had Harry A. Koch as XLR-99 programme manager and Robert W. Seaman as project engineer but Wesley Schilling was the lead designer. Two significant areas of concern were addressed at the outset: propellant combination and the start-up/shut-down procedures. While the company had experience with engines of this thrust rating, it had less knowledge about the coolant requirements. Moreover, the molecular nature of anhydrous ammonia would give it rough running and combustion instability, the latter common in most rocket motors of the period.

Several fuel additives were tried in an attempt to ease these conditions, including methylamine and acetylene but these were dangerously unstable, although the instability problem was eventually solved through improved injector design. The injector configuration itself proved difficult to settle, some 15 different arrangements being tried in the process. Combustion instability was related to the injector problem, in that it usually followed the accumulation of unburned propellant.

This was solved by incorporating a continuously running igniter, in effect a small rocket thrust chamber, to overrun the main combustion phase after shutdown to burn the residual propellants remaining in the chamber. It was also necessary to ensure that the flammability characteristics of LOX and ammonia were not exceeded before start-up and that the control sequence of the engine would go through a series of electrical interlocks, removing the need for separate controls to deliver the propellants into the chamber.

The ignition sequence was in two phases, the first involving three surface-gap spark plugs which ignited the incoming gaseous oxygen and liquid ammonia propellants and began the combustion process at a low level to minimise the risk of pre-ignition and burn up any expelled fuel. These combusted propellants ignited the second phase which introduced the propellants into the combustion cavity through an impinging jet injector, with the fuel flow being used to regeneratively cool the second stage chamber, allowing a build-up of pressure in the combustion chamber. Pressure switches in both igniters ensured that there would be no propellant delivery unless pre-set levels were achieved. The mixture ratio was maintained within the flammability range by a cavitating venturi located in each of the second stage propellant lines to restrict the flow under transient conditions.

With this basic design concept the engineering team got to work on what would soon become one of the most complex rocket motors of its time. Initial studies determined that it would be necessary to first develop the engine to operate within the 50-100 per cent thrust range and then to open up the throttle range down to 30 per cent. The development of a system to provide electrical interlocks proved a valid safety feature and operated on a decision-based protocol rather than a pre-set sequence of events.

The combustion chamber had a throat diameter of 21.9cm (8.64in) and an expansion skirt diameter of 99.8cm (39.3in) which provided a nozzle area ratio of 9.8:1. The chamber was regeneratively cooled with ammonia on a return flow system where the pipes were arranged so that it flowed down the walls in one tube and up in the adjacent tube in the opposite direction. The 196 tubes in the 'spaghetti' bundle were manufactured from AISI 347 stainless steel, furnace brazed, with each tube having a diameter of 0.9cm (0.375in) and a wall thickness of 0.084cm (0.033in).

A number of injector designs were examined before selection of the so-called, multi-spud type made from age-hardened Inconel X which provided ease of manufacture and stable injection characteristics. The assembled injector head had 18 elements, the spuds arranged in two rows, 12 in the first row, six in the second and set within a single hemispherical

Below left: The turbopump and associated systems were mounted to the main combustion chamber of the XLR-99 in a compact but relatively light structure. *Author's collection*

Below right: Constrained by the internal dimensions of the aft fuselage and thrust box, the XLR-99 was difficult to work on due to limited access through the integrated elements. Note the white turbopump exhaust pipe. *Author's collection*

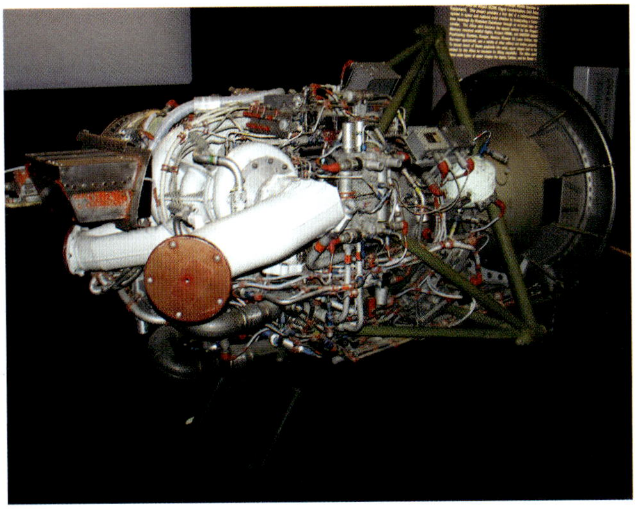

Above left: With an expansion ratio of 9.8:1, the exit nozzle had a diameter of 99.8cm (39.3in) and was built for multiple restarts. *Author's collection*
Above right: The turbine exhaust folded back around the side of the XLR-99's combustion chamber and exited in the upper right quadrant of the aft housing in the rear fuselage. *Author's collection*

dome. This differed from the showerhead design of the XLR-30 and to test the new design engineers fitted it to a test engine, possibly the XLR-10 delivering 22.24kN (5,000lb) of thrust to measure performance and fine-tune the design.

Several different spud designs were tested in this way before the dual-row configuration was selected. Spray adjustments to the outer ring were necessary to reduce heating levels in the throat area tubes. To fully evaluate the new design changes and the overall layout of the operating engine, Siemens decided to set up a breadboard engine, an arrangement of all the assemblies and working parts but linked together to see how they all interacted rather than assembled as a finished engine in three dimensions. This way of evaluating the design before building it into a working engine got the support of NAA who promptly offered tanks, propellant lines and pressurisation systems then being developed for the airframe to enhance the test experience.

Another problem was encountered with the bundle tubes where several different materials were examined, including nickel, aluminium and stainless steel before the latter was selected based on its high melting point, strength and high thermal conductivity. Nevertheless, some 30 different tube patterns were tried out and analysed for their heat transfer characteristics. During the examination of overall thermal properties it was decided to coat the interior of the combustion chamber with a ceramic layer, which was also selected from a wide range of possibilities to protect the interior of the chamber face from the 2,760°C (5,000°F) temperature of the combustion process. The final choice was Rokide Z (zirconium) and a special applicator was developed by RMI's Kenneth Gaddis who fabricated a tool to apply it evenly using a derivative of an acetylene gun over the top of a Nichrome flame-sprayed undercoat, 0.0127cm (0.005in) thick.

Provided by the Norton Company of Massachusetts, the Rokide Z material provided a hard surface with excellent heat protection properties. A surface layer of 0.05-0.10cm (0.02-0.04in) thickness was applied, although in practice the coating was found to erode quickly and it was replaced with a graduated Nichrome coating. Nevertheless, this application of Rokide Z was highly appropriate, as the company had provided precision grinding wheels to Robert H. Goddard who, in March 1926 had been the first man to successfully launch a liquid propellant rocket.

The turbopump was a particular challenge since it would have its own gas supply and would also be responsible for adjusting the thrust level of the engine itself. Much effort was expended on determining the optimum gas supply for this turbine, which would drive the two propellant pumps. The system eventually chosen was based on 90 per cent hydrazine peroxide in monopropellant decomposition across a silver screen catalyst. This produced a gas with a temperature of 737°C (1,360°F) upstream of the nozzles so that the gas impinged upon the turbine blades, which transmitted that energy to a single shaft driving the two pumps.

The LOX pump operated at 13,000rpm and was developed from that used on the XLR-30 while the fuel pump, which was mounted to the same drive shaft, operated at 20,790rpm. The outlet pressure was around 8,274kPa (1,200lb/in^2) delivering 1,118kw (1,500hp). The combined propellant flow rate was 5,897kg (13,000lb) per minute, using up all the X-15's 8,165kg (18,000lb) of propellant in 85 seconds. Thrust output was controlled by altering the speed of the turbopump upstream of the catalytic bed by a throttle valve.

A major problem in handling these large quantities of propellant was their very different temperatures. It posed engineering problems common to all rocket engine designs but the use of these in an aircraft of this size were unique. The ammonia had an input temperature of -45°C (-50°F) and -33°C (-28°F) while the LOX had an input temperature of -193°C (-316°F) to -170°C (-275°F) and the hydrogen peroxide had a temperature between 10°C (50°F) and 49°C (120°F). Technical solutions were of value not only to the X-15 programme but to other projects which had similarly demanding requirements.

A primary concern to the design and development engineers was to build up the motor in such a way that there could never be an unplanned mixing of LOX, anhydrous ammonia and hydrogen peroxide. Also, to ensure that all shafts for the

Above: A close-up shot of the interior of the combustion chamber and its regenerative cooling tubes. Note the facing plate with propellant injectors. *Author's collection*

common turbopump, oxidiser, fuel and turbine had dual seals with provision for overboard disposal of any residual materials. Helium was injected into the drain cavities at engine shutdown to clear any leaks, an important consideration not only for ensuring a complete evacuation of the lines but also for making the vehicle safe after landing.

RMI's Component Development Laboratory developed ground-breaking methods of ensuring that the electrical functions of the engine, as well as all other elements of the system, were in accordance with the man-rating standard. This was becoming a universal requirement for all Air Force and NASA rockets designed to carry humans. The XLR-99-RM-1 was self-diagnostic to the extent that it was designed to operate automatically through self-monitoring and fail-safe procedures. The pilot did not have sufficient instrumentation to make rapid decisions about malfunctions other than basic operating parameters. Man-rating was applied to Redstone and Atlas rockets for the Mercury programme and it would be applied to the Titan rocket when, from late 1961, it was decided to use that for two-man Gemini missions.

The design of the engine itself affected the design of the airframe, in that the acoustic effect of the rocket motor firing would impose high sound levels on the structure, potentially causing damage and reducing fatigue life. A maximum of 163db (decibels) was recorded at a distance of 7.6m (25ft) behind the aircraft with a peak of 156db recorded on the horizontal stabiliser. The survivability of the airframe depended upon a continuous operational match between the acoustic levels which would be incurred and the structure of the aircraft itself.

Trials and troubles

Within a year of beginning work on the engine, RMI notified the Air Force on 10 July 1957 that they would need an extension of the delivery schedule, citing a nine-month delay. There was also a suggestion that if they could be allowed a loaded weight growth to 379kg (836lb) they could deliver on time and the company did report that they could offer an airframe weight reduction because they now calculated an 89kg (197lb) reduction in the quantity of helium required. The Air Force agreed to the increased weight.

By 11 December that year RMI reported that despite these efforts the engine development was six months behind schedule and concern grew so that on 7 January 1958 the Air Force requested a detailed schedule and a revised timeline for completion, which was duly delivered to the Wright Air Development Center within a week. It advised that a further five and

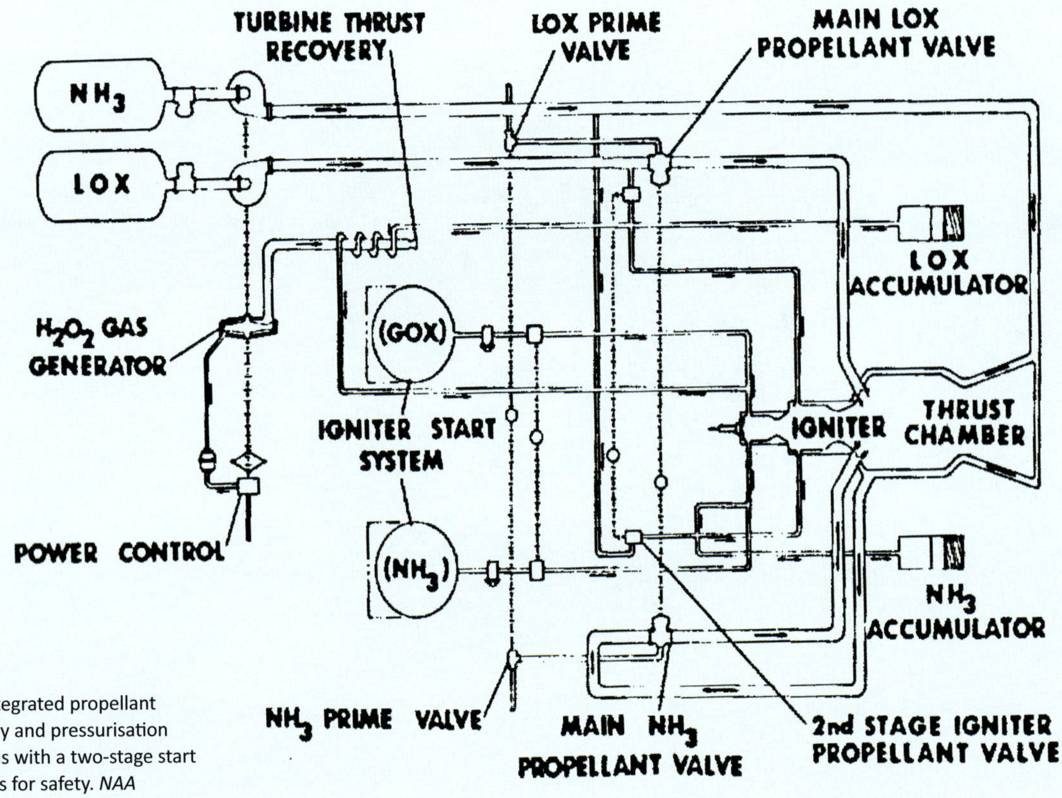

The integrated propellant delivery and pressurisation systems with a two-stage start process for safety. *NAA*

a half months would have to be added to the schedule and that costs had doubled since the most recent estimate the previous July. It was at this critical point in the development programme that the XLR-11 was introduced as a stop-gap measure to get the aircraft flying until the XLR-99-RM-1 was flight ready, a request which had been considered almost two years earlier by Walter Williams.

The Air Force responded to these delays by applying extra resources to RMI, paying the additional money and setting up an advisory group to monitor progress. These delays began to seriously affect relations between RMI and the customers along with politicians keen to get the rocket plane into the air and out of the atmosphere, seeing in its capabilities a measure of national pride, a heightened urgency due to Soviet space successes. The launch of Sputnik 1 in October 1957 saw the NACA metamorphose into NASA (National Aeronautics and Space Administration) on 1 October 1958.

Engine testing began in the latter half of 1958 with eight flight-worthy motors produced for the development programme. A destructive failure during a firing on 24 October was caused by inadequate components, which were already scheduled to be replaced but which were not thought to have the potential to fail catastrophically – another lesson in the dangers of pushing the envelope and pushing too hard! But this early period helped forge a solid basis for the final stages in qualifying the engine for flight. The airframe was already being prepared for flight and the engine was still some way behind.

A critical milestone, the Preliminary Flight Rating Test (PFRT) was achieved on 18 April 1959 with four engines permanently assigned, two of which were considered flight engines. From this there were expectations that the FRT itself would be completed by 1 September that year. Edwards AFB received the first ground test engine on 7 June and the first flight engine arrived less than two months later. There had been 10 engines under the initial contract with six spare injector assemblies and a further flight-rated engine would be added at a later date.

Static tests were conducted at RMI's facilities which, because they were sited on the Naval Research Test Station, Lake Denmark, New Jersey, had to receive the permission of the Navy Department. Ten engine runs were made in a special chamber at the US Air Force Arnold Engineering Development Center, Tullahoma, Tennessee, simulating an altitude of 21,336m (70,000ft). Static tests were also conducted on the Propulsion System Test Stand (PSTS) at Edwards AFB, a facility completed in June 1959. This was where engine checks would be completed before a flight and where pilots and ground crew would receive familiarisation training. RMI would use one part of the PSTS for engine tests and the Air Force test engines installed in X-15 airframes in another.

The Flight Rating Test conformed to the MIL-E-6626 specification and this cleared the engine for its use in a manned vehicle. Two engines were used for endurance testing, each one completing more than one hour of operating time with one engine firing for 108 minutes on routine maintenance checks. A total of 93 engine tests were made to ensure that it would respond to simulated emergency conditions, verifying its ability to react and shut down in a fail-safe mode. A total of 234 engine tests were completed in achieving the PFRT, which

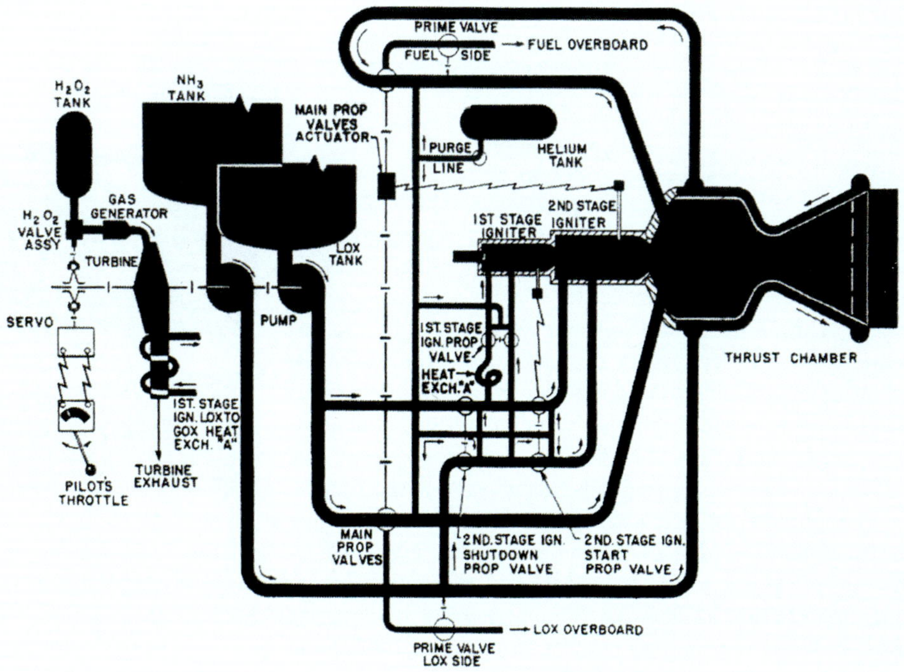

Ignition began with the first of the two-stage start system igniting a mixture of oxygen and ammonia producing energy to start the second stage, ignition in the combustion chamber, as clearly defined on this working diagram. *NAA*

was achieved within four months. There were 192 full scale firings with 42 comprising system and element tests which did not require combustion.

Pre-flight testing was declared complete by RMI general manager Raymond Young on 18 February 1960. The first of several ground runs of the engine was made in X-15-3 on 2 June 1960, with the aircraft held firmly to the test rig. Several minor hitches were encountered, including losing the back end of that aircraft during the third run five days later – with Scott Crossfield in the cockpit. But the fault was in ground equipment and not with the engine itself. Crossfield made the first powered flight with the XLR-99-RM-1 on 15 November 1960 but that and subsequent flights with this engine are covered later. Testing was all important, for the first 53 flights each XLR-99 being run for 188 minutes before being flown for 75 minutes in all.

This was a time of great optimism in the aerospace world at large and in high-altitude, high-speed flight in particular but great changes were underway and challenges were there to be met. In aviation, the six-engine Mach 3 XB-70 strategic nuclear bomber had just been demoted to a research and development programme and several high-speed interceptor projects were under threat as both the government and some defence officials believed the missile would replace the manned aircraft.

But propulsion was at the heart of it all. The application of a rocket motor to manned flight appeared to be the way of the future and the technology that was pioneered in the development of this advanced engine for the X-15 was believed to hold great promise for successive generations of manned hypersonic aerospace vehicles. It was, nevertheless, a time when great public expectations were aroused by the selection of seven Mercury astronauts in April 1959 to fly into space aboard a one-man space capsule.

Many feared that this effort would be eclipsed by the Russians, their concerns vindicated on 12 April 1961 when Yuri Gagarin became the first man to orbit the Earth. Few at the time, however, believed that this single event would stir the courage of a nation to place humans on the Moon by the end of the decade – people propelled through the atmosphere and into space by rocket motors. But there was certainty in the conviction that rocket powered aerospace planes would eventually eclipse the one-shot spectacle of a space capsule for the more certain future of manned trans-atmospheric vehicles carrying people to great speed in the atmosphere and to destinations beyond.

RMI had been so convinced of their technology that there was high confidence that the XLR-99 would be developed further into the primary propulsion system for aerospace vehicles such as Dyna-Soar, believing, with some justification, that they could get the jump on Aerojet and Rocketdyne already expanding their businesses on the rising wave of orders for ballistic missiles and space launch vehicles. RMI even considered that this throttleable motor would be suitable to power a lunar landing vehicle as it descended to the Moon, hovering like a helicopter in the final stages of descent as the pilot selected an appropriate landing spot. Such a motor would in fact be needed but not from RMI.

To fulfil these expectations, consideration was given to alternative propellants with greater energy, combinations such as LOX/hydrazine, nitrogen tetroxide/hydrazine, LOX/hydrogen and hydrogen/pentaborane. These ideas were discussed in the RMI booklet *Space Technology* with a concept portrayed employing a lightweight, 290kg (639lb) throttleable XLR-99 using storable propellants and producing a thrust of 300kN (67,445lb) for manned lunar landings. There was talk of a much more powerful engine in design stages, a throttleable motor based on the XLR-99 design which could offer up to 672kN (150,000lb) of thrust with the same tubular bundle for regenerative cooling and with a total height of

Right: The XLR-99 programme included a wide range of tests under different conditions and throttle settings where the performance of the motor and the consequences of different operating modes were evaluated prior to – and during – the flight phase. *Author's collection*

more than 1.8m (6ft).

Perhaps astonishingly, the fate of this and other large-scale aspirations was decided by legal counsel supporting litigation from disgruntled residents of New Jersey who filed for damages they claimed had been caused to their properties by the testing of the X-15 motor. Judgements set down by the Supreme Court of New Jersey decreed that '...the testing of rocket motors on the ground may be abnormally dangerous and that the defendants' activities were not negligent but ultra-hazardous and therefore the defendants were absolutely liable for property damages caused to homeowners near the sites'.

The intrusive and expanding suburbanisation of the area had encroached upon industry facilities which, given the associated effects of testing these large rocket motors – sometimes up to 10 times a day – had brought damage to properties and caused the company to pay out large sums of money in compensation. By this time RMI had been bought out by Thiokol and it became a division of that company, which majored on solid propellant motors and their technology, most notably receiving the contract on 20 November 1973 for the Solid Rocket Motors, integral to the Solid Rocket Boosters for the Space Shuttle.

But the limitations of scale worked against what was now the Rocket Motors Division (RMD) of Thiokol and with ideas outclassing their facilities they pleaded for money from their parent company so that test facilities could be built on the West Coast away from urban development. With big players such as Aerojet and Rocketdyne able to mobilise resources and facilities, the addition of RMD in the equation was

Below: Technicians from the Plasmokote Corporation apply a layer of Rokide Z zirconia coating to the interior of the expansion skirt. *Rocketdyne*

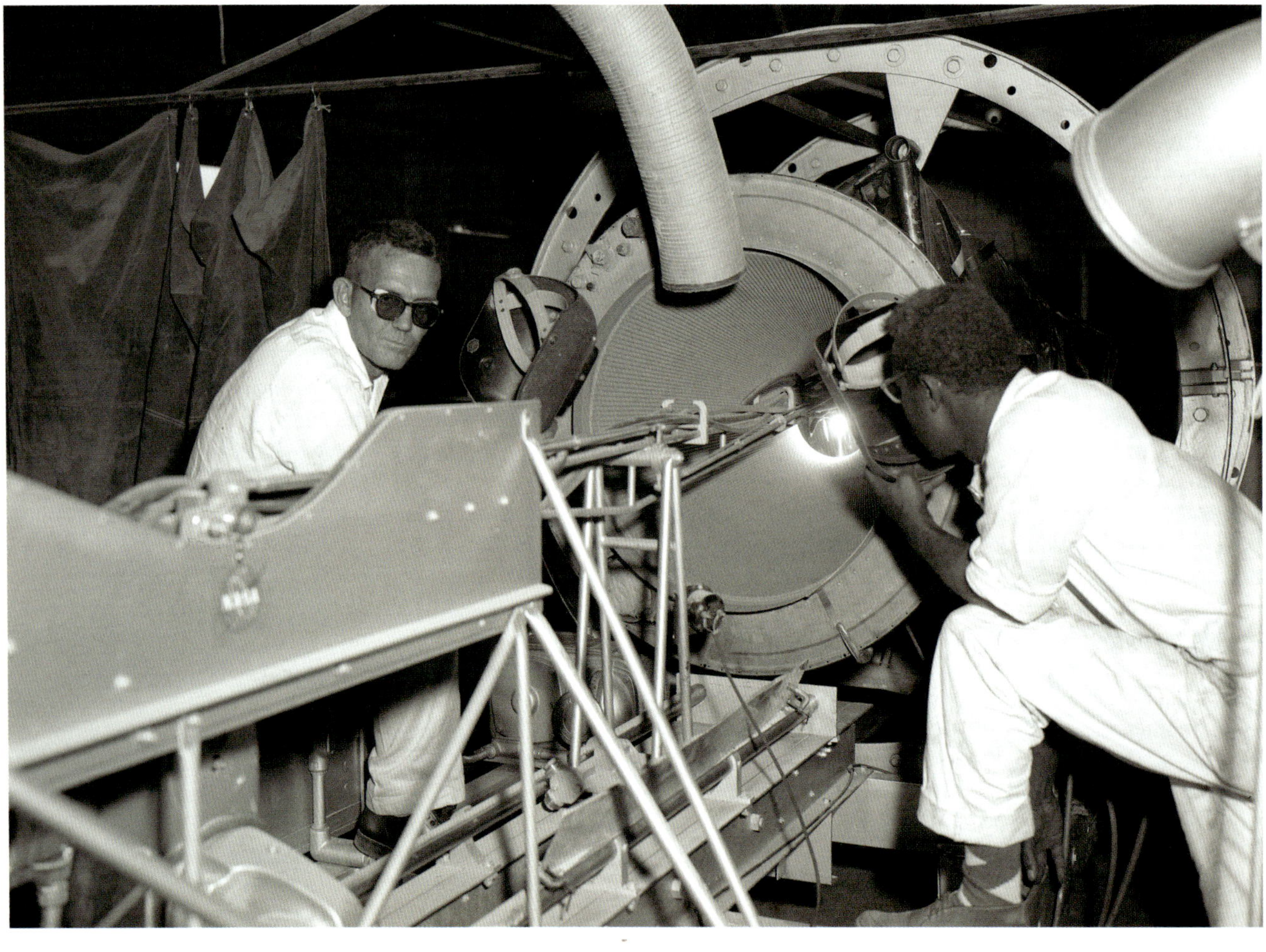

Right: Technicians, engineers and managers get a tutorial, assisted by mimeographs, charts and chalkboards. The XLR-99 represented a major step up from the relatively conventional XLR-11 and would educate a new breed of rocket engineer. *NAA*

considered too high a risk, so they pursued contracts for small motors. Much of their work had gone to the Navy for the development of liquid rockets but with the Vietnam War under way this work fell off and Thiokol could see no future role for the company in big engines.

RMD did some fine work and their products made it to the Moon, not as a lander engine for manned missions as they desired but as the descent engines for the seven unmanned Surveyor spacecraft, five of which successfully landed on the lunar surface between 1966 and 1968. In the last days of the company they were machining artillery shells under subcontract and in 1970 Thiokol began to quietly phase out RMD's operations. RMD ceased to exist in June 1972, bringing to an end a phase in American rocketry which had begun at the very dawn of pioneering endeavours and ended with little rocket motors sitting on the Moon.

But the price for the development of the first throttleable rocket motor, man-rated and reusable, unique in the development of rocketry, was very high. The development costs for the XLR-99 continued to soar throughout its protracted history. By June 1959 the cost had gone from an initial estimate of \$10.478million to \$68.373million, with each of the 10 engines under contract estimated to cost \$1million. Most aerospace projects suffer from underestimates on cost at the time of contract award but much of the growth in the development of this engine came from a learning curve that built up as the project progressed. It was RMI's misfortune that they were unable to directly capitalise on the hard-won investment in technology that could have seen them survive for several more decades.

An interim solution

Because the XLR-99-RM-1 would not be ready by the time the X-15 was available for powered flight tests, the addition to adopt the XLR-11 for early flight trials would ensure minimum delay on getting aerodynamic data about the aircraft. Moreover, there was little impact from the different fuel carried for the XLR-11 and minimal impact on handling and control mechanisms. The first two X-15s would be initially powered by the XLR-11, each aircraft having two quad-units stacked one above the other within the structural cradle designed for the XLR-99 but suitable for the interim motors as well. As built, the frame structure for the more powerful motor was bolted straight in to the rear fuselage and the only interface changes necessary were to attach the two XLR-11s to the frame. Some ballast was also required but in all other respects the substitution was a relatively easy task.

In aligning the motor packs, the upper set was canted down slightly while the lower pack was canted up to converge the thrust line with the X-15's centre of gravity. As installed, the two packs protruded farther aft than the single XLR-99 and this required some additional cover extending back from the rear fuselage, giving this configuration a distinctly unique appearance. Because each pack was, in effect, a completely separate engine, it was possible to start up both sets at the same time with no effect on the structure of the airframe. Although, with eight combustion chambers, it was possible to achieve full thrust in eight incremental steps.

Identified as RMI 6000 C4 motors, each new quartet of combustion chambers had a thrust at altitude of 35,586N (8,000lb), the dual package producing a maximum thrust of 71,172N (16,000lb), 30 per cent more than that available from the standard XLR-11 used on the X-1 and Skyrocket programmes and 30 per cent of the thrust which would be available from the XLR-99. The motors were assembled at

Right: A test chamber at the Arnold Engineering Development Center (AEDC), Arnold AFB, Tennessee. *AEDC*

Edwards from spares remaining on site. The cluster of four chambers at the top were identified as pack No. 1, those beneath as pack No. 2. After installation, the fuel pump was situated on the right side with the oxygen pump on the left with the chambers numbered 1 to 4 in a clockwise direction starting at the top and facing forward. Each quartet of motors carried a turbopump exhaust outlet pipe between the Nos 3 and 4 motors.

Each of the two XLR-11 packs had a length of about 1.52m (5ft), a height of 0.91m (3ft), a width of 0.61m (2ft) and a weight of 156.5kg (345lb). The 293.3lit (77.5USgall) hydrazine tank for turbopump fuel installed for the XLR-99 was retained for the dual XLR-11 packs but, due to the reduced requirement, only 155.2lit (41USgall) was loaded. Support systems built in for the XLR-99 were retained for the smaller motors, items such as pressurisation, fire suppression and compartment walls being common to the two.

Most of the dual packs were built up from spares and leftovers from the earlier X-1 series and the motors themselves were maintained by the Air Force Flight Test Center with support from Reaction Motors Incorporated. There was a great degree of familiarity with these motors. They had been used throughout the X-1 and Douglas D558-2 series and as an integral JATO pack for the XF-91 Thunderceptor programme, the XLR-11 replacing the Curtiss-Wright XLR-27 which failed to perform satisfactorily. The XLR-11 would also power some lifting-body aircraft tested at Edwards during the 1960s.

Modifications to the propellant utilisation system to accommodate the ethyl-alcohol and water fuel for the substitute engines were minimal, there being virtually no difference in the consistency and operating temperature compared to the anhydrous ammonia for the XLR-99. Each rocket chamber could be started within two seconds, all four chambers in a single quartet starting up in sequence within eight seconds. As two packs were installed they operated as separate units, it being possible to start up single chambers in both packs at the same time. Two chambers could be turned off and on again after all four had been running for a minimum of 10 seconds. But if all four chambers were shut down it was necessary for the pilot to wait 20 seconds before a re-ignition sequence could begin.

The first powered flight with the XLR-11 took place on 17 September 1959 with X-15-1 and the last with this interim propulsion system occurred on 7 February 1961 with the same aircraft. In that period 30 flights were made with the XLR-11, which had powered the first two aircraft, the fastest speed being 3,660kph (2,275mph) or Mach 3.5 with Robert White at the controls of the final flight with this propulsion system. The highest altitude achieved with the XLR-11 was on 19 May 1960 when White reached 33,222m (108,997ft). X-15-2 was removed from the roster after its flight on 26 May 1960 for the XLR-99 to be installed. From that date, flights with the XLR-11 packs were made with X-15-1 for the nine months remaining until X-15-1 stood down for installation of its XLR-99.

Below: Heavily instrumented for tests, an XLR-99 at the AEDC during the extensive development phase. *AEDC*

Chapter Thirteen

Engineering the X-15

Paradoxically, given its speed and altitude performance, the general appearance of the aircraft was of a conventional mid-wing monoplane with low aspect-ratio wings, a large dorsal wedge-shaped tail and a ventral wedge-tail, with a circular cross section fuselage on to which were grafted full length side-wall tunnel chines. Almost uniquely for the aircraft industry, however, the real difference lay in the materials employed in its construction, which were selected on the basis of strength, temperature and thermal properties, resistance to corrosion and processing requirements.

Chief structures engineer Dr. R. L. Schleicher recognised early in the design phase that a large percentage of the wetted area, defined in aeronautical terms as the surface in contact with the air flow and derived from the nautical term for that portion of the hull in contact with water, would experience high temperatures. He calculated that most of the surface would experience temperatures of 427-649ºC (800-1,200ºF) and that the high strength required could only be met by titanium and nickel-based alloys. None of the exotic structural material derived from rare elements had yet been developed, limiting to some extent the flight envelope that aircraft of this type could fly.

Schleicher was concerned that even steel and titanium would lose strength in these temperature regions and the only solution for the hottest areas was to employ Inconel X and, due to its stability it was selected by him for the entire exterior surface. He was intrigued by its behaviour under temperatures which would see other alloys weaken, recognising that by being oxidation and corrosion resistant it would maintain high levels of structural value under these extremes. Under thermal stress, Inconel forms a passivating oxide layer which protects the surface and arrests degradation. In the 1950s it was the ultimate high-technology material. Over time, across several industries, Inconel would have a very wide range of applications from rocket motor chambers to 3D printers.

The X-15 was designed for +4.0-g and -2.0-g during thrust runs and +7.33-g and -3-g after shut-down. The high g-loading was required by a flight profile which anticipated descent from a peak altitude of 76,200m (250,000ft) and a speed of 6,911kph (4,295mph) for a maximum angle-of-attack re-entry with two optional pull-outs. One called for a maximum alpha entry with speed brakes remaining closed and pull-out beginning at a predetermined altitude (which would be the highest permitted for 7.33-g lift and control power). The other applied where speed brakes were deployed at peak altitude and the 7.33-g recovery was conducted at a point not to exceed a maximum dynamic pressure (max-q) of 119.7kPa (2,500lb/ft^2). This recovery dynamic pressure limit

Above: The X-15 adopted the same landing gear geometry as that on the Bell X-2, with a single nose leg and two aft skids and the definitive design remained close to that of the proposal. *NASA*

Right: Attention to accessibility was evident from the side fairings where conduits, cabling and plumbing were located, with access to subsystems and additional equipment such as experiments and electronics. *NAA*

was believed to represent the re-entry at the lowest altitude for successful recovery but consistent with appropriate safety margins for adequate terrain clearance.

The engineering design of the X-15 had been carefully measured against these representative flight profiles. Once the aircraft had been evaluated and the pilot's handbook written, most research flights would follow variables based on these two flight plans, although there would be considerable margin to accommodate special trajectories arising from observations and measurements made in more routine fights. In setting the g-load bands, engineers determined that the limiting max-q would represent the lowest altitude for recovery and that these pull-out manoeuvres would be conducted only once on each flight. During this kind of manoeuvre the X-15 would slow down appreciably and heat up quickly. Because of this, if a second pull-up manoeuvre was necessary it would be executed at a lower rate of acceleration to avoid overloading the structure with thermal input.

The design of the fuselage employed a mix of monocoque and semi-monocoque structures based around frames and bulkheads for load distribution with Inconel X for the outer skin, which was stabilised through frames and bulkheads using J-section frames, and with longitudinal stiffeners in selected areas. The structure had been developed as a stiff unit capable of overload conditions due to the relatively unknown environment in which it was to operate, and to accommodate

X-15 – Side Elevation

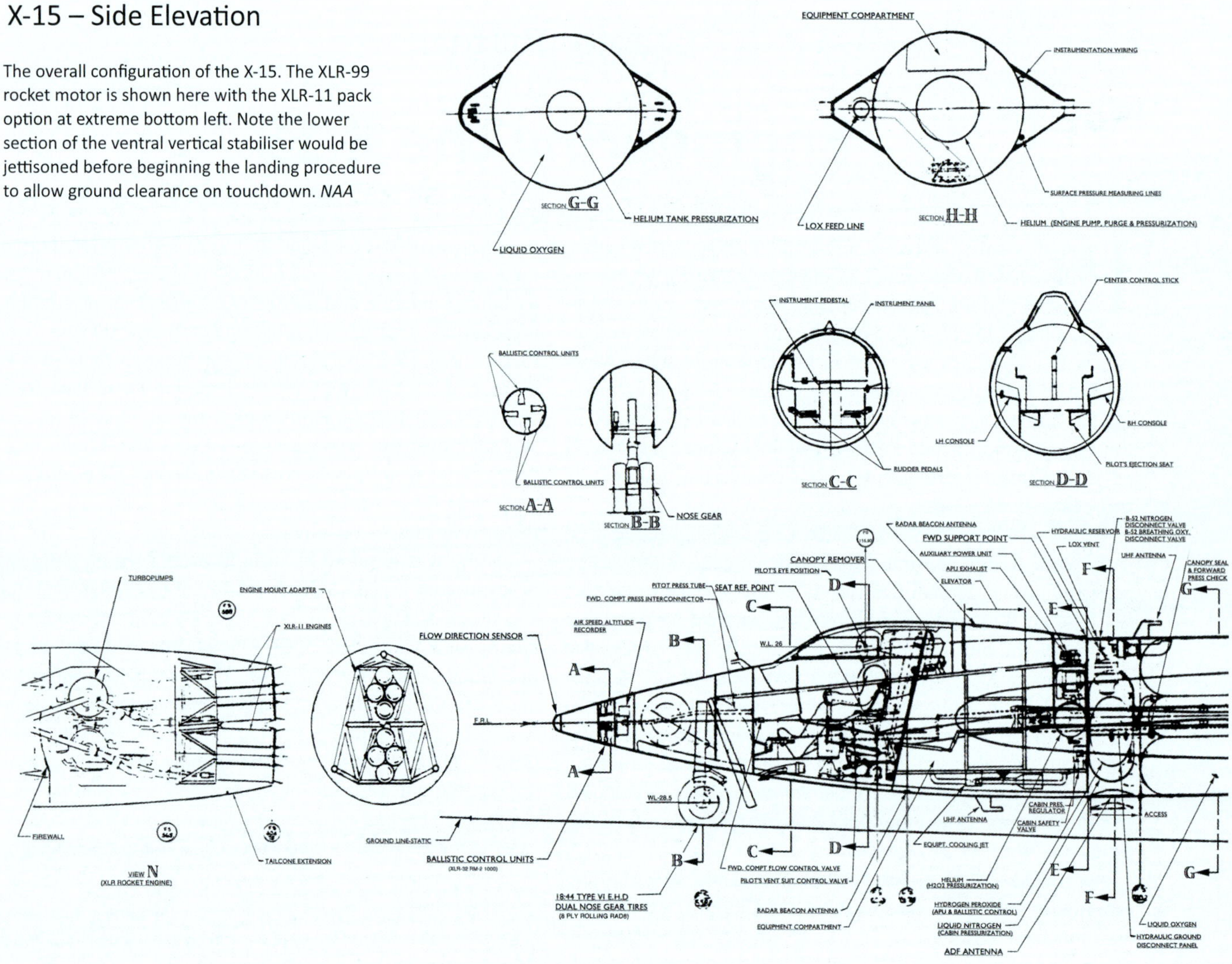

The overall configuration of the X-15. The XLR-99 rocket motor is shown here with the XLR-11 pack option at extreme bottom left. Note the lower section of the ventral vertical stabiliser would be jettisoned before beginning the landing procedure to allow ground clearance on touchdown. *NAA*

an engine with a considerably high thrust/weight ratio (1:0.75) affording a wide range of research possibilities.

The entire forward section of the fuselage was of semi-monocoque construction and included the cockpit and equipment compartment, nose wheel assembly and forward sensor package. The flight test instrumentation and the sensor boom used on early flights was supported in this section, as well as the nose ball introduced later. The extreme forward section, back as far as the forward section of the nose wheel bay, was pressurised as Equipment Bay No. 1 and had insulation and radiation blankets where appropriate.

The cockpit and Equipment Bay No. 2 were of shell construction with riveted Inconel X skin over an inner shell made of 2024-T4 aluminium alloy, which also formed a pressure barrier. The void between the two shells was filled with spun-fibreglass insulation and a radiation shield and the intercostals connecting the two were fabricated from titanium alloy. Aft of the No. 2 Equipment Bay was the compartment for the two auxiliary power units (APUs).

The fuselage centre section was a monocoque construction consisting of two main propellant tanks with circular cross section. Equipment Bay 3 was located between them at the centre of gravity. The outer skin was of welded Inconel X except for three mechanical joints to ease assembly. The forward liquid oxygen tank formed the forward section of the centre fuselage and consisted of a set of toroidal frames with an Inconel X skin. The end toroidal frames were also made from Inconel X while three radial intermediate frames were fabricated from aluminium alloy to serve as load bearers. These also doubled as slosh baffles, preventing the sudden movement of large quantities of propellant causing attitude excursions or structural damage during acceleration and g-forces. The end toroidal frames were welded directly to the skin with the aluminium baffles riveted to the Inconel shell.

A separate core tank inside the LOX tank was located along the length of the toroidal frame and served as a helium storage vessel. Two other spherical helium tanks were located left and right of the wing root fairing tunnels outboard of the engine. All three helium tanks were interconnected and provided pressure for purging the engine chambers, for useable-gas and for emergency jettison. The 0.198m³ (7ft³) helium vessel in the LOX tank incorporated the 2,482kPa (3,600lb/in²) LOX tank pressurisation line and was of negligible weight.

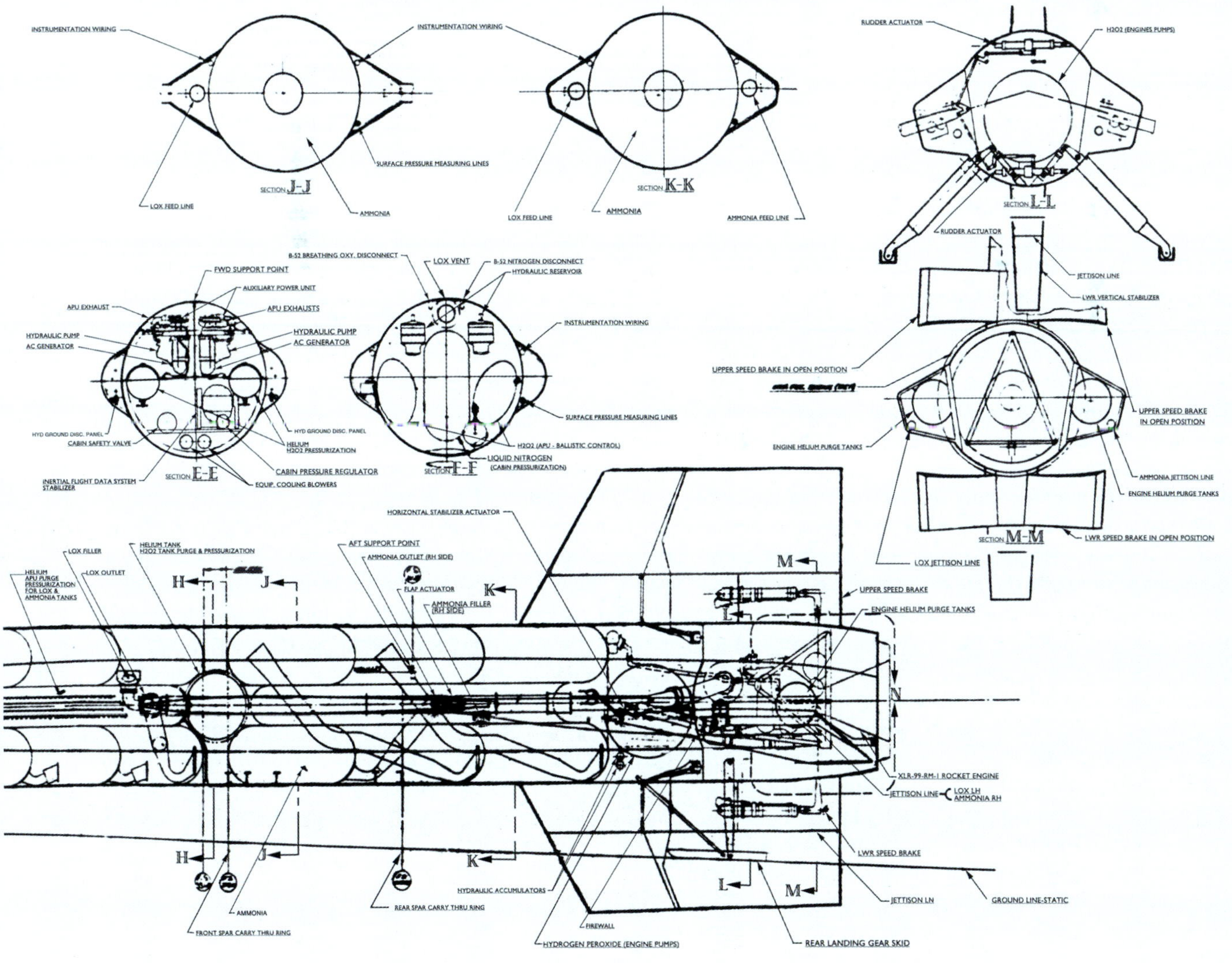

X-15 – General Arrangment

An annotated diagram of the primary systems and subsystems and relative location of key equipment in the X-15 as built. *NAA*

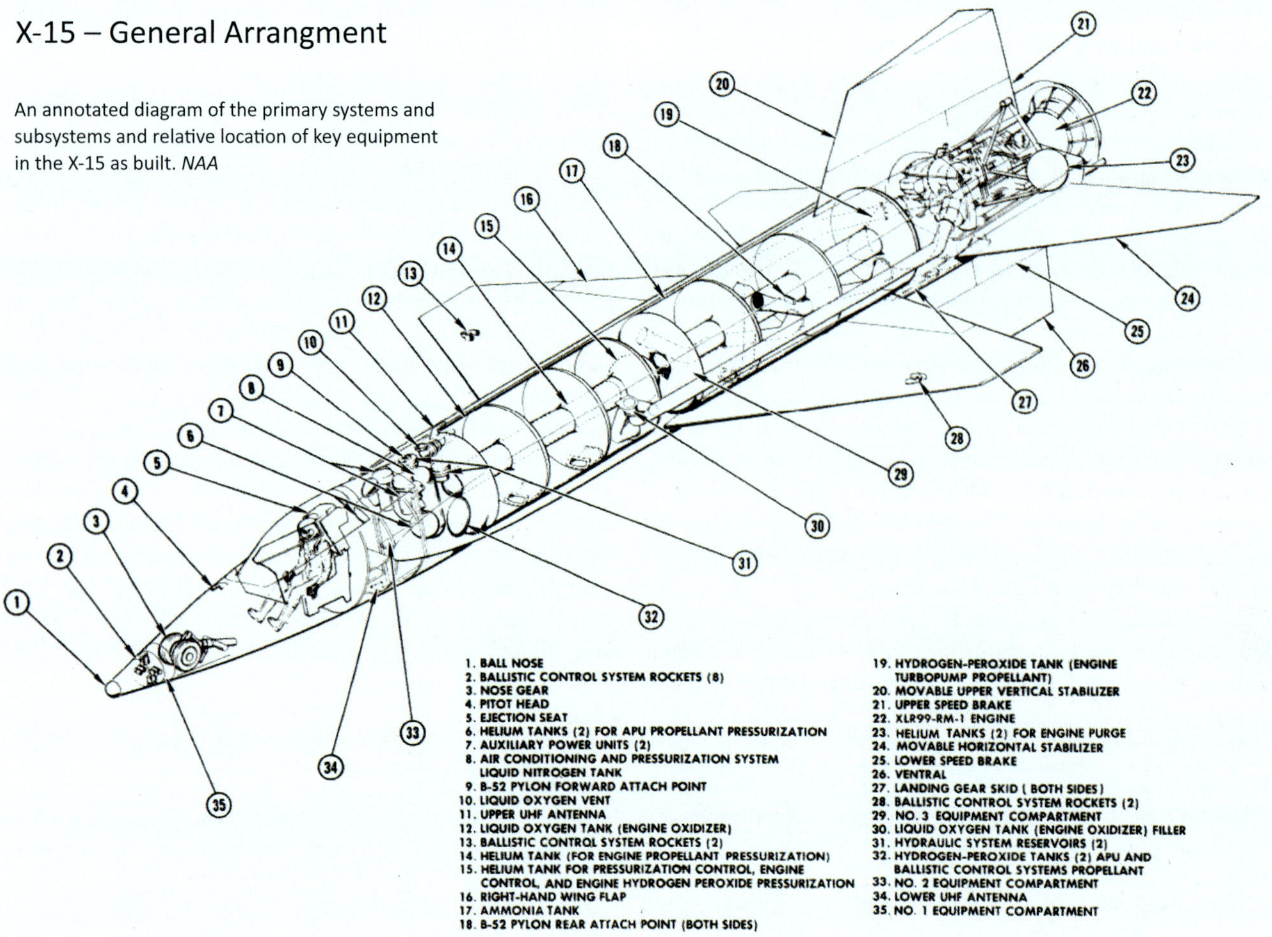

The LOX tank had a total volume of 4,088 litres (1,038USgall) with a propellant mass of 4,717kg (10,400lb). Of this, 53lit (14USgall) were residual at a pitch of 38deg and 71.9lit (19USgall) were vented and used as ullage (the boil-off void between the liquid oxygen and the fixed volume of the tank). Filling was conducted on the ground by a service tanker through the carrier-plane, with a fluid sensor providing automatic top-off during flight. On the ground the tank could be serviced through a filler located on the top of the wing fairing tunnel, or chine, leading edge.

The anhydrous ammonia tank was located aft of the LOX tank and had a similar construction but comprised an annular tank and a core tank containing more fuel. These tanks also provided added structural rigidity to the fuselage. The ammonia tank had a capacity for 5,469 lit (1,445USgall) with a fuel weight of 3,810kg (8,400lb). The maximum pressure in the fuel tank was the same as that for the LOX tank but with a minimum temperature of -31°C (-24°F). The filler for the fuel tank was situated on the underside of the right tunnel near the trailing edge of the wing.

Initially, the design of the LOX tank for the centre fuselage had been designed to sustain an ultimate internal pressure of 765.kPa (111lb/in^2) for critical external loads. These included calculations for normal shear, axial and torsional loads, after which an internal lower collapse pressure was calculated of 41.37kPa (6 lb/in^2). Areas which would experience high loads included the upper and lower Inconel X segments which had a thickness of 0.16cm (0.063in), stiffened with J-section ring frames with an area of 0.22cm^2 (0.0355in^2) at an average spacing of 15.24cm (6in). The temperature range in the LOX tank, as measured at the hemispherical end dome and the cylinder, was -145°C (-230°F) to 152.8°C (307°F).

A separate spherical, 387kg (854lb), 0.283m^3 (10ft^3) diameter hydrogen peroxide tank was located aft of the ammonia tank and this had a capacity of 293.3lit (77.5USgall). It was used to pressurise the LOX system to 331kPa (48lb/in^2). A swivel-type pickup line ensured a positive feed, irrespective of the attitude of the aircraft, and the top of the tank supported a combination pressure and vent valve. When the engine was operating the system was pressurised by helium gas which forced the hydrogen peroxide to the gas generators providing steam for driving the turbines. When the engine was not operating the system vented to the atmosphere.

The centre of gravity of the aircraft was maintained by a propellant transfer system whereby LOX and ammonia were expelled to the delivery lines from opposing directions: the oxidiser outflow was to the aft of the (forward) LOX tank and the fuel was to the front of the (aft) ammonia tank, thus preserving a shift in c-of-g of only 3.5 per cent at most. The LOX tank had a top-off capability fed from the carrier-plane, which

Right: Designed for low weight and structural integrity, fabrication of the forward section of the monocoque fuselage incorporating the cockpit, ejection seat rails and nose leg well. *NAA*

Right: The main structural monocoque section of the central fuselage, aft of the forward section and designed to carry the propellant and pressurisation tanks. *NAA*

carried two liquid oxygen tanks. The so-called climb tank had a capacity of 3,785 lit (1,000USgall) which was fed to the mated X-15 during take-off and the climb to drop height. Float levels shut the top-off supply when the boil-off had been replenished and the tank was full. A 1,892.5 litre (500USgall) cruise tank provided replenishment from 30 minutes before launch so that it was colder and had greater density. These tanks could support a two hour flight to the drop point.

Tanks, wings and tail

The decision to adopt monocoque propellant tanks had been the source of much debate and not a little opposition. Engineers obtained their decision by starting with the more conventional semi-monoque concept. Working to the logical certainty that for every material experiencing a given heat input there was minimum skin thickness for the structure to maintain integrity, the design team recognised that with a semi-monocoque design the skin thickness would be calculated for dynamic loads alone, while the underlying structure would be configured to absorb pressurisation. NAA engineers concluded that by increasing the thickness of the outer skin, the inner skin could be eliminated completely while accommodating thermal, dynamic and pressurisation loads.

By adopting a monocoque design, turning the propellant tank into the body of the structure itself and thus creating a wet fuselage, thermal stress would be reduced because the structural material itself was integral with the surface and the temperature gradient would quickly reach unity. The negative aspect of a monocoque design was that the skin was thicker, and therefore heavier. But that was compensated by the elimination of the under-skin and the net balance was a weight reduction. However, the aft fuselage reverted to a semi-monoque assembly which supported the tail elements, the main landing skids and the propulsion system.

Heavy titanium frames were located in this section to accommodate the severe loads which would pass through the structure. The Inconel X skin was riveted to the frames. The tubular steel mount in the engine bay was capable of accepting either the XLR-11 or the XLR-99 and which held it, together with the turbopump assemblies, independent and completely isolated from the structure of the fuselage itself. A firewall separated the propulsion bay from the centre fuselage and a fire seal was installed to prevent heat or jettisoned propellants from feeding back into the aft section. Provision was made for purging the entire area with helium to extinguish flames and serve as a coolant.

The wing for the X-15 was of trapezoidal shape, a modified NACA 66005 aerofoil without dihedral but with a thin (5 per cent thickness/chord) section and a 2.5:1 aspect ratio. The leading edge of the wing had a 25deg sweep at quarter-chord and was thin but not sharp, while the blunt trailing edge was 5.1cm (2in) thick at the root and 0.95cm (0.375in) at the tip. It was modified at the 17 per cent chord line to graduate to a constant slope from the 67 per cent line rearward, culminating in a 1 per cent blunt trailing edge. The wing was clean, without flying control surfaces, except for a small, hydraulically actuated flap at the inboard trailing edge. In several respects the wing was of standard construction being of multi-spar box beam design. Reinforced Inconel X skins were the material of choice, withstanding creep and providing strength to the calculated maximum temperature of 649°C (1,200°F). The skin varied in thickness, from 0.23cm (0.09in) at the root to 1cm (0.40in) at the tip of the upper surface, and 0.165cm (0.065in) to 1cm (0.40in) at the tip of the lower surface.

Throughout, internally the structure was built up in A-110AT titanium alloy sheet with extrusions. Flat web chan-

Right: Calibrating strain gauges and test components, the High Temperature Loads Calibration Laboratory at the Flight Research Center incorporated a programmable heating system with infrared quartz lamps producing a variable range of temperatures up to 1,649degC (3,000degF). Here, a horizontal stabiliser is subjected to stress and various temperatures. *NASA*

nel sections were chosen for the front and rear spars with intermediate spars of corrugated web attached to the external skin through separate angles. Three ribs were adopted for the main wing box of the same general construction as the front and rear spars and these were attached with A-286 rivets. The tip rib formed the exposed wing tip and was fabricated from Inconel X. Seventeen spars were located between the root and the mid-span rib, with nine spars outboard of that position.

The leading and trailing edges of the two wings were of multi-rib design with the size of the panel determined by the stiffness required. The entire forward leading edge was machined from a block of Inconel X so that it would serve as a heat sink. Initially, this was fabricated in five separate sections but when flight conditions demonstrated certain anomalies in the way it was effectively acting as a barrier, this was increased to nine segments. The gap between adjacent segments was 0.127cm (0.05in).

During the design phase the two-position wing flaps were of conventional titanium rib-type construction with Inconel X front spar and skins. However, wind tunnel tests revealed panel flutter and the outer skin was corrugated with an Inconel X inner skin. The position of the flap was determined by the pilot through an electromechanical actuator which had two electric motors coupled together by differential gears. The output powered a cable system that opened valves in the dual flap actuators to position the flap up or down. There were no intermediate positions. If one motor failed, flap extension was still possible but at half speed from the normal 8-10 seconds deploy time. Hydraulic relief valves set to respond to aerodynamic loads would close the flaps at speeds above

Below: X-15-1 hangs in the National Air and Space Museum, Washington, DC, where the clean lines and conformal blending of the side fairings with the fuselage and the wings were highly praised by the selection committee in deciding upon the definitive design. *NASM*

Right: The speed brakes are shown open in this view of the rear fuselage section where side fairing access panels have been removed revealing internal conduits and plumbing. *NASA*

463kph (288mph). There was no feedback indicator in the cockpit to notify the pilot of deployment, the feel of the controls and verification from the chase pilot providing confirmation of that event.

Considerable effort went on wing stress analysis and a lot of feedback from the previous experimental rocket planes provided the basis for this work. The basic design approach was one of simple beam theory and the solution solved a root problem as well. From approximately mid-span outboard, the construction followed a cantilever eight-cell beam concept for determining load stresses. Inboard of the mid-span point, the wing was divided into nine individual box beams and a single cell torque box. To this were directed the redundant shears and moment forces propagated from the structure around the wing root rib.

Designing the windshield for the X-15 was a challenging prospect, given the environment in which the aircraft was designed to operate. As initially conceived, it comprised a triple pane structure with a single outer pane and two double inner panes. It was made from soda-lime tempered plate to a specified requirement for withstanding temperatures no greater than 399°C (750°F). Early results in the initial phase of the development revealed that this had been significantly underestimated. Fresh calculations indicated that on some flights temperatures could go as high as 537.8°C (1,000°F), for which the original glass was deemed inadequate to protect the pilot. A new alumino-silicate 0.952cm (0.375in) thick outer pane replaced the original one but the inner planes continued to use the soda-lime glass throughout the flight phase.

All the glass used throughout was supplied by Corning with special tests conducted to show the resilience of their product under these extreme circumstances. One test devised by the scientists at Corning required a 21.3 x 71.1cm (8.4in x 28in) portion of this glass to be heated to 287.8°C (550°F) in a salt bath for three minutes and then plunged into tap water at room temperature. But a disaster was narrowly avoided when a panel of soda-lime glass, incorrectly fitted as an outer panel to X-15-2 for a flight to 66,142m (217,000ft) on 11 October 1961, cracked during the descending leg with near-fatal results.

Then a panel of alumino-silicate glass in the right window of X-15-2 shattered on its next flight on 9 November 1961 while decelerating from Mach 6.04 through Mach 2.7. The latter incident was caused when the retaining frame buckled close to the centre of the upper edge and focused thermal energy in that area which caused the failure. This brought a change in the frame material from a 0.1cm (0.05in) thick piece of Inconel X to a 0.25cm (0.10in) thick piece of 6Al-4V titanium alloy.

Further concerns about the windshield arose when plans were being made to push the X-15A-2 on to Mach 8 so an elliptical window with three panes was installed on the right side of the canopy. The outer pane was a 1.65cm (0.65in) thick panel of fused silica. The middle pane was 0.95cm (0.375in) thick alumino-silicate and the inner pane was a 0.74cm (0.29in) thick piece of soda-lime glass. A possible recurrence of the earlier problem with the buckled frame was avoided, at least in theory, by redesigning it into a flush-mounted alignment with the glass.

The attachment assembly for the wing/fuselage juncture was bi-metallic with Inconel X wing and side fairing covers and titanium alloy (5Al-2.5Sn) forgings and extrusions

Right: Upper and lower speed brakes open, the arrangement of the two XLR-11 rocket motors and the eight combustion chambers being clearly visible within the holding frame. *NAA*

forming an A-frame assembly. During the fabrication and assembly phase many items such as beads, lightening holes, scallops and corrugated webs reduced internal loads to a minimum and relaxed the thermal loads. This reduced the overall strain on the response of the wing to low and high mechanical loads.

The two horizontal stabilisers had the same aerofoil section as the wings, with a 5 per cent thickness/chord ratio, and these were mounted to the aft end of the rear fuselage chine with 15deg of anhedral. They could be moved symmetrically for pitch control, differentially for roll inputs, or in compound motion for complex attitude and pointing angles. This was unique among contemporary high-performance aircraft, although the all-moving horizontal stabiliser for pitch control had been a feature of the early X-1 series but not for differential movement. The structure of the stabilisers consisted of an integral main spar in Inconel-X positioned at the 57 per cent chord line, a front spar in aluminium (A-286) just aft of the leading edge and a titanium trailing edge. The structure had Inconel X ribs ahead of the main spar with 8Mn titanium alloy ribs aft and a 0.127cm (0.050in) Inconel X skin. The leading edge was fabricated from 40.6cm (16in) spanwise segments to lower potential expansion from stagnation-point temperatures.

To facilitate differential operations, each tail section was mounted on its own spindle which was an integral part of the main spar and attached to the fuselage next to the side chines. The main spar was designed to convey normal bending loads along the entire span and the front spar closed out the torque box which terminated at the rib root. As with the wing, the leading edge of the stabilisers was formed from sheet stock filled with weld material which doubled as a heat sink. Hydraulic cylinders attached to an arm in line with the outboard bearing were employed for actuation of the stabilisers.

Above and above right: The aft section of the rear fuselage on X-15-1 in the National Air & Space Museum provides a comparative view of the XLR-99 expansion skirt and the various jettison and vent lines either side of the fairings. *NASM/NAA*

There was some debate about the temperature differences, albeit small, which were seen and to accommodate this it was proposed that the skin gauge was increased and the stiffener spacing was decreased in an attempt to avoid buckling. But this process would increase the weight by a considerable amount, at least an additional 88.45kg (195lb). It was decided to accept that some thermal buckling would occur during the short period during re-entry when maximum temperatures were experienced. But permanent buckling was not acceptable and the skin thickness was retained without stiffeners.

The vertical stabilisers were attached above and below the rear fuselage and supported a 10deg wedge shaped cross-section to enhance stability in the hypersonic regime. The rudder comprised the upper and lower sections of the vertical tail units. During design and for initial flight tests, the ventral stabiliser was considered prudent for high-alpha (angle of attack) pointing where the forward fuselage could mask the air flow and neutralise the effectiveness of the dorsal stabiliser in yaw. The design included a fixed section attached to the fuselage and a moving section acting as a rudder for both dorsal and ventral stabilisers.

The vertical stabilisers were formed from fixed box structures with titanium and Inconel X, the latter also used for skins. A single speed brake attached to the aft root section of

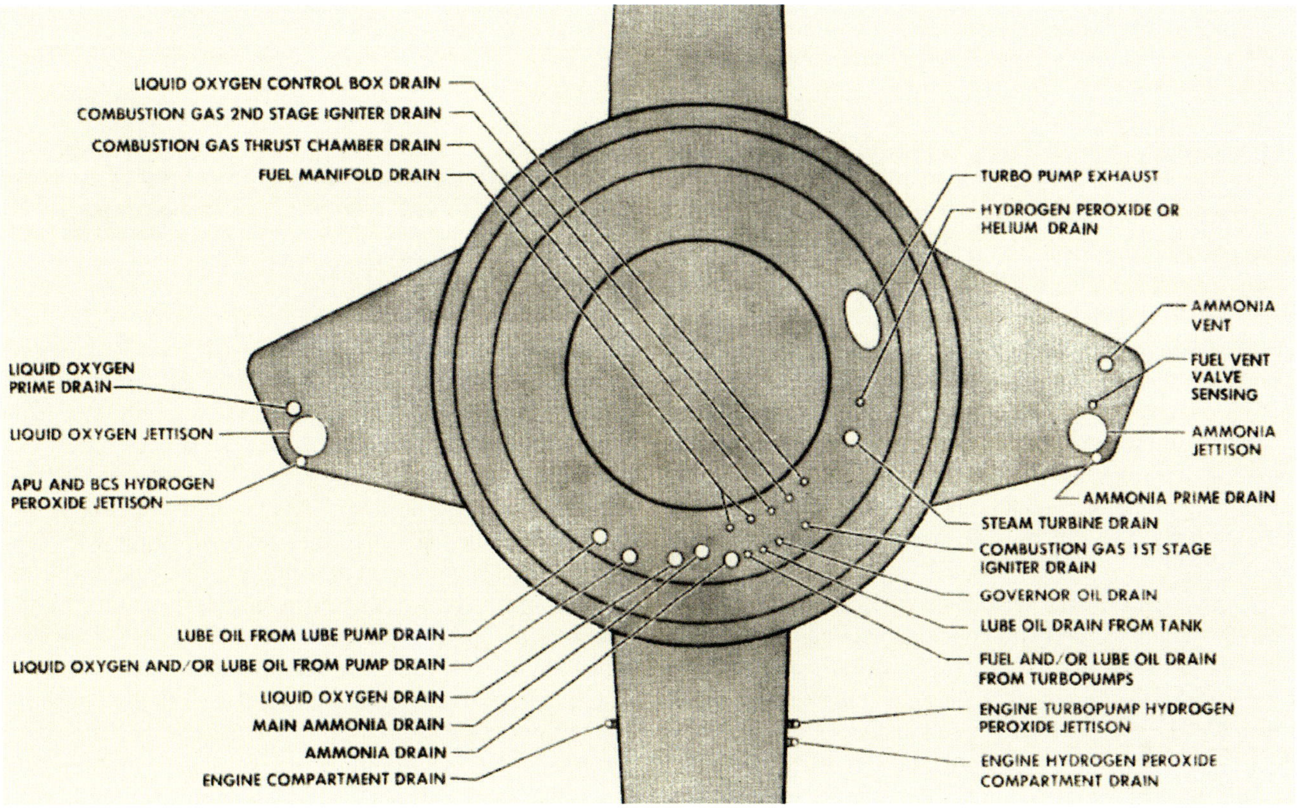

each stabiliser was hinged from the fixed portion, each pair actuated by a hydraulic strut. The brakes were fabricated from Inconel X and reinforced by a corrugated inner skin and ribs. The all-moving rudder was fabricated entirely from Inconel X with front, main and rear beams, the main and rear beams providing a sixth beam for attachment to the fixed vertical stabiliser. The attachment was secured by a spindle support with two bearings 43.2cm (18in) apart, with the moveable portion actuated by a hydraulically-operated strut.

In operation, the ventral rudder had to be jettisoned prior to landing because it protruded below the landing skids when they were deployed. For releasing the ventral rudder the pilot actuated a jettison button which electrically fired four explosive bolts and a piston which also contained an explosive charge. A mechanical system was available as a back-up. After separation, a parachute was deployed to lower the rudder to the ground for reuse. Flight experience revealed that the ventral tail contributed to instability at hypersonic speeds at high angles of attack and it was removed for 73 flights, 126 completed with it attached.

Below: The design evolution of the vertical stabilisers was largely determined through wind tunnel tests which here can be seen in mid-1956 displaying the early shape and the minimal ventral stabiliser. *NASA*

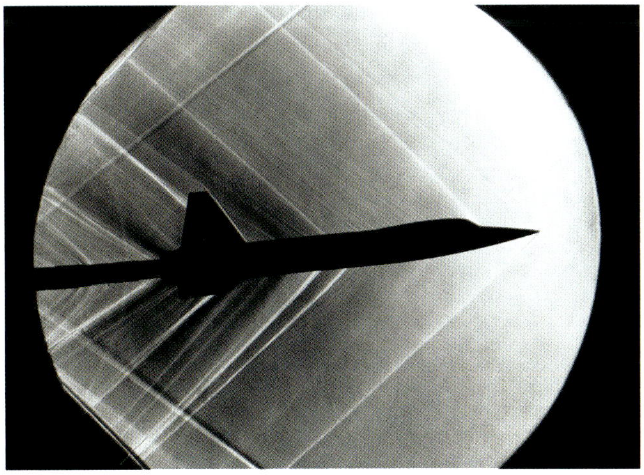

The speed brakes were essentially two symmetrical panels hinged at the front end with one segment powered by the No. 1 hydraulic system, the other by the No. 2 system. Any one hydraulic system could operate the speed brakes but at a reduced rate under specific air loads. The pilot could place the brakes in any position from fully open, at an angle of 35deg, to fully closed. The speed brake actuator consisted of two handles on the left side of the cockpit wall, the inboard handle controlling the ventral brake, the outboard handle controlling the dorsal brake. A lock pin between the two handles prevented the two brakes from being moved asymmetrically but on one flight the pin was removed for testing asymmetric handling. The position of the brakes could be determined by the pilot from a scale showing position in 5deg increments.

Getting grounded

The landing gear design for the X-15 was very different to that employed by the X-1 series and its derivatives or by the Douglas Skyrocket. Those first-generation rocket planes adopted a tricycle undercarriage and were nose-sitters. The X-15 adapted the design chosen for the X-2, which had a nose leg and wheel arrangement with two skids deployed from the rear of the fuselage. The X-15's nose leg was housed in a conventional wheel

Right: When the X-15-2 was reworked into the X-15A-2 with extended fuselage, the configuration was tunnel-tested using this model displaying the ventral stabiliser without the jettisonable lower section. *NASA*

well with two boat-shaped skids stowed externally within the aft side bays. The legs were rigid but some degree of outward play was possible through an air/oil shock absorber which was attached to the upper end. The skids were located to the far aft of the fuselage and there would be modifications to this arrangement as the programme progressed.

The design of the landing gear was based upon an aircraft weighing 4,990kg (11,000lb) at touchdown with a sink rate of 2.7m/sec (9ft/sec), touching down on the skids at 303-370kph (188-230mph) with an angle of attack of approximately 6deg. While the design remained frozen the empty weight of the aircraft grew and this would bring problems during the flight tests and later during the research missions, as described in Section 3.

To save space it was decided that the nose leg should be stowed in a fully compressed condition with nitrogen gas being used to extend it after rotating down for landing. There were some design problems with this arrangement when it was discovered that the gas trapped under compression produced a mixed gas/oil foam inside the cylinder, making the first one-third of the stroke ineffective. The higher loads imposed bringing the nose down brought a modification whereby the strut was fitted with a floating piston to keep the gas and the oil separate.

The dual nose wheels were forged from cast magnesium and had aluminium rims to which were attached standard 10-ply aircraft tyres inflated to 1,655kPa (240lb/in^2). As flight activity progressed a change was made in 1966 to some flights carrying cast aluminium wheels fitted with 12-ply tyres at the higher pressure of 2,034kPa (295lb/in^2) with the intention of increasing the margins during landing and rollout. Modifications to the nose leg too were required after it was discovered during preparation for a flight with X-15-1 on 3 March 1967 that it was binding during an attempt to compress it for retraction. NAA conducted an examination of the leg and discovered that the strut was bent. A similar incident had occurred with the same aircraft on 12 July 1966 but in neither case were there any unreasonable loads imposed on the leg.

Concerned at the reason, and with the safety of the pilot and the aircraft in mind for what was in any event a tricky part of an X-15 flight, engineers made a comparison with X-15-3, which had no history of any such occurrence. The only difference which could be found was that X-15-1 had been flying with the new tyres, which had greater weight and inertia, while the third aircraft had the old 10-ply tyres. Because the newer tyres were thought to be inducing drag loads during spin-up, X-15-1 reverted to the older tyres on the older wheels. With higher landing weights and loads, X-15A-2 retained the 12-ply tyres and the aluminium wheels.

The rear gear comprised two 4130-steel skids with an Inconel X strut on each side of the fuselage chine. They were attached with trunnion fittings and bell cranks to the shock struts attached to the inside of the fuselage. These fittings allowed the shoes to rotate in pitch and roll but not in yaw so as to maintain longitudinal alignment. Drag braces were attached to the fuselage in front of the trunnions and to the skids at the attachment pin. Bungee springs helped keep the skids in a forward-facing direction prior to touch-down. In the retracted position the skids were folded up and forward against the lower fuselage.

As the flight programme progressed there were concerns about the ability of the rear landing gear to accommodate higher landing weights. The X-15-1 and X-15-3 aircraft would be rated to a new maximum landing weight of 7,257kg (16,000lb) and an emergency weight of 7,711kg (17,000lb). Plans existed for rotation of the horizontal stabiliser on landing to reduce the loads on the main skids but they would also require modification for the increased weight. The preferred mode was to relocate the nose gear trunnion on these two aircraft as had been done for X-15A-2. Another option was to add a third skid to the underside of the ventral fin, which would redistribute landing loads and relieve the stress on the entire landing gear. The decision was taken to add a third skid, installed on X-15-3 for its flight on 18 June 1966, and to X-15-1, for its flight on 22 March 1967. There was some consideration given to adding a third skid to X-15-A2 for flights involving the ramjet mock-up but this was never implemented.

Control of the landing gear was via a T-shaped handle on the left wing of the main instrument panel in the cockpit, linked via cables to the main gear uplocks and the nose gear and wheel well door uplocks. The handle would be pulled a

Left: Tunnel tests with 10cm (4in) models of the X-15 were conducted in the Hypervelocity Free-Flight Facility at the Ames Research Center, opened in 1964 offering a unique capability for testing aeroballistic devices in mediums other than air and sub-atmospheric pressures. *NASA*

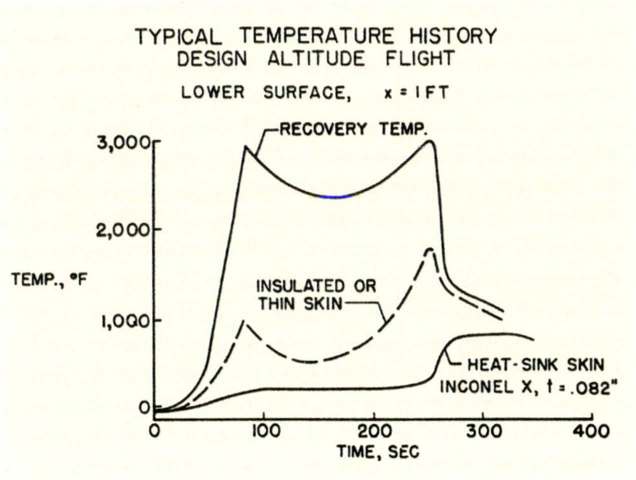

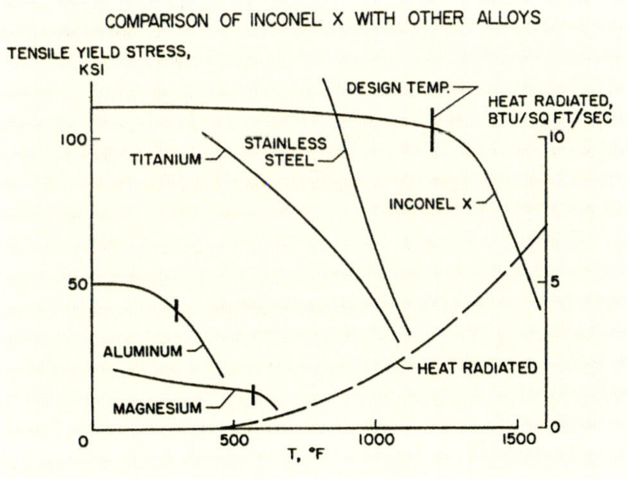

Above: Chart showing the temperatures experienced by the exterior of the X-15 during a typical high altitude flight compared to an insulated or thin-skin structure. *NACA*

Above right: Tensile yield stress in thousands of pounds per square inch (KSI) are here expressed across a range of temperatures at which the materials concerned resist restoration and fracture. The heat radiated is vital in determing when failures might occur and shows the resilience of Inconel X in meeting the design temperature requirements. *NACA*

full 27.9cm (11in) rearward, releasing the uplocks and allowing a spring-loaded scoop door in the main door to swing down and into the airstream. This in turn would fire the initiator to actuate a piston which would force open the door against flight loads which previously would have held the door closed. After the gear was released a switch on the left main gear would activate a charge triggering release of the ventral stabiliser and, as with the speed brakes, confirmation that the gear was down would come from the feel of the aircraft and from the chase pilot.

On many aircraft the design of the landing gear is critical to its operation and with research aircraft, compromised in their configuration by the requirements of their mission, it is often a difficult design challenge. The X-15 landing gear engineering effort had a smooth run. Three test programmes were implemented, including a dynamic test for stability using a model, a nose wheel shimmy test, and a full scale main gear test on the dry lakebed at Edwards. These were followed by a full scale nose shimmy test at the landing test facility at Langley where a wide range of speed runs were made on a diverse set of test tracks including muddy, dusty, wet paved` and dry surfaces. Blocks were intentionally placed in the path of the rolling nose gear to test for deflections or shimmy tendencies. The results were highly positive, showing there was no need for dampers or torque links.

Skid tests were conducted at Edwards, with replica devices attached to a retractable carriage fastened to the back of a trailer and pulled along by a truck at speeds of up to 113kph

Right: A clear view of the landing skid which would be deployed prior to touchdown. Also shown are the fixed portion of the ventral stabiliser and various access points on the aft fuselage. *NASA*

Below: As a means of measuring theoretical thermal transfer rate against flight results, the dimensionless Reynolds number (in the abscissa) as the ratio of momentum forces, balancing these against given flow conditions. The Cfi (ordinate) is defined by Blassius' equations as the 'incompressible friction coefficient'. Boundary layer predictions derived from theoretical extrapolation are within these coordinates and the X-15 falls across the convergence of predicted skin friction. It was this information which greatly assisted the Apollo and Shuttle programmes. *NACA*

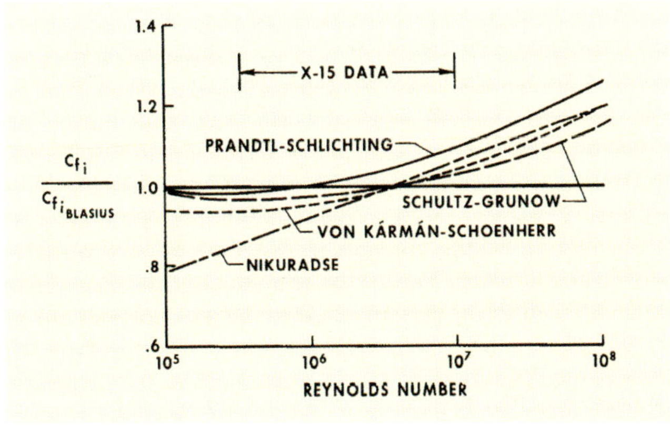

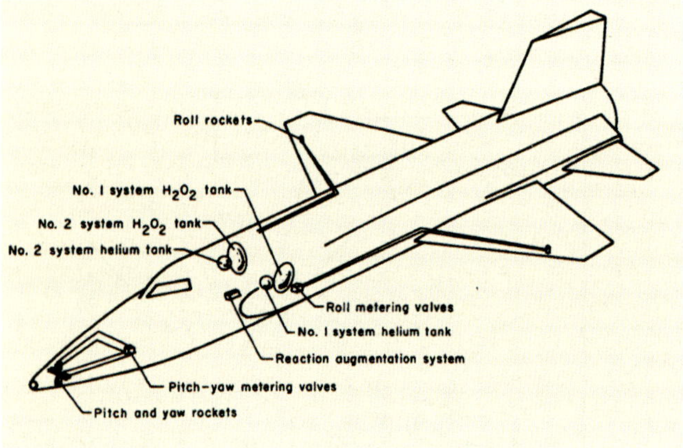

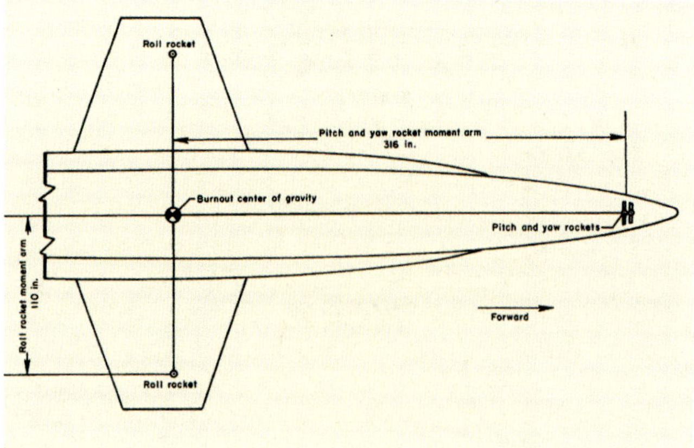

Above: The Ballistic Control System (BCS) was the first of its kind applied to an operational programme, more than five years before the first humans went into space. The exoatmospheric thrusters were disposed around the nose and on the wing tips. The BCS reaction line was placed through the X-15's centre of gravity (above) for pitch, yaw and roll control. *NAA*

(70mph). The tests with the skids worked through a release mechanism that operated as the truck began to slow down, releasing the shoes to drop to the lakebed. The response of the skids was recorded by high speed cameras on the truck. Various sensors measured the vertical and drag loads, measuring strut stroke and various parameters to verify that the landing gear could operate satisfactorily in a wide range of conditions. One concern, subject to simulation in these tests, was the ability of the gear to remain effective under side loads imposed by a 'skidding' motion either side of the centreline after touch-down.

Minor modifications to the landing gear well would take place during the flight programme. One of which was to add a seal to the nose gear door after it had been noticed on X-15-1 on 4 October 1961 that hot boundary layer air had seeped into the nose gear well causing damage to some tubing and a small part of the structure. None of this compromised the effectiveness of the aircraft or its gear but it did pose a potential threat for future high-temperature flights. Later, on two separate flights, Maj. Robert A. Rushworth was flying above Mach 4 when the nose gear lowered, which caused some interesting flight characteristics and burned through both tyres. It was eventually deduced that the fuselage was expanding due to the heat and, because the cable had insufficient slack to compensate, it pulled it free at entirely the wrong time. Engineers increased the slack, requiring the pilot to pull the stick 35.6cm (14in) to drop the gear.

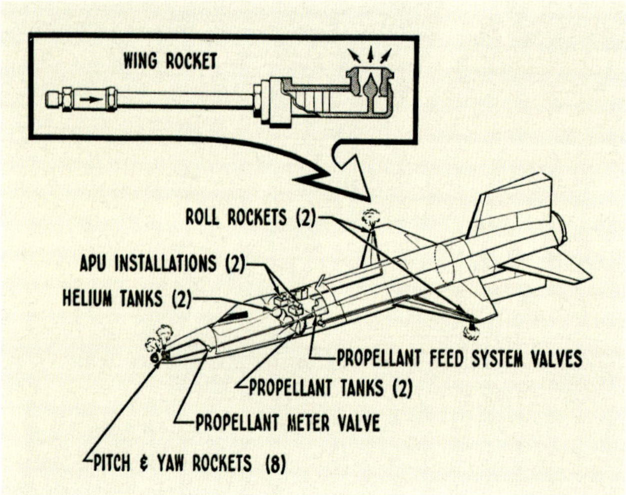

Attitude and orientation

Flight control for an aircraft designed to exit the aero-effective regions of the Earth's atmosphere was the responsibility of the Ballistic Control System (BCS), Developed by Bell, the BCS for the X-15 would be specified where dynamic pressure was below 1.197kPa (25lb/ft²) which was at an altitude of 54,864m (180,000ft). In practice many pilots began to use it at 30,480m (100,000ft) where the pressure was 2.394kPa (50lb/ft²). Nevertheless, at the lower, recommended, pressure for switching over from aerodynamic to thruster control, the overall effectiveness of the two systems balanced out. Development and test of the BCS for the X-15 ran parallel to work being conducted by Langley-PARD for attitude control and flight orientation in the Mercury spacecraft, inherited by NASA in 1958 as the lead agency for what had previously been an Air Force project for placing men in space.

For the X-15, two independent systems were installed, both using hydrogen peroxide monopropellant which was decomposed into an effective force by converting it to steam over a silver screen. The steam was transferred to small thrusters in the nose and in the wing tips. The hydrogen peroxide was drawn from the same supply as that used for the two Auxiliary Power Units (APUs), the No. 1 system being supplied from the No. 1 APU tank and the No. 2 system from the No. 2 APU tank. Later in the flight programme a transfer system was installed whereby residual monopropellant from the turbopump could be used by the APUs after engine shutdown. This system was eventually installed in all three aircraft, activated by a switch on the upper right side of the main instrument panel.

Eight jets were installed in the nose of the X-15, each with a thrust of 503N (113lb) in pairs pointing in opposing directions at four locations arranged at 90deg intervals. Two 178N (40lb) thrusters were located in each wing tip, one up and one down. The entire system was divided into two separate rings:

Left: The relative location of the BCS thrusters with associated propellant storage vessels. *NAA*

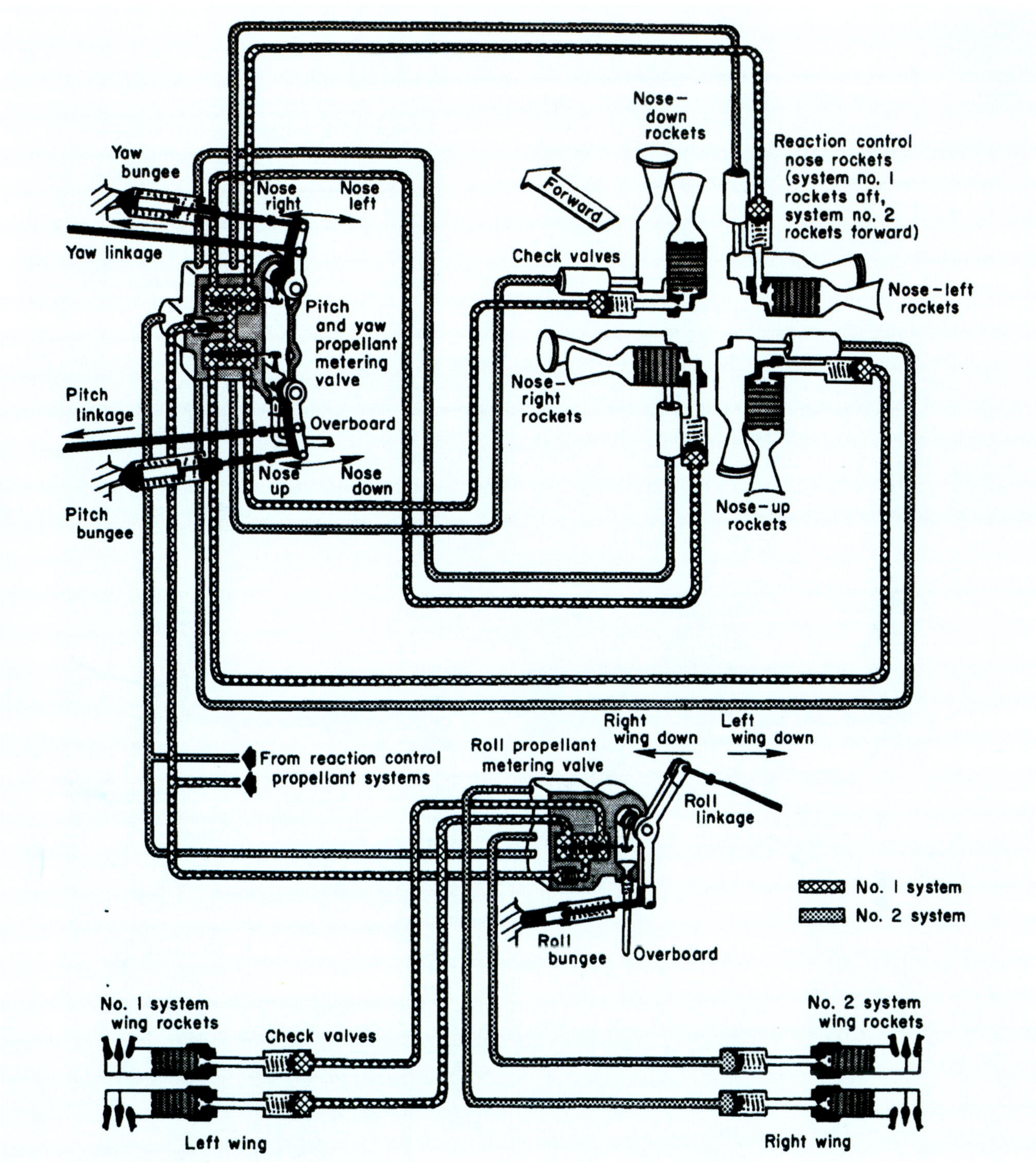

Above: This operating schematic for the BCS flight control system shows the activating valves for the monopropellant, fed across a silver screen for decomposition of the hydrogen peroxide into steam and directed through a thruster jet creating a force and inducing a reaction. *NAA*

the No. 1 system operating four nose thrusters and the two thrusters on the port wing tip; the No. 2 system operating the rest. This arrangement ensured redundancy for maintaining attitude control at all times during exo-atmospheric flight.

Each nozzle had a 3.5cm (1.4in) orifice in the skin, with a maximum flow rate of 0.227lit (0.06USgall) per second for the pitch thrusters and 0.078lit (0.02USgall) per second for the roll thrusters. On most high altitude missions, where the X-15 was outside the atmosphere for several minutes, the consumption total would be approximately 7.57lit (2USgall). Effective operation of these thrusters was crucial to the safety of the vehicle. Prior to independent flight, just before the launch, the thrusters were fired for about three seconds to ensure they worked correctly. The wing tip thrusters were on a line directly through the X-15 centre of gravity, which was 8m (26.3ft) aft of the nose thruster centreline.

Operation of the thrusters was counter-intuitive for pilots used to aerodynamic controls. After an attitude excursion had been commanded, in the near vacuum of near-Earth space the aircraft would continue moving in roll, pitch or yaw until a further thruster input in the opposing direction was made to arrest the motion. A pitch-up command would activate the down-pointing thrusters in the nose to begin an attitude motion pointing the nose upward which would be arrested by a brief blip on the upward-pointing thrusters. Likewise, a yaw to right or left would be started with thrusters initiating the excursion followed by a reverse command to halt the motion. Much of the learning process would be acquired through simulators.

A sidestick controller was installed on the left side wing of the cockpit display panel. The natural tendency to follow flight control functions required that the system be configured so that a yaw to the right required a right movement on the stick, a pitch-down motion being commanded by moving the stick forward, and reverse movement of the controller for opposite excursions. Quite familiar to astronauts, in the early 1960s it was a unique system for a spaceplane, relevant only to very high altitude flights. Late in the research programme, the BCS was removed from X-15A-2 when its flight plans no longer carried it to very high altitude.

Before the final decision on the precise handling configuration for the BCS, several engineers, as well as test pilot Scott Crossfield, felt that a rate damping system would be helpful in avoiding an over-distraction by the pilot on what was still a very unfamiliar way of controlling a winged vehicle in flight. For that reason a Reaction Augmentation System (RAS) was installed in X-15-1 and X-15-2 during 1963 but for X-15-3 the MH-96 adaptive flight control system was installed, obviating the need for the RAS. It worked by damping out attitude excursions to anticipate the need for compensatory thrusting to avoid the override mentioned previously.

The RAS had a rate gyro sensor which measured the angular rate about all three axes and, with a pre-set angular rate installed, it automatically fired the proper thruster to reduce the sensed angular acceleration. It began to fire the opposing thruster in a sequence of small bursts so that it would bring the attitude excursion to a halt. In practice the pilot would have to make small 'tweak' bursts of thruster fire to precisely align the attitude with the desired pointing angle in pitch or yaw. The pilot had the ability to switch off augmentation

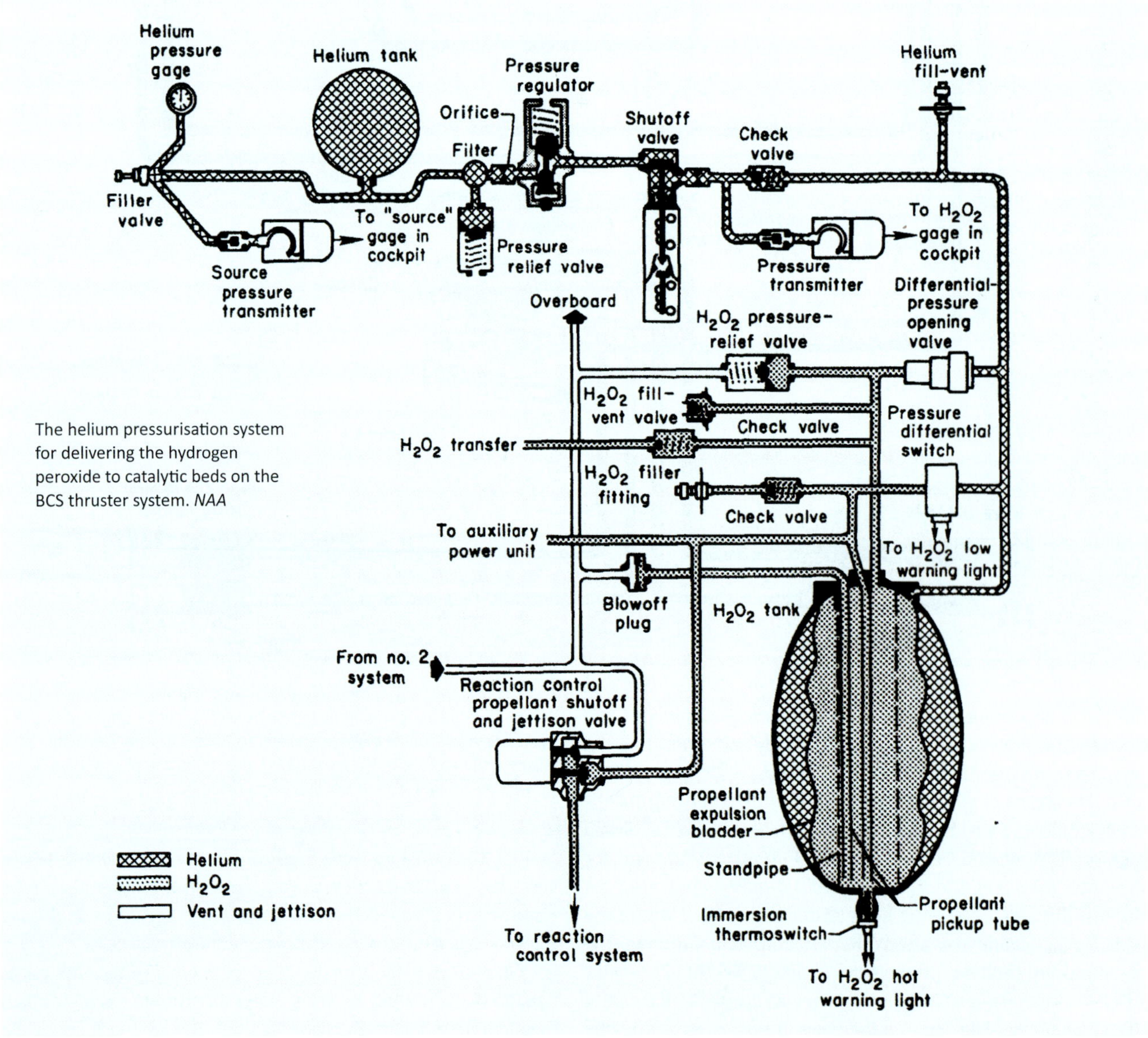

The helium pressurisation system for delivering the hydrogen peroxide to catalytic beds on the BCS thruster system. *NAA*

about any axis as desired and the system disengaged completely and automatically when the X-15 entered the denser levels of the atmosphere.

Hydraulic and electrical power for the X-15 was provided by two 29.8kw (40hp) Auxiliary Power Units (APUs) operating on decomposed hydrogen peroxide driving a hydraulic pump and electrical generator. Built by General Electric they operated quite independent of the rocket motor(s) and were installed, side-by-side, in a dedicated compartment ahead of the LOX tank. Separate dedicated feed systems were fitted for each APU with helium used to pressure-feed the monopropellant, each APU contributing approximately half the required power level. In the event of a single APU failure the aircraft could be operated by the working APU securing critical functions, albeit for a restricted flight.

Each APU was turned on or off using a switch in the cockpit, start-up activating a solenoid valve which released a flow of monopropellant through the gear case for cooling before it was routed to the unit itself. The hydrogen peroxide was released to the APU through a flow control valve which operated to control the speed of the APU, normally 51,200rpm. A sensor would command automatic shutdown if the speed reached 56,000rpm. From this valve the monopropellant would pass across a series of silver and stainless steel screens which would decompose the hydrogen peroxide into superheated steam. This would enter the turbine through five nozzles pointing at the turbine wheel. The turbine proper worked through a reduction gear to transmit power to the electrical generator and the hydraulic pump.

The X-15 employed an alternating current for electrical power with direct current power systems. The ac system was produced by a 200/115volt, 400-cycle three-phase generator attached to each of the two APUs. The 28volt dc system was powered from the ac system through two transformer-rectifiers. In emergencies it could also be powered by a 24volt battery. This was designed specifically for the X-15 but later batteries were scavenged from the Lockheed F-104 programme since they were the same size and produced slightly more power. They were also available off-the-shelf and because of that were available at less cost. Electrical power on both ac and dc circuits could be supplied from ground units before take-off through a plug attachment on the top of the fuselage aft of the cockpit canopy. In the air, electrical power was supplied from the carrier-plane until the APUs on the X-15 were started.

The hydraulic systems installed in the X-15 provided power for operating the aerodynamic controls, including the rudders, stabilisers, wing flaps and speed brakes, and for the ball nose. Two independent hydraulic systems were installed, with dual tandem actuators so that failure in either one would not deny use of any critical functioning items. Each hydraulic actuator was designed to hold half the maximum design hinge moment which engineers considered adequate for control of the aircraft. The system selected was a standard Type III with 20,685kPa (3,000lb/in^2) operating in parallel and with the emergency system as a back-up. Fluid for the hydraulic system was provided from a reservoir, with the pressure maintained at the correct level by a variable high-displacement pump and a constant low-displacement pump secured directly to each APU.

Each reservoir held 3lit (0.8USgall) of fluid, with the total per system being 4.9lit (1.3USgall) while the maximum flow rate was 60.6lit/min (16USgall/min). For almost all the time (at least 90 per cent) the flow rate was less than 5.7lit/min (1.5USgall/min) and this resulted in an arrangement whereby an E-14101-A pump maintained a fixed outflow of 6lit/min (1.6USgall/min) for all normal requirements. A second, 3913 variable-volume, pump was available for a surge requirement of 60.6lit/min (16USgall/min) with check valves in place to act as a regulator by switching off the higher capacity pump when not required.

Designed and developed by Sperry Rand Corporation Vickers Division, it was fabricated by that company and brought an energy-efficient solution. The advantage with this design, which was unique to the X-15, was that it required less power from the APU and put less heat into the fluid. On the ground the hydraulic system had a temperature of -29°C (-20°F) increasing to -17.8°C (0°F) during the climb to the cruise and 10°C (50°F) at launch. This would rise to 204.4°C (400°F) in the eight minutes it took to fly a high-speed profile. For this type of flight a period of 22 minutes would be spent in heat-soak after touch-down. On 15 flights the fluid remained at this temperature for 7.5 hours.

A number of optional fluids were evaluated for the X-15, including MIL-O-55606, which was the standard US Air Force hydraulic fluid, General Electric F-50, Monsanto OS-45-1, Oronite 8200, and Oronite 8515. The decision over which to use for various applications hinged on its ability to maintain viscosity at the maximum temperature of 204.4°C (400°F). Any reduction in viscosity could cause leaks from seals and valve assemblies but thermal stability, lubrication properties and its ability not to degrade seals and other materials was critical. So critical were the judgements over use that two Oronite products were set up to compete against each other: Oronite 8200 was acceptable but was found to have a degrading influence on Neoprene WRT seals; Oronite 8500 had the same general qualities but without affecting the seals, so that became the logical choice.

Information about the aircraft's angle of attack and sideslip, vital for flying the aircraft on instruments, was problematical in the high supersonic and hypersonic regime, where high temperatures would make it impossible to equip the X-15 with ordinary vane-type sensors. Moreover, for the high-altitude flight profile the conventional sensors would be useless in the airless void above the atmosphere. To solve the problem NAA turned to the Nortronics Division of the Northrop Aircraft Corporation for the conceptual design and construction of a ball nose device which would remain protected from the external temperatures. In doing so it helped pioneer a new way of determining attitude orientation and α-angle as well as the β-drift (sideslip) and in so doing began the convergence of technology and information systems for manned aircraft and electronic digital systems for guided missiles.

Officially known as the Hypersonic Airflow Direction & Pitot-Pressure Sensor (HADPPS), the ball nose for the X-15 weighed 35.4kg (78lb) and was 37.75cm (16.75in) in length with a diameter of 34.92cm (13.75in) at the base, where it was attached to the front face of the forward fuselage section, constituting the nose of the aircraft proper. Half the weight was accounted for by the thick Inconel X outer skin faces. Thirteen chromel-alumel thermocouples were installed in the centre of the nose to measure skin temperature. Being nickel-based they have good corrosion resistance and some of the widest temperature range sensitivity available, offering a range from -270°C (-454°F) to 1,260°C (2,300°F) and a melt point of 1,400°C (2,550°F). They are known for their reliability across a wide range of rugged and environmentally challenging environments. Five other thermocouples measured various internal temperatures.

Expanded nitrogen was used to cool the sensors in the ball nose and connections through to the main body of the forward fuselage were made through male couplings that automatically engaged with female receptors. The core of the nose itself was a 16.5cm (6.5in) diameter Inconel X sphere with two pairs of 0.477cm (0.188in) orifices, each located 42deg from the stagnation point. One pair was aligned with the vertical plane, the α orifices, the other pair were in the horizontal plane, the β orifices, while a total pressure measurement for the X-15 was obtained with a 1.27cm (0.5in) orifice located at the stagnation point.

The sphere was rotated around the α and the β axes by hydraulic power, which was obtained from the X-15's hydraulic services, and driven to a null point of equality for all sensor ports. From that point it was orientated directly to the relative wind vector and two transducers detected the position of the sphere with respect to the airframe. This signal was sent to the cockpit instruments, to the on-board recorders and to the telemetry system streaming data to the ground. Because the dynamic pressure during flight could range from 0.04877kPa (1lb/ft²) to 119.7kPa (2,500lb/ft²), adjustments were necessary in the servo loop to keep it stable and maintain accuracy. The ball nose could sense angles of attack from -10deg to +40deg and measure sideslip of +/-20deg. It was capable of operating with a skin temperature of 649°C (1,200°F). The angular accuracy of the sensor was within +/-10deg for dynamic pressures above 0.4788kPa (10lb/ft²).

For all its sophistication and precision, the means to test it prior to approving installation was anything but high-tech. Needing to find a means of exposing the intricate, and delicate piece of instrumentation to the temperatures it would experience in flight, the NACA had a solution: put it up close to the afterburner of a North American Aviation F-100 Super Sabre and turn the engine on! The first trial effort was made on 20 January 1959 and it worked. At least for a while, until one of the tests exposed a curling lip on a ball nose under test, caused, it was discovered, by the engine being run for too long and exposing the HADPPS to temperatures in excess of 1,316°C (2,400°F), compared to a planned temperature of 1,038°C (1,900°F).

The ball nose was highly effective for flight profiles using the basic X-15 but high-speed runs with the X-15A-2 required a different material for the outer skins for it to survive temperatures experienced by the air vehicle at Mach 8. The NACA's Lewis facility had developed a new sphere fabricated from TAZ-8A cermet and this was manufactured by the Rohr Corporation and delivered to Edwards in mid-1966. Tests initially proved troublesome and cast doubt on the new ball but after further work at Rohr it performed satisfactorily. This too was tested up the rear end of an afterburner – this time on a more powerful – and hotter J79 on an F-104 Starfighter. It was carried by X-15A-2 for the first time on 21 August 1967.

For taking total pressure readings during subsonic flight a pitot head was located on the forward fuselage ahead of the cockpit canopy but this was changed for the high-temperature environments destined for the X-15A-2. For that aircraft the normal static locations were covered with the MA-25S ablative insulation. A special vent was fitted behind the cockpit, tested on X-15-1. The normal dog-leg shaped pitot tube in front of the cockpit was replaced with one that could be retracted when the temperatures were at their highest and extended when the aircraft was below Mach 2. This pilot-actuated mechanism was the precursor to a similar system adopted for the NASA Space Shuttle.

The ball nose was connected to the X-15's hydraulic system and was cooled with nitrogen. To test its resistance to the heat of high speed flights, technicians installed it close to the exhaust pipe of a J79 jet engine – with not unsurprising results! *NAA*

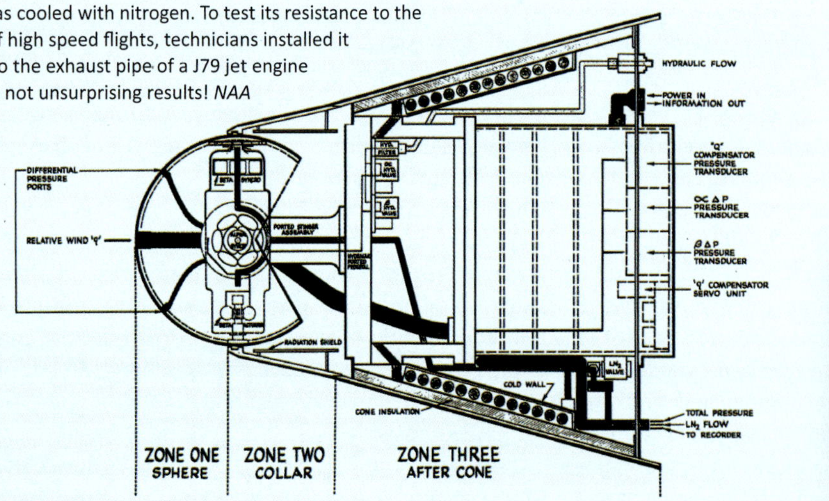

Chapter Fourteen

Systems and Subsystems

With unprecedented performance, the need to determine the X-15's altitude and speed at all times during independent flight brought unusual challenges and this proved one of the more problematical areas of development. It was implicit within the original work requirement for the aircraft and was addressed by all the airframe contenders. In fact, it was to be one of the first attempts to provide what the NACA defined as a 'stable platform', from which these essential parameters could be determined. Difficult to envisage in today's world of high-speed electronics and ring-laser gyroscopes, in the mid-1950s the development conducted around the requirement for a stable platform on the X-15 was a precursor to the introduction of such systems in the 1960s. In fact, the X-15 was to be part of the development cycle for that equipment.

In one respect the X-15 bridged two eras and different systems found their way into the X-15 programme: an analogue system and a digital system, both of which used similar inertial measurement units (IMUs). Paradoxically, problems encountered during development of the analogue system were greater than those encountered by the digital system. This was because the analogue system was the first of its kind and was developed in parallel with the configuration design

Above: As explored in Chapter 13, the Ballistic Control System and its thruster units (shown here in the nose section) pioneered the use of control systems in a winged vehicle designed for exoatmospheric flight. It called for a particularly unusual form of adaptive flight control system. *NASA*

of the flight system. It was these problems that led to a decision to switch to a digital system which allowed programming through the computer and was therefore more flexible.

When the system design was finalised in June 1957 the analogue system was the only one available and a contract was awarded for six systems. Weight, power, reliability and performance were still problematical areas and much of the technology was still very new. Nevertheless, solid-state electronics were selected with extensive use of electromechanical systems. While still being very new, transistors were capable of providing the reliability and power requirements commensurate with the specification written for the analogue system. But as written, the specification was beyond existing capabilities and although early flight tests displayed reasonable performance, it was clear by early 1963 that it was failing to meet the necessary requirements.

The original specification for the analogue system required a total velocity range of 0-2,134m/sec (0-7,000ft/sec) with an accuracy of +/-30m/sec (+/-100ft/sec), a rate of climb of 0-305m/sec (0-1,000ft/sec), with an accuracy of +/-21m/sec (+/-70ft/sec), and a geometric height of 0-152,400m (0-500,000ft), with an accuracy of +/-1,524m (+/-5,000ft) at 300 seconds and +/-3,048m (+/-10,000ft) at 500 seconds.

By 1963 doubts surfaced about the performance of the system, which was believed to be woefully inadequate and falling far short of the specification. In the November, efforts accelerated to obtain a new system for the X-15. With the cancellation of the X-20 (formerly Dyna-Soar) a new digital reference system became available and while this was still not state-of-the-art, because it used a computer dating to 1959, there were clear advantages to putting it in the X-15 programme. The final decision was made in April 1964 to modify the X-20 device and use it as a replacement for the analogue system. It was installed on X-15-1 for a checkout flight on 15 October 1964 and later it was fitted to X-15-3, although not without some problems due to the MH-96 adaptive flight control system. The X-15-2 continued to fly with the analogue system

The analogue system comprised two parts: a reference system installed in the carrier-plane and the Inertial Flight Data System (IFDS) installed in the X-15, configured to provide altitude, rate of climb, total velocity and attitude information by measuring accelerations of the vehicle relative to an inertial frame with subsequent interrogations for velocity and position. The equipment in the carrier-plane included a flight control panel, a Doppler radar and an N-1 gyro-stabilised magnetic compass. The Doppler radar provided ground velocity drift angle to the flight control panel and the N-1 furnished magnetic heading.

The circuitry in the control panel resolved total radar velocity into range and cross-range components and also monitored the performance of the X-15 system, displaying position, velocity errors and gyroscopic drift rates to the operator in the B-52. The IFDS in the X-15 consisted of an IMU, an analogue computer and a set of displays for the pilot. It was designed from the outset to operate without any external input from the moment the aircraft was released from the carrier-plane.

The stable platform for the X-15 was provided by the Sperry Gyroscope Company and was essentially a Schuler-tuned system slaved to the Earth. Schuler-tuning is used in aircraft, submarines and ships to take account of the curvature of the planet and to determine direction with respect to axes pointing north, east and down, which will change as the vehicle moves around the curvature of the Earth. It was explained first by the German engineer Maximilian Schuler in 1923. Attitudes, together with velocity and height data, were provided to the pilot. The platform weighed 79.8kg (176lb) and occupied a volume of 0.17m^3 (6.03ft^3). It drew 600w of electrical power and was cooled with nitrogen gas.

The inertial reference in this system was a four-gimbal platform to maintain the orientation of three force-rebalanced accelerometers with respect to the local vertical and a predetermined azimuth through any attitude or orientation of the X-15. The specified parameters were a non-acceleration sensitive drift of 1deg/hr (0.17rad/hr), an acceleration sensitive drift

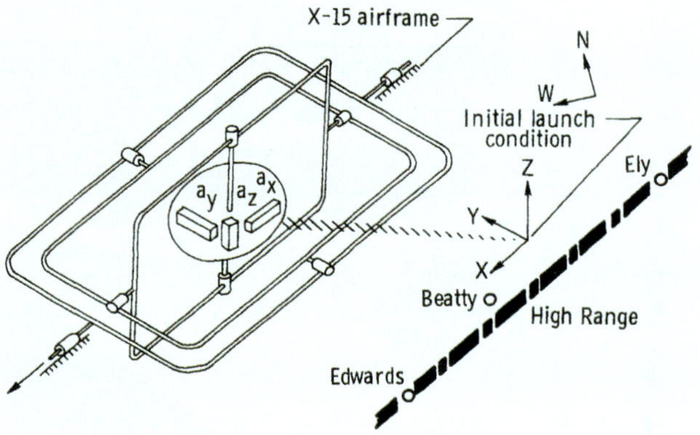

Above: As discussed in Chapter 18, accurate information on attitude orientation and directional stability was crucial for effective flight operations. The stable platform for the X-15 was developed and manufactured by Sperry Gyroscope, the conventional design involving outer, middle and inner gimbal rings for relative axes. New to manned aircraft, the inertial platform had many problems until a derivative, the FRC-66, was introduced. Below the photograph is a generalised and simplified diagram showing the IMU and the relative position for azimith at launch to the High Range tracking systems. *NASA*

X-15 – pitot tube details

Later flights replaced the nose-boom probe with the ball nose, relocating the pitot tube to the upper forward fuselage. For early flights, air data was obtained from the nose-boom and pitot probe shown below with dimensions. *NASA*

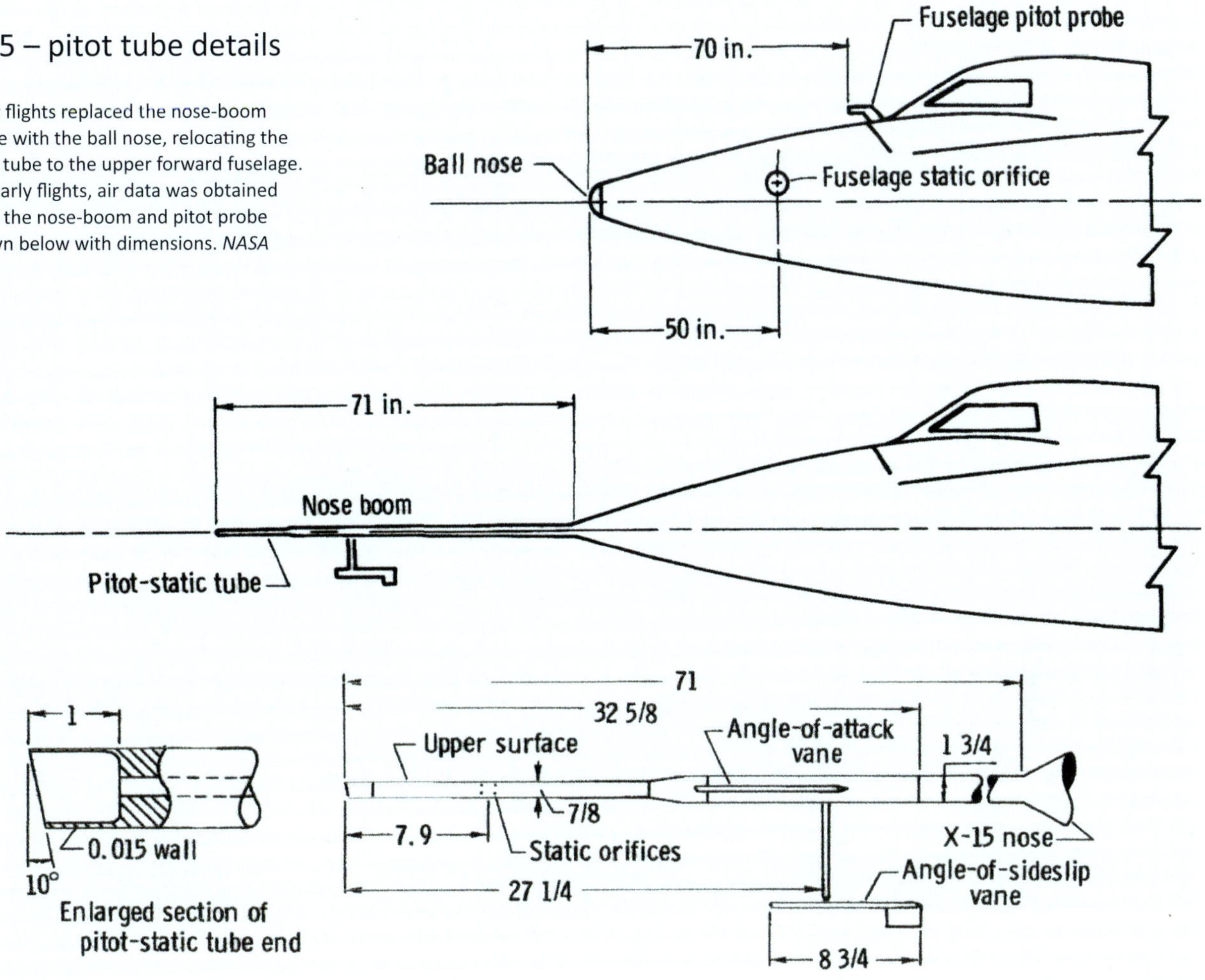

of 0.1deg/hr (0.017rad/hr), a random drift of 0.03deg/hr rms (0.005rad/hr rms), and an anisoelastic drift of 0.1deg/hr/g^2 rms (0.0002rad/hr/g^2). The accelerometer range was +/-10deg, a linearity of 3×10^{-5}g (or 0.01 per cent, whichever was the greater), and a threshold <1×10^{-5}g. The stabilisation electronics and the power supply were mounted within the IMU, using the gimbals as heat sinks for the power transistors and the covers as heat exchangers. The IMU was pressurised and there was no transfer or mixing with the air in the instrument bay.

The analogue computer converted the sensed inertial accelerations into appropriate output velocity and position about the three coordinate reference axes and also provided torqueing signals to the IMU which would maintain local vertical and azimuth orientation. Position, velocity and erection integrators were required for this as well as the necessary power supplies. The three integrator packages were electromechanical in design, each containing a single integrator with one for each axis.

Pilot displays were pitch, roll and heading presented on a three-axis attitude indicator, or '8-ball'. This took the form of a pictorial display combining attitude and azimuth within a universally mounted sphere providing background for a miniature reference aircraft which remained fixed relative to the cockpit. The sphere itself was controlled by the stable platform and could rotate 360deg in pitch, roll and azimuth. The miniature aircraft always remained in proper physical relationship to the simulated Earth, horizon and sky of the background sphere.

The attitude display was driven by synchro-signals from the IMU while the inertial-height display was driven by synchro-signals originating in the analogue computer. The total-velocity indicator performed a computation, the square root of the sum of the squares, to convert the components of the measured velocity into total velocity, displayed through a servo follow-up circuitry. The rate-of-climb indicator was a simplified dc meter receiving signals direct from the computer.

The digital IFDS comprised four separate subsystems: an IMU, a Coupler Electronics Unit (CEU), a digital computer and appropriate pilot displays. It used a gyro-compassing technique and was subject to a complete erection and alignment cycle while on the ground and while mated to the carrier-plane. The IMU was similar to that used for the analogue system, essential differences being in the electronics which were mounted within the CEU rather than within the inertial platform itself. There was also a significant reduction in the amount of cooling required, provided that the temperature inside the instrument bay remained below 21°C (70°F). The gyroscopes were similar to those employed by the analogue system, the accelerometers being of electromagnetically restrained floating pendulum design.

The specification for the gyroscopes in the digital system stipulated a non-acceleration sensitive drift of 3deg/hr (0.52rad/hr), an acceleration sensitive drift of 0.5deg/hr (0.0087rad/hr), a random drift of 0.02deg/hr (0.0003rad/hr), and a anisoelastic drift of 0.02deg/hr/g^2 rms (0.0003rad/hr/g^2 rms). The accelerometer range was ±10deg, a linearity of 30x10^{-5}g (or 0.03 per cent, whichever was the greater), and a threshold of 1x10^{-5}g. The specified system volume available was 0.167m^3 (5.29ft^3), a weight of 104.8kg (231lb) and a power drawdown of 450w.

The CEU provided coupling and electrical interface between the IMU and the digital computer as well as providing all essential power regulation, malfunction detection tasks, gyroscopic coupling and accelerometer rebalancing. The computer was a dual-function device which had a Digital Differential Analyser (DDA) section and a General-Purpose (GP) section which contained a drum memory of 1,664 x 24-bit words. The GP section performed solutions of the complete guidance equations, each solution being independent of the previous one. This was generally acceptable under conditions where uninterrupted solutions to a number of different parameters was required.

Real-time computation was accomplished with a section of integrators using individual incremental computational techniques. The DDA section mechanised the equation dz = ydx with only increments of the variable for x, y and z being transferred from one place to another within the DDA. In this way, using proper computing techniques, the combination provided an efficient capability with periodic solutions from the GP section and continuous updating from the DDA. The cockpit displays used with the digital system were mechanised and different to those for the analogue system. The total-velocity indicator, rate-of-climb indicator and inertial-height indicator were all positioned through feedback from the digital shaft encoder.

The analogue system was referenced to a line extending from the axis of the Edwards High Range, which had the disadvantage of complicating equations for the Earth rate corrections, in the solution of the accelerometer equations, because Earth rate terms appear in all three coordinates. Because a separate heading angle must be maintained in the computer at the same time, the mechanisation was simplified as a result of the limited range restrictions.

The digital system, however, was very different. Aligned to true north and the geocentric vertical, a frame of reference was established in the north-east and local vertical directions whereas Earth rates in terms were entered only in the north and vertical axes. The analogue approach was a simple integration for velocity, with a feedback for centrifugal and Coriolis acceleration corrections, and a second integration for position with the necessary mass-attraction feedback to the velocity integrators. In the digital system the acceleration signals were converted to ΔV (velocity change with direction) pulses by the pulse rebalance electronics located in the CEU. The ΔV pulses were continuously summed in the DDA section which was updated every three seconds. New direction cosines were computed in the GP section. Position changes in the north, east and vertical distances were also summed in the DDA along the direction cosines computed within the GP.

The inertial system was designed to operate only when cooling air was supplied and because insufficient provision had been made for storable coolant the system was only turned on when the carrier-plane reached an altitude of 10,058m (33,000ft). At that point ram air was used for cooling and this usually occurred 30 minutes after take-off and 15 minutes prior to the drop. This left insufficient time for the system to erect itself and it was necessary to add more coolant capacity to the carrier-plane in the form of a liquid nitrogen system. Only then could the system be turned on and erected continuously from take-off.

After the cooling problem had been solved, other problems emerged. Because of the dynamic conditions under which the erection was taking place calibration in the air was incompatible with the time constraints on the gyroscopic drift rate compensation loops. This required some modification to the compensation loops but after that was put in work it was decided that a better way of obtaining more accurate calibration of the gyroscopic drift rate would be undertaken on the ground.

This also necessitated further modification so that the system could be turned on, erected and calibrated prior to taxiing for take-off. The procedure allowed the drift-rate potentiometers to be locked with compensation for torque variation rates by horizontal and vertical position, accomplished by trimming the basic drift term. After take-off, the system would receive continuous updates in velocity and heading from a reference system and periodic updating in position from the control panel during flight on the carrier-plane. But this procedure itself brought problems caused by ambient air being introduced to the liquid nitrogen cooling and pressurisation system during the ground operations.

The temperature of the gaseous nitrogen was about -4°C (-40°F) and when the outside air was mixed in it condensed out and froze, producing frost which tended to collect in narrow passages in the cooling ducts and even in the heat exchangers themselves. It was not infrequent for the cooling airflow to become completely blocked causing the system to overheat. The problem was only finally resolved by delaying the start-up time until after the pilot was in the cockpit with the canopy closed to reduce the amount of moisture-laden air sucked in.

Additional value was garnered from this procedure when it was found that the gyroscopic drift-rate stability and repeatability was sufficiently good to allow compensation on the day before a flight, followed by erection on the day itself. Further improvements were possible through a concerted effort to eliminate 'ground loops' in the electrical circuits – improper grounding techniques – which made it possible to shorten the ground erection time to under 20 minutes. This allowed ground erection of the system with the pilot in the cockpit to be adopted as a standard procedure.

All these modifications and procedural changes were made slowly during late 1961 and early 1962 and were followed the following year by a reasonably reliable inertial system. But the accuracy of the system was still far short of the desirable and frustration was compounded by the pace of the flight schedule. The intensity of activity forced upon the flight engineers by an ambitious set of research goals allowed very

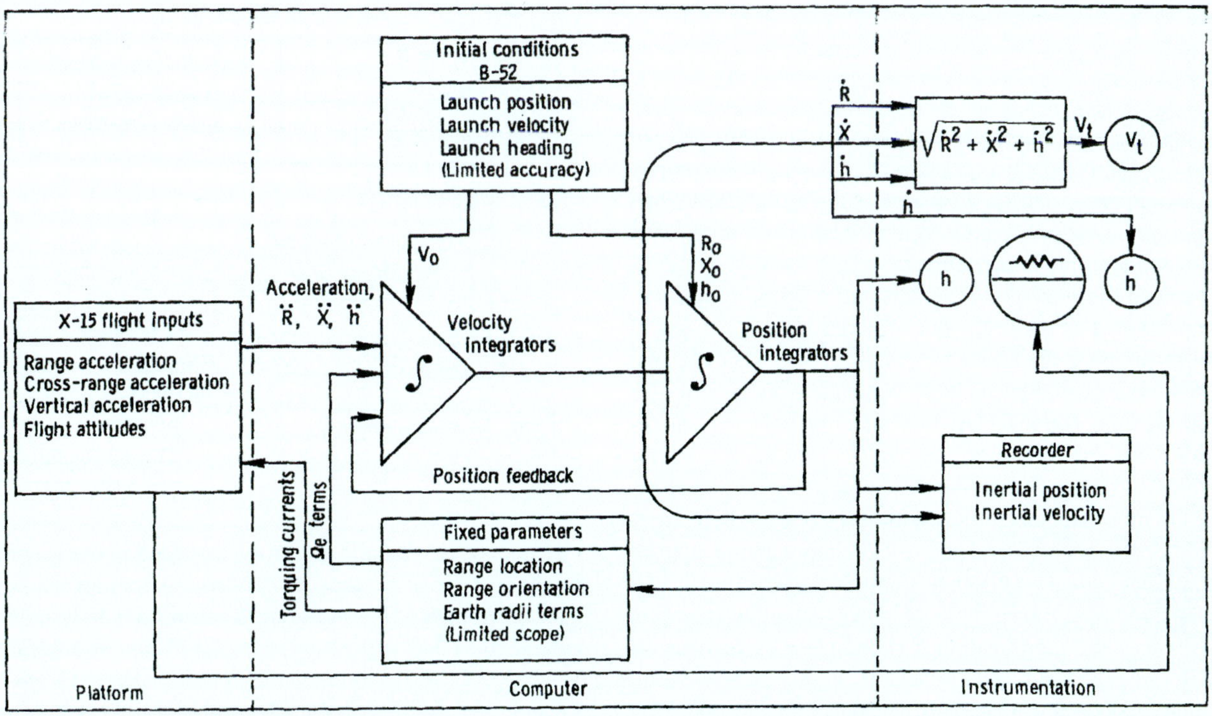

Above: The analogue flight data system between the B-52 and the platform, computer and instrumentation for the X-15 in shown here. *NASA*

Below: The digital Flight Data System (FDS) integrating information flow from, to and between the platform, computer and instrumentation. *NASA*

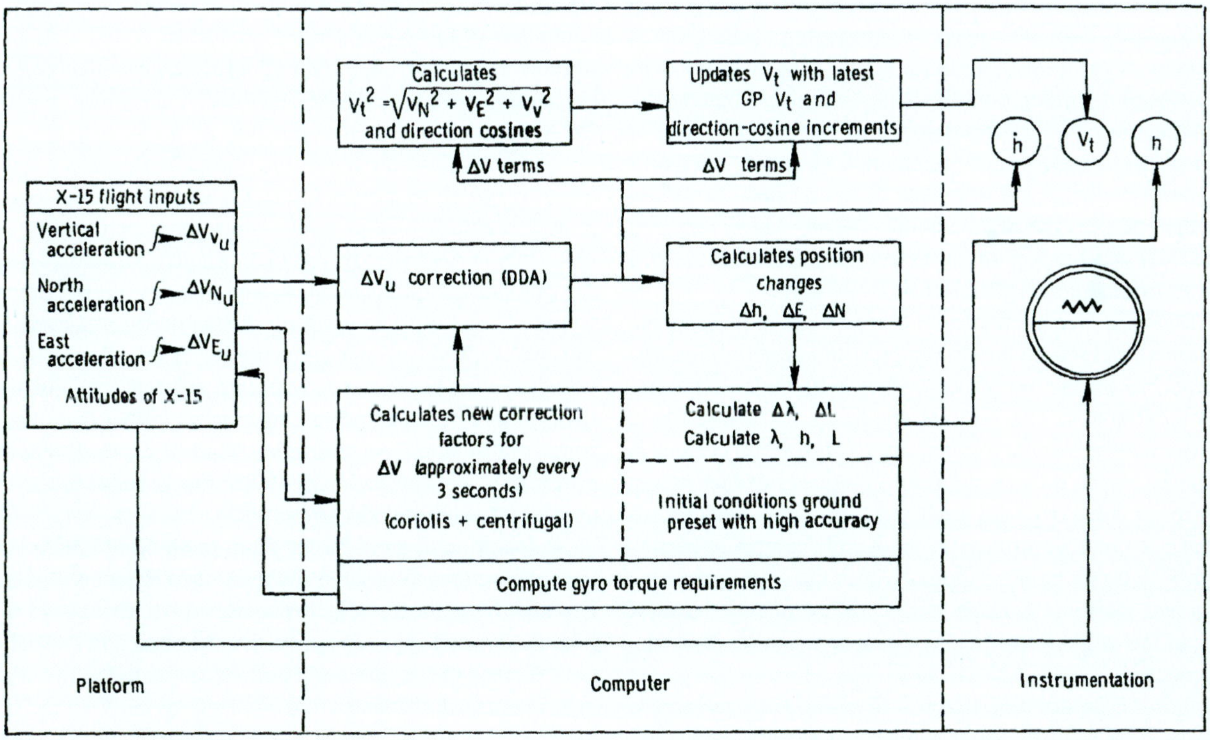

little time for doing systems upgrades or for installing new items of equipment.

Flight data system

The X-15 was both a development programme and an operational research vehicle and the rigid flight schedule combined with expansion of the flight envelope did not allow time for significant changes either in equipment or procedures. Priority was given to presenting vehicle attitudes and total velocity and in supporting the attitude, altitude and velocity parameters to ensure they were sufficiently reliable for the existing systems to be retained. But that began to change when an extensive follow-on programme was agreed, with the flight

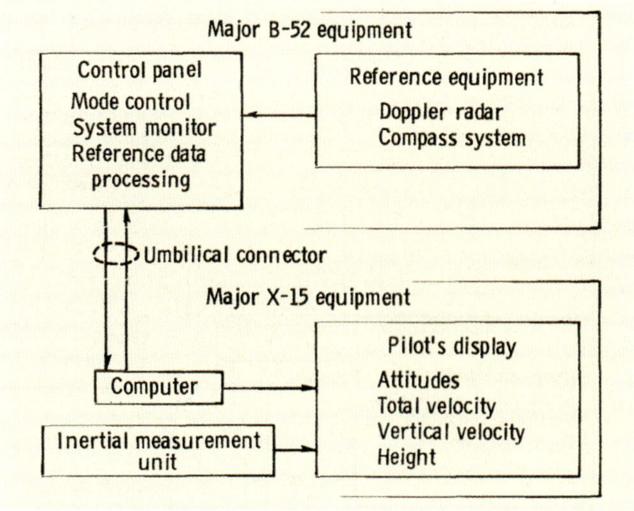

Right: Integrated elements of the Inertial Flight Data Systems (IFDS) are included on this simplified block diagram showing the links between the X-15 and the B-52. *NASA*

phase being approved for several more years. At the start of the X-15 programme it was expected that the flight operations phase would run for three years and subsequent extensions both compromised an ageing system and drove unplanned updates and systems improvements.

The need for precision flight data and reliability improvements prompted a new flight data system for the X-15 and in opting to improve the analogue system it was believed that time was now available for improvements to the electronics with priority on the IMU. At first attention focused on improving the circuits and the hardware in the accelerometer loops and in the power supplies. The accelerometers were replaced by more advanced ones with self-contained electronics with rebalance loops and pick-off excitation being integral with the basic unit. This eliminated much of the original hardware and reduced the number of power supplies required. This phase of the modification was complete by delivery of one IMU in July 1964. On the next 16 flights there were no anomalies and greater accuracies. The new unit was matching the original specification for the first time and so a second unit was acquired which itself was better than the original.

Next came improvements to the gyro-heater amplifiers which, while the circuitry was not responsible for any malfunctions, did affect the voltage levels causing fluctuations in the output of the gimbal torque motors. This redesign was successful and further modifications continued right to the end of the programme. A result of these improvements was to enhance the stability and regularity of power delivery throughout the IMU and to reduce power dissipation. While more than 50 per cent of the cooling gas previously required by the IMU was blocked off as unnecessary, heaters were still required for maintaining operating temperature.

While time was available for carrying out modifications, attention turned also to the computer, with new amplifiers being procured for the integrator together with their electromechanical choppers. The original amplifiers had caused heat dissipation even without a signal due to high idling current in the transistors but the new amplifiers reduced this dissipation by approximately 10w for each unit. This new design also provided a great improvement in overall computer performance with better power supplies within the unit. With these timely and welcome changes and modifications the requirements of the original specification were met and in some cases exceeded.

The X-15 programme had the advantage of accepting a digital system from the X-20 which had already received a considerable amount of development and test before it got to the hypersonic research aircraft. Environmental testing had been conducted by the Air Force and a complete flight test programme had been carried out using a Lockheed F-101. The computer itself had been applied to several other airborne programmes and so it was with a degree of relief that personnel at the Flight Research Station accepted the new digital system.

However, two significant problems stood in the way of its adoption for the X-15, the first concerning cooling. The specification stipulated that the system could operate in an environment of -1.1°C (30°F) to 21°C (70°F) and at an ambient pressure of 101.3kPa (14.7lb/in^2) to 24.1kPa (3.5lb/in^2). Blowers were installed at the inlet port and at the exhaust port of the computer to circulate gas from the instrument bay but it was discovered that when the temperature of this gas fell below 4.5°C (40°F) the operating cycle of the computer was affected – but only by a small amount. It was found that some computers of this type operated satisfactorily and without noticeable effect but others would experience a change in the clock rate which would speed up the computational rate in the DDA, producing erroneous results.

The second problem was the digital computer's susceptibility to switching power transients in circuitry designed to protect memory loss at power shut-down or during power transients. NASA discovered that circuitry on some computers was not operating properly and numbers in the memory would change without warning due to high-level transients. This was solved by a wiring change to ensure memory retention during power transfer, when transients were most likely to occur as a result of normal operations, rather than through some malfunction. In addition, X-15-1 experienced large power transients on the main 400Hz bus because of the large number of experiments carried.

Preparation of an X-15 for flight required pre-planning so that analogue and digital flight control systems could be checked out in the air vehicle concerned but about a week before the mission. The next check on the analogue system was to take place the day before the flight and with the two air vehicles mated. In this check the connections between the IFDS in the X-15 and the control panel in the carrier-plane were verified and the computer calibrated with the Doppler radar. The heading reference used was a precision synchro-transmitter set to the heading of the carrier-plane as determined by bench marks scribed into the pre-flight area hardstand. After this calibration a simulated inertial run was made to determine the performance of the system under static conditions.

On the morning of the flight the analogue system would be switched on and erected after the pilot was locked in to the

X-15 cockpit. This erection was fast because the gyro-drift compensation potentiometers would have been calibrated and locked during the previous checks, which lasted 20 minutes. The system operated inertially until sufficient altitude had been gained, usually around 1,524m (5,000ft) for operation of the Doppler radar. Erection resumed using the carrier-plane's reference systems. This mode was usually retained until the X-15 was launched, after which the system was operated in the inertial mode for the remainder of the flight.

After the initial check one week prior to flight, the digital system would not be turned on again until the morning of the mission. Flight tapes would have been loaded into the computer at the end of hangar tests and, when switched back on, the first requirement was for preheat and final alignment. This task was carried out while the pilot was entering the cockpit and starting his close-out procedures. Prior to switching power from the carrier-plane to internal power on the X-15 the system was switched to flight mode and remained thus throughout the flight. The altitude loop was clamped to the pressure altitude until 60 seconds before launch when it was unclamped for the system to operate in flight mode throughout.

Support requirements for the inertial flight data system were very different for the X-15 to those for any other aircraft; indeed they are for any research aircraft required to perform in a very different, almost unique, environment to that of a production-line aircraft destined either for military or commercial service. One outstanding reason is key also to understanding why the attention to individual computer performance was so meticulous and seemingly protracted in resolution. In the late 1950s and early1960s, computers were hand-made machines and each had peculiarities bequeathed by the individual working on assembly, or the team working to test it. Moreover, for the X-15 programme they were prototypes from which much else would flow and through which engineering analysis and evaluation was as much about how they functioned as to how they did their required tasks.

For the X-15 programme an extensive laboratory support structure was required, and put in place. Gone had been the dream of having support for the IFDS carried out in the field by one technician, one NASA engineer and one contractor field manager. The level of maintenance required was to be reduced to a simple module replacement cycle and adjustment of the power supply. A facility was set up to conform to this and to handle all servicing requirements but with only six systems available, and with the high component failure rate experienced, this became wholly inadequate.

The number of people assigned went from three people to 10 – five technicians and five engineers – with the level of maintenance increased to cover complete computer rebuild and IMU repairs, including gyroscopes, accelerometers and slip-ring replacement. The surge was key to keeping the system running in the very early stages of the flight qualification phase and until the improved analogue system was available. With the arrival of the digital system the laboratory area had to be substantially expanded with a large influx of test equipment, spares and people. Manpower for the two systems went up further, to six technicians and five engineers. This field support group was augmented by links to people at the digital

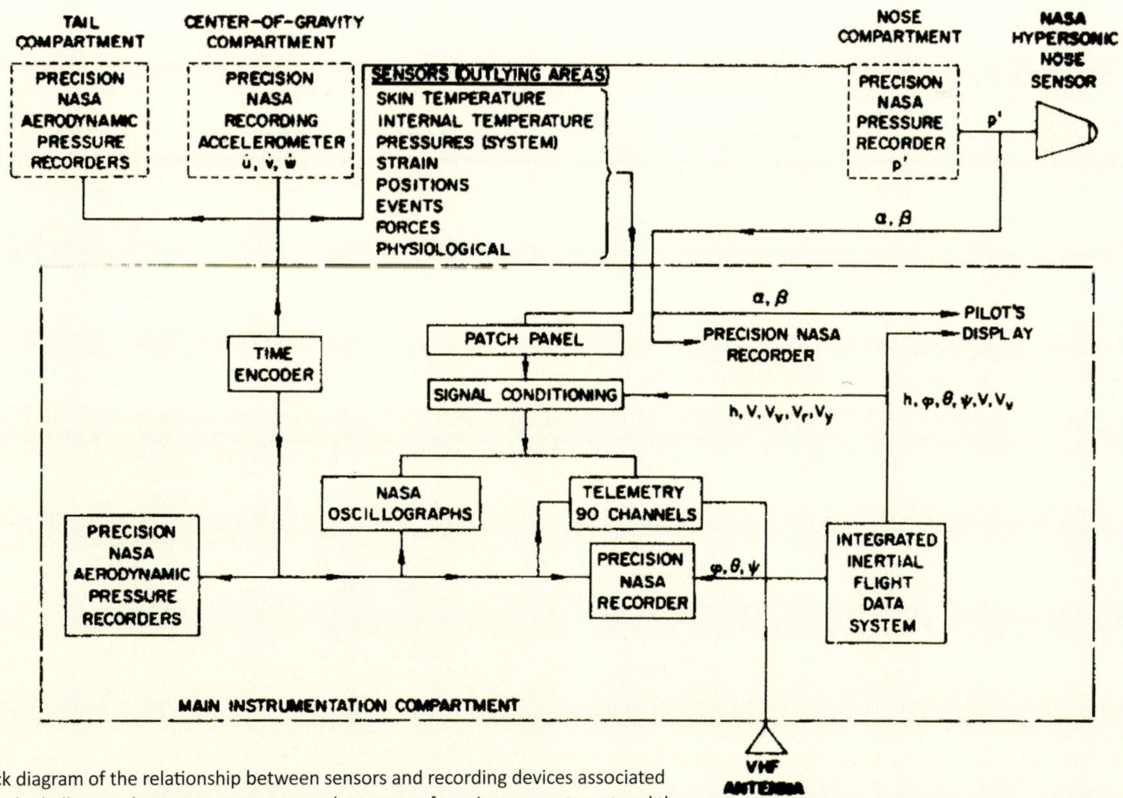

Block diagram of the relationship between sensors and recording devices associated with the ball nose, the nose compartment, the centre-of-gravity compartment and the tail compartment as integrated with the IFDS and telemetry requirements. *NASA*

system contractor facility consisting of a systems engineer, a computer programmer and various levels of associated support and back-up.

Any comparison between the analogue and the digital flight data systems has to take account of the period over which each system had been developed, the financial investment in each programme and the amount of integration time required for the analogue system, which was essentially the same as that required for the digital system when that was introduced.

Development of the analogue system began in June 1957 when the definitive requirements of the programme had been agreed and finalised. Design and development of the digital system started in December 1960, which was before the integration of the analogue system into the X-15. Costs for the analogue system were about $4.5million but costs for the digital system amounted to $28.3million plus an additional $1.2million for modifications and for associated computer programming. Many of the integration problems for the analogue system, such as the cooling and related modifications, were applicable to the digital system as well and that helped ease it into service.

In comparing the analogue and digital systems on performance, the digital equipment provided smaller mean errors which were repeatable during successive flights and with higher reliability. Because of its ability to support re-programming, the digital system was more flexible and could be tuned to specific requirements on particular flights. In this it was more flexible than the analogue system, where equation mechanisation is hard-wired and therefore offered very little flexibility. Moreover, analogue systems in general have errors that accumulate as a result of tolerance imperfections within each manufactured component. As computer users even today accept, no two machines are identical.

The limitations of the analogue system necessitated the use of reference systems in the carrier-plane so as to provide a continuous erection of the inertial system up to the point of launch. Degraded performance of these reference systems resulted in further degradation being propagated to the inertial system. The digital system was not prone to these same error sources since, with the exception of the vertical loop, it was a self-contained navigation system. While the analogue system was adequate to perform specific tasks the digital equipment was more suited to handling a wide variety of tasks where high precision was required.

Talking to the ground

Monitoring the performance of the X-15 using on-board systems was only part of the measurements and tracking requirements of the programme. In flight the X-15 could cover a ground range of approximately 555km (345mls), passing through a wide portion of the Earth's atmosphere, operating in excess of Mach 6 and at altitudes of up to 106,700m (350,000ft). Monitoring a flight of this type required the establishment of a radar tracking range, which was known at the NACA as High Range. It consisted of three radar ground stations with the NACA/NASA flight research facilities at Edwards as the prime control station. The Edwards control room received real-time velocity and altitude from the three radar stations, with altitude and ground track displayed on large plot boards and velocity indicated on a meter for the use of the ground controller.

Mod II radars, which were really modified SCR-584 radars, were installed at all three stations and consisted of an automatic angle and range-tracking system designed to provide azimuth, elevation angle and slant-range data. They operated on S-band frequencies and had a 740km (460ml) range capability. Tracking was in the form of azimuth, elevation and range, obtained from two optical encoders and one electromechanical encoder attached directly to the antenna and the range shafts. A 16-digit parallel code was obtained for azimuth, elevation and slant range at a rate of 10 samples per second, with digital information from the encoders recorded on magnetic tape.

Due to the flow field around the aircraft, on-board measurements of the ambient atmospheric temperature were difficult for the X-15 to make. Meteorological information was obtained through sounding data used to correct radar data for free-stream conditions. This data was used to obtain the free-stream velocity, Mach number and dynamic pressure. As an example, radar data was corrected to free-stream values by adding or subtracting horizontal wind components. Balloon sounding data was used from the ground up to an altitude of about 30,480m (100,000ft) with data extrapolated above that level for flights which did not exceed 38,100m (125,000ft).

For each flight an AN/AMT-5B rawinsonde balloon was released by the Air Force Weather Service at Edwards AFB as the carrier-plane took off. The package transmitted signals received by an AN/GMD-1A rawin set which was recorded on tape for data reduction later and for integration with the flight measurements from the returning X-15. For flights above 30,480m (100,000ft), meteorological sounding rockets provided data and information on prevailing winds. Between 1 October and 15 March each year, winds from this altitude up to 60,960m (200,000ft) were rated at monsoon level with

Below: This general overview of the locations for key ranging and tracking locations also shows the Tonopah Test Range and associated military airfields. *Finlay McWalter*

Left: Dr James A. Van Allen poses with a LOKI sounding rocket of the type used for obtaining meteorological data fired from the Tonopah Test Range in Nevada. Information would be used to provide temperatures and pressures in the upper atmosphere. Van Allen provided the science instruments for the first US satellite, Explorer I launched on 31 January 1958. *Author's collection*

a strong westerly flow. From 1 June to 15 August the prevailing winds are weaker and easterly. Between these periods, short and transitional periods of weak and variable wind conditions prevail.

Data for X-15 flights was obtained from LOKI and ARCAS meteorological sounding rockets fired from the Tonopah Test Range in Nevada, the test range for the Atomic Energy Commission, and from Point Mugu Naval Air Station, California. LOKI wind soundings were made by radar tracking of metallised-nylon chaff while ARCAS soundings were obtained by tracking a parachute which deployed automatically at an altitude of 60,960m (200,000ft). Wind data above this level were extrapolated from the lower-altitude data. The ARCAS package carried a 10-mil bead thermistor for the measurement of ambient temperatures, useful up to about 45,720m (150,000ft) but hopeless for measurements at higher altitudes.

At altitudes above 60,960m (200,000ft) pressure and temperature values were obtained from standard atmospheres held by NASA for all reference conditions but precise detail was lacking due to the absence of meteorological data above that height. From the beginning of the programme it was accepted that the flight planning would have to live with this uncertainty and extrapolation of the balloon and rocket data was the best it was ever going to get. At least until more precise data became available from a host of technologies which transformed the science of meteorology and weather data gathering.

One aspect which was a unique problem for the X-15 programme was the accurate measurement of Mach number at high altitude. This was due to some degree because sound transmission becomes meaningless in the near vacuum conditions of the outer atmosphere and the free-stream specific-heat ratio is very difficult to determine. For X-15 scientists and engineers working the physics of very high altitude flight, 'space' begins at 91,440m (300,000ft), or 91.4km (56.8mls). For this reason, all data sheets and logs purporting to show a Mach number for very high altitude flights, the figure is not a measured value but merely an extrapolation assuming that the specific-heat ratio is constant.

While related specifically to the aerodynamic control of the X-15 the Stability Augmentation System (SAS) had an important role to play in serving as a bench mark from which successive evolutions emerged. Each would greatly influence the wider range of modern combat aircraft, eventually finding its way into the commercial sector. X-15-1 and X-15-2 were fitted with the Westinghouse SAS for providing damping input to the all three control axes. X-15-3 was fitted with the adaptive flight control system – the MH-96 – which is explained later.

The Stability Augmentation System had three separate and independent channels. Each had a working circuit which took commands from the gyroscopic assembly in a specific axis and sent an operating command to the relevant servo. The separate monitoring circuits received identical and parallel commands and passed them to the malfunction detector. This compared the two and if a limit was exceeded, which was pre-set into the detection system, it disabled the circuit and removed the SAS from control of that axis.

Electrical signals were sent to the electrohydraulic transfer valve on each side of the servo cylinder piston from the working circuit and this controlled hydraulic pressure on each side of that piston. The No. 2 hydraulic system powered the pitch-

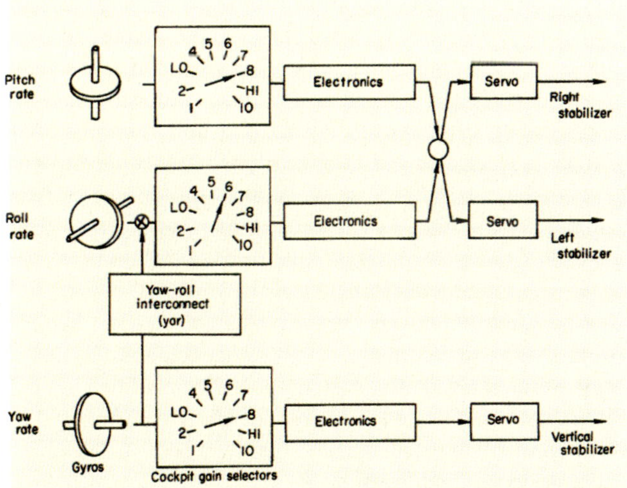

The functionality in each of the three axes of the Stability Augmentation System with cross-over command links between the electronics and the servos for pitch and roll rates through the horizontal stabilisers. *NAA*

Reaction Augmentation System (RAS)

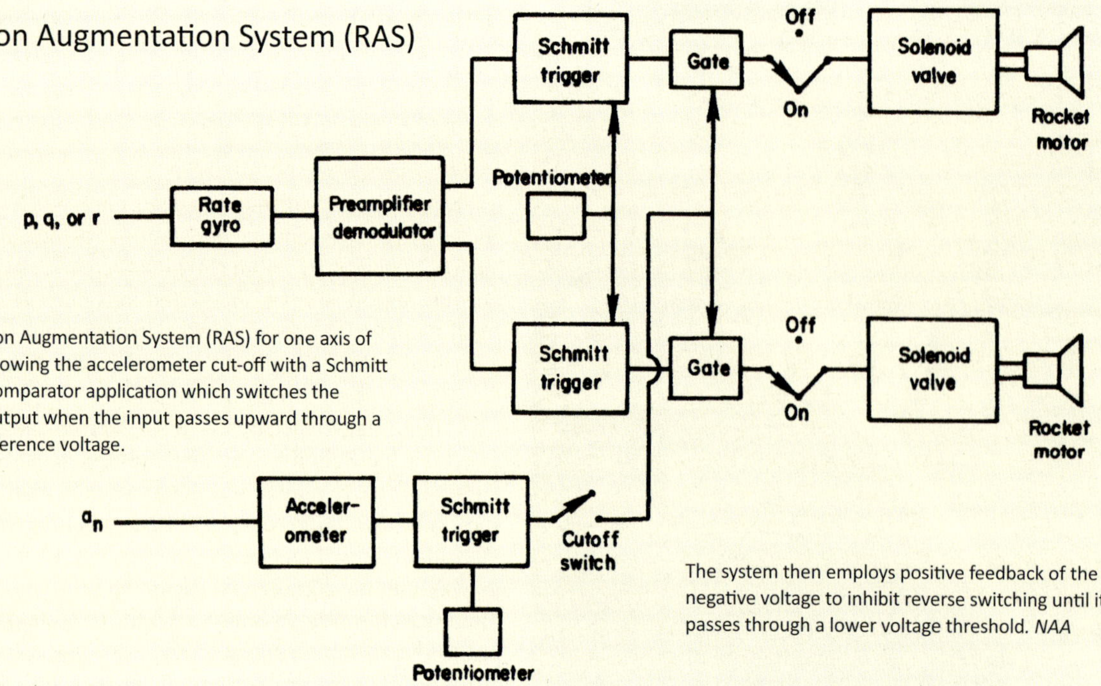

The Reaction Augmentation System (RAS) for one axis of the X-15 showing the accelerometer cut-off with a Schmitt trigger, a comparator application which switches the negative output when the input passes upward through a positive reference voltage.

The system then employs positive feedback of the negative voltage to inhibit reverse switching until it passes through a lower voltage threshold. *NAA*

roll servo cylinders and were connected to the horizontal stabiliser control linkages by mixer bell cranks. Any loss of that hydraulic system would engage the emergency back-up and any sudden loss of pressure in the No. 2 system would require manual re-setting of the pitch and roll damping channels by the pilot. The yaw servo cylinder was slaved to the No. 1 hydraulic system and this was mechanically linked to the vertical stabiliser through a mixer bell crank. There was provision for interaction of yaw and roll damping working surfaces, which would deliver signals from the yaw axis of the gyroscope to the roll circuit, thus augmenting roll damping.

In the configuration of the early X-15 controls the pilot had an SAS function switch for each axis with positions designated STDBY and ENGAGE. In the standby mode the input signals to the servo cylinder control valves and hydraulic pressure to the servo cylinders were disconnected, while the working channel was still functioning. There was also a function switch for the interaction of yaw and roll damping which allowed the pilot to disengage the cross-coupling function. A special rotary-knob gain selector was provided for control of the ratio of the damping signal to the servo cylinder displacements. Ten positions were scribed on each knob with position No. 3 considered low and No. 9 rated as high. In general, pilots preferred the No. 4 setting for each pitch, roll and yaw axis.

When the Alternate Stability Augmentation System (ASAS) was installed these controls changed and the rotary knobs were removed. The switches too were modified to read STDBY, LO-GAIN and HI-GAIN. The last two positions here were approximately equivalent to the No. 3 and No. 9 settings in the previous configuration but they differed in that they could be adjusted on the ground to pilot preferences. Pilots reported serious concerns when it was understood that excessively high landing loads were being imposed unnecessarily by the SAS, several landing gear failures occurring not as a result of bad landings but by the automated system itself. A disengagement switch was added for the pilot to turn the system off immediately after skid contact with the ground.

In April 1962 X-15-1 and X-15-2 were fitted with the Alternate Stability Augmentation System (ASAS), which comprised a working circuit only without selectable gains. It provided pitch-roll damping in the event of a failure to the primary SAS roll channel. When this was armed it would automatically take over in the event of a failure in the SAS. The yaw channel remained the same and continued to serve its original purpose. In early 1967 the ASAS fitted in X-15-2 was modified to include the yaw axis for an additional margin of safety above Mach 6 and this was later applied to X-15-1 also.

There were several examples in the X-15 programme where the Air Force ran tests and obtained results relevant to its Dyna-Soar/X-20 programme, and there was at least one example of where the X-15 programme benefited from the cancellation of that project in 1963. However, one piece of technology which had been developed at the instigation of the Air Force was transferred to the X-15 programme for evaluation long before cancellation, when the suborbital/orbital spaceplane was still a viable endeavour.

The Air Force wanted to develop a system which would deliver truly invariant aircraft response to pilot control commands and they made this a design goal for Dyna-Soar. With the advent of supersonic, and potentially hypersonic, aircraft the Air Force was concerned that flight control systems then in existence were not capable of fulfilling requirements. Existing systems lacked the ability to control the aircraft under all operating conditions and it was taking a great deal of time to develop unique systems for individual aircraft. With the non-linear aerodynamic link between control surfaces and the stability of the aircraft, flight control systems were only as good in what they could do as the projected requirement of the system assumed by the designer; and flight control systems could only operate within the conditions predicted by the engineer who built them. The Air Force made it a primary goal to remove the effect of this non-linear link and develop self-adaptive systems.

Adaptive flight control

The Air Force defined a fully adaptive system as 'one which has the capability of changing its parameters through an internal process of measurement, evaluation, and adjustment to adapt to a changing environment. Such a system would automatically adapt to flight conditions of varying aerodynamic control effectiveness without recourse to air-data sampling'.

During the first half on the 1950s the development of self-adaptive systems was considered essential for existing combat aircraft. In 1956 the Air Force agreed that there was a sufficient level of technical and theoretical knowledge available to provide such a device for its new generation of high-altitude/high-speed aerospace vehicles. The following year a development programme began which would involve a range of conventional aircraft for concept and breadboard evaluation. The flight test programme involved the Lockheed F-94 Starfire and the McDonnell F-101 and by 1958 the Air Force was sufficiently convinced of the viability of such a system that it initiated a programme for flight demonstration in the X-15.

This was believed necessary to fully explore the envelope open to existing and future aircraft and to stress the concept so as to better understand the advantages of an adaptive system. Most of the pre-1958 work had been carried out by the Office of Air Force Scientific Research, the Air Research & Development Command and at the Wright Air Development Center. Several NASA centres had been involved in this work, notably the Ames facility, and there was a considerable degree of industrial participation, particularly from the Massachusetts Institute of Technology and Minneapolis-Honeywell.

Removing the need for air data sampling was key to providing adaptive flight control for a wide range of aerospace vehicles such as those anticipated by the Air Force for the following decade or so. The decision to advance the test environment was made by choosing the X-15 because the rate of change and the range of its stability and control parameters, for instance the effectiveness of the control surfaces, short-period damping and frequency would force a robust check on the system.

In June 1959 the Air Force awarded a contract to Minneapolis-Honeywell for the development of the Adaptive Flight Control System (AFCS) for the X-15, stipulating that it must include dual redundancy for reliability, integration of the aerodynamic and BCS control systems, rate command control and simple outer-loop hold modes in attitude and angle of attack. The MH-96 AFCS was essentially an improved version of the E-10 autopilot developed in 1958 for the Lockheed

Adaptive Flight Control

Right: The instrument compartment was rebuilt with considerable work required for it to accept the MH-96 and its electronics box, which provided a different configuration of X-15-3's data recording equipment. *NASA*

Below: The Dyna-Soar boost-glide programme bequeathed to the X-15 the MH-96 adaptive flight control system (AFCS) shown on this simplified schematic. It provided stability augmentation in all three axes and was introduced after the rebuild of X-15-3. *NASA*

Below right: The typical electrical and mechanical elements of the pitch plane sensor with the hypersonic flow direction sensor at the Pt2 position. *Northrop*

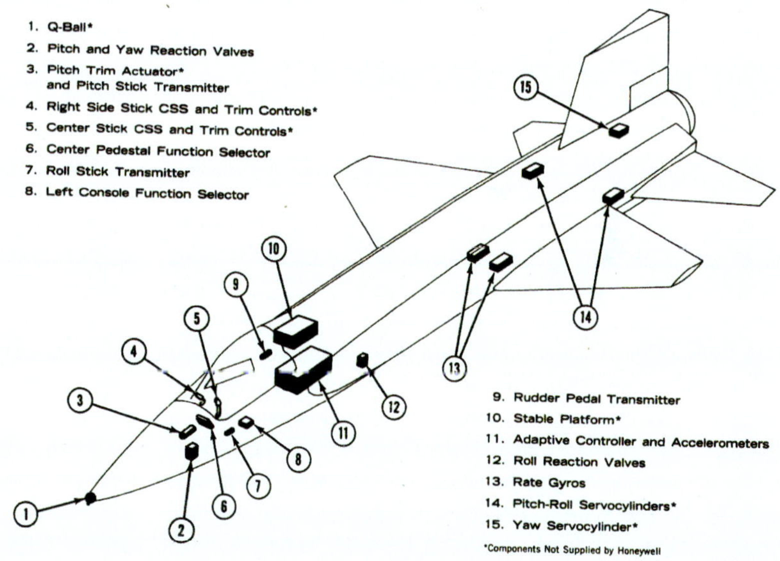

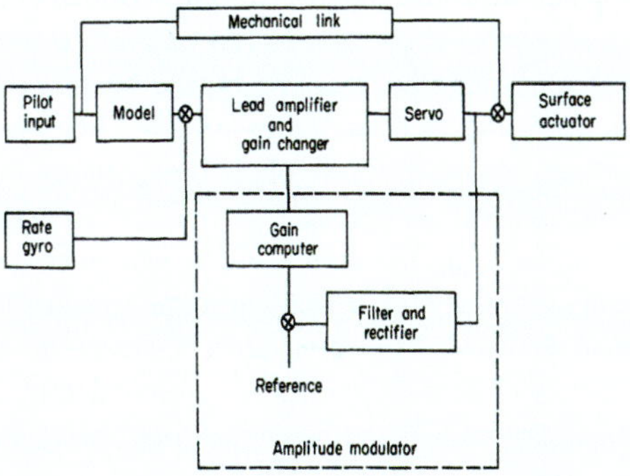

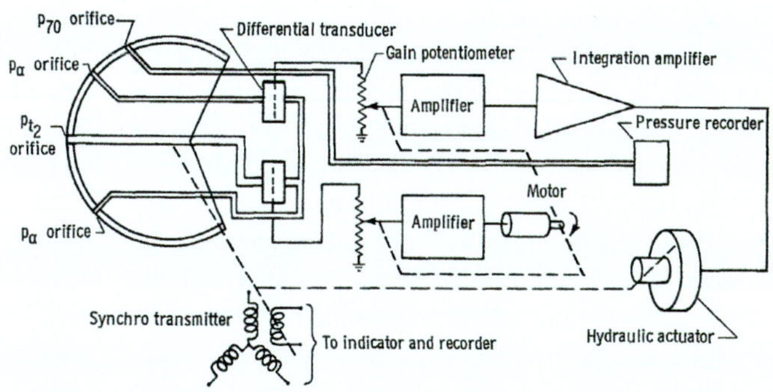

F-94C, the first adaptive flight control system to fly in a maned aircraft. The resulting prototype of the MH-96 was tested on an X-15 simulator and it was also subject to initial evaluation on the F-101. The AFCS was installed on X-15-3 in mid-1961 in time for its first flight with test pilot Neil Armstrong on 20 December 1961.

The MH-96 replaced the Westinghouse SAS installed on the other two aircraft and would provide stability augmentation in pitch, roll and yaw. However, installing the system was harder to achieve than the commitment, the device having to fit in to the reconfigured lower instrument elevator shaft where the smaller SAS equipment had been located. Commands to the system were in the form of electrical signals proportional to the movement, or displacement, of the right side-controller or to the centre stick and the rudder pedals. There was provision to electrically trim the pitch and roll axes, although this brought some difficulties because the MH-96 had been placed on line with X-15 systems equipment rather than equipment it had been designed for.

In operating the system the pilot encountered certain difficulties caused by the way the AFCS worked. In attempting to null the pitch servo-motors, the follow-through systems employed a low-rate trim motor which, in adjusting to the centre point of the pilot's stick, would move the stick to a precise position. If the pilot was using the stick for a specific manoeuvre it would slip out of phase with the manual actuation of the controls and, having become saturated, oscillate for several seconds at a low amplitude. This in itself was of no great significance but it required the pilot to retain a mental picture of his desired (manual) movement of the stick while absorbing the consequences of the variable driven by the trim motor. In such a situation it was easy for the pilot to induce compensating movement of the controller out of proportion to the requirement.

A central tenet of the AFCS was redundancy, driven by the belief that reliability was a vital part of a successful re-entry because it would require controls damping. This conflated with the fail-safe philosophy permeating all aerospace systems, indicative of a feed-back loop from unmanned missiles and rocket systems. Much that would be developed in manned operations, both lifting and ballistic, would soon come to dominate both air and space systems design. Fail-safe operation was essential, it was believed, because any minor transient in a high-dynamic environment could very easily cause the loss of the vehicle. As designed, the MH-96 had two parallel channels and either one was adequate to fully control the vehicle through all its operations.

The nature of the circuitry allowed a single channel to go down with virtually no impact on the system because the gain charger would increase to align with the limit cycle. Because the two gain computers were interlocked during operations there was no possibility of hard-over failures caused by limit-cycle problems and this satisfied both redundancy and the fail-safe design. It came at a price, which was to reduce the effectiveness of the system and impose some restrictions on the flight envelope. In trying to achieve flexibility, engineers provided parallel fixed-gain channels with fail-safe passive circuitry which limited the minimum gain for adaptive operation. These circuits had to be sufficiently powerful for emergency operation throughout the flight envelope but that conflicted with it having to be lower than the critical levels in high-dynamic regions of the envelope.

Above: Development of a fully adaptive flight control system began with trials involving the Lockheed F-94C and these led to the MH-96, installed in X-15-3 in which Armstrong made its first flight in December 1961. *USAF*

After the flight test programme began with X-15-3 in January 1961 success was quickly achieved in running down any deficiencies or abnormalities with the system. The first seven flights were part of the acceptance test programme with the last three of these serving as demonstration and acceptance runs. Following this, the AFCS was used on 58 flights with a maximum altitude of 107,960m (354,200ft) being achieved and with dynamic pressure environments from 90.446kN/cm^2 (1,889lb/ft^2) to near zero. There was no opportunity to optimise system performance or to define total capability but considerable value was gained from the comments of pilots on the rate-command feature rather than the adaptive aspects.

Interestingly, reports back in from the pilots failed to comment on the invariant response characteristic, because they tended to subjectively ignore response through stick deflection and were insensitive to the subtle manifestation of the invariant rate-command. Nor did the pilots report awareness of the compensating variables provided by the AFCS when physical changes were made to the overall configuration of the wetted area, through landing gear deployment, flap deployment, use of speed brakes, etc.

Trim changes were automatically made by the adaptive system, as were variations in the longitudinal centre-of-gravity because here too the trim changes were automatic and subtle. Trim changes through the transonic region were similarly unobserved by the pilots, who were somewhat disorientated by the smoothness of actual events normally cued to the pilot by physical sensations but masked by the adaptive nature of the system. Some characteristics of the AFCS were distinctly unnatural to pilots schooled on conventional non-adaptive flight control systems.

A classic example being the action of the rate-command feature, which denied the AFCS conventional response to changes in airspeed or dynamic pressure. Because the aircraft's attitude did not change unless it was commanded by the pilot, the neutral stick position did not fall through as it ordinarily would be expected to as airspeed decreased and it did not pitch up as speed increased. Because of this, as perceived

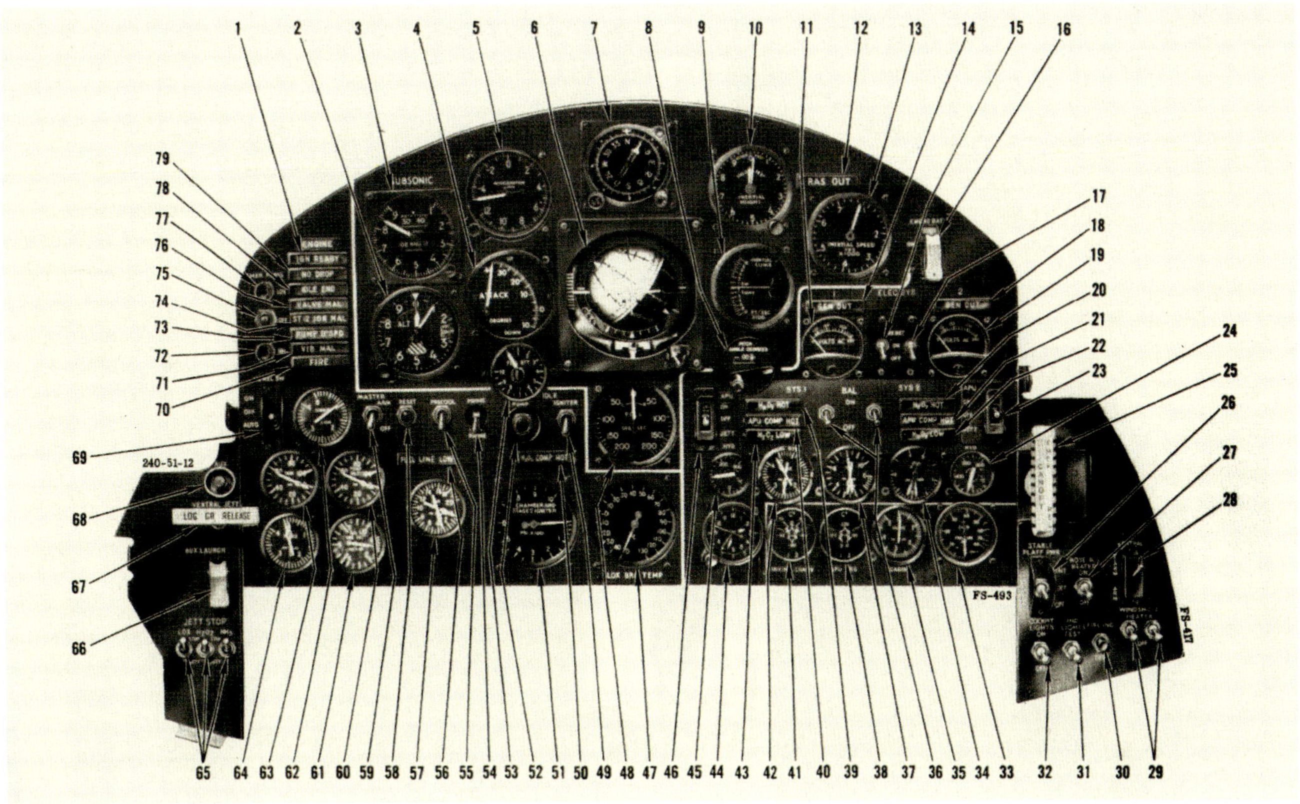

Above: The initial X-15-1 cockpit configuration with instrument layout and displays on the central control panel. *NASA*

1. IGNITION-READY CAUTION LIGHT
2. ALTIMETER
3. AIRSPEED INDICATOR
4. ANGLE-OF-ATTACK INDICATOR
5. ACCELEROMETER
6. ATTITUDE INDICATOR
7. AZIMUTH INDICATOR
8. PITCH ANGLE SET CONTROL
9. VERTICAL VELOCITY INDICATOR
10. INERTIAL HEIGHT (ALTIMETER) INDICATOR
11. NO. 1 GENERATOR VOLTMETER
12. RAS-OUT INDICATOR LIGHT
13. INERTIAL SPEED (VELOCITY) INDICATOR
14. NO. 1 GENERATOR-OUT LIGHT
15. NO. 1 GENERATOR SWITCH
16. EMERGENCY BATTERY SWITCH
17. NO. 2 GENERATOR SWITCH
18. NO. 2 GENERATOR-OUT LIGHT
19. NO. 2 GENERATOR VOLTMETER
20. NO. 2 APU HYDROGEN PEROXIDE OVERHEAT WARNING LIGHT
21. NO. 2 APU COMPARTMENT OVERHEAT CAUTION LIGHT
22. NO. 2 APU HYDROGEN PEROXIDE-LOW CAUTION LIGHT
23. NO. 2 APU SWITCH
24. NO. 2 HYDRAULIC TEMPERATURE GAGE
25. CANOPY INTERNAL EMERGENCY JETTISON HANDLE
26. STABLE PLATFORM SWITCH
27. NOSE BALLISTIC ROCKET HEATER SWITCH
28. VENTRAL ARMING SWITCH
29. WINDSHIELD HEATER SWITCHES (2)
30. FIRE-WARNING LIGHT TEST BUTTON
31. INDICATOR, CAUTION, AND WARNING LIGHT SWITCH
32. COCKPIT LIGHTING SWITCH
33. CABIN PRESSURE ALTIMETER
34. HYDRAULIC PRESSURE GAGE
35. CABIN HELIUM SOURCE PRESSURE GAGE
36. NO. 1 AND NO. 2 BALLISTIC CONTROL SWITCHES
37. HYDROGEN PEROXIDE TANK PRESSURE GAGE
38. APU BEARING TEMPERATURE GAGE
39. NO. 1 APU HYDROGEN PEROXIDE OVERHEAT WARNING LIGHT
40. NO. 1 APU COMPARTMENT OVERHEAT CAUTION LIGHT
41. MIXING CHAMBER TEMPERATURE GAGE
42. APU SOURCE PRESSURE GAGE
43. NO. 1 APU HYDROGEN PEROXIDE-LOW CAUTION LIGHT
44. CLOCK
45. NO. 1 HYDRAULIC TEMPERATURE GAGE
46. NO. 1 APU SWITCH
47. LIQUID OXYGEN BEARING TEMPERATURE GAGE
48. RATE-OF-ROLL INDICATOR
49. IGNITER IDLE SWITCH
50. H O COMPARTMENT-HOT CAUTION LIGHT
51. CHAMBER AND STAGE 2 IGNITER PRESSURE GAGE
52. TURBOPUMP IDLE BUTTON
53. FUEL QUANTITY GAGE
54. ENGINE PRIME SWITCH
55. ENGINE PRECOOL SWITCH
56. FUEL LINE-LOW CAUTION LIGHT
57. PROPELLANT MANIFOLD PRESSURE GAGE
58. ENGINE RESET BUTTON
59. ENGINE MASTER SWITCH
60. PROPELLANT PUMP INLET PRESSURE GAGE
61. H O TANK AND ENGINE CONTROL LINE PRESSURE GAGE
62. PROPELLANT SOURCE PRESSURE GAGE
63. PROPELLANT TANK PRESSURE GAGE
64. H O SOURCE AND PURGE PRESSURE GAGE
65. JETTISON STOP SWITCHES
66. AUXILIARY LAUNCH SWITCH
67. LANDING GEAR HANDLE
68. VENTRAL JETTISON BUTTON
69. HELIUM RELEASE SELECTOR SWITCH
70. FIRE-WARNING LIGHT
71. ENGINE VIBRATION MALFUNCTION CAUTION LIGHT
72. AMMONIA TANK PRESSURE-LOW CAUTION LIGHT
73. TURBOPUMP OVERSPEED CAUTION LIGHT
74. STAGE 2 IGNITION MALFUNCTION CAUTION LIGHT
75. PROPELLANT EMERGENCY PRESSURIZATION SWITCH
76. VALVE MALFUNCTION CAUTION LIGHT
77. LIQUID OXYGEN TANK PRESSURE-LOW CAUTION LIGHT
78. IDLE END LIGHT
79. NO-DROP CAUTION LIGHT

by the pilot, the aircraft had no obvious speed stability, a characteristic which would, in itself, not have been too disorientating from the usual cues expected. But there was another unsettling characteristic.

Natural to an experienced pilot, one cue was the absence of a change in stick force, which did not occur at all with an active AFCS. This effect was especially noticeable during landing. During a normal approach, airspeed decreased at a constant rate of approximately 7.4kph (4.6mph) during and after the flare. In X-15-1 and X-15-2, equipped with the fixed-gain control system, the pilot worked continuously with a positive stick force, pulling back and occasionally re-trimming as the speed bled away during level deceleration after the flare. With X-15-3 and its AFCS the pilot had no need to pull back on the control stick as speed decreased because, as the flare was completed, the aircraft was in a near-level flying attitude with the control system automatically maintaining that orientation.

At the instant of completing the flare the pilot had to push back sharply on the control stick to prevent the aircraft ballooning, as it would be at a higher angle of attack and therefore a higher pitch attitude than necessary to maintain a 1-g flight. If the pilot released the stick the AFCS would have maintained that attitude and started to climb. To prevent that, after the flare the pilot would be working a negative stick-force slope and this would create an unnatural sensation and a distinct feeling of uncertainty. With the standard rate-command system, the pilots trimmed to a nose-down pitch rate before the flare to preload the control stick and this did gain some semblance of speed stability. Pilots also reported a distinct lack of ground effect, due to the invariant response of the AFCS.

Cockpit

With the decision to conduct early powered flights with the dual-motor XLR-11 and with the air-data probe, the layout of the cockpit was different to that where the single XLR-99 and the ball nose were installed. These panels went through several revisions in the course of the programme, some being for reconfiguration of instruments and some for better ergonomics or visual clarity. Also, the MH-96 adaptive flight control system installed in X-15-3 introduced another displays change and that panel became the subject of a major rework from Lear-Siegler.

It was always in the nature of the programme that the X-15 would receive frequent reconfiguration of displays, as scientific

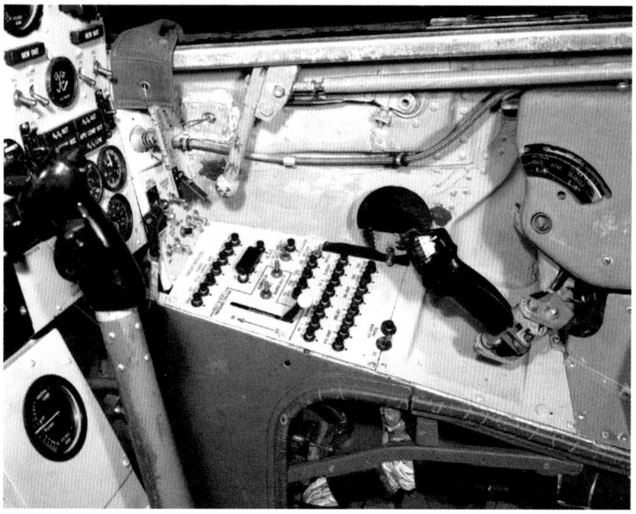

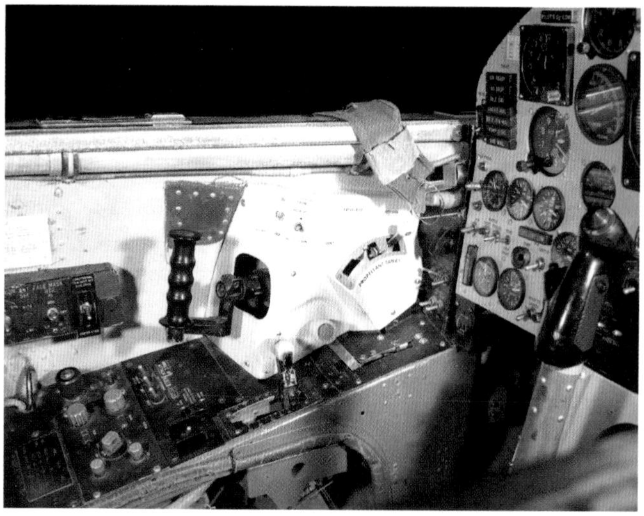

instruments were added or changed and specialised items of research equipment installed. Nevertheless, there were a number of attempts to provide a standardised cockpit layout, separating the functionality of the aeroplane from the hybrid mix of missions and tasks for which it was frequently adapted.

The early flights were made with a flat black panel, functional groupings of instruments, displays, switches and toggles sectioned off with white lines. In 1963, this was changed to a white panel which afforded sharper visual detail with toggle switches replacing rotary knobs for the Stability Augmentation System and again when the Alternate Stability Augmentation System was fitted. X-15-1 retained a more conventional layout while X-15-3 received several modifications and got the definitive display when Lear-Siegler provided a vertical-tape instrument.

Central to all the displays, however, was the '8-ball' attitude indicator which obtained its information from the Inertial Flight Data System (IFDS) and provided a pictorial display to which the pilots flew the aeroplane. This in itself caused some serious concerns when the natural tendency to align with conventional flying attitudes were compromised to some extent by the nature of the X-15's flight profile. Controls for the aircraft were of a conventional layout with the exception of the location of the centre stick and the right console hand controller,

Left: The early cockpit configuration showing the angled side panels and central control stick for low-g flight with aero-surfaces reveals the progress made in cockpit design and adaptability for the new-generation X-15. The aerodynamic control stick was carried on the right side of the cockpit which was an option for high-g manoeuvres. It also contains circuit-breakers for the APU, among other systems. The left side of the cockpit provides control switches for the XLR-99 including a single throttle lever below the white enclosure housing the propellant controls. The BCS control stick is positioned in front of this enclosure. *NASA*

which served the same function, and the left side-stick controller for operation of the BCS thrusters.

In conventional fashion, the centre stick was used for all normal flight conditions except for periods of high acceleration when high g-forces prevented the pilot from performing this function with an extended arm. It offered pitch and roll capability through inputs summed by mixer bell cranks and applied to the horizontal stabiliser actuator valves. The stick also incorporated a microphone button and alternate pitch trim switch on the grip handle. The right side-stick controller was located on the right console, angled so as to provide a rest for the pilot's arm, enabling him to control the aircraft during high longitudinal accelerations. It was coupled to the centre stick linkages and had hydraulic augmentation to reduce the force required to operate the flight controls. It too had a microphone switch and a trim switch with a knob graduated from +3deg to -25deg in the leading edge travel of the stabiliser.

The left side-stick controller was for flight control using the BCS system and was located above the left angled console and provided yaw control by appropriate left or right use of the stick, with roll effected through rotation of the handle about its spindle. Pitch could be controlled by moving the stick up or down and was ergonomically designed so that the pilot could use it with minimum physical movement during periods of high acceleration.

The Reaction Augmentation System (RAS) was fitted to X-15-1 and X-15-2 in 1963 to help the pilot avoid over-compensation when using the Ballistic Control System and the jet thrusters. When the BCS side-stick controller was in the neutral position the rate gyro sensed the angular rate in the three axes and, responding to a manually pre-set angular rate, it fired the relevant No. 1 system thruster to reduce the angular acceleration. This is described earlier in the section discussing the BCS.

The only standard flight control device unchanged from a more conventional aircraft was the rudder pedal. These were mechanically linked to the yaw system mixer bell cranks, where the movement of the pedal and the SAS were summed. This transmitted a signal to the stabiliser actuator assembly control valves for positive operation. However, unlike a conventional aircraft there were no brakes on the X-15 and so the rudder pedals had no toe-brake component.

The cockpit canopy designed into the X-15 had good visibility forward and sideways for the pilot and consisted of a pneumatically counterbalanced section with mechanical lockdown and a rear hinge line allowing it to open 45deg. It could be locked from inside or outside with a seal set into the rim for full cockpit pressurisation. The head support was retractable and could be lowered from the top of the canopy to provide better head restraint during deceleration.

Above: A completely revised panel was developed by Lear Siegler incorporating vertical-scale displays for enhanced situational awareness. Although they represented the style of display being introduced by the US Air Force, X-15 pilots in general disliked the new configuration after it was introduced on X-15-3 in 1966. *Lear Siegler*

The canopy could be jettisoned by an initiator triggered by the seat armrests being raised but it could also be explosively released by activation of a T-handle inside the cockpit. A second handle was provided in a special housing on the starboard side of the fuselage for use by ground personnel in emergencies. The cockpit itself was lit by two floodlights installed on the inside of the canopy with their beams pointing down and forward. These could be controlled by a switch on the right side console. The instrument panel was filmed during flight by a movie camera which provided direct information on instrument readings for post-flight analysis and on some flights the canopy also served as a support for experiments.

Instrumentation

The design requirement for instrumentation and measuring systems was required to record the data on the aircraft because, as seen previously, the telemetry systems were still evolving and had very low bandwidth. This changed as the programme evolved but developments in obtaining, recording and transmitting data were not able to benefit the aircraft to any major extent through to the end of flight operations in November 1968. The NACA and NASA initially required at least 1,000 data points in the aircraft. NAA's accepted design incorporated 1,050 consisting of 588 thermocouples, 64 strain gauges, 28 control surface position indicators, 136 aerodynamic surface pressures, 22 basic flight parameters such as angle-of-attack, and 212 aircraft condition monitors.

The design requirement for the X-15 to carry 362.8kg (800lb) of instrumentation was greatly exceeded by the actual capacity for carrying 589kg (1,300lb). Most of that would be carried in a removable elevator inside the instrumentation compartment behind the cockpit. The design allowed engineers to readily access the compartment and associated cabling and wiring for flight-by-flight changes in equipment, should that be necessary. Other recesses were used for instruments, including a compartment between the two propellant tanks and a primary instrument compartment in the nose, all of which were pressurised and with temperature controls.

As built by NAA, the X-15 had 656 thermocouples, 112 strain gauges, 140 pressure sensors and 90 telemetering pick-ups. Each thermocouple consisted of 30-gauge chromel-alumel leads which were spot-welded to the inner face of the external skin. To reduce resistance in the thermocouple loops, leads connecting them were of 20-gauge extensions with the added advantage of minimising errors due to changes in resistance. These were installed by NAA on the basis that they need never be replaced for the life of the aircraft. To achieve that, silicone-based fibreglass braids covered the leads and the extensions but this did have its disadvantages. If exposed to a sudden increase in temperature to 648.9ºC (1,300ºF) it could ignite the outgassed material and cause an explosion. For this reason, NASA gradually built up the high-temperature flights, for operational reasons but also to gradually condition the material. Not so durable were Bakelite strain gauges which degraded as the structural temperatures increased but over time these were replaced with Formex. Eventually, Micro-Dot provided strain gauges of a weldable type with static pressure taps comprising tubing with an outside diameter of 0.79cm (0.329in) set flush into the exterior skin.

The majority of the instrumentation was carried on the starboard side supplemented with a few sensors on the port side and across the vertical stabiliser. It was assumed that the symmetry between the right and left sides of the X-15 would make no difference to the measurements and as built there were none near the two propellant tanks or on the horizontal stabilisers. Some did get installed on the stabilisers and later in the programme new stabilisers were provided by NAA with integral pressure transducers, loads sensors and thermocouples.

Obtaining visual information about a flight in progress was well-nigh impossible with the extant technology of the 1950s/1960s but NAA provided four camera bays known as 'bug-eyes', two on the top of the fuselage and behind the cockpit and two under the centre of gravity compartment. A single 16-mm motion picture camera was located in each bay to provide views of the fuselage, the wings and the stabilisers. Film of X-15 flights showing the view looking rearward is common on YouTube channels and in documentaries. Interestingly, the National Geographic Society provided cameras for some of those shots. As the programme progressed, other items of equipment replaced the cameras but they were not always utilised, flush plates being attached over the bug-eyes instead.

Supporting its latter role as an experiment-carrier, in August 1962 NAA began development of an additional box-shaped compartment which could be carried above the top of the fuselage immediately behind the upper, wedge-shaped vertical stabiliser. Eventually, two different box shapes and sizes were provided, one of which had a stabilised platform for specific and accurate alignment, the other did not. These boxes were adaptable for X-15-1 and X-15-3, while X-15A-2 did have its own box but that was used for containing additional helium for the propellant system.

In all cases, design and production of the boxes was only sanctioned after following a detailed analysis as to potential problems with flow patterns and shock waves. The boxes fitted to the width of the vertical stabiliser and as high as the speed brakes with a length back to the end of the fuselage. Fabricated from Inconel X, the boxes had no pressurisation or thermal control and the simpler of the two only contained provision for supporting experiments that did not require a stable platform. The other box offered a removable panel which enclosed the aft-facing side to prevent ingestion of rocket motor exhaust products.

There was also provision for experiments which required exposure to the environment at extreme altitudes and for those a special hatch was provided behind which was a small compartment for instruments. The hatch was redesigned from the original specification to provide two doors each 50.8cm (20in) long by 20.3cm (8in) wide, meeting on the centreline on top of the fuselage and opened from either side to expose instruments on equipment inside. Known as the 'Skylight' hatch, it was integrated with the rebuild of X-15-2 after McKay's accident and later installed on X-15-1.

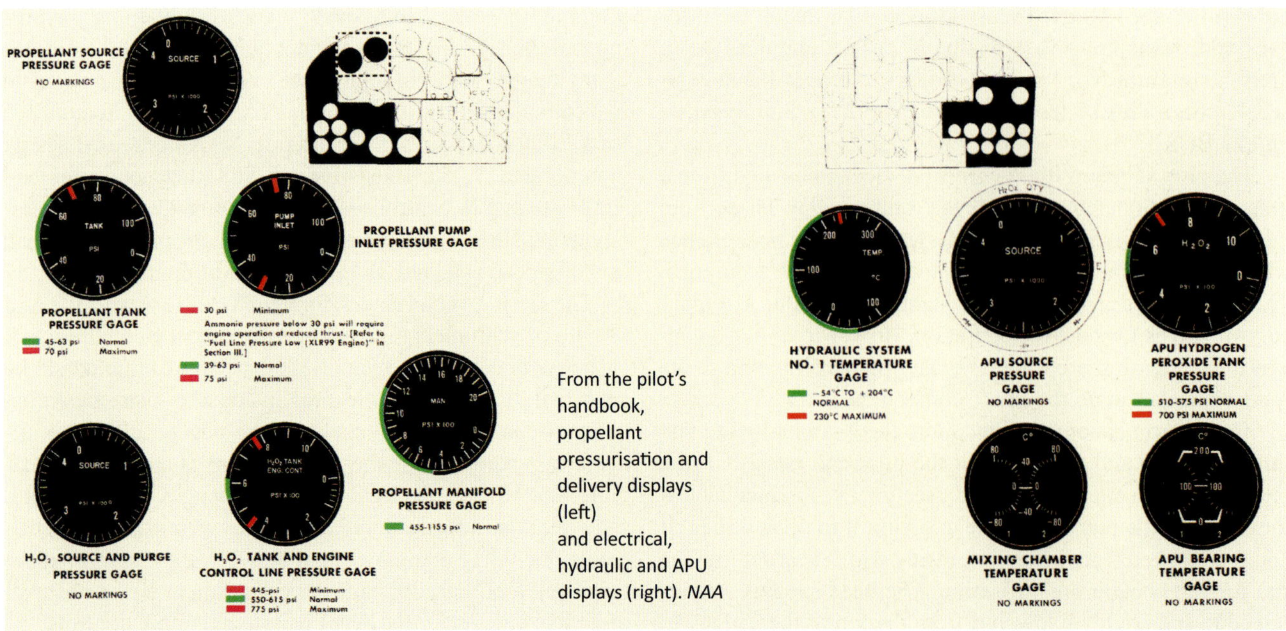

From the pilot's handbook, propellant pressurisation and delivery displays (left) and electrical, hydraulic and APU displays (right). *NAA*

Chapter Fifteen

Human Factors

The NACA and the Air Force had encountered the challenges of keeping pilots physiologically alert and fit when flying in the rarefied regions of the upper atmosphere since the early days of planning for the X-1 and X-2 series. It was the Air Force, however, that carried out research in human physiology, as that related directly to their interests in seeking to better understand the environment in which its pilots would be operating with other hypersonic vehicles then planned, such as the Dyna-Soar/X-20. Begun before any direct plans had evolved at the NACA for human space flight, this work played a major role in helping NASA with its manned space flight programme from 1958.

The need for a pressurised environment was driven by known physiological responses to reduced pressure levels and to depleted oxygen in the human body. Considerable scientific research had been conducted in many countries during the 1930s and early 1940s in an attempt to find a solution to problems with high altitude flight. The history of pressure suit design is long and its story not appropriate here but the basic physiological parameters are helpful in understanding the pioneering work conducted through the X-15 programme. In some respects, an unsung legacy for the sometimes quite similar suits worn by aircraft pilots and astronauts in the following decades.

The effects of diminishing atmospheric pressure are felt

Above: Surrounded by heat lamps in a thermal vacuum chamber, Scott Crossfield tests the XMC-2-DC for thermal properties. *NASA*

Above: Developed out of the S-1 partial-pressure suit worn by Yeager when flying the X-1, Joe Walker displays the US Air Force T-1 suit which was originally designed for high-flying B-36 crew. *NASA*

by human subjects at heights of approximately 3,000m (10,000ft) above median sea level, where the brain registers a reaction through difficulty concentrating and some sleepiness. At this height the oxygen pressure in the arterial blood is 8.2kPa (1.2lb/in^2) but if the subject is using a breathing mask delivering pure oxygen, that effect is delayed until a height of 12,200m (40,000ft) is reached. Early on, it was found that the psychomotor effects could be delayed through the use of an oxygen mask at a pressure greater than that of the surrounding air pressure – known as positive pressure. If the altitude of the aircraft increased to 13,100m (43,000ft) the arterial oxygen in the blood would fall to 6.0kPa (0.9lb/in^2) but if the oxygen pressure delivered through the mask was increased to 2.0kPa (0.3lb/in^2) above the surrounding atmospheric pressure the arterial pressure would be restored to 8kPa (1.2lb/in^2).

But there were limits. As the pressure increased, the amount of blood returning to the chest would be reduced, resulting in a reduction in the volume of blood flowing back from the heart with consequential effects of unconsciousness. Furthermore, while breathing in, the oxygen would be pushed back into the lungs through positive pressure but to push it back out would require muscular action. This effect could be alleviated to some extent by increasing the pressure on the outside of the chest through a pressure-vest similar to an anti-g suit where an air-filled bladder applies pressure to the lower torso and limbs.

Developed initially in 1943 by German-born Dr. James Paget Henry at the University of Southern California after travelling to America from England, a pressure suit was provided which applied partial pressure to most of the body. During tests on himself the following year, Dr. Henry noticed that at a simulated altitude 17.7km (58,000ft) and wearing a partial pressure suit, his hands swelled to twice their size, caused probably by boiling of tissue fluid. He found a solution by wearing tight-fitting gloves. Under normal conditions, the blood boils at 100°C (212°F) but if the atmospheric pressure drops to 6.3kPa (0.9lb/in^2), as it does at 19.2km (63,000ft), it

Above: Tested on 14 October 1957, the first XMC-2-DC suit under evaluation. With its silvered finish for thermal protection, this suit evolved into the type worn by astronauts on the 1961-63 Mercury flights. In the public's eyes, it became the archetypical image of 'space-men'. *NASA*

will boil at 37°C (99°F). But his work also showed that there is no direct correlation between the specific altitude and pressure at which a fluid will boil and that this is dependent on a wide range of variables.

The partial pressure suit was effective for short durations of up to 10 minutes but in 1953 the Air Force had a requirement to provide full protection for aircrew flying at altitudes of 15,240-21,336m (50,000-70,000ft) as anticipated for the B-52. It was concerned that loss of pressure would require the crew to maintain altitude for an hour or two to evade attack, for which only a full pressure suit would be sufficient. Work on this type of suit had been underway for two decades already, the more famous of which was the experimental tests by aviator Wiley Post with the B F Goodrich Company of Akron, Ohio, in the mid-1930s. During the war, several other companies became involved, including Bell Aircraft, the Goodyear Rubber Company and the US Rubber Company.

Partial pressure suits and suitable helmets were in development for the initial X-1 flights and Henry's suit formed the basis for that worn by 'Chuck' Yeager when he exceeded Mach 1 in October 1947. Dr. Henry had worked with the Air Force and fine-arts graduate Alice King Chatham, to design and fabricate a partial pressure suit designated S-1 with a soft, full head helmet which obviated the need for a separate oxygen mask. It was while wearing this that Yeager achieved his historic flight and that led to the T-1 with a two-piece, clamshell helmet for broader operational use, including for flight crews on high-flying B-36 missions. By the early 1950s, the CIA became interested in a full pressure suit for pilots flying the Lockheed U-2 spyplane and, later still, the SR-71.

With some experience to hand and the expanding requirements of high-performance combat aircraft, the Air Force defined the requirement for a full pressure suit capable of providing 12 hours of protection at a minimum pressure of 34.475kPa (5lb/in^2) at altitudes in excess of 16,764m (55,000ft). All for a suit weighing less than 13.6kg (30lb). Two contenders were reviewed: the XMC-2-DC from David Clark and the XMC-2-ILC from the International Latex Corporation. The ILC suit was cumbersome, containing convoluted joints and was bulky as a result, despite a lot of development having gone into that under a Navy contract.

The breakthrough came with the David Clark slip-knit suit incorporating an inner, gas-impermeable, pressure bladder fabricated from nylon with an outer restraint layer made from nylon cords woven in a link-net pattern and slightly bigger than the inner layer. When inflated, the inner bladder prevented the suit from ballooning while the outer garment allowed it to deform according to body shape. Where previously candidate full pressure suits had incorporated several convoluted joints for hips, knees and elbows, only a single neck ring was required with the David Clark suit to attach the helmet, with wrist locks restraining the gloves.

The David Clark Company of Worcester, Massachusetts, had provided partial pressure suits for the Bell X-1 programme and full pressure suits for the D-558-2 Skyrocket. There was no attempt to provide full dexterity or independence of movement but the unique construction of the suit would serve as a template for all suits which were to follow. When the requirement for the X-15 programme was first announced, the company put up the XMC-2-DC. It was world-class in type and function as the first effective full-pressure suit and, at 15.8kg (35lb) was only a little above the specified weight in the Air Force requirement. A proposed contender from North American had weighed 49.9kg (110lb)!

The prototype S794 David Clark suit became a development programme in itself, increasingly stringent requirements extending its application as the world's first full-scale spacesuit. New materials and various compositions of rubber and nylon layers were incorporated for what was now referred to as a Link-Net structure. Two production-level suits were fabricated for tests, with separate paths of modified construction and distribution of materials. Much of the development work had the support of Scott Crossfield, who had always been a strong advocate of the full pressure suit. Great importance was placed on suit development, to the extent that a requirement for this was issued to NAA on 2 March 1956 with a similar directive to the David Clark Company on 8 April to produce such a garment for the X-15.

Below: Neil Armstrong suits up for a flight in X-15-1 on 30 November 1960 and displays the standard elements that would define suits used in the air and in space for decades to come: torso protection with separate helmet secured by a neck ring and separate gloves and boots. At this date no human had flown into space. Less than nine years later he would walk on the Moon. *NASA*

And therein began the heated debate between the NAA and the Air Force advocating a partial pressure suit and the NACA and Scott Crossfield for a full pressure garment. It reached a peak confrontation at the 20-22 June 1956 gathering where the Air Force began to recede under convincing argument and the backing of the Aero Medical Laboratory which judged that a full pressure suit was well within the state-of-the-art and could be successfully developed for the X-15. Full scale development was adopted and reviewed on 12 July 1956 and at the cockpit mock-up review on 7-13 October 1957 the proposed suit configuration (the S794-3C) was evaluated.

Weighing 16.8kg (37lb), it was sent to the Aero Medical Laboratory and tested in the centrifuge at Wright Field for two runs at 7-g before some modifications and adjustments were required, resulting in the S-794-4 suit which, after further tests, led to the S-794-5 suit, regarded as the prototype for the MC-2 model for the X-15. This was evaluated in a Lockheed T-33 and then a Lockheed F-104B, logging several hours of trial and analysis measuring its suitability for rocket flights. After further minor changes and adjustments the design was closed on 3 May 1958 but a sequence of frustrating but relatively minor delays began to threaten the X-15 flight test programme. Crossfield received his flight suit on 17 December.

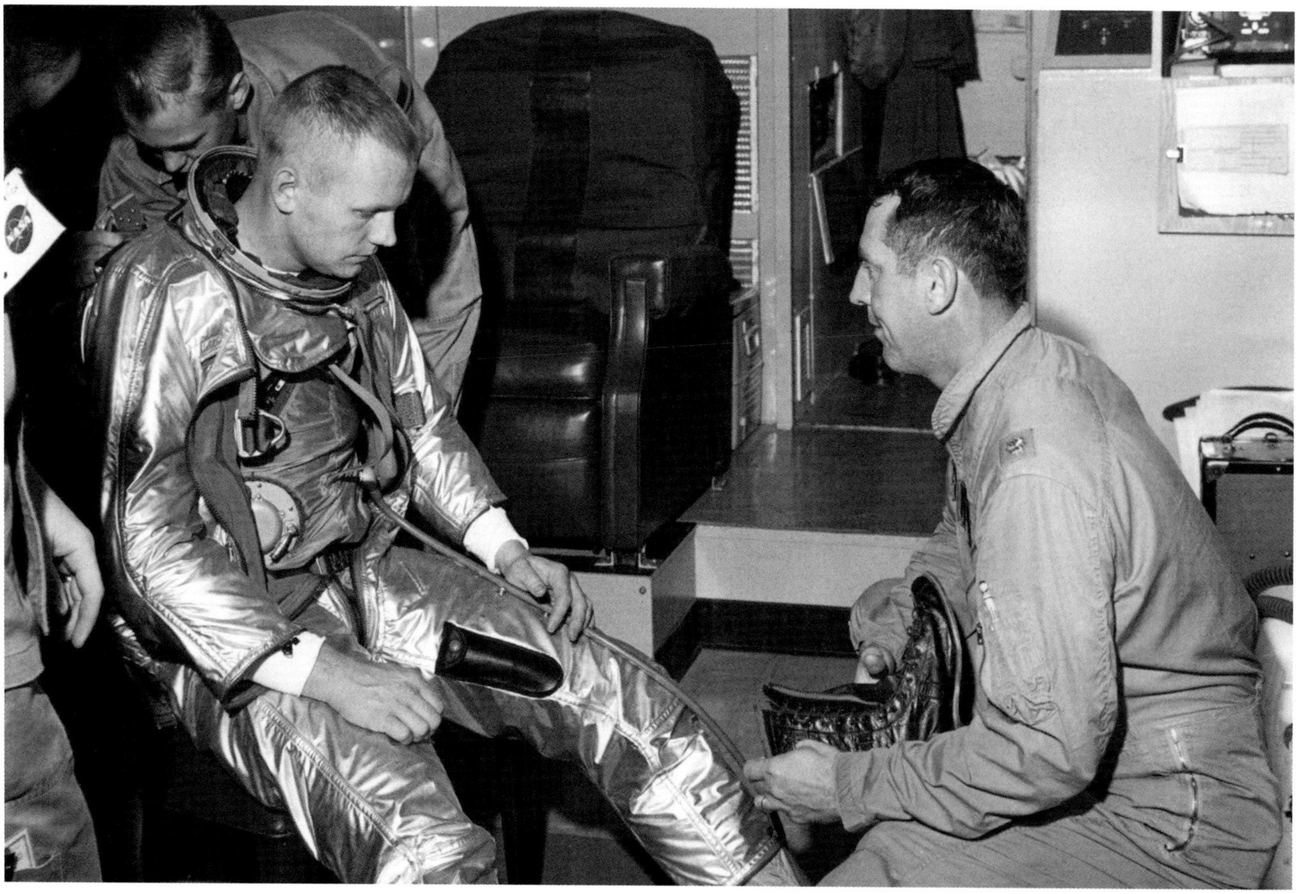

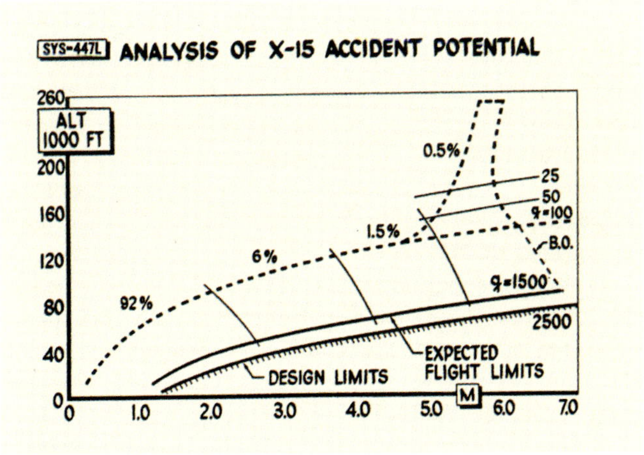

Above: This chart displays the calculated probability of an accident as a percentage of total catastrophes set against altitude and speed regimes with dynamic pressure indicated. Design and flight limits are shown set against height and Mach number. Note that this does not imply a probability of an accident but rather the zones where accidents that do occur are likely, inferring here that most risk is at the lower end of the altitude/speed spectrum. *NASA*

Suited for speed

Tailored for each pilot, the MC-2 consisted of a ventilation layer, upper and lower rubberised garments and upper and lower restraint garments. The ventilation portion included a porous wool garment and the two components of the rubber garments formed a seal at the waist area with their edges folded over three times. The lower half featured an anti-g layer which borrowed the concept from the standard Air Force suit for protection rated up to 7-g. The suit was pressurised below the neck level with gaseous nitrogen fed directly from the aircraft supply and it offered provision for various orifices and leads connected to the biomedical sensors.

The novel feature of the David Clark design was the fabrication of the link-net restraint layer which inhibited the ballooning that had characterised other suit designs. The link-net was a brilliant piece of creative design engineering in that it worked similar to a torsion net which provided a lightweight and non-rigid restraint. As the pressure increased the link-net would shorten the longitudinal dimension and any tendency to elongate was compensated by a tendency to increase in circumference. In this way the overall dimension of the suit remained the same.

The outer layer of the suit consisted of a reflective garment applied more as a scuff protector than for any practical reason. It also provided some insulation against high temperatures but its aluminium-silvery appearance became a trend-setter for movies and the popular press who took this as the new look for the Space Age. It was a reputation endorsed when Mercury astronauts appeared in their silver suits during flights between 1961 and 1963. The MC-1 outer layer contained the various restraints and harnesses described earlier and it would have also given a little extra protection for the undergarments during ejection.

The only slightly modified MA-3 helmet was built up from a fibreglass shell with special head liner and a visor with a conductive coated lens preventing fogging through electrical resistance heating. Communications equipment included moulded ear cups together with standard AN/AIC-10 earphones and a microphone. These appendages were positioned on the inner face of the helmet, thus avoiding any protrusions during ejection. The helmet was attached to the suit by a lightweight and detachable lock with a sealed rotating bearing for full head mobility.

With a dome-shaped Plexiglass helmet and an occupant breathing pure oxygen, the Goodrich suit was capable of maintaining a constant pressure equivalent to an altitude of 10,668m (35,000ft) – 23.8kPa (3.46lb/in^2), compared to a sea-level pressure of 101.36kPa (14.7lb/in^2) – all the way to space. This pressure is close to the minimum pressure of oxygen the body requires for proper function. Although the body can operate effectively for up to a month without nitrogen, a factor which would limit the duration of Gemini and Apollo missions, the consistent supply of oxygen is essential for retaining at least adequate brain function. The Goodrich suit was bulky and stiff and brought many complaints from pilots involved in tests, but as one observer stated laconically: 'We are in favour of being alive and stiff rather than dead and stiff!'

Despite its futuristic appearance the MC-2 suit was little more than a prototype for improvements which were inevitably part of the development programme. Bulky and uncomfortable, the MC-2 required high maintenance and could prove troublesome for pilots when a sudden change in breathing could reverse the normal flow of nitrogen to the suit and oxygen to the helmet! But to alleviate the physical difficulty of donning the suit, David Clark integrated the various layers into a one-piece garment with a pressure-seal zipper. The silver over-cover was retained but it hosted a series of modifications to improve the overall acceptability to the wearer, and to improve maintenance. Each suit was still tailored for each pilot.

Much as with the aeroplane itself, the pressure suit developed as the programme went along, the David Clark A/P22S-2 (company model number S1023) integrating the separate layers linked to a single zipper. That arrived at Edwards on 27 July 1959 for initial tests and within a year it had been integrated with flight trials on a Convair JTF-102A alongside cockpit evaluations and simulator runs. NAA also conducted wind tunnel tests with the suit to evaluate its effectiveness against air pressure, which would be essential for keeping the pilot alive in the event of an ejection.

Welcomed by the men flying the X-15, the A/P22S-2 was first worn in the air by Joe Walker on 21 March 1961 when X-15-2 failed to drop due to problems with telemetry. It was worn nine days later when Walker flew X-15-2 to Mach 3.95 and an altitude of 51,510m (169,600ft). In all, the A/P22S-2 was worn on 163 X-15 flights. Along the way, improvements were made to the biomedical connectors and to the entire electrical interface for physiological data. But welcome as it was, a few modifications advanced the technology with rotating glove rings, a better and more efficient helmet/neck-ring connector, new redundant suit zipper and an improved face seal around the cheeks.

The MC-2 and A/P-22S-2 formed the basic design from which all future suits for NASA and the US Air Force were developed. A wide range of USAF pilots, including those who flew in the SR-71, wore the David Clark suit in whatever designated form it existed at the time of flight. And there were several versions and variants of that. The Navy had chosen B F Goodrich as the source for its own suits, the full pressure but bulky Mark I, the modified Mark II and the lighter Mark III. By 1958 the Navy had accepted the Mark IV suit as standard for its pilots flying fast jets at high altitude.

The Mark IV was accepted by NASA as their first astronaut suit, receiving the designation XN-1 to XN-4 which were used on the six Mercury space flights between 1961 and 1963. But improvements to the David Clark A/P22S-2 was the foundation suit from which NASA had the company develop the G-3C, G-4C and G-5C suits for the Gemini astronauts on 10 flights between 1965 and 1966. The ILC suit was adopted for the Apollo A-7LB suit but the Navy switched to the David Clark Company when the Air Force Life Support Special Project Office took over responsibility for all pressure suits for the US armed services.

The environment in which the X-15 pilot existed during flight was the same in both the cockpit and the suit and the regulator maintained that at 24,132kPa (3.5lb/in^2), which was close to the lowest level permissible and the same as that which NASA would accept as the baseline for spacewalks during the Gemini (1965-66) and Apollo (1968-1975) flights. Physiologists required that the X-15 pilot's skin temperature was kept below 37.7°C (100°F) and flight results would show that this was ensured by the environmental control system. To monitor this, a set of biomedical data would provide the flight surgeon with an ECG reading, oxygen flow rates, pressure differences between the suit and helmet and between the suit and the cockpit and the pilot's skin temperature at four body locations. The difference in pressure between the helmet and the suit also indicated respiration.

While much of the data acquired was expected to provide vital information on a pilot's ability to operate in conditions of weightlessness, only a limited amount of time was spent by the X-15 under microgravity conditions. With space flights in the Gemini programme extending to two weeks by the end of 1965, this information was quickly superseded. However, vital data on the physiological effects of piloting a winged aircraft back through the outer reaches of the atmosphere was unequalled prior to the first Shuttle flight in April 1981 and proved of value to that programme until it began to assemble its own database. In that regard, the X-15 results were significant.

Some physiologists likened a typical X-15 flight profile to a compressed space flight lasting less than 10 minutes and sought to extract correlations from the data on that basis. But this was not possible due to the different flight profiles, pilot tasks, equipment integrated with flight plan activities and the almost unique nature of each individual flight. Physicians were initially surprised by the difference between patterns of physiological response in military pilots in general and by the X-15 pilots in particular. They found no relaxation of heart rate, respiration or the general conditioning through familiarity between pilots on their first or their last X-15 flight.

It was generally found to be the case that frequent exposure to the same cycles of potentially dangerous activity in military aviation brought a sense of reassurance reflected in lower heart and respiration rates. This was not so with the X-15 programme, probably because each flight was approached by its pilot as though it were a completely new experience. Psychologically, this was interpreted as the brain setting up a defence against unexpected situations brought about through a malfunction or an unexpected phenomenon. It was a potential advantage, in that it heightened the response since none of the 'new' flight profiles were interpreted as having happened before, despite the majority of activities required being the repeat of a previous flight.

It was the need to condition the pilot against a range of assumptions that fed across to the NASA manned space flight programmes. On the known certainty that behavioural familiarity breeds contempt, it pushed pre-flight preparation into an acceptance of the unexpected. In this way, uncertainty, and the ability of a pilot to handle that, drove the manned programme towards a grindingly punishing ordeal of simulator runs where pilots – and crews – were conditioned to believe that handling problems, contingencies, emergencies and unfamiliar situations were preferable to a continuously repetitive practice of the same procedures. It was the underpinning reason why astronauts almost always find the actual pre-launch and launch experience less stressful.

In a technical simulator run the brain always engages with the body to mimic the psychophysiological reactions of an actual flight, inducing the same brain waves, heart, respiration and perspiration levels as the real-world event. Which is why biomedical evidence shows that astronauts always relax when a flight begins, because in both their brain and their mind, but not physically, they have already experienced the worst that can happen. This has also fed across into the world of military aviation and while the X-15 programme did not fully engage with these techniques, NASA did use the data as a baseline for how to train astronauts and in that regard is one of the lesser-known products of the programme.

Ejection seat

The safety of the X-15 pilot invoked a special set of studies and engineering tests because, before the project began, nobody had seriously examined the prospect of routinely flying men at hypersonic speeds. When considering the way a pilot could escape from an aircraft out of control at Mach 5 or above, only two options were available: capsule or ejection seat. We have seen that test pilot Scott Crossfield was in favour of ejection but a cursory note of the way the two options emerged clarifies the logic of that decision.

As the performance of combat aircraft entered the supersonic regime in the 1950s, the design of the ejection seat was required to meet challenges very different from those associated with subsonic aircraft. Essentially a seat ejected by small rocket charge from the fuselage of a doomed aircraft, the ejection seat concept had first been demonstrated in 1929 when Romanian inventor Anastase Dragomir tested his system at Orly airport, Paris. In 1944 the Heinkel He 162A became the

X-15 Ejection seat

The X-15 ejection seat (right) emerged from the sometimes bitter fight to exclude the escape-pod concept pushed by the Air Force, a standard design choice for its Mach 3 aircraft. Scott Crossfield campaigned tirelessly to get the ejection seat, being dismissive of the separable nose section. In its day, the X-15 seat was considered the most advanced of its type, predicted after numerous tests to be effective at altitudes up to 36,570m (120,000ft) and speeds of up to Mach 4. The effectiveness of these tests helped forge the way for ejection seats, rather than the Launch Escape System used on Mercury and Apollo, to be selected for the Gemini spacecraft, an application which was potentially flawed and problematical. *NASA*

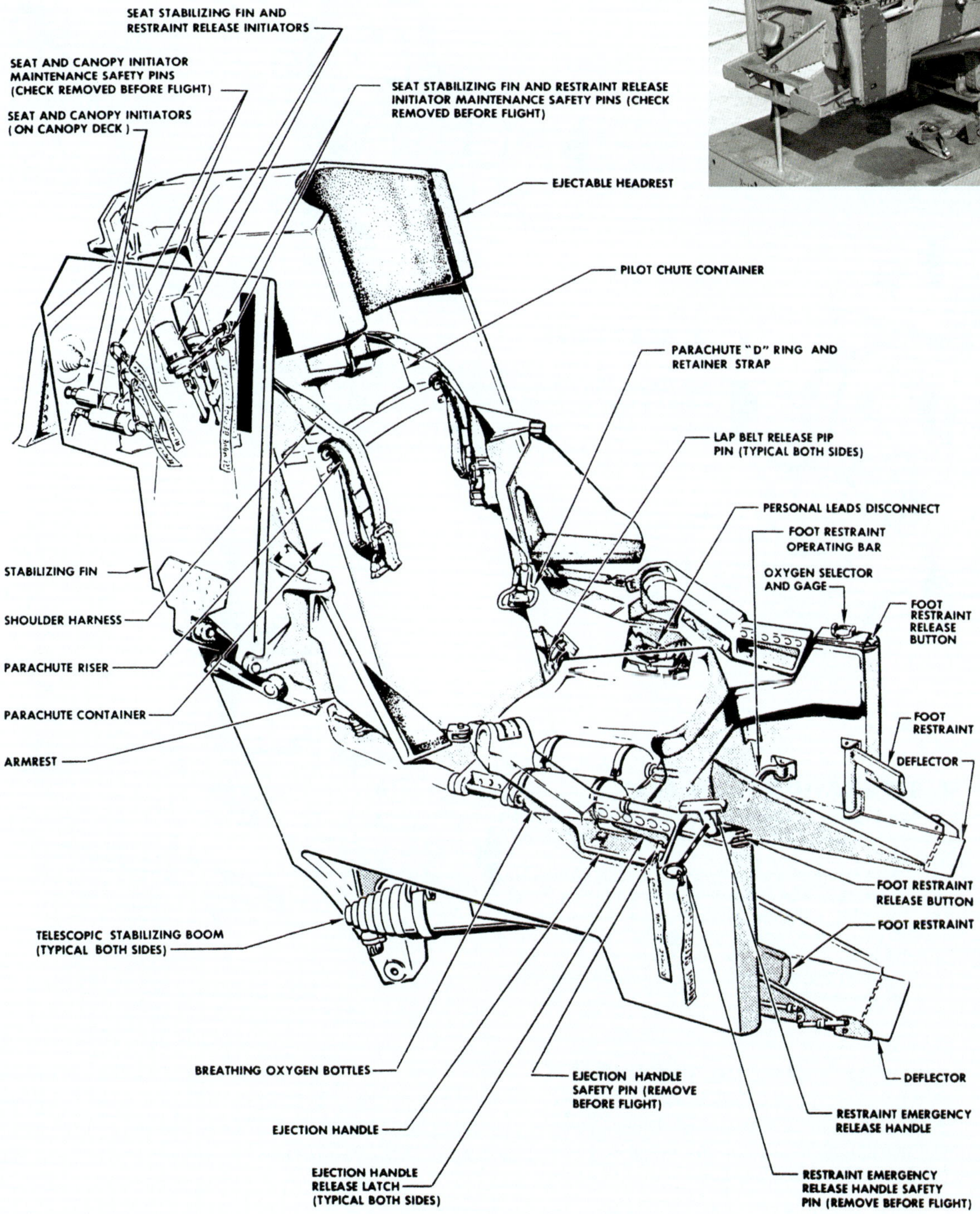

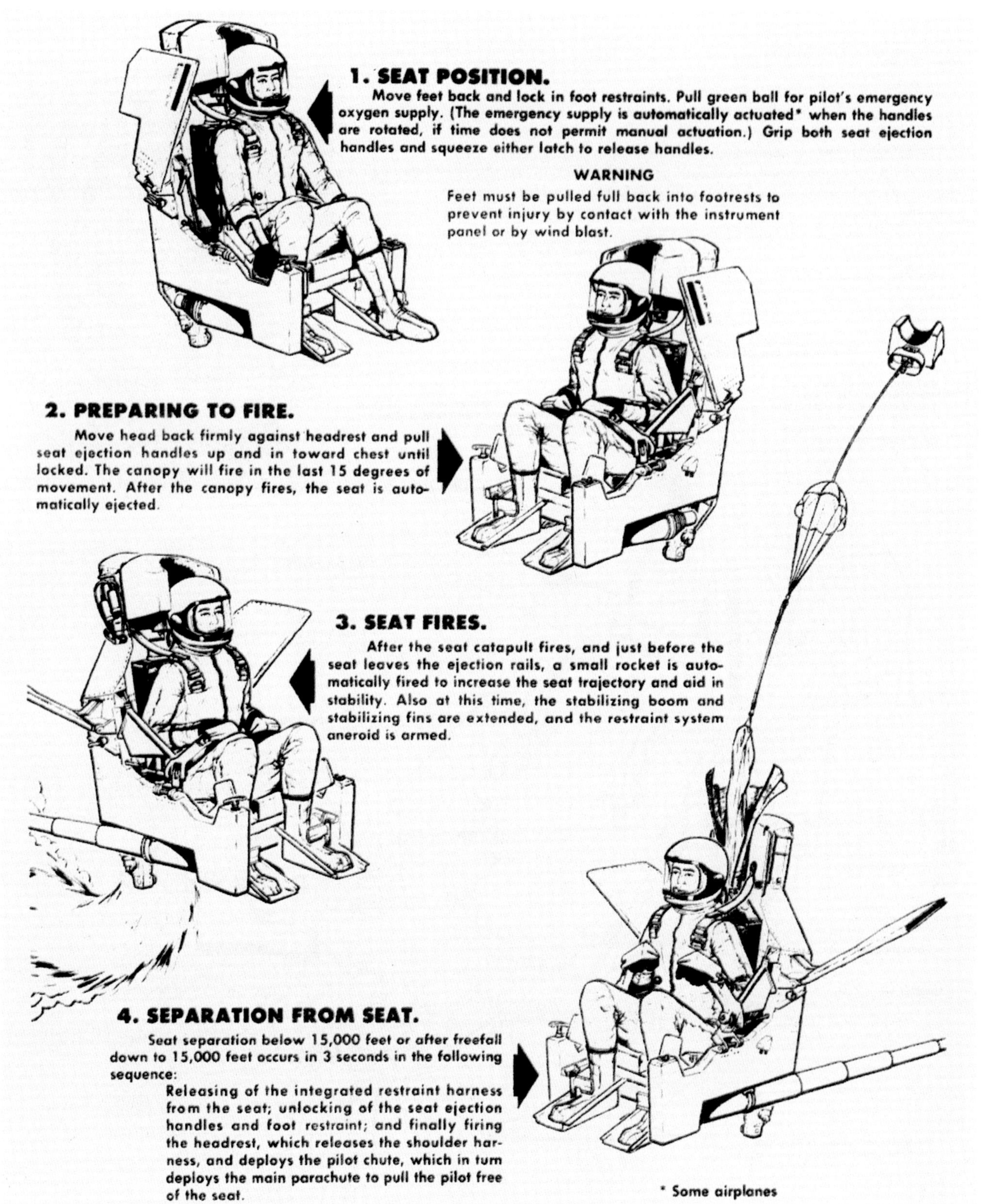

first aircraft to enter service with an ejection seat fitted as standard but other types were quick to follow and in the post-war race for turbojet-powered combat aircraft it became an essential safety feature on every new aircraft of that type.

As aircraft speeds increased there was a move toward capsule escape systems, whereby the crewmember was encapsulated in a pod comprising a folded enclosure which would snap shut on ejection and protect the crewmember from the supersonic slipstream. It would open to allow the seat and pod structure to fall away, the pilot descending by parachute. Other designs had the crewmember remain encapsulated, riding down to the ground enclosed in the capsule which would deploy a parachute at subsonic speed and in some cases air bags to cushion the impact.

Left: The operating sequence of the seat ejection cycle to the point of separation from the X-15. *NASA*

A hybrid system would involve a jettisonable forward section of the fuselage, tipping the pilot out after separation, but this was considered by many pilots likely to incur physical stresses which could just as easily kill the escapee as save him. One such was the escape capsule designed for the Douglas D558-2 Skyrocket. Wind tunnel tests indicated a strong possibility that the ejecting pilot would be killed by the g-force incurred. NACA test pilot Scott Crossfield decided from the outset that he would never use this, preferring instead to ride down to subsonic velocities and bale out in the conventional manner. He was never called upon to do so.

As described earlier, the Bell X-2 also had an escape system, one which several pilots also disliked. It was designed as a detachable nose section and cockpit for attachment as the forward fuselage. On 27 September 1955, inexperienced X-2 rocket plane pilot Milburn Apt lost his life when using the separation device. Crossfield had always believed that it was a killer system and Apt demonstrated that this was the case – with his life.

However, most engineers working on the programme were in favour of some form of encapsulation and this was indeed the favoured design trend in the 1950s. The Mach 3 Convair B-58 Hustler had a crew capsule system whereby each of three crewmembers could escape individually and depart the capsule for a conventional parachute descent after separating from a clamshell enclosure. It was a natural engineering solution favoured by engineers. But the pilots differed and there was considerable lobbying by them in opposition to the anticipated decision favouring capsules.

The one strongly negative aspect about the crew capsule was weight. Analysis showed that it would raise the weight of the X-15 from 14,062kg (31,000lb) to 18,144kg (40,000lb) and while the empty weight would grow the proportionality of capsule to structure remained the same. Moreover, an open ejection system would be consistent with the design philosophy implicit throughout the programme: that the design and systems selected for the X-15 should be as simple and as conventional as possible, ensuring minimum risk and granting maximum reliability and safety. It was one occasion where the engineers and the pilots agreed!

But the Air Force was not convinced and at the 2-3 May 1956 meeting held at Wright Field they pressed upon the assembly of scientists, engineers and pilots the weakness in the

Below: A rocket sled at Edwards South Base was used to test the seat firing sequence, initially empty, then with a dummy and finally a volunteer test subject wearing the David Clark MC-2 full pressure suit. *NASA*

Above: The South Base rocket sled demonstrates a full ejection sequence and deployment of stabiliser fins. *NASA*

ejection seat, maintaining that encapsulated ejection, or separation from the main body of the air vehicle was a sure means of protection from the extreme conditions of leaving the aircraft at high speed and high altitude. Scott Crossfield, an engineer himself who understood the rationales given for safety and simplicity, likened the aircraft itself to a capsule capable of protecting the pilot until it descended, or slowed down, to more favourable conditions for ejection.

The Air Force wanted capsules for another reason. They saw the X-15 as a precursor test vehicle for a range of separate systems which could be applied to operational combat aircraft and, just perhaps, to expanded roles for an operational military version of the aircraft itself. Capsules would be fitted to the Mach 3 XB-70 and capsule escape had figured large in the design of the Dyna-Soar spaceplane. Nevertheless, the NACA got its way and the pilots won the argument.

A formal cockpit inspection held in July 1956 had included an ejection seat, specially designed for the X-15 and with a new type of pilot restraint harness together with small winglets so that it would operate like a shuttlecock and stabilise when taken by the slipstream, preventing it tumbling or oscillating. The seat ejection rocket motor had a propulsive thrust of 13.34kN (3,000lb) to propel the seat well clear of the fuselage.

The detailed design of the seat required it to be operable up to Mach 4 or to a maximum altitude of 36,576m (120,000ft), the zone where the X-15 was most likely to encounter an emergency situation. To fire the ejection seat the pilot had first to release the cockpit canopy, the restraint devices tightening on his arms and legs at ejection altitudes above 4,572m (15,000ft). When ejecting below this altitude there would have been a three second delay before the sequence began.

The seat itself contained interface connections and control devices for pilot operation in normal flight. Oxygen was contained in a cylinder attached to the underside of the seat and was used when the aircraft was launched from the carrier-plane, prior to which the feed would come direct through the attachment shoe on the starboard wing. The pilot could switch between supplies by use of a selector valve and gauge on the left side of the seat.

Personal leads for oxygen and the ventilated suit were attached to a quick-disconnect block attached to a fitting on the left, inside the seat bucket. The seat itself also had a quick-disconnect receptacle to plug in to the pilot's biophysical instrumentation wiring harness, located at the top of the seat pan in the forward right-hand corner. Manually adjustable shoulder harness straps were fastened to the integrated parachute restraint harness, these also equipped with quick-disconnect fittings. During the ejection sequence the shoulder harness was released when the headrest was ejected.

Above and right: The ejection seat installed in X-15A-2 as it appeared at the Museum of the US Air Force while the aircraft was being prepared for display. The position allowed a good ergonometric arrangement for the crew controls, display panels and clearance for access.
Museum of the US Air Force

The main parachute was housed in a container attached to the harness with a pilot parachute in a separate container, the pilot parachute being released along with the headrest. After a fall from high altitude the operation sequence would have been activated by an aneroid device at 4,572m (15,000ft) by firing three initiators that ejected the headrest and released the seat belt, personal leads, ejection handles and all restraints to allow the pilot to depart the seat and fall free.

To fire the ejection seat the pilot raised either of two ejection handles on the seat to within 15deg of its full travel, at which point the canopy was jettisoned. As it departed the aircraft it would fire the seat catapult initiator which in turn fired the two-stage seat catapult. The ejection handle release latch was in the top portion of each handle and would be actuated when either ejection handle was grasped. The two handles were physically connected by a link to a torque bar, so raising either one also raised the other, locking into position until unlocked by the restraint release system. If the canopy had been lost for some reason, the ejection sequence would not work until the ejection handles were raised.

As the pilot separated from the seat the ejection handles would automatically unlock to swing outboard, allowing the pilot to fall away. Several modifications were carried out on the seat itself, allowing automatic actuation of the pilot's emergency oxygen supply when the handles were raised and a cable would pull the pin from the emergency oxygen supply valve. The pilot's personal parachute was housed in a fibreglass container attached to the integrated harness at top and bottom. The main parachute could be either a 7.3m (24ft) or 8.5m (28ft) type. A second container housed the pilot parachute which, along with the parachute container lids, closed out the top of the container. The pilot parachute container was held in place during ejection by a retaining pin which locked into the manual ripcord pin. On the top of the container a retainer pin fitted into the ejection seat headrest which pulled out the main parachute.

As this was deployed a rescue beacon in the parachute container would automatically begin transmitting at a frequency of 244.4MHz through an antenna attached to one of the parachute straps. When the pilot separated from the seat the parachute container remained with the pilot. The riser quick-release buckles also fastened the shoulder harness and parachute container to the pressure suit fittings on the pilot's chest, just below the shoulders. The ripcord 'D' ring was attached to a strap fastened to the left side of the parachute container and this too had a quick-release buckle attached to a fitting on the left side of the integrated restraint harness just below the arm.

The lap belt portion consisted of two straps, one over each hip. These were fitted with hooks which snapped into a ring portion on the lap belt release fitting either side of the seat, which attached the pilot to each side of the seat itself. Adjuster straps allowed the pilot to cinch in the harness to a tight fit.

The modified pressure suit had restraint straps and parachute harness designed as an integral part of the garment. A neck seal was provided to keep the nitrogen pressurisation and oxygen breathing supply separate. This supply of breathing oxygen was activated automatically and provided sufficient gas for approximately 20 minutes after the pilot separated from the ejection seat.

There was some conjecture about the appropriate size of parachute for the programme, the initial choice being the C-9 which had a diameter of 8.5m (28ft) but this was not considered suitable for the aircraft due to the limited packing space available and the requirements of the suit itself. A new 7.3m (24ft) parachute was designed and used in the initial phases of the programme. Following some concerns by physicians about the impact speed with the smaller diameter design, in October 1960 North American was contracted to test a redesigned parachute of the larger diameter and this was eventually cleared for use through trials at the National Parachute Range. The type of parachute actually used was left to the preference of individual pilots.

In June 1965 NASA contracted with NAA for five new larger diameter parachutes to replace the smaller ones because they had reached the end of their useful life. The new parachutes had a modified disconnect device which allowed the pilots to release half the shroud lines as they descended but they still had the bulk of the former, larger diameter, issue and were much less comfortable to use. Fortunately, no pilot ever ejected, or used his parachute during the programme. The one pilot who should have been in a position to use his parachute was Michael Adams, killed when X-15-3 crashed to Earth on 15 November 1967.

Below: X-15 pilot John McKay in front of the open cockpit to X-15-3 displaying the window area and head rest. *NASA*

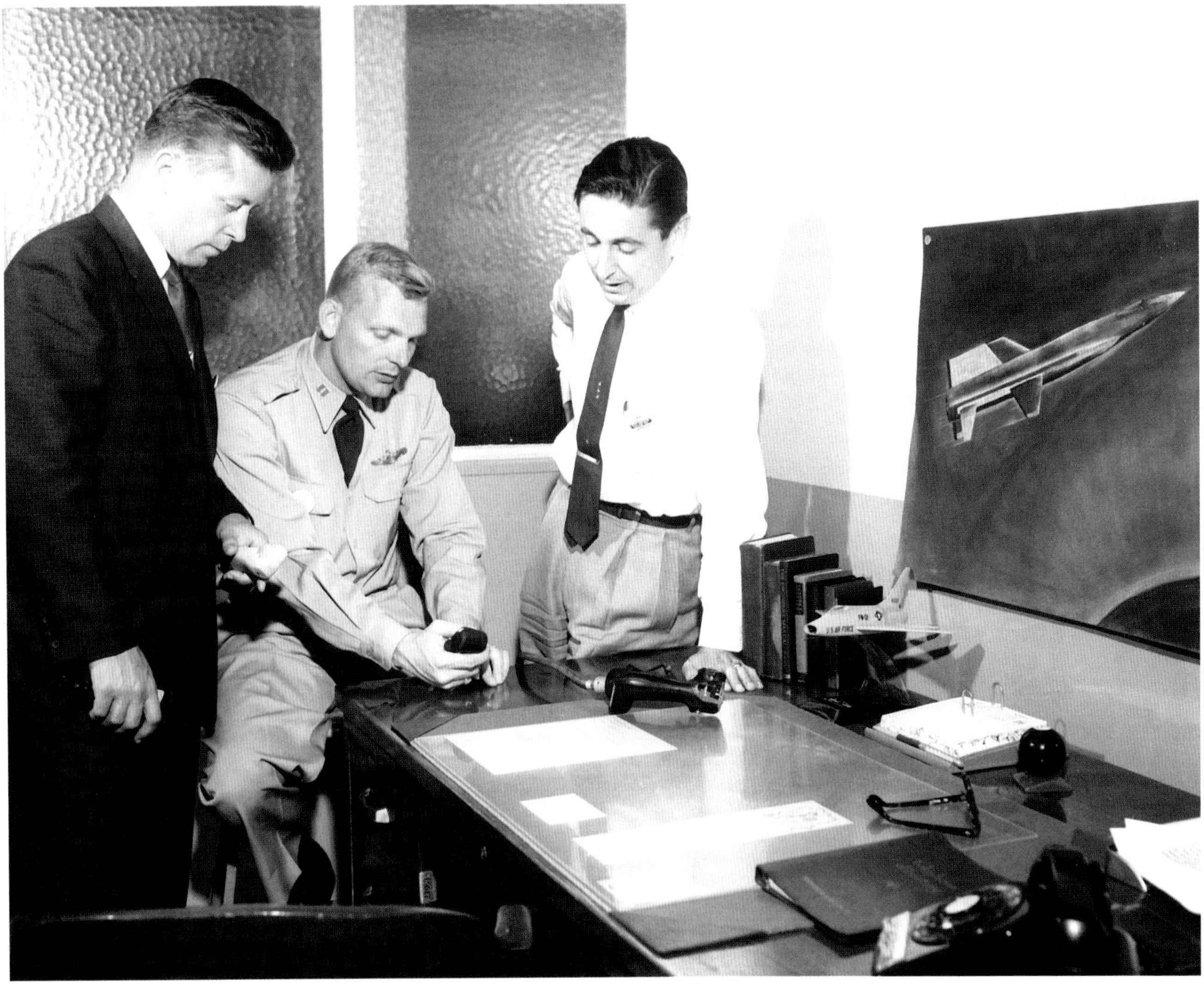

Chapter Sixteen

Flight Simulation and Tracking

The use of simulators in the NACA/Air Force flight research programmes was introduced shortly after the Second World War and resulted in some successful applications for the later flights in the X-1 programme and with the X-2. The phenomenon of roll-coupling and flight control problems around Mach 3 were evaluated and worked in the analogue simulators then available but the demands of the X-15 programme and the enhanced requirements for those more challenging flights demanded better solutions. Their use bred a new cadre of individuals, 'flight planners' who calculated the precise details of a flight path or trajectory with profound knowledge of the capabilities of the X-15 and its vicissitudes. They were a largely unsung, but vital group who would bequeath to the nascent US manned space programme a level of unique expertise.

During the development phase of this aircraft, engineers and assigned pilots used a fixed-base simulator at NAA's Inglewood factory. This was fundamental not only to understanding the way the aircraft could be flown but of predicting control responses and even of establishing recovery routines for in-flight problems or malfunctions. It consisted of a duplicated cockpit, and an 'iron bird' layout of flight controls, push-rods, linkages, connectors that mirrored the real aircraft, equipped with a full Stability Augmentation System and the MH-96 flight control system when that became available. The simulator was connected to three PACE 231R analogue computers provided by Electronics Associated Inc.

Above: Bob White (left), Iven Kincheloe (centre) and Scott Crossfield pause for the photographer while discussing the design and operation of the Ballistic Control System. Although assigned to fly the X-15, Air Force pilot Kincheloe was killed in a flying accident on 26 July 1958. *NASA*

The choice of an analogue system was forced upon the simulation team because the digital systems of the day were incapable of providing the necessary computations at the speed required. It incorporated 380 operational amplifiers, 101 generators, 32 servo amplifiers and five electronic multipliers. When it began operation in October 1956 it was capable of 5-degrees of freedom, eventually being modified to handle all six degrees, including roll, pitch and yaw and accelerations in each of those three axes. It was also capable of simulating flight envelopes from Mach 0.2 to Mach 7 and from ground level to an altitude of 322km (200mls). It was able to show a capability for the X-15 to safely re-enter the atmosphere from a peak height of 167.6km (104.2mls), subject to a very precise entry corridor.

The fixed-base simulator also played a significant role in helping with the design of the aircraft itself, replacing the fixed dorsal tail with the dorsal/ventral design it ended up with. But there were certain limitations and initially it was only able to work with one of three parameters at a time: atmospheric exit, ballistic flight and re-entry. Various improvements and upgrades would expand that to a significant portion of a flight in an integrated flight simulation of a written profile. Within a year of its introduction, it was capable of covering a complete flight from drop to touchdown. By mid-1958 it had logged more than 2,000 simulated flights and 3,500 'flying' hours and provided the pilots – Crossfield in particular at this early stage – with an ability to liaise with the flight planners and make recommendations on individual flight profiles based on experience in the air.

The Inglewood simulator was employed to evaluate new instruments, the MH-96 being an excellent example, a task on which Neil Armstrong spent a considerable amount of development time. As its use continued into the flight phase of the X-15, techniques or routines evaluated in the simulator were tried out in the air first and the results fed back into the simulator for analysis. Many aspects of handling and operational control of the aircraft in the air were evaluated and demonstrated in the simulator before they were installed in the X-15 and many items of equipment, modified even in a minor way, were first proof-tested on the 'Iron-Bird'.

The Inglewood simulator was the only one of its type and

Below: The analogue simulator consisted of a crude cockpit mock-up used for initial support at the Flight Research Station. Provided by North American Aviation, it was an improvement on the simulator at its Inglewood facility when the computers and the cockpit were placed in the same room. This was renamed the Air Vehicle Flight Simulation Facility and was located in Building 4800, later repurposed as the office for the centre director. *NASA*

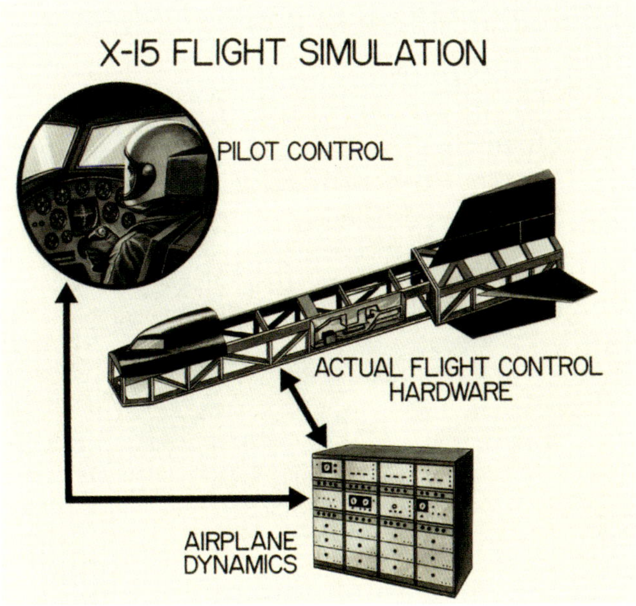

Left: The 'Iron-Bird' hydraulic rig transferred from North American to Edwards. Electronics Associates Inc, produced the PACE 231R computers, three of which were used to control the simulator set up at Edwards to familiarise pilots with the X-15 control functions. Each had 380 amplifiers, 101 function generators, 32 servo amplifiers and five electronic multipliers. *NASA*

the only other facility engaged with the X-15 project for this type of work was the centrifuge at the Naval Air Development Center, Johnsville, Pennsylvania, where a cockpit mock-up was used for acceleration tests. By now known as the Flight Research Center (FRC), the NASA facilities at Edwards AFB did not get their simulator operational until 3 January 1961, the first 20 X-15 flights relying exclusively on the Inglewood simulator. But this comprised only the cockpit mock-up and limited simulator capability provided by various computers over time, including the Model 31R, the 131R and the 231R. It became known as the Air Vehicle Flight Simulation Facility but was a poor substitute for the Inglewood 'Iron-Bird'.

NAA was contractually obliged to move their fixed base simulator to the FRC but were reluctant to do so until they had fully integrated, and evaluated, the MH-96 adaptive flight control system and this delayed its arrival until April 1961. NAA was installing the MH-96 into the third X-15 (X-15-3) and its qualification for flight required the use of the 'Iron-Bird'. Various upgrades were made to it over time, a malfunction-generator being of particular value for providing pilots with simulated failures. These included malfunctions to major aircraft systems, providing the pilot with a range of options for fail-safe recovery and pre-flight experience with contingency options.

This aspect of the X-15 project was exported to several other NASA programmes along the Edwards flight line, and also to the emerging manned space programme in which short flights with a single astronaut were quickly evolving into complex orbital operations with two men in a single spacecraft. By the time the 'Iron-Bird' was getting into its stride at Edwards, NASA was being tasked with sending three men to the vicinity of the Moon and two down to the surface before the end of the decade. The complexity of such operations and the sophistication of the spacecraft required to achieve these goals was made progressively more efficient, and effective, through the use of simulators built on the experience with the iron-bird and its successors.

Fault detection and failure mitigation became the hallmark of activities with the X-15 simulator, aspects inherited by the NASA people at the Manned Spacecraft Center in Houston and at the Marshall Space Flight Center in Huntsville. The procedures and protocols with the X-15 wrote the book on how those activities would be conducted, right down to the flight planning directorates and the contingency and emergency procedures routines written up for every manned space flight. Aspects of these are all too frequently overlooked when heaping praise on the men and women who put astronauts on the Moon, many of whom worked on the X-15.

An intriguing aspect of the flight simulation capability enabled engineers to remove and test items of equipment which proved troublesome in checkout on the ground or in flight. Several components from the X-15 were evaluated, and either replaced or upgraded, as a result. The addition of readout displays in the form of strip-charts or plot-boards pointed the way toward full calibration of output and data. The full-scale plotter was duplicated in the flight control room and at the various ranges where the flight was being tracked and monitored. The addition of a digital computer, the recently devel-

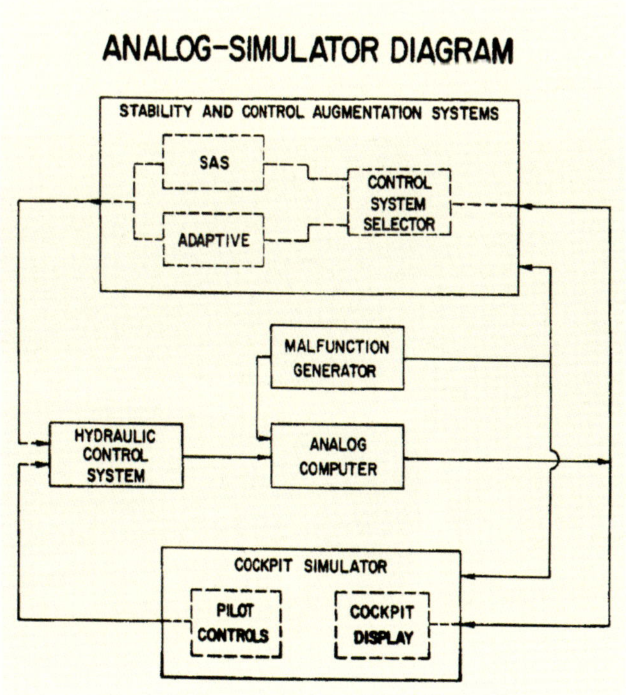

Right: The NAA Inglewood facility had fixed-base simulators which consisted of four major elements at the heart of which was the analogue computer and a malfunction generator providing sequencing and control of other related systems. The hydraulic simulator ('Iron-Bird') had the more complex suite including a complete Stability Augmentation System. *NAA*

oped SDS 930 in 1964, allowed real-time operation with non-linear coefficients generated for the X-15A-2.

But there were early issues with the SDS 930 and for a while the hybrid computer at the Air Force Flight Test Center was used instead for initial flights with this rebuilt aircraft. During 1965 and 1966 these limitations affected not only preparation of the X-15A-2 flights but also the installation of the MH-96 on the X-15-3. That forced modification to the SD 930 where it was given two magnetic tape units with a line printer assisting with energy-management simulations. And all the while, successive modifications and upgrades to the 'Iron-Bird' simulator continued.

The simulator at the Flight Test Center had been developed to examine the handling characteristics of the proposed Dyna-Soar boost-glide system, re-designated X-20 when the operational development of the type was cancelled at the end of 1963. It was six months later that the digital computer arrived for that simulator and it was eventually adapted for work on the X-15 flight expansion programme seeking to explore the flight envelope out to Mach 8. But it was never used for pilot training as its primary purpose, although some pilots did receive familiarisation on it. Instead, with the demise of the X-20 programme, it was adapted for a wide range of Air Force aircraft and was used for predicting heating conditions on re-entry profiles for the NASA Shuttle Orbiter.

A limitation with both analogue and digital simulators was that, being fixed base, they could not be used for landing training, lacking the visual cues essential for out-the-window approach, flare and touchdown dynamics. But modifications to a four-degree-of-freedom simulation did allow some landing loads to be calculated and this made a contribution to improving the design of the landing gear during the early design phase of the X-15. Some simulations were conducted on the three-axis, motion-base device at the Ames facility but only to evaluate the g-loading on the pilot, used in 1961 by Rushworth, Walker and White.

Above: The CRT display consisted of a videoed paper chart from a horizontal plotter providing a guide of the 'view' out the window, in this case to Joe Walker on 10 July 1963. Primitive by the standards of just a few years later, the efforts to produce these aids had been driven by Felt, Storms and Williams. They provided the base from which future simulators would evolve with increasing rapidity, providing an enabling aid for the advanced space missions of the later 1960s. *NASA*

In several ways a silent partner in the X-15 project, the US Navy made a major contribution through its Aviation Medical Acceleration Laboratory (AMAL), which had been established at Johnsville on 24 May 1949. The Navy was an early convert to the need for a physiological research facility, arguably perhaps because it was already heavily involved in evaluating the consequences of extreme environments due to its submarine programme. And this, a lot earlier than the Air Force. The AMAL was geared for a major contribution through research conducted with its large centrifuge. Its sheer complexity delayed its first use until 2 November 1951, test-

Below: Dubbed the 'Iron Cross', the fixed-base simulator was provided at NAA and Edwards AFB with a layout approximating that of the X-15 with stabilising arms to prevent it from tipping over. *NASA*

Above: The 'Iron-Bird' simulator attached to a mock-up of the forward section of the fuselage and pictured (right) with canopy. Located at the Flight Research Center, it duplicated a similar one at North American with analogue computers, mechanical linkages, bell cranks, cable push rods and hydraulics. It had a complete Stability Augmentation System and would eventually host the MH-96 Adaptive Flight Control System. *NASA*

ed on that date for the first time by Capt. J. R. Poppin, the director of the AMAL.

The facility did not open officially before 17 June 1952 but it was already a world-class facility without parallel, capable of replicating accelerations of up to 40-g. Suspended on a double-arm gimbal system, a gondola could be configured for a variety of tests with its angular motions capable of any articulated angle for accelerations in any axis. Several unique tests were undertaken on this device, including a shared programme with the Air Force in 1956 which demonstrated that chimpanzees could withstand an acceleration of up to 40-g for one minute. A test two years later demonstrated that a human occupant could withstand 37.5-g for five seconds. This human centrifuge facility was integrated with Langley's computer simulator, integrating a mock-up of the X-15 cockpit with the Naval Air Development Center's Typhoon digital-analogue computer.

Dynamic testing of this type was crucial to the design of controls in the X-15 cockpit and in addition it allowed pilots to simulate the accelerations likely to be encountered under various unplanned attitude excursions during re-entry. Tests

Above: The US Navy Aviation Medical Laboratory at Johnsville, Philadelphia, housed the world's largest centrifuge, imposing accelerations of up to 40-g on equipment under test. The gondola was carried on a dual-gimbal fixture allowing rotation up to right angles from the direction of rotation. Here, NASA astronaut Walter M. Schirra prepares for a ride. *USN*
Below: The Johnsville centrifuge was equipped with a cockpit and controls to give X-15 pilots experience at simulated g-loadings, using an oscilloscope and a central control column, upgraded later with side-stick controllers. *USN*

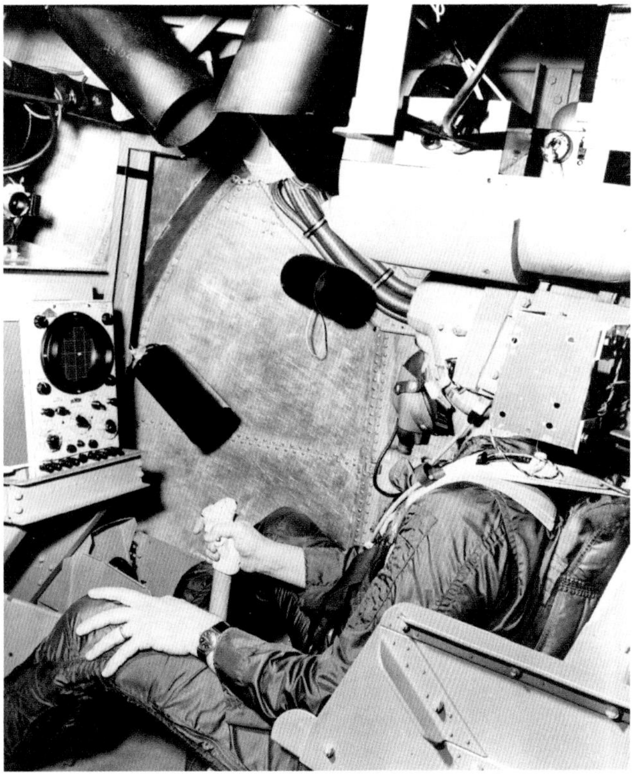

like these showed the accelerated forces likely to be encountered with respect to the pilot's ability to operate the stick controllers under adverse conditions. Test subjects wore anti-g suits to provide a more realistic simulation but on one of these Crossfield blacked out when his suit partially failed. Nevertheless, it allowed pilots to anticipate unexpected difficulties in flight with a motion-based simulation which they had already experienced.

When linked to the Typhoon computer, the centrifuge became a real-time motion simulator, as the mocked-up cockpit could be used by the pilot to 'fly' the replicated mission and receive the same angular accelerations as directed by the duplicated controls. Because these motions were limited to pitch, roll and yaw, some operators criticised the system as being unrepresentative of the dynamic motions in flight. The pilots disagreed and found value in those rides. A compromise was found whereby the teaming with Langley allowed NASA engineers at the Virginia facility to control the motion of the centrifuge while the computer presented the appropriate displays in the 'cockpit'. Further to this, X-15 pilots Armstrong, Crossfield, Kincheloe, McKay, Walker, Al White and Bob White logged collectively 755 simulations in which the centrifuge was static, and the gondola used for simulations, and 287 dynamic tests with an active centrifuge. These were designed to proof the pilot in responding to an abnormal re-entry with failed dampers.

In-flight simulation

The teaming across facilities and different government agencies involved in fixed-base and motion-based simulation produced vital development work on the layout of the cockpit and the flight controls under high accelerations. It disproved the

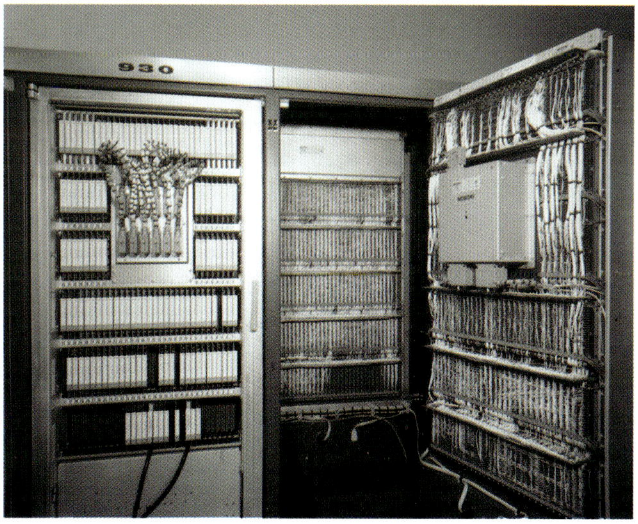

Right: Of great assistance with establishing real-time simulation, the large SDS-930 digital computer proved troublesome at first but redeemed itself when it facilitated nonlinear coefficients produced for the X-15A-2. *Scientific Data Systems*

naysayers who believed that pilots would never be able to control a fast-moving vehicle in air and through space. The further applications of these tests and simulated flight conditions is defined in earlier sections describing flight control systems and cockpit layout. But the work on the Johnsville centrifuge provided simulation experience for the seven Mercury astronauts selected in April 1959. The results also fed directly in to the cabin layout and conformal couch concept for that spacecraft and, later, for the two-man Gemini capsule.

But the ground-based simulators and centrifuge runs were incapable of providing in-flight experience for practising, and evaluating, landing procedures, for which an F-104 was able to provide. In an appropriate configuration to simulate the descent rate by idling the engine, extending the landing gear, deploying the speed brakes and using a drag-chute deployed in flight, the similarity in wing loading between the two enabled pilots to get some idea of the X-15's landing characteristics.

To get some feel for the stability and control characteristics of the X-15 during re-entry, Cornell Aeronautical Laboratory applied its modified, two-seat NT-33A with an F-94 bloated nose section. Cornell engineer Jack Beilman installed a programmable, non-linear function generator to change the gains of 32 sensed aerodynamic and rigid-body feedback variables. The front cockpit was modified to duplicate the X-15's ballistic controls and, with the flight control sensitivity continuously changing, a simulated re-entry could be made. The aircraft would enter a dive at 5,182m (17,000ft) and pull up for a zero-g trajectory for one minute duration, at which point the flight control sensitivity would change so as to simulate the shift from flight outside the atmosphere to the rapidly changing dynamic of atmospheric flight.

To reproduce the effect called for a carefully orchestrated deception in which the pilot, his face covered by a hood preventing him seeing anything other than the displays, would operate the ballistic side controller as though he were changing

Below: Cornell Aeronautical Laboratory's Flight Research Department provided the X-15 programme with a variable stability trainer, the NT-33A, a modified Air Force T-33A-1-LO training aircraft (51-4120). Originally used by Lockheed, the Allison Division of General Motors and the WADC, it had the larger-volume nose of an F-94A for test equipment and tip tanks with electro-hydraulically actuated drag petals. *USAF*

Right: Another trainer used by the X-15 programme was a converted F-100C-1-NA (53-1709), the first tri-axis variable stability aircraft, at Ames from 4 September 1956 and assigned to Langley on 2 November 1960 as NASA 25. *NASA*

the attitude orientation of the aircraft. In fact, that motion only changed the displays in his cockpit and not the orientation or flight path of the NT-33A. Only the rear-seated 'instructor' would know the actual attitude and orientation of the aircraft. To the pilot, he was flying a steep decelerating descent but in reality he was not. The simulator biased the attitude indicator to a bank angle of 75deg and a deceleration of 5-g as the front-seat pilot used his BCS controller to achieve what he believed was a wings-level flight path. This sophisticated simulation was used from May 1960 by Armstrong, McKay, Petersen, Rushworth, Walker and White.

One other adapted aircraft played a part in flight simulation, a modified JF-100C (53-1709) on strength at Ames from 4 September 1956, assigned to NASA-Langley on 2 November 1960 and to the FRC in 1962. It was employed for variable-stability training to simulate a different aspect of the flight profile to that which had been provided by the NT-33A from Cornell. The primary difference was that the JF-100C was a single-seat aircraft and the pilot was on his own. By adding two analogue computers, the aircraft was able to provide technicians with the ability to change the variable-stability gains and provide motion traces similar to those from the ground-based X-15 simulator. By 1962 it had been retrofitted with the vertical stabiliser of the F-100D. Tested out and calibrated by Walker and White, the first flight was conducted on 24 March 1961 and the last of 104 flights took place on 11 March 1964.

Another, more abstract form of simulation was the use of Lockheed's IBM 7094, at the time an impressively powerful tool found increasingly throughout the emerging aerospace industry, to predict heating equations. To these were added two programmes developed by NAA for simulating structural heating values across the airframe under designated flight profiles. As flights progressed, the data obtained from actual flights was compared with the predicted values and checked out on the fixed base simulator to obtain accurate values. The results were digitised and used extensively for the X-15 and other programmes. The positive feedback loop allowed predictions and actual flight results to flow back into the fixed base simulator, which was progressively tweaked to improve its predictability and accuracy.

Left: Introduced in 1954, at the core of planning and flight profile preparation was the increasing use of digital computers, such as the IBM 704 electronic data processing units. It consisted of several elements integrated into a single operating unit using fixed or floating point arithmetic and operated on the binary number system, each register having a capacity of 36 bits and sign. *IBM*

Keeping track

The preparation of pilots for assignment to the X-15 was an essential aspect of the flight research programme and there were unique challenges with that. Equally challenging was the requirement placed upon ground facilities and infrastructure to support each flight and to track the aircraft and acquire the data generated. It called for unprecedented preparation and planning, with new equipment grafted on to an existing test range ideally suited to the expanding requirements of the X-15. Frequently ignored, the improvements and changes made necessary were expansive and costly but without them the programme would not have delivered the results it sought.

Under the new naming protocols when the NACA became NASA, on 27 September 1959 the High Speed Flight Station became the Flight Research Center (FRC), a name which it would retain until 1976 when it became the Hugh L. Dryden Flight Research Center (DFRC). Co-existing with an ever-expanding facility operated by the US Air Force as Edwards Air Force Base, NASA expanded its presence there as the focus for flight test operations with the X-15. Before the renaming ceremony in 1959, Walt Williams had gone to the Mercury programme and would set up manned space flight operations at Cape Canaveral, his replacement being Paul F. Bickle from 15 September 1959. For a more complete history of the facility, see Appendix 2.

Range support for the X-15 programme was planned from the beginning, the agreement for the NACA and the Air Force to work together noted in a letter between the two bodies dated 7 April 1955. The Air Force Flight Test Center under Brig.

Gen. Benjamin S. Kelsey wanted a major role in X-15 operations and the following month it was proposed that the Air Force would set up the required installations and prepare the site for the NACA to operate it as an integrated flight research station. For some the argument as to which body should have overall control of operations mouldered along, while the NACA put together a plan to build upon the initial efforts for providing telemetry applied in the X-1 series.

It was agreed that the Air Force Model II radar already operating across the Atlantic Missile Range would be set up at Edwards and that telemetry should include flight parameters and research data in addition to the engineering data which had been obtained with the earlier programmes. It was debate over the type of, and specification for, the new range radar and telemetry acquisition sites that resurrected discussion as to which organisation should have control over operations. This was the topic of a meeting on 16 November 1955 during which the Air Force pitched for full control of the expanded range conceding that it could be used by the NACA. The latter pointed out that the return of data was not only desirable for the joint programme but that the safety of the X-15 and its pilot would depend upon clear and distinct lines of command and control over flight operations. In the end it was a hybrid decision, with the Air Force in overall charge of the site but the NACA, and later NASA, totally responsible for X-15 flight operations.

The NACA's Gerald Truszynski laid out the broad requirements for these activities and defined the necessary size of the range, saying that it would have to be at least 644km (400mls) long and incorporate three radar sites for obtaining accurate flight data on trajectory and path. This was considerably greater than anything prepared for existing flight programmes and again brought up concerns about sonic booms, from the X-15 and its coterie of chase planes over populated areas. The flight corridor selected would also have to avoid commercial flight paths and training zones for military aircraft. Radar site locations had to be placed carefully so that the line-of-sight to the fast-moving aircraft was unobstructed by the highly undulating, mountainous and desolate terrain, irrespective of flight path.

The zone selected for what would be officially named the High Altitude Continuous Tracking Range (HACTR) – most popularly known as the High Range – would include three States, beginning at Edwards AFB in California, extend across Nevada with radar stations at Ely and Beatty and on to Wendover in Utah. With most flight profiles taking the X-15 over Death Valley, flights would terminate with a landing at Rogers Dry Lake in a swath 80.4km (50mls) wide with tracking clearance to an altitude of 152.3km (94.7mls). Designated by the Air Force as Project 1876, the range would be constructed by the Electronic Engineering Company of Los Angeles. The final understanding held that the Air Force would retain ownership to facilities outside the areas assigned to NASA and that full control and operation of the High Range would reside with NASA until completion of flight activity, or earlier if the 'National Situation so decrees'.

Finding a suitable location for the radar sites brought its own difficulties and frustrations, the Ely site compromised by commercial copper developments, poor angles of sight and lack of roads or accessibility. Finally, a site was found known as Rib Hill, a 9.1km (5.65ml) spur road off Highway 50 being all that was necessary to afford access, being only 16.1km (10mls) southeast of the small town of Ely and its adjacent airport. But there was a compromise when electrical power and the local water supply was not as effective or as efficient as required. But the radar site at Beatty was more readily located, 9.6km (6mls) northwest of Springdale, Nevada, only 4.8km (3mls) west of Highway 95 and at an elevation of 1,493m (4,900ft). For the Edwards site, all that was needed was an extension of the existing facility, an addition to Building 4800.

Rationale for the equipment required at the three tracking sites was transferred from the Atlantic Missile Range and included the SCR 584 radar units with modifications for accuracy in range, azimuth and elevation, in addition to the Model II. The radar units were aligned with a remote optical tracker passing the elevation and azimuth of the target. They incorporated two range settings of 701km (436mls) and 350km (218mls) utilising a 3m (10ft) diameter dish transmitting on a beam 2.5deg wide and operating on a pulse-repetition frequency of 205-1,707pps. The dishes could slew at 5deg/sec in azimuth and 2.5deg/sec in elevation. The physical operating parameters were factored in to the selection of locations where the X-15 would be released for flight and the location of contingency landing sites.

Data from the three sites would be recorded on magnetic tape using equipment compatible with the IBM-704 (first introduced in 1954) which produced geometric altitude, plan position, trajectory position and the velocity. A second IBM-704 located at the Flight Research Center would process data from the X-15 oscillograph and photo-recorders on to IBM punch cards via manually operated film recorders. The cards would generate the tapes. The automatic processing of data in this way was known as Project Datum and run by the Air Force Flight Test Center at Edwards.

While each of the two remote tracking stations had a plotting board showing the flight path, Edwards had the results from all three stations and was able to plot the flight path along its full trajectory but the way data was moved from one site to another, and the amount of data which could be transferred, was limited by the technology of the time. As the flight programme progressed, however, innovative processes were able to bypass these limitations and provide adequate tracking capability. Real-time data readouts were available for telemetry coming in to all three sites and this allowed some support to the pilot, information on the monitoring consoles being available as bar graphs or on oscilloscopes which permitted an assessment of whether the observed parameters were within pre-planned expectations.

Voice communications with the X-15 were conducted through the AN/CRC-27 UHF set, although at first an interim Collins set was found to operate effectively with the AN/ARC-34 transceiver installed in the X-15. Communications between the three sites was ensured by two UHF transmitters and receivers, one operating as a back-up. The three sites were interconnected so that an operator keying a transmitter

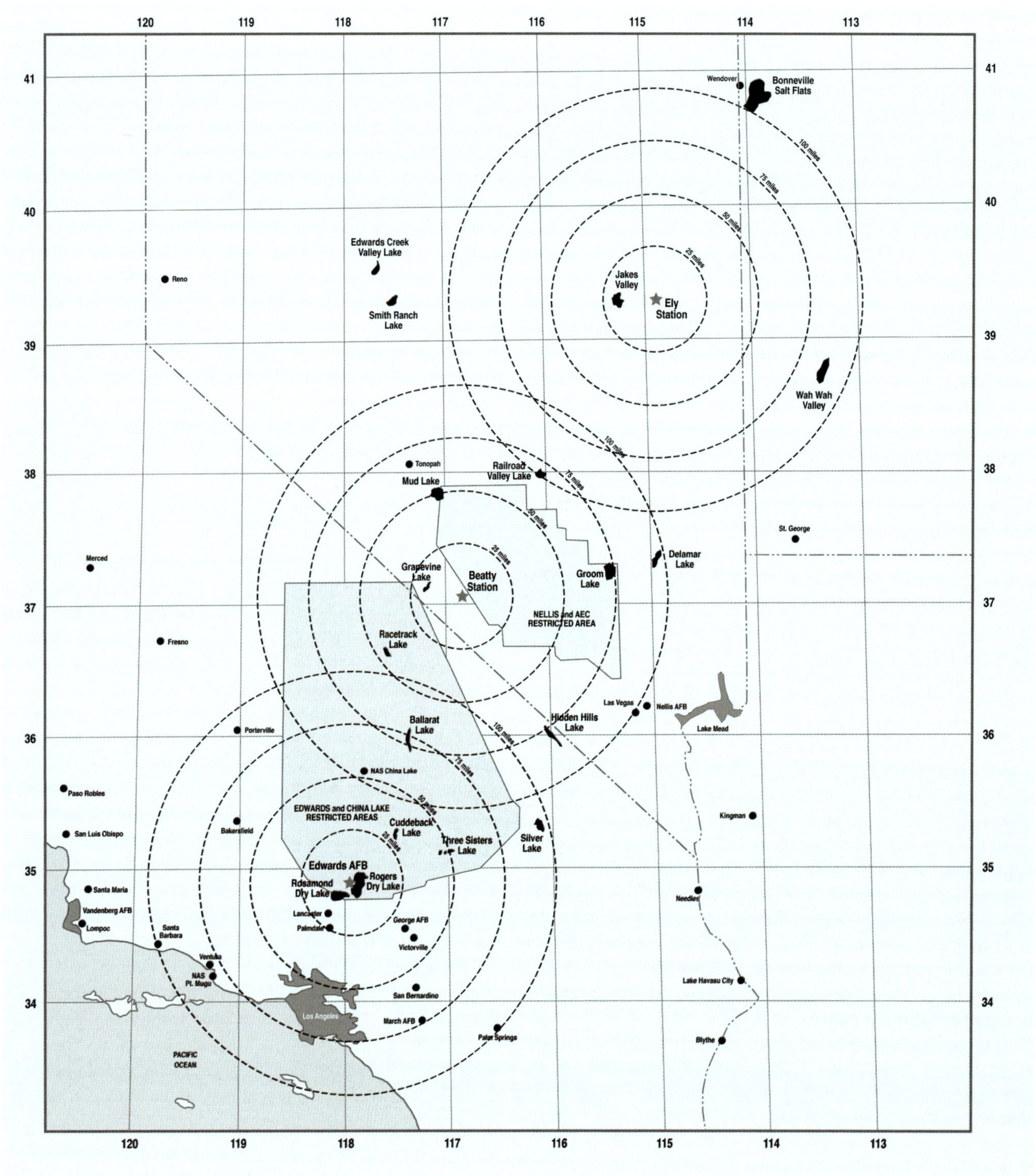

Above: The area across which X-15 flights would take place encompassed three states and a lot of rugged terrain, with tracking stations at three High Range locations. Areas restricted to commercial and general aviation are shaded but on days when flights would take place the entire area was a prohibited zone. *NASA*

from a single location would have that automatically appearing at the other sites simultaneously. These were backed up by station-to-station links for communications between any two sites. This did have some problems due to the simultaneous keying of the audio tone at all locations, averted by slightly offsetting the transmitted frequency while remaining within the bandwidth of the receiver.

To evaluate the effectiveness of the VHF communication system, the NACA had a B-47 fly from Los Angeles to San Francisco at a height of 4,572m (15,000ft), making the return flight at a height of 12,192m (40,000ft) while technicians monitored the system via six ground stations. The effectiveness of the High Range network at high altitude was a major concern in that the additional intermediate ground stations, added in to the test compared with the three across the High Range, were suspected of potentially incurring interference.

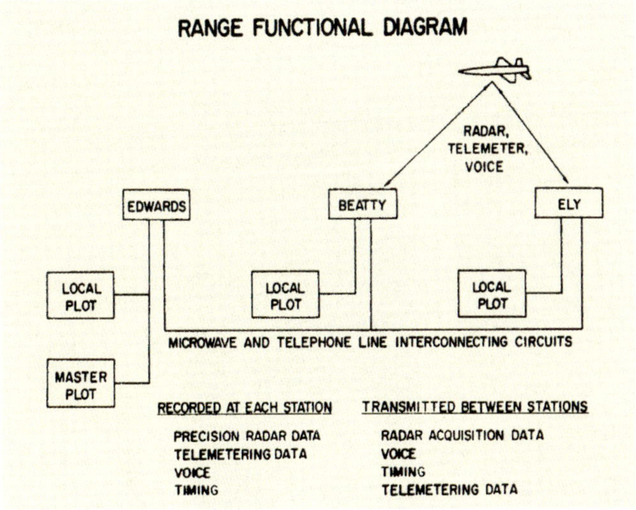

Left: In addition to that at Edwards AFB, California, High Range tracking stations were situated at Beatty and Ely, Nevada. Set up in 1955, each had a unique plot allowing it to track the X-15. Built by Gerald Truszynski, the entire system was applied in greatly expanded form to the Minitrack stations for America's first satellites and to the network used for manned Mercury flights. *NASA*

However, they proved not to be disruptive and monitors were happy with the result, which included pre-recorded tapes played from the aircraft to simulate a busier communication path than would be realised on X-15 flights.

Home on the range

Over the first several years of X-15 flight operations the High Range received improvements and some modifications, the Model II at Ely being replaced with the MPS-19C unit from March 1967 and the Flight Research Center got one too. Manufactured by Reeves, it operated on a frequency of 2,700-2,900MHz with a power output of 500Kw. It was mounted some distance away from the location of the original Mode II, which had been on the top of Building 4800 where it was subject to some vibration that the MPS-19C could not tolerate. Also in March 1967, the microwave communication system between Ely and Edwards was upgraded to receive higher Pulse-Code Modulation (PCM) data at 144Kbps from the X-15-3.

Any further considerations regarding the operational flexibility of the High Range was increasingly compromised by the use of the various dry lakes for launch and landing.

Selection of places over which to drop the X-15 would always have to take account of the possibility that any one of those could be required to support an unpowered glide to the ground and that contingency landing strips would have to be available for both unpowered and powered flights.

Operations were going to be very different to those conducted by all previous X-craft, be they aiming for high-speed, high-altitude or some other research profile. Across the High Range were a variety of possible contingency sites, suitability depending on their location and visibility to tracking sites, availability down to private owners and other government agencies unwilling to relinquish use, even for only emergencies.

Three phases of the X-15 programme would define the effort and energy in selecting launch and landing sites: the initial test phase; the high-speed profiles; the high-altitude profiles; and the advanced higher-Mach flight goals of the X-15A-2 programme with external tanks. Each would require a suitable landing site 30.5km (19mls) from the drop point, which would be on a flight path 22.5km (14mls) abeam of a downwind landing pattern where a glide to touchdown would require a 180deg turn. At the beginning of 1957, NAA, the Air Force and the NACA conducted a survey of potential locations for five contingency and five emergency landing sites, each 48-80km (30-50mls) apart. It took several years to gain permissions, complete purchase or get legal approval for use-rights on those 10 sites.

Various locations were requested but refused for a variety of incontestable reasons. The Air Force had asked for Jakes Lake and Mud Lake at the same time. Both sites were in Nevada and they had wanted Groom Lake as the launch site rather than Mud Lake. But the level of security required to access the Groom Lake site – 'The Ranch' as it was known in service-parlance – prevented that. The location for CIA programmes with the highest classification, 'Area 51' as it became known, was unable to play host to the X-15 and its associated personnel. Different obstructions also prevented the use of the candidate Jakes Lake site, a sprawling area of 1,011ha (2,500acres) and home to several ranchers whose cattle grazed the area assigned as public domain – a very 20th century equivalent of open-range versus fenced-in homesteaders!

The alternative option, Mud Lake's 3,748ha (9,262acres) was already in use as the Las Vegas Bombing and Gunnery Range. Requisitions of this site required approval from the House Armed Services Committee and that took time while a repurposed effort claimed use on Cuddeback, Jakes and Mud due to a slight reduction in area claimed, thus removing it from the House legislature! But this ran into further problems. Mud happened to lie in the northwest corner of a restricted area used by the Sandia Corporation for work it had under contract with the Atomic Energy Commission. Approval was granted on a non-interference basis for activities under way there in return for Sandia not planning its own operations at that location when alerted to an X-15 flight.

Preparation for landings at the various sites bordered on the bizarre – and sometimes the macabre. Due to its use for bombing practice, various dummy 'targets' littered the area at Mud Lake with debris, rocks, bomb cases, posts, fencing and shattered remains of exploded munitions and gunnery rounds. But clearing the area for its use as a potential landing site was not enough. The hardness of the lakebed was important for proofing the bearing strength of the surface material, and a process which became standard practice was to take a steel ball weighing 8.16kg (18lb) and drop it from a height of 1.8m (6ft) and on finding a penetration 'crater' of no more than 7.6cm (3in) in diameter, it was deemed satisfactory.

Other sites brought problems of a different kind. For launches over Silver Lake the flight path would be inside the

Above: Mod II oscilloscopes presented tracking data to operators with information processed on large paper charts tracing flight paths on pre-printed maps. NASA

scope of the Federal Aviation Authority (FAA) in its management of airspace. The X-15 would only use this location when equipped with the XLR-11 rocket motors and as part of a 161km (100ml) sector which ran from this place back to Edwards. Part of that would marginally encroach on public airspace open to use by private pilots logging a suitable flight plan but without the requirement to consult for partial or temporary closures. The prospect of a Piper Cub running headlong into an X-15 performing a 180deg turn prior to landing was unacceptable. The FAA issued a waiver so that, upon notification, that small region of airspace would be closed to commercial and general aviation and promptly reopened at the end of the flight.

Left: The presentation of information through the Mod II system used separate colours for the ground trace of the aircraft and for its altitude plotted on the paper charts. NASA

Waivers too were required to get the various sites allocated within contingency or emergency categories and Cuddeback Lake was one of those, borderline for use in emergencies due to its high penetration when subject to the gravity-ball test. In this case, it produced an 11.4cm (4.5in) depression at one end of the candidate runway and an acceptable 7.6cm (3in) penetration at the other. In other locations, unmapped sinkholes were discovered, an abandoned railhead, evidence of mining and activity from the 19th century which left deep ruts and rusted iron bars and uncharted, rutted wagon tracks from some long abandoned project.

The magnitude of this activity grew in size and scope with personnel from NAA and the Air Force conducting surveys at more than 50 potential sites in lakebeds across the three States. Candidate locations were also surveyed regarding the changing nature of the surface from season to season, chart-

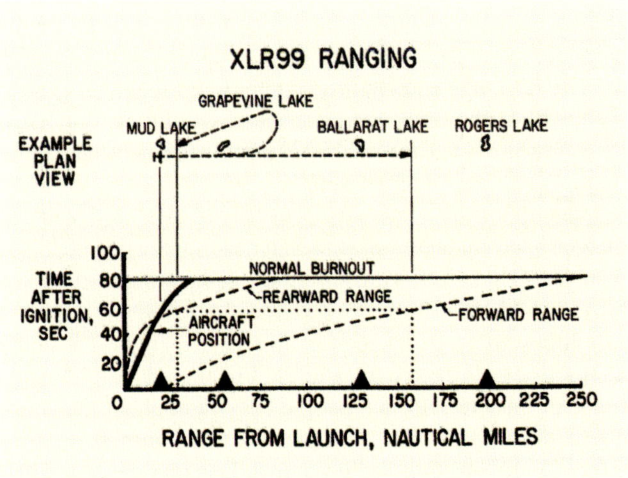

Right: Designated landing sites according to the burnout time of the XLR-99, showing the range from the launch point and the time after ignition. *NAA*

ing the effects of rain and generally inclement weather which, even for the limited flight distances of the X-1, Skyrocket and X-2 series had proven an obstacle to year-round flying. Several sites were added when the more powerful XLR-99 was installed and full-performance flights began carrying the X-15 further away from Edwards. Initially, flights would use Silver, Hidden Hills (California), Mud (Nevada) and Wah Wah (Utah) and a range of intermediate lakes were selected, each providing crash vehicles, recovery trucks, medical vehicles and all their support personnel. But there were problems with obtaining legal permissions for many and only a few were earmarked for use in extreme emergency, Wah Wah being one of those temporarily deleted from that list.

Of the 10 launch locations selected, Delamar supported 62 flights, followed by Hidden Hills supporting 50 drops, Mud with 34, Rosamond with 17, Silver for 14, Smith Ranch for 10, Palmdale eight, Railroad for two and Cuddeback and Lancaster one each. During the total flight programme, Rogers Dry Lake would host 188 landings, with four at Mud, two at Cuddeback and one each at Delamar, Rosamond, Silver and Smith. One flight failed to land when X-15-3 broke up in flight on 15 November 1967. As the programme geared up through the XLR-11 flights and then with the XLR-99, and as the rebuild of the X-15-2 into the X-15A-2 expanded requirements, the fluid nature of the site selections evolved and matured. Initially, the NACA had wanted unacceptably abundant resources from the Air Force, equipment and personnel which were simply unavailable, and as the flights got higher and faster, moving operations further up the High Range, the demands increased.

All flight operations involving military aircraft require considerable planning and a great deal of paperwork. More so for test flights and some readers will be familiar with the tedium of those procedures. But experimental aircraft require a lot more and involve considerable resources and a broad range of assets to make them possible. Not only for planned operations but for optional alternative flight operations, for contingencies and for emergencies. For the X-15 operating across the High Range, these were considerable, as defined through one request from the NACA to the Air Force in October 1960 for resources on the ground and in the air to support a single flight.

Beatty and Ely ground stations required eight people at each location with transport arranged to get them out and back to cover the drop. Only the high-speed runs used Wah Wah Lake as the drop site and the request was an example of the optimum requirement, all the more pressing as high-speed flights were planned at approximately weekly intervals. The X-15 would be released 32km (20mls) north of Wah Wah supported by two chase aircraft. On the ground there, a team of two Air Force fire trucks, an H-21 helicopter, eight firemen, an Air Force pilot as controller, an Air Force crew chief, doctor, pressure-suit technician and an X-15 technical specialist in case of an immediate landing. Between Wah Wah and Delamar would be a NASA Jeep and three X-15 specialists in case it had to set down at an intermediate location.

At Delamar, Nevada, the next contingency landing site about 193km (120mls) away, would be one Air Force fire truck, four firemen, four Air Force flight crew, two paramedics and a NASA X-15 specialist with a Jeep carrying nitrogen purge equipment. Between there and the next landing site, an Air Force F-104 would be circling to provide chase support should the X-15 have to slow down unexpectedly. Next on was Hidden Hills, 185km (115mls) further back towards Edwards, where the primary emergency landing site was supported by two F-104s ready to act as chase aircraft on the X-15 and a C-130 standing by to evacuate the pilot, an Air Force fire truck, four firemen, two pilots, four Air Force flight crew, two paramedics and a NASA X-15 specialist.

At Edwards where the flight was planned to end, a NASA radio van, a single H-21 helicopter, the NASA lake controller, two fire trucks, eight firemen, a flight surgeon, pressure suit technician and a NASA X-15 specialist would be waiting. In addition, post-flight aircraft recovery crews and their equipment, including vehicles, added to the general resource inventory. Of course, this optimised wish-list was never accommodated in full but it is representative of the requirements set down for a typical flight, one of 199 between 1959 and 1968,

Right: Introduced in 1962, the IBM 7094 was an advanced, solid-state computer with twice the processing speed of its predecessors, double-precision floating point operations and seven index registers. *Arnold Reinhold*

an average of one flight every 16 days; fewer days if all the planned but aborted launches are considered (see Appendix 4). The Air Force had too few resources to fill all the requirements all of the time, but the general requirement as listed here was provided for in the majority of these flights. But there was a time factor as well.

The allocation of personnel to on-site availability meant that they stayed overnight at local hotels, supporting the flight from early the following morning anticipating a 09:00hrs NB-52/X-15 take-off from Edwards. Moreover, site selection was followed up by lakebed familiarisation flights for pilots of H-21 or C-130 recovery aircraft. Fluctuating requirements too kept the site selection people busy throughout the entire operational phase. For a while, attention turned back to Groom Lake as a preferable site over Delamar and some discussions were held about that. But the seamless transition in testing of the U-2 and the SR-71, and the addition of other highly classified projects, ensured that this would never happen, despite best efforts of NASA and the Air Force.

When flight profiles for the advanced performance capabilities of the X-15A-2 were plotted it became desirable to expand the list of available contingency and emergency landing sites. With the planned release of the drop tanks at an altitude of 19,812m (65,000ft) and a speed of Mach 2.2, the dispersion ellipse was wide. Considering the absence of precise detail over aircraft attitude, separation angle, deflection due to wind effects and potential inconsistencies with the parachute deployment at 4,572m (15,000ft), they would fall at different rates and to different locations. The heavier tank would descend at 27kph (17mph), the lighter tank at 22.5kph (14mph). The plan was to recover the spent tanks by helicopter and lift them to a flatbed truck for return to Edwards.

Above: Mountain tops were favoured locations for optimum look-angles for radar and telemetry receivers. Beatty (above) was closed when the X-15 programme ended. There is nothing there now except for concrete slabs to mark the place where so much data was received. *NASA*

Below: The Air Force station at Ely was returned to its original owners after X-15 flights ceased and was eventually closed in 1992. *NASA*

The significant reduction in acceleration levels due to the heavier tanks redefined the optimum location of contingency and emergency recovery sites. The fixed base simulator was used to study flight profiles and trajectories involving full and premature engine shut-downs, including and excluding the tanks. Optimised for high-speed runs, the planned flight trajectories were simulated to an altitude of 30,480m (100,000ft), the maximum anticipated for these flight paths. Only 346km (215mls) from Edwards, Mud was eliminated as being too close while Smith was too far for the glide profile. A survey to find a suitable intermediate location got under way in May 1965 with attention drawn to Edwards Creek Valley Dry Lake which John McKay had discussed as a general possibility for the earlier flights in March 1961.

Located approximately 37km (23mls) from Smith, Creek Valley was not suitable for planned emergency or contingency touchdowns but it would allow for a straight-in approach in the event of an engine shut-down at the least desirable part of the thrust profile and it could be used for an emergency descent if a malfunction occurred at the point of tank jettison. For planned flights to Mach 8, various alternate thrust profiles were tested in the simulator and two possibilities emerged for an emergency, continuing forward or turning back to reverse the descent. Moreover, should a failure occur at the point of tank release, it was found desirable to have the pilot arrive over the contingency site at an altitude of 6,096m (20,000ft).

Carefully overlaying the worst-case probability with the relative location of potential sites, the cusp of the choice between going forward or turning back would be at a thrust duration of 53sec, when the pilot could either go on to Grapevine Lake, arriving there at an altitude of 13,106m (43,000ft) or reverse direction through a 180deg turn and arrive over Mud Lake at a height of 3,353m (11,000ft). There was a dead-man zone at 29-31sec where it would be impossible to reach either location at the required altitude in excess of 6,096m (20,000ft). And there was a further window of 4-7sec duration where it would be impossible to reach either at a height of greater than 1,524m (5,000ft). For these reasons, high-speed runs with the X-15A-2 would begin from either Mud Lake or Creek Valley.

The initial flights would begin over Mud Lake due to the distance between that location and Edwards, with later flights anticipated to launch out of Creek Valley taking advantage of better glide performance than had been expected. That removed most of the gaps revealed in the simulators but the exercise was a valuable lesson in balancing calculations, actual flight performance and trajectory profiles run through the simulator. In reality, there were only four flights with the external tanks attached, all of which originated from Mud. Except for one, a qualification flight with empty tanks out of Cuddeback.

Section 3

Tests and Operational Flight Results

Chapter Seventeen

Powered Trials

In an entirely coincidental event just two weeks and a day after the formation of NASA, on 15 October 1958 the first X-15 (56-6670) was rolled out of the Inglewood assembly facility with much celebration and not a little nod to the encroaching era when humans would regularly, but perhaps not routinely, fly into space. To the aviation and space press eager to witness the event, it epitomised the Space Age, the X-15 looking every bit as it should for the goals it had been designed and built to achieve. It was a singular achievement for North American and for the more than 200 subcontractors, vivid testament to the bold vision barely four years earlier that had made this day possible.

It was a big event for NASA, the Air Force and for North American Aviation, whose president and general manager of the Los Angeles division, Raymond Rice, played host to an impressive list of guests and VIPs. Officials from the ARDC, the FTC and Harrison Storms, the project's chief engineer, accompanied test pilots Neil Armstrong, Scott Crossfield, John McKay, Robert Rushworth, Joseph Walker and Robert White. Speeches were made, senior political leaders including Vice-President Richard M. Nixon made profound statements and displays of space suits and rocket motors attracted attention. It was NASA's first public showcase. America had already launched five probes into space and exactly one week before the X-15 roll-out, NASA had formally started work on Project Mercury to put the first American in orbit.

But the X-15 was here and now, and in its age a portent – that in the near future humans were at long last set to leave the Earth and its fragile atmosphere and place their first toehold on what a future president (John F. Kennedy) would identify as 'this new ocean of space'. As we have alluded to earlier, while developed as a research tool for hypersonic flight, testing the aero-thermal and near-space environment, others saw in the X-15 a philosophical representation of humankind's driving urge to cross known boundaries and assail

Above: Two weeks after NASA officially succeeded the NACA, on 15 October 1958 the first X-15 was rolled out of North American Aviation's Inglewood facility to a fanfare of publicity heralding the new age of hypersonic flight and space exploration. *NAA*

Left: With two XLR-11 engines stacked one above the other, X-15-1 exhibits the wedge-shaped tail surfaces with symmetrical or differentially operated horizontal tail surfaces. *NAA*

new frontiers – of technology and human knowledge.

The roll-out attracted artists, poets and writers to mark the event as a landmark in human achievement. Newspapers lauded the event across the nation, sounding brass for a country finally extricating itself from the doldrums of Soviet 'firsts' in space. There were now more American than Russian satellites in orbit and visible plans for US astronauts soon to follow them. People were already speaking openly about future missions to the Moon, perhaps within the next two decades, while the technical and trade press in the US and across Europe and the UK reported on the latest developments, including the giant Saturn I rocket emerging from the drawing board.

In a pragmatic way, the Air Force (and to some extent, the Navy too) envisaged it as a much-needed research tool for future manned combat aircraft. Others, with a more far-reaching vision, saw the X-15 as an intermediate step between the X-1, Skyrocket and X-2 series and the BoMi and RoBo concepts, even then eagerly anticipated as the roadmap to put the Air Force in space. A more comprehensive discussion of those plans can be found in a later chapter, where legacy concepts such as a delta-wing X-15 variant are also described.

After the brouhaha over its unveiling, the X-15 was moved back inside its assembly facility, only to emerge again on the night of 16 October and, sheeted down with a protective cover, make its way on the back of a flatbed truck to Edwards AFB. There, it was to receive final pieces of test equipment, subject to numerous checks and tests before preparations could begin for the first mated flight. The Air Force anticipated around 300 flights for the three X-15s and while the development and production phase had been designated System 644L, the initial phase of flight operations would proceed under System 605A authority. It was expected that the flight phase would start in July 1959 and last for five years.

Initial operations would be the contractor's responsibility for demonstrating flight capabilities above Mach 2. The pilot for those company trials was Scott Crossfield. The three aircraft were assembled to be identical, the first two being fitted with the XLR-11 rocket motors, the third with the XLR-99. The first two aircraft would be turned over to the Air Force after their contractor tests, with X-15-3 making a couple of flights with the XLR-99 before it too joined the first two. The more powerful XLR-99 would then be retrofitted into the first two airframes and similarly subject to contractor check-out flights.

These plans would change in June 1960 (which see later) when X-15-3 blew its back end off during a static firing at the Edwards test facility, NAA handing the rebuilt aircraft over to the Air Force without ever flying it. But plans for the Air

Below: The roll-out of X-15-1 was attended by Vice President Richard M. Nixon, whose administration under President Eisenhower had received criticism for flagging response to the Soviet challenge in space. Two days later the X-15 was at Edwards Air Force Base. *NAA*

Right: The initial group of X-15 pilots appear in front of the Flight Research Center at Edwards Air Force Base. Left to right: Forrest S Petersen, A. Scott Crossfield, Robert M. White and Joseph M. Walker. *NASA*

Force to take over flight operations was contested, largely on the grounds that its poor performance handling the Bell X-2 envelope-expansion programme left it ill-qualified to participate in the X-15. Before he left to take charge of Mercury flight operations planning, Walt Williams in particular was an outspoken critic of Air Force management. It was a bitter issue for some time until the shared handling was eventually smoothed out.

The Air Force assigned Iven Kincheloe as its first and prime X-15 test pilot, with the Flight Test Center's Richard J. Harer as flight engineer. It did little to help ease the matter when Kincheloe told Walt Williams that he did not want the Air Force involved, believing them to be insufficiently qualified on the type to handle it. Which, to some extent was true, as the NACA had been reluctant to share everything they knew with the Air Force. But all this was long before the rollout and would eventually be remembered only in the reflections of project veterans and disgruntled diehards who would forever regret that it was not a 'wholly-owned' NACA/NASA programme. Kincheloe never got the chance to fly the X-15, being killed in a tragic air accident on 26 July 1958, his place taken by Robert Knight.

Perhaps surprising to all but those on the inner face of the programme, the way in which the initial flights would take place and precisely what they would achieve was open to conjecture and considerable change over time. There was a general air of business-as-usual permeating the programme, personnel routinely meeting technical, planning and managerial challenges in a routine manner. Gone were the days of excitement, absent was the sense of drama and leatherneck-personnel whooping it up at the Pancho Barnes' *Fly-Inn* drinking den as Chuck Yeager had on the night before he exceeded Mach 1. That was more than a decade before. Now, Crossfield had reached Mach 2, the X-2 had already exceeded Mach 3 and there was a sniff of the familiar, turning uncertainty into a new sense of confidence and assuredness.

If only for managerial, operational planning purposes and accounting, the anticipated evolution of capabilities and flight activity was laid out on eight separate phases. The first phase would conduct contractor demonstration flights with the XLR-11 and piloted by Scott Crossfield. The second phase would consist of familiarisation flights with NASA and Air Force pilots evaluating the aircraft with its initial rocket motor. Phase three would proceed along with phase two and provide back-up pilots Petersen, McKay, Rushworth and Armstrong with qualification flights. Phase four would be a series of contractor flights to check out the XLR-99.

Phase five would begin customer flight operations with the XLR-99 and take over operations from North American. Phase six would introduce and check out the MH-96 adaptive flight control system in X-15-3 and explore the design flight envelope with this equipment. Phase seven would explore the full capabilities of the aircraft on high-altitude and high-speed flights, providing research data to fulfil the more ambitious expectations of the programme. Phase eight would employ the aircraft for carrying experiments within the defined corridor of its potential, utilising the X-15 as a carrier for experiments rather than as an experiment in hypersonic flight in its own right.

None of this occurred in the precisely orchestrated sequence laid down and changes were made as operations pro-

Right: Compared with the earlier B-29/B-50 carrier-planes, use of the B-52 improved, but also made more complex, procedures for attaching the X-15 to the pylon shoe on the inner starboard wing. It required the pilot, Crossfield here, to ingress the cockpit ahead of rollout to the runway and to remain in the aircraft until released, usually around 40 minutes after take-off. *NASA*

gressed. Added later, after the landing accident to X-15-2, phase nine would modify the aircraft into the X-15A-2 configuration for flights with drop-tanks and an attempt at Mach 8. In its initial assessment, NASA believed it would take only 17 flights to progress to Mach 6 and a design altitude of 76,200m (250,000ft), several flights being committed to familiarising pilots with the aircraft.

At the time of rollout, the first phase (contractor flights) was divided into four separate segments which would begin on 31 January 1959 with 'Lightweight Captive Flight Evaluation', whereby the mated configuration would be flight tested without propellants and fluids but with all the procedures, including simulated fuel jettisoning, taking place. This would be followed on 9 February with the 'Lightweight Glide Flight Evaluation', verifying launch procedures, release from the carrier-plane and handling characteristics prior to landing. Next would be the 'Heavyweight Captive Flight Evaluation', taking the mated configuration into the air for full evaluation of a fuelled X-15 and full propellant jettison procedures. The final phase would be the 'Powered Flight Evaluation' scheduled for 2 April in which the X-15 would flight-test the XLR-11.

With this schedule intact, X-15-1 checked in at Edwards on 17 October 1958 and was joined by X-15-2 (56-6671) in April 1959. The first aircraft was thoroughly checked out and numerous grounds runs with the APUs, installed at Edwards, were conducted. Far from building a sense of satisfaction, this period extending to several weeks were 'sheer agony' according to Scott Crossfield. Numerous breakdowns occurred, APU bearings over-heated, connectors leaked and turbines seized. It took high management people from NAA and APU manufacturer General Electric to get hold of the problem and sort it all out. A quick engineering fix relocated the mounting points for the APUs onto separate bulkheads, which removed vibrations transmitted between the two and this appeared to solve the problem.

Feeling the air

Anticipating, as any seasoned test pilot might, that the first mated flight would be subject to a blizzard of minor technical issues and problems to delay the day's events, Crossfield was pleasantly surprised to find the first captive flight get off at 10:00hrs on 10 March 1959. It was only three hours later than expected, a mere 39 days later than the scheduled date written five months previously. The mated aircraft achieved a height of 13,716m (45,000ft) and a speed of Mach 0.85. As anticipated, the cockpit pressure bled down as the NB-52 climbed, the suit inflated as required and Crossfield ran through a range of checks and activations, actuating levers and valves to test simulated fluid jettisoning, and lowering the landing gear in a simulated touchdown while still in the mated configuration.

The next flight would test the X-15 in free flight, albeit unpowered, and that attempt occurred on 1 April but a failed radio called an abort. Using the flight profitably, the mated configuration remained airborne to carry out a range of further checks and tests before landing. A second attempt on 10 April was also called off, when another radio failure and problems with the APUs frustrated efforts. Another attempt to get a drop on 21 May was similarly aborted when the SAS failed in the X-15 and one of the APUs overheated. Problems with the APUs continued and throughout this early period became the principle cause of delays and failures to achieve

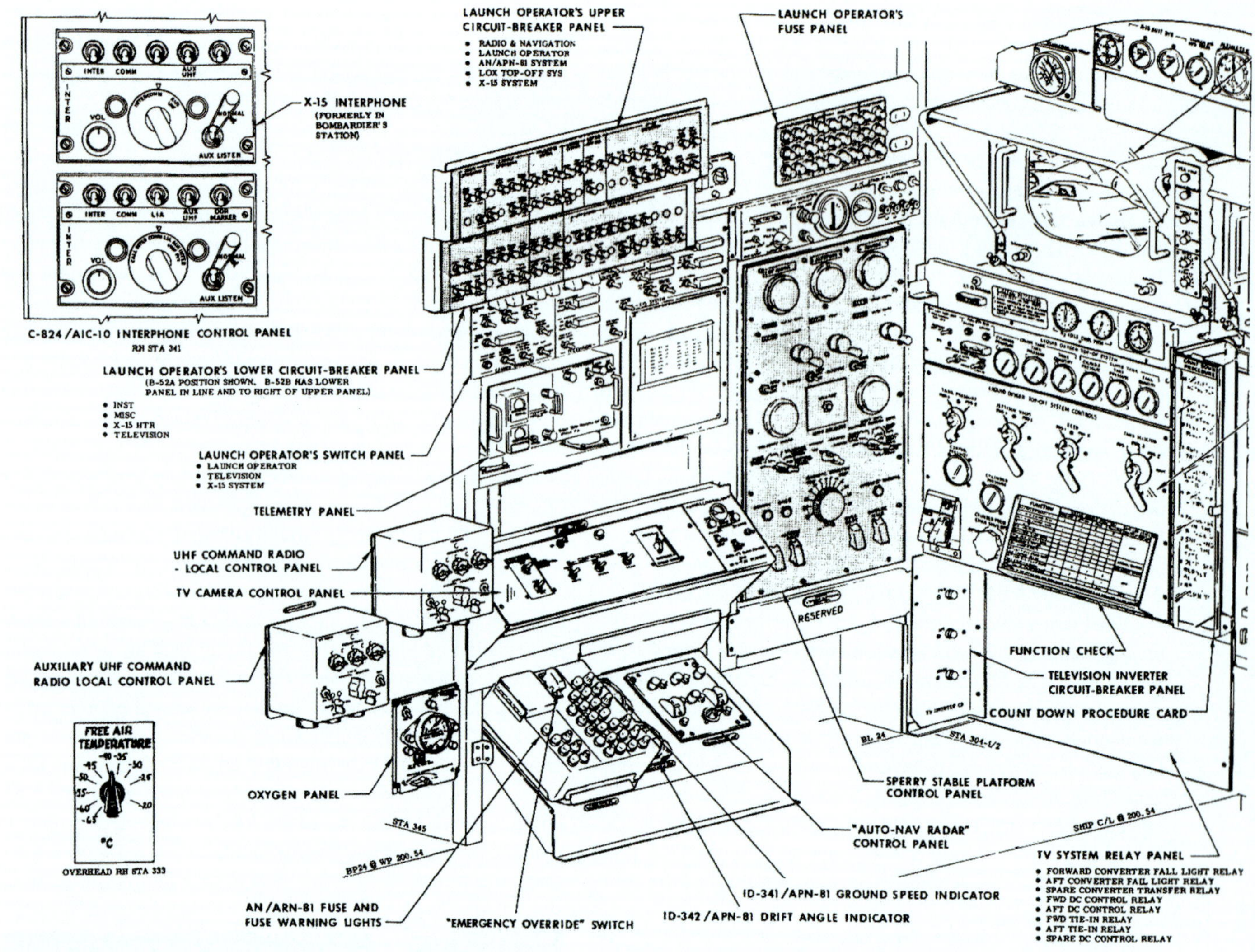

flight results.

The day after the second failure to get an unpowered drop, X-15-2 fired up its XLR-11 on the ground at Edwards, the first time this motor had been tested after installation. Crossfield was in the cockpit for that, as he was for the third attempt at a drop flight with X-15-1 on 5 June. It was called off when Crossfield reported smoke in his cockpit, even before the mated configuration got airborne; a ventilation fan motor had overheated. But the delays and frustrations bought time for technicians to work on solving many minor problems, making some adjustments to internal systems and generally acquiring a steep learning curve regarding the vicissitudes of this machine. To good avail.

The long anticipated drop test took place on 8 June 1959 when Crossfield separated from the NB-52 at an altitude of 11,445m (37,550ft) and a speed of Mach 0.79. It was a close call, the SAS pitch damper failed but Crossfield was not about to get carried back to Edwards a third time. Rolling to the right at 30deg, the X-15 flew away cleanly and stable, Crossfield electing to conduct some unscheduled manoeuvres as he gained confidence in the aircraft's characteristics. As he neared the ground, to his surprise Crossfield encountered severe porpoising, which only got worse as he hunted after each pitch up and down, veering toward a classic case of pilot-induced-oscillation (PIO). Landing safely at 278kph (173mph), X-15-1 came to a halt in 1,189m (3,900ft).

The problem was not one of PIO but of Crossfield's preference to use the side-stick controller rather than the centre stick and that had restricted authority so the solution was to widen that by adding a small orifice to the hydraulic cylinder. Some problems had been encountered which would need attention and what would evolve into an almost continuous attention to technical issues, not uncommon with any aircraft, began to unfold. But the pace began to pick up when X-15-1 was wheeled across to the hangar at Edwards where it would receive propellant connections and associated plumbing and electrical conduits for its XLR-11.

Despite its history and the successful application of this engine to the X-1 and Skyrocket series, the XLR-11 showed a fickle side during preparation for tests preceding the first powered flight attempt. During a purging of hydrogen peroxide lines in the aft bay of X-15-2 following a standard ground

Right: Captive-carry flights preceded glide drops followed by powered runs in a flight test strategy exported to other research programmes and eventually to the Shuttle programme more than a decade later. *NASA*

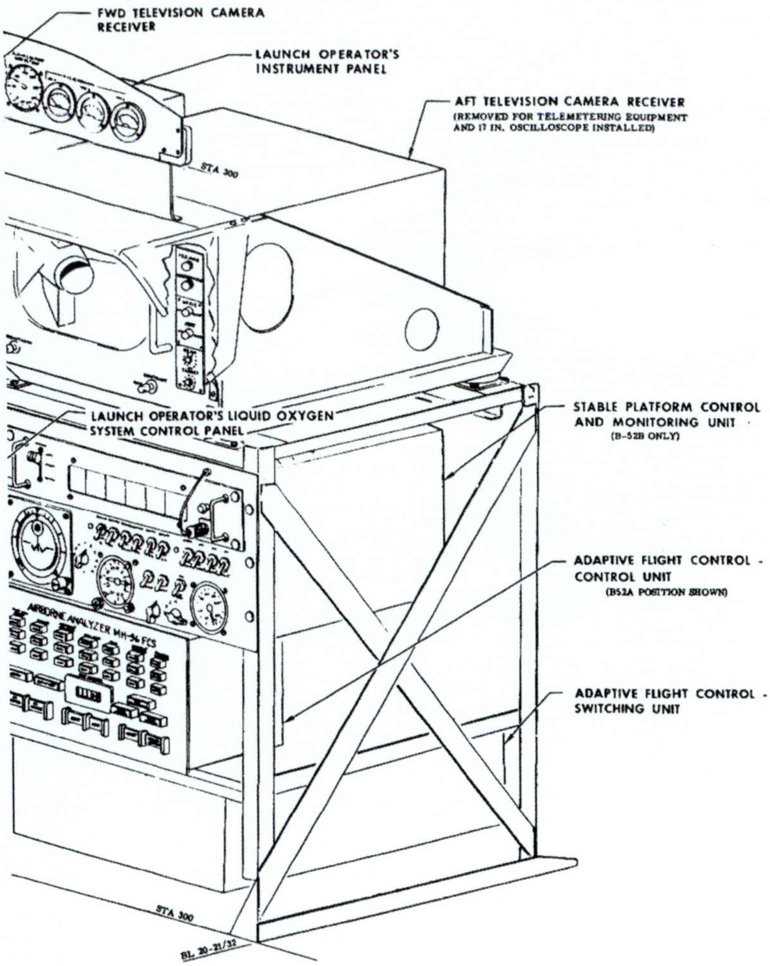

The spacious interior of the B-29/B-50 generation was diminished in the somewhat cramped confines of the B-52, given over as it is to a capacious bomb bay. The launch operator's station was at the right rear seat position, on the same side as the X-15. The exact configuration of the pilot's controls used for launching the X-15 was slightly different but required no re-familiarisation briefings. *Boeing*

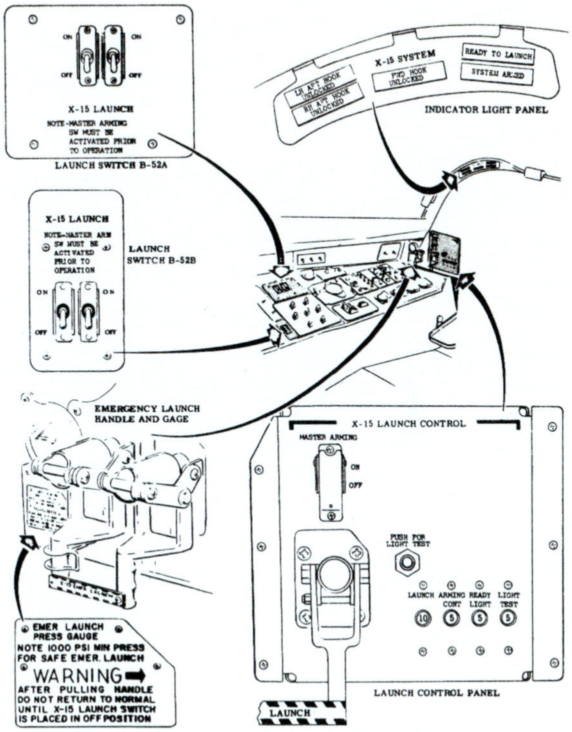

test, a hose contaminated with a very small residue of oil caused an explosion in the engine bay and a fire which was quickly dowsed. There was no serious damage, although it took some time to clean up and restore lines and conduits. But it was a further delay to plans for Crossfield to make the first captive-carry flight with X-15-2. With full propellant tanks, that took place on 24 July 1959, during which top-off tests with the NB-52 were conducted and propellant jettison completed, the actual times being 140sec for the hydrogen peroxide and 110sec for the LOX and ammonia.

Attempts to get the first powered flight with X-15-1 were continuously frustrated by a series of problems, including trouble with the APUs, failed regulators and problems with the hydraulics. This began to cast doubts about the X-15 programme among the press and the politicians, eagerly waiting for an exciting success story to validate confident assertions made at rollout that this was the dawn of new era for American technology. It took some direct pressure applied to North American by the Air Force for the issue to come to a head. It did, however, expose the Air Force once again as pushing hard for success when caution was the only true path to a safe success.

In the end it fell to North American's chairman of the board, James H. 'Dutch' Kindelberger, to argue the case for staying the course of carefully constrained preparation and rigid safety standards, rather than pressing on regardless and losing both aircraft and pilot. But further pressure was not necessary as attention turned to the second X-15 for the first powered flights, while work continued on X-15-1, fitting it out with the XLR-11 and its associated support installations.

On 17 September 1959, Crossfield took X-15-2 to a speed of Mach 2.11 and an altitude of 15,953m (52,341ft) in a powered duration of 3min 44.3sec. It took Crossfield 9min 11sec, after being launched at a height of 11,460m (37,600ft) and a speed of Mach 0.8 (2,241kph/1,393mph), to get back down on the ground. There had been several technical issues but nothing to cause overdue concern, despite a small fire in the rear caused by heat on the fuel pump diffuser case which, after

Above: Almost eight months after rollout, with Scott Crossfield in the cockpit, on 8 June 1959 X-15-1 makes its first drop flight. Caught in the wash of the B-52's wings, the X-15 falls away and rolls to the right then back up to the horizontal shortly before the carrier-plane makes a turn to the right. *NASA*

Left: The event is celebrated by staff at the Flight Research Center. *NASA*

landing, required the aircraft to go back to Inglewood for repairs. Back in the air on 10 October for another powered flight, that attempt was aborted before launch when several propellant and communication troubles arose. Similarly aborted before the drop was another attempt four days later due to a flurry of technical issues.

The second powered flight for X-15-2 was accomplished on 17 October, achieving a speed of Mach 2.15, this time with a burn duration of 4min 14.5sec, but the third flight on 5 November was not so successful. Dropping away at an altitude of 13,411m (44,000ft), Crossfield started procedures to light up the XLR-11s when one chamber in the lower engine blew up, the ensuing flames and visual damage to the rear end of the aircraft spotted by two of the three chase pilots. Electing to set down at Rosamond Lake, Crossfield entered a steep dive which inhibited propellant jettison and, leaving some inside the tanks, increased the weight to 6,866kg (15,138lb). Touching down nose high, the wheel leg bottomed out and the fuselage snapped in two at mid-point, just forward of the LOX tank, bringing the crippled aircraft to a slithering halt in 457m (1,500ft), less than a third of the usual distance. It was the first in-flight emergency and the first landing at a location other than Rogers Dry Lake.

Returned to NAA's Inglewood facility for repairs and additional fasteners and doubler-plate at both top and bottom of the fuselage, Crossfield was convinced it was a manufacturing flaw waiting for the inevitable consequence. Indeed that may have been so but the overall configuration of the landing gear placed dependency for a safe touchdown and rollout on a stiff nose leg taking the transfer of energy from the centre of gravity to the extreme forward section of the fuselage as the nose came down for contact with the surface. It would not be the only problem caused by this arrangement. As if to add punishment to embarrassment, in the final attempt of 1959, X-15-1 was taken aloft on 16 December for its first powered flight only to have that aborted due to low LOX tank pressure and, again, problems with the radios.

With X-15-2 off-line for repairs at Inglewood, X-15-1 made its first powered flight at the first attempt in 1960 when Crossfield achieved a speed of Mach 2.53, 2,685kph/1,669mph), on 23 January. This was the first use of the NB-52B (008) and the first time the stable platform had been installed in the X-15. With an urgency to get the X-15 into its design operating environment, and to satisfy the new and very public face of aerospace achievement driven by the need to show technological superiority to a watching world, it was designed to coincide with its hand-over to the Air Force. That occurred on 3 February, the date North American officially handed over the X-15 to the government. The Air Force would place it on 'loan' to NASA for flight operations and conduct its own test flights during this year, when the programme got into its stride and real-world results began to show its capabilities.

Exploring the envelope

With an enhanced sense of optimism, work continued to evaluate the basic characteristics with another flight by X-15-2 planned for 4 February, now back from Inglewood, rebuilt and with a stronger fuselage and replacement nose leg. But low LOX tank pressure and radio trouble aborted that. There

Below: Scott Crossfield in X-15-1 returns from an early contractor flight, often the start of a lengthy period of data analysis and report-writing. *NASA*

Right: Engineers and managers pore over engineering data, in this particular instance after the first glide flight where the X-15 flew independently for the first time but a scene to be repeated many times over the next nine years. *NASA*

were problems too with the Ballistic Control System, installed in X-15-2 for the first time because preceding flights had not been at a sufficiently high altitude to require that. But it was proving troublesome and it was decided not to install that for early flights with the X-15-3 aircraft.

Three successful flights in successive attempts with X-15-2 were piloted by Crossfield on 11 and 17 February and 17 March, the first marred solely by the new landing leg bottoming-out after touchdown. During the second flight the upper XLR-11 engine shut down prematurely, limiting the speed to Mach 1.57, although the engine was successfully re-ignited. The third flight investigated manoeuvrability with the dampers on, achieving Mach 2.15 and giving Crossfield an opportunity to perform a 360deg roll and a 6-g turn. The following day another launch attempt had to be aborted when fuel leaked and the windshield delaminated less than a minute before release.

And then, some said in a release of good fortune but realistically due to an increased familiarity with attending to the aircraft and pre-flight nuances, between 25 March and 19 April 1960 the two X-15s successfully completed five consecutive launch attempts. For the first of these, Crossfield was one of three chase pilots as Joe Walker piloted X-15-1 during the first government flight on behalf of NASA. But it was not auspicious as the upper engine required two re-starts, the roll damper was inoperable and the stable platform malfunctioned. Crossfield flew the next flight in X-15-2 four days later and conducted a cold-soak mission to simulate environmental conditions. On 31 March, Crossfield flew the same ship to evaluate SAS gains and check manoeuvrability.

On 13 April, Maj. Robert M. White made the first Air Force flight when he flew X-15-1 to a speed of Mach 1.9 (2,017kph/1,254mph) and suffered a hydraulic hose failure in addition to a film drum malfunction which prevented any landing data being recorded. This was followed by Walker's second flight for NASA on 19 April, reaching Mach 2.56 in X-15-1 despite another hydraulic failure. It was NASA's first performance build-up flight, launched after one of the eight engines on the NB-52 (003) had to be shut down. Walker also demonstrated that the rudder could be used to steer the aircraft on rollout after touchdown. Crossfield tried to get in a further flight with X-15-2 on 5 May but APU-1 shut down and the hydrogen peroxide failed to jettison, calling an abort.

The following day, Bob White took X-15-1 on his second launch and achieved Mach 2.2 despite a roll damper failing at launch before a successful reset, the ventral stabiliser failing to jettison as planned but doing so when the back-up kicked in at gear deployment. Speed and altitude runs were

High Range tracking and telemetry stations are shown with an early design of the landing pattern, the launch altitude shown here being somewhat lower than the 12,190m (40,000ft) adopted later in the flight programme. *NASA*

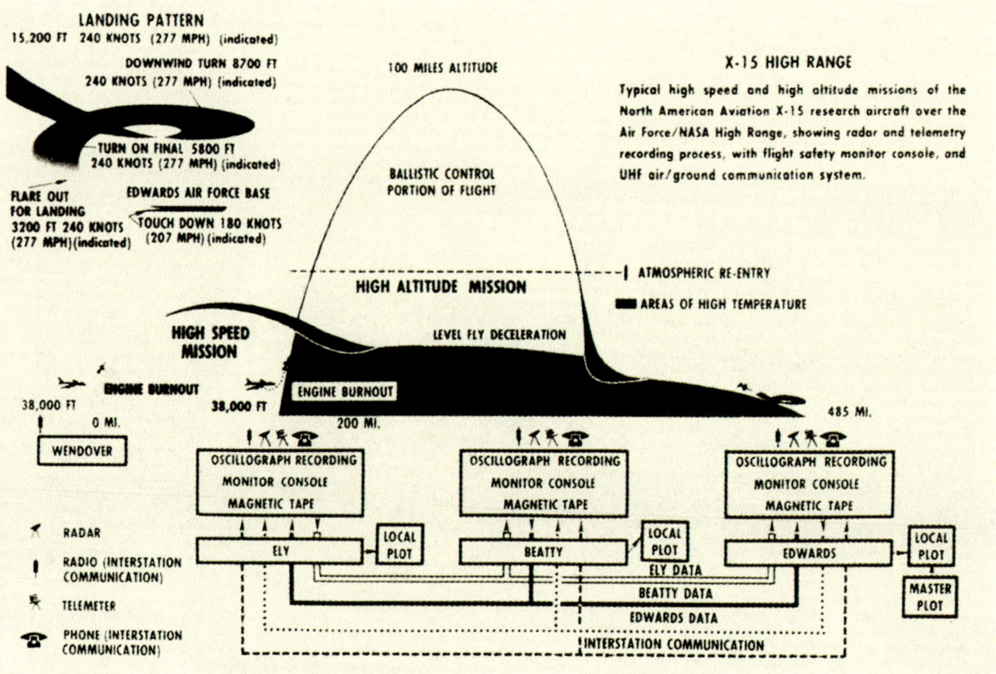

significantly below the potential of the aircraft due to the installation of the XLR-11 motor packs but on the next flight, 12 May, Joe Walker was assigned to launch out of Silver Lake for the first time; all preceding flights had been out of Rosamond. The BCS was absent as intended due to pending decisions over its suitability and use and the stable platform was inoperative. The learning curve was still in an ascending trajectory.

The flight began with the release of X-15-1 from the NB-52 at 13,655m (44,800ft) and a speed of Mach 0.83. Both rocket motors fired and Walker put the flight path on an 8deg ascent to reach 23,738m (77,882ft) before levelling off and beginning a shallow dive at which point, the acceleration being greater than expected, he shut down three of the eight cylinders. The marked acceleration caused cavitation in the propellant pumps which promptly closed the other five chambers. Nevertheless, Walker logged a speed of Mach 3.19 (3,396kph/2,111mph) but on the way down he elected not to conduct a planned series of tests with the side-controller when he found that it required 'a very strained arm position'.

White got the next flight with X-15-1 on 19 May which took him to 33,222m (108,997ft) on what was tagged as an altitude build-up flight, and a speed of Mach 2.31. Seven days later Crossfield took X-15-2 on an evaluation flight to test the BCS, reaching Mach 2.2, but reported vibrations in the control system which occurred after touchdown. The next attempt on the following day was the first of three attempts by Walker to launch in the X-15-1 but telemetry failure and a problem with the power supply prevented that. As it did also 3 June when the APUs lost hydraulic pressure. On 8 June yet another attempt was aborted before launch when nitrogen gas leaked, preventing the necessary pressurisation for continuing the flight.

Above: Robert Rushworth returns after the 25th free flight of the X-15, the 16th with X-15-1. *NASA*

From the outset, X-15-3 was slated to receive the considerably more powerful XLR-99 engine, which had itself given considerable trouble during development. With the XLR-11 twin-packs installed, the first two X-15s had only begun to explore the aircraft's speed and altitude capabilities. Nevertheless, the flights so far had demonstrated basic handling characteristics and provided pilots with some experience, comparing the simulators with the actual vehicle in the air. And it had provided ground crew, technicians, engineers and managers with a period in which the processes for flight and the procedures for mission operations, had begun to develop.

X-15-3 had arrived at Edwards, without its engine, on 26 August 1959 and before powered flight operations began with X-15-1. The first ground-test model of the XLR-99 had

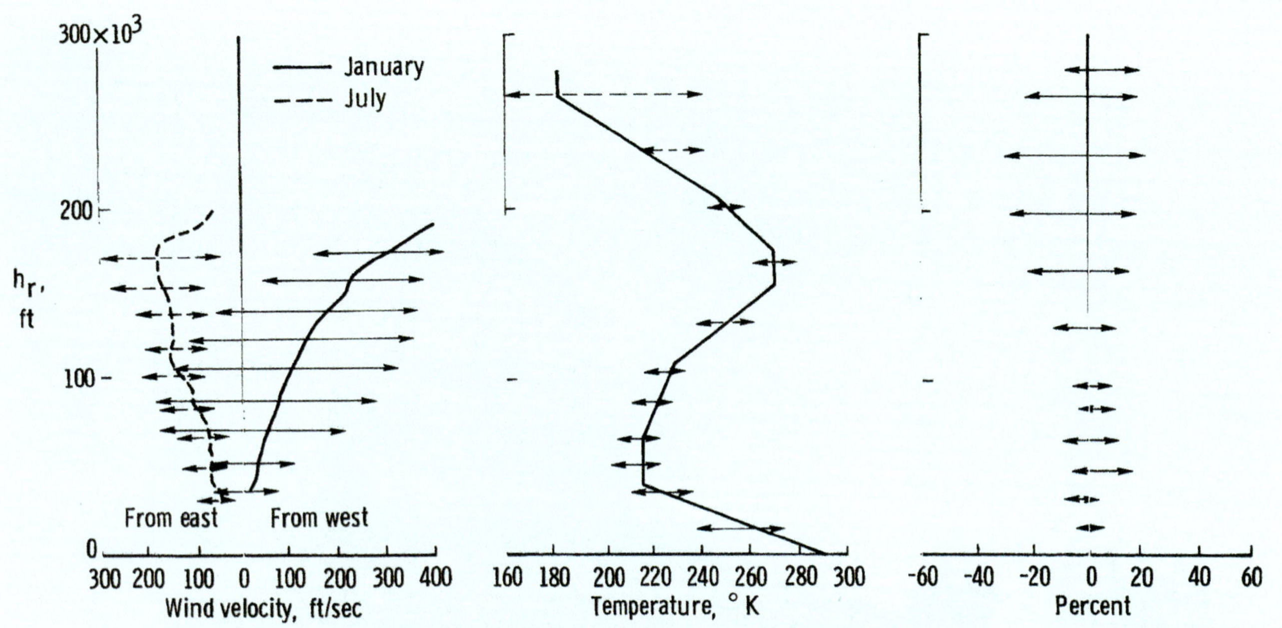

(a) Mean January and July zonal winds for 30° N.

(b) Range of systematic variability of temperature.

(c) Departure from standard density.

NASA used the 1962 standard Atmosphere model to baseline wind, temperature and density parameters, values from which specific control of the X-15 would be determined for unique flight profiles. Temperature and wind data (below) were collected from several sources prior to each flight, the data being integrated with the flight plan. *NASA*

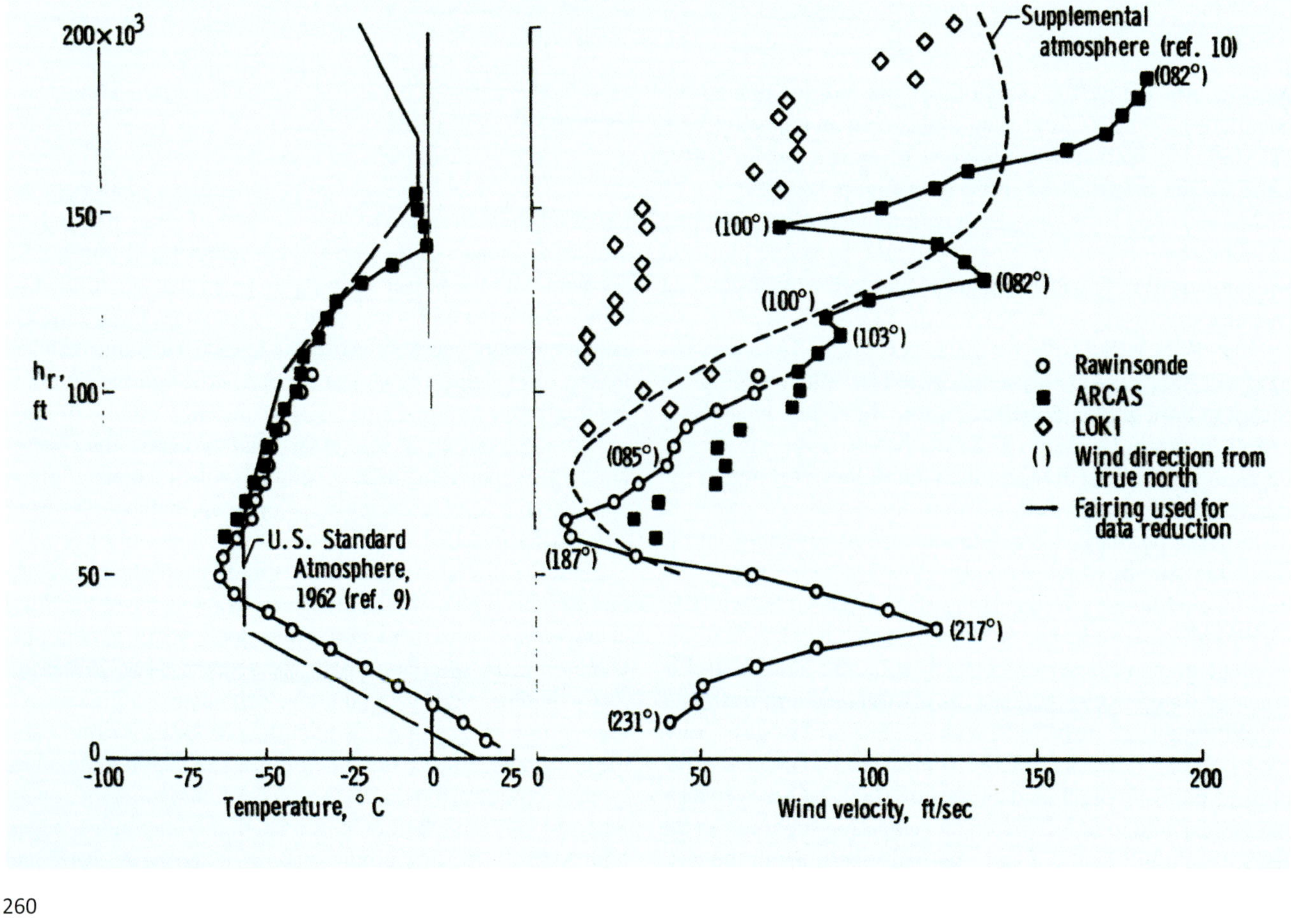

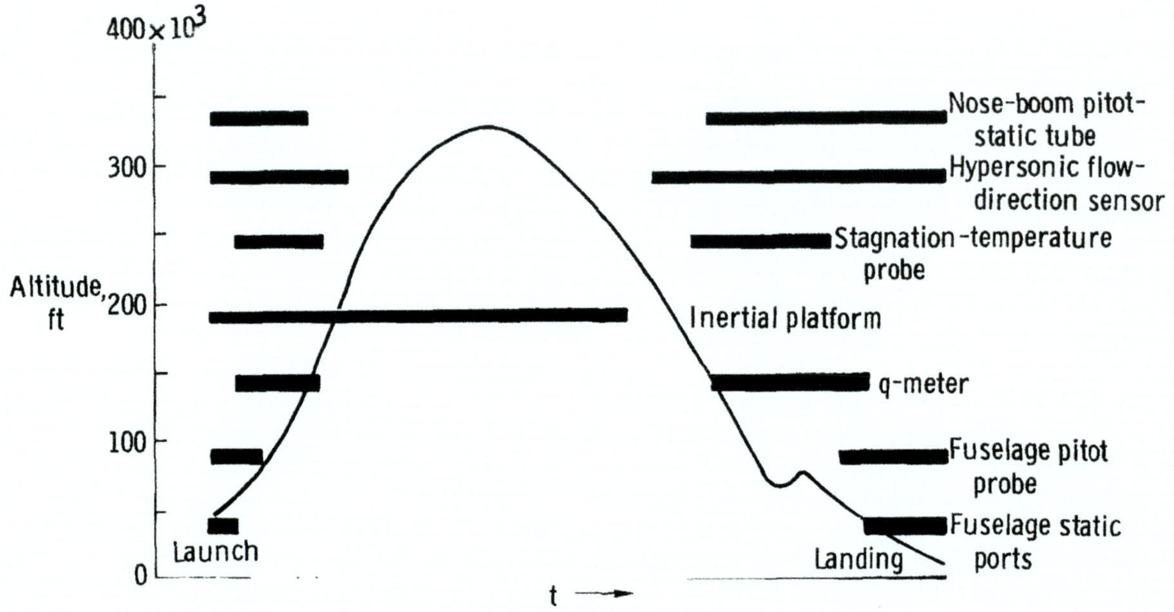

Sensors on the X-15 were used for different flight objectives, the allocation on a timeline for high altitude flights shown above with low altitude flight sensor allocations below. *NASA*

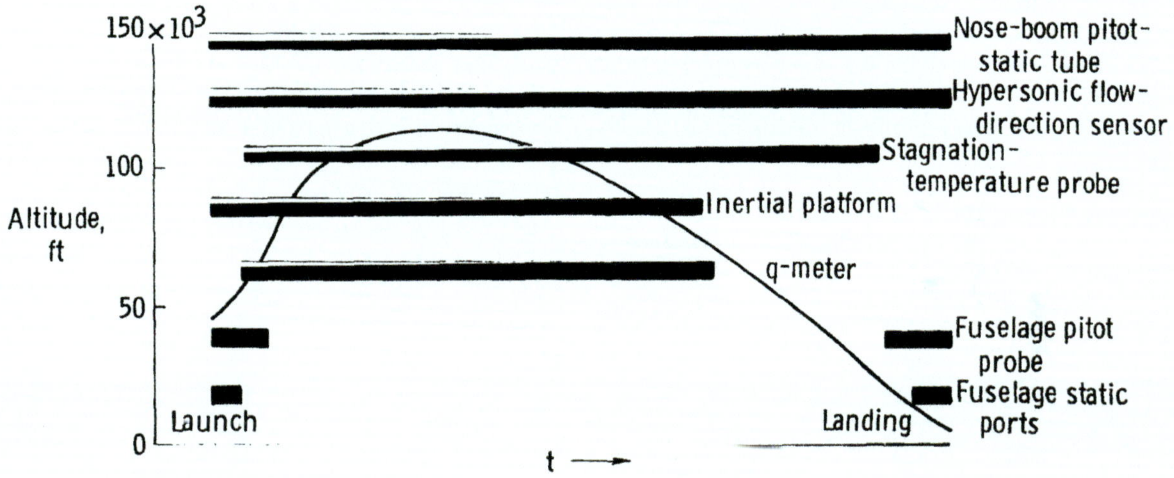

been there since 7 June 1959 and the first hot-fire test was conducted at the Rocket Engine Test Facility (RETF) on 26 August. With a desire to get the XLR-99 retrofitted in to the next aircraft, X-15-2 was withdrawn from flight activity on 26 May 1960 after Crossfield's BCS test in anticipation of that. The first ground-run of the XLR-99 in X-15-3 was conducted on 2 June. Crossfield was in the cockpit because it could only be started by the occupant. The monitoring crew were in the blockhouse and only the fire-crews were close to the X-15 in case of an accident. Some damage was noted to the LOX inlet line brackets but repairs were made and a successful run completed.

With general engine operating sequences proved out and satisfactory, the next step was to check the shut-down and restart capability, together with the throttle settings. That took place on 8 June during the early evening hours, the day Walker returned from his third successive launch abort. Crossfield started the engine and moved the throttle to the 50 per cent position and verified that the pressure had stabilised before advancing the throttle to the 100 per cent notch. This was a powerful engine, with a thrust equal to that of the German V2 ballistic rocket, and it presented an impressive sight.

Five seconds later, Crossfield moved the throttle to idle, set it there for a further five seconds and shut it down. Fifteen seconds later he advanced the throttle to 50 per cent at which point the turbopump spun up, the two stages of the combustion process occurred as planned and all looked good. As it stabilised, the thrust fell away and it shut itself down, a valve warning light in the cockpit came on and Crossfield returned the throttle to the off position. The light went out. Using standard procedure, Crossfield reset the auto-safety systems with a view to restarting the motor at which moment an enormous explosion ripped the fuselage in two and propelled the section ahead of the engine, with Crossfield inside, 9.1m (30ft) forward.

Crossfield acted instinctively, throwing all the circuit-breakers and tried calling the blockhouse but the communications were severed. Fire trucks were on site within 30 seconds and dowsing the entire area with water. Pitching full-tilt into a forensic investigation of what had happened, personnel began a meticulous search for all the items, however miniscule, that had been blasted apart, finally removing the engine from X-15-3 five days later. The airframe was destined for NAA's Inglewood facility, arriving there on 15 June, where it would be rebuilt. The entire aft section had to be replaced, as did the four dorsal, ventral, left and right stabilisers, the speed brakes, landing skids and both propellant tanks. The wings were repairable and the APUs and the stable platform – expensive items – were retained during the rebuild.

The investigation found no flaw in the design of the aircraft or the XLR-99 but certain procedures and equipment employed at the site specifically for the test firings needed to be changed. It had all been caused by inadvertent over-pressurisation of the ammonia fuel tank. But it came at greater cost than the delays incurred to readying the more powerful engine and the third X-15 for flight operations. The annual budget for the year that began 1 July 1960 had been reduced and the cost of rebuilding X-15-3 was an unwelcome addition to expenditure. The test site too had incurred expensive damage which took time to repair. Nevertheless, X-15-3 was going to be a much welcome addition, including the MH-96 adaptive flight control system from the Dyna-Soar programme. The Air Force wanted to test that before flying it in the boost-glider. North American said it could deliver the rebuilt aircraft to Edwards in August 1961, ready to begin flight operations two months later. That estimate was off by only two months which, for a programme of this complexity, was pretty good.

Meanwhile, preparations were made to install the XLR-99 in X-15-2 and Joe Walker and Bob White continued flying X-15-1, on 12 August achieving the highest altitude powered by the XLR-11 when White reached 41,605m (136,500ft) in a flight lasting 11min 39.1sec. Walker was making high-speed runs routinely over Mach 3, and on 19 August holding at that speed for thirteen seconds. It was time to expand the pilot base. The US Navy put its own pilot in the cockpit for a run with X-15-1 on 23 September when Cdr. Forrest S. Petersen achieved Mach 1.68, curtailed by premature shut-down of the XLR-11s and two unsuccessful restart attempts. John B. McKay made his first flight on 28 October followed by Robert A. Rushworth on 4 November.

On that date NASA had attempted two flights, preceding Rushworth's flight with a planned launch to re-qualify X-15-2 and make the first powered demonstration with the XLR-99 installed. Crossfield was unable to launch when APU-2 failed and hydrogen peroxide leaked. North American was required to conduct three demonstration flights with the more powerful engine before handing it over to the government. The second attempt on 15 November was more successful and launched at 14,020m (46,000ft) and Mach 0.83. As the X-15 fell away, Crossfield settled the throttles at 50 per cent and in 2min 17.3sec had accelerated to Mach 2.97 (3,153kph/1,960mph). Crossfield achieved a maximum altitude of 24,750m (81,200ft) and was back on the ground 8min 28.4sec after the drop. The only notable anomaly was a small hydraulic leak.

Post-flight, and on detailed inspection of the XLR-99, concerns were raised about the Rokide coating on the inside of the expansion chamber, which appeared to have degraded uniformly across the interior face of the bell-shaped nozzle.

Below: Positioned with the aft end facing the blast deflector and with the control room housing test engineers and technicians, preparations are made to fire up the XLR-99. *NASA*

Below right: On 8 June 1960 Scott Crossfield was in the cockpit for a live test of the XLR-99 when the aft end was blown off in an explosion. *NASA*

LAKE	RUNWAY LENGTH	HEADING	ELEV	T A C A N STA	CHAN	RAD	N MI
Bonneville	7-8 mi	3-21	4250	BVL	70		
Delamar	2.5	0-18	4000	MLF	58	215	110
Edwards	7-8 5 6 5 4	17-35 18-36 5-23 7-25 9-27	2300 (X-15) (North) (South) (Navaho Trail)	EDW	68		
Grapevine	2	1-19	4000	BTY	94	300	30
Hidden Hls	3	15-33	2000	LAS	116	250	40
Mud	5	6-24	5000	OAL		90	35
Silver	2	12-30	1000	LAS	116	215	65
Smith's	4	4-22	5700	NFL	82	90	55
Three Sis (W) (E)	2.5 2.5	3-21 5-23	3500	LAS	116	210	110
Wah Wah	3.5	2-20	4500	MLF	58	290	20

MISC. LAKEBED INFORMATION

Left: Reference sheets were handed to pilots giving information on the various abort sites and runway information together with distances and radio/telemetry channels for specific regions. *NASA*

NAA's Harrison Storms got involved in the decision whether to continue with the contractor flights or ground the aircraft and by implication all flights with the XLR-99, or make an informed judgement and proceed. In consultation with Air Force FTC commander Brig. Gen. John Carpenter, Storms got a unanimous decision to proceed. It was an object lesson in rational decision-making within a complex technical project.

In 'X-15 Hardware Design Challenges', Storms defined the boundaries of an educated judgement in engineering thus: '…there is a very fine line between stopping progress and being reckless. That the necessary ingredient in this situation of solving a sticky problem is attitude and approach. The answer, in my opinion is what I refer to as "thoughtful courage". If you don't have that, you will very easily fall into the habit of "fearful safety" and end up with a very long and tedious-type solution at the hands of some committee. This can very well end up giving a test program a disease commonly referred to as "cancelitis", which results in little or no progress.'

With the decision made, Crossfield flew the third powered contractor flight with the X-15-2 on 6 December 1960 and successfully demonstrated power settings and throttle levels, achieving all that was required for handing the project and its three progeny, to the Air Force and to NASA. The total engine run time was 2min 8.9sec, propelling X-15-2 to Mach 2.85 (3,026kph/1,881mph) and a maximum altitude of 16,268m (53,374ft). This was Crossfield's last flight in the X-15, his fourteenth since the first glide drop on 8 June 1959 and the last of his more than 130 rocket flights.

Expanding the envelope

With the programme handed over to the Air Force/NASA government team, a significant amount of work remained on changing out the engine in X-15-2 and making it ready to resume flight operations, which it would do two months after Crossfield's last flight. Meanwhile, on 9 December, NASA test pilot Neil Armstrong made the first flight with the Q-ball replacing the nose boom on X-15-1, and on 7

Left: NASA put great store in the X-15 programme and made several films about the aircraft and its activities. All three aircraft are lined up 23 April 1965 for filming *Research Project X-15*, a highly recommended NASA documentary which can be seen on YouTube. *NASA*

February 1961, Bob White made the last flight with XLR-11 rocket motors, achieving Mach 3.5 (3,660kph/2,275mph) and an altitude of 23,820m (78,150ft). The aircraft was returned to Inglewood the following day for it to receive an XLR-99, the same date X-15-2 was delivered back to Edwards. For the next six months, flight operations would be exclusively with this aircraft.

There was much to learn, information delayed due to the initial XLR-11 rocket packs being incapable of pushing the X-15 faster than Mach 3.5. Data regarding the aerothermal environment at high Mach numbers in the hypersonic region was denied until the more powerful XLR-99 became available. That began to change as envelope expansion was explored, beginning on 7 March 1961 when Bob White took X-15-2 to Mach 4.43 (4,674kph/2,905mph) and a height of 23,606m (77,450ft). The powered phase lasted 2min 7sec and from launch to touchdown the flight lasted 8min 34.1sec.

Much public attention was attracted to the programme in the first few months of 1961, particularly April and May. On 12 April Russia's Yuri Gagarin had become the first human in space when he made a single circumnavigation of the Earth. Responding to that, President Kennedy directed Vice President Lyndon Johnson to come up with ideas on how to beat the Russians. On 5 May, NASA successfully launched its first astronaut, Alan Shepard, in a Mercury capsule carried on a ballistic trajectory by a Redstone rocket lasting little more than fifteen minutes from launch to splashdown.

On 25 May, the day Walker flew X-15-2 to a record speed of Mach 4.95 (5,320kph/3,307mph), Kennedy addressed a joint session of Congress and directed NASA to land astronauts on the Moon by the end of the decade. Anything to do with space was hot news and the X-15 received its fair share. White extended the envelope still further on 23 June, achieving Mach 5.27 (5,797kph/3,603mph) with the XLR-99 providing thrust for 1min 18.7sec. Another milestone was passed on 10 August when Petersen took the X-15-1 into the air to check out its new XLR-99 engine, which, despite him grabbing the speed brake handle instead of the throttle on launch, propelled him to Mach 4.11 (4,400kph/2,735mph). Walker took the same ship past Mach 5 for the first time on 17 October 1961.

X-15-3 was back at Edwards in time to attempt its first flight on 19 December 1961 with Neil Armstrong at the controls but the Q-ball suffered a malfunction, aborting the launch and preventing him from checking out the MH-96 flight control system. With better luck next day, Armstrong took it on its first flight and reached Mach 3.76 (4,025kph/2,502mph). The MH-96 system dropped out at launch then kicked back in but the yaw limit cycle went to fixed gain during the powered phase, which lasted 1min 46.3sec. As the final flight of the year, X-15-3 had advanced the programme and expanded the potential for flight operations to come.

The high-speed flights with Walker and White in X-15-1 and X-15-2 had taken winged flight into the hypersonic regime and begun to open a window on heating effects and the aerothermal environment beyond Mach 5. A second objective had been to investigate the structural effects of high-temperature flight on the X-15, and a third had sought to obtain measurements of stability and control during re-entry from high altitude. Important too were the physiological responses of the pilots to flying on these frontiers. The Air Force sought this data for its Dyna-Soar boost-glide programme and saw information from the X-15 as feeding directly into experimental projects which it hoped to translate into programmes for future manned space flights.

In this year of 1961, the X-15 and the Mercury space programmes were gearing up for their primary objectives and, although the latter would go on achieve a grander objective – orbital space flight – than the winged X-15 was capable of, a natural banter grew between the X-15 pilots and the astronauts. X-15 pilots were proud that they physically controlled their vehicle and that they alone were responsible for control of their rocket-ships; the astronauts were keen to point out that in the coming year they would be circling the globe far above the useable atmosphere. It was an attractive prospect and Neil Armstrong applied for the astronaut corps during the 1962 selection and within seven years would become the first man to walk on the Moon, having survived the only on-orbit abort which occurred during the Gemini VIII mission in March 1966.

The qualities that made good X-15 research pilots were similar to those required for astronaut assignment: an ability to conduct a pre-planned set of manoeuvres, rehearsed in a simulator, and carried out with precision and control while confident of contingency options should the evaluation be compromised by a malfunction or an unexpected response. And there is a distinction between the research pilot and a test pilot, the former being interested and attracted to the science of the task rather than being drawn exclusively to the engineering of the machine he is flying; a desire to provide highly accurate data rather than explore the performance or operating capabilities inherent in the aircraft he is testing.

The research pilot requires a high level of discipline, because he is seeking the optimum manner in which data and measurement can be obtained for purposes which may be

outside his speciality. He must never divert from his task on a whim, attracted by the opportunity to try something different he perceives, in the air, as being better than the sequence tested and verified in ground-based simulators. Thus did the engineers and the scientists on the X-15 programme require a range of inputs, including angle-of-attack changes, rudder pulses, control dynamics and roll and yaw excursions. Conducted as pre-planned and necessary for the information sought and not as a sense of inquiry spontaneously created by the pilot experiencing a test flight. The spectrum of investigation and research required the aircraft to be a tool for selected experiments, mapping the aerodynamic performance of the X-15, its lift-to-drag ratio, aerothermal loads in a variety of flight conditions, and the precise effectiveness of controls and stick inputs.

High-speed flights had shone a light on the tendency for buckling in the fuselage tunnels but these were not structural members and merely covers for a surfeit of conduits, pipes and cables running down the sides of the aircraft, Nevertheless, some changes were made to the allowance for movement in the skin to prevent undue effects of the heating from reforming the exterior contour of the aircraft. As noted, the temperature difference between the side panel skin and the primary structure was 269ºC (500ºF) but improvements were effected in a wide range of minor ways. For instance, on 30 March 1961 Walker's flight was the first use of the much improved A/P22S-2 suit, reportedly better to wear, more comfortable and with improved vision for the occupant.

During that flight, Walker had reached 51,694m (169,600ft), giving him two minutes of near zero-g, a record for the X-15 in altitude and an all-time record for the weightlessness experienced. In fact it would quickly be eclipsed by the first ballistic Mercury flight with Alan Shepard on 5 May. It did, however, demonstrate a case of structural resonance when vibration in the vertical and transverse axes at 13cps aligned with the first bending mode of the horizontal stabiliser. This was caused by a sympathetic oscillation induced by a motion sensor oscillating at a common frequency. It was, in this case, caused by the pitch-rate gyro detecting motion in some other part of the structure, commanding an actuator to follow at the same frequency, thus perpetuating the effect.

Above: X-15-2 aloft under the starboard wing of its carrier-plane. *NASA*

Apart from the engineering analysis of the way the X-15 behaved in flight and the scientific investigation of the aerothermal environment, certain groups within the Air Force and in other government agencies were keen to know Walker's impressions of observations during his flight. At this date the Dyna-Soar strike and reconnaissance programme was very much alive as the third step in the evolution of supersonic and hypersonic systems leading to orbital flight. Coming several weeks before the short, ballistic hop of Alan Shepard in his Mercury capsule, there was keen interest in how well a pilot at such extreme altitude could discern objects on the ground.

Written in response to a request for Walker to describe how well he could observe features on the surface of the Earth, his published comments mirrored other debriefing sessions in which a body of specialist opinion doubted the ability of a pilot to usefully distinguish objects from such an altitude. Scepticism on the ability of a man to see and interpret surface features would extend well into 1962 and 1963. To directly address this, Mercury astronauts conducted visual tests of their ability to make out surface features and to identify markings previously placed on the ground.

Walker was adamant that, from his vantage point, there was indeed much that could be seen, asserting that he had 'No difficulty is experienced in observing and identifying geographical features...particularly in areas with which one is familiar. An outstanding aspect of this is the appreciation of relative heights or elevations; different levels of the surface. Mountains still stand out as mountains and looking down into the Los Angeles Basin, I could tell the smog as distinct from some low stratocumulus clouds along the seacoast. Areas which are heavily forested or under agricultural development could be separated from those areas where nothing was growing, and once again, if one were familiar with the territory, this is even easier to pick out'.

Physiologically, results from the X-15 programme served to indicate the stresses which might be encountered by Mercury astronauts. Air Force and NASA physicians monitored the basic parameters of the pilot's body and noted significantly increased stress levels, primarily on heart rate, compared to responses the same pilots presented on test flights with conventional aircraft. Heart rates on X-15 missions routinely peaked at 145-185 beats per minute (bps) compared with 70-80bps when testing jet aircraft. It was found that pre-flight anticipation was the primary cause, not post-flight physical stress from g-loads or other factors.

Before the Mercury flights began the X-15 high-altitude flights allowed periods of weightlessness to be experienced of up to two minutes in duration at extreme altitude, and this helped to increase confidence that the Mercury astronauts would have no problems either. It had always been accepted that the X-15 would provide support for the manned orbital programme, although when it began in 1954 that was anticipated to be through a boost-glide system such as the later Dyna-Soar programme.

Pitching it right

A significant part of the X-15's work was in the area of flight dynamics, understanding how winged vehicles could be controlled manually and with the aid of equipment such as the SAS or, later the AFCS. NASA-Langley had been responsible for much of the work into how to conduct a re-entry flight profile so as to limit the g-loads from acceleration and balance heat load versus heat rate. Integrating wind tunnel tests, and theoretical calculations based on existing experience, and matching that with simulated runs prior to a flight, indicated to flight planners that a constant angle-of-attack at the top of the re-entry path was preferable. Dynamic pressure would increase and raise the g-level and at some point the pilot would ease the nose down toward level flight. As the maximum altitude increased and re-entry began at greater height, the angle-of-attack would have to increase to keep the structural forces within design limits.

Initial tests indicated that an alpha-angle of 15deg was possible at entry interface with the SAS switched off but above that the X-15 could be uncontrollable, particularly with the dampers off. The simulators were fed with this data and the pilots 'flew' mission profiles in which the horizontal stabilisers were at zero-deflection. When simulator runs were made with the stabilisers at a leading-edge down at 15-20deg, instability became uncontrollable. All indications showed that the maximum deflection would be 8deg and that limited altitude flights to no higher than 60,960m (200,000ft), an unacceptable restriction.

To explore solutions, engineers examined the control logic of the SAS itself and how it operated the dampers. It had two channels, one operating as a working channel and another as a monitoring channel for each axis. If the moni-

Below left: The flight path for a standard landing pattern from the high-key altitude of 8,808m (28,900ft) and 555kph (345mph) rolling to a 45deg banked turn to a low-key, 190deg heading to touchdown. *NAA*
Below: Alternate high-key landing approaches from an alternate altitude of 6,860m (22,500ft) at 444kph (276mph) rolling to a 30deg banked turn. *NAA*

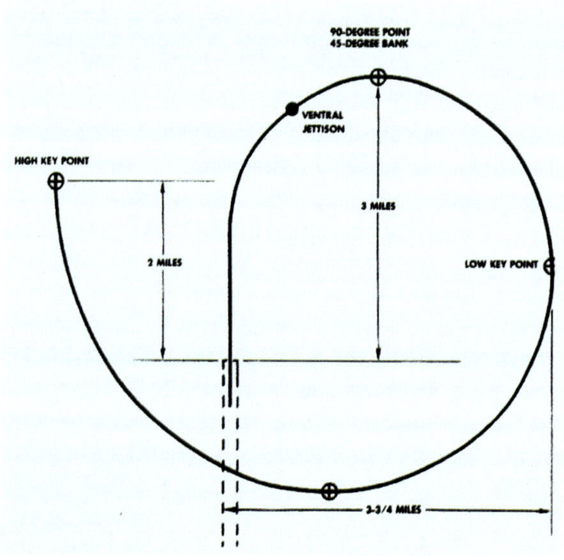

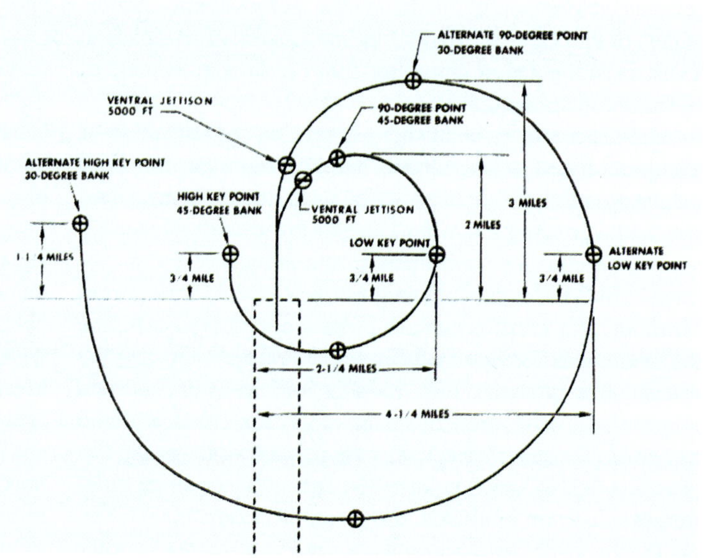

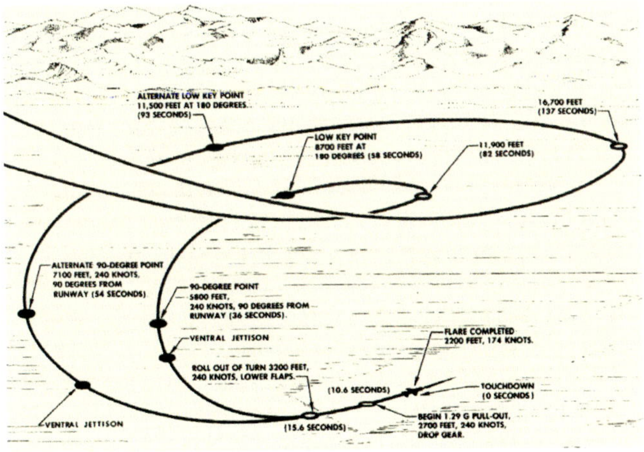

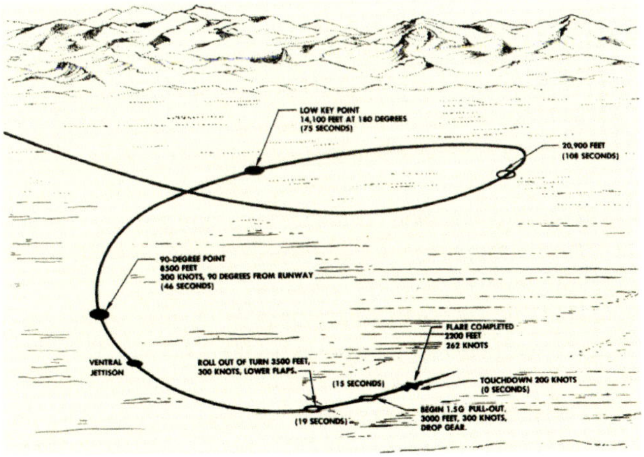

Above: The low-key flight pattern approach path from an altitude of 4,298m (14,100ft), some 75 seconds before touchdown. *NAA*

Above right: The flight patterns from primary and alternate low-key departure points. These nominal and alternate flight paths were evaluated, tested and rehearsed in the simulators by each pilot. *NAA*

toring channel was in disagreement with the working channel it shut down the relevant damper on that axis. Initially, the SAS had not been designed to run as a fail-operational system to save weight but as the flight operations moved into areas where this was becoming a real concern, engineers looked again at the way it operated. Technically, it was believed that if the roll channel damper failed approaching re-entry it could be catastrophic.

There was uncertainty as to the validity of these conclusions and the flight on 19 August flown by Joe Walker had been made from a relatively benign altitude of 23,159m (75,982ft) and with the roll dampers switched off. As he increased the angle of attack, Walker picked up the lateral oscillations predicted by the simulator and verified that the problem was real. The origin of the problem lay within the early design assumptions made by the engineers at NAA. In assuming that the aircraft would be flown wings-level for most of the time, only the re-entry pitch-up angle was considered relevant to the high-altitude flights.

The solution was to develop a back-up damper, the ASAS, its development and application being covered in Chapter 14. It was considered a back-up system and was regarded as such by the pilots and operated on a fixed-gain level, pre-set by the pilot before the flight. It was strictly for fail-safe only use and was installed in X-15-1 and X-15-2 during April 1962, with a modification introduced five years later in X-15A-2 to also include the yaw axis to cover contingencies with flights involving the dummy ramjet engine. This was also retrofitted to X-15-1 but was unnecessary in X-15-3 as this aircraft had the MH-96 system with its built-in redundancy.

As the flight programme unfolded and a broader understanding of the aircraft's dynamic characteristics became known, consideration of flying the aircraft at high angle of attack returned, following issues about these re-entry profiles. Engineers were concerned that the ventral vertical stabiliser compromised handling at high angles of attack. It appeared that the stabiliser was too large and it was decided to find out what would happen if it was reduced in area. Which was no problem at all as it did not require the redesign of a ventral stabiliser since the lower section was jettisoned anyway at the end of each flight. It could be left off for an evaluation flight. But there were concerns. Scant time and wind tunnel effort had been done on such a configuration at high-Mach speeds despite an abundance of data on low-speed handling with the lower ventral portion removed, as it always was for landing.

With suitable protection for thermal effects on the exposed undersurface of the fixed, upper portion of the ventral stabiliser, the first flight in that configuration was flown by Bob Rushworth on 4 October 1961, where he reached Mach 4.3 and a maximum altitude of 23,774m (78,000ft). No significantly noticeable effects were observed but the handling qualities were better in this configuration at an 8deg angle of attack. Thus began a major research project at Langley to test in wind tunnels the entire speed range with the lower portion of the ventral stabiliser removed. Results confirmed the information already obtained from flight data and matched wind tunnel tests that allowed fully mechanised tests on the simulators.

Further, extensive wind tunnel tests were conducted and on 28 September 1962 Jack McKay took X-15-2 on a run to Mach 4.22 and an altitude of 20,787m (68,200ft) with the lower ventral removed. The following 88 flights with the X-15 were conducted in this configuration, until it was reinstated for X-15A-2 using external fuel tanks for a flight on 3 November 1965 and on six successive launches. In total, 73 flights were conducted with the lower ventral on and 126 with it off. The overall effect was greatly beneficial, increasing the L/D ratio from 4.25 to 4.5 and moderately improving range, allowing re-entry from Mach 6 at trajectories of up to 26deg and flight path angle of up to -38deg.

As the flight programme approached two years of operating experience, several incidents revealed a great truth about the fundamental lesson in developing a vehicle of this capability, that 'what are minor and unimportant features of a subsonic or supersonic aircraft must be dealt with as prime design problems in a hypersonic airplane', according to John Becker, adding 'This lesson was applied effectively in the precise design of a host of important details on the manned space vehicles'. The inherited legacy of the first two years of X-15 experience played directly into the Mercury manned space programme and added greatly to confidence in the Dyna-Soar project, although that would survive barely two more years.

Experience was unique, however, in operating the XLR-99 as it demonstrated the difficulties here too with a new and unique form of rocket propulsion, with throttle and restart capabilities at a time when these requirements were hard to translate into engineering success. Very few flights had not experienced some form of failure with this engine, whether on start-up, during running, at shutdown or on restart. The engine was always reliable in starting a second time on the same flight but problems occurring after shutdown were more difficult to understand. There was a simple reason. By putting the engine through the same cycle of accelerations, engineers discovered that under very specific flight conditions, the lubrication pump would cavitate for two seconds, triggering an auto-shutdown.

A solution was found by putting in a delay timer on the malfunction circuit to delay the shut-down command for a further four seconds, by which time cavitation would have settled down. That solved the problem but there were still persistent inconsistencies with ignition. And the supply of hydrogen peroxide for the XLR-99 turbopump was tapped into after Bob White, in a flight on 11 October 1961, appeared to run close to the limit on propellant for the BCS during a flight to 66,141m (217,000ft). After this, a fluid transfer system was installed in all three aircraft to prevent a recurrence.

During the second half of 1961, the Air Force Flight Test Center gathered data for a study of failure analysis in the first two years of operation and reached some compelling conclusions. They appeared to justify the argument for putting a man in the loop and for designing vehicles with redundant systems, for a range of different applications. It would have been possible to build a remotely controlled research aircraft capable of all the performance objectives of the X-15, short of those specifically requiring a human on board. Nobody was suggesting that this should have been the case, but there was a broader debate over operational systems, whether for research or deployment, involving manned or unmanned vehicles. More specifically, over the value of redundant systems with manned vehicles compared with unmanned systems built to a cost and lacking redundancy.

In examining the first 44 launches and two planned captive X-15 flights to the end of October 1961, factoring in the 30 aborts it was possible to assess the impact of having a pilot on board. In the 44 launches, it was determined that 43 (97.7 per cent) were successful as flown by the requirements of respective flight plans. These flights were compared with an equivalent, manned vehicle but without systems redundancy, in which only 27 (61.3 per cent) of those flights would have been successful. In a comparative vehicle with no pilot but redundancy, 24 (54.5 per cent) would have been completed as planned. In an unmanned vehicle with no redundancy only 23 flights (52.3 per cent) would have been successful. Only 19 flights (43 per cent) had no issues at all related to whether it had a pilot or redundant systems.

The bigger lesson from the analysis showed that in a vehicle with a pilot but no systems redundancy, 14 (31.8 per cent) of the 44 missions would have resulted in the loss of the aircraft. As an illuminating comparison, Boeing performed a similar study looking at the Bomarc air-defence system, an unmanned ground-launched missile with no redundancy in a bid to save costs. Supporting the analysis from the Flight Research Center, but disarmingly worrying for potential customers, it too found that exactly 43 per cent would be successful compared to a parallel system with redundancy and a pilot.

Albeit derived from a theoretical analysis, the data input was obtained from real-world cases – at least for the X-15 – and the lesson propagated into the next generation of defence and space-related programmes in which deleting redundancy was no cost-saving decision at all, rather a guarantee of failure in the majority of operational uses. Analyses such as these provided the groundwork for determining acceptable levels of failure allowed in manned and unmanned systems. It pushed the art to a new state, in which failure could be accepted as inevitable, but managed internally and inherently within the design of the component, the system or the vehicle.

This matured during the late 1960s when design considerations of reusable shuttlecraft-type vehicles based decisions over redundancy built on the mean-time-between-failure (MTBF) value expressed in hours, first of components and then of the on-board systems, which underpinned the design philosophy for the Space Shuttle. This in turn grouped risk into the sequential flow categories of fail-operational/fail-operational/fail safe, in that an initial malfunction would allow the mission objectives to be fulfilled while a second failure would secure the vehicle for an intact abort. Another example of how the X-15 pioneered a lot of the procedures and processes which became aerospace design standards over time.

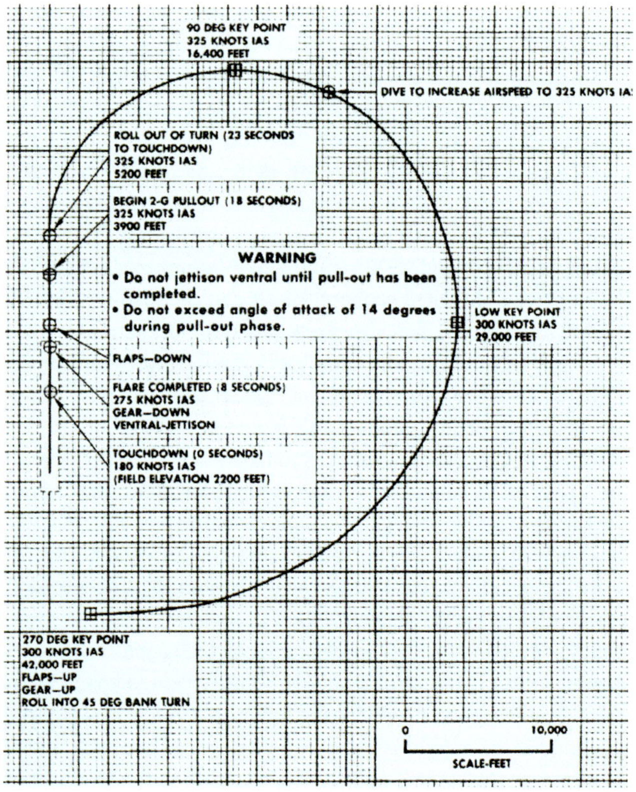

Below: A page from the X-15 Pilot's Handbook defining forced landing pattern limits to be adhered to following an emergency or an abort. *NAA*

Chapter Eighteen

Faster and Higher

The third X-15 industry conference was held in November 1961, the first since 1958. Closed to a public audience, it hosted 442 attendees from government agencies and a wide range of aerospace companies, universities and laboratories who heard 24 papers covering the first two years of flight operations. Research results were presented, along with status reports on the technical and engineering performance of the three vehicles and on the way the programme would continue to expand opportunities for flight research. There were also several comparative papers linking wind tunnel tests with in-flight results.

Many, listening to the scientists' and engineers' reported findings, were keen to know what had been learned about the boundary layer transition, at various speeds and different angles of attack. Early data proved that the level of heat transfer was much higher in the turbulence of the boundary than on a laminar wing. Information had been obtained by thermocouples and translated into heat transfer coefficients but later a special heat-sensitive paint applied to large areas had been used. With thermocouples on the starboard side and the paint on the port side, information was compared and the paint shown to be especially helpful as it presented a visual gradation in colour at the different temperatures.

The distribution of thermal maps clearly preserved in the various colour hues presented under different temperatures indicated that the spars and ribs served well as heat sinks, the expansion joints on the leading edge of the wings being concentrated heat zones. The paint proved especially useful on areas where it was difficult to mount thermocouples and after its first application for a flight with X-15-1 on 4 August 1960, it provided qualitative and highly useful information. For instance, it revealed wedge-shaped temperature patterns where the expansion joints caused temperatures of 537°C (1,000°F) as a result of the turbulence. Inconel X shields only 0.02cm (0.008in) thick were attached and this was shown to reduce the wedges but not to completely eradicate them.

An additional effect of the thermal wedges caused buckling behind the expansion joints and several solutions were offered, including additional fasteners which could be applied near each gap, or slot, and additional expansion slots, each with its own shield, which would be applied to various segments of the wing leading edge. There were technical and cost concerns with this because NAA had designed the wing with shear ties attached to the expansion slots and the optimum solution would have required a substantial re-engineering of the wing. Nevertheless, the limited shear tie modifications were effective and limited the amount of leading edge

Above: The NB-52 takes off with X-15-3 at the start of its flight with Bob White to an altitude of 95,936m (314,750ft) on 17 July 1962. *NASA*

buckling as measured.

The consequences of high temperatures on various parts of the structure were profound, given the increased heat load, eight times as high at Mach 6 as it is at Mach 3. This information was of very great interest to manufacturers with several supersonic projects on hand and a couple of hypersonic missile projects in development. Unanticipated temperature effects, first experienced on the side-fuselage fairing panels, had surprised some engineers, flight results showing unexpected results. It was apparent that different volumes of propellant remaining in the tanks at engine shut-down significantly affected the thermal gradients across the structure. This, in turn caused unexpected buckling and distortions, solved as the programme evolved with additional stiffeners and ties.

These modifications and structural measurements revealed areas where buckling might cause unacceptable deformations, with consequent impact on air flow and thermal gradients because of changes to the surface undulations, the boundary layer and its impact on adjacent laminar flow zones. To these areas too, heat-sensitive paint was applied and further flights helped define the magnitude and the variable nature of the challenge. Some areas were more affected than others, the speed brake actuators in particular, while localised heating was burning out wires in the wing roots and the tail surfaces.

It was also a concern that slight gaps in the nose landing leg doors were causing heat to penetrate and flow to hit the bulkhead dividing that compartment from the cockpit wall. In a particularly disturbing incident to X-15-2 on 23 June 1961, piloted by Bob White to a maximum Mach 5.27, the bulkhead heated to 288°C (550°F) and began to burn, sending smoke into the cockpit. To prevent a recurrence, an Inconel seal was applied to the rear face of the nose gear door with a baffle plate fixed to the bulkhead. There were prescient warnings here regarding the insidious manner in which hot air flow can penetrate even the smallest gap and cause interior damage potentially catastrophic to the vehicle itself and to the pilot.

The conference had been timely and looked forward to the next phase in which the MH-96 AFCS could be fully integrated and its performance analysed. It still held great relevance to future boost-glide vehicles and was only one of the reverse-transfers from the more ambitious Dyna-Soar programme which was itself expected to benefit from X-15 data. So far, the programme had kept pace with expectations, if not to the schedule initially laid down by the Air Force, the Navy and the NACA. Now, there were many more projects clamouring for funds and managers debated the next important steps.

Under the operations schedule, most personnel on the programme expected it to run to the end of 1964 and to log around 300 flights, significantly more than the 100 it had been expected to support at the beginning. Very few going back to work from the November 1961 conference would have predicted that it would survive for a further four years beyond

Right: NASA test pilot Neil Armstrong immediately after a flight in X-15-1, attended by technicians securing data cassettes and engineers eager to examine the condition of the vehicle, each flight a test of the X-15 itself. *NASA*

Below: Gathered around a recently returned X-15, technicians and engineers group together for a photo-record of their work on the programme. *NASA*

that predicted end date. By the end of 1961 the programme appeared in good shape, with X-15-3 on the flight-line and much research still to do. But 1962 would see a significant shift in the programme and bring an opportunity for advancing the state-of-the-art across engineering, technology and science.

The longest flight

The coming year was to see varied fortunes in the operational life of the X-15, beginning on 10 January 1962 with the only powered flight not to exceed Mach 1. On that day, Forrest Petersen launched from the B-52 over Mud Lake shortly after midday and proceeded to light up his XLR-99. It failed to fire and he could not get it to start on a second attempt.

Below: As the team sought ever-higher altitude flights it encountered the transition zone between aerodynamic and BCS attitude and directional control authority. Here on this chart, q expresses aerodynamic pressure and shows the boundary beyond which the BCS was to be used. The altitude is matched against speed in feet/second with the shaded zone denoting use of aero-surfaces for flight control. *NASA*

Below right: In further expression of the boundary between aero-surface and BCS control, the ordinate shows elapsed time for a high altitude flight and the solid line shows height over time. The dashed line expresses aerodynamic pressure (q) in pounds/square foot with the shaded section displaying the transition parameters. *NASA*

The objective had been to conduct a high angle-of-attack flight for aerodynamic heating tests but X-15-1 only achieved Mach 0.97 and came back to a landing at the contingency site of Mud Lake, the first time an X-15 had not returned to Rogers Dry Lake.

Petersen was already on assignment elsewhere and he left the programme as a career move and not at as a result of this aborted flight, which was not his fault. It had been the last flight of the X-15 by a Navy pilot and drew it further away from active participation in flight operations. X-15-1 was retrieved on the back of a truck and was returned to Edwards three days after the aborted flight. Checks showed no clear reason why the XLR-99 had twice failed to ignite but a minimal amount of repair was necessary and plans were laid to try another launch on 23 January. A ground run four days before that date prepared the aircraft and its engine but a day later Edwards was hit with rain and eventually snow.

Meanwhile, Neil Armstrong had flown his fourth launch on the type when he barrelled X-15-3 to Mach 5.51 after launch at Mud on 17 January and returned to Rogers. This was the last for more than two months as adverse weather set in, laying 30.5cm (12in) of snow across the lakebed but providing an opportunity to get all three X-15s in the hangar for maintenance and some sundry modifications. The weather worsened during mid-February and flight attempts did not resume before 29 March, the first of three successive attempts to launch on three consecutive days by Neil Armstrong in X-15-3. On two of those attempts, the launch had aborted due to minor technical issues with the platform and the MH-96.

Armstrong managed to evaluate these systems on his fifth attempt, with a successful launch on 5 April but only after a second attempt to ignite the engine for a test of the Q-ball at low and high dynamic pressures. Next on the flight-line, Walker flew X-15-1 on 19 April after an aborted attempt the day before, achieving Mach 5.69 but delivering no landing data as chase-pilot McKay had to abort. Next up was Armstrong's sixth flight, the first with X-15-3 carried by B-52 008 and one which notched another record, for the longest flight from launch to landing.

It began with take-off at 10:34hrs on 20 April followed by

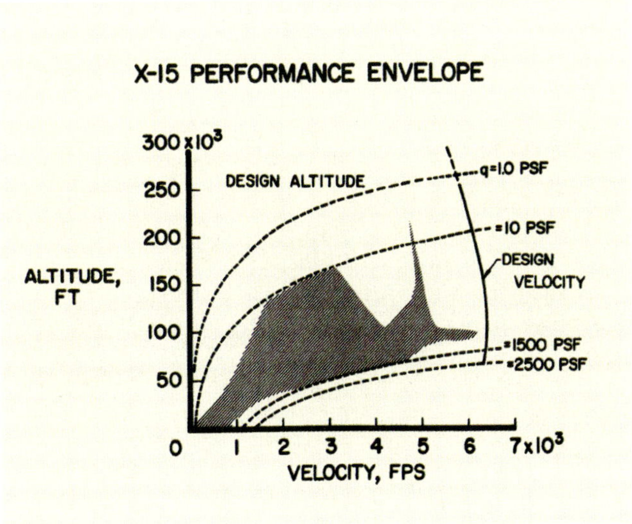

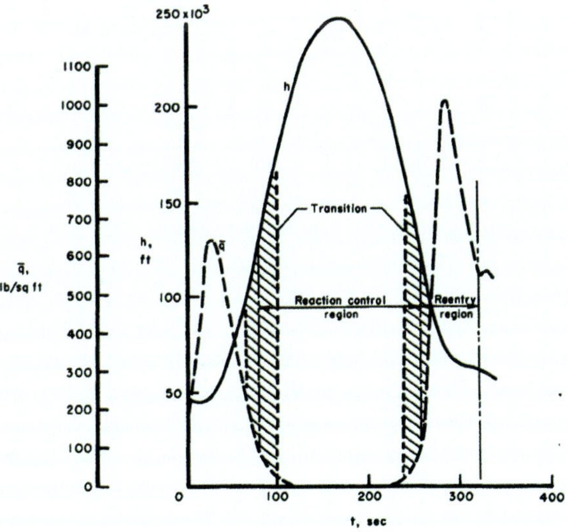

Above: A unique attempt to mount two launches in the same day on 4 November 1960 with Scott Crossfield in X-15-2, carried by *High and Mighty*, and Robert Rushworth in X-15-1 carried by *The Challenger*, failed when Crossfield experienced an APU-2 malfunction. Rushworth got in a productive flight. *NASA*

a launch at 11:26:58 over Mud Lake. Armstrong reached Mach 5.31 (6,096kph/3,789mph) and an altitude of 63,246m (207,500ft) to begin a standard re-entry profile to evaluate the MH-96 during a pre-planned sequence of manoeuvres. As he would report after the flight, Armstrong was impressed with its performance, asserting that the 'aircraft control and damping during ballistic flight and entry were outstanding, and considerably [smoother] than had been expected'. As he descended through 48,768m (160,000ft) the thruster jets' hydrogen peroxide supply low-level warning light came on at which point Armstrong switched to the transfer bleed supply from the APU turbopump supply.

As his altitude dropped through 35,052m (115,000ft), and he began a pull-out, Armstrong noticed that he was increasing altitude, albeit on a very shallow climb. Radar data showed this and Joe Walker instructed Armstrong to make a hard turn to the left, to lose speed and height and keep within the Rogers capture ellipse for a safe landing back at that location. But the X-15 failed to respond and after a second instruction to make another turn, Armstrong noticed that he was still climbing slightly and flying further away from Edwards. Very soon he was flying 30,480m (100,000ft) over Edwards at Mach 3 and heading in the wrong direction.

Confused, but calm, Armstrong waited for the X-15 to settle back down into the atmosphere. What he had experienced was a bounce back off denser layers of the atmosphere at the low angle-of-attack held on re-entry. This skip-effect would be used on hypervelocity re-entry trajectories for Apollo spacecraft returning from the Moon, effectively reducing the heat rate and spreading the load over a longer period. But if the angle was too shallow, it could cause the re-entry body to lift back out of the atmosphere, effectively causing it to bounce back into space. What Armstrong had experienced was a re-entry too shallow to allow the atmosphere to slow the X-15, effectively turning it into a flat stone sent at a shallow angle across the surface of a lake.

At the point where Armstrong was able to settle back into the denser layers of the atmosphere, the X-15 was 72km

Right: Frequently overlooked, the large contingent of support equipment and personnel to mount a single flight attracted a critical eye from administrators and budget managers. Here NASA's *Gooney Bird*, a Douglas R4D assigned to X-15 operations and but one of a relatively large fleet of support aircraft. *NASA*

Right: Neil Armstrong attends a test of the lake bed to ensure its ability to support the weight of an X-15 at touchdown as a steel ball is dropped from a height of 1.8m (6ft) to ensure a depth of no more than 7.3cm (3.25in) was created. *NASA*

(45mls) south of Edwards but with only just sufficient energy remaining in the vehicle to make it back to Rogers. But only through judicious energy-management after pondering the option of diverting to nearby Palmdale. That was undesirable due to the concrete runway, unforgiving on the X-15's landing skids and likely to cause a serious accident. Deciding on Rogers, Armstrong set up for a touchdown on the southernmost spot available, 19km (12mls) from the usual runway marked across the northern edge of the Lake.

Alerted to a potential accident, crash trucks and fire crews raced at breakneck speed across the distance separating the two locations as Armstrong calmly settled the X-15 down on runway 18 in a very normal and uneventful landing. But he had established two records: the longest miss-distance from the pre-planned touchdown point on a non-emergency flight, and the longest time an X-15 had been airborne: 12min 28.7sec. It had also flown a total of 461.1km (286.6mls) since launch.

Flights came and went over the next couple of months as operations took advantage of the useful period of the year when the weather was benignly quiescent and the landing lakes were accessible and open, important criteria for getting a launch. But 1962 will be remembered for several reasons, both in the X-15 programme and within the broader world of NASA's general activities. On 20 February, John Glenn became the first American to orbit the Earth, circling the globe three times.

The pressure was on to show politicians the progress being made across several activities and on 2 May X-15-3 was flown to Eglin AFB, Florida, for a live-fire demonstration for President Kennedy, the X-15 being placed on display as a further indication of national commitment to technological achievement. It was flown back on 5 May. Just 19 days later, Malcolm Scott Carpenter repeated Glenn's three-orbit flight around the Earth. On that flight he came close to running out of attitude control propellant, a reminder of how crucial it was to monitor quantities remaining in the tanks – for both spacecraft and spaceplanes!

June was a busy month for X-15 operations, six launches accomplished on six attempts, with the first launch from Delamar on 1st of the month, a test of manoeuvres planned for manned spacecraft returning from orbit on the 7th, further evaluation of the BCS on the 12th, the contractor's demonstration of the MH-96 on the 21st, an unofficial absolute speed record of Mach 5.92 on the 27th and a heating analysis at low angle-of-attack and low Mach number on the 29th.

Three aborted attempts by White followed, on the last of which another attempt was made to get two flights off on the same day. It was frustrated by the first but followed during the afternoon of the same day (16 July) with success when Joe Walker flew the programme's 61st launch in X-15-1. This

Above: X-15-2 turns on to finals around the alignment cylinder, the imaginary circle in the sky followed by the descending leg on an incoming trajectory to the flare point. *NASA*

flight was the first to accommodate the new instrument panel, which was now identical to the panel in the fixed base simulator, on a checkout of the SAS. It was also the last time an F-100 was used as chase with the X-15-1. Launched over Mud, it landed at Rogers but the ventral parachute failed.

High achiever

Throughout the programme, pilots continued to gain valuable insight on issues relating to visual acuity, attitude-sensory orientation between eye, brain and instrument displays and their intuitive awareness. No better example of that can be had than the successive attempts by Bob White to get an accurate attitude profile to replicate the pre-launch plan. Briefed at great length, it all became a little harder for X-15 pilots to precisely follow the speed/altitude/pitch, roll and yaw attitude orientations they had practised and simulated on the ground. White's flight was a classic case of dislocated orientation between physiological sensors in the human body and information displayed by a cockpit instrument.

During a flight in X-15-3 on 12 June 1962, Bob White was on course for a peak altitude of 62,789m (206,000ft) and all went well during the first part of the climb at a 32deg angle to the horizontal. Despite the instrument ball showing the correct climb angle, White was convinced that the X-15 was continuing to increase its pitch and climb angle. He responded to an overwhelming conviction that the aircraft was pitching at an ever increasing angle and that he had to get the nose down immediately. As he said later: 'I couldn't resist the urge just to push [the controller] on back down until the light blue of the sky showed up. I never did get to the horizon, but I was satisfied that it wasn't happening.'

In reality, White was climbing at the correct angle and maintaining 32deg, but in overriding the logic of a measured read-out he peaked out at 56,266m (184,600ft), far lower than the pre-planned profile, because he overrode the logic of his instrument displays and switched on his sensory responses. This had been foreseen to some extent by the physicians training Mercury astronauts, the intuitive awareness that sensory-driven responses would frequently override mechanical read-outs, potentially causing disorientation and coupled interactions between physical responses and measured information.

On the second attempt little more than a week later, White fought that inclination and reached 75,194m (246,700ft) but did note that it was 'reassuring again to hear ground saying

Right: X-15-3 venting in free flight. *NASA*

you're right on profile and track' and felt that this 'eliminates any concern on the pilot's part'. But he was still 1,005m (3,300ft) below the required altitude for this flight. On the third flight associated with this altitude phenomenon, on 17 July White had a height objective of 85,953m (282,000ft). In an attempt to overcome the under-runs on the first two flights, he pitched up to a slightly greater angle and had the advantage of an engine which produced a little above nominal thrust and burned a little longer at the assigned setting.

Those minor differences produced an altitude of 95,935m (314,750ft) which was acknowledged by the Fédération Aéronautique Internationale (FAI) as an international altitude record for atmospheric flight by a rocket-powered, winged flying machine. The Air Force had been striving for an altitude run above the height at which it qualified its pilots for astronaut wings and it got it, the first achieved with the X-15 and the first astronaut wings awarded to the pilot of a non-ballistic vehicle.

It was an achievement acknowledged the following day from the lawn of the White House when President Kennedy awarded the Collier Trophy to four X-15 pilots: Scott Crossfield, Forrest Petersen, Joe Walker and Bob White, each representing the four government agencies invested in the X-15 of which only the last two pilots were still in the programme. On that day too, White received his astronaut wings at a special event in the Pentagon. NASA hosted a dinner that evening for all four men during which Vice President Lyndon Johnson awarded each one with the Distinguished Service Medal and where administrator James Webb complimented the team on 'a classic example of a most effective way to conduct research'.

But there is a footnote. All 'astronaut' claims barring two flights made by Joe Walker above 80.45km (50mls) in 1963 were disallowed by the FAI, which decided that the neatly rounded altitude of 100km was the qualifying height for that category. Nevertheless, the Air Force and NASA still hold to the 80.45km (50mls) qualifying altitude. Strangely, NASA was reluctant to officially induct these into its official log of space flights, while admitting the two ballistic flights of Shepard and Grissom in 1961. Astronauts, it seems, do not ride rocket planes! But each flight involved a team and while the pilots got the trophies, they themselves were one part of a well-knit group who made these flights possible. Not only on the ground but in the air too.

Those usually side lined in popular histories of the X-15 include the valued team of chase pilots, without whom at least a few X-15 flights would not have ended successfully. A typical X-15 flight would involve four chase aircraft, with each covering specific segments and locations: Chase-1 would cover the pre-launch phase from take-off to the pre-launch systems and control surfaces checks; Chase-2 would support the launch of the X-15 and any abort; Chase-3 would be over the landing site covering pre-flare and flare and relaying any advisories; and Chase-4 was assigned to the Edwards landing area for following the descending aircraft, verifying ventral jettison, landing gear deploy and giving height to ground call-outs.

Various aircraft were assigned to these duties, Chase-1 would take off with the NB-52, usually flying an F-100 during the early flight tests, occasionally a F4D Skyray. Chase-2 and Chase 3 would invariably be found in an F-104 and would normally be an X-15 pilot or a NASA test pilot. Chase-4 would require an F-104 to keep up with the X-15 as it came around the alignment cylinder and on to the flare on the way down to a landing. It was during this period that the F-100 chase-plane was retired, replaced with the T-38 which had conducted a detailed simulation of that role against the NB-52.

There was a distinct advantage in the switch; the F-100 was unable to perform a right turn at 13,716m (45,000ft) because, at the release pattern, it was on the inside of the turn and that could only be conducted at a comparatively slower speed. The preferred left turn allowed the F-100 to keep pace by flying on the outside of the curve but in doing that it blocked telemetry signals until approximately two minutes prior to launch. The T-38 was not so compromised, allowing left turns without occulting the radio signal.

The first operational flight with the new T-38 was with X-15-1 on 26 July 1962, from which date it was almost always the prime chase plane. This was the last flight by Neil Armstrong in the X-15 before he departed for training as an astronaut. After this flight, X-15-1 was returned to Inglewood for modifications and for KC-1 camera equipment to be installed for optical degradation tests. It would not return for flight until April 1963.

On 9 November 1962 pilot Jack McKay flew X-15-2 on what should have been a heating research flight to Mach 5.55 and 38,100m (125,000ft). Commanding the throttle open to 100 per cent, McKay realised that the thrust level was stuck at 35 per cent and he shut it down at 70.5sec into the planned 90sec burn. Jettisoning most of the remaining propellant, he turned back to conduct an emergency landing at Mud Lake, a well-rehearsed procedure and one which should have seen a satisfactory landing. As he came in the flaps would not lower and he touched down at 476kph (295mph) which caused the left landing skid strut to dig in, collapse and turn the aircraft sideways, flipping it over. As it rolled, McKay jettisoned the

Above: Returning from a heating research flight in X-15-2 on 9 November 1962, John McKay had throttle problems with the XLR-99 and jettisoned propellants. In descending to an emergency landing at Mud Lake he was unable to deploy the flaps and touched down fast causing a skid to dig in and flip the aircraft over. *NASA*

Right: Suffering injuries that would remain with him for life, John McKay was extricated from beneath the upturned X-15-2 by digging out lakebed material. *NASA*

canopy but his head struck the ground first, compressing his spine, crushing several vertebrae and permanently reducing his height by 2.54cm (1in).

It was a lucky escape. Fire trucks and crash teams were quickly on the scene but toxic ammonia fumes venting from the crashed aircraft prevented them from getting to McKay until an H-21 pilot used the downwash from its rotating blades to keep the air clear where they worked. The teams dug a hole in the surface of the lake and pulled McKay out from underneath the forward fuselage. A C-130 landed nearby with paramedics who administered aid and flew McKay back to Edwards for hospitalisation. This was the only emergency rescue conducted during the programme.

An accident review board was appointed on 15 November and X-15-2 was returned to North American for a rebuild. The aircraft had completed its 31st flight, a log during which it had accumulated a flight time of 4hr 40min 32.2sec, with plenty of life remaining. The intention was to return it to flight readiness according to the original specification. But the Air Force had other ideas. It wanted to adapt the X-15 to extend the flight envelope from a design goal of Mach 6 to Mach 8, some 2,438m/sec (8,000ft/sec), and to modify the rebuilt X-15-2 vehicle to a platform for flight testing a hypersonic scramjet.

To achieve this higher speed the aircraft would have to carry more propellant for extending the burn duration of the XLR-99 rocket motor from 90 seconds to around 150 seconds. It was proposed that this additional propellant could be carried in two tanks, one either side of the fuselage and below each wing so that they could be jettisoned after the propellant they contained had been consumed before the internal tanks. Moreover, the aircraft would need to be longer by 73.7cm (29in) to accommodate a new compartment at the centre of gravity between the two inboard propellant tanks. The scramjet motor would be carried below the ventral fin and this would require extension of the landing gear skid

Above: By February 1964 the rebuilt X-15-2 was back at Edwards AFB under the re-designation X-15A-2, with a launch mass of 22,517kg (49,604lb) and the fuselage extended by 73.7cm (29in). *NASA*

legs to provide ground clearance at touchdown. The proposal anticipated that eventually the scramjet would operate at hypersonic speeds.

New targets

While NAA reworked the X-15-2 vehicle into a more capable research vehicle, NASA got on with the planned research programme and used the time to carry out some improvements and a few modifications which did not require a return to Inglewood of either aircraft. One of the problems concerned an in-flight failure of an APU on a flight with X-15-3 piloted by Rushworth on 4 October 1962 and again on the same aircraft piloted by Walker on 17 January 1963. These events are noteworthy since they were the only serious technical failure in the entire programme, prompting a special investigation by the Air Force, NASA and General Electric. The problem was discovered to be worn turbine shafts operating in a non-pressurised box at high altitude, solved by pressurising that area.

Improvements too were overdue in the configuration of the cockpit displays which, after modifications to match the simulator, was improved to ease the pilot's workload. Over time, from mid-1963 several changes were visibly noticeable, including the colour to a grey rather than the black panel on initial displays. This did improve visual acuity and helped pilots distinguish the instrument readings with greater clarity and speed, the latter being an important rating used by physiological testers to rate an individual's ability to respond quickly and accurately to changes on the displays. Optometric studies indicated that eyeball contact would achieve the same result within 0.3 seconds compared with an equivalent reading against a black panel of 0.7 seconds.

During the 1960s, pilots and astronauts held ratings through a 'blink-box' test in which the subject immerses his head inside a black box, the only illumination being a light panel which can be controlled from the outside to flash at different durations measured in fractions of a second and with various brightness and contrast levels. Inside the box, the representative instruments can only be seen when lit from the panel. This tests the speed at which the subject's brain can react, defined as the ability of the subject to remember and note down what they saw as a measure of accuracy and perspicacity.

Physiologists observed that the ability to register instrument readings in a fraction of a second is an innate reaction and pilots are broadly divided into separate categories: those who see the entire range of instruments but can recall each with an error of +/-20 per cent of the true value, and those who see only a few selected instruments but with an error of +/-2 per cent. It was found that the majority of the latter category can control their attention when focused on to selected instruments but that those who 'see' a wider distribution of dials cannot train themselves to focus on just a select group whenever the light comes on.

During the early 1960s, physiologists at the Lovelace Clinic tested both men and women candidates for test pilot and astronaut selection and divided these groups into male and female test subjects. The majority of women recorded a wider range of visual cues but, in recall, had less accuracy on

Above: The X-15-2 suffered a burst tyre on touchdown after the nose leg deployed at Mach 4.2 on 14 August 1964, leaving two disc-cutters to lay grooves in the desert floor. *NASA*
Above right: Heat tests on a redesigned nose leg on X-15-2. *NASA*

any one, while men tended to have fewer visual cues that they could recall yet see certain selected fields with greater accuracy. The ability to train the eye-brain coordination to focus attention on to selected instruments provided an opportunity to align that onto intuitive hand movements with the control stick or side-controller.

None of this had been examined when the X-15 programme began but a decade on, and with particular emphasis on human physiology in high-performance vehicles, there was a two-way transfer of knowledge to better understand the way the eye, the brain and the subjective performance decisions made in the cockpit would improve the performance of the pilot. This was one of several research activities conducted during early learning, in which it was believed that routine flights in and out of the atmosphere would be commonplace by the 1970s.

In a more direct sense, adhering to the fundamental objectives of the programme, the X-15 continued to explore the aerothermal environment and sometimes exposed certain flaws in the original design. One of those concerned the introduction of a Reaction Augmentation System (RAS) which, along with the SAS, was seen to be an advantage when tested in the fixed base simulator, as briefly discussed in Chapter 13. This was a classic example of reviews and decisions made before the flight programme began which had to be modified and significantly changed with accumulated flight experience. Installed in X-151-1 and X-15-2 during 1963, most of that year and the next were spent in filtering out any sympathetic frequencies in the X-15 itself.

As had been assigned to Bob White in the previous year, in 1963 Joe Walker was tasked by the Air Force with obtaining flight results from very high altitude runs to a peak of 109,728m (360,000ft). Some debate had surrounded the proposition that the X-15 would be capable of executing a re-entry from 121,920m (400,000ft) and a margin was built in to compensate for an engine over-burn or a higher thrust than calculated pre-flight. These errors could attract dangerous consequences and White's 1962 attempts at high altitude flight had demonstrated the amount which had still to be learned from pilot perception and precision flight profiles.

The actual altitude achieved, versus that planned before the flight, had greater determinants than variables through human error, however. A one-second overrun on the predicted engine burn would increase altitude by a further 1.219m (4,000ft) and a change in the climb angle of one degree would increase height by 2,286m (7,500ft). That latter altitude surge was the same amount which would be added to the planned height if the thrust dispersion was only half as great as that experienced on previous flights, where some engines provided an additional 13,344N (3,000lb) of thrust.

A significant flaw within the X-15 operating envelope was the unpredictability of the engine in both thrust level and controllability. It was during this period that considerable development work was under way to provide restartable and throttleable rocket motors for critical space missions, most notably the two main propulsion systems on the Grumman Lunar Module for going down to the surface of the Moon and for returning to lunar orbit for rendezvous with the Apollo spacecraft. There was great interest from engine manufacturers on the performance of the RMI XLR-99 and its operation was viewed with more than a little interest. But that is another story.

All three factors of overrun, change in climb angle and a thrust dispersion converged for Walker's first attempt in X-15-3 on 19 July 1963 when he was aiming for 96,012m

(315,000ft) and overshot by 9,997m (32,800ft). Launched from Smith Ranch due to the distance which would be flown, 464.2km (288.5mls), the engine ran hot for 84.6sec and the climb angle was 0.5deg too high. Three more attempts in the first half of August were aborted due to weather problems and some technical malfunctions. But the attempt did launch on 22 August when Walker made his last flight in the X-15 aiming for a peak altitude of 109,728m (360,000ft).

The flight was routine with no significant anomalies, except when one of the BCS thrusters iced up, as Walker achieved an all-time X-15 record altitude of 107,960m (354,200ft). The return through the outer atmosphere produced the usual 5-g deceleration while the aircraft flew down a 45deg flight path before Walker levelled out at around 21,336m (70,000ft). Consistently, the Air Force had worked with NASA on re-entry profiles supporting trajectories for piloted, winged, air vehicles. Much of this was to support plans for an era of boost-glide vehicles such as the X-20 but that vehicle was cancelled five months after Walker's flight. The two events were unrelated but at the time of its cancellation, X-20 pilots were aligned with checkout flights on the X-15.

In just over a month after Walker's flight in X-15-3, X-15-1 was back on the flight-line for a launch on 7 October 1963. Employed in its traditional role checking out a new pilot, Joe Engle conducted a flight to Mach 4.21 (4,560kph/2,834mph). Next up was Milton Thompson's first checkout flight in X-15-1 on 29 October. Along with Rushworth, these two pilots would conduct all X-15 flights until joined by McKay in March 1964. Those four were exclusively assigned to the type until joined by Bill Dana and Bill Knight toward the end of 1965 and Mike Adams in October 1966.

When the X-15 programme began there were assumptions made about the operational life of the programme and many thought that it should be supported through 1964 and probably no longer. But the accident to McKay and the rebuilding of X-15-2 gave new purpose to a programme in which the distinction between the three airframes was becoming greater with each passing year. The overall body shape of all three remained the same but there were differences under the skin which provided unique capabilities with each vehicle; now that X-15-2 was being repurposed for higher speeds, those difference were more noticeable.

In several respects, the aircraft was bearing the scars of high temperature, high speed and high altitude flights and each was displaying patches and reworked outer skins which bore the hallmarks of those demanding objectives. Along the way too, several adaptations were necessary to improve the data-rate for the wide range of measurements from its increased performance. Various recording devices designed in to the original airframes were becoming increasingly incapable of capturing all the required parameters. Because all the recorders were analogue devices, and because there was limited space for optimum equipment, tape recorders were frequently used instead. When larger oscillograph devices were installed there was better quality of data, with greater accuracy, but less of it.

An addition during 1964 was not exclusively aligned with the X-15 programme but it was stimulated by the expanding amount of work into measuring flight loads on aircraft designed for supersonic and hypersonic speeds. Known as the High-Temperature Loads Calibration Laboratory, it was installed in Building 4820 and provided for a wide range of loads and temperatures applied to structural component test sections or to complete aircraft. The facility was 45.7m (150ft) long, 36.5m (120ft)wide and 12.2m (40ft) high with an entrance door 41.4m (136ft) wide and the full height of the laboratory. It incorporated the latest advancements in control techniques and data acquisition equipment and closed-circuit TV.

With hydraulic systems, 34 actuators for applying loads to structures, it was equipped with infrared quartz lamps with heating systems capable of imposing temperatures of up to 1,649°C (3,000°F) on a wide range of materials and airframe sections. Its primary function was to calibrate strain-gauge installations and test components but it played a useful role in the XB-70 and SR-71 programmes, where high loads and temperatures were anticipated. It proved its worth late in the operational flight test phase where it was used to prepare for very high temperature runs with the redefined X-15A-2.

Envelope expansion

Throughout 1963 and much of 1964, the flight programme planned for an expanded operational capability, raising the speed through the significant changes made to the X-15-2. This radical upgrade in performance capability was strongly opposed by many NASA engineers and programme personnel but the Air Force pressed their case and approval was given to ask the contractor to modify the aircraft during rebuild so that it would be capable of carrying out this advanced evolution. On 13 May 1963 North American Aviation had been awarded a contract worth $4.75million to return the original aircraft to flight status with modifications.

It was delivered back to the Flight Research Center on 15 February 1964 as X-15A-2. Between those dates a very different X-15 was produced as the most significant technical evolution of the entire programme. Much of what the Air Force anticipated was a vehicle capable of testing an air-breathing Hypersonic Research Engine (HRE). The performance requirement stipulated a speed of 8,777kph (5,454mph) at an altitude of 30,480m (100,000ft), anticipating a maximum dynamic pressure of 47.5kPa (6.9lb/in^2) and a maximum temperature of 712°C (1,315°F).

The overall dimensions of the X-15A-2 were the same as the other aircraft, except the fuselage was 73.6cm (29in) longer produced by a plug at the centre of gravity between the two integral propellant tanks. The most significant visual difference, however, were the two jettisonable propellant tanks, one either side of the fuselage, which would provide 70 per cent more propellant and an additional 60 seconds of burn time at full throttle. It also incorporated three helium tanks with a total capacity of 0.238m^3 (8.4ft^3) for pressurisation, located inside the aft sections of the extended side fairings. An extra spherical helium tank was installed to the rear of the vertical stabiliser for pressurisation. Changes were also necessary

Above and right: X-15A-2 would make eleven flights without drop tanks from 14 August 1964, the first with the tanks attached taking place on 3 November 1965 as a qualification of the jettison procedure. Despite the amount of work carried out to rebuild the airframe and provide additional propellant capacity, the aircraft came up against the thermal effects of high-Mach flight which would limit its capabilities. *NASA*

to accommodate higher temperatures on the windshield, the trapezoidal frames on the original X-15-2 being replaced with elliptical windows consisting of three panes of glass: the outer pane of 1.65cm (0.65in) fused silica; the middle pane of 0.95cm (0.375in) alumino-silicate glass; the inner pane a 0.74cm (0.29in) laminated soda lime glass block.

NAA also extended the rear landing gear struts by 17.1cm (6.75in) which provided an 83.8cm (33in) clearance between the bottom of the ventral fin and the ground. These struts were also capable of withstanding an additional landing weight of 454kg (1,000lb). Addressing concerns that this aft leg extension would cause potential problems when the nose came down on touchdown, the nose gear leg trunnion was mounted 22.9cm (9in) lower, thus compensating for the higher aft end.

The fuselage was modified to incorporate two doors, 50.8cm (20in) in length and 21.6cm (8in) wide, opening upward to allow access to a compartment immediately behind the cockpit where cameras and a range of instruments could be located. There was also provision for additional data recorders, five 36-channel oscillographs, eight 3-channel oscillographs, two 14-track tape recorders, one 24-cell manometer and a cockpit camera. All this was supported by an 86-channel PCM telemetry system for sending data to the ground.

The drop-tanks were each 7.16m (23.5ft) in length with a diameter of 95.88cm (37.75in), attached to the fuselage by fixtures within the side fairings. Propellant and gas disconnect lines carried fluids from the tanks to the interior of the fuselage, secured by disconnects after the tanks had been jettisoned, which had to take place before the aircraft reached a speed of Mach 2.6. The left tank attached to the port side of the fuselage had an empty weight of 521.6kg (1,150lb) and carried 3,001lit (793USgall) of liquid oxygen for an all-up weight of 4,046kg (8,920lb). The right tank on the starboard fuselage side weighed 294kg (648lb) empty and held 4,087.8lit (1,080USgall) of fuel with a loaded weight of 3,107kg (6,850lb).

The desired performance increment from the additional burn time was partly diminished by the additional mass carried to provide the extra speed, reducing the estimated maximum velocity to between 2,316m/sec (7,600ft/sec) and 2,347m/sec (7,700ft/sec), 91.4-122m/sec (300-400ft/sec) be-

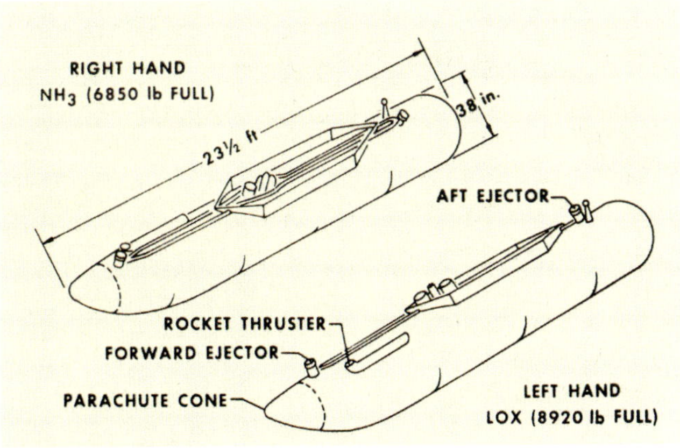

Above: The external tanks contained an additional 70 per cent of propellant for the XLR-99, increasing burn time from about 90 to 150 seconds. *NAA*

low the desired value. With the ventral HRE taking the place of the lower rudder, the associated drag would reduce the speed still further to a maximum 2,194m/sec (7,200ft/sec). Instead of achieving a desired 8,775kph (5,454mph), calculations showed that the X-15A-2 would do well to reach 7,898kph (4,909mph). Nevertheless, the additional velocity increment would carry the ramjet test platform to a significant percentage of the optimum speed sought by the Air Force.

When the re-designated X-15A-2 was accepted by the Air Force on 17 February 1964 and delivered back to Edwards from North American's Inglewood facility, it was about 350.6kg (773lb) overweight. It had a launch mass of 22,517kg (49,640lb) of which 14,629kg (32,250lb) was in propellant, 42 per cent of which was carried in the external tanks. Without the external tanks, it made a new captive flight on 15 June, followed 10 days later by its first launch in the new configuration, a flight piloted to Mach 4.59 by Rushworth using only 77 per cent thrust output. The new external propellant tanks would not be attached until November 1965 but Rushworth reported the handling characteristics to be close to those of the unmodified aircraft, with longitudinal trim relatively unchanged at up to 15deg angle of attack.

The second powered flight of the X-15A-2 exposed an unintended consequence of pushing against the heat barrier when thermal expansion of the airframe caused the landing gear release cable to stretch and deploy the nose leg prematurely. The pilot was Robert Rushworth and the incident occurred on 14 August as he was decelerating through Mach 4.2, on his way back from Mach 5.23 and a maximum altitude of 31,486m (103,300ft). Rushworth felt a jolt similar to that experienced at gear deploy just before a normal landing but he was not immediately aware that this was the reason. Nevertheless, as smoke began to fill the cockpit he was aware that the gear door must be open and that some part of the aircraft was melting as heat bled in through the gap.

Rushworth was concerned to get the aircraft down as soon as possible but advice from chase pilot Bob McKay was to stay at high altitude as long as possible and allow the front end to cool down. Descending toward the Rogers landing site Joe Engle flying Chase-3 in an F-104 confirmed the state of the nose leg, seemingly down and locked but with almost no tyres remaining. Uncertain as to what would happen when the nose leg came down, Rushworth made a near perfect landing, cutting four very neat grooves in the desert floor where the rim walls of the two wheels cut furrows as the leg remained undamaged.

Undeterred by his experience, Rushworth returned the X-15A-2 to flight on 29 September, but this time the nose gear scoop door came open at Mach 4.5! As a result, several modifications were made to the nose gear and equipment. On 17 February 1965 Rushworth was again in the cockpit when the right main skid deployed at Mach 4.3 descending through 25,908m (85,000ft). He made a good landing, got out and kicked the aircraft. Thermal expansion had again exposed a vulnerable part of the design.

In all, eleven flights were made with the X-15A-2 before empty jettisonable propellant tanks were attached for an evaluation flight on 3 November 1965 with the tanks jettisoned at Mach 2.25 as planned and a landing at Rogers Dry Lake after a peak speed of Mach 2.31. In an attempt to reuse the jettisonable tanks, each had a drogue parachute and a main descent parachute designed to release on activation at an altitude of 2,438m (8,000ft). On this flight, the tanks appeared not to execute a nose-down attitude when released. Tumbling as they fell, the drogue retardation parachute on the LOX tank failed to deploy resulting in its loss on impact. Nevertheless, the fully mated assembly checked out and preparations got under way to begin the expansion phase into the high-Mach regime.

Ablative barriers

The fourth X-35 industry conference was held on 7 October 1965 which, judging by its size reflected less interest in the programme, although 500 people turned up to the event. However, only 13 papers were presented covering about 150 flights where the X-15 had accomplished most of its objectives and

Right: Robert Rushworth and X-15A-2 prepare for the first flight with external tanks attached for a dash to Mach 2.31. The two tanks separated as planned and the ammonia tank was recovered but the LOX tank was destroyed when its parachute failed to deploy. *NASA*

Right: Heat-sensitive paint applied to the vertical stabiliser provided a thermal map to show, in greater definition than was possible with point-sensors, the graduated changes in temperature caused by friction with the atmosphere. *NASA*

Below right: The thermal paint was applied to the left side of the aircraft with thermocouples on the right side to provide comparative data. *NASA*

since 1963 the aircraft had itself been a carrier for science and engineering experiments. Representatives from NASA field centres were there as well as several Air Force organisations but this was the last X-15 industry conference, although papers would continue to emerge as the results were analysed and increasingly incorporated in additional research activity.

By the end of 1965 operations at Edwards were deterred by high levels of precipitation, the annual cycle of bad weather affording opportunity for some modifications and improvements to all three X-15s. Included was a new instrument panel from Lear Siegler incorporating vertical-scale displays and changes were made to the wiring. The new displays received mixed responses from the pilots, not all happy with the new configuration. Other changes included wiring for wing-tip experiment pods and a third skid to accept the higher weights anticipated by the increasing range of science payloads.

Major maintenance was required on the NB-52B carrier-plane and this was sent off to Tinker AFB for that and after it returned to Edwards on 8 April, NASA and the Air Force spent a couple of months equipping it for the heavier X-15A-2. At this stage of the programme, each X-15 was limited to altitude ceilings defined by analysis of simulations at their different, increased weights and maximum dynamic pressure. X-15A-2 would be limited to a maximum altitude of 76,200m (250,000ft), X-15-1 to 80,772m (265,000ft) and X-15-3 to 109,728m (360,000ft). These were largely academic as the high-altitude flights had for the most part been completed, except for the additional tests sought for X-15-3 with the MH-96.

Launched on 1 July 1966, Rushworth's last flight in the programme was the first flight with full external propellant tanks. The engine received propellant via on-board tanks, fed from the external tanks until they were depleted and could be jettisoned. Simulation of a worst-case scenario held that if propellant from one of the tanks began to transfer and not the other it would cause an irrecoverable roll calling for the pilot to jettison both tanks. Having verified that propellant jettison was working from the external tanks, Rushworth dropped away.

Seconds later, Jack McKay in Chase-1 reported that the ground could not see any fuel flow into the fuselage tank. Rushworth shut down the engine and jettisoned the flanking tanks and prepared for an emergency descent into Mud Lake. The tanks were not supposed to be jettisoned full but a faulty electrical circuit caused that to happen, the fuel tank briefly hanging up on the fuselage and scarring the side as it rotated and broke the fixture. Rushworth's departure came after he had flown 34 launches in six years. After four flights by William McKnight in X-15A-2, Rushworth was replaced by Maj. Michael J. Adams who would make his first flight on 6 October 1966.

That winter, the flight programme stood aside as the weather did its annual rotation, sending rain and puddles to the 'dry' lakes. But 1967 would prove eventful for two reasons, each of which stand out as seminal flights: the only re-entry flown without any dampers after a total loss of electrical power, and the introduction of a thermal ablative coating on X-15A-2 for its high-speed runs.

The first of these occurred on 29 June when Knight was launched in X-15-1 on a flight planned to achieve Mach 5.7 and a maximum altitude of 76,200m (250,000ft), the type's 73rd flight. It began at 10:22hrs when B-52 008 took off and climbed to the drop altitude followed by a launch at 11:27:51.2hrs over Smith Ranch followed by the start of the powered run. As he climbed through 24,384m (80,000ft) and noted a speed of 3,401kph (2,113mph) the engine suddenly quit, 67.6sec after ignition. In his post-flight report, Knight reported how he felt comfortable with the flight and had settled in to the climb:

'Things were looking real good and I was really enjoying the flight. All of a sudden, the engine went "blurp" and quit. There could not have been two seconds between the engine quit and everything else happening because it all went in or-

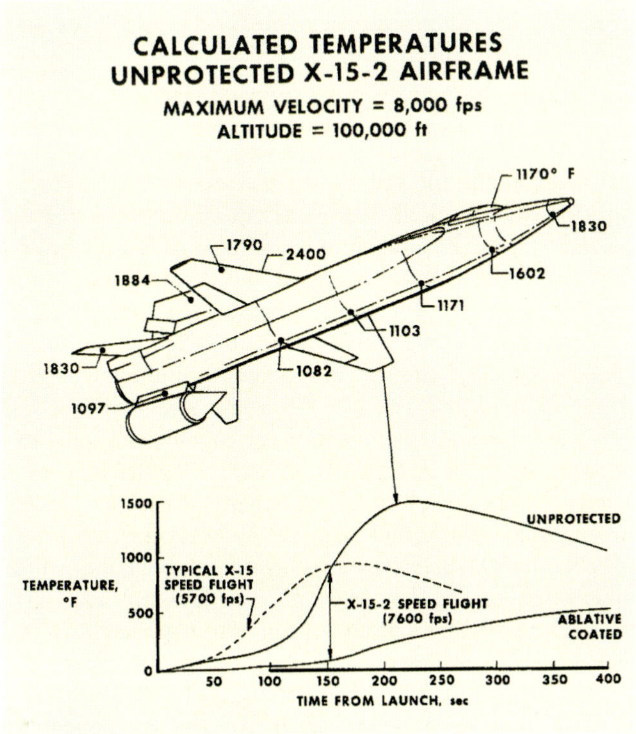

Above: Expanding the envelope to include flights above Mach 7 would require thermal protection from an ablative coating applied to the entire external area. *NASA*

der. The engine shut down. All three SAS lights came on. Both generator lights came on and then there was another light came on, and I think it was the fuel low line light. I am not sure. Then after all the lights got on, they all went out. Everything quit. By this time, I was still heading up and the airplane was getting pretty sloppy. As far as I am concerned both APUs quit.'

The nightmare scenario for X-15 pilots was a total power shut-down, including hydraulics, without any means of controlling the aircraft and this, it seemed, was what had happened. As the aircraft rolled slightly Knight could see the Mud Lake emergency site below and was considering when he should eject. Peaking at 52,730m (173,000ft) he began to fall back through the atmosphere and tried regaining control with the BCS. Unsure whether the thrusters were working, he switched to the emergency battery and tried to restart the APUs.

One APU came back on line and Knight flew a 6-g turn onto the eastern end of the emergency landing point, setting the aircraft down for what appeared to all the world as the perfect end to a normal flight! Rolling to a stop and unattended by ground crew, after several attempts Knight managed to get the canopy open but then had trouble removing the connectors with the head rest installed. Removing his helmet he pulled the emergency release which caused the rest to eject, strike the canopy and fall back down on his unprotected head!

Another day at the office…

Meanwhile, preparations were nearing completion with X-15A-2 for an evaluation of the ablative coating. Before that, the first flight in which full tanks operated as planned occurred on 18 November 1966 when Knight reached Mach 6.33 with instrumentation verifying the propellant flow quantities. Following this, a new cover was installed over the window in the left side of the canopy and a dummy scramjet shape was prepared and installed on the lower vertical stabiliser, the jettisonable portion of which had been removed to allow sufficient ground clearance with it installed.

Temperature simulation was an important factor in predicting the thermal load which would be imposed by the higher Mach number and this task was aided by use of the Dyna-Soar simulator at the Air Force Flight Test Center. This allowed engineers to observe the temperature effects from aft of the nose gear door for a simulated flight to Mach 7.6 at 30,480m (100,000ft) and to compare those results with known temperature levels experienced by an actual flight to Mach 6.

The thermal map thus provided was sobering to view. Designed to run to a maximum of Mach 6.5, the total thermal load on the underside of the nose at this speed was about 2,424kj/hr (2,300Btu) with the leading edge of the wing absorbing 10,013kj/hr (9,500Btu). At Mach 8 these figures would rise to 13,700kj/hr (13,000Btu) and 28,985kj/hr (27,500Btu) respectively. Flights to verify the new configuration would initially be conducted with empty tanks and then with full tanks before the high-speed runs could begin. For those flights the aircraft would need some additional thermal protection.

During the decade prior to the modifications to X-15A-2, scientists and engineers had experimented with heat-sink versus ablative thermal coatings for ballistic missile warheads and for manned space vehicles. The Dyna-Soar concept had employed heat-sink materials while the manned Mercury capsule used both heat-sink and ablative shields. Long before the accident to X-15-2, the programme had tested various ablative samples, starting with a patch of Avcoat No. 2 attached to the leading edge of the starboard wing for a flight to Mach 4.3 on 4 October 1961. A derivative would be selected for the heat shield on the Apollo spacecraft. An ablative covering

Right: An ablative coating developed by The Martin Company was applied to the ventral stabiliser on X-15A-2 for a test on 18 May 1966 piloted by Robert Rushworth. *NASA*

Above: Meticulous attention to the depth of the applied ablative coating was essential to maintain weight growth within calculated limits.
Below: The ablation coating gave the X-15A-2 a unique appearance, but this was soon to be hidden by application of the thermal emissivity layer. *NASA*

over the entire exterior surface of the X-15 would be the solution to its survival above Mach 6.5.

Initially, NAA chose a material produced by Emerson Electric known as Thermolag 500. It could be applied with a spray gun and came in considerably below the weight of 181.4kg (400lb) allowed for the thermal protection system over the whole aircraft. While passing all the required criteria, and proving it could provide satisfactory thermal protection, it was rejected due to the extended curing time which was unfavourable for its application over such large areas.

A joint NASA/Air Force evaluation team set up in late 1963 examined 15 contenders and samples of these were tested on the other two aircraft. A separate NASA ablator was developed at the Langley facility as a back-up and some surprises surfaced when flight results showed up deficiencies in a large number of products, particularly when the gap between ground testing and flight testing was, once again, seen to be too long. It took some time to work through the evaluations, three commercial contenders and the NASA material in the final run, before a product from Martin Marietta was selected in January 1966.

Known as MA-25S it had a density of 448kg/m^3 (28lb/ft^3) and could be sprayed and cured at room temperature.

Developed by the company over several years before the need arose for the X-15 programme, MA-25S had been used as a gap-filler for seams and access panels, which were sealed prior to flight, on re-entry research vehicles such as the X-23A PRIME. A few samples were flown in strategic locations on an X-15A-2 flight to Mach 5.43 on 18 May 1966 and proved satisfactory, although some sensors installed to record critical data failed.

Application of the ablator required the aircraft to be thoroughly cleaned, with all gaps, joints and seams tightly sealed, a task which required significant quantities of solvent to remove the black lacquer, stencil marks and any other applications to the skin of the aircraft. Powdered cleaner was applied and tape was laid down to mask seams and seals which would have to be broken open in preparing the vehicle for flight. For ablator application the entire surface had been divided up into nine areas, polythene sheets covering eight of those while individual sections were worked on. A commercial spray gun was then used to coat the aircraft, a major difficulty emerging with control of depth and density during application. As the team worked on through each section, their effectiveness improved and the work got easier.

When the entire aircraft had been covered the masking tapes were removed, but not without a little difficulty, and the ablative material was allowed to cure at room temperature for several hours. Overall, the thickness tolerance was a staggeringly thin +/-0.051cm (+/-0.020in) but still the aircraft came out with the ablator weighing 56.7kg (125lb) more than expected, which further reduced the predicted speed with scramjet attached to about Mach 7. Preparation was completed after the surface was sanded and a layer of Dow Corning DC90-090 RTV applied to the entire surface, sealing in the ablator. The MA-25S had a pinkish hue when dry and the sealant gave the aircraft an overall white appearance, although in low sunlight some areas retained a hint of pink. NASA requested another layer to give a better and more uniform white appearance, justified on grounds of thermal emissivity.

The first flight with the full ablator was made on 21 August 1967 with Knight at the controls and the external tanks off but with the scramjet simulator installed. Some fogging of the right window pane occurred due to outgassing from the ablator as the aircraft hit Mach 4.94. Some damage was recorded to a few sections of the ablator but it clearly worked as expected and Martin Marietta technicians readied the surface coating for the start of the programme's expansion phase, the high-speed runs for which it had been prepared. That flight occurred on 3 October 1967 which, although unsuspected at the time, would be the last flight of the X-15A-2, but not without consequences.

The flight began with the NB-52B carrying X-15A-2 to a height of 13,335m (43,750ft) for an early afternoon launch. It weighed 23,640kg (52,117lb). Knight ignited the XLR-99 at 12deg angle of attack and, holding right deflection on the stick to prevent it rolling over to port from the heavier LOX tank, slowly pitched back to a 35deg angle. Little more than a minute after the drop the aircraft was accelerating through Mach 2.4 and 22,037m (72,300ft) as he slowly nosed over,

Below: August 1967 and the definitive white coating is complete as X-15A-2 is posed for a shot outside the hangar at Edwards AFB. *NASA*

Above: With a dummy scramjet shroud attached, the X-15A-2 begins a run after release from the NB-52A on 21 August 1967, the first time in full ablative coating with drop tanks. *NASA*

jettisoned the external tanks and, accelerating more rapidly now, levelled out at 31,090m (102,100ft), shutting down at a burn duration of 140.7 seconds, the radar data confirming a maximum speed of Mach 6.7, or 7,273kph (4,520mph).

Throughout this phase, and unknown during the flight, the aircraft had been severely damaged and the hydrogen peroxide light came on prompting a request from the ground for him to jettison the remaining amount. Then he found it impossible to jettison the residual propellants from the on-board tanks and, high on energy, he began his descent, finding no verification that he had safely jettisoned the dummy scramjet. Jettisoned propellant was the way a chase pilot got a visual, identifying the tiny aircraft at the head of a streaking plume of bright vapour. He would be coming in hot, high and alone and with chase advising on the condition and the gear deployment.

As the crew converged on his aircraft after a successful landing and rollout they raced to the back of the X-15 where substantial parts of the ventral fin had burned through and skins had been rolled back in the intense heat. It transpired that shock waves from the dummy scramjet had impinged on the ventral fin and focused thermal energy on the outer surface. But the dummy scramjet was nowhere to be seen. It was found later where some careful calculations predicted it to be.

The high-speed run had been a close-run brush with disaster. Parts of the aircraft had begun to melt away, the shock waves had burned through the leading edge of the lower ventral fin setting off fires in the engine bay and heat had fired the scramjet separation charges at Mach 1, sending it to the ground from 9,753m (32,000ft) over the Edwards range. Heat had destroyed the helium lines preventing the propellant from being jettisoned and a large amount of damage had been caused by buckling as the structure resisted the enormous amount of heat generated when the vehicle passed through the air at almost seven times the speed of sound.

Left: The second and last flight of the X-15A-2 with full ablation and carrying external tanks was completed on 4 October 1967. Knight achieved Mach 6.7, the highest speed in the programme, but came back with a partially melted ventral stabiliser. *NASA*

Chapter Nineteen

Tragedy and Closure

After Knight's record-breaking flight on 3 October 1967, a considerable amount of analysis went into the post-flight examination of both the flight and the X-15A-2 itself. Much information had not been recorded during the flight that could have been of immense value in these processes. The inadequacy of the technology extant in the late 1960s and the burn-through of several sensor points on that vehicle added to the challenge of piecing together the details. The flight had gone according to plan for the trajectory and the flight plan had run close to the pre-flight prediction. But a series of failures due to unforeseen interactions between the shock waves and the thermal effects of high speed altered the sequence for descent and landing. And that brought concern when the physical state of the aircraft had been examined.

The contractor Martin Marietta expressed the honest judgement of its scientists and engineers in what was an admission of inadequate modelling: 'The actual flight environment in the area of the modified ventral fin proved to be much more severe than anticipated. The condition was directly attributable to interaction effects of the shock waves generated by the dummy ramjet, the ventral, and the pressure probes. The ablator applications in this area were inadequate to protect the structure under these flow conditions, and the vehicle suffered localized damage in the area.'

This had been the result of erosion in the ablator on the ventral stabiliser and damage to the skin had been caused by high heat loads in the areas of shock impingement. The leading edge of the ventral fin had burned through and on either side of the torque box assembly. Wiring and pressure lines had been destroyed but the thermocouples indicated that much of the first 140sec of motor burn caused a progressive erosion and that at 160sec all protection had gone and that the structure was burning through. Particle debris from the destroyed areas of ablator directly impinged on layers further away causing damage there too. All ablation material had burned away from the lower speed brakes and there was considerable erosion of the material on the underside of the fairing tunnels.

Because of the pitched-up attitude of the flight vector, the underside of the fuselage and the wings had greater exposure to higher temperatures than the upper surfaces, the obverse being the case with the horizontal stabilisers. Patterns of ab-

Above: Together on 4 August 1967, two aircraft which would end up in the National Museum of the US Air Force but which, for a while, were united in a concept to fly the X-15 (foreground) off the top of the XB-70. *NASA*

Above: Maj. Michael J. Adams had his first flight in the X-15 on 6 October 1966 and made his seventh flight on 15 November 1967 when he was killed. *NASA*

lation were easily spotted adjacent to orifices causing disruption to flow and local stagnation, for instance where the pressure orifices in the ball nose were located and around the openings for the BCS thrusters. Also affected were stacks and vents causing heating problems, with stagnation and trailing-wake damage from doors and access panels. There was blistering at the wing tips and charred patches on the upper surface of the wings.

The ablator had worked in some areas and the concept was generally considered worthy of further study but the results from examination of the material and the structure were surprising. The overall concept had been compromised by the measurements that showed the thermal protection had increased, rather than decreased, the interior temperatures as it inhibited the soak-factor in moving heat into cooler zones. The original plan had been for Martin Marietta to fix any areas of ablator showing erosion and to do that for three flights. That was now out of the question and directed them instead to remove the remaining ablator so that X-15A-2 could be returned to North American for repair. The comment of one engineer was telling: 'If there had been any question that the airplane was going to come back in that shape, we could never have flown it.'

Little more than a month after Pete Knight made his record-breaking run on 3 October 1967, Michael Adams completed 23hrs of simulator runs for his own flight in X-15-3, primarily to evaluate a new guidance display system developed by NASA's Ames Research Center. Adams had already flown six flights, his first on 6 October 1966 when the fuel bulkhead ruptured causing a shutdown at Mach 3 and a landing at Cuddeback. During his third flight the cabin pressure failed, inflating the suit and making it difficult for him to fly the aircraft properly in the bulky garment. He claimed he had suffered vertigo, a disorientation where a pilot can incorrectly feel he is spinning.

Adams' seventh flight was profiled to take him to 76,200m (250,000ft) along with seven experiments including one for solar spectrum measurements at high altitude to aid scientists at the Jet Propulsion Laboratory designing instruments for planetary research. He had worked for more than 23 hours in the simulator rehearsing procedures and contingencies for this one flight. The flight itself was delayed several days and on the morning of the successful launch, 15 November 1967, Adams' wife and mother were watching from the viewing

Left: The wreckage of X-15-3 after it crashed near Johannesburg, California, attempting to reach Cuddeback after reaching a speed in excess of Mach 5 but experiencing control difficulties. *NASA*

room outside the control room as the X-15 was hauled to the drop altitude of 13,716m (45,000ft), where X-15-3 was released at 10:30:07.4hrs.

Shortly after the aircraft fell away, rolling first to the right and then back to wings-level, Adams ignited the engine but as he passed through 25,908m (85,000ft) an electrical short, probably in one of the experiments, caused the MH-96 dampers to drop out. X-15-3 had a blended aero-surface/BCS-thruster capability through the right-hand controller but the display for attitude had a dual purpose, selection of which required the pilot to make a conscious decision as to which was required. Correctly set during ascent to an alternate display mode, vernier attitude errors were displayed over the attitude indicator, pitch errors showing up on the α-needle and bank errors on the β-needle. Adams would have been expected to switch back to the α/β mode for re-entry.

The electrical spike fooled the MH-96 system into interpreting a higher dynamic pressure than the X-15 was experiencing and this initiated the system into locking out the thrusters and maintaining authority through the aero-surfaces. As he climbed toward his peak altitude, realising that the aircraft was not responding to his inputs through the right-hand controller, Adams sought to regain BCS control, and the thrusters which were the only means of controlling attitude at this height. As he continued climbing it appears he suffered a bout of vertigo again and began flying as though the display was showing sideslip while it was in fact showing roll vernier attitude.

This part of the flight plan required Adams to rock the wings so that an ultraviolet plume experiment could sweep the horizon and record data. But due to the incorrect display setting, the roll became excessive and the aircraft began to drift until, at peak altitude of 81,077m (266,000ft), it was in a 15deg sideslip to the right. As he began to descend the drift began to worsen and the X-15 reached 90deg to the flight path when it encountered denser air. Yaw motion worsened until the aircraft had turned completely round and was facing backward but nobody on the ground could detect the real position of the aircraft. Less than four minutes after dropping away from the carrier-plane, Adams reported that he was in a spin and descending through 39,624m (130,000ft) and still above Mach 5.

No one had ever calculated the effects of being in a spin at these speeds and altitudes. It was not thought possible for it to happen and the means of getting out of it were totally unexplored. There had been no simulation to rehearse appropriate procedures because the physics of the phenomenon were unknown. The only communication from the aircraft was a series of groans as the pilot was subject to very high g-forces but Adams managed to get it under control as the aircraft descended through 36,576m (120,000ft) using both aero-surfaces and BCS. At Mach 4.5 the now inverted aircraft was in a dive toward the ground at an angle of 40-45deg. As the pilot attempted to gain control, inputs from the MH-96 were inducing severe oscillations which only compounded the problem. Chase pilots Hugh Jackson and Bill Dana believed the X-15 could still make it. Assuming that Adams was heading for the emergency landing strips at Ballarat or Cuddeback they set off for those locations to be in position to talk him down.

With the aircraft now experiencing unacceptable loads and forces oscillating +/-13-g, the aircraft began to buckle and finally broke up, passing through a height of 18,897m (62,000ft) at 10:34:57.5hrs and falling upside down at Mach 3.93. Impact occurred near the town of Johannesburg. The wreckage was scattered across a wide area and it was some time before the forward part of the fuselage, its pilot still inside, was found. As a result of the detailed analysis and review of the accident it was concluded that Adams had become disorientated and had not understood that when he was fighting sideslip he was actually commanding roll angle. The electrical spike had caused a reduction in the overall effectiveness of the flight control system and that the erratic performance of the MH-96 had directly contributed to the disaster.

Several recommendations, some written up and others not, followed this tragic incident, the only loss of life in the entire 10-year flight programme. Specifically, the investiga-

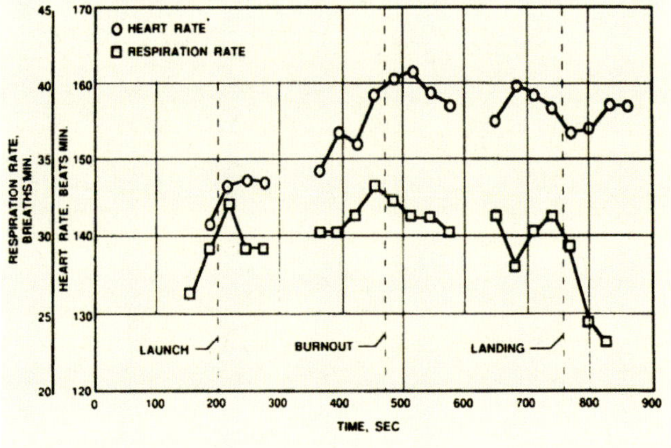

Right: Frequently defined as a marginal bonus of the X-15 programme, physiological monitoring of pilots as they transitioned to weightless flight in the vacuum of space was an essential part of its very existence. Heart rates of 160 beats/min and high respiration levels were measured by body sensors, information which was highly relevant to the emerging space programme. *NASA*

tion recommended that the control room should have a heading indicator so that the flight controller could see immediately the actual orientation of the aircraft, something that had not been provided. It also recommended that future pilots be screened for 'labyrinth sensitivity', or vertigo. But unwritten was a general consensus view that one instrument, so critical to attitude orientation should not be used for other indications as well, especially during periods of intense cockpit activity. By posthumously awarding Mike Adams astronaut wings, the Air Force recognised that he had just nudged the boundary into 'space'.

There were now only two X-15s remaining and the loss of X-15-3 came in a year of sombre reflection over the dangers of this business. On 27 January, astronauts Grissom, White and Chaffee had been killed in a fire while inside their pressurised Apollo Command Module less than a month before the first manned flight in that programme. Four days later, two Air Force technicians had been killed in another flash fire, inside an altitude chamber at Brooks AFB, Texas. On 24 April Russian cosmonaut Vladimir Komarov lost his life when the first manned Soyuz spacecraft fell to Earth, killing him. And only a few weeks before Mike Adams lost his life in X-15-3, Pete Knight had almost been killed when X-15A-2 took brutal heat and fire damage.

It is easy to conclude that the X-15 fell foul to the two unexpected incidents in 1967 which led to the programme's termination the following year. But although understandable, that is not correct and usually never is. The Apollo programme returned to flight status better and more capable than it was before. The Soyuz spacecraft was redesigned and came back to be a reliable vehicle. Yet, aerospace history is replete with examples of catastrophic events occurring to a project or programme, subsequently interpreted as the reason why it was cancelled shortly thereafter. It was thus too with the frequently quoted reason for cancellation of Concorde operations less than three years after the fatal crash of 25 July 2000. And so it could be with the X-15. The real story is more nuanced. As related previously, there had been several times beginning in 1963 when the programme faced closure.

During 1966 the X-15 programme again came under threat of retirement when the Aeronautics and Astronautics Coordinating Board (AACB) sought to find a date beyond which flight operations could no longer be sustained. The AACB had been set up on 13 October 1960 with responsibility for coordinating programmes between the Department of Defense and NASA. Since the X-15 was already in existence when the AACB was formed, it fell under the auspices of the Research Airplane Committee (RAP), which had operated the project since its inception in 1954. But the RAP itself came under the authority of the AACB and their deliberations were significant, if only because of that. The Air Force had interest in the X-15 for its advanced legacy derivative re-builds such as the delta-wing version but the AACB had different views.

With the Air Force assessing that it would end its experiments on the existing X-15 by the end of 1967, the AACB decreed that from 1 January 1968 it was going to be the sole responsibility of NASA to fund and operate it. Either by

Below: X-15 pilots pose for a photo-shoot. Left to right: Joseph Engle, Robert Rushworth, Jack McKay, Pete Knight, Milt Thompson and Bill Dana. *NASA*

Left: Three civilian NASA pilots were awarded Astronaut Wings in addition to four military pilots (left to right): Bob White (USAF), Bill Dana (NASA) Neil Armstrong (NASA) and Joe Engle (USAF). Families of deceased NASA pilots Jack McKay and Joe Walker were also granted Astronaut Wings. USAF pilots Robert Rushworth and Pete Knight had already received their wings. *NASA*

coincidence or conviction (of the need to support continued flights) it quickly emerged that the Air Force would not finish its work with the X-15 by the end of 1967. Only as late as 24 August 1967 was a solution found whereby the Air Force would continue to pay the bills – for continued support from NAA, Reaction Motors and for other contractor support services – while NASA would reimburse them for those costs. With NASA's budget ten times what it was at NACA when the X-15 began, it would have been disingenuous to do otherwise. However, the Air Force would pay for the carrier-planes and for elements of the programme they had instituted themselves.

The meetings also resolved some pending issues, such as dissolving the Research Airplane Committee and all its activity; oversight would migrate to the Aeronautics Panel of the AACB. It was agreed that the research programme would continue until at least the middle of 1968 and on 26 October a new agreement between the Air Force and NASA was signed, finally retiring the understanding that had been in place since 1954. But the inevitability of bringing the X-15 programme to an end was enshrined in a written caveat that support from outside NASA would only continue until the last two Air Force experiments had been completed.

There were many dissenting voices to oppose the retirement of the X-15, its value to aviation unquestionably still current, but very few of those were ultimately responsible for employee pay cheques and national budgets. In mid-1967, NASA was about to start fiscal year 1968 and there were pressing challenges across the agency. The total NASA budget was already in sharp decline, with uncertainties regarding the future direction of aeronautics programmes. And that occurring within a mix that had already so highly prioritised space projects and President Kennedy's Moon goal to the detriment of many other aspirations and forgotten goals for aviation and aeronautical science.

The Air Force made its decision to pull from the X-15 programme and announced on 13 March 1968 that it would withdraw funding at the end of that calendar year. This effectively ended the programme and sealed its fate. But there were still many who fought for its retention. The shuttlecraft concept was emerging as a solution to cost-saving for a post-Apollo era in which budgets would be low, Moon bases would be put on hold, grand visions for planetary exploration would be a dream and Earth-orbiting science bases and space stations would be the new goal - eventually. There was much, said its advocates that the X-15 could still do to support development of a winged, reusable shuttlecraft – a 'civilianised' X-20. There was never a majority for that argument.

Closure

X-15A-2 was returned to Edwards on 27 June 1968 but it never flew again. After the Adams tragedy, only X-15-1 remained on the flight-line and it would make only eight more launches. Immediately after the loss of X-15-3, the programme stood down for findings from the accident review board and for re-grouping across the winter months at Edwards.

Flights would go on, however, and Bill Dana was assigned to take X-15-1 up on 6 February 1968 for a captive check on electrical systems renovated since Knight's complete electrical failure on this aircraft in June 1967. The following day's planned drop was cancelled when the cabin pressurisation system failed and the SAS yaw channel failed a check. It failed again on 27 February and metal fragments were found in the test box after the X-15 had been removed from the carrier-plane. Dana finally got to fly his twelfth X-15 ride on 1 March when he launched for a Mach 4.36 flight to 31,973m (104,900ft) lasting 7min 35.1sec.

Two more attempts were aborted during March and early April before another launch occurred with X-15-1 on 4 April when he reached Mach 5.27 and a peak altitude of 57,150m (187,500ft). Some problems were encountered with a couple of the experiments and this flight also carried the wingtip pods for instruments, first carried on 15 October 1964. It also carried patches of different types of insulation applied to Saturn launch vehicles, five previous flights having conducted this investigation on X-15-3. When that vehicle was destroyed the experiment switched to X-15-1, with 16-mm movie cameras in wing pods recording the effects of supersonic speed and high dynamic pressure on insulation across the speed brakes.

The wingtip pods were an innovative means of carrying various experiments and instruments and each consisted of a container 147.3cm (58in) in length with a diameter of 20.3cm (8in) and a maximum loaded weight of 43.6kg (96.2lb). The first use had been with X-15-1 on 15 October 1964 when McKay reached Mach 4.56 and 25,877m (84,900ft). The pods had doors, opened in flight to expose sensors or camera lenses and others carried micrometeoroid detectors. Pilots found the pods had little effect on handling although a vibration at the same frequency as the wing bending mode did cause some to comment on buffeting. A second set of pods was manufactured for interchangeability with X-15-3 but the use of all pods was compromised to a degree by efflux contamination from the wingtip thrusters.

Bill Knight took the next flight, launched on 26 April 1968, largely a repeat with the same instruments as the previous launch, reaching Mach 5.05 and 63,886m (209,600ft). Dana was back in the cockpit of X-15-1 for a planned flight on 23 May but weather aborted that attempt. The weather was acceptable for the following flight, launched on 12 June to Mach 5.15 and 67,086m (220,100ft), carrying experiments but constituting an altitude build-up flight. A series of delays caused by weather, planning and a few technical issues kept the X-15 and Bill Knight from getting airborne as planned on 8 July and from being launched seven days later, when the BCS test failed prior to the drop.

Logging a 'first' by dropping over Railroad Dry Lake, Knight finally got a launch on 16 July but during the powered phase the hydraulic gauge failed on the way to Mach 4.79 and a peak altitude of 67,513m (221,500ft), which changed the flight trajectory. Again, tip pods were carried but Knight reported severe vibration all the way back down to 19,812m (65,000ft), not uncommon returning from high altitude flights. Next up was Bill Dana, on 21 August to a peak altitude of 81,534m (267,500ft), some 5,334m (17,500ft) above the target sought but the last above the atmosphere and into space, at least as defined by the Air Force.

The penultimate flight of the X-15 programme and, as it turned out, the last flight for the Air Force, took place on 13 September when Bill Knight logged Mach 5.37 and an altitude of 77,450m (254,100ft). At 482km (299.8mls), it was this pilot's farthest flight in distance, lasted 9min 23sec and was his sixteenth launch. Bill Dana was assigned to fly the very last X-15 flight and was scheduled for a launch on 12 October coordinated with a Minuteman missile test from Vandenberg AFB up the coast but delays to that brought a postponement. It was to be a synchronised event to gather information about the ICBM in flight using equipment on the X-15, the first that this had been carried out under the Western Test Range Launch Monitoring Experiment.

That last flight began when the B-52 took off from Edwards at 08:56hrs on Thursday 24 October 1968. Dana launched from Smith Ranch at 10:02:47.3hrs and fired the XLR-99 for 83.8sec, achieving a speed of Mach 5.38 and a peak altitude of 77,724m (255,000ft). Several experiments were attempted but the majority failed, including a sky-brightness test which stopped when the rocket motor shut down. X-15-1 landed on Rogers Dry Lake at 10:14:15.6hrs, having travelled a distance of 478.6km (297.2mls). The B-52 followed, touching down at 11:02hrs. It had accounted for 81 flights, more than either of the other two aircraft, and it had qualified its pilots for astronaut wings and exceeded Mach 6, only the X-15A-2 flying faster.

At the time Dana landed, nobody knew that this was the last flight in the programme. At least one last flight was scheduled, the next planned for 26 November piloted by Bill Knight. The X-15-1 and its B-52 008 carrier-plane were hooked up the day before but the flight had been put back a day or so. When Knight climbed aboard and did preparatory checks he found the right yaw rocket in the BCS was steaming, rendering it inoperable and preventing the flight from getting off the ground. The X-15 was separated from the B-52 so that it could participate in other tests in another programme. B-52 003 was supporting a Lifting Body flight which occurred on 9 December when the HL-10 was dropped on its fourteenth free flight, which delayed the X-15 flight.

Lifting Body vehicles had been flying off the B-52 since the M2-F2 on 12 July 1966, joined by the HL-10 and the X-24. There was increasing interest in the programme, both as a set of configurations capable of deadstick landings following re-entry from space and in ways to get manned spacecraft back to conventional landings and in so doing cut costs. Reusability was becoming the key factor in planning for a post-Apollo space programme and attention was already focused on concepts integrating both reusable launch vehicle and spacecraft combined into a single system. Later to emerge as the Space Shuttle.

With the HL-10 launched, X-15-1 was mated to B-52 003 on 9 December but the following day bad weather scrubbed the planned flight, as it did the following day. On 12 December the mated configuration got airborne but the inertial system failed before launch. This was the last time an X-15 was taken aloft. More bad weather cancelled an attempt the following day and on 17 December a C-130 support aircraft essential to back-up was required elsewhere. The following day poor weather again scrubbed the possibility of getting off the ground and on 19 December plans were made to launch the next day using telemetry systems from Hidden Hills Dry Lake.

At last, it seemed, the flight would finally get off. The weather reports were not good for 20 December but there was a window of opportunity, all the recovery and rescue vehicles, the helicopters were available and the transport network was in place. That morning, the aircraft were already mated and Knight climbed in to the X-15, carried out the lengthy checks and the B-52 crew prepared to taxi out. It never got to the runway. Paul Bickle, head of the NASA facility, was in the control room and called the crew to let them know that the flight was scrubbed – it was snowing hard at Edwards AFB and the helicopters were grounded. His tone said it all: 'Someone is trying to tell us something. It's time to wrap up the programme.'

There would not be another attempt, the funding would only last until the end of the year and it was five days to Christmas. For senior management there were mixed emotions. For some, a sense of relief that the programme could finally close the book on NASA's hypersonic project without further loss of life. The X-15 had been asked to do many things, probably a few too many, and had lasted far longer that had been anticipated in 1954. Its list of accomplishments was long and there was great pride in what it had achieved, expanding the flight envelope and providing incentive for further research.

For the public, awash with Moon pictures from Apollo 8 and anticipation of a lunar landing the following summer, the gloss had gone off the hypersonic programme and even the public affairs officers at Edwards, related facilities (especially Langley) and at headquarters were at pains to remind the taxpayer of the achievements they had funded.

For the engineering fraternity that had designed, developed and nurtured it through 199 flights and 10 years of

X-15 – Operational data

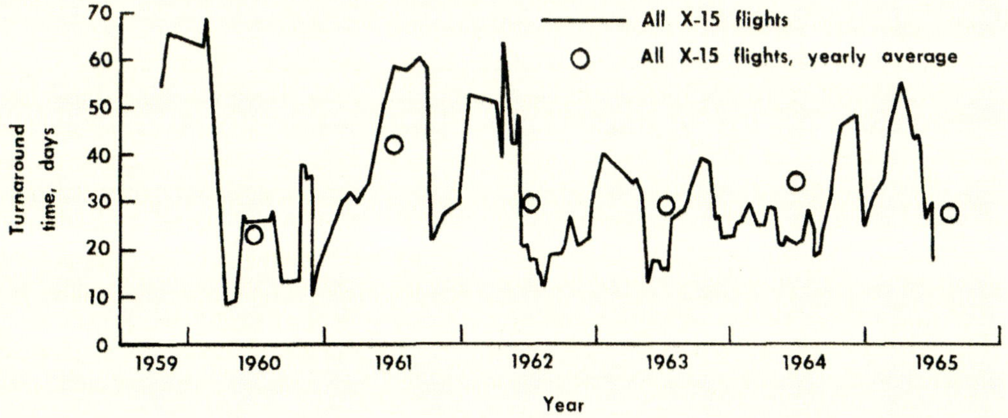

Operationally, the X-15 averaged around 30 days between flights although frequency was not the aim, rather a sustained adaptability to different flight requirements. *NASA*

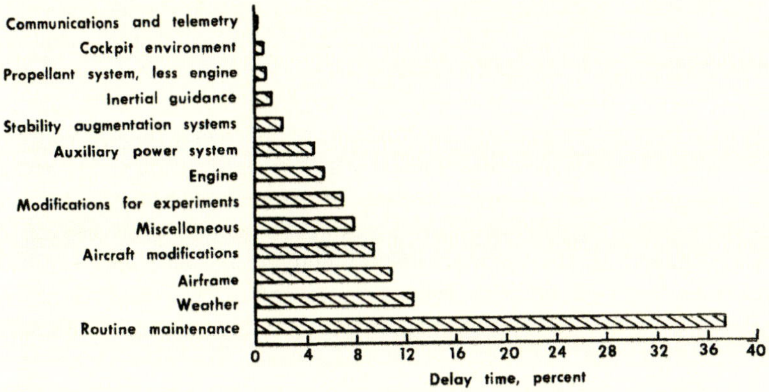

The reason for flight delays are here defined by functional requirements where maintainability was responsible for around one-third of all factors. As a prescient forewarning of troubles to come, maintainability and 'turnaround' emerged as the major cause for delays with the Shuttle programme. *NASA*

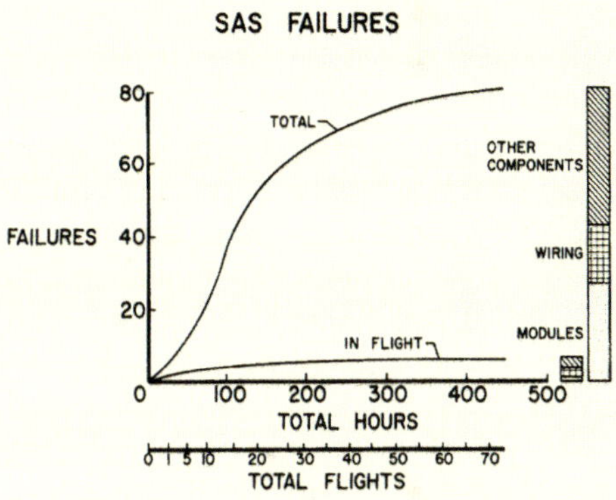

The failure rate for the Stability Augmentation System (SAS) was high and is recorded here for the first 70 flights. *NASA*

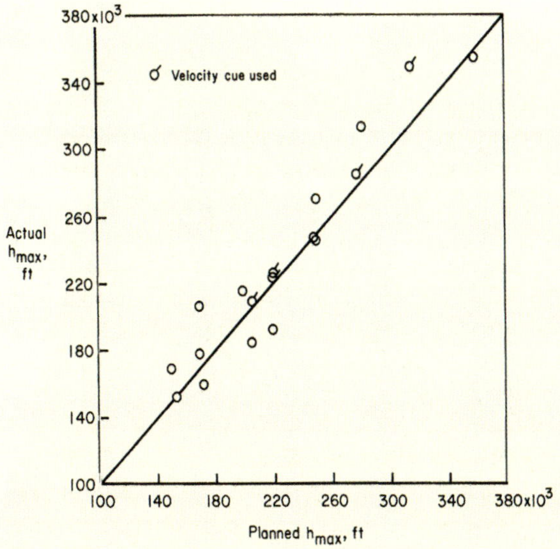

Concerns about the ability of the throttleable XLR-99 to maintain a close match between projected and achieved altitude marks were laid to rest by the data, although there were disparities. *NASA*

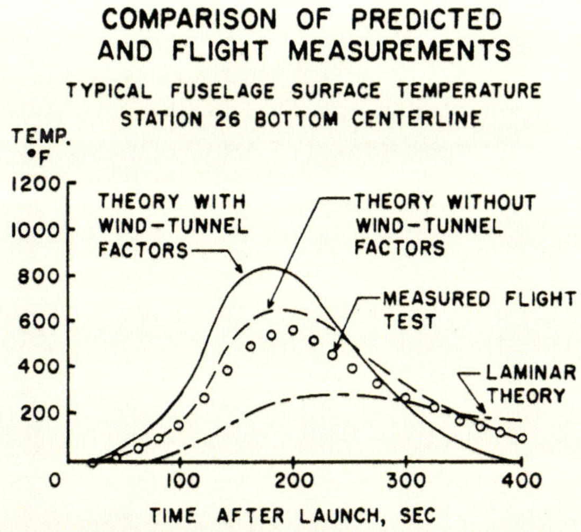

Confirming the assertions of engineers who viewed the X-15 as providing more accurate data than that extrapolated from wind tunnel tests, data showed the precise thermal curve at speed and altitude which differed markedly from that expected by calculation alone. *NASA*

operations, it was a programme none of the participants would ever see equalled. It had generated 766 technical, engineering and scientific reports, providing a central focus for hypersonic research in much the way the X-1 and X-2 programmes had done for supersonic flight. It had never achieved Mach 7 but the three X-15s had spent a few minutes faster than Mach 6, an hour above Mach 5, almost six hours above Mach 4, close to nine hours above Mach 3, twelve hours above Mach 2 and eighteen hours faster than Mach 1.

Its significance to the technicians, support pilots flying the B-52s, the chase-plane pilots, the transport and rescue aircraft as well as the helicopter crews and the fire, rescue and medical personnel was great. They had participated in one of the last great high-speed/high-altitude research programmes, forged under a combined NACA/Air Force/Navy banner and metamorphosed from an aerothermal test vehicle into a hypersonic research tool. Much of the success had been due to the two B-52s, 003 flying 93 launches, 008 flying a total of 106, and to the myriad of personnel assigned essential but unsung roles.

On this last day of the programme there was little to do but gather at Juanita's saloon in Rosamond and party. There to reflect, chat, tell stories, swap jokes, exchange banter, express gratitude and relive the days when three sleek portents of future flight had soared faster and farther than any other winged aeroplane in history – or ever would again – manually flown by pilots. For a long time, Betty Love had been chronicling the logs of each aircraft, meticulously recording the flight data and assembling the detailed timelines of each flight, whether launched or not. Those logs were closed now, with her simple, reflective words: 'This ends an era in flight research history.'

But there was one last corrective, for NASA to acknowledge that its X-15 pilots had made it into space and were deserving of astronauts wings. Three NASA research pilots had qualified for the same recognition accorded Air Force pilots: Bill Dana, John McKay and Joe Walker. Sadly, only Bill Dana was alive when the wings were handed out at a special ceremony at the Dryden Flight Research Center on 23 August 2005. They were presented by the chief of the astronaut office, Navy Captain Kent V. Rominger, The families of Jack McKay and Joe Walker were on hand to accept the wings posthumously on their behalf.

The two surviving aircraft were available for museums but the cost of restoring them and making them fit for display would cost money at a time when NASA was finding ways not to spend it. Nevertheless, the decision was taken on 20 February 1969 for X-15-1 to be prepared for display at the Smithsonian Institution, Washington DC, which had been seeking rights to it since 1962 and the appropriate processes were put in work. It was finally transferred to the National Air & Space Museum (NASM), of the Smithsonian, on 7 July 1971. It was moved around on loan before it was unveiled to public view at the NASM on 1 July 1976.

The National Museum of the United States Air Force took possession of X-15A-2, which had been repaired and restored to the finish it had before the thermal ablative coating had been applied. As mentioned previously, the two carrier-planes were committed to the Lifting Body programme and when that ended in November 1975 the NB-52A was retired to the Pima Air & Space Museum near Tucson, Arizona. The NB-52B continued to serve, supporting the X-38 and X-43 programmes but in 2005 it was replaced with a B-52H, which ran out of tasks and was returned to Air Force deployment the following year.

Below: On 28 November 1961, President Kennedy received this model of the X-15 which was presented to him in the Oval Office a few minutes after the 1960 Harmon International Trophy for Aviators had been presented to Crossfield, Walker and White. *The John F. Kennedy Presidential Library and Museum*

Chapter Twenty

Experiments

The X-1 series, the X-2, the Skystreak and the Skyrocket experimental research aircraft had been designed and built to explore various aspects of high performance flight, be it in speed or altitude. None had been developed as platforms for science experiments and as carriers for a range of instruments exploring facets of the environment in which they flew. Some of these aircraft had carried instrument packages pursuant to their primary role but the X-15 was very different in that there was always the belief that it could do more than serve to explore corners of the high-speed/high-altitude envelope. It was possible for it to lift to completely new and unexplored regions a wide range of instruments, sensors and measuring devices. Not only to take the pulse of the new environment but to observe, measure and record new devices for more advanced aircraft, even satellites and space vehicles.

The official records of the X-15 programme show that the introduction of experiments was discussed from a very early period in the programme's history and only formalised through an information release dated 13 April 1962: 'The hypersonic X-15 will become a "service" airplane to carry out new experiments in aeronautical and space sciences, in a program planned to make use of its capabilities for extremely high speeds and altitudes beyond Earth's atmosphere. The new program adds at least 35 flights … and may take two years to complete.' An understatement revealed through the comprehensive sequence of experiments conducted over the life of the programme.

Discussions about this opportunity began in the middle of the previous year when both the Air Force and NASA proposed to the community that the X-15 be used for science experiments which had not been conceived when the specification had been written in 1954. Some of the potential experiments included instruments to support existing NASA programmes, the Orbiting Science Observatory (OSO) being one. There were other potential users, some of whom saw the X-15 as a suitable carrier for an experimental hypersonic

Above: In 1953, the year before the X-15 was formally approved, a gathering of research aircraft at the Flight Research Center epitomised the era in which aircraft were flown to define the characteristics of the high-speed/high-altitude environment. From left, clockwise: three Skyrockets and a Skystreak in front. The X-15 would push the boundaries further and provide a platform for a wide range of engineering and science experiments. *NASA*

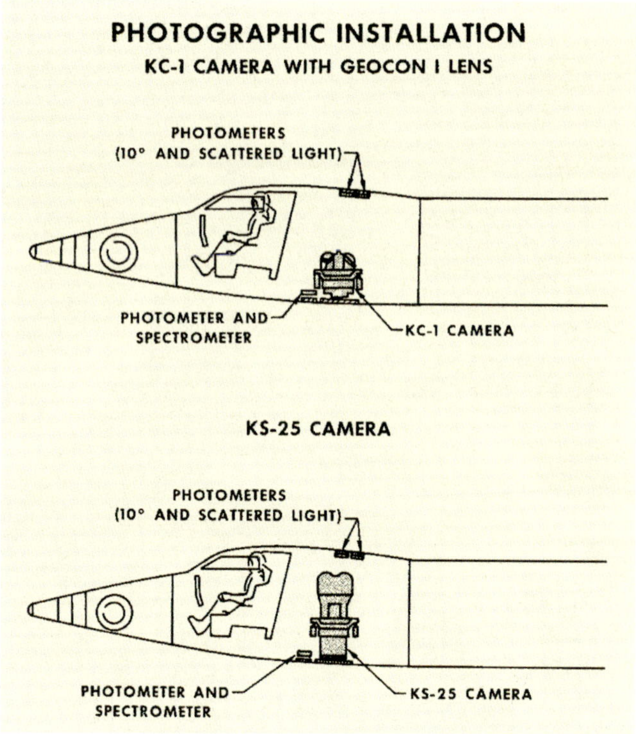

Right: Operating as a carrier for experiments, this Photo-Optical Degradation Experiment (PODE) provided data on the effects of supersonic and hypersonic shock waves on the optical quality of various cameras. Equipped with a GEOCON I mapping lens for low distortion, the KC-1 provided low-distortion images but the KS-25 was more sensitive and flew on the second of six flights between April 1963 and June 1964. *USAF*

ramjet engine contributing to air-breathing studies, others which supported initial work on the Aerospace Plane, or ASP.

Another early exponent of the X-15 for supporting research was arranged by the Air Force in cooperation with North American Aviation. In 1961, NAA was developing the Mach 3 XB-70 Valkyrie and wanted to find ways of suppressing its infrared signature. At this time, engineers were beginning to think about what today are referred to as 'stealth' technologies and Lockheed was already working to find ways to reduce the radar signature of its own Mach 3 family of fighter and reconnaissance concepts leading to the SR-71 Blackbird. Accordingly, the X-15 was considered a suitable platform for evaluating appropriate coatings.

NAA had already developed concept coatings to counter IR detection equipment used by Soviet devices and two candidates were on trial, each appropriate to a specific temperature band. Had these coatings been applied to an operational successor of the XB-70, they would have given the aircraft a flat silver finish rather than the white paint used on the prototypes. To test one of these coatings, a patch was applied to the vertical stabiliser of X-15-2 for the flight piloted by Bob White on 7 March 1961. This was the first Air Force flight and the coatings showed no peeling or erosion during the run to Mach 4.43, which was the first flight by any aircraft above Mach 4.

The Air Force was an early exponent of the research opportunities and followed with a radiation detection package from the Special Weapons Center at Kirtland AFB, New Mexico. It flew on 4 October 1961 when Rushworth flew X-15-1 to an altitude of 23,774m (78,000ft). The instruments included a Geiger tube, an ion chamber, two scintillators and a multi-channel tape recorder. The 4.5kg (10lb) package was installed inside the cockpit on the left side console and results from this and subsequent flights showed that the pilot received only the normal dosage levels of radiation and that flights to greater altitude would not present any physiological harm.

Further data-gathering equipment in the form of film strips was flown between 1961 and 1963 to determine levels of cosmic rays encountered above 15,240m (50,000ft), with parallel measurements obtained by the carrier-plane for relative comparison. Later, NASA's Goddard Space Flight Center (GSFC) sponsored cosmic ray detection packages installed on the aft ends of the fuselage side-fairings for measurements at extreme altitude. Some of the earlier Air Force experiments had been in support of the anticipated boost-glide programme expected to follow X-15, while the GSFC measurements sought further definition of the atmosphere and regions of near-Earth space to support its programmes for science payloads on satellites.

During the 1960s, scientists were engaged in a major programme of data-gathering about all aspects of the Earth's environment and near-Earth space. Major discoveries from the first satellites launched in 1958 had provided scientists with a very different view of the Earth's environment to that which had pertained when the X-15 was conceived and nobody could have imagined the wealth of new knowledge which would accrue from research and observation in this age of space exploration. Utilising the payload-carrying capacity of the X-15, a range of physical experiments helped expand the knowledge base.

Left: The forward experiment bay of X-15-1 where a Singer scanning radiometer is being installed, with an Iratran IV window in the lower fuselage to provide an Earth-facing view. It would measure reflected solar radiation and that emitted from the surface of the Earth to test imaging instruments at Mach 3-5. *NASA*

Left: John McKay flew X-15-2 to 47,518m (155,900ft) on 22 June 1965 carrying the Hycon HR-236 camera which provided this view of the southwest United States. Most of the photographic tests conducted by the X-15 eventually supported military applications. *NASA*

One of those was to help define the requirements for instruments designed for the Orbiting Astronomical Observatory series of Earth-orbiting satellites. To help with that, astronomers needed to know the UV levels of intensity in the sky background and NASA installed a photomultiplier in one of the bug-eye ports, flown with X-15-1 on 19 April 1962. It had been planned to install a bespoke UV star-tracker and horizon scanner in the skylight compartment on X-15-2 but that was delayed when the aircraft was damaged. It eventually flew in X-15A-2 on 18 May 1965 and was carried again on 13 more flights, the last on 12 August 1966.

Defence experiments involved a series of Air Force measurements of the total Earth background radiation so as to develop an operational early-warning system for missile launches. An initial idea envisaged a series of spectrometers installed in the bug-eye orifices which would obtain information from above the UV absorption levels at 40,233m (132,000ft). Scientists believed that most of the UV radiation would be absorbed by the atmosphere and that the plume of a missile in flight would stand out as a bright light. Technical and funding difficulties prevented the experiment from being deployed but not until after the basic instrument had been developed and applied to a subsequent experiment for measuring the UV exhaust plume of the XLR-99 rocket motor.

That test began with the X-15-3 flight on 23 April 1965 piloted by Joe Engle. Known as the Barnes UV scanning spectrometer and solar-blind radiometer, it obtained useful data. A later flight was planned to carry a Millikan dual-channel radiometer and this flew on X-15-3 launched on 14 September 1966 piloted by Bill Dana. A failed heater prevented any useful data and a vacuum UV spectrometer was planned for flight later that year but there is no evidence that it was ever flown. What was flown, however, was a NASA experiment to determine whether horizon phenomena were sufficiently stable to be included in the set of navigation references for the Apollo Guidance & Navigation System (GNS) under development at the Massachusetts Institute of Technology (MIT).

That experiment involved a radiometer installed in the tail-cone box attached to X-15-3, incorporating a 16-mm motion film camera. First flown on 2 May 1963, it was useful for MIT's development of the photometers for the GNS and it was carried aloft on seven additional launches, the last on 8 July 1964. There were plans to fly it several more times but by then it had been superseded by a more sophisticated experiment which was flown on X-15-1. Nevertheless, the information garnered by the X-15-3 flights helped to define the horizon profile to within 4km (2.48mls) and this was applied to evolving technology for the Gemini and Apollo missions.

The more advanced measurements of horizon-intensity profiling depended on three specially developed instruments from MIT flown on five X-15-1 flights with a fixed platform in the tail box supporting a photomultiplier photometer, a solid-stage photometer and an aft-facing camera. These were followed by a set of more sophisticated equipment including a spectral photometer, camera and star tracker attached to a tri-axis stabilised platform also situated in the tail box. Isolated from the motion of the X-15 it was designed to acquire the star Polaris with the gimbal system capable of adjusting the horizon scan rates. A door was also provided which would open above 30,480m (100,000ft) as the X-15 departed the atmosphere.

The investigative programme was vital to the success of the Apollo programme in that it would allow astronauts to conduct back-up triangulation of their position using selected stars and Earth horizon measurements to calculate their position with a high level of precision. This would be vital if communications with Earth were lost. The initial phase of the X-15 experiments began with a checkout of the equipment by John McKay on 6 May 1966 with the last of four operational data-collection launches on 8 September 1966, but results were spasmodic due to technical issues. A further four flights took place with good results.

Below: An Apollo Horizon Experiment pack filled the tail-cone box below the dorsal stabiliser, carried at various times by X-15-1 and X-15-3 for a wide and diverse range of experiments and associated equipment. Designed to provide calibration and test of tweaked sensors, two different housings were utilised as required. *NASA*

Above: From 15 October 1964, X-15-1 flew the first bespoke experiment pod, 20.3cm (8in) in diameter and 147cm (58in) long for carrying equipment on the wing tips and outside the flow field. Here, the Atmospheric Density Measurements Experiment is seen with its probe deployed. Pods were also flown on some X-15-3 flights. *NASA*

The second phase of this advanced experiments programme incorporated a Barnes infrared edge tracker which had been added at the behest of the NASA Manned Space Center. It was intended to provide data for spacecraft attitude stabilisation in the Apollo Applications missions, which eventually morphed into the Skylab programme flown in 1973-74. The experiment instrument was a telescope with a 6.1cm (2.4in) silicon lens attached directly to the elevator on the skylight hatch on X-15-1. Installed during early 1967, it made a single checkout flight and four data-gathering runs between 26 April 1968 and 13 September 1968. It delivered dubious results and was not satisfactory. Nevertheless, the concept was in the flight plans for Apollos 8, 10 and 11 for verifying sextant checks on the Earth's horizon, which in that application proved accurate and reliable.

Supersonic eyes

One of the more direct applications of the X-15 as a research platform emerged during the 1950s after engineers became concerned about the effects of turbulent boundary layer effects on optical cameras and other electromagnetic sensors carried by supersonic reconnaissance aircraft. Not long after the beginning of the X-15 programme, and before the final selection of a contractor, scientists had been concerned about the convergence of free-stream Mach number and the density of the stream. Known as 'light spread' it was known to influence the accuracy of star trackers and to affect the evaluation of terrain in photographs taken by an RF-101 Voodoo reconnaissance aircraft flying at Mach 1.4. By the late 1950s, the Army Corps of Engineers sought a formal definition of this problem so that it could be circumvented by an appropriate technology.

The Army asked the Itek Corporation's Vidya division for

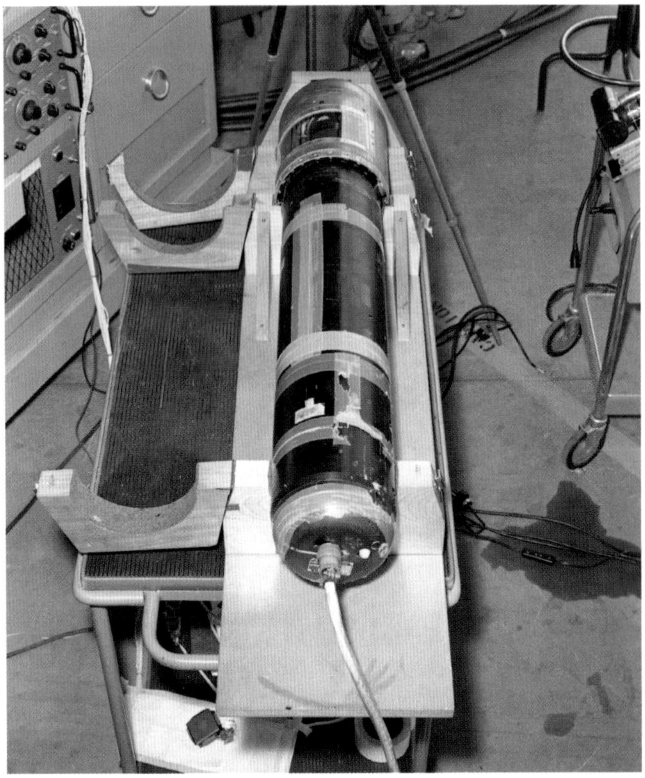

Above: One example of the several different experiments carried in the left wingtip pod of X-15-1 and X-15-3 was the High Altitude Brightness Experiment measuring the sky with a resolution of 2 angstroms for guiding development of future star trackers. *NASA*

a solution and the Navy sought help from MIT. The problem had broad implications and NAA was concerned about the impact this could have on its XB-70. The programme examined effects on supersonic and hypersonic platforms and looked to the X-15 as a data-gathering source. The Fairchild KS-25, high-acuity camera set and the Fairchild KC-1 cartographic camera were selected as optical test instruments, the Army being more interested in the latter while the Air Force was specifically interested in the tactical and strategic aerial reconnaissance programmes already a bedrock of national defence.

The Air Force funded a major investigation of this problem and under Project 6220 it issued a contract to NAA via the Reconnaissance Division of the Air Force Avionics Laboratory. To mount the cameras in the X-15, Aeroflex Laboratories provided a stable mount and Vidya conducted the experiment and the ensuing analysis of results. Fairchild provided the KS-25 camera and the Hycon manufacturing company came up with the lenses. To rate the effect, targets were designed and the ground layout provided by Cornell Aeronautical Laboratory.

The investigation envisaged three separate flight profiles, covering high speed, high altitude and one which flew an anticipated XB-70 profile. The target areas would have to be laid out well in advance and sympathetic to the flight trajectories of the X-15s, each supporting between six and 10 targets laid out along the flight path. After extensive evaluation, Delamar and Smith Ranch were selected in a line back to-

ward Edwards AFB and comprising specified three-bar target shapes in single or triple patterns for location identification against a pre-set map. The sites were selected to cover flight altitudes from atmospheric re-entry to high-speed runs lower down. Each pattern conformed to standard photo-calibration targets, modified to help identify visual acuity by having particularly sharp edges.

On the ground, Scripps Institute of Oceanography provided a photometric van equipped with photometers for sky radiance measurements and for surface target radiance. Meteorological data was obtained locally to calibrate the context in which the measurements were made, atmospheric information being provided by radiosondes launched by the Air Force. As with all scientific measurements, context was all-important and essential for understanding the conditions under which the optical camera film was obtained from the X-15.

The KC-1 camera had been provided with a specially modified lens to minimise distortion while providing high visual acuity. The total experiment package weighed 70.7kg (156lb) to which was added about 40.8kg (90lb) in camera and film, occupying a volume 40.6cm (16in) long, 45.7cm (18in) in length and with a height of 53.3cm (21in). It was situated at the bottom of the instrument compartment facing directly down below the fuselage. The new lens had a focal length of 15.24cm (6in) with an aperture of f/5.6, sufficient for a resolution of 37 lines/mm (0.039in). The circular viewing window flush with the lower fuselage skin was 45.7cm (18in) in diameter and 3.8cm (1.5in) thick. Each Super-XX film image was 22.86cm (9in) square, the usual film load being 118.8m (390ft).

Above: Initially installed on X-15-2 and then X-15-1, a 'skylight' allowing exposure of sensors and other devices to free space allowed direct and unobstructed viewing without the use of optical windows. The device shown here is the Ultraviolet Stellar Photography Experiment. *NASA*

Six X-15-1 flights were flown in this initial configuration between 11 April 1963 and 18 July 1963, the first and the last piloted by Bob Rushworth. Film was removed from the X-15 at Edwards and shipped out to Westover AFB, Massachusetts for processing and analysis. The results remain classified to this day. The value of these flights extended to operational planning for the SR-71 and the XB-70 programmes and were synonymous with techniques used by the RB-57D and by high-altitude balloons.

The second series of experimental tests focused on the KS-25 but these were integrated with the same stabilised platform as that for the KC-1 tests, with the addition of a small analogue computer connected to the X-15's stable platform for image-motion compensation. It also carried seven down-looking photometers for monitoring the spectral changes in light compared to attitude, with two additional, up-pointing photometers for monitoring the level of light in the upper atmosphere. An additional measurement was taken as to whether the flow was boundary-layer or laminar and its thickness measured so that this could be compared with the photographic images obtained at that time.

Compared to the KC-1, the KS-25 was larger and heavier, requiring a space 33cm (13in) in length, 25.4cm (10in) wide and 106cm (42in) high. As he had for the KC-1, Dr. J. Baker built the lens for the KS-25, which had a focal length of 61cm (24in) and had a relative aperture of f/4, providing a resolution of up to 90 lines/mm (0.039in) on Super-XX film. The frames were 11.4cm (4.5in) square and the magazine held 72.2m (150ft) of film. The camera itself, which incorporated several modifications for installation in the X-15, weighed 147.4kg (325lb) in addition to the experiment support package for a total weight of 218kg (481lb). To test its ability to withstand accelerations, it was tested in a centrifuge located at the Rocket Propulsion Laboratory at Edwards.

To set up the experiment within an environmental context, the Air Force flew the range with a RB-47 to carry out the same coverage anticipated for the X-15. Of the high-speed and high-altitude flights flown with the X-15-1, four in particular were singled out as providing useful results. These were launched on 5 December 1963 and 27 March, 8 April and 29 April 1964 on flights between 30,784m (101,000ft) and 53,340m (175,000ft) and speeds between Mach 5.01 and Mach 6.06. As with the preceding tests with the KS-1 camera, a RB-47 was used to take photographs of the site targets for comparative analysis.

As a result of various tests, the use of near-infrared colour film, an innovative 'first' at the time, proved valuable in demonstrating its potential for observing hot-spots hidden by camouflage or foliage. This spurred development of operational near-IR films which were introduced later in the decade in South-East Asia and during the Vietnam War. In the very high speed runs, results were mixed and some smears and obscuration showed up on film which spoiled the images but a lot of that was caused by the quartz window covering the experiment compartment. It was also found that there was little effect from the boundary layer and that it did not materially degrade the results.

Above: The 'skylight' hatch on X-15-1 with the Western Range Launch Monitoring Experiment installed with the intention of tracking the trajectory of a Minuteman missile launched from Vandenberg AFB, California. *NASA*

The results from this second phase remain classified but sufficient has been placed in the public domain to show the value of these experiments with the X-15 as the carrier for investigations which would not have been possible without it. But that was then and there is some doubt as to whether the current photo-reconnaissance cameras with a much narrower field of view, down to 0.5arc-sec or less compared to 6arc-sec for the KC-1 and KS-25 cameras, would tender the same results. Nevertheless, these tests proved the worth of the X-15 for wide-ranging experiments of use outside the programme itself and how new technologies were developed from the results obtained.

These tests had been preceded by an Air Force experiment flying two separate camera systems in X-15-2 at the same time. One was a vertical camera with a focal length of 30.4cm (12in) and the other an oblique camera with a 15.2cm (6in) focal length, located in the centre-of-gravity compartment between the propellant tanks. The objective was to find out how effective reconnaissance photography would be from a supersonic platform and the first flight was on 9 October 1962 when the oblique camera took shots of Las Vegas in black-and-white film. Colour film was used in both cameras on 22 June 1965, the oblique camera taking shots of Las Vegas

Left: Installed primarily to test adhesives for use with the thermal insulation on the Saturn V launch vehicle, white samples were flown on the upper speed brakes of X-15-3's penultimate flight, 31 October 1967. After the loss of this aircraft, similar patches were flown on X-15-1. *NASA*

Left: The test pilots who flew the X-15 were involved in engineering analysis and frequently collated data through the technical reports they were required to write, as with Milt Thompson in 1956 not long after he had been hired by the NACA as an engineer. *NASA*

while the vertical camera shot Indian Springs AFB, both using infrared Ektachrome. This sequence of tests also used Kodak SO-90 film which was especially suited to this work.

Toward the end of December 1965, the Hycon camera was replaced with a Maurer 500 on X-15A-2 for a flight on 30 August 1966 piloted by Bill Knight to Mach 5.21 and a peak altitude of 31,150m (102,200ft). Despite problems with the camera mounting the results were satisfactory and two additional flights were flown. The Maurer was replaced with a Hycon KA-51A camera for a flight on 21 August 1967 to a speed of Mach 4.94 and an altitude of 27,736m (91,000ft). The following flight on 3 October 1967 carried a 16-mm, aft looking Milliken camera for taking pictures of the dummy ramjet installed for that run to a record-breaking Mach 6.7.

Dyna-Soar and the SST

While X-15 engineers supported experiment and instruments dedicated to fields outside the general remit of this research aircraft, several were associated with exploring facets of its own operation. And of obtaining information about how its own systems were operating and to what level further improvements could be made to this and its successors. The learning curve that came with repeated use of systems and equipment brought changes driven by comments, observations and complaints from the pilots. Significant among which was an issue with the mechanical side-control stick which had attracted ergonomics specialists for its application to small cockpits and to possible future high-g combat aircraft and to aerospace vehicles such as Dyna-Soar.

As installed, the side-controller was linked mechanically to the centre stick and to the actuators on the control surfaces. Pilots found that this had an unnatural 'feel' when operated, and that it had an adverse response due to the absence of a mechanical link to the flight control system. A development programme began in an effort to install an all-electrical link, such as would be incorporated in later fighters, and in 1962 NAA test-flew an adapted F-100C which had an electric side-stick control system. This work progressed only on the basis that it was applicable to Dyna-Soar but when that was cancelled in late 1963, so too was the electric stick.

The unique high-performance capability of the X-15 allowed engineers to test a range of different high-temperature leading-edge surfaces of potential value on future aerospace vehicles. Readers may recall the debate over interchangeable wing and stabiliser leading edge segments at the beginning of the programme, an option supported by Ames but not incorporated in the selected configuration. After the envelope expansion flights had been completed, thoughts turned again to different leading edge shapes as alternative to the rounded profile engineers adopted in an attempt to reduce temperatures. Total replacement of the wing leading edge was too complex and expensive but the ventral rudder posed a likely candidate and X-15-3 became subject to a modification.

The standard rudder had a leading edge with a 1.27cm (0.5in) radius of curvature on the forward 1.52cm (0.6in) of the chord. A sharp-edged candidate for test had a leading edge extension of 13.1cm (5.16in) producing an overall chord of 2.74m (9ft). The leading edge had a radius of 0.038cm (0.015in) at the tip which was fabricated from stainless steel. Special boundary layer tips were set along one side of the rudder and applied as spot welds, 0.31cm (0.125in) in diameter and 0.05cm (0.020in) high about 12.7cm (5in) back from the leading edge.

Measurements were to be obtained with eleven 30-gauge thermocouples spot-welded to the inside of the skin and six 0.63cm (0.25in) pressure orifices nearby and connected to the standard manometers in the side fairing. Baseline data was collected from a similar set of sensors on the blunt leading edge of the ventral rudder on X-15-2. The first flight with X-15-3 thus modified occurred on 7 November 1963 with Bob Rushworth at the controls for a flight to Mach 4.4 and the adapted rudder was retained on 11 flights with this aircraft through to the final launch on 26 August 1964, after which it was removed to make way for other instrumentation on the next launch. It was, however, reinstalled for the flight after that and retained through to the last flight of X-15-3. It provided valuable data on theories regarding heat characteristics of various leading-edge radii.

The Air Force wanted to measure the infrared signature of the X-15's exhaust products to compare the ammonia/LOX combination with other measurements it had made of IR signatures from the Atlas and Titan ICBMs. This information would feed in to the development of early-warning satellites monitoring the surface of the Earth for hostile missile launches. To get this data, the X-15 would carry a set of detectors provided by the Cambridge Research Laboratory and installed in the tail box of X-15-3. These included an infrared radiometer with a calcium-fluoride lens and a range of different filters. The instrument was flown on seven flights in 1963 and 1964 but technical problems plagued attempts to get useful data, which was obtained on only one flight. As with the camera experiments, the results from these launches remain classified.

Above: In 1962 Milt Thompson had been the only NASA pilot assigned to fly the X-20 and he then joined the Lifting Body programme to take his experience with the X-15 to another level. Here he is seen climbing in to the M2-F2 in which he made five flights during 1966. *NASA*

As a further development of this activity, the Air Force Research Technology Division installed a Singer scanning radiometer in the lower section of the X-15-1 instrument compartment in 1965, 'looking' out through an Iratran window situated in the lower fuselage to measure levels of solar radiation reflected from, and emitted by the Earth. Six flights were flown between 26 March and 30 September 1965 with this installed, the last one being the first familiarisation flight for Knight. It had been planned to remove this equipment but poor results on the preceding flight prompted researchers to leave it on. Despite the profile intentionally not following that required for previous data-gathering flights, it did return good results and useful too, since it demonstrated the practicality of obtaining infrared data at supersonic speeds.

This period saw a considerable amount of research effort through airborne and ground-based experiments which aimed to find out how effective infrared imaging could be. Several operational production aircraft were mustered in for these tests and the X-15 played a crucial role in that it provided a very high speed platform for these experiments. The work conducted by X-15-1 stimulated development of infrared line scanners which were introduced on equipment for production combat aircraft, initially in the form of the Texas Instruments AN/AAS-18. It also stimulated NASA into the development of the Earth Resource Technology Satellite (ERTS) programme, which launched its first satellite – Landsat 1 – on 23 July 1972, the first in a sustained line of global environmental monitoring satellites which provided free access for countries around the world and still does. Moreover, Meade developed small scanners for use in General Aviation for monitoring local pollution in urban and rural areas.

Another Air Force test concerned the degradation in the optical qualities of transparent windows when exposed to very high temperatures. NASA instrumented the window seals between the outer pane and the frame and between the separate panes in the window on X-15-2 to measure precise temperature data. This was vital to the safety of the X-15 as well as potential uses on other vehicles and several flights were made in 1963 with this installed. Expanding upon this, attempts were also made to get X-20 window samples flown on the fixed portion of the ventral stabiliser for six flights in 1964 but the experiment was cancelled after the X-20 was

Right: Objectives for the X-15 included the need for experience with manned vehicles in space, evaluation of materials, the study of human factors and research into atmospheric re-entry. All of which came together in a series of highly focused programmes which would culminate in the Shuttle. Here, a group of models for testing various configurations at Edwards AFB are displayed. They were operated using radio control sets from model hobbyists. The 'mother-ship' for dropping the models is at the top. Left to right: Richard C. Eldredge, Dale Reed, James O. Newman and Bob McDonald. *NASA* abandoned. There were, however, measurements made of a sample window attached to the fixed portion of the ventral stabiliser on X-15A-2 to determine the effects of smoke from the heated ablative material causing lasting effect, and this was found to be so.

At the time the X-15 was expanding its flight profile and beginning to service experiments and research projects outside an analysis of its own performance and systems capabilities, the US government became interested in a national supersonic transport (SST) programme. The X-15 supported that effort. Major US manufacturers had been looking at such a concept for several years, beginning with tentative design concepts in the early 1950s. By 1963 the US government formally announced a design competition, a significant spur to that being the agreement signed between France and the UK for development of an Anglo-French Concorde supersonic airliner.

Supporting both this and the impending development of Mach 3 military reconnaissance and bomber aircraft, the Air Force Research Technology Division began a programme to study the mechanical loads and the thermal stresses which would be experienced by very large aircraft of this type. The experiment matured out of a study by Republic Aviation concerning analytical procedures it had developed for determining these factors on box beams and frame structures. Samples of those would be flown on the X-15 as a means of verifying the loads analyses. Ambitious plans to emplace 360 strain gauges and thermocouples in the wing/fuselage attachment points were put forward to the Federal Aviation Administration (FAA).

This was unusual, as a regulatory body the FAA was not usually involved in conducting detailed research and engineering projects. It believed that NASA should pay for these experiments and thought that verification of Republic's analytical processes would not be best served by this approach. But the interests of the Flight Research Center prevailed, money was found and the tests proceeded.

Initially, it was decided to install a few measurement devices on a set of horizontal stabilisers on X-15-3 for basic reference data. Flights were made in this configuration between 18 July 1966 and 20 July 1967. Some inexplicable anomalies were noted but the cause was elusive. In a more advanced series of tests, a new set of horizontal stabilisers was fabricated by NAA and installed on X-15-3, the starboard side of the X-15 carrying 128 strain gauges and 125 thermocouples, prepared and tested in the High Temperature Loads Calibration Laboratory after which they were installed on X-15-3 for a flight on 25 August 1967.

Several precisely defined manoeuvres were flown at specific Mach numbers and angles of attack but with conflicting and ill-defined results. Other tests were made using symmetrically positioned panels under the centre fuselage and on the wing tips, one of which would have a discontinuity by way of steps and wavy surfaces for sinusoidal distortions. These were integrated with the second, more advanced phase using the new stabiliser forms but the results were still providing puzzling results when the aircraft was lost, along with all further hope of transferring the work to one of the others.

Large aircraft designed for sustained cruise at high supersonic speeds were the primary focus of analysis for another experiment involving the X-15, this time more specifically based around the flight profile of a cross-country SST. It had been noted that aircraft cruising at Mach 3 appeared not to produce a noticeable sonic boom and some measurement had been made of Apollo spacecraft up to Mach 16 but with inconclusive data in that regard and certainly not representative of future shuttlecraft.

On 22 March 1967, Mike Adams flew X-15-1 to Mach 5.59 over special instruments set up at Mud Lake on a flight expected to record the pressure wave at Mach 5.3 and an altitude of 28,041m (92,000ft). At 0.0162kPa (0.34lb/ft²) the overpressure was less than some had expected and gave only a slight atmospheric distortion. In further application, microphone arrays were laid down around Goldstone and Cuddeback. Without atmospheric measuring stations located nearby, the meteorological data was recorded back at Edwards. In another flight of the same type, the X-15 arrived over the Goldstone area at Mach 4.8 with the engine throttled to 50 per cent thrust with speed brakes extended. When it was over Cuddeback at Mach 3.5 the engine had shut down and the speed brakes had been retracted. The results followed similar test patterns from an SR-71 flight and the calculations regarding diminished overpressure had been proved correct.

Measuring the environment

The X-15 was the perfect platform for discovering more about the environment in which it, and potential successors, would operate. But it was also fundamental to the design of long-range ballistic missiles. It had been hoped to provide an ionisation gauge in a wingtip container for measuring the atmospheric density above 30,480m (100,000ft), not the pod designed as a universal experiment container which was used later for follow-up tests. Lacking a suitable location on which to place the gauge, the ball nose and stable platform were used instead to acquire data on pressure, velocity and altitude. Two flights were flown for this purpose in 1961 and four in 1963. These flights were coordinated with launches of ARCAS rocket sondes sent up from Point Mugu, and the

Above: Between 1966 and 1970 the Northrop HL-10 Lifting Body made 37 flights, powered by a single, four-chamber XLR-11 rocket motor for supersonic flight and launched off the NB-52B. Here, Bill Dana watches after a successful touchdown while Bill Reeves is preoccupied at the cockpit. *NASA*

results generally showed a slightly greater density than had been calculated for altitudes between 33,528m (110,000ft) and 45,720m (150,000ft).

Following this, the Air Force Geophysics Research Directorate organised a programme to utilise the starboard wingtip pod container on X-15-1 by installing a densatron ionisation gauge in the nose section. The instrument was provided by the College of Engineering at the University of Michigan and two flights checked out the device on 15 and 30 October 1964. Three further flights were made but the device never produced satisfactory results. In fact a combination of factors revealed the difficulty in planning and programming a test run without full awareness of interference, in this case from a combination of the bow shock-wave at lower altitudes and the BCS thruster efflux above 73,152m (250,000ft). But some stoic researchers did believe they got some useful data from measurements taken at intermediate altitudes!

The same Air Force directorate also conducted a micrometeoroid experiment to support an agencies-wide investigation into the potential danger in small micrometeoroid particles travelling at great speed encountering aerospace vehicles and satellites in low-Earth orbit. The X-15 was capable of carrying samplers to the very outer edges of the atmosphere but not into space. In 1965 NASA launched very large micrometeoroid detector panels into orbit attached to the spent upper stages of the last three Saturn I rockets and numerous research programmes sought definitive information about the size distribution of individual particles and the population density.

The micrometeoroid research programme stimulated the design of the wingtip pods and occupied the port tip pod on X-15-1. It was designed with a lid which would open at the rear and rise to a vertical position, rotating upward and swivelling so that the underside faced the fuselage. Thus exposed to the airstream, it would open a collection surface located in the side of the unit, the unit itself rotating to six different positions with a time indication marking when each step occurred. Several problems were encountered with the first flight when the door opened prematurely, on 15 October 1964. A flight on 10 December was made to calibrate the amount of contamination incurred at installation.

The experiment was also prepared for attachment to X-15-3 but there were various malfunctions and further attempts with X-15-1 to get satisfactory results. The equipment frequently failed, was arguably too complex and took little account of the inappropriate use of the X-15 for tasks compromised by the aircraft's operating systems. Especially the BCS thrusters which contaminated the sampler and rendered the results suspect. But six flights did return findings which proved marginally useful and helped to add additional data points to an increasingly broad compilation of information about micrometeoroid particles in near space and entering the outer atmosphere.

Further use of the X-15 served directly the needs of the Air Force in measuring the brightness of the sky at altitudes above 60,960m (200,000ft). To do this with the X-15, they modified an existing contract for a spectrophotometer, being built by Northrop Nortronics for the U-2 spy-plane programme, so as to measure the sky in the spectral range of 3,500-7,500A (angstrom) and with a resolution of 2A. This was to assist with future development of star trackers being developed for aircraft and spacecraft and, in some development programmes, for re-entry vehicles on ballistic missile warheads for trajectory adjustments and enhanced accuracy. Researchers used the U-2 data and extrapolated upward to predict what the X-15 would find and then compared that with the actual observations starting at 12,192m (40,000ft).

Known officially as the High-Altitude Sky Brightness Experiment, the spectrophotometer was placed in the port wingtip pod, flown on X-15-1 flights launched on 15 October 1964 and 26 February 1965 for initial checkout, for the first full data run on 6 May 1966, which provided no useful data due to the emergency landing. Good data was obtained on 28 July but on 11 August a blown fuse prevented useful measurements, a malfunction which brought on a major effort to find out why these were consistently failing. The solution lay in a power connector which was modified. The X-15-3 proved more successful with this experiment, the first of two profitable runs taking place on 1 November 1966 before the experiment was retired.

Related to these experiments, albeit in a tangential manner, were several investigations to measure X-ray air density through a series of solid-stage cells attached to the forward section of the starboard wingtip pod. These measured the backscatter to identify air density through a series of flights in 1967 and 1968 but with no successful results. The need for qualitative information about the upper atmosphere and the various air density levels at different altitudes was crucial to the development of supersonic and hypersonic rockets and missile systems as well as to the development of spectral sensors for fast jets and, particularly, combat weapon systems.

In an unrelated experiment sponsored by the Jet Propulsion Laboratory (JPL), the rear section of the port-side wingtip pod on X-15-1 was equipped with 12 sensors attached to a spectrometer for measuring solar spectral levels. These were considered useful in determining the energy levels of the Sun, the degree of atmospheric absorption and to evaluate the effectiveness of solar cells for simulated environments. Initially, the experiment required a hatch to expose the sensors but this was changed to a quartz window and installed on X-15-3 to make use of the new PCM telemetry that it carried. The first of three flights took place on 26 April 1967 but results from that were disappointing due to its brief duration following a premature shutdown.

Several experiments were started and cancelled, either through an inability to fashion the necessary hardware due to technical limitations or to unsuccessfully finding an effective way of using the X-15. Some experiments, however, looked to use existing systems to explore the opportunity for getting this information without the need for purpose-built hardware. One such experiment involved the use of an evolution of the existing ball nose to test whether it would be possible to use it for measuring air data parameters. It was an experiment created by Rodney K. Bogue and John P. Cary at the Flight Research Center.

Known as the fixed-alpha nose, the evolved derivative was a fixed sensor to determine the angle of attack. Flown as an experiment, it was installed in the port wingtip pod and consisted of a ported sphere, 11cm (4.36in) in diameter with a total sensor length of 47.6cm (18.75in) which protruded as an extension. One of the ports was located 5deg below the zero angle of attack axis with the remaining four ports arranged symmetrically around that in the vertical and horizontal axes. The vertical ports measured angle of attack with the horizontal ports providing data on sideslip motion, although these were never employed as such. The experiment was carried by X-15-1 flown once, piloted by Bob Rushworth on 26 March 1965.

From this single flight researchers judged the fixed-alpha sensor to be acceptable, although specific measurements, compared to the aircraft's existing ball nose as a reference, were compromised by flow disturbances and shock-wave impingement. There was some perturbation caused by suspected wing deflections and some rotational flow around the sensor package. But overall, the ball nose was considered an acceptable alternative and a slightly modified model was attached to X-15-1 for a further set of tests on six of its last seven flights. NASA was encouraged by the results and a developed version was incorporated into the Apollo Launch Escape System for air data information in the event of an abort. It also provided the base concept for a further development employed by the Shuttle as the Shuttle Air Data System (SADS) for flights between 1986 and 1991.

While this and many other experiments provided the basis for future developments with projects such as the Space Shuttle, there were hopes that some could be carried across from cancelled programmes in the hope that they could provide some value for new ventures. One of those involved the Garrett AirResearch heat exchanger from the cancelled Dyna-Soar boost-glide vehicle. The idea was to put it in the X-15's instrument compartment and conduct tests to determine its efficiency and effectiveness at high altitude and in zero-g conditions such as that experienced in parabolic flight. The first model arrived at Inglewood in November 1964 and was subjected to centrifuge tests at the Rocket propulsion Laboratory at Edwards the following month. It was further tested in a parabolic flight on a KC-135 in early 1965 with plans to place it aboard X-15-1.

To cool the equipment, a large compressor was needed and this would have required more start-up power than that available either on the X-15 or the NB-52, although it was felt that the latter could have supported a larger alternator for such a purpose. To do this the wiring on both aircraft would have required an upgrade to handle the higher power levels and that could have been prohibitive due to its impact on other systems. It might have been possible to power up the compressor using ground equipment, relinquishing the operating power to the X-15's APUs, which were capable of doing that. However, power loads would be compromised and the device was never installed; it was passed across to the Apollo Applications Program for some of its more advanced requirements but that never happened either.

In retrospect, some of the proposed experiments appeared bizarre by definition yet contained sensible research objectives. Of those, the wake-flow investigation stands out. Set up by the Flight Research Center, it aimed to measure the density of the atmosphere at 76,200m (200,000ft) and the drag characteristics of a towed balloon at that altitude. It had a secondary purpose in that it contributed to the suggestion that a towed, inflatable body could be used as a decelerating device on a re-entry body. This was associated with a proposed experiment for the Mercury orbiting spacecraft but changes were made with the intention of releasing a Mylar balloon from the tail-cone box on X-15-3 above 76,200m (250,000ft) rather than have it towed.

As defined, the experiment settled on two planned X-15 flights above 91,440m (300,000ft) using the same balloons, specially fabricated and produced for the Mercury programme. Two flights were planned for high altitudes with four follow-on tests above 76,200m (150,000ft) but only two were flown. The first, on 19 July 1963 where Joe Walker reached 106,000m (347,800ft) and the second which reached 107,960m (354,200ft) on 22 August 1963. Both attempts were unsuccessful and resulted in cancellation of further efforts, the wake-flow investigation resorting to a flow transducer mounted on the forward part of the port wingtip pod. It was a fall-back substitute and flown only a few times in 1966 and 1967 on X-15-1 and X-15-3.

Arguably another in the 'bizarre' category was a proposal from NASA's Langley Center to set up an X-15 experiment in which an inflatable device would be carried to high altitude, separated and pressurised to see how well inflatable structures would work in the vacuum of near-space. It was to be photographed so that researchers could evaluate whether such a concept was feasible. An initial proposal had it folded into a compact package and carried instead of the ventral rudder but then an external store position was suggested. Even as it was in discussion, it appeared somewhat unrealistic, in that the complexity was probably too great for the limited time spent at extreme altitude.

But the idea would not go away and it was adopted by proponents of the decelerator model in which deployed balloons or other devices could be released on tow to achieve that drag result. Everything from self-inflating supersonic parachutes to ballutes, cones and inflatable spheres was considered and some preparatory tests were conducted on an F-104 in April 1965, dropped from 17,373m (57,000ft) and a speed of Mach 1.8. Some X-15 hardware was built in late 1966 but it was never flown. Yet both inflatable structures in space and supersonic parachutes became major technologies which would find use in space and with hardware, although the former would wait several decades. Proponents were, however, encouraged by the two Echo inflatable balloon passive communication satellites which had been launched into orbit on 12 August 1960 and 25 January 1964, precursors to the active communications relay satellites which would soon follow.

These and several other experiments, proposed but never flown, testify to the broad-based range of scientific and engineering investigations made during the X-15 flight programme and reflect the value of that capability. In several respects, the requirements outgrew the capabilities of the X-15 to accept an increasingly sophisticated set of proposals and requests, many more than could be accommodated. They reflected the relevance of the X-15 but also exposed its inability to satisfy all-comers. These research programmes and the projects which they stimulated were but a precursor to the more advanced successors, many of which would ride into space on satellites, spacecraft and manned space vehicles. Nevertheless, the X-15 played a seminal role in helping develop the technologies which would underpin the space programme. That is as much its legacy as the purposes for which it was designed.

Below: On display at the National Museum of the US Air Force, in pure performance the X-15A-2 with its jettisonable drop tanks was incapable of unleashing its potential due to significant thermal problems on the aero-structure. *Author's collection*

Chapter Twenty-one

Context and Legacy Concepts

Embracing the bigger picture, at a classified level the origin of the X-15 programme was associated with a strategy involving advanced aerospace concepts which, for obvious reasons, did not appear in the literature of the time. Much of the debate about the true value of the X-15 was polarised by two opposing views regarding its value. The desire on the part of the Air Force to test a vehicle capable of maturing into a combat system and on the part of the NACA for a pure research vehicle to continue the work they had been doing since the First World War – advancing knowledge and the scientific understanding of flight and flying, especially at high speed and high altitude.

As a way of putting this all into relevant context, by March 1954, when the ad hoc group was formed at Langley to plan the way it could gain approval for the new aircraft, research into this area had been granted more than eighteen months earlier. If approved, said the group, the new hypersonic research programme would fill the gap between what was referred to as Round One types (the original X-series) and Round Three (Dyna-Soar), filling the void known as Round Two with the rocket plane which would become the X-15 and a series of potential derivatives.

Before the world's first satellite, Russia's Sputnik 1, was launched on 4 October 1957 it was assumed that humans would access space through reusable spaceplanes, or trans-atmospheric vehicles, with wings and lifting re-entry bodies

Above: Preceded by Round 1 types such as the X-1 series/X-2 and Skyrocket, the X-15 was seen as Round 2 and a precursor to Round 3 with the Dyna-Soar and its derivatives. Here depicted with the Transtage second stage of the launch vehicle, Dyna-Soar could have produced a very different future for manned space flight than the one which unfolded. *Author's collection*

Right: The general arrangement of the Dyna-Soar/X-20 was constrained by the performance and weight-lifting capabilities of the rocket with which it was to be launched on a ballistic trajectory. *USAF*

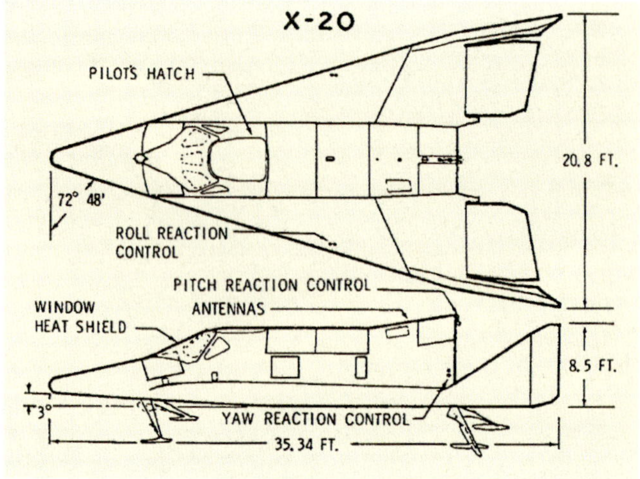

returning to a pre-selected landing site. That evolutionary step was to evaporate over the next three and a half years and metamorphose into ballistic capsules launched by conventional rockets. But in that interval, ideas which had been in gestation since the end of the Second World War crystallised into Dyna-Soar.

Dyna-Soar grew out of several previous projects which formally began as BoMi, an acronym for bomber missile, in 1952. It was proposed by those in the Air Force who believed they could combine the ballistic missile with the manned bomber to create an unstoppable strike system, operating as a strategic bomber or a reconnaissance system. Formal BoMi studies had been completed by late 1955, although some further work would continue, and by early 1956 another concept – Brass Bell (Reconnaissance System 459L) – was being studied as a Mach 15 reconnaissance version of BoMi. By the middle of that year a further requirement had been defined for a combined reconnaissance/bomber version called RoBo.

The ability to have a manned strike/reconnaissance system was attractive, the advantages of a call-back capability was highly beneficial and avoided the possibility that an order to launch a nuclear strike could not be revoked. A missile could not be recalled after launch, or destroyed before it reached its target because ballistic missiles of the future could not be made vulnerable to electronic intervention from anyone, especially an enemy. But the lack of knowledge about high Mach-number flight resulted in a decision in November 1956 to develop a research successor to the X-15 called Hywards, capable of Mach 18 and an altitude of 109,728m (360,000ft). Already under development by then, the X-15 was designed to reach Mach 7 and 76,200m (250,000ft) and to slot in to the research programme as a precursor to Hywards.

At this date, the X-15 was expected to begin operations in 1959 and Hywards would follow with flights from 1965. But there were concerns that the latter would fly too soon after its predecessor for it to gain anything in its design evolution from X-15 flight results. Moreover, with a severe cap on defence spending during the Eisenhower administration, and an overlap between Brass Bell, RoBo and Hywards, there was a pressing need to consolidate requirements and slim down the programme to a research programme which could also serve in the role of operational precursor. In October 1957 the Air Research & Development Command brought these three separate programmes together under

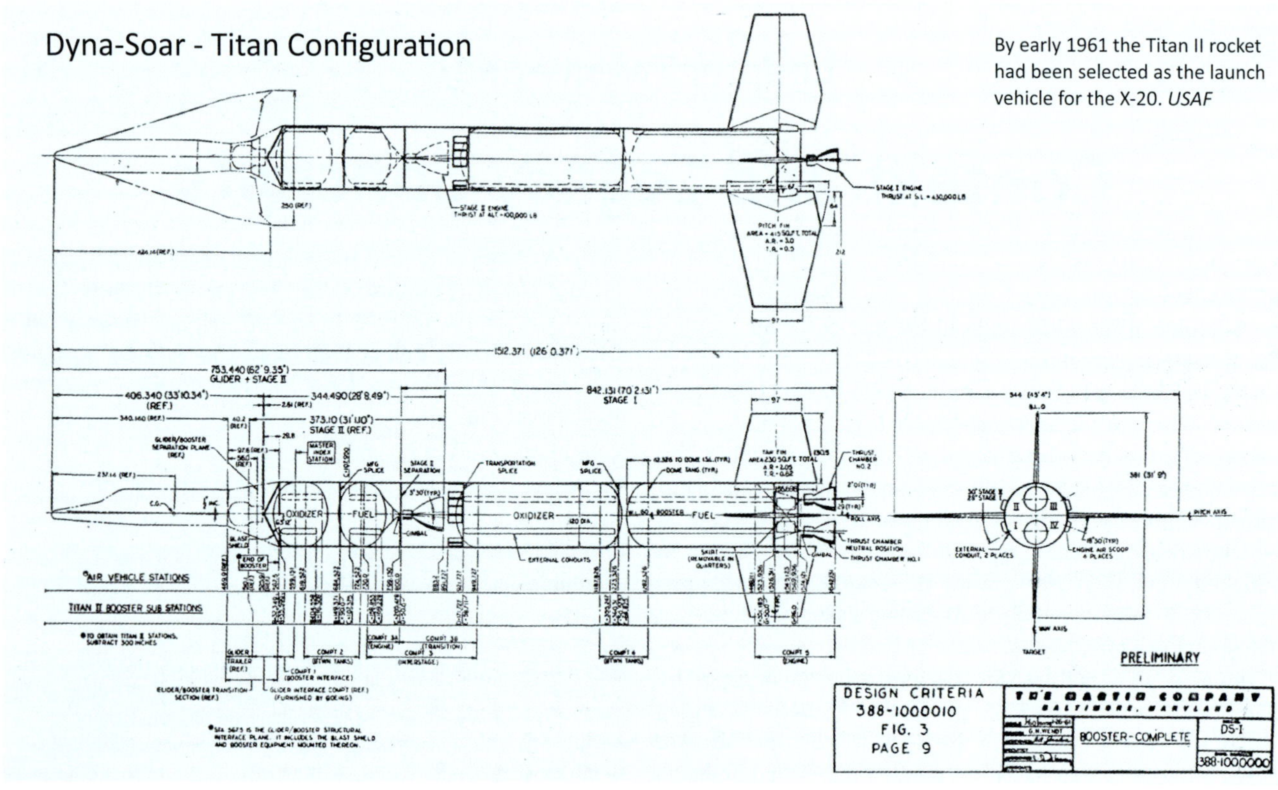

By early 1961 the Titan II rocket had been selected as the launch vehicle for the X-20. *USAF*

Left: With development of the Titan and the enhanced performance from solid rocket boosters, the X-20 would have had the benefit of the Titan IIIC, imagined here in an artist's rendition. *Author's collection*

System 464L, the three-phase project Dyna-Soar.

All three phase vehicles would be launched by man-rated rockets developed from ballistic missiles. Derived from Hywards, Step I would be a research vehicle for test flights beginning in 1965. Step II would fly from 1969 and provide a capability not dissimilar to Brass Bell, with a range of up to 18,500km (11,500mls) and a maximum speed of 24,240kph (13,200mph). Step III would fulfil the RoBo mission from 1974 and be capable of reaching 91,440m (300,000ft) and a top speed of 24,135kph (15,000mph). In its developed configuration, it would be a fully operational orbital bomber, capable of reconnaissance and eventually of identification, inspection and neutralisation of enemy satellites in space.

After a design competition, in June 1958 Boeing was selected from nine companies bidding to build Dyna-Soar and Martin Marietta was selected to provide the man-rated Titan rocket to launch it. This was immediately the result of a joint NASA/USAF agreement to conduct it as a joint programme. But over the next several years the defence of manned versus unmanned systems tipped in favour of satellites and space vehicles rather than winged spaceplanes and it became increasingly hard to justify Dyna-Soar.

When the Kennedy administration came into office in January 1961, it took an early position to downscale the programme. But on 16 November of that year the Manned Military Space Program study decided to upscale the programme to an orbital capability with 10 flights conducting single-orbit circumnavigation of the globe. Later the following year two multi-orbit flights were added within the 10-flight programme and the decision made to use the Titan III launcher.

It was about this time that the X-15 pilots became heavily involved in Dyna-Soar, with Milton O. Thompson assigned, at that time, as the sole NASA pilot-consultant to the programme in 1959. Eventually, a further six pilots were assigned, including Neil Armstrong and Bill Dana from NASA and Jim Wood, Russ Rogers, Hand Gordon and Pete Knight from the Air Force Flight Test Center. Wood was assigned as permanent chief consultant pilot at Boeing with the pilots rotating there on a monthly basis. They were a vital element in the design of the vehicle and on the cockpit ergonomics, instrumentation and displays, flying endless hours in the simulator and developing re-entry control procedures and handling techniques. When Dana left the programme he was replaced with Albert H. Crews.

A particularly intriguing aspect of their work was to demonstrate, and effectively develop, the ability for Dyna-Soar pilots to control the Titan III launch vehicle all the way up to separation from the second stage. But the Air Force view that all winged vehicles should have at least one pilot in charge of controlling them, ran counter to the logic explained by rocketeers from NASA and men such as the legendary Wernher von Braun. The Titan was an Air Force project and von Braun received howls of criticism when he proposed to a meeting of the Society of Experimental Test Pilots that they would not have to develop techniques for doing that. Rocket engineers would build in to their launch vehicles automated flight controls, with greater safety and higher reliability than any pilot could achieve, he said.

The integration with experimental test pilots brought greater possibilities to the Dyna-Soar programme and it could have seen winged vehicles operating in space at least 10 years earlier than the Shuttle. But it did not exist just be a 'first', rather to be a generic evolution to Stage 3 of the long-term plan for an operational military system. The von Braun approach won the day over automated versus manual control of powered flight, but it was too late for Dyna-Soar.

The Kennedy administration reduced the programme to an experimental status and in June 1961 its designation changed to X-20, retained as a research vehicle for expanding upon the X-15 flight envelope. The first drop test within the atmosphere was now scheduled for January 1965, the first ground launch being planned for November 1965 and the first piloted launch scheduled for May 1966. The last of the experimental flights would be in September 1967.

The X-20 would consist of a glider weighing 5,556kg (12,250lb) of which 453kg (1,000lb) was for payload, attached to a 2,608kg (5,750lb) transition section, 4.5m (15ft) in length and with a maximum diameter of 3m (10ft) divided into a propulsion section and an equipment section. The overall length would have been 10.75m (35.3ft) with a maximum wing span of 6.3m (20.8ft) and a height of 2.7m (8.9ft). The maximum landing weight of the glider was to be 5,307kg

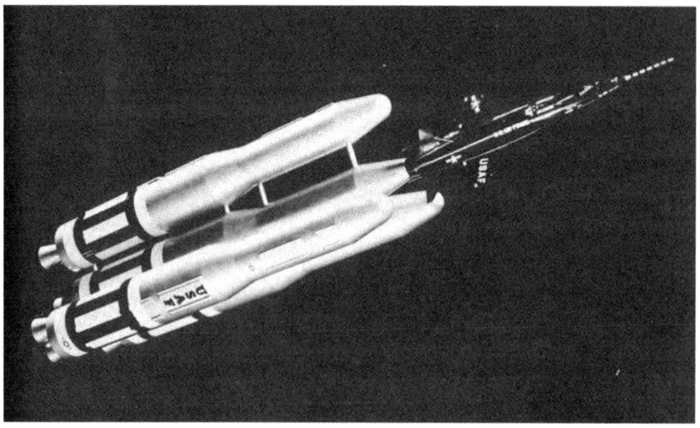

Right: As an alternative to Navaho boosters, clusters of Titan I stages would have propelled a redesigned X-15B into orbit. *Author's collection*

(11,700lb). As with the cockpit of the X-15, the X-20 would be pressurised with nitrogen and the payload section would provide 2.1m³ (75ft³) of volume for science instruments and measurement systems.

In those intervening years, the Dyna-Soar programme had changed markedly. The various phases had been redefined and reworked while the defence strategy and rationale for strategic systems had evolved. A lot of this was driven by the evolving technologies, not only in shifting the pendulum away from manned to unmanned system; the increasing use of transistors and semi-conductors would change it even further, shifting the bias toward highly sophisticated and complex machines operated remotely without the extra cost or the risk to human life inherent with manned vehicles.

This was both a logical and a pragmatic decision: logical because it would cost less and pragmatic because specialists, whether in a cockpit or on the ground, represent a great deal of financial and resource investment. If they could be kept out of harm's way, the investment would reap a valuable return. And perhaps uncomfortably, that rationale increasingly seemed relevant to the piloted X-15 when manned combat aircraft operating at these speeds were unlikely to become operational. It was perhaps only to be expected that Defence Secretary Robert McNamara gave the Air Force a simple choice – to develop Dyna-Soar into a fully operational system or use NASA's two-man ballistic Gemini spacecraft for the manned military mission in space, linked to the Manned Orbiting Laboratory. Gemini won out, but that didn't work out either. Again, another story.

Nevertheless, the X-20 was cancelled in December 1963 and the Air Force took up the Manned Orbiting Laboratory programme, in which Gemini spacecraft would be used to convey the crew and to operate its advanced optical reconnaissance equipment. That too was cancelled in 1969. The story of the integrated and phased plan to explore opportunities with winged orbital and re-entry vehicles operated by pilots and conducting a wide range of operational duties from orbit has largely disappeared from all but the most engaged enthusiasts and aerospace historians. The X-15 is largely central to decisions regarding those possibilities with projects and programmes abandoned in the wake of the 'faster-cheaper' method of using capsules and expendable rockets.

Lost also to many amid the publicity and fame attached to the Mercury, Gemini and Apollo astronauts and Moonwalkers, pilots for the Dyna-Soar/X-20 programme were the first 'spacemen' selected by the United States. They included four who flew the X-15 (Neil Armstrong, William Dana, Pete Knight and Milton Thompson), and some of the tasks from the original mission spectra for that vehicle were looked at for X-15B and the delta-wing variant. Just seven years after the cancellation of the X-20, the Air Force requested adaptation of the X-24A lifting-body into the X-24B, a delta-wing vehicle powered by an XLR-11 rocket motor of the type used with the Bell X-1, for evaluation of a delta-wing which it had been unable to apply to the X-15.

With its 78deg, double-delta planform the X-24B proved it would fly well and with a near-2.5:1 lift-to-drag ratio it proved that the Dyna-Soar concept would have worked too. NASA's Shuttle, with its double-delta, flew equally well on flight paths trailed by the X-15 and the X-24B. The Air Force waited a very long time to get its own wings into space but that was achieved on 22 April 2010 when the Boeing-built X-37B was carried into orbit on an Atlas V from Cape Canaveral. That series is still flying and remaining in space for increasingly lengthy periods, more than a year on some missions.

As a sequel to the evolutionary story of the X-15, to Dyna-Soar and, to some extent, to the Aerospace Plane (ASP), the Space Shuttle emerged for very different reasons and for completely separate functions. Attempts have been made to claim that the X-15 was merely a precursor to the Shuttle, or that the Shuttle was a natural successor to the X-15. It could be said that neither is true, for the following reasons.

While a considerable amount of information vital to the successful design of the Shuttle Orbiter was obtained by the X-15, the purpose of that earlier vehicle was very different, as it served as a research tool for characterising what was, at the time, a completely unknown and alien environment. The Shuttle was an attempt to produce a reusable, logistics and crew supply vehicle for orbital assets based around a manned space station and all the supporting infrastructure that this required. It was intended to be a fully operational space transportation system and under the criteria applied to all such systems it came very close to being that.

It could be argued that the Shuttle could not have been built had it not been for the X-15, and that is probably true insofar as the acquisition of that vital data would had to have been obtained by some other means in a different way. But the X-15 was crucial to designing with confidence, a flight control system capable of bringing a Shuttle crew back safely. And to understanding the dynamics of flight trajectories and the balance between energy and thermal protection. It is best remembered for that alone.

The X-15B proposal

For a short while after the dawn of the Space Age, which began with the launch of Russia's Sputnik 1 on 4 October 1957, some military planners in the United States were convinced that a human presence in orbit was vital to the national security interest. The continuing pressure on the political leadership

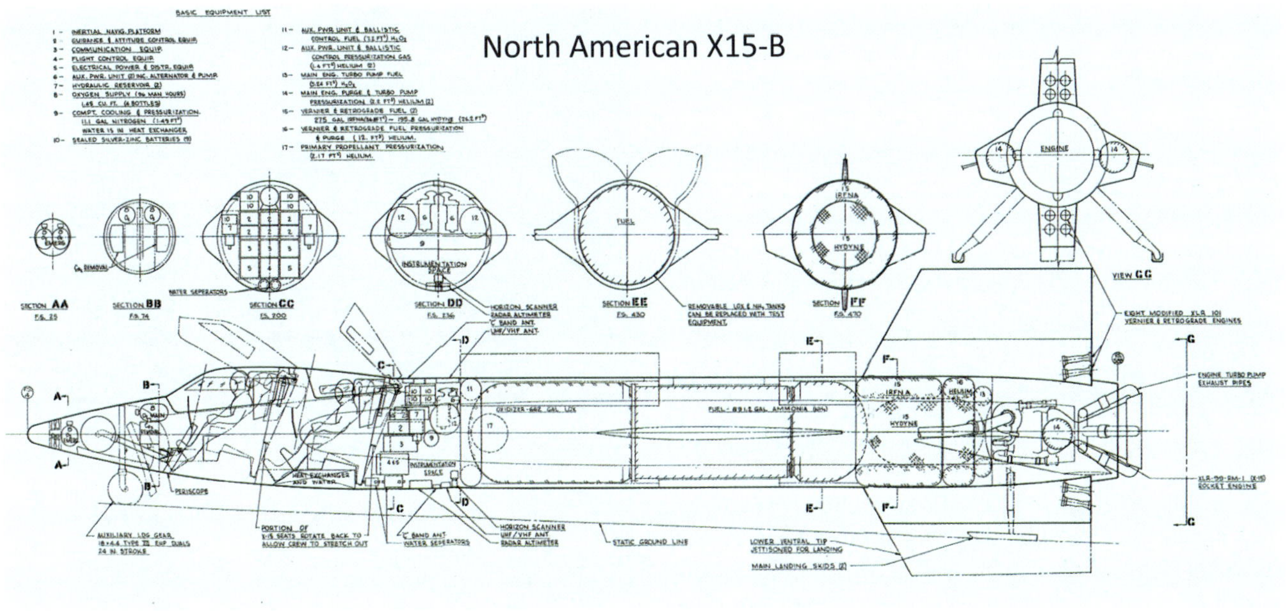

Above: With XLR-101 vernier and retrograde rocket motors, the revised two-seat X-15B would have achieved orbital flight prior to Dyna-Soar, as depicted in this 1959 engineering layout. *Parker Temple, restored from the original by Ms. Betty Temple*

to place the Dyna-Soar space vehicle in orbit was a big step up from existing capabilities and left a gap between supersonic research and conditions Dyna-Soar would encounter. By the late 1950s support began to grow for a technology demonstrator which could serve as a precursor to the semi-operational Dyna-Soar and verify certain assumptions which had been made regarding the winged spaceplane.

Clearly, the X-15A was unable to achieve orbital flight from the propulsion system it had and the thermal protection system was inadequate for the challenging environment of re-entry from orbit. Moreover, it was considered essential to have a second crewmember on board and, taking the two-seat idea of the original X-15 concept supported by the US Navy, the Air Force examined a version known as the X-15B which could accommodate a research engineer or second pilot. But the adaptation of the X-15 into a true spaceplane originated very much earlier than the two-seater supporting the Dyna-Soar programme.

Below: While the X-15B was being seen as an operational development precursor to the three-phase Dyna-Soar progamme, the latter was viewed as a development vehicle for establishing a military presence in orbit. In the late 1950s, the Air Force considered satellites as interim, stop-gap solutions to the need for advanced intelligence gathering. *Boeing*

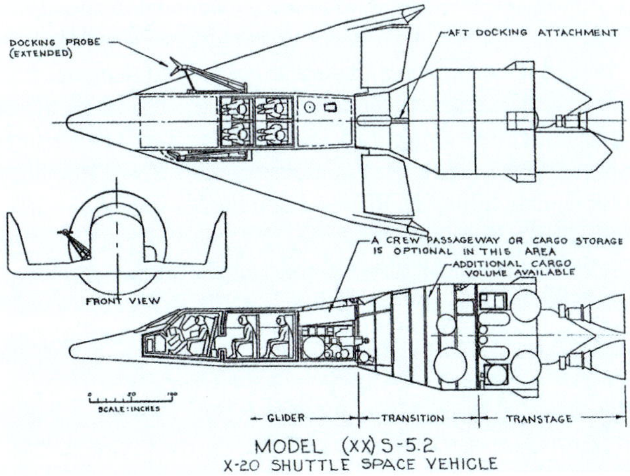

The basic idea for the X-15B evolved from the original North American proposal in February 1956 for the US Air Force Manned Ballistic Rocket Research System (Project 7969), a Space Age precursor to place a man in orbit, when very few seriously believed the Russians could do anything like that. The plan for a military man-in-space programme was overtaken by the shock of Sputnik 1 and the government's reaction to near-hysteria which gripped America, terrified of Soviet technological supremacy. But Project 7969 survived the turbulent reaction to Sputnik and continued on through the period of intense Congressional debate about how to respond.

Industry proposals for Project 7969 were tendered in January 1958, the NAA concept being a version of the X-15. Of the 10 proposals evaluated at Wright Field, six companies proposed capsules in various configurations and only four proposed winged vehicles. NAA proposed a stripped-down X-15 which could be launched on a two-stage rocket from Cape Canaveral to a single orbit of the Earth with an apogee of 122km (76mls) and a perigee of 72km (47mls). While being effectively outside Earth's atmosphere for lifting flight, even at these altitudes the modified X-15 would be on a suborbital trajectory because the perigee was too low for it to remain in orbit.

To provide for this suborbital flight around the Earth engineers would have reduced the empty weight to 4,490kg (9,900lb) for a fuelled weight of 13,300kg (29,400lb). It would have been launched from Cape Canaveral on four solid propellant booster rockets, three clustered as a first stage and one forming a second stage. The X-15's integral XLR-99 would have comprised the third stage. The rocket stages were based on the propulsion system for the Navaho, an air-breath-

Right: A fanciful depiction of a Saturn IB lifting the X-15A-2 toward orbit. In reality, the X-15B would have been the only derivative capable of orbital flight. *Parker Temple*

ing supersonic cruise missile launched by two powerful XLR-83-NA-1 booster rockets, each delivering a thrust of 1,800kN (405,500lb) from three rocket motors nested together at the base of the propellant tanks. For single-orbit flight the X-15 with three clustered Navaho boosters and their nine motors would have a lift-off thrust of 5,410kN (1.216million lb) and a second stage thrust of 1,800kN (405,500lb).

This spaceplane version of the X-15 would have employed a René 41 alloy shingle heat shield and a thicker Inconel X hot section but there would be no de-orbit propulsion required as the suborbital trajectory would lower the vehicle back into the atmosphere on a shallow re-entry path after one circumnavigation of the Earth. Using its cross-range capability, the X-15 would ditch in the Gulf of Mexico after the pilot ejected over land. As an expendable spaceplane it was hardly suited to a sustained research programme and served the need for a stunt rather than a protracted development effort leading to a sustainable capability.

While the US government organised a metamorphosis of the NACA into NASA, the direction of the man-in-space programme would shift to civilian ownership under the new organisation. Project 7969 became Man-In-Space-Soonest (MISS) to accelerate plans by the USAF for it to be the first to place a human in orbit. But when NASA was formed out of the NACA on 1 October 1958, MISS became Project Mercury and the new space agency got the job of recruiting astronauts and launching them into space.

Nevertheless, the Air Force continued to study modified X-15 vehicles as a means of consolidating the military mission in space. While the modified and leaner X-15 had been part of the Project 7969 proposal in January 1958, a parallel proposal was being rushed out by North American Aviation under the designation X-15B. Much bigger than the hypersonic X-15, and with a two-man crew, its XLR-99 would have been replaced by a Rocketdyne LR105 rocket motor with a thrust of 200.16kN (75,000lb) or 364.29kN (81,900lb) in the vacuum of space.

The LR105 was the central sustainer engine for the Atlas ICBM and used liquid oxygen and kerosene propellants rather than the LOX/anhydrous ammonia propellants of the XLR-99. Accordingly, the X-15B would have been larger than the basic aircraft and carried a beefed-up thermal protection system together with legacy systems and subsystems. Propulsion for launch would have been provided by a pair of XLR-83-NA-1 boosters, delivering a thrust of 3,602kN (810,000lb), connected together at the base but spaced so that one-third up, nestled in the space between them, was another Navaho booster stage projecting forward on top of which would be mounted the X-15B.

For launch, the paired boosters would fire for 80sec and be jettisoned before ignition of the single booster/X-15B combination which would carry the stack to a height of 121,920m (400,000ft) at which point the LR105 would take over and propel the winged spaceplane to a speed of almost 28,962kph (18,000mph). Mission planners anticipated a three-orbit flight before re-entry and a controlled landing at Edwards Air Force Base, the terminal phase to touchdown being in the same manner as the X-15A.

There was so little knowledge about the upper atmosphere, and so much ignorance about the aerothermal environment to which the X-15B would have been exposed that there would have been no possibility for the spaceplane, as built, to have survived re-entry. Like so many proposed concepts of its day, the technical ideas exceeded reality. Nevertheless, the Air Force persisted and studies continued on the North American proposal, quietly and in the background. This was a difficult time for Dyna-Soar as mission modes and flight planning were in a state of flux. The much more aggressive attack on orbital flight problems revealed significant challenges far beyond the capabilities of any X-15 derivative.

No doubt encouraged by the early test flights of the X-15 being conducted by Scott Crossfield, several alternative X-15B booster configurations were examined during 1959. One even envisaged a cluster of two-stage Titan I ICBMs arranged with three in a triangular configuration enclosing a fourth in the centre, to the top of which the X-15B would be attached. The first stage of a Titan I was powered by a pair of Aerojet LR87-3 delivering a thrust of 1,467kN (330,000lb). The launch thrust of this configuration would have been 5,871kN (1.32million lb).

With the cancellation of the Navaho cruise missile in 1957 and the priority on Air Force ICBM deployment being given to the Atlas and Titan programmes, there was little hope

Right: Theoretically applicable to both the X-15B and delta-wing versions which were soon to be proposed, a Mach 3 launch off the top of an XB-70 Valkyrie would have greatly extended operational capabilities. *NAA*

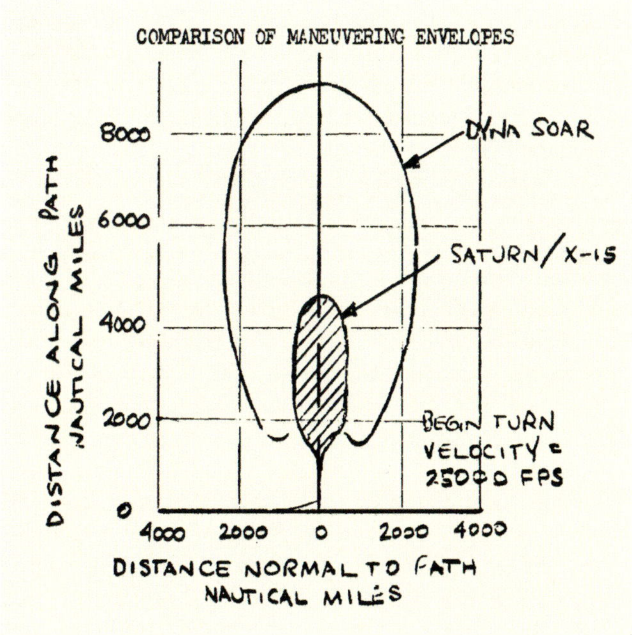

Left: Both the Air Force and North American Aviation worked up proposals for an interim X-15B to bridge the gap as a Round Two link between early high-speed/high-altitude research aircraft and the Dyna-Soar. *NAA*

of getting those propulsion systems for use in a research programme. The natural booster for the X-15B was the Saturn C-1 rocket under development at the Army Ballistic Missile Agency in Huntsville, Alabama. With a thrust of more than 5,782.4kN (1.3million lb), the Saturn was transferred to NASA in October 1959 and would be readily available for the Air Force. Still more than 18 months away from the decision by President Kennedy to send astronauts to the Moon, the prioritisation on Project Apollo was yet to unfold. In 1959, the Marshall Space Flight Center, as the Huntsville facility was renamed, could do with the expanded requirement for this super-booster to justify continued development. The more customers the better.

Saturn-rider

While the proposed X-15B appears to have had the same dimensions as the X-15A, in addition it carried eight small XLR-101 retro-rockets for de-orbit in two quads located in the dorsal and ventral fins just above and below the fuselage. But this conflicted with obvious changes forced by the greatly extended life of the vehicle in flight. With two crewmembers the original bottle oxygen would be inadequate and the X-15B would have required a regenerative system of some sort. A major change involved the addition of a clamshell payload bay across the top of the fuselage capable of containing science instruments or equipment, or up to 2,268kg (5,000lb) of additional propellant.

There was also provision for a rendezvous radar, clearly with the intention of supporting missions involving a second object, manned or unmanned, with which the X-15B would have approached for station-keeping. No provision was made for docking. This aspect surrounding rendezvous mirrored other highly classified plans for space rendezvous, allowing a spacecraft or spaceplane to home in on potentially threatening hostile satellites and destroy them. It was synonymous with the original expectation of the early Dyna-Soar mission

requirement.

In the late 1950s the military role in space was evolving at speed, far from the general gaze of public scrutiny and outside the surge in NASA activity. Killer-satellites were an early proposition in the lexicon of military concepts for space. In 1959, under the classified programme Bold Orion, a rocket launched from a Boeing B-47 intercepted the Explorer 6 satellite in Earth orbit. Within a few years the SAINT (an acronym for SAtellite INTerceptor) programme was under way and concerted efforts to produce an operational anti-satellite system supported a broad-based effort.

Several concept drawings appeared with these various proposals for a spaceplane derivative of the X-15, one of which shows a space-walking crewmember exiting the second cockpit position behind the pilot and carrying out maintenance on a satellite dish-shaped antenna. None of these had any chance of becoming viable and were prepared in the hope of placing potential applications under the eyes of Air Force recipients. In the 1950s and 1960s, confidential proposal brochures turned up on the desks of procurement officers, politicians and advocacy groups such as the Rand Corporation with greater frequency than confetti at a wedding.

Nevertheless, the X-15B was clearly an integral part of the long-anticipated military mission in space and four specific flight profiles were developed to define its requirements. These included low-altitude short-duration flights to long duration flights lasting up to two days and reaching altitudes of up to 965km (600mls). Trading payload for altitude, the spaceplane would have been capable of reaching 3,057km (1,900mls) into space. Re-entry was problematical and engineers recognised the significant challenge posed by the thermal loads encountered due to kinetic energy produced through friction with the atmosphere.

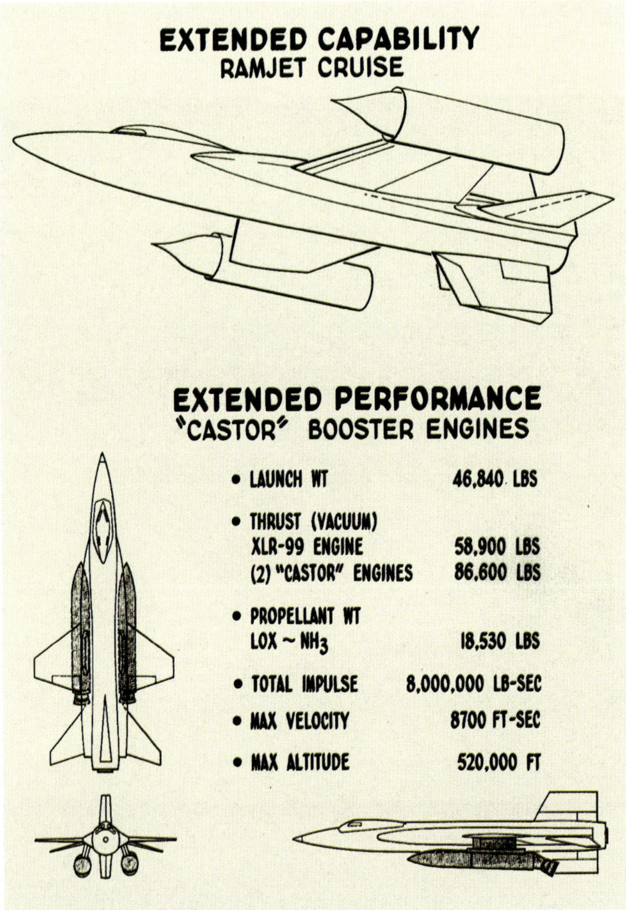

Left: In 1960 pressure was applied in an unsuccessful effort to get ramjet engines installed on the X-15 wingtips as a research effort for this type of propulsion. Also in 1960, it was suggested that two Castor solid rocket motors could boost performance to Mach 8.5 and an altitude of 158km (98mls). *NAA*

One way of solving the re-entry heat-load problem was to trade payload for fuel and effect a thrusting re-entry rather than an aero-braking mode. Paying the price with higher heat load, the X-15B could lift an additional 748kg (1,650lb) to 965km (600mls) but these trade-offs brought complications. It all hinged on heat-rate (the time it took to reach maximum temperature) versus heat-load (the total amount of thermal energy handled by the shielding). Knowledge about the upper atmosphere was scant at best and these were vague, theoretical approaches.

Using existing models, it was calculated that the X-15B would experience a nose temperature of 649°C (1,200°F), while the wing leading edges would experience peak temperatures of 2,704°C (4,900°F). The basic X-15 experienced wing temperatures no higher than the nose temperature on the re-entry model. Because of this the basic structure of the X-15 was woefully inadequate for its proposed role as a spaceplane. The mixed monocoque/semi-monocoque structure, its titanium frames for accommodating engine thrust and the tubular steel structures in the engine compartment would all see unacceptable temperatures.

NAA proposed a hot skin and carried out extensive research from a materials, and not a structures, standpoint and this work contributed greatly to the future success of several unmanned re-entry bodies which would evolve through the combined efforts of the Air Force and industry to produce survivable vehicles. This would also contribute greatly to the development of the Shuttle, a NASA commitment to which was made only 10 years after the X-15B proposal and only a few months after the last flight of the X-15.

While engineers studying a derivative suborbital X-15 considered René 41 and beryllium oxide for thermal protection, by the time it got to the level of a Saturn-launched orbital vehicle the analyses had progressed and were more sophisticated. A great amount of research was going on to find suitable materials for protecting re-entry warheads for ballistic missiles as well as for protecting the next generation of manned vehicles. By 1959 NASA was already thinking about manned missions to the Moon involving high-velocity return trajectories.

The research carried out for the these projects and for the Mercury spacecraft fed back across to the X-15B concept and forced proposals to use highly exotic and toxic materials, including ceramics such as thorium oxide at the wing root. Mid-span materials would include beryllium oxide while protection of the wing and tail leading edges would use columbium, effective against temperatures up to 1,538°C (2,800°F).

Other materials also being considered were molybdenum (1,649°C/3,000°F), graphite (2,093°C/3,800°F) and tungsten (2,621°C/4,750°F). These materials were considered only for their chemical properties and their ability to maintain integrity at high temperature.

The methods necessary to fashion and employ such materials on an aerospace vehicle were completely unknown in 1959 and even the titanium being worked for the Lockheed A-12 had required special tooling to be invented for forming and machining, a process unique to that aircraft. Nevertheless, while nickel alloy was felt to be acceptable for most of the wing trailing edge, the structural box was to have been coated with molybdenum. Thermal management of the load would have required completely new engineering concepts. It should be said that a lot of materials research conducted in this period fed directly to the benefit of reusable shuttlecraft studies in the late 1960s.

Throughout the relatively short life of the X-15B proposal the standard reference for the spaceplane launcher was the Saturn C-1 (later Saturn I) but an optional S-II stage being designed for the Saturn V and providing a thrust of 3,558kN (800,000lb) was mooted. In its developed form, the S-II stage would use uprated J-2 engines with a stage thrust 25 per cent greater than this. The S-I stage of the C-1 had eight H-1 engines, which in its evolution would eventually deliver a thrust of around 6,672kN (1.5million lb). With an added second stage in the form of the liquid oxygen/liquid hydrogen S-IV powered by six RL-10 engines delivering a total thrust of 400.3kN (90,000lb), it had the lifting potential to put the X-15B in orbit. For this application it would retain the XLR-99 as a third stage. At various times in that brief period during 1959, other upper stages were suggested, including the second stage of the Titan ICBM.

Air-launched concepts were also considered. While the B-52 would continue to serve as an air-launched carrier for flight tests with the X-15B, the prospect of launching it into space required a very different platform. For this function the North American Aviation XB-70 was discussed. This Mach 3 prototype bomber was being developed as a nuclear bomber and reconnaissance system but it would not fly until 1964. In 1959 it was considered to be a suitable platform for the X-15B, capable of carrying it to a height of 21,300m (70,000ft) at which point it would be released. But the energy available would only permit the X-15B to carry out a suborbital flight and not a full orbital mission. This did, however, introduce a pseudo-operational role for the X-15B in which it could have been considered for high-speed reconnaissance functions, albeit with a limited set of landing sites.

It appears from the proposal documents that considerable effort was given over to studying the trade-off between aerodynamic re-entry and powered re-entry, without a very satisfactory conclusion being reached. Basically, the more payload it carried the more aerodynamic heating would be imposed on the vehicle. Conversely, the lower the re-entry velocity, due to a higher impulse from the retro-rockets, the less heat load would be imposed. These trade-offs were wrestled with and not entirely resolved because the uncertainties were outside the margins required to constrain the decision about thermal protection concepts. It was a dilemma which floored the Dyna-Soar design and, fortunately, it rendered the orbital X-15B untenable.

Above: Playing the role of first-stage in an air-launched satellite concept, the X-15 would have sent a Blue Scout into space carrying a satellite destined to orbit the Earth. This was one of several proposals for launching Blue Scout into space. *NAA*

The December 1959 proposal for a space-capable X-15 anticipated detailed design completion by February 1962 followed by fabrication completed eight months later and first systems tests by January 1963. Glide tests from the B-52 carrier-plane would begin in May that year toward vertical test launches commencing shortly thereafter with orbital flights starting in June 1964. Dyna-Soar I was now expected to fly into space beginning in July 1962, rendering superfluous a legacy hypersonic research aircraft designed a decade earlier. Instead of demonstrating technologies essential for Dyna-Soar, it would lag far behind its purported successor.

Scramjets and satellites

But even as these momentous decisions were being wrestled with, several more applications of the X-15 were proposed. In November 1960, a year after the Saturn I/X-15B proposal had surfaced, NAA and the Air Force looked into the possibility of attaching scramjet (supersonic ramjet) engines to the wing tips to provide a hypersonic cruise capability. Another proposal at the same time envisaged the use of a Castor solid propellant rocket attached to each side of the fuselage beneath the wings. With two Castor motors providing an additional 385.2kN (86,600lb) of thrust, increasing total impulse by 147 per cent, the modified X-15 could have reached a speed of 9,541kph (5,930mph) and an altitude of 158,500m

(520,000ft), 158km (about 98mls). At this time the Castor motor was being adopted for the Thor missile in its use as a space launch vehicle and for what would become the Delta rocket, developed exclusively for launching satellites. In its application to the X-15 it would have been used for reaching high altitude rather than speed.

Whether the X-15 would have been capable of attaining such altitude would have depended upon the energy management of the re-entry phase, for this would have transformed the hypersonic research aircraft into a suborbital spaceplane. The specific function of a vehicle of this capability was not sufficiently evident to warrant it for serious consideration and the imminent demise of the Dyna-Soar/X-20 programme supported the view that the Air Force was getting out of the business of piloted spaceplanes. The technology for unmanned systems was clearly already in existence.

One further possible application of the X-15 presented it as the intermediate stage of a small satellite launch system. The Air Force was looking at the possibility of a launch-on-need capability for placing small satellites in orbit rapidly and without assigning a launch pad at the Kennedy Space Center or Vandenberg Air Force Base. It was from these two facilities, on the East Coast and West Coast respectively, that US military satellites were launched. The Scout programme was a NASA launch system consisting of a stack of separate solid propellant stages for placing small satellites in orbit. Under the Blue Scout programme, the Air Force would use this system for their own purposes.

Blue Scout was a generic name for a range of possible stage combinations and, for its application to the X-15, two versions were planned. Both were posited by a joint proposal from NAA and the Aeroneutronic Division of Ford Motor Company. This involved the B-52 as the first stage, the X-15 as the second stage and the Blue Scout cluster of solid propellant motors as the third stage. Under the direction of project manager Roland P. Bergeron, Aeroneutronic did all the running on this proposal, claiming large cost savings over conventional pad launches.

One version of the X-15/Blue Scout would have used the Hercules ABL X258 and ABL X259 rocket motors in tandem. Unguided flights would use the ABL X259 with an Aerojet 30 KS 8000 (AJ10) motor together with the Naval Ordnance Test Station NOTS 100A, a spherical motor used for orbit injection. The assembled weight would be 1,360-2,268kg (3,000-5,000lb) and the rocket combination would be attached to the X-15 on a 227kg (500lb) trapeze beneath the fuselage. The only other modification to the X-15 would be a shift in the thrust vector of the XLR-99 downwards by 2.5deg to compensate for the shift in the centre of gravity of the mated configuration. This system would be capable of placing a 22.7kg (50lb) satellite in a 1,480km (920mls) orbit or 45.4-68kg (100-150lb) to orbits of 555-724km (345-520mls). These figures relate to an East Coast launch, launches to polar orbits from California would have a slight payload decrement due to the absence of planetary rotation for assisting with orbital speed.

To execute a typical satellite launch the B-52 would climb to 13,700m (45,000ft) and release the X-15, carrying the Blue Scout assembly on the trapeze. At 47,749m (156,000ft) and a speed of up to 5,920kph (3,680mph), the X-15 would drop the rocket stack and coast on up to an apogee of 91,440m (300,000ft) while the Blue Scout stages fired sequentially. Ascent trajectories could launch the Blue Scout at 10-60deg angle of attack, depending upon the requirement of the mission. The sequence of operations would be controlled by the X-15 pilot through the test conductor working at a checkout console on the B-52.

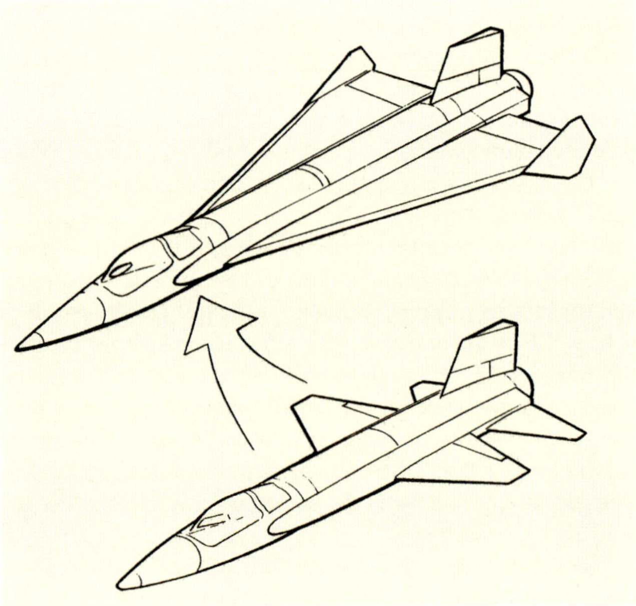

Above: Not long after flights began with the X-15, proposals were raised for a delta-wing adaptation of the original design. *NAA*

As plausible as this was, the concept never grew out of the definition phase as other and less complex means of placing small satellites in orbit evolved, including the use of submarines to launch satellites direct from firing tubes, originally configured to fire missiles with warheads. The Air Force also developed a range of small satellites launched piggy-back from rockets delivering bigger satellites to orbit. But there was one application which came very close to reality, the only one for which significant modifications to the basic aircraft were required.

Delta-wing X-15

In 1964 there was increasing support for transforming the function of the X-15 into a tool for hypersonic cruise research. In parallel with increasing emphasis on military applications, the possible use of hypersonic vehicles for transport and commercial applications, plus the concept of winged rocket stages recovered for re-use, NASA was keen to study the possibility of giving the X-15 a delta-wing configuration. A formal meeting was held at the Flight Research Station on 9-10 December 1964 in which Paul Bickle affirmed that '...a delta-wing X-15 program could establish a baseline of confidence and technology from which decisions regarding the feasibility and design of advanced air-breathing vehicles could be realistically made...'.

The FRC followed this in 1965 with a request for North

American Aviation to carry out a detailed study on this concept which was required to incorporate a 'slender hypersonic wing substituted for the present wing and horizontal tail'. NASA wanted the wing to support sustained flight at Mach 7 with brief periods at Mach 8 and the basic structure of the aircraft to remain the same as for the original aircraft equipped with the trapezoidal wing.

Other aspects required a design load limit of 5-g and a maximum dynamic pressure of 95.76kPa (2,000lb/ft^2). Consideration was to be given to lengthening the fuselage by 2.44m (8ft) for increased propellant capacity, and a possible thermal shield replacing the ablative coatings of the X-15A-2. NASA also raised the possibility of relocating the wing attachment from mid-fuselage to a position flush with the bottom, increasing dynamic load to 119.7kPa (2,500lb/ft^2) and structural loads of up to 7.33-g. These factors were to include the external propellant tanks and relocation of the nose gear.

When the cost estimates came in for the thin-wing delta X-15 it amounted to $29.75million required between fiscal years 1967 and 1973, of which 83 per cent would go to the contractor and the balance would go on NASA expenses. With no clear and unambiguous reason to keep the X-15 flying, however, there was a prescient warning that should the Air Force decline funding to maintain the programme, costs could increase by a further $17million. The development plan anticipated a request for proposals which would be issued in August 1966 followed by a contract award in March 1967, modification of X-15-3 between December 1967 and October 1968 and a first flight in January 1969. There were to be two test drops followed by 37 research flights completed by the end of 1972.

The RFP (Request for Proposals) finally went out in

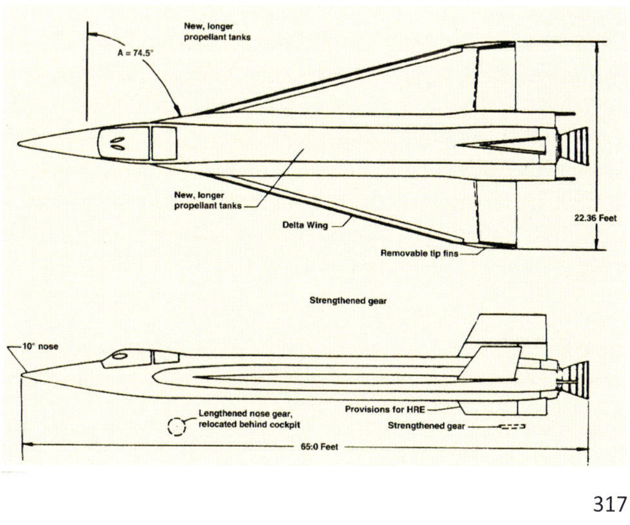

Above: NASA Langley Research Center conducted several wind tunnel tests on a range of alternate delta-wing X-15 configurations. *NASA*
Right: A thin-wing delta held promise and led to further refinement, defined by the type of experimental work envisaged. *NAA*

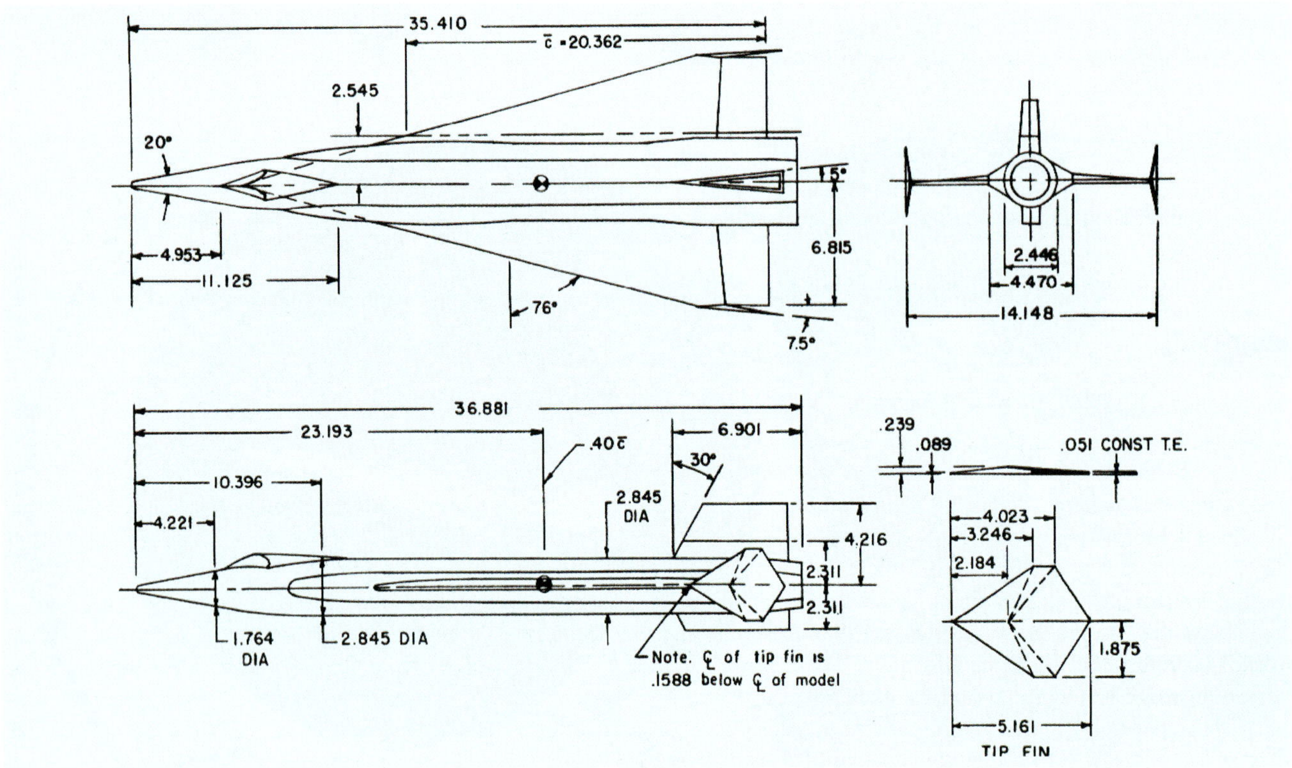

Above: Further refinement to a wind tunnel model differed from earlier options by changes to the vertical wing tip fins. By 1967, with the loss of X-15-3, work had largely stopped on these different configurations. *NAA*

March 1967, with several aircraft manufacturers expressing interest in bidding for the contract. Keen to secure the work, NAA funded wind tunnel studies of delta configurations and Langley Research Center used its 50.8cm (20in) hypersonic tunnel to conduct studies on 1/15th and 1/50th scale models at a range of speeds from Mach 0.2 to Mach 6.9. Overwhelmed by the intensity of their work, none of the other manufacturers bid on the proposal and, with a 500-page report presented to NASA, NAA outlined what would be a substantial rework of the basic aircraft.

To maintain conformity with the NB-52 carrier-plane, NAA proposed retaining the same wing span, for a 56m² (603ft²) planform with a leading edge sweep of 76deg. The single elevon at each wing trailing edge had an area of 2.86m² (30.8ft²) with a +4.5deg/-5.0deg deflection capability for roll and longitudinal control. Dorsal and ventral stabilisers and new wing tip fins would control directional stability, with the dorsal rudder providing directional control. The wing tip fins could be adjusted on the ground to evaluate various levels of directional and lateral stability but they would primarily provide these functions at high alpha-angles when the vertical stabilisers were blanked from the airflow.

The wing structure was crucial to the thermal conditioning of the vehicle in high-temperature flight regimes. Ideally, a heat sink structure should adopt a monocoque shell comprising a single skin integrally stiffened with a minimum number of restraining spars and ribs, their caps exposed to aerodynamic heating to reduce the heat rate. But this was counter to the convention where monocoque structures were devoid of these stiffeners, scalloped spar and rib designs proving sufficient for stability of the covering panels and still providing sufficient shear strength.

The hypersonic cruise mission required an additional propulsion system known as the Hypersonic Research Engine (HRE) which it was proposed would be carried on the ventral fin. But the aircraft had to be aerodynamically stable without the HRE, which was expected to weigh 454kg (1,000lb). To accommodate test flights of the delta-wing X-15 without the HRE, a separate ballast compartment was provided which

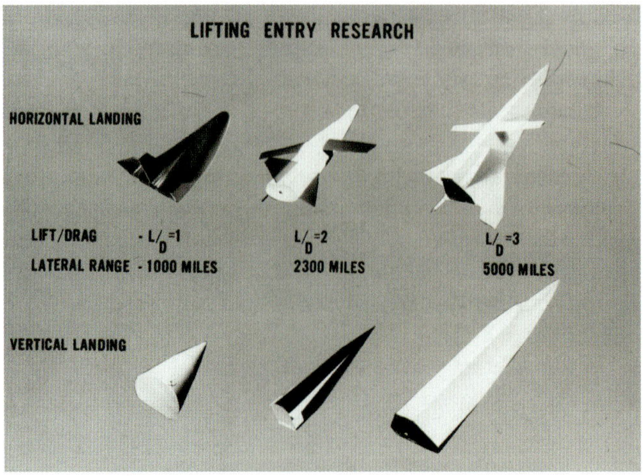

Right: By 1968 NASA was focusing on lifting-body concepts for winged flight into space and evaluated a range of different designs offering various cross-range capabilities. With the Air Force X-20 cancelled, it fell to NASA to develop a new form of space transportation applicable to both military and civilian payloads. *NASA*

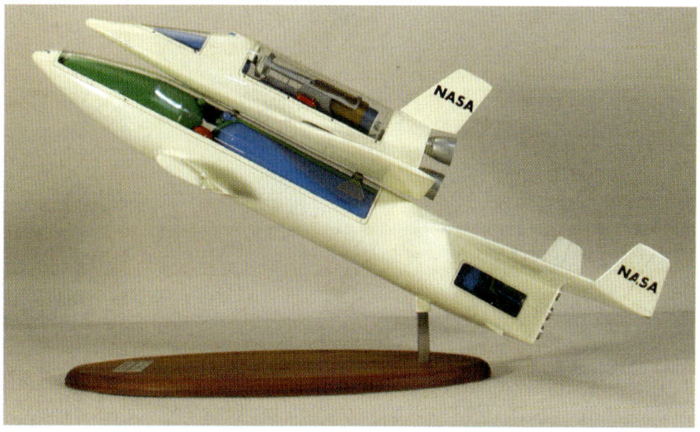

Right: By 1968-69, several contractors were preparing studies of different configurations to carry winged vehicles into orbit, coining the name Space Shuttle. By 1970 the preferred configuration was a fully reusable system with fly-back booster lifting an orbiter to altitude from where it would carry on to achieve orbit. *The Martin Company*

would also double as an experiment chamber when the engine was not installed.

The shape of the wing too was crucial to how the aircraft behaved both aerodynamically and thermodynamically and the contour of the leading edge was given careful consideration. The consensus was that this would have little or no effect on the performance of the aircraft since lift would come primarily from positive pressure on the undersurface of the wing itself. But it was left as an open issue, little understood at the time and one slated for NASA wind tunnel tests to obtain the necessary data. Nevertheless, all agreed that the leading edge contour would significantly affect low speed handling and in particular the landing phase.

The thermal environment was not nearly as severe as the profiles for suborbital or orbital X-15B re-entry profiles but the leading edge would, nevertheless, experience a temperature of 1,204°C (2,200°F) and NAA did some tests on a wing segment fabricated from columbium, already a chosen material for Dyna-Soar, at 1,315°C (2,400°F) with positive results. Which was just as well as there was no other material available which could operate as a heat sink at this temperature.

Immediately aft of the leading edge on the undersurface of the wing, NAA proposed a 61cm (24in) wide strip of metallic heat shield with thermal stand-off clips covering a sandwich of low-density insulation. Aft of this area it was felt that Thoria-Dispersion (TD) nickel would suffice to protect the wing structure. TD nickel is a strengthened steel producing high yield and tensile strength.

The wingtips on the delta-wing X-15 were originally to have been upswept to provide directional stability in the absence of a ventral rudder and this followed the majority of later X-15 flights where high angles of attack were normal. But the delta-wing model would fly the majority of its profiles on low-alpha angles due to its cruise-orientated research programme, where sustained level flight was more usual. But those early wind tunnel tests conducted by NAA revealed an inadequacy above Mach 6 and so vertical fins were added, protruding above and below the wing immediately inboard of the tip, which tests in the Langley 50.8cm (20in) tunnel proved to be more workable. There was provision in the final NAA proposal for these wing tip fins to be removed should the tunnel tests prove incorrect.

The overall length of the delta-wing aircraft was extended by 3.05m (10ft) to 19.03m (62.43ft). While retaining a little of the existing aircraft structure from immediately aft of the cockpit forward, the mid and aft sections of the fuselage were a completely new design, accommodating a propellant section increased by 231cm (91in) and carrying new attachment and support fittings. A test specimen of the mid fuselage region was manufactured from René 41 and Inconel 718 to evaluate which was preferable but no decision had been made when the project was scrapped.

The ballast/experiment compartment was a 73.7cm (29in) section added behind the ammonia tank while the instrument section between the fuel and oxidiser tanks was retained. This aft section would house the fuel for the HRE and provide systems equipment monitoring sensors. The forward fuselage would give up the ogive cross-section for a 20deg included-angle conical section, a semi-monocoque structure fabricated from René 41 and either Inconel X or Inconel 718. Consideration was given to replacing the air-data nose ball, standard on the conventional aircraft, with a Litton 7-port sensor.

To provide the necessary thrust to sustain cruise at Mach 7 and achieve brief flights at Mach 8, several different propulsion systems were considered as replacements for the XLR-99. The purpose of this engine would be to carry the X-15 in a sustained hypersonic cruise so that one or more configurations of HRE, attached to the ventral fin, could be tested much like the scramjet on the basic X-15. The primary candidate for this purpose was the Aerojet YLR91-AJ-15 which used a form of N_2O_4/UDMH (nitrogen tetroxide/unsymmetrical dimethyl hydrazine – a mixture for this combination known as Aerozene-50) propellants.

Developed as the second stage of the Titan II ICBM, with a 25:1 nozzle it would produce a thrust of 444.8kPa (100,000lb) and have been capable of propelling the aircraft to a maximum speed of 9,590kph (5,960mph), far beyond the design requirement of the delta-wing X-15. This assumed a drop weight of 23,807kg (52,485lb) and a thrust termination weight of 8,611kg (18,985lb). With the HRE engine attached, the theoretical maximum velocity would be 9,155kph (5,690mph).

In examining the cruise potential, some thought was given to providing an additional engine for extended cruise capability but the integration of such a system in the mid and aft sections of the fuselage, into what was already a tight and highly compact piece of engineering, made that an almost impossible task. It was proposed that the growing interest in providing good flight data for sustained Mach 7 flight might be applied to the operational capabilities of intercontinental strike and reconnaissance aircraft which were being considered at the time.

But the YLR-91 never made it through to the final set of deliberations, a greatly modified XLR-99 being selected instead. Reaction Motors was confident that they could increase the thrust of the existing engine to 369.18kPa (83,000lb) at 30,480m (100,000ft) with a capability to throttle back to a

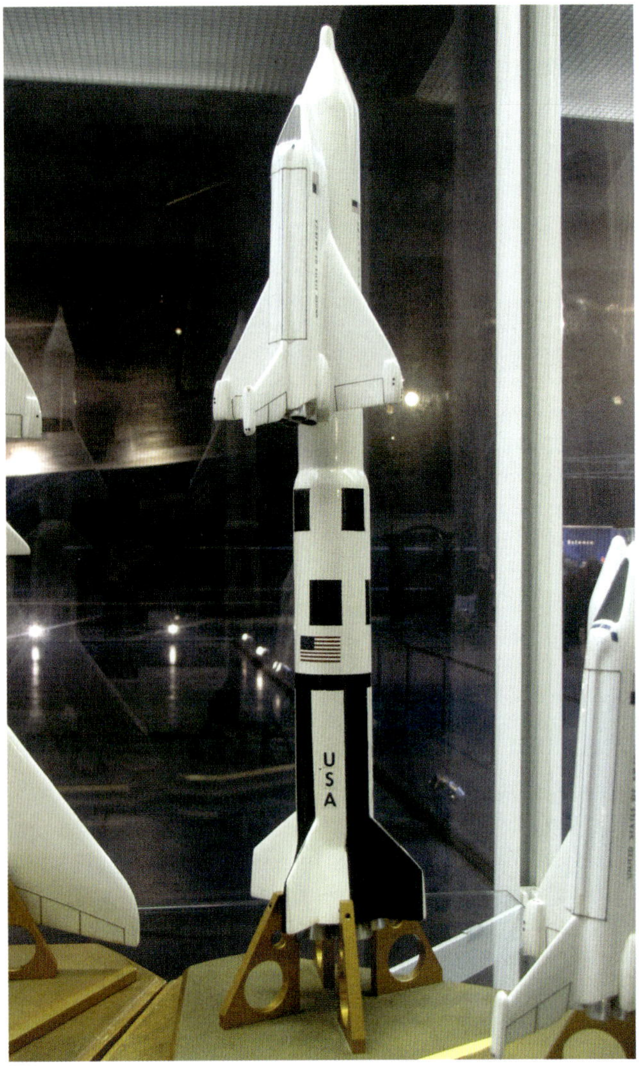

Above: When it was deemed that a piloted, reusable booster would be too costly, it was suggested that the orbiter and an external propellant tank could be launched by an expendable S-IC stage from the Saturn V programme. *Ben Schumin*

thrust of 35.6kPa (8,000lb) for sustained cruise at Mach 6.5. With an additional propellant tank on the centreline of the fuselage the delta-wing vehicle could achieve Mach 8. However, given the difficulties already experienced with that engine, doubts were raised regarding these claims.

Several other changes were necessary, both to accommodate the additional weight and to compensate for the changes in the centre of gravity. The most obvious being the relocation of the forward nose leg to a position behind the cockpit, the original set of instruments from that compartment being transferred to the void created by the change of location. There were other more subtle changes of which several had great potential for the further development of flight control systems. The MH-96 adaptive control system had been fitted to X-15-3 in parallel with the original mechanical linkages, but the delta-wing derivative was to have a fly-by-wire system without conventional back-up. This alone would have made the delta-wing version unique for its day.

When the final configuration and wind tunnel results were in – over 300 hours having been accumulated with scale models – it was apparent that only a few elements of the original X-15 would be retained and that the delta-wing version was a completely new aircraft utilising very few parts from the original design. But even as interest in this hypersonic cruise vehicle waned in both NASA and the Air Force, even more exotic roles for a derivative aircraft were envisaged. One suggestion was that the delta-wing aircraft should be equipped with a scramjet engine from the outset.

There had been much speculation about the Aerospace Plane, a hypersonic air-breathing, hydrogen-fuelled, air vehicle which would use a scramjet motor as its primary propulsion system. The ASP, as it was known, was highly classified and incorporated a range of technologies but the environment in which it would be operating was little understood. There was also an increasing number of studies underway on re-entry vehicles with conventional wings or with a blended wing-body structure. These so called Lifting Bodies, and the desire to provide spent rocket stages with a fly-back capability, kept alive scientific and engineering interest in the hypersonic environment.

Nevertheless, a full commitment to the delta-wing X-15 derivative was difficult to find, despite support from NASA's John Becker, at the Langley Research Center, and among engineers and scientists at the Flight Research Center. The proposal was still moving forward when Mike Adams lost his life along with X-15-3 on 15 November 1967 and that brought the curtain down on what could have been a completely new lease of life for the aircraft. By this date the trend toward hypersonic flight was drifting away and the concept appeared too far ahead of its time. But the ASP concept had one more throw-over to the X-15 as it existed.

As defined, ASP would evaluate a variety of different propulsion concepts including the LACE (Liquid Air Collection and Enrichment) engine which would collect air as it flew, extract the oxygen, chill it to a liquid phase and use it to combust fuel carried integrally. A quantity of oxygen would be stored on board and used to mix with the fuel when the air thinned beyond use. This was highly attractive because oxygen is very much heavier than hydrogen and takes up a substantial amount of volume and weight in any rocket system. If only sufficient oxygen was carried to get it off the ground and up to hypersonic speed, the remaining amount required for propulsion at the edge of the atmosphere and into space could be collected on the way.

Some engineers examined the possibility of refuelling the ASP as it cruised in the atmosphere at Mach 6 and turned to the X-15 for a way of making this happen. They proposed a Hypersonic In-flight Refueling System (HIRES) which envisaged two X-15 vehicles flying in formation at Mach 6 and demonstrating such a capability. It was never pursued but the idea was supported by ASP contracts which, in addition to NAA working on this highly classified project, included Douglas and Convair. The thought of two aircraft of this type, launched on the same day, flying in formation with interconnecting fuel transfer lines is a bizarre idea and, along with nuclear-powered aircraft and hydrogen-fuelled spy-planes, one firmly rooted – and abandoned – in the era in which it was discussed.

Appendix 1

X-15 Specification

Physical Characteristics of the Basic X-15 and X-15A-2

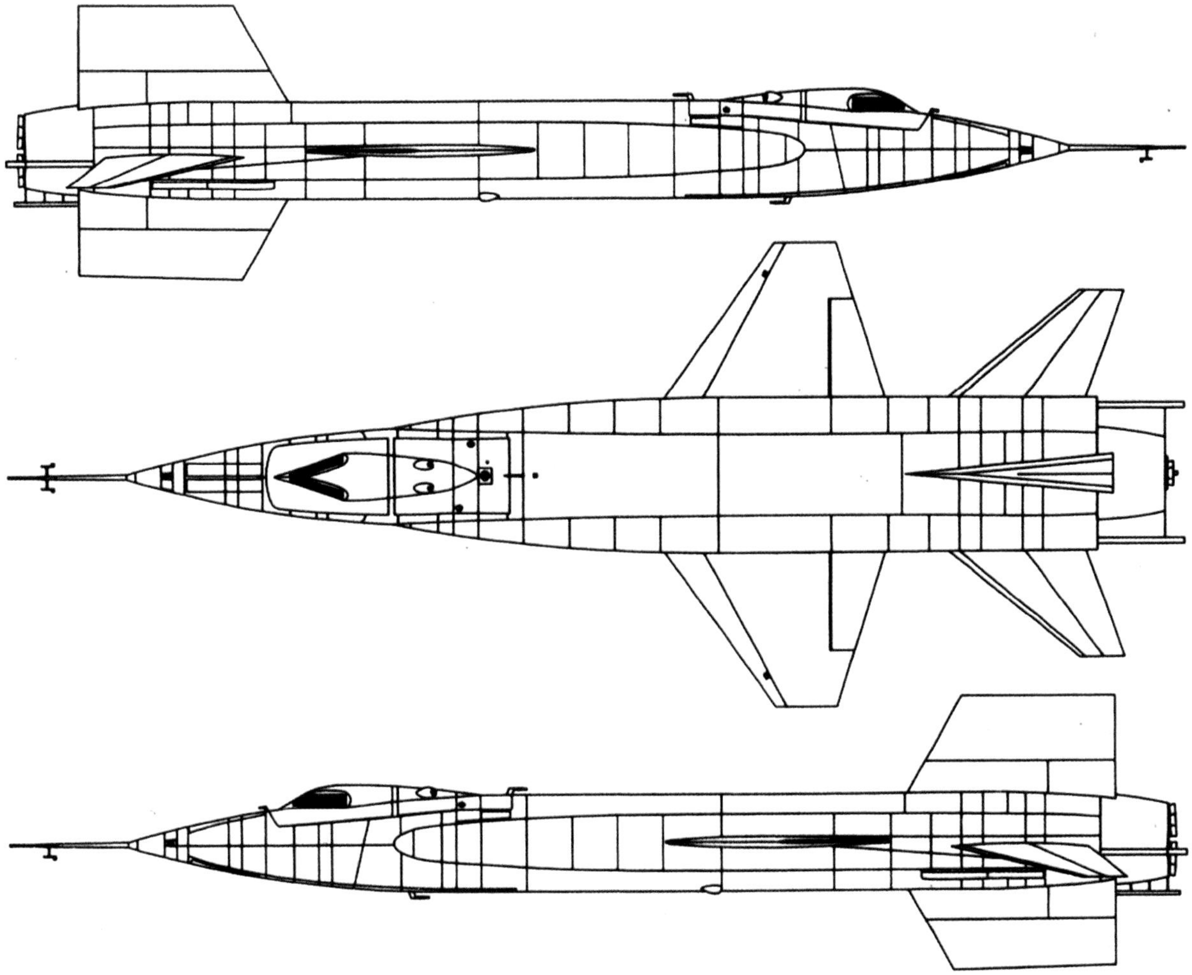

Fuselage

Length X-15 with XLR11, no pitot boom, ft: 49.50
Length X-15 with XLR99, no pitot boom, ft: 50.25
Length X-15A-2, ft:..52.42
Maximum width, ft:..7.33
Maximum depth, ft: 4.67
Maximum depth over canopy, ft: 4.97
Side area (X-15-1, -2 and -3 total) ft^2:....................................215.66
Side area (X-15A-2 total) ft^2:..221.38
Fineness ratio: 10.91
Ground line angle at rest, deg:..2.35
Height (skid to vertical fin tip), ft:..11.62

Wing

Aerofoil section: ....NACA 66005 (modified)
Total area
(includes 94.98 ft^2 covered by fuselage), ft^2: 200.00
Span, ft: 22.36
Mean aerodynamic chord, ft:..10.27
Root chord, ft: 14.91
Tip chord, ft: 2.98
Taper ratio: 0.20
Aspect ratio: 2.50
Incidence, deg: 0.0
Dihedral, deg: 0.0
Sweep at 25 per cent chord: 25.64
Aerodynamic twist, deg:..0.0
Loading, lb/ft^2:...66.50
Loading X-15A-2, lb/ft^2: 280.65

Flap

Type:...Plain
Area (each), ft^2:...8.30
Span (each), ft: 4.50

Inboard chord, ft: 2.61
Outboard chord, ft: 1.08
Deflection, down (nominal design), deg: 30
Ratio flap chord to wing chord: 0.22
Ratio flap span to wing semi-span: 0.40
Trailing-edge angle, deg: 5.67
Travel down, deg: 30.00

Horizontal tail

Airfoil section: NACA 66005 (modified)
Total area
(includes 63.29 ft^2 covered by fuselage), ft^2: 115.34
Span, ft: 18.08
Mean aerodynamic chord, ft: 7.05
Root chord, ft: 10.22
Tip chord, ft: 2.11
Taper ratio: 0.21
Aspect ratio: 2.83
Sweep at 25 per cent chord line, deg: 45
Dihedral, deg: -15
Movable surface area, ft^2: 51.77
Ratio horizontal-tail area to wing area: 0.58
Deflection: Longitudinal, up, deg: 15
Longitudinal, down, deg: 35
Lateral differential (pilot authority), deg: ±15
Lateral differential (autopilot authority), deg: ±30
Control system: Irreversible hydraulic boost with artificial feel

Upper vertical tail

Aerofoil section: 10deg single wedge
Total area, ft^2: 40.91
Span, ft: 4.58
Mean aerodynamic chord, ft: 8.95
Root chord (at chine intersect), ft: 10.21
Tip chord, ft: 7.56
Taper ratio: 0.74
Aspect ratio: 0.51
Sweep at 25 per cent chord line, deg: 23.41
Ratio vertical-tail area to wing area: 0.20
Movable surface area, ft^2: 26.45
Deflection, deg: ±7.50
Control system: Irreversible hydraulic boost with artificial feel

Tip chord, ft: 7.56
Sweepback of hinge line, deg: 0

Lower vertical tail

Airfoil section 10º single wedge
Total area, ft^2 34.41
Span, ft 3.83
Mean aerodynamic chord, ft 9.17
Root chord, ft 10.21
Tip chord, ft 8.00
Taper ratio 0.78
Aspect ratio 0.43
Sweep at 25-percent-chord line, deg 23.41
Ratio vertical-tail area to wing area 0.17
Movable surface area, ft^2 19.95
Deflection, deg ±7.50
Control system: Irreversible hydraulic boost with artificial feel

Speed brake

Area (each), ft^2: 5.37
Mean span (each), ft: 1.60
Chord (each), ft: 3.36
Frontal area at maximum deflection, ft^2: 13.8
Deflection, deg: 35

Base area

Fuselage, side fairing, vertical fins, wings, horizontal tail, landing skids), ft^2: 34.1

Total frontal area

Maximum, including wing and horizontal tail
at 0^0 deflection angle, ft^2: 38.8

Landing gear

Skid track, ft: 9.65
Nose gear to skid tread, ft: 39.67

Weights (representative)

Empty, lb: 11,374
Empty, X-15A-2, lb: 18,340
Launch, lb: 31,275
Launch, X-15A-2 lb: 56,130

Acknowledgement for this information goes to aerospace engineer and historian Dennis R. Jenkins, with grateful thanks.

Appendix 2

Edwards Air Force Base

Home of the X-15

Above: Seen from high altitude, the facilities at Edwards AFB blend into the dry lake bed where the Air Force and NASA share flight test facilities. *NASA*

As flight testing grew quickly in the second half of the 1940s, the Muroc facility began to take on a progression of new identities, defined by names reflecting the growth and expansion of activity at the dry lake site. As related in the main narrative, on 30 September 1946 Walt Williams headed the first group of five NACA engineers to arrive at what was then known as the Muroc Army Air Base. The place was known as Rogers Dry Lake at the edge of the Mojave Desert and the NACA shared some of that space with the Army as the Muroc Flight Test Unit (MFTU), which had been given permanent status by NACA director Hugh L. Dryden on 7 September 1947.

By the end of 1948 the MFTU had grown to have 60 personnel and the work expanded greatly. With the growth of flight activity funded primarily out of the Langley and Ames research centres, the MFTU was given a level of independent authority when, on 14 November 1949 it was renamed the NACA High-Speed Flight Research Station (HSFRS), now with around 100 permanent staff. On 27 January 1950 the Air Force renamed the host facility as the Edwards Air Force Base in honour of Capt. Glen W. Edwards, killed on 5 June 1948 in the crash of a Northrop YB-49 flying-wing bomber prototype.

On 1 July 1954 the NACA personnel which had previously occupied what was referred to as South Base, where training units were located, moved to permanent facilities midway between that location and North Base, where Air Force flight testing took place. Now with some 250 employees, the NACA facility was to be known as the High-Speed Flight Station (HSFS). Following the metamorphosis of the NACA into NASA, on 27 September 1959 the HSFS became the Flight Research Center (FRC) at which date it had around 340 people. At this time the biggest research programme under way at the site was the X-15. Soon, the Lifting Body programme arose which itself played a vital role in combining data from the X-15 programme to inform designers working up the initial operating envelope for the Space Shuttle.

The FRC got a further change of name on 26 March 1976 when it became the Dryden Flight Research Center in honour of the late Hugh L. Dryden, former head of the NACA and deputy administrator of NASA until his death on 2 December 1965. It now had some 560 people on strength. A further expansion of roles and responsibilities came when it was reconfigured as a landing field for 13 captive and active Air Launched Tests with the Space Shuttle Orbiter and its adapted Boeing 747 carrier-plane in 1977.

That role expanded to support operations from 1981-2011 as a landing field for Shuttle orbital operations and to sustain readiness to act as an emergency landing facility on missions assigned routinely to land at the Kennedy Space Center in Florida. The latest change occurred on 1 March 2014 when fittingly it became the Armstrong Flight Research Center in honour of Neil Armstrong, who in July 1969 became the first man to walk on the Moon. Armstrong was a pilot-engineer of great natural talent possessing a high instinct for the nuanced qualities of a test and research pilot par excellence.

Over time, the NACA and NASA presence there had grown from support for Air Force and Navy test operations to a converging association by NACA-dedicated flight research activities with aircraft it had itself developed. That grew to embrace aircraft specifically designed by the NACA, most notably the X-15 hypersonic, high-altitude research aircraft, the first winged vehicle to carry humans into space.

At a less ambitious level, the use of aircraft to conduct real-world flight tests with appropriately instrumented aircraft

Above: National Advisory Committee for Aeronautics Director Hugh L. Dryden formally established the Muroc Flight Test Unit at Muroc Army Air Base on 7 September 1947. *NACA*

Above: On 27 January 1950, the Muroc Army Air Base was re-named Edwards Air Force Base, after test pilot Glen W. Edwards who lost his life on 5 June 1948 flying the YB-49 flying-wing prototype bomber. *NACA*

Above: A collection of NACA research aircraft as of August 1953. Grouped around the Douglas X-3 Stiletto, rotating clockwise from bottom left: Bell X-1A, Douglas Skystreak, Convair XF-92A, Bell X-5, Douglas Skyrocket and Northrop X-4. *NASA*

was a great step forward and underpinned the tremendous strides taken in high-performance capabilities. Less known is the more mundane, arguably larger contribution it has made to general and commercial aviation as well.

X for 'diversification'

Under the X-series designation, and working cooperatively with the NACA at a level it had never done before, through the recognition of vital interests shared with the civilian scientists the Air Force supported a gradual but significant expansion of Muroc. In a very few years it would exceed the facilities and the responsibilities of Wright Field, the historic centre of US military aviation originally placed at Huffman Prairie as the site where the Wright brothers began the development of their flying machines in 1904. Adopting various names, Wright Field was officially unveiled as such on 12 October 1927 and through further name changes became Wright-Patterson Air Force Base on 13 January 1948.

After the Second World War, the Air Force looked outside its own research activities to cooperate in the development of transonic and supersonic aircraft, most notably of course with the NACA on the X-1 series and the X-2. Ever keen to establish speed and altitude records, the Air Force at Edwards AFB achieved the first flight through Mach 1 and, with the X-2, through Mach 3. Seeking to probe the exotic flight environment above Mach 3, as related elsewhere it would suffer a short and tragic operational life. Nevertheless, the Air Force ensured that its participation in the X-15 would be rewarded by an Air Force pilot (Maj. Robert White) exceeding Mach 4, 5 and 6 for the first time just as Yeager had for Mach 1. The NACA's Scott Crossfield had, of course, been first through Mach 2.

Not all the early X-series were committed to fundamental data-gathering devoid of a direct correlation with proposed requirements or design bids. One, however, realised an unusual set of possibilities which did, eventually, result in an operational aircraft which would never have been built, let along placed in production, had it not been for an X-series aircraft. That project was the X-3, aptly named Stiletto for its highly streamlined and long, extended nose section and needle-point tip. Ironically, it was designed and built to a requirement pre-dating any of the X-craft.

Above: Never matching speed expectations, the X-3 did much to pioneer the use of new materials, including titanium, and provided considerable data on stability and flight loads. *Author's collection*

Above: Not all aircraft tested at Edwards were piloted, the X-10 being a test vehicle for the design configuration of the North American SM-64 Navaho cruise missile. *Museum of the USAF*

Douglas had been in discussion with the Air Force since 1941 for a jet-powered aircraft capable of taking off and landing under its own turbojet propulsion and of achieving Mach 2 at 9,144m (30,000ft). That work had been realised with authorisation dated 30 December 1943 for the detailed investigation of such an aircraft. The initial proposal had been approved on 30 May 1945. It would be funded under Project MX-656, designated X-3 and designed for the Westinghouse J46 turbojet. Douglas knew it as the Model 499 and two flying prototypes were ordered but the engine failed to live up to its promises and was replaced with two Westinghouse XJ34-WE-17 engines.

The X-3 eventually flew for the first time on 20 December 1952. Diminutive in size, defined in appearance by its extended fuselage and extremely thin and narrow-span 4.5 per cent thickness-chord wings, only one was ever built. It never went supersonic in level flight, although it could slip through Mach 1 in a dive. But it had a profoundly successful legacy (at least in production numbers) in the F-104 Starfighter, beneficiary of the type when Lockheed took wind-tunnel data from the X-3 and applied that to an unsolicited bid for a supersonic interceptor. The Air Force generated a requirement for what, despite its supersonic capabilities, became one of the most hotly contested combat aircraft programmes of the time. In all, more than 2,500 were built.

Liked by some but loathed by many among the broad range of NATO countries that bought the type, the F-104 Starfighter remained with the US Air Force for eleven years before it was retired in 1969. Intriguingly however, when equipped with a 26,688N (6,000lb) Rocketdyne Ar-2 rocket motor and sporting extended wings and modified tail surfaces, it could reach altitudes slightly above 39,624m (130,000ft) and would serve as a test platform. Stimulated by an X-series research project, the F-104 went full circle and ended up applied to advanced research capabilities at Edwards.

Above: Based on data from the X-3 programme, Lockheed produced the XF-104A interceptor which utilised a very thin, low aspect-ratio wing for high speed. *USAF*

X for 'application'

But this was just the beginning of a line of X-craft that endures to this day. The X-3 had been a further exploration of design configurations for high-speed flight, while the X-4 was the first type not designed for investigating the supersonic regime, being a tailless design capable of high subsonic speeds. Another product of the late 1940s, the Bell X-5 was a demonstration of the variable-geometry wing on lightweight, subsonic fighter designs and emerged directly out of German research. Officially approved in July 1949, it first flew two years later and operated as a research platform for three years.

Subsequent numerical X-series research projects broadened greatly from the regimen of piloted aircraft, X-6 through X-12 being either speculative concepts never built or a succession of different rockets and missiles with little attachment to Edwards AFB. Diversification and application had been added by the involvement of the Defense Advanced Research Projects Agency (DARPA), formed in 1958 by order of President Eisenhower. He wanted an organisation for the development of advanced and exotic technology, specifically for military needs in the longer-term. As such it served all the armed services but when NASA was formed in 1958, much of its personnel and resources, including its budget, went there forcing a redefinition of its role.

Piloted flight returned to the X-series with the Ryan X-13 Vertijet, a conceptual vehicle designed to evaluate the possibility of a vertical take-off capability. Only two were built and flight trials lasted less than two years before cancellation in September 1957, a full translation to horizontal flight and back for a vertical landing having been accomplished at Edwards

AFB on 11 April 1957. It was emblematic of innovative design solution for operating combat aircraft away from conventional and highly vulnerable airfields in wartime. The successful way in which that was achieved fell to the British with the eventual development of the Harrier V/STOL aircraft. But the search for a successful V/STOL capability threw up another X-craft, the Bell X-14, first flown in 1957. Only one was built but a wealth of data was acquired on the flight control and handling characteristics of those types.

Concurrent with several of these programmes, the X-15 emerged during the mid-1950s and took its place in an increasingly busy test schedule and flight line at Edwards AFB with growing demand on the NACA facilities and resources.

Above: Flight tests at Edwards embraced new concepts developed with an eye on operational deployment, including the Ryan X-13 V/STOL research delta. *NASA*

It followed the first and second generation high-speed/high-altitude research projects but had to fit within an increasingly busy series of projects and programmes, many exploring the potential in applying new and innovative technology to research requirements.

The X-16 was a ghost allocation to deflect attention from a highly classified military reconnaissance programme which was never developed, the functional requirement being satisfied by the Martin RB-57. The X-17 was a re-entry

Above: Contemporary with the X-15, Lifting Body research programmes included the Air Force X-24A, one of three configurations exploring powered and unpowered flight with unconventional shapes. *NASA*

Above right: Rebuilt from the X-24A into a slender delta planform, the X-24B emerged from the Air Force Flight Dynamics Laboratory in 1973. *NASA*

Right: Development of the Shuttle programme in the 1970s followed the era of high-speed/high-altitude X-series research aircraft and required new facilities supporting air-launched Orbiter glide flights and emergency landings from orbital missions between 1981 and 2011. *NASA*

test rocket while the X-18 was an experimental tilt-rotor, a V/STOL cargo aircraft only one of which flew in November 1959. It was followed by the X-19, another tilt-rotor experiment which provided interesting data but no further development. As mentioned frequently throughout this book, the X-20 was the designation applied to the Dyna-Soar boost-glide vehicle when it was deferred due to a lack of enthusiasm for its original objective.

The next several X-projects contemporary with the X-15 included the X-21, a sizeably reworked Douglas B-66 conducting boundary-layer research with a configuration in which the underwing engines were replaced by a different type and located in the rear fuselage. Multiple span-wise slots sucked turbulent boundary-layer air from the upper surface. Two aircraft were built but the surface orifices were easily blocked, clogged or filled with ice from the chilled air of the upper atmosphere. The Bell X-22 was a ducted fan tilt-rotor with four engines on four wings in a Navy project designed to reduce take-off and landing runs.

By the mid-1960s, NASA was getting interested in Lifting-Body concepts and after the unmanned Martin X-23 manoeuvrable atmospheric re-entry vehicle, the X-24A and X-24B provided an extensive evaluation of blunt-body and streamlined configurations in a joint programme with the US Air Force. Two more programmes were contemporaries with the X-15 and arguably at the extreme end of the performance spectrum: the experimental X-25 Benson autogyro and the X-26 sailplane used by the US Navy to give new pilots experience with handling the challenges of yaw/roll coupling.

All these programmes ran concurrently with the types described in detail in this book and give a rough picture of the extent and diversity of aircraft handled at Edwards by the Air Force and NASA. In addition, a broad collection of new military production aircraft were delivered to the site and tested there both before and during service introduction. And a wide range of in-service types rotated through for one-off tests and trials of new equipment, benefiting from the extensive data collection and tracking facilities available and noted elsewhere in this book.

At the time of writing the latest X-craft is the X-62, an adapted Lockheed Martin F-16 originally designated the NF-16D and carrying a multi-axis, thrust vectoring engine nozzle. Now operated by the Test Pilot School, it also incorporates computerised flight control software to make optimum use of the ability of the pilot to maintain full control through and beyond a conventional stall.

Right: One of the latest experimental types at Edwards, the Dynetics X-61A Gremlins emerged from DARPA as a recoverable sensor platform powered by a small turbofan engine. Up to eight can be controlled simultaneously. *Dynetics*

Appendix 3

X-15 Research Pilots

Journeying to the Edge of Space

The following biographical details of X-15 pilots have been listed according to the chronological order in which they made their first flight in the type. Three others were assigned to fly the X-15 but for various reasons were denied that opportunity. They are listed in alphabetical order as the last three entries in this Appendix.

Above: Milt Thompson experienced the dangers of flight testing before he came to fly the X-15, going on to play a major role in the development of Lifting Bodies – aero-vehicles that trade drag for lift to demonstrate the plausibility of landing winged spacecraft without power. *NASA*

Albert Scott Crossfield

Born: 2 October 1921
Deceased: 19 April 2006, age 84
First X-15 flight: 8 June 1959
Last X-15 flight: 6 December 1960
Total X-15 flights: 14

Born in Berkeley, California to a farming family, Crossfield began studying engineering at the University of Washington, Seattle, in September 1940 but left in May 1942, without completing his course, to join the Navy and fight for his country. He served as a fighter and gunnery instructor before being assigned to a field post in Hawaii in early 1945 where he began training with a carrier air group assigned to the Second Marine Division for the invasion of Japan. After the war ended in September, Crossfield was ordered back to Seattle in November 1945.

In early 1946 he was instrumental in starting up a reserve squadron, VF-74, flying F6F Hellcats and F4U Corsairs. Later that year, Crossfield returned to his university and studied for a B.Sc. degree in aeronautical science, graduating in June 1949 and obtaining his M.Sc. the following year. In 1950, Crossfield joined the NACA at its High Speed Flight Station. During the next five years he flew a wide range of jet and rocket-powered research aircraft, making 87 rocket-powered flights in the X-1 and Skyrocket, plus an additional 12 jet-only flights in the latter.

Crossfield also flew the X-4, X-5, XF-92A and Skystreak at Edwards AFB and it was while flying the Skyrocket on 20 November 1953 that he became the first pilot to exceed Mach 2. In 1955 he left the NACA and joined North American as the X-15 project test pilot, making an enormous contribution to the engineering design of the cockpit and to the development of the flight control system. Crossfield achieved a maximum speed of Mach 2.97 and a peak altitude of 26,857m (88,116ft).

After his involvement with the X-15 programme he spent a further five years in charge of the systems tests and the quality control engineering programme for the Hound Dog stand-off missile. It was built by North American and deployed from underwing pylons on the B-52 from wing positions at the same location as utilised previously for the X-15. Crossfield was also involved with the Paraglider programme, with the Apollo spacecraft and the S-II cryogenic second stage of the Saturn V launch vehicle. Before leaving North American, Crossfield spent two years as their technical director of research engineering.

From 1967 Crossfield was an executive with Eastern Airlines and from 1974 he spent two years as senior vice president with Hawker Siddeley Aviation, with the last sixteen years of his professional life as a special consultant to the House Committee on Science and Technology. He died in a crash flying his Cessna 210 in a violent thunderstorm over Georgia. Among his many honours and awards is the NASA Distinguished Public Service medal, recognising more than 50 years of service to aeronautics.

Joseph Albert Walker

Born: 20 February 1921
Deceased: 8 June 1966, age 45
First X-15 flight: 25 March 1960
Last X-15 flight: 22 August 1963
Total X-15 flights: 25

'Joe' Walker was born and bred in Washington, Pennsylvania, graduating from Washington & Jefferson College in 1942 with a B.A. in physics. He joined the Army Air Forces and saw service in North Africa flying twin-boom Lockheed P-38 Lightnings where he was awarded the Distinguished Flying Cross and the Air Medal with seven oak leaf clusters. He joined the NACA's Aircraft Engine Research Laboratory in March 1945 where he worked on icing research, flying into extreme weather over the Great Lakes region.

In 1951, Walker moved to the HSFS at Edwards AFB and rose to become chief pilot in 1955. His assignments as project pilot included the Skystreak, Skyrocket, X-1, X-3, X-4 the X-5 and service types such as the F-100, F-102, F-104 and the B-47. Walker also participated in the development of reaction controls, frequently flying a JF-104A to 27,432m (90,000ft) where the indicated airspeed was less than 55kph (34mph) with no effective control from aerodynamic surfaces. Moving to the X-15 programme, where reaction controls proved essential, he used his earlier experience to reach a maximum speed of Mach 5.92 and an altitude of 107,960m (354,200ft) – peak height for the programme.

Walker was killed when the F-104 he was flying during a formation photo-shoot with the XB-70A was caught in the slipstream of the prototype Mach 3 bomber and hurled across its two vertical fins. Even so, his 25 flights in the X-15 ranked him third among those who flew the most research flights. In 2005 Joe Walker's family received a set of NASA Astronaut Wings for his flights above 80.45km (50mls), which is recognised by the Air Force and NASA as the height at which the space domain begins.

Robert Michael White USAF

Born: 6 July 1924
Deceased: 17 March 2010, age 85
First X-15 flight: 13 April 1960
Last X-15 flight: 14 December 1962
Total X-15 flights: 16

New York-born 'Bob' White joined the Army Air Forces at the age of 18. Fifteen months later, in February 1944, he received his wings, then joined the 354th Fighter Squadron flying P-51s. He was shot down during his 52nd combat mission in February 1945 and spent two months in a German POW camp. Back in the United States after the war, he went to New York University and in 1951 obtained his B.Sc. degree in electrical engineering.

With the outbreak of war in Korea he was recalled as a pilot and engineering officer with the 514th Troop Carrier Wing at Mitchel AFB, New York, from where he was assigned to the 40th FS in Japan as a flight commander flying F-80 jet fighters until mid-1953. After the war he became a systems engineer at Rome Air Development Center, New York. In January 1955 he graduated from the Experimental Test Pilot School and stayed on to test the F-86K, F-89H, F-102A and F-105B fighters and fighter-bombers.

As deputy chief of the Flight Test Operations Division and assistant chief of the manned spacecraft branch, on the death of Iven Kincheloe on 26 July 1958, White became the prime Air Force X-15 pilot. On and off, he also had considerable association with Project Dyna-Soar and the Air Force sought his expertise with the X-15 to integrate it with the new boost-glide programme.

Though he made comparatively few flights, White collected the greatest number of 'firsts' in the X-15 programme, piloting the first manned flights through Mach 4, Mach 5 and Mach 6, and also becoming the first to exceed 60,960m (200,000ft) and 91,440m (300,000ft). These were logged after flying the fastest (Mach 3.5) and the highest 41,453m (136,000ft) flights in an X-15 powered by the XLR-11. He also obtained, and still holds, the FAI altitude record for a piloted aircraft, at 95,936m (314,750ft) – not the highest achieved by the X-15, but the highest in certified world records.

Posted to the 36th TFW at Bitburg in Germany as operations officer in October 1963, White moved on to command the 53rd TFS, returning to the USA in August 1965 where he attended the Industrial College of the Armed Forces in Washington. While there he also obtained a science degree in business administration from The George Washington University. In May 1967 he became deputy commander for operations at the 355th TFW, flying 70 combat missions during the Vietnam War.

Back at Wright-Patterson in June 1968, White was appointed the director of the F-15 Systems Program Office and on 31 July 1970 took command of the Air Force Flight Test Center. From there, on 17 October 1972, he became commandant of the Air Force ROTC, and rose to chief of staff of the 4th Allied Tactical Air Force in March 1975.

Bob White retired in February 1981 with the rank of Major-General. A joint recipient of the 1961 Robert J. Collier Trophy, presented by President Kennedy in July 1962, he continued to receive national and international awards throughout his life.

Forrest Silas Petersen USN

Born: 16 May 1922
Deceased: 8 December 1990, age 68
First X-15 flight: 23 September 1960
Last X-15 flight: 10 January 1962
Total X-15 flights: 5

A native of Holdrege, Nebraska, 'Pete' Petersen graduated from the Naval Academy in June 1944 and served with the USS Caperton, a Fletcher-class destroyer, during its campaigns in the Philippines, Formosa and Okinawa. Switching to the air side of the Navy, Petersen graduated from flight training in 1947 and was assigned to CF-20A before two years of study at Naval Post Graduate School, graduating with a master's in engineering in 1953. During 1956 he attended the Naval Test Pilot School and after graduating he stayed on as an instructor.

In August 1958 he was assigned by the Navy to be their X-15 pilot and worked with NASA, piloting five flights, until January 1962 when he left to serve as commanding officer of VF-154 at Naval Air Station Miramar. He was then assigned to be the director of the Division of Naval Reactors at the Atomic Energy Commission, where he assisted with nuclear power training. In January 1964 Petersen joined the USS *Enterprise*, serving as executive officer until April 1966 during which time the carrier completed its first combat tour in the Vietnam War.

After a brief stint as assistant to the director of naval programme planning, Petersen assumed command of the attack transport USS *Bexar*, later serving as deputy chief of naval operations for air warfare and then as commander of Naval Air Systems Command. Vice Admiral Petersen retired from the Navy in May 1980 and died of cancer in Omaha, Nebraska ten years later.

John Barron McKay

Born: 8 December 1922
Deceased: 27 April 1975, age 52
First X-15 flight: 28 October 1960
Last X-15 flight: 8 September 1966
Total X-15 flights: 29

Born in Portsmouth, Virginia, McKay served in the Navy during World War Two and graduated from Virginia Polytechnic Institute in 1950 with a B.Sc. in aeronautical engineering. He joined the NACA in 1951 and was employed at Langley as an engineer shortly before moving to the HSFS. There, he flew F-100, YF-102A, F-102A, F-104, YF-107A, Skystreak and Skyrocket, the X-1B and the X-1E. In that time he logged more time on rocket-powered aircraft than any other pilot after Scott Crossfield, completing 46 flights by the time he was assigned to fly the X-15.

McKay flew two flights with the XLR-11 powered X-15 and the remainder with the XLR-99, reaching Mach 5.65 and a peak altitude of 90,098m (295,600ft). He made three emergency landings, one of which nearly cost him his life after a bad landing on 9 November 1962. On that day, X-15-2 flipped over on its back after one of the landing skids dug in, crushing him underneath. The accident compressed his spine, reducing his height by 2.54cm (1in), and crushed several vertebrae. He returned to flight on 25 April 1963 and went on to make 22 more flights in the X-15 despite his injuries.

McKay's experience with the X-15 afforded the opportunity for demonstrating skills which were lauded by fellow pilot Milton Thompson, who regarded him as 'an excellent stick-and-rudder pilot, possibly the best of the X-15 pilots'. He retired from NASA in October 1971 and succumbed to complications from his earlier accident less than four years later.

Robert Aitken Rushworth USAF

Born: 9 October 1924
Deceased: 18 March 1993, age 68
First X-15 flight: 4 November 1960
Last X-15 flight: 1 July 1966
Total X-15 flights: 34

A native of Madison, Maine, Bob Rushworth graduated from Hebron Academy in 1943 and served with the Army Air Forces during World War Two flying C-46 and C-47 transport aircraft. In 1951, he received a B.Sc. degree in mechanical engineering from the University of Maine and in 1954 secured another degree in aeronautical engineering from the Air Force Institute of Technology. He became a test pilot at Wright Field two years later.

Graduating from the Experimental Aircraft Test Pilot School, he moved to the fighter operations branch at Edwards AFB before becoming operations officer in the manned spacecraft section, which included flying the X-15. He also flew the F-101, TF-102, F-104, F-105 and F-106.

Rushworth completed two flights powered by the XLR-11 and 32 flights with the XLR-99 – 17% of all X-15 flights and the greatest number logged by the same pilot. He achieved a maximum speed of Mach 6.06 and an altitude of 86,868m (285,000ft). His many contributions to the programme included making the first flight with the ventral fin removed for stability tests and completing an emergency recovery after the nose wheel deployed at close to Mach 5, for which he received the Distinguished Flying Cross.

After leaving the programme, Rushworth graduated from the National War College in August 1967 and moved to the F-4 combat crew training facility at George AFB, California. The following March he went to Cam Ranh Bay Air Base in Vietnam as the assistant deputy commander for operations at the 12th TFW where he flew 189 combat missions. Between April 1969 and January 1971, he was the programme director for the AGM-65 Maverick missile and in February 1971 he became the commander of the 4950th Test Wing at Wright-Patterson AFB.

With the rank of General, Rushworth served the Air Force as inspector general for the Air Force Systems Command from May 1973 and in February 1974 returned to command the Flight Test Center. In November 1975 he became the commander of the Air Force Test and Evaluation Center at Kirtland AFB, New Mexico, retiring from the Air Force in 1981 as vice commander of the Aeronautical Systems Division at Wright-Patterson.

Neil Alden Armstrong

Born: 5 August 1930
Deceased: 25 August 2012, age 82
First X-15 flight: 30 November 1960
Last X-15 flight: 26 July 1962
Total X-15 flights: 7

Born in Wapakoneta, Ohio, Neil Armstrong had a natural aptitude for mathematics and engineering that he would hone as a test pilot and later as a research pilot. He applied for one of the US Naval College Program's four-year scholarships having logged twenty hours of solo flying at his own hard-earned expense, and entered Purdue University before going solo for the first time as a Navy pilot on 7 September 1949. After carrier qualification training on the F8F Bearcat at Naval Air Training Command, Pensacola, Midshipman Armstrong reported for duty.

On 21 June 1951, Armstrong's unit, VF-51, shipped out aboard the USS *Essex* to join the Korean War, where he flew combat air patrols in the comparatively sluggish F9F Panther. With his college career on hold, Armstrong had the option of staying with the Navy or returning to higher education. On 1 February 1952 the Navy terminated his regular commission but reappointed him as an ensign in the Naval Reserve. Armstrong then resumed his course at Purdue and graduated in January 1955 with a B.Sc. in aeronautical engineering.

After a brief stint with the NACA Flight Propulsion Research

Laboratory, Armstrong jumped at a vacancy in the High Speed Flight Station at Edwards flying experimental aircraft. At first he was employed as an aeronautical research scientist, then as a pilot, which saw him fly as project pilot on the F-100A, F-100C, F-101 and the F-104A. He flew the X-1B, X-5, F-105, F-106, B-47, KC-135 and the Parasev, accumulating 2,400 flying hours.

In 1960 Armstrong became part of the NASA team working in liaison with the Air Force on the Dyna-Soar project. This led him to make seven flights with the X-15, during which he attained a maximum speed of Mach 5.74 and a maximum altitude of 63,246m (207,500ft). In 1962 he applied to the NASA astronaut corps and was accepted, after which he was assigned to the two-man Gemini and the three-man Apollo programmes aimed at a lunar landing by the end of the decade.

A consummate research-engineer/pilot, Armstrong applied an intuitive awareness of the characteristics of whatever craft he was flying toward its use as a platform for scientific investigations. His role within the astronaut corps was to do that with the Apollo spacecraft and the Lunar Module, in which he commanded the Apollo 11 mission. He made the first manned landing on the Moon in July 1969, accompanied by Buzz Aldrin, and became the first person to walk the lunar surface.

After a year travelling the world on a publicity tour, on 18 May 1970 NASA announced that Armstrong would become deputy associate administrator for aeronautics at the Office of Advanced Research and Technology (OART), at NASA headquarters in Washington, DC. While there he urged the Flight Research Center to investigate digital fly-by-wire (DFBW) rather than persist with analogue systems. When asked why, Armstrong pointed out that he had used just such a fly-by-wire system to land on the Moon, which led directly to the DFBW programme involving an adapted F-8C Crusader.

In August 1971 Armstrong left NASA to take up a position as professor of engineering at the University of Cincinnati. Although he never studied for a Ph.D., he was awarded one on the basis of presentations he gave on Apollo. However, on 1 January 1980, having grown tired of academia, he left to become chairman of Cardwell International Ltd, and in 1982 he moved on to chair Computing Technologies for Aviation for 10 years. Along the way he also served in a wide range of board and consultative positions and continued to fly and explore the capabilities of new aircraft.

Armstrong made a seminal contribution to aeronautical engineering, firstly through his work for NASA on experimental aircraft at Edwards AFB and later by integrating his practical experience of spaceflight into the more general world of aeronautical engineering. After his death from complications following a routine heart operation, NASA renamed its Dryden Flight Research Center in his honour.

Joe Henry Engle USAF

Born: 26 August 1932
First X-15 flight: 7 October 1963
Last X-15 flight: 14 October 1965
Total X-15 flights: 16

Born in Abilene, Texas, Engle graduated from the University of Kansas at Lawrence in 1955 with a B.Sc. in aeronautical engineering. From there he joined Cessna Aircraft as a flight test engineer and was commissioned in the Air Force ROTC programme. He began flying training in 1957 and a year later earned his pilot's wings, being assigned to the 474th FS (Day) on F-100s and then with the 309th TFS at George AFB, California.

Engle graduated from the Aerospace Research Test Pilot School (ARTPS) in 1962 at which time he was assigned to Edwards for training as a military astronaut. At this date the Air Force was pressing hard for a military role in space when it was considered essential to have a man in the cockpit for orbital flight. In June 1963 he joined the X15 programme to continue toward a seat flying the X-20, the re-designated Dyna-Soar boost-glide programme. It would see him persist in a career orientation toward winged spaceplanes and associated orbit and re-entry vehicles ending with the Shuttle.

As a pilot with the X-15 programme for two years, Engle achieved a maximum speed of Mach 5.71 (6,255kph/3,888mph) and a peak altitude of 85,526m (280,600ft). With the X-20 cancelled in 1963, after his stint in the X-15 programme Engle applied to become a NASA astronaut and in April 1966 was accepted as its youngest inductee, age 33. Assigned to the Apollo programme, Engle served on the support crew for Apollo 10, rotating to back-up Lunar Module pilot for Apollo 14 and then to LMP for Apollo 17.

When NASA succumbed to pressure from a wide range of

scientific bodies in the United States clamouring for a professional scientist to work on the lunar surface before the end of Moon flights, it decided to replace him with scientist-astronaut Harrison Schmitt. But it did have its compensations. As Engle might have said, 12 men walked on the Moon but only one would ever fly both the X-15 and the Space Shuttle.

That 'first' came when he was assigned as commander of one of the two crews to fly approach and landing tests with the Shuttle Orbiter *Enterprise* in 1977 and made two flights in that programme. In November 1981 he commanded the second flight of the Shuttle when he flew *Columbia* and conducted a manually controlled re-entry and landing. During that flight he conducted 29 designated manoeuvres to test the control systems, another 'first' which has never been repeated with a winged vehicle returning from orbit.

Flying the Shuttle for the fourth time, the second time in orbit, Engle commanded *Discovery* in August 1985 on the twentieth Shuttle mission during which satellites were deployed and a previously failed communications satellite was secured and repaired in orbit on two space-walks.

Engle's contribution to the X-15 programme is best seen in the work he conducted before his 16 flights in that vehicle and, as a consequence,the valuable learning that he took with him to the Shuttle programme. Engle was the only pilot to have flown both vehicles and the only one to have manually flown a winged vehicle all the way down from orbit.

Milton Orville Thompson

Born: 4 May 1926
Deceased: 6 August 1993, age 67
First X-15 flight: 29 October 1963
Last X-15 flight: 25 August 1965
Total X-15 flights: 14

Milton Thompson hailed from Crookston, Minnesota and began a flying career with the Navy in early 1944, serving in China and Japan during the Second World War before assignment as a fighter pilot with carriers off the Pacific and Atlantic oceans. Released from active duty in November 1949, he enrolled at the University of Washington, Seattle, to finish engineering studies and graduated with a M.Sc. degree in 1953, at which point Thompson joined Boeing as a structural flight test engineer on a range of projects, including the B-52.

On 19 March 1956 Thompson joined the NACA's High Speed Flight Station and was assigned as a research pilot in January 1958, joining the four already there: Joe Walker, Stan Butchart, Jack McKay and Neil Armstrong. Although his first flight there was in a C-47, Thompson and that small group of test pilots would eventually fly 14 different types, including the X-1B and the X-1E, while awaiting the X-2 – which never did arrive due to its cancellation after the fateful crash – and the X-15.

In the programme at its operating heart, Thompson helped prepare the site and its facilities for flight operations and inevitably, in 1959, got caught up in the Dyna-Soar/X-20 programme, as well as the Rogallo Parasev inflatable wing concept for landing ballistic capsules back on a conventional runway. He was also assigned to the Lifting-Body programme, on 16 August 1963 becoming the first person to fly the M2-F1. After nine years as a test pilot he would fly a total of 23 different types of flying machine.

As one of the earliest entrants to the world of the X-15, Thompson joined the NACA right at the time it was gearing up to become NASA and take upon itself the mantle of the national space programme. Arriving in the weeks just before the first US satellite launch, when NASA emerged at the end of the year he experienced the educational programme it instituted as a way of briefing its nationwide facilities in the science and engineering of space flight. To experienced hands at Edward AFB and the HSFS, it was heady stuff and soon led to encouragement from the Mercury managers to join them in the programme to get the first American in orbit.

Walt Williams was initially dismissive of the ballistic capsule and, while being offered the chance to join that group out of NASA-Langley, he cautioned them to think again before applying, insinuating that as test pilots they would find the job unsatisfying. After Williams was appointed to head flight operations at the Mercury programme, he never lost his high regard for the flight activity at Edwards AFB. When Thompson was assigned to human factors research and appointed to brief the Mercury-Seven astronauts on physiological responses to the space environment, Williams introduced him in a manner unlikely to garner favour from these silver-suited elites: 'Now here is a real test pilot!'

During his assignment to the X-15, Thompson achieved a personal maximum speed of Mach 5.48 (5,990kph/3,723mph) and an altitude of 65,257m (214,100ft). Aside from that project, Thompson was a major contributor to the Lifting-Body programme, making 47 flights in the M2-F1 and the first five flights with the M2-F2. Thompson's active career ended in 1967 and two years later he became chief of research projects. In 1975 he became the chief engineer at Dryden and remained so until his death.

Along the way he had served on the NASA Space Transportation System Technology Steering Committee, in which he campaigned to get rid of the Shuttle Orbiter's air-breathing engines and save weight. To qualify this judgement, he assisted greatly with the design of the Orbiter for making power-off landings which, for some time early in the design phase, was considered unwise. His X-15 experience was an invaluable input in this regard and he campaigned tirelessly for new avenues of opportunity with unpowered re-entry vehicles and landings on conventional runways.

William J. Knight USAF

Born: 18 November 1929
Deceased: 7 May 2004, age 74
First X-15 flight: 30 September 1965
Last X-15 flight: 13 September 1968
Total X-15 flights: 16

'Pete' Knight was brought up in Noblesville, Indiana, enlisted in the Air Force in 1951 and graduated with his wings in 1953, being assigned to the 438th FIS flying an F-86D. A year later he won the prestigious Allison Jet Trophy Race at the National Air Show, in Dayton, Ohio.

Knight graduated from the Air Force Institute of Technology in 1958 with a degree in aeronautical engineering and went directly to the Experimental Test Pilot School at Edwards AFB, serving as test pilot in fighter operations.

In 1960 he was assigned to the USAF's Dyna-Soar programme as a pilot-consultant and would eventually become a designated Dyna-Soar pilot before the project was cancelled in 1963, at which point he attended the Aerospace Research Test Pilot School.

After graduation from the ARTPS in 1964, Knight was assigned to the X-15 from 1965. Much of the conditioning for Dyna-Soar assignments mirrored the exhausting and undignified hardships endured in test rigs and physiological chambers, also imposed on the original Mercury astronauts. These included many hours in the Johnsville centrifuge, a unique facility where mocked-up cockpits and instrument panels sought to find the weaknesses in test subjects and the possibilities of novel control opportunities with new techniques.

Knight achieved the highest speed recorded by an X-15 pilot, reaching Mach 6.7 (7,272kph/4,520mph) in X-15-2 on 3 October 1967 and a personal altitude record of 85,496m (280,500ft). In 1969 he was transferred to Southeast Asia and to service in the Vietnam War where he flew 253 combat missions in the F-100, following which he served as test director for the F-15 System Program Office at Wright-Patterson AFB. In 1979 he took up a post as vice commander of the Air Force Flight Test Center and retained currency through assignment to the F-16 Combined Test Force.

Pete Knight retired from the Air Force in 1982, having logged in excess of 7,000hrs flying time on more than 100 different types of aircraft. Two years later he entered politics and was elected to the Palmdale city council, becoming the city's first elected mayor in 1988. Four years later he served in the California state assembly and in the California state senate from 1996.

Like so many of his peers, Knight received numerous awards and recognition for his service, one of only eight X-15 pilots who qualified for astronaut wings by flying higher than 80.45km (50mls). He died from cancer.

William Harvey Dana

Born: 3 November 1930
Deceased: 6 May 2014, age 83
First X-15 flight: 4 November 1965
Last X-15 flight: 24 October 1968
Total X-15 flights: 16

Born in Pasadena, California, 'Bill' Dana graduated from Military Academy in 1952 with a B.Sc. degree, joined the Air Force and served four years as a pilot, flying a stint in the Korean War on F-84Fs. At the cessation of hostilities, he resigned his commission and went back to school, graduating from the University of Southern California in 1958 with a master's degree in aeronautical engineering. That same year he joined NASA and started a career as a research pilot in September 1959. He was assigned to the Dyna-Soar programme and worked with Neil Armstrong and Milton Thompson as pilot-consultant for three years, spending a lot of time on the mock-up with Boeing in Seattle.

Dana spent nearly three years logging his 16 flights on the X-15, during which he twice exceeded the qualifying altitude for astronaut wings and reached a personal peak altitude of 93,543m (306,900ft) and a top speed of Mach 5.53 (6,270kph/3,897mph). Dana's most notable contribution was with the Lifting-Body programme for which he received the NASA Exceptional Service Medal. He had special responsibility for the control systems on the M2-F3. In 1976 he was appointed chief pilot at the Flight Research Center before becoming chief of the Flight Operations Directorate.

Dana made further contributions to aeronautical engineering when he became the project pilot on the F-15 Highly Integrated Digital Electronic Control (HIDEC) research programme and co-pilot on the F-18 High-Angle-of Attack (HAA) development activity. Both programmes would grow into an operational capability as well as providing high-alpha research results of more general application.

In August 1993 Dana became chief engineer and remained in that position until he retired in 1998, receiving his astronaut wings for the two high-altitude X-15 flights.

Michael James Adams USAF

Born: 5 May 1930
Deceased: 15 November 1967, age 37
First X-15 flight: 6 October 1966
Last X-15 flight: 15 November 1967
Total X-15 flights: 7

Born in Sacramento, California, Michael Adams joined the Air Force in November 1950, graduating with his pilot's wings and a commission on 25 October 1952. He was assigned to a fighter-bomber unit in Korea, where he flew 49 combat missions in four months before spending 30 months with the 613th FBS at England AFB, Louisiana. After that came six months ROTC at Chaumont Air Base in France. But Mike was a natural student and ambitious for a broader range of opportunities

Still in the Air Force, he graduated from Oklahoma University in 1958 with a degree in aeronautical engineering and completed 18 months of astronautics studies at Massachusetts Institute of Technology (MIT) in 1962. Attending the Experimental Test Pilot School at Edwards AFB, he was awarded the Honts Trophy for best in class before graduating with honours in December 1963. Assigned to the Manned Orbiting Laboratory (MOL) programme at Edwards, he requested a transfer to the X-15 programme, to which he was admitted in the summer of 1966.

During his time at the ARPS in 1963, Adams had a near fatal incident while flying with David Scott in an F-104 making a simulated X-15 approach. The aircraft suddenly lost power, which rapidly increased the descent rate. Electing to stay with the aircraft, Adams waited for the F-104 to impact the runway before ejecting; had he done so earlier, the ejection sequence during the rapid descent rate would not have given him sufficient vertical velocity to reach the necessary altitude for the parachute to open. The F-104 slammed down hard, ripped off its landing gear and the engine was propelled forward, crushing the cockpit where Adams had been a moment before. Scott was trapped in the burning aircraft and had to use emergency cable cutters to release his feet from the wreckage and leap free.

Adams was a popular pilot and in his seven flights in the X-15 he achieved a personal top speed of Mach 5.59 (6,149kph/3,822mph) and an altitude of 81,077m (266,000ft). The conditions under which Mike Adams lost his life, in the only X-15 fatality of the programme, have been described elsewhere in this book. The Air Force awarded him posthumous astronaut wings for the last flight on which he exceeded the threshold considered the beginning of the space environment. In 1991, his name was added to the Astronaut Memorial at the Kennedy Space Center listing those who had lost their lives on duty.

Iven Carl Kincheloe Jr USAF

Born: 2 July 1928

Deceased: 26 July 1958, age 30

A native of Detroit, Michigan, Kincheloe enrolled at Purdue University and joined the Air Force ROTC, through which he studied aeronautical engineering and graduated in 1949 with a B.Sc. Two years later he received his pilot's wings from Williams AFB, Arizona, and in 1952, as a captain, joined the 25th FIS. Flying 131 missions in Korea, was credited with shooting down five MiG-15 fighters – enough to qualify him as an official 'ace'.

Back in the United States, Kincheloe was appointed as gunnery instructor at Nellis AFB, Nevada. In 1953 he was admitted to the Empire Test School in Farnborough, England, gaining an M.Sc. in aeronautical engineering from Oxford in 1954. Returning home once more, he was named chief of the manned spacecraft section of the Fighter Operations Branch at the Flight Test Operations Division, Edwards AFB and soon after became the first Air Force project pilot for the X-15. On 17 September 1956 he flew the troublesome Bell X-2 to a record altitude of 38,465m (126,200ft).

Kincheloe lost his life in July 1958 when the F-104 he was flying suffered an engine failure and he ejected too low for his parachute to open. By this time he had logged 3,573hrs flying a total of 70 different types of US and foreign aircraft and had received many prestigious awards, one of which the Society of Experimental Test Pilots named after him. The Air Force later renamed Kinross AFB, Michigan, Kincheloe AFB in his memory.

John A. Manke

Born: 13 November 1931

Deceased: 31 January 2019, age 87

Manke was born in Selby, South Dakota, and after being selected for the NROTC programme in 1951 he graduated with a B.Sc. degree in electrical engineering from the Marquette University, Milwaukee in 1956. He entered flight training and served as a fighter pilot with the Marine Corps but left in 1960, after which he worked for Honeywell until 1962.

Manke joined NASA in May 1962 as a flight research engineer and worked on planning X-15 operations. Together with Mike Adams he completed preliminary 'schooling' on the type and sat in for a test run at the Rocket Engine Test Facility. He was assigned to fly the X-15 but the programme ended before he got that opportunity. Manke also made 42 flights in the HL-10 Lifting-Body vehicle, the first on 22 May 1968, and after the retirement of the X-15 he became chief of flight operations at the FRC until he retired on 27 April 1984.

Alvin Swauger White

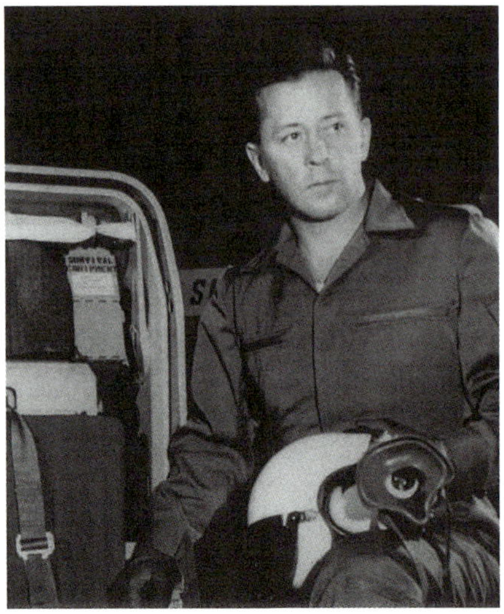

Born: 9 December 1918

Deceased: 29 April 2006, age 87

Raised in Berkeley, California, Al White studied electrical engineering at the University of California at Davis before transferring to the Berkeley campus in 1938. Three years later he enlisted in the Army Air Corps and graduated from flight school at Williams Field, Arizona in May 1942. Following two years as an advanced flying instructor he joined the 355th FG in England, flying two tours on combat duty from D-Day to the end of the war in Europe eleven months later.

After the war White returned to the University of California and graduated with a degree in aeronautical engineering in 1947. The following year he re-enlisted in the Air Force and served at Wright-Patterson AFB for almost three years on parachute research before graduating in 1952 from the Air Force Test Pilot School at Edwards and joining the fighter test section. He left the Air Force in May 1954 to become a test pilot for North American Aviation.

During his time at NAA he was the second contractor pilot (after Scott Crossfield) assigned to fly the X-15. He also worked on the Johnsville centrifuge programme and the fixed base simulator as well as logging eleven F-100 and F-104 flights as chase pilot for X-15 launches. White logged 8,500hrs flying time in 125 different aircraft. He never did get to fly the X-15 himself but in 1957 he became the project pilot for the XB-70 and moved full-time to that after X-15 contractor flights were completed. He was the sole survivor of the crash of the second prototype XB-70 on 8 June 1966 when it was struck by the F-104 flown by Joe Walker. After retirement, White became a well regarded aviation consultant.

Appendix 4

X-15 Flight Log

Flights and False Starts

The information from which the following table has been compiled originated in the flight logs of the pilots concerned; in the flight plans filed prior to the launch and post-flight reports filed by NASA; and by personnel at the facility which since 2014 has been known as the Armstrong Flight Research Center, in honour of Neil Armstrong, X-15 research pilot and NASA astronaut.

However, special mention should be made of the outstanding research work of Michelle Evans, who has meticulously examined both the published flight records and the plot charts which were used to form graphs from which some corrective material was obtained. It is from her work, homologated with other records, that the following can exist at all and thanks for that work are granted accordingly.

In the table, the three X-15 aircraft are labelled as -1 (56-6670), -2 (56-6671), and -3 (56-6672) and the B-52 carriers are identified by the last three digits of their tail numbers (003 or 008). Launch date is in day, month and year. Drop times are given in hours, minutes and seconds and flight times and burn duration for the X-15 are in minutes and seconds. Speed, altitude and flight distance from launch to landing are given in mph, feet and miles, respectively. The flight number is the cumulative total of free drops.

Flights bearing no mission number indicate where an X-15 was carried into the air but not launched. Chase names are those of the chase pilots for each drop flight and supplementary comments are added to provide additional detail. The main text of this book should be consulted via the index for further description of a particular flight.

Above: As a civilian test pilot for NASA, Neil Armstrong had skills in decision-management and an ability to resolve multiple problems for a solution. It was these, not his flying skills, that gained the approval of the astronaut selection board and sent him on a path to the Moon. *NASA*

PILOT	DATE	FLIGHT NO.	X-15	B-52	FLIGHT DETAILS				
					Launch Time	Drop Lake	Burn Time	Landing Lake	Flight Time
Crossfield	10/03/59		-1		Scheduled captive flight. Failed SAS, B-52 power supply, frosted windshield.				
Crossfield	01/04/59		-1		Radio failed, APU-2 shut down, lost pressure suit cooling.				
Crossfield	10/04/59		-1		APUs shut down and upper panel of the vertical stabiliser cracked.				
Crossfield	21/05/59		-1		APUs failed. Liquid nitrogen source pressure too low.				
Crossfield	08/06/59	001	-1	003	08:38:40.0	Rosamond	00:00.0	Rogers	04:56.6
Crossfield	24/07/59		-1		Scheduled full fuel captive test. Low LOX pressure. Radio failed.				
Crossfield	04/09/59		-1		Fluctuations in LOX tank pressure due to vent leakage.				
Crossfield	17/09/59	002	-2	003	08:08:48.0	Rosamond	03:44.3	Rogers	09:11.0
Crossfield	10/10/59		-1		Problem with LOX pressurisation. Leak in helium source.				
Crossfield	14/10/59		-1		Problem with LOX pressurisation. High cabin pressure. Fuel valve failure.				
Crossfield	17/10/59	003	-2	003	10:13:07.0	Rosamond	04:14.5	Rogers	09:37.7
Crossfield	22/10/59		-2		Pilot oxygen system failure. Frosted windshield.				
Crossfield	31/10/59		-2		Bad weather.				
Crossfield	05/11/59	004	-2	003	09:39:28.0	Rosamond	00:13.9	Rosamond	05:28.0
Crossfield	16/12/59		-1		Low LOX pressure.				
Crossfield	23/01/60	005	-1	008	16:17:05.0	Rosamond	04:27.2	Rogers	09:53.8
Crossfield	04/02/60				Fuel tank pressure loss and APU-2 failure.				
Crossfield	11/02/60	006	-2	008	10:15:04.0	Rosamond	04:11.2	Rogers	10:15.5
Crossfield	17/02/60	007	-2	008	09:41:32.0	Rosamond	05:09.4	Rogers	10:35.9
Crossfield	17/03/60	008	-2	008	08:31:25.0	Rosamond	03:53.5	Rogers	08:39.5
Crossfield	18/03/60		-2		Fuel leak and delaminated windscreen triggering abort 60sec before launch.				
Walker	25/03/60	009	-1	008	15:43:23.0	Rosamond	04:32.0	Rogers	09:08:0
Crossfield	29/03/60	010	-2	008	09:59:28.0	Rosamond	04:04.2	Rogers	09:10.5
Crossfield	31/03/60	011	-2	008	08:42:05.0	Rosamond	04:14.5	Rogers	08:56.5
White	13/04/60	012	-1	003	09:15:11.0	Rosamond	04:13.7	Rogers	08:52.7
Walker	19/04/60	013	-1	003	08:51:44.0	Rosamond	04:20.6	Rogers	09:58.6
Crossfield	05/05/60		-1		APU-1 shut down. Hydrogen peroxide vent failure.				
White	06/05/60	014	-1	003	09:53:19.0	Rosamond	04:06.5	Rogers	09:23.2
Walker	12/05/60	015	-1	003	08:47:37.0	Silver	04:16.3	Rogers	10:10.3
White	19/05/60	016	-1	003	08:46:47.0	Silver	04:34.7	Rogers	11:24.6
Crossfield	26/05/60	017	-2	008	09:08:36.0	Rosamond	04:03.4	Rogers	09:14.4
Walker	27/05/60		-1		Telemetry and power supply failure.				
Walker	03/06/60		-1		No hydraulic pressure to APUs.				
Walker	08/06/60		-1		Nitrogen leak leaving insufficient pressure.				
Walker	04/08/60	018	-1	003	08:59:13.0	Silver	04:24.2	Rogers	10:22.6
White	11/08/60		-1		Nitrogen fuel leak.				
White	12/08/60	019	-1	003	08:48:43.0	Silver	04:16.2	Rogers	11:39.1
Walker	18/08/60		-1		APU failed to start.				
White	02/09/60		-1		Telemetry failed.				

FLIGHT DETAILS (contd.)					
Speed	**Mach No.**	**Max. Altitude**	**Distance**	**Chase**	**Notes**
522	0.79	37,550	023.9	White/Wood/Roberts	This was the only scheduled glide flight and the shortest flight of the programme. Pitch damper failed at launch.
1,393	2.11	52,341	088.4	White/Walker/White	First powered flight. Turbopump case failed. Fire in hydrogen peroxide compartment. Flaps extended to only 60%.
1,419	2.15	61,781	092.4	White/Walker/White	
660	1.00	45,462	034.5	Baker/White/Walker	Roll damper failed at launch and bottom XLR-11 exploded. Structural failure on landing forward of LOX tank. Nose gear failed on touchdown.
1,669	2.53	66,844	108.2	Baker/Walker/White	Late take-off caused by telemetry problems.
1,466	2.22	88,116	114.4	White/Walker/White	Nose gear bottomed out on touchdown.
1,036	1.57	52,640	097.3	White/Walker/White	Premature shutdown on upper XLR-11 but reignited.
1,419	2.15	52,640	087.5	White/Walker/White	Performed 360-deg roll and 6-g turn with dampers on and off.
1,320	2.00	48,630	092.8	Crossfield/White/McKay	
1,293	1.96	49,982	092.1	White/Knight/Rushworth	
1,340	2.03	51,356	092.2	White/Rushworth/Knight	
1,254	1.90	48,000	093.1	White/Walker/Rushworth	
1,689	2.56	59,496	107.2	Rushworth/McKay/Knight	
1,452	2.20	60,938	105.9	Knight/McKay/Rushworth	Roll damper failure at launch but reset. Ventral tail jettisoned by backup.
2,111	3.19	77,882	127.9	White/Rushworth/McKay	Inoperative stable platform. All five motor chambers shut down when only three so commanded.
1,590	2.31	108,997	138.8	Knight/Rushworth/McKay	Altitude progression flight.
1,452	2.20	51,282	094.4	White/White/Petersen	
2,196	3.31	78,112	135.5	White/Rushworth/Petersen/ Knight	Stability and control check and aerodynamic thermal build-up. Burned canopy seal.
1,772	2.52	136,500	137.1	Rushworth/Petersen/Looney	Altitude test with XLR-11 motors.

PILOT	DATE	FLIGHT NO.	X-15	B-52	FLIGHT DETAILS			FLIGHT DETAILS (contd.)	
					Launch Time	Drop Lake	Burn Time	Landing Lake	Flight Time
Petersen	20/09/60		-1		APU-2 failed to start.				
Petersen	23/09/60	022	-1	008	09:52:06.0	Rosamond	02:26.6	Rogers	07:09.6
Petersen	11/10/60		-1		Hydrogen peroxide pressure regulator ran amok.				
Crossfield	13/10/60		-2		APU-2 leak. First attempt with XLR-99.				
Petersen	20/10/60	023	-1	008	09:30:27.0	Rosamond	04:45.4	Rogers	09:26.1
McKay	28/10/60	024	-1	008	09:43:56.0	Rosamond	04:27.5	Rogers	09:05.3
Crossfield	04/11/60		-2		Hydrogen peroxide leak. APU-2 malfunction.				
Rushworth	04/11/60	025	-1	008	12:43:33.0	Rosamond	04:31.0	Rogers	08:46.3
Crossfield	15/11/60	026	-2	003	09:59:00.0	Rosamond	02:17.3	Rogers	08:28.4
Rushworth	17/11/60	027	-1	003	12:43:07.0	Palmdale	04:21.9	Rogers	08:58.2
Crossfield	22/11/60	028	-2	003	13:25:55.0	Rosamond	02:05.1	Rogers	07:31.7
Armstrong	30/11/60	029	-1	008	10:42:43.0	Rosamond	05:09.1	Rogers	09:53.8
Crossfield	06/12/60	030	-2	003	15:29:30.0	Rosamond	02:08.9	Rogers	08:07.2
Armstrong	09/12/60	031	-1	008	11:52:40.0	Palmdale	04:30.1	Rogers	10:49.0
McKay	15/12/60		-1		Hydraulic system pressure failure, aborted 30sec prior to launch.				
McKay	11/01/61		-1		Hydraulic pressure abort.				
McKay	01/02/61	032	-1	008	10:47:32.0	Rosamond	04:23.7	Rogers	10:47.7
White	07/02/61	033	-1	008	12:56:10.0	Silver	04:36.1	Rogers	10:27.8
White	21/02/61		-2		Inertial system failure. No cabin pressure.				
White	24/02/61		-2		Attitude gyroscope malfunctioned.				
White	07/03/61	034	-2	008	10:28:33.0	Silver	02:07.0	Rogers	08:34.1
Walker	21/03/61		-2		Electrical power from B-52 failed.				
Walker	30/03/61	035	-2	008	10:05:00.0	Hidden Hills	01:21.9	Rogers	10:16.5
White	21/04/61	036	-2	003	10:05:17.0	Hidden Hills	01:11.6	Rogers	10:03.4
Walker	19/05/61		-2		No APU pressure, problems with cabin pressurisation and drop aborted two seconds prior to launch.				
Walker	25/05/61	037	-2	003	12:16:35.0	Mud	01:14.3	Rogers	12:08.1
White	20/06/61		-2		Misidentified LOX spillage as hydrogen peroxide from APU drain.				
White	23/06/61	038	-2	003	14:00:05.0	Mud	01:18.7	Rogers	10:05.7
Walker	12/09/61	040	-2	008	14:40:17.0	Mud	01:55.0	Rogers	08:43.9
Petersen	28/09/61	041	-2	008	09:50:25.0	Hidden Hills	01:27.1	Rogers	08:41.6

Speed	Mach No.	Max. Altitude	Distance	Chase	Notes
1,108	1.68	53,043	062.4	Looney/Walker/Rushworth	Early shutdown of all eight XLR-11 chambers and two unsuccessful restarts.
1,280	1.94	53,800	099.6	White/Rushworth/Arm-strong	Evaluation of stability and control.
1,333	2.02	50,700	096.8	Looney/White/Petersen	Ventral parachute failed to open.
1,287	1.95	48,900	101.2	Looney/White/Armstrong	Second of two air-lifts this day, first attempt at two flights.
1,960	2.97	81,200	093.7	White/Walker/White	First flight with XLR-99. Hydraulic leak.
1,254	1.90	54,750	097.8	Looney/Walker/Knight	Premature XLR-11 shutdown with sluggish start to APU. Launched over Palmdale and not a dry lake, repeated only on flight 031.
1,656	2.51	61,900	085.0	White/Walker/White	First in-flight restart on XLR-99 and with throttle settings tested at 50%. 75% and 100%. One BCS thruster leaked.
1,155	1/75	48,840	102.0	Looney/Petersen/Walker	One chamber on upper XLR-11 failed to ignite.
1,881	2.85	53,374	085.2	White/Petersen/White	XLR-99 shut down on first of two restart attempts. Final contractor flight.
1,188	1.80	50,095	108.2	Daniel/Petersen/White	First flight with Q-ball replacing nose boom.
1,211	1.88	49,780	098.3	White/Petersen/Wood	Arm side-controller checkout. Last launch from Edwards flight area.
2,275	3.50	78,150	139.3	Daniel/Knight/Petersen/ Rushworth	Last flight with XLR-11. X15-1 returned to contractor for XLR-99 installation on 8 February.
2,905	4.43	77,450	150.5	Rushworth/Walker/ Petersen/Looney	Initial flight for X-15-2 with Q-ball replacing nose boom. First USAF flight with XLR-99. Only time F4H used as chase and flown by Petersen.
2,760	3.95	169,600	180.5	White/Knight/Petersen/ Rushworth	First NASA flight with XLR-99 and restart. First use of T-38 as chase-plane.
3,074	4.62	105,000	169.3	Looney/Walker/Rogers/ Wood	Restart on XLR-99. Pitch damper dropped out at ignition. Cabin pressure fell back to 14,020m (46,000ft).
3,307	4.95	107,500	228.5	Looney/Daniel/Petersen/ Rushworth	First launch from Mud, SAS dropped out at launch but re-engaged. Cabin pressure fell to 15,240m (50,000ft).
3,603	5.27	107,700	230.3	Looney/Daniel/Crews/ Walker	First flight past Mach 5. Cabin pressure fell to 17,068m (56,000ft), inflating pressure suit.
3,618	5.21	114,300	210.3	White/Petersen/Daniel/ Rushworth	Fuel pressure loss at launch. Engine throttled back to 50% and then to 75%. Cabin pressure leak.
3,600	5.30	101,800	158.5	Daniel/McKay/Rogers	

PILOT	DATE	FLIGHT NO.	X-15	B-52	FLIGHT DETAILS			FLIGHT DETAILS (contd.)	
					Launch Time	Drop Lake	Burn Time	Landing Lake	Flight Time
Rushworth	04/10/61	042	-1	003	10:40:50.0	Silver	02:02.0	Rogers	08:31.3
White	11/10/61	043	-2	003	12:20:00.0	Mud	01:22.5	Rogers	10:14.7
Walker	17/10/61	044	-1	003	10:57:33.0	Mud	01:24.6	Rogers	10:11.7
White	27/10/61		-1		Weather overcast at Mud Lake launch site.				
White	02/11/61		-1		Cabin pressure failure.				
White	03/11/61		-1		Malfunction to XLR-99 ignition system, aborted with 10sec to go.				
White	09/11/61	045	-2	008	09:57:17.0	Mud	01:26.9	Rogers	09:31.2
Armstrong	19/12/61		-3		Q-ball malfunction.				
Armstrong	20/12/61	046	-3	003	14:45:50.0	Silver	01:46.3	Rogers	10:25.4
Petersen	10/01/62	047	-1	003	12:28:16.0	Mud	00:03.3	Mud	03:45.7
Armstrong	17/01/62	048	-3	003	12:00:34.0	Mud	01:37.4	Rogers	10:27.7
Armstrong	29/03/62		-3		Overheating on stable platform heat exchanger. Fire detector warning light.				
Armstrong	30/03/62		-3		Engine cooling gas circuit breaker failed to close, launch aborted at zero seconds.				
Armstrong	31/03/62		-3		MH-96 failed.				
Armstrong	05/04/62	049	-3	003	10:04:25.0	Hidden Hills	01:19.2	Rogers	11:17.0
Walker	18/04/62		-1		Obscuring cloud over Mud Lake area.				
Walker	19/04/62	050	-1	003	10:02:20.0	Mud	01:24.3	Rogers	08:58.9
Armstrong	20/04/62	051	-3	008	11:26:58.0	Mud	01:22.4	Rogers	12:28.7
White	25/04/62		-2		Cloud cover prevented launch.				
White	26/04/62		-2		Engine ignition problem.				
Walker	27/04/62		-1		Poor weather.				
Walker	30/04/62	052	-1	008	10:23:20.0	Mud	01:21.6	Rogers	09:46.2
Rushworth	08/05/62	053	-2	008	10:01:28.0	Hidden Hills	01:37.9	Rogers	08:50.5
Rushworth	22/05/62	054	-1	003	10:04:46.0	Hidden Hills	01:15.3	Rogers	09:16.2
White	25/05/62		-2		Planned test of SAS but platform overheated.				
White	29/05/62		-2		B-52 stable platform not operating.				
White	01/06/62	055	-2	008	10:51:15.0	Delamar	01:26.0	Rogers	10:01.9
Walker	07/06/62	056	-1	003	10:29:20.0	Hidden Hills	01:21.5	Rogers	08:24.2
White	12/06/62	057	-3	008	12:04:00.0	Delamar	01:21.9	Rogers	09:35.4
Walker	27/06/62	059	-1	003	13:08:10.0	Mud	01:28.6	Rogers	09:32.4
McKay	29/06/62	060	-2	008	10:41:47.0	Hidden Hills	01:52.4	Rogers	08:53.4
White	10/07/62		-3		B-52 landing gear retract failure.				

Speed	Mach No.	Max. Altitude	Distance	Chase	Notes
2,830	4.30	78,000	135.6	Daniel/McKay/White	Lower ventral removed for test of stability and control.
3,647	5.21	217,000	237.1	Daniel/McKay/Wood/ Rushworth	BCS and re-entry evaluation. Outer panel of left windshield shattered at 21,336m (70,000ft).
3,900	5.74	108,600	201.1	White/McKay/Daniel/Knight	Pressure and air friction research without SAS.
4,093	6.04	101,600	211.7	Rushworth/Walker/Gordon/ Daniel	First flight above Mach 6. Outer panel of right windshield shattered at Mach 2.7.
2,502	3.76	81,000	150.9	Daniel/Petersen/Rushworth	MH-96 disengaged at launch but re-engaged at ignition. Yaw limit cycle at fixed gain during propulsion phase.
645	0.97	44,750	032.0	Daniel/Walker/McDivitt/ Rushworth	Engine failed to ignite on two attempts and first to land away from Edwards area. Last US Navy flight.
3,765	5.51	133,500	223.5	Gordon/Petersen/McDivitt/ Rushworth	
2,850	4.12	180,000	181.7	Daniel/McKay/Rushworth	Engine failed to ignite on first attempt. Q-ball tests at low and high pressures.
3,866	5.69	154,000	218.5	Dana/Rushworth/Daniel/ Knight	
3,789	5.31	207,500	286.6	White/McKay/Gordon/ Rushworth	By maintaining g-limit, aircraft 'bounced' back up into rarefied atmosphere and went 72km (45mls) south of Edwards before turning around. Longest flight in programme.
3,489	4.94	246,700	231.6	Daniel/White/Dana/ Rushworth	Specifically mounted to exceed Soviet altitude record and verified by the FAI.
3,524	5.34	70,400	143.5	Daniel/McKay/Rushworth	First test of XLR-99 at 30% throttle setting.
3,450	5.03	100,400	143.0	Daniel/Dana/Rogers	Boundary layer flow study. Engine shut down prematurely and left roll out of trim.
3,675	5.42	132,600	224.5	Daniel/Dana/Rogers/Collins	100th air-lift for an X-15. Vibration noted at 30% thrust.
3,672	5.39	103,600	168.6	Daniel/McKay/White	Air flow research. Engine vibration. Almost 90deg right turn made over Daggett to evaluate manoeuvrability of a spacecraft returning from orbit.
3,517	5.02	184,600	249.0	McDivitt/McKay/Collins/ Gordon	Pilot checkout flight and BCS test.
4,104	5.92	123,700	223.2	Rushworth/McKay/Knight/ Daniel	Ventral parachute lost. Pitch damper went inoperative during pull-up.
3,280	4.95	83,200	167.0	Rushworth/Armstrong/ Daniel	Heating rates at low alpha and low Mach number.

PILOT	DATE	FLIGHT NO.	X-15	B-52	FLIGHT DETAILS			FLIGHT DETAILS (contd.)	
					Launch Time	Drop Lake	Burn Time	Landing Lake	Flight Time
White	16/07/62		-3		Loose B-52/X-15 umbilical connector.				
Walker	16/07/62	061	-1	008	14:09:25.0	Mud	01:23.9	Rogers	09:37.8
White	17/07/62	062	-3	003	09:31:10.0	Delamar	01:22.0	Rogers	10:20.7
McKay	19/07/62	063	-2	008	09:53:45.0	Hidden Hills	01:46.2	Rogers	08:23.8
Armstrong	26/07/62	064	-1	003	11:22:30.0	Mud	01:22.8	Rogers	10:21.4
Walker	01/08/62		-3		Failure in fuel tank pressurisation.				
Walker	02/08/62	065	-3	003	09:56:15.0	Mud	01:20.0	Rogers	09:14.0
Rushworth	08/08/62	066	-2	008	10:08:35.0	Hidden Hills	01:35.8	Rogers	07:42.8
Walker	10/08/62		-3		Broken wire at BCS control system.				
Walker	14/08/62	067	-3	003	10:41:35.0	Delamar	01:24.2	Rogers	09:04.9
Rushworth	20/08/62	068	-2	008	10:08:40.0	Hidden Hills	01:26.5	Rogers	08:38.2
Rushworth	29/08/62	069	-2	008	10:36:03.0	Hidden Hills	01:32.0	Rogers	08:47.1
McKay	27/09/62		-2		Pilot tripped ejection handles in error.				
McKay	28/09/62	070	-2	008	10:04:55.0	Hidden Hills	02:08.2	Rogers	09:27.5
Rushworth	04/10/62	071	-3	008	10:10:11.0	Delamar	01:43.2	Rogers	09:50.5
McKay	09/10/62	072	-2	003	10:58:32.0	Delamar	01:19.5	Rogers	09:40.3
Rushworth	23/10/62	073	-3	008	11:30:40.0	Mud	01:18.0	Rogers	09:46.3
McKay	09/11/62	074	-2	008	10:23:07	Mud	01:10.5	Mud	06:31.0
White	13/12/62		-3		Nitrogen pressure systems loss and failure with low pressure relief vent.				
White	14/12/62	075	-3	008	10:44:07.0	Mud	01:17.7	Rogers	09:37.1
Walker	20/12/62	076	-3	008	11:25:04.0	Mud	01:21.0	Rogers	08:54.3
Walker	17/01/63	077	-3	008	10:59:16.0	Delamar	01:21.2	Rogers	09:43.9
Walker	18/04/63	079	-3	008	12:16:17.6	Hidden Hills	01:19.0	Rogers	07:13.2
McKay	25/04/63	080	-1	008	14:03:38.3	Delamar	01:26.3	Rogers	10:32.3
Walker	02/05/63	081	-3	008	09:59:54.0	Mud	01:19.2	Rogers	09:17.2

Speed	Mach No.	Max. Altitude	Distance	Chase	Notes
3,674	5.37	107,200	227.8	Daniel/Dana/Engle/ Rushworth	New instrument configuration compatible with simulator and to check out SAS. Ventral parachute failure.
3,832	5.45	314,750	268.3	McDivitt/McKay/Dana/ Thompson	Weather switched launch from Smith Ranch. FAI recognised altitude record.
3,474	5.18	85,250	161.2	Rogers/Dana/Rushworth	Heating rates at low alpha and high Mach number.
3,989	5.74	98,900	214.8	Rushworth/Collins/Daniel/ White	Aerodynamic stability and drag. Lost lower vertical door. Hydraulic leakage. Smoke in cockpit.
3,438	5.07	144,500	223.5	Daniel/McKay/Collins/ Rushworth	Evaluation of MH-96 modifications to rectify previous yaw problem.
2,943	4.40	90,877	143.9	McDivitt/McKay/Engle/ Collins	Aerodynamic heating evaluated at moderate velocity and low altitude.
3,747	5.25	193,600	231.7	Rushworth/Dana/Engle/ White	MH-96 roll mode inoperative with some instability in all three axes. Low engine fuel pressure. Ventral removed for subsequent X-15-3 flights.
3,534	5.24	88,900	154.2	Gordon/McKay/Engle/Daniel	Evaluated heat rates at high speed and moderate alpha angle. SAS tripped out. Small detonation in engine.
3,447	5.12	97,200	160.6	White/Walker/McDivitt/ Knight	Evaluation of heating effects at high alpha angle and high Mach number. Intermittent SAS. Speed brake vibration. Subsequent flights with X-15-2 flown with lower ventral removed until flight 155.
2,765	4.22	68,200	144.2	White/Walker/Engle/ Rushworth	Longest engine burn to date.
3,493	5.17	112,200	229.6	Rogers/Collins/Walker/ Gordon	APU-1 stopped operating 5min after launch.
3,716	5.46	130,200	235.3	White/Dana/Rushworth/ Rogers	Second stage igniter exploded. Subsequent flights limited to 01:19 burn time until problem resolved.
3,764	5.47	134,500	235.3	Rogers/Dana/Thompson/ Knight	B-52 initiated launch due to popped circuit-breaker in X-15. APU exploded.
1,019	1.49	53,950	45.4	White/Walker/Evenson/ Daniel	Failed engine governor valve reduced thrust output to 30% and fuel starvation. Multiple issues caused roll-over on landing, retiring X-15-2 for a total rebuild and conversion to X-15A-2.
3,742	5.65	141,400	227.5	Rogers/Dana/Evenson/ Knight	Entry flown at 22deg alpha.
3,793	5.73	160,400	226.6	Rushworth/White/Daniel/ Gordon	Explore control system limits at high dynamic pressure.
3,677	5.47	271,700	246.2	White/Dana/Gordon/Daniel	APU-1 failure four minutes after launch. Q-ball shutdown due to hydraulic pressure loss. Rudder servo failed two minutes before touchdown. Altitude build-up flight with no ventral.
3,770	5.51	92,500	147.5	White/Dana/Sorlie/Rogers	First test of new Q-sensor for measuring maximum dynamic pressure. Nose gear door opened at Mach 3.4.
3,654	5.32	105,500	234.0	White/Thompson/Wood/ Knight	SAS disengaged at launch, alternate engaged. KC-1 camera test.
3,488	4.73	209,400	216.3	White/Dana/Rogers/Knight	High altitude APU checkout. New nose gear doors and main skid oleo legs.

PILOT	DATE	FLIGHT NO.	X-15	B-52	FLIGHT DETAILS			FLIGHT DETAILS (contd.)	
					Launch Time	Drop Lake	Burn Time	Landing Lake	Flight Time
Rushworth	14/05/63	082	-3	008	12:11:56.0	Hidden Hills	01:26.9	Rogers	07:33.1
McKay	15/05/63	083	-1	003	10:50:46.0	Delamar	01:24.1	Rogers	10:20.5
Walker	29/05/63	084	-3	008	10:43:22.0	Delamar	01:24.3	Rogers	11:42.5
Rushworth	18/06/63	085	-3	008	10:34:21.0	Delamar	01:19.3	Rogers	09:40.3
Walker	25/06/63	086	-1	003	09:53:50.0	Delamar	01:32.8	Rogers	09:59.3
Rushworth	27/06/63	087	-3	008	09:56:03.0	Delamar	01:20.0	Rogers	10:28.0
Walker	03/07/63		-1		Communication equipment failure.				
Walker	09/07/63	088	-1	008	12:12:12.0	Delamar	01:23.6	Rogers	08:57.7
Rushworth	17/07/63		-1		X-15 pilot oxygen mask disconnected.				
Rushworth	18/07/63	089	-1	003	10:07:20.0	Mud	1:25.2	Rogers	09:23.9
Walker	19/07/63	090	-3	008	10:20:05.0	Smith Ranch	01:24.5	Rogers	11:24.1
Walker	06/08/63		-3		Overheating computer and weather wave-off.				
Walker	13/08/63		-3		APU-1 failed after four seconds of operation.				
Walker	15/08/63		-3		Weather abort but APU-1 also failed again.				
Walker	22/08/63	091	-3	003	10:05:57.0	Smith Ranch	01:25.8	Rogers	11:08.6
Engle	04/10/63		-1		Communication equipment failure.				
Engle	07/10/63	092	-1	008	12:22:56.0	Hidden Hills	1:58.9	Rogers	07:37.8
Rushworth	14/10/63		-3		Inertial platform malfunction.				
Rushworth	25/10/63		-3		Inertial platform malfunction.				
Thompson	29/10/63	093	-1	008	12:42:34.0	Hidden Hills	02:06.1	Rogers	08:43.0
Rushworth	07/11/63	094	-3	008	10:11:14.0	Hidden Hills	01:47.2	Rogers	08:51.7
Engle	14/11/63	095	-1	008	11:19:21.0	Hidden Hills	01:24.6	Rogers	07:46.5
Thompson	19/11/63		-2		Weather wave-off.				
Thompson	27/11/63	096	-3	008	12:17:40.0	Hidden Hills	01:29.0	Rogers	07:04.3
Rushworth	05/10/63	097	-1	008	11:04:36.0	Delamar	01:21.2	Rogers	09:34.0
Rushworth	18/12/63		-1		Camera system incorrectly wired.				
Engle	08/01/64	098	-1	008	12:10:31.0	Mud	01:16.6	Rogers	08:50.7
Thompson	16/01/64	099	-3	008	10:03:30.0	Hidden Hills	01:24.2	Rogers	08:17.0
Rushworth	28/01/64	100	-1	008	12:11:36.0	Delamar	01:17.2	Rogers	10:25.5

Speed	Mach No.	Max. Altitude	Distance	Chase	Notes
3,600	5.20	95,600	149.2	Sorlie/Dana/Daniel	Engine failed to ignite on first attempt due to vibration. Evaluation of skin heat transfer rates.
3,856	5.57	124,200	242.9	Rushworth/Dana/Evenson/ Daniel	Tested a traversing probe which extended every four seconds to measure air flow. Gear box pressure lost five minutes after launch. Nose gear scoop door opened at Mach 5.2. Fire in nose compartment. Both tyres disintegrated on landing. Forward fuselage buckled.
3,858	5.52	92,000	232.9	White/Dana/Knight/Rogers	Heat transfer rate measurements. Inner panel on left windshield shattered at engine cut-off.
3,539	4.97	223,700	235.0	Gordon/Dana/Ward/Rogers	Altitude build-up flight.
3,911	5.51	111,800	248.4	Daniel/McKay/Wood/Rogers	Heat build-up evaluation with traversing probe and optical degradation instruments. Left fuselage forward fairing cracked at buckle spot from flight 083.
3,425	4.89	285,000	236.6	Daniel/McKay/Wood/Rogers	
3,631	5.07	226,400	240.8	Daniel/McKay/Rogers/Wood	Optical degradation evaluation. Traversing probe inoperative after engine burnout. Cork ablation tested on lower right speed brake.
3,925	5.63	104,800	214.8	Rogers/Dana/Evenson/ Gordon	Malfunction in second stage igniter, engine shut down manually. Ablative test patches on speed brakes and leading edge of lower fixed ventral fin.
3,710	5.50	347,800	288.5	Crews/Dana/Rogers/Daniel/ Wood	Towed balloon test for Mercury spacecraft MA-9 mission.
3,794	5.58	354,200	293.4	Wood/Dana/Gordon/Rogers	Towed balloon experiment. Initial test of altitude predictor sensor.
2,834	4.21	77,800	138.5	Sorlie/Thompson/Rogers	Ablative test on speed brakes. Pilot performed an unauthorised roll on descent.
2,712	4.10	74,400	144.2	Sorlie/Walker/Rushworth	New Emerson Electric ablative materials tested on lower right speed brake.
2,925	4.40	82,300	145.8	Gordon/Thompson/Sorlie	Initial tests with razor-sharp upper vertical stabiliser leading edge. Heat transfer evaluation and stability with damper off.
3,286	4.75	90,800	146.5	Rushworth/Dana/Rogers	Ablative materials removed for optical degradation mission.
3,310	4.94	89,800	145.9	Rushworth/Dana/Sorlie	Inertial system inoperative at launch.
4,018	6.06	101,000	233.7	Wood/Sorlie/Dana/Engle	
3,616	5.32	139,900	219.3	Rushworth/Dana/Wood/ Sorlie	Evaluated high angle-of-attack stability without SAS. Inertial platform malfunctioned at peak altitude.
3,242	4.92	71,000	145.8	Gordon/Peterson/Crews	Heat transfer test with upper vertical razor edge. Stability and control test with damper off. Skids coated with cermet.
3,618	5.34	107,400	238.7	Engle/Dana/Crews/Wood	Stability and control evaluation with upper speed brakes prior to installation of redesigned lower ventral fin for scramjet project. Repeated SAS roll failure.

PILOT	DATE	FLIGHT NO.	X-15	B-52	FLIGHT DETAILS			FLIGHT DETAILS (contd.)	
					Launch Time	Drop Lake	Burn Time	Landing Lake	Flight Time
McKay	13/03/64	102	-3	003	09:46:27.0	Hidden Hills	01:45.2	Rogers	07:29.0
Rushworth	17/03/64		-1		Computer failure.				
Rushworth	27/03/64	103	-1	003	10:10:18.0	Delamar	01:25.0	Rogers	09:52.4
McKay	31/03/64		-3		Failed inertial guidance system.				
Engle	08/04/64	104	-1	003	10:02:27.0	Delamar	01:19.9	Rogers	09:45.7
Rushworth	29/04/64	105	-1	003	10:00:27.0	Delamar	01:22.3	Rogers	09:34.6
McKay	11/05/64		-3		Over pressurised LOX tank regulator.				
McKay	12/05/64	106	-3	003	09:51:46.0	Hidden Hills	01:48.6	Rogers	08:11.3
Engle	19/05/64	107	-1	003	10:26:28.0	Delamar	01:18.7	Rogers	09:01.2
Thompson	21/05/64	108	-3	003	09:39:34.0	Silver	00:42.9	Cuddeback	07:56.5
Thompson	11/06/64		-1		Multiple technical malfunctions.				
Rushworth	15/06/64		-2		Verification of modifications but multiple failures.				
Rushworth	23/06/64		-2		APU-2 shut down unexpectedly.				
Rushworth	25/06/64	109	-2	003	09:34:47.0	Hidden Hills	01:18.2	Rogers	08:44.7
McKay	30/06/64	110	-1	003	09:49:40.0	Delamar	01:23.4	Rogers	11:26.7
Engle	02/07/64		-3		MH-96 malfunction prevented launch.				
Engle	08/07/64	111	-3	003	13:02:52.0	Delamar	01:18.9	Rogers	09:56.4
Engle	28/07/64		-3		Depleted cooling gas.				
Engle	29/07/64	112	-3	003	11:55:19.0	Hidden Hills	01:33.5	Rogers	07:49.0
Thompson	12/08/64	113	-3	003	10:12:33.2	Hidden Hills	01:22.0	Rogers	06:42.8
Rushworth	14/08/64	114	-2	003	09:54:19.0	Delamar	01:20.9	Rogers	12:06.3
McKay	26/08/64	115	-3	003	10:42:07.0	Hidden Hills	01:34.4	Rogers	07:19.7
Thompson	03/09/64	116	-3	003	09:54.54	Hidden Hills	01:32.2	Rogers	06:18.1
Engle	23/09/64		-3		Cabin pressure failure.				
Rushworth	29/09/64	118	-2	008	13:00:13.0	Mud	01:19.7	Rogers	09:51.0
McKay	02/10/64		-1		SAS malfunction.				
McKay	15/10/64	119	-1	008	13:15:40.0	Hidden Hills	01:12.9	Rogers	08:40.9
Thompson	29/10/64		-3		Planned captive flight to check nose gear door changes.				
Thompson	30/10/64	120	-3	008	09:51:52.2	Hidden Hills	01:14.4	Rogers	07:10.8
McKay	06/11/64		-2		Planned captive flight to check nose gear door changes.				
McKay	16/11/64		-2		Planned captive flight to check nose gear door changes.				

Speed	Mach No.	Max. Altitude	Distance	Chase	Notes
3,392	5.11	76,000	151.5	Rogers/Peterson/Engle	Heat transfer, skin friction and boundary layer noise.
3,827	5.63	101,500	228.7	Gordon/Peterson/Adams/ Engle	Investigation of induced turbulence.
3,468	5.01	175,000	227.2	Gordon/Thompson/Crews/ Rogers	Optical degradation experiment. APU fire caused by overheating but cause never resolved.
3,906	5.72	101.600	233.7	Sorlie/Dana/Crews/Rogers	Optical degradation experiment. Inner pane of right windshield shattered. Smoke in cockpit.
3,084	4.66	72,800	155.6	Sorlie/Peterson/Engle	Inertial guidance computer failure denying pilot information on velocity, altitude, rate-of-climb. SAS pitch and roll channels tripped off. Speed brakes only opened to 30%.
3,494	5.02	195,800	221.6	Sorlie/Gordon/Dana/Daniel	Optical degradation experiment. Altitude build-up.
1,865	2.90	64,200	087.0	Rushworth/Dana/Sorlie	Faulty fuel line switch shut down engine at 41 seconds and failed to re-ignite on two attempts. Emergency landing.
3,104	4.59	83,300	159.9	Engle/Peterson/Rogers/ Sorlie	First flight in X-15A-2 configuration. Right roll noted out of trim and right horizontal stabiliser warped, replaced with stabiliser from X-15-3.
3,334	4.96	99,600	226.4	Engle/Peterson/Sorlie/ Rogers	Power for stable platform failed at launch and alternate mission profile flown.
3,520	5.05	170,400	242.7	Sorlie/Dana/Smith/Rogers	Ablative test patches on lower ventral and speed brakes.
3,623	5.38	78,000	151.6	Sorlie/McKay/Rogers	Measured heat transfer rates and evaluated ablative patches.
3,535	5.24	81,200	136.9	Rushworth/McKay/Sorlie	Vibrations with speed brakes at high aerodynamic pressure.
3,590	5.23	103,300	227.4	Knight/Dana/Engle/Sorlie	Nose gear deployed at Mach 4.2. Tyres failed to rims at rollout.
3,863	5.65	91,000	157.5	Sorlie/Peterson/Knight	Experiments with heat transfer, skin friction and boundary layer.
3,615	5.35	78,600	140.9	Knight/Walker/Rogers	Tested heat transfer and turbulence over distorted panels.
3,542	5.20	97,800	210.3	Sorlie/Thompson/Parsons/ Engle	Stability and control evaluation. Nose gear scoop door opened at Mach 4.5. Star tracker system check.
3,048	4.56	84,900	153.5	Rogers/Peterson/Knight	Initial flight with 90kg (200lb) wing pods. Micrometeorite experiment opened going transonic. Evaluated X-20 inertial guidance system.
3,113	4.66	84,600	142.1	Rushworth/Peterson/Engle	Tested nose gear door modification and centre control stick. Boundary layer and shear layer experiments. Fire warning light 54sec after engine shutdown.

PILOT	DATE	FLIGHT NO.	X-15	B-52	FLIGHT DETAILS			FLIGHT DETAILS (contd.)	
					Launch Time	Drop Lake	Burn Time	Landing Lake	Flight Time
Engle	04/12/64		-1		Fuel vent valve malfunction.				
Thompson	09/12/64	122	-3	008	10:36:17.0	Hidden Hills	01:41.4	Rogers	06:25.7
Engle	10/12/64	123	-1	003	11:10:26.0	Delamar	01:20.5	Rogers	09:44.7
Rushworth	22/12/64	124	-3	003	10:44:52.0	Hidden Hills	01:28.0	Rogers	07:49.9
Thompson	13/01/65	125	-3	003	10:51:06.7	Hidden Hills	01:38.5	Rogers	06:47.8
McKay	26/01/65		-1		Inertial system failure.				
Engle	02/02/65	126	-3	008	12:50:14.6	Delamar	01:21.4	Rogers	09:58.3
Rushworth	15/02/65		-2		Scheduled captive flight to check main landing gear but camera gear failed.				
Rushworth	15/02/65		-2		Successful check on main landing gear modifications.				
Rushworth	17/02/65	127	-2	008	10:44:59.6	Mud	01:19.8	Rogers	09:19.8
McKay	19/02/65		-1		APU-2 malfunctioned.				
McKay	25/02/65		-1		Bad weather.				
McKay	26/02/65	128	-1	008	11:45:55.0	Delamar	01:23.2	Rogers	09:26.0
Rushworth	26/03/65	129	-1	008	11:01:59.2	Delamar	01:19.6	Rogers	11:04.3
Engle	23/04/65	130	-3	008	19:44:16.7	Hidden Hills	01:31.4	Rogers	07:42.1
McKay	28/04/65	131	-2	008	12:26:20.9	Hidden Hills	01:18.9	Rogers	07:52.5
Thompson	11/05/65		-1		Problems with SAS, APU and cabin pressure.				
McKay	13/05/65		-2		Unable to pressurise cabin.				
McKay	18/05/65	132	-2	008	09:56:38.0	Mud	01:18.9	Rogers	09:42.0
Thompson	25/05/65	133	-1	008	10:12:07.5	Mud	01:21.1	Rogers	09:02.5
Engle	28/05/65	134	-3	008	09:43:51.0	Delamar	01:22.5	Rogers	09:35.4
McKay	08/06/65		-2		Loss of helium pressure.				
McKay	11/06/65		-2		Loss of helium pressure.				
Engle	16/06/65	135	-3	003	10:26:33.0	Delamar	01:17.80	Rogers	9:46.4
Thompson	17/06/65	136	-1	008	09:40:31.2	Delamar	01:22.2	Rogers	08:54.0
McKay	22/06/65	137	-2	008	09:44:43.9	Delamar	01:25.3	Rogers	09:47.7
Engle	29/06/65	138	-3	008	10:21:17.6	Delamar	01:21.0	Rogers	10:32.5
McKay	02/07/65		-2		Inertial platform failure.				
McKay	08/07/65	139	-2	003	09:16:55.8	Delamar	01:22.9	Rogers	09:33.4
Rushworth	13/07/65		-3		Cabin pressure regulator malfunctioned.				

Speed	Mach No.	Max. Altitude	Distance	Chase	Notes
3,723	5.42	92,400	142.1	Rushworth/Peterson/Sorlie/ Twinting	Skin friction, boundary layer noise and ablatives test.
3,675	5.35	113,200	227.2	Sorlie/McKay/Parsons/ Rogers	X-20 guidance evaluation with dampers off for directional control. SAS pitch malfunction after launch. Carried air density experiments.
3,593	5.55	81,200	148.4	Twinting/Mallick/Knight	Ablative samples carried but roll oscillations after launch.
3,712	5.48	99,400	147.7	Smith/Dana/Rushworth	Heat transfer, boundary layer noise, skin friction evaluation. Malfunction to roll damper on pull-up manoeuvre.
3,885	5.71	98,200	230.6	Sorlie/Peterson/Stroface/ Rushworth	Boundary layer noise and skin friction data-gathering. MH-96 fixed-gain test. Radar beacon intermittent performance.
3,511	5.27	95,100	207.2	Sorlie/Dana/Thompson/ Engle	Evaluation of landing gear modifications. Engine briefly lost power at T+23sec. Right main landing skid extended at Mach 4.3. Inertial attitude failed.
3,750	5.40	153,600	236.9	Knight/Peterson/Stroface/ Engle	Guidance system and BCS evaluation. Air density and sky brightness experiments.
3,580	5.17	101,900	230.8	Engle/Dana/Gentry/Knight	Inertial guidance system check and infrared scanner photography.
3,580	5.48	79,700	148.7	Rushworth/McKay/Knight	Heat transfer and boundary layer noise tests with evaluation of ablative samples.
3,273	4.80	92,600	154.1	Sorlie/Thompson/Engle	Evaluation of stability and control. Inertial attitude rate failure.
3,541	5.17	102,100	215.9	Sorlie/Mallick/Gentry/Engle	Completed landing gear modification checkout. Experiments with star tracker and stability and control.
3,418	4.87	179,800	211.9	Rushworth/Peterson/ Stroface/Knight	MIT scanner tests.
3,754	5.17	209,600	243.4	Sorlie/Haise/Parsons/Knight	Boundary layer noise experiments. Horizon scanner attached above engine exhaust on upper ventral.
3,404	4.69	244,700	232.1	Wood/Mallick/Sorlie/ Twinting	Ultraviolet radiation measurements through scanner in tail. Boundary layer noise evaluation. APU-2 shut down after engine start, restart successful.
3,541	5.14	108,500	218.2	Twinting/McKay/Stroface/ Engle	IR scanner and reflected solar radiation measurements. Two SAS pitch and roll failures before launch, reset and failed after launch. Alternate SAS used.
3,938	5.64	155,900	245.0	Rushworth/Peterson/ Gentry/Knight	Redirected from planned Mud launch due to thunderstorms. Landing gear evaluation and star tracker tests.
3,432	4.94	280,600	239.2	Wood/McKay/Gentry/ Parsons	Boundary layer noise, horizon scanner and radiometer tests along with re-entry techniques.
3,659	5.19	212,600	245.5	Adams/Peterson/Gentry/ Knight	RAS failed to work. Landing dynamics investigated.

PILOT	DATE	FLIGHT NO.	X-15	B-52	FLIGHT DETAILS			FLIGHT DETAILS (contd.)	
					Launch Time	Drop Lake	Burn Time	Landing Lake	Flight Time
Thompson	23/07/65		-1		Leak in pressure suit faceplate.				
Thompson	27/07/65		-1		Malfunction in radio equipment.				
Thompson	28/07/65		-1		Q-ball was incorrectly wired causing malfunction.				
Rushworth	03/08/65	141	-2	008	12:40:05.7	Delamar	01:22.4	Rogers	09:32.0
Thompson	06/08/65	142	-1	008	09:41:46.7	Delamar	01:23.0	Rogers	10:13.0
Engle	10/08/65	143	-3	003	11:24:21.7	Delamar	01:22.1	Rogers	09:51.8
Thompson	20/08/65		-1		Failure to cabin pressure regulator.				
Thompson	24/08/65		-1		Inertial system failure.				
Thompson	25/08/65	144	-1	003	09:54:46.8	Delamar	01:24.5	Rogers	08:51.5
Rushworth	26/08/65	145	-3	008	09:52:12.1	Delamar	01:18.6	Rogers	10:27.6
McKay	02/09/65	146	-2	008	09:40:05.6	Delamar	01:24.0	Rogers	09:09.8
Rushworth	09/09/65	147	-1	008	09:55:50.7	Delamar	01:22.1	Rogers	11:10.2
McKay	14/09/65	148	-3	008	10:01:06.0	Delamar	01:20.9	Rogers	09:58.1
Rushworth	22/09/65	149	-1	003	10:58:39.7	Delamar	01:22.0	Rogers	10:53.9
McKay	28/09/65	150	-3	003	10:07:37.6	Delamar	01:20.8	Rogers	11:56.6
Knight	30/09/65	151	-1	003	09:43:55.3	Hidden Hills	02:7.4	Rogers	08:22.6
Engle	08/10/65		-1		BCS leak.				
Knight	12/10/65	152	-3	008	09:43:13.2	Hidden Hills	01:06.2	Rogers	07:07.8
Engle	14/10/65	153	-1	003	003	12:46:32.6	Delamar	01:24.8	09:18.4
Dana	02/11/65		-1		Cabin pressure regulator failed. No telemetry.				
Rushworth	03/11/65	155	-2	003	09:09:10.7	Cuddeback	01:24.1	Rogers	05:01.6
Dana	04/11/65	156	-1	008	09:11:31.0	Hidden Hills	02:04.2	Rogers	08:45.1
Rushworth	13/04/66		-2		Failed inertial system prior to launch.				
Rushworth	20/04/66		-2		SAS yaw channel failed to engage following APU start.				
Rushworth	05/05/66		-2		SAS yaw channel failed to engage following APU start.				
McKay	06/05/66	157	-1	003	13:30:12.8	Delamar	00:35.4	Delamar	06:02.7
Rushworth	18/05/66	158	-2	003	10:24:00.3	Mud	01:21.9	Rogers	08:56.8
McKay	02/06/66		-1		Inertial system failure.				
McKay	10/06/66		-1		Inertial system failure.				

Speed	Mach No.	Max. Altitude	Distance	Chase	Notes
3,602	5.16	208,700	249.2	Sorlie/Dana/Whelan/ Stroface	BCS stability checks with star tracker experiment. Minor problem with roll trim.
3,534	5.15	103,200	235.6	Rushworth/Haise/Living-ston/Engle	Stability and control evaluation. Flew with replaced SAS wiring. Q-ball replaced.
3,550	5.20	271,000	246.9	Sorlie/Dana/Gentry/Stroface	Evaluated re-entry techniques but yaw damper disengaged and had to be reset 20 times.
3,604	5.11	214,100	237.1	Rushworth/McKay/Merrett/ Parsons	Experiments with horizon scanner. Poor pitch control on touchdown.
3,372	4.79	239,600	230.0	Sorlie/Haise/Livingston/ Parsons	Boundary layer noise and radiometer experiments.
3,570	5.16	239,800	242.4	Rushworth/Peterson/ Stroface/Knight	Airframe x-rayed by USAF prior to flight. Star tracking and landing dynamics tests.
3,534	5.25	97,200	234.0	Wood/Peterson/Livingston/ Parsons	Tests of ablative material on lower fixed ventral and speed brake surfaces. Infrared horizon scanner tests.
3,519	5.03	239,000	239.2	Rushworth/Haise/Everson/ Knight	Boundary layer tests and infrared scanner experiments. Bad data on MH-96 caused by failed trim motor pitch filter.
3,550	5.18	100,300	232.7	Sorlie/Dana/Adams/Engle	Infrared scanner tests. Venting on LOX tank induced pitch-down after engine firing.
3,732	5.33	295,600	290.5	Rushworth/Peterson/Haise/ Engle	Boundary layer noise experiment.
2,718	4.06	76,600	143.7	Sorlie/Peterson/Engle	Infrared scanner test and evaluation.
3,108	4.62	94,400	140.7	Sorlie/Haise/Engle	APU-2 shut down prematurely after launch and restarted 90 seconds after engine shutdown.
3,554	5.08	266,500	237.4	Sorlie/McKay/Parsons/ Knight	MIT Horizon Photometer and Pace transducer test. Yaw damper reset twice after tripping out.
1,500	2.31	70,600	54.4	Knight/Haise/Engle	First flight with external tanks, demonstrated successful jettison. Lower ventral lost when parachute failed. Only launch from Cuddeback.
2,765	4.22	80,200	141.8	Sorlie/Peterson/Knight	Pilot checkout flight. Three attempts at engine ignition, 25 seconds late and 1.2sec overburn on planned duration.
1,434	2.21	68,400	62.2	Knight/Curtis/Peterson/ Gentry/Stroface	Engine shut down short of planned 01:22 burn due to pump failure and ruptured case. Planned atmospheric density measurements and micrometeorite collection and sky brightness experiment.
3,689	5.43	99,000	211.7	Sorlie/Dana/Peterson/ Gentry	Test of ablative materials on nose gear door, horizontal stabiliser and lower ventral. Fuel leak caused 2.1sec underburn with a planned Mach 5.38 over-achieved.

PILOT	DATE	FLIGHT NO.	X-15	B-52	FLIGHT DETAILS			FLIGHT DETAILS (contd.)	
					Launch Time	Drop Lake	Burn Time	Landing Lake	Flight Time
Rushworth	27/06/66		-2		Scheduled captive flight to check full external tanks.				
Rushworth	01/07/66	159	-2	008	11:02:36.1	Mud	00:33.2	Mud	04:48.6
Knight	12/07/66	160	-1	003	11:32:15.7	Mud	01:23.2	Rogers	08:36.0
Dana	13/07/66		-3		Inertial system failure.				
Dana	18/07/66	161	-3	003	11:38:24.1	Hidden Hills	01:35.5	Rogers	07:30.6
Knight	20/07/66		-2		Bad weather.				
Knight	21/07/66	162	-2	003	12:02:03.1	Delamar	01:21.3	Rogers	08:51.0
McKay	28/07/66	163	-1	008	10:01:12.1	Delamar	01:25.4	Rogers	09:43.0
Knight	03/08/66	164	-2	008	08:45:26.3	Delamar	01:21.8	Rogers	09:05.5
Dana	04/08/66	165	-3	008	09:54:43.7	Mud	01:18.9	Rogers	08:28.0
McKay	09/09/66		-1		Inertial system failure. BCS propellant leak.				
McKay	10/08/66		-1		No rescue helicopter on station.				
McKay	11/08/66	166	-1	003	09:44:13.1	Delamar	01:24.8	Rogers	09:22.2
Knight	12/08/66	167	-2	003	08:39.4	10:25:33.0	Delamar	Rogers	01:21.7
McKay	25/08/66	169	-1	003	09:49:11.2	Delamar	01:23.4	Rogers	10:16.2
Knight	30/08/66	170	-2	008	09:51:37.2	Mud	01:20.5	Rogers	08:49.9
McKay	08/09/66	171	-1	008	10:39:16.8	Smith Ranch	00:45.5	Smith Ranch	06:24.5
Dana	13/09/66		-3		Radio failed.				
Dana	14/09/66	172	-3	003	12:01:29.5	Delamar	01:19.3	Rogers	08:58.6
Adams	28/09/66		-1		Bad weather.				
Adams	04/10/66		-1		Cabin pressure failed due to faulty canopy seal.				
Adams	06/10/66	173	-1	003	12:16:59.8	Hidden Hills	01:29.9	Cuddeback	08:26.4

Speed	Mach No.	Max. Altitude	Distance	Chase	Notes
1,061	1.70	44,800	35.2	Knight/Peterson/Curtis/Sorlie	Handling evaluation with full external tanks but faulty indicator showing no fuel flow prevented ablative tests and local flow measurements in ramjet region at planned Mach 6. Engine shutdown short of planned 02:12 burn time but successful tanks separation at half-full quantity.
3,652	5.34	130,000	209.8	Curtis/Dana/Hoag/Gentry	Pilot checkout flight, electrical loads survey and checkouts on inertial system, new window shade and stick-kicker.
3,217	4.71	96,100	146.1	Curtis/Manke/Gentry	First with the new Lear Siegler cockpit display and third landing skid.
3,568	5.12	192,300	231.9	Curtis/Manke/Sorlie/Gentry/Peterson	Pilot altitude build-up flight, star tracker checks, test of Martin ablative material, base drag study. Right roll out of trim.
3,702	5.19	241,800	253.4	Curtis/Peterson/Sorlie/Gentry	Pace transducer test, micrometeorite collection and horizon scanner checks. Computer malfunction and pitch trip-out due to electrical transients on alternator-2.
3,440	5.03	249,000	231.1	Curtis/Manke/Parsons/Sorley	Pilot altitude build-up flight with star tracker and base drag study. Inertial attitude read incorrect throughout the flight.
3,693	5.34	132,700	212.4	Curtis/Manke/Parsons/Gentry	Boundary layer noise data, horizontal tail loads, heat transfer panel experiment. Optical background experiment.
3,590	5.21	251,000	239.5	Sorlie/Manke/Everson/Gentry	Highest dynamic pressure recorded for any X-15 flight (15.182kPa/2,202lb/in^2). Power transients caused SAS dropouts. Wing tip pod flutter investigation.
3,472	5.02	231,100	231.4	Sorlie/Mallick/Smith/Adams	Star tracker and base drag measurements. Alternate pitot static checkout.
3,543	5.11	257,500	253.4	Adams/Manke/Smith/Knight	Micrometeorite collection, horizon scanner and rarefied gas experiment with wing pod flutter evaluation. All telemetry lost five minutes after launch. Computer malfunction degraded cockpit displays during re-entry through to landing.
3,543	5.21	102,200	209.3	Curtis/Manke/Hover/Stroface	Maurer camera system carried for the first time. Ventral parachute deployed before ventral jettison. Pitch and roll SAS dropouts. Ablative tests, temperature and base drag studies. M=8 computer checked out.
1,602	2.44	73,200	67.5	Curtis/Manke/Stroface/Gentry	Horizon scanner evaluation, electrical loads survey and horizontal stabiliser angle of attack study. Fuel tank regulator failure caused indicated low line pressure and premature engine shutdown from planned duration of 01:25.5.
3,582	5.12	254,200	235.8	Curtis/Manke/Hover/Stroface	Altitude build-up flight, micrometeorite collection, solar spectrum analysis and dual channel radiometer test. Engine thrust misalignment caused right yaw during burn phase. Energy management computer too cold to turn on.
1,977	3.00	75,400	112.8	Sorlie/Dana/Gentry	Pilot checkout flight. Rupture to forward fuel tank bulkhead caused premature engine shutdown from planned burn duration of 02:09.

PILOT	DATE	FLIGHT NO.	X-15	B-52	FLIGHT DETAILS			FLIGHT DETAILS (contd.)	
					Launch Time	Drop Lake	Burn Time	Landing Lake	Flight Time
Knight	19/10/66		-2		Failed ammonia tank.				
Dana	01/11/66	174	-3	003	13:24:12.8	Smith Ranch	01:22.8	Rogers	10:43.9
Dana	18/11/66		-3		Transformer malfunction.				
Knight	18/11/66	175	-2	008	13:24:07.2	Mud	02:16.4	Rogers	08:26.8
Adams	23/11/66		-3		APU bearing temperatures too high.				
Adams	29/11/66	176	-3	003	11:38:32.6	Hidden Hills	01:37.9	Rogers	07:56.2
Knight	22/12/66		-2		Planned captive flight for thermocouple checkout.				
Adams	15/03/67		-1		Bad weather. Radio failure.				
Adams	21/03/67		-1		Inertial system malfunction.				
Adams	22/03/67	177	-1	003	09:52:04.5	Mud	01:19.7	Rogers	09:27.9
Adams	20/04/67		-1		Bad weather. Inertial system over-chilled.				
Dana	26/04/67	178	-3	008	11:20:17.3	Silver	00:23.2	Silver	05:10.3
Adams	28/04/67	179	-1	003	09:23:32.6	Delamar	01:22.0	Rogers	09:16.0
Knight	05/05/67		-2		Bad weather.				
Knight	08/05/67	180	-2	008	12:27:38.8	Hidden Hills	01:16.9	Rogers	08:26.8
Dana	17/05/67	181	-3	003	10:45:48.0	Silver	01:36.1	Rogers	06:55.6
Adams	26/05/67		-1		Inertial system failure.				
Adams	01/06/67		-1		Inertial system failure.				
Adams	14/06/67		-1		Radio failure 15 seconds before launch.				
Adams	15/06/67	182	-1	003	11:09:28.3	Delamar	01:21.4	Rogers	08:21.0
Dana	22/06/67	183	-3	008	14:57:17.2	Hidden Hills	01:33.2	Rogers	07:06.3
Knight	29/06/67	184	-1	008	11:27:51.2	Smith Ranch	01:07.6	Mud	10:07.0
Dana	20/07/67	185	-3	008	10:11:00.8	Hidden Hills	01:32.1	Rogers	07:36.5
Knight	07/08/67		-2		Planned captive flight to check effects of cold-soak on ablative coating.				
Knight	11/08/67		-2		Suit vent heater failed.				
Knight	16/08/67		-2		Pressure loss in helium supply.				
Knight	21/08/67	186	-2	008	10:59:16.0	Hidden Hills	01:22.2	Rogers	07:40.0
Adams	25/08/67	187	-2	003	13:27:28.0	Hidden Hills	01:11.3	Rogers	07:37.0

Speed	Mach No.	Max. Altitude	Distance	Chase	Notes
3,750	5.46	306,900	292.1	Adams/Peterson/Stroface/ Gentry	Micrometeorite collection, duel channel radiometer check, tip-pod accelerometer data, sky brightness experiment, cockpit displays evaluation.
4,250	6.33	98,900	204.3	Adams/Peterson/Curtis/ McKay/Gentry	Evaluation with full external tanks, Martin ablative sample test, local flow evaluation and base drag study.
3,120	4.65	92,100	149.2	Knight/Manke/Gentry	Pilot checkout flight with tip pod accelerometer data but radio failed at launch and contact not resumed until Cuddeback.
3,822	5.59	133,100	222.2	Gentry/Peterson/Evenson/ Knight	Pilot build-up flight, stabiliser angle-of-attack evaluation. Ablatives test patches on left stabiliser.
1,163	1.80	53,400	42.3	Gentry/Manke/Knight	Frozen fuel pressure sensor line initiated premature shutdown short of planned 01:43 burn time.
3,720	5.44	167,200	235.3	Sorley/Manke/Evenson/ Cuthill	Altitude build-up flight with technical checks and IRIG timer checkout. Pitch attitude malfunction and erratic inertial velocity.
3,193	4.75	97,600	166.9	Sorlie/Evenson/Dana/Adams	Stability and control check with dummy ramjet installed but Last flight before full ablation applied. Eyelid test on left window but when opened aircraft pitched up, rolled right and yawed right.
3,177	4.80	71,100	124.5	Sorlie/Manke/Evenson/ Cuthill	Simulated lifting-body glide approach.
3,606	5.14	229,300	236.9	Gentry/Manke/Davey/Hoag	Pilot altitude build-up with IRIG timer checkout, horizon scanner test and horizontal stabiliser alpha data. Stick kicker inoperative.
3,611	5.34	82,200	139.7	Knight/Manke/Krier/Gentry	Cold wall heat transfer data and PCM checkout.
2,870	4.23	173,000	169.9	Cuthill/Dana/Jackson/ Evenson/Hoag	Horizon scanner and horizontal stabiliser alpha data plus ASAS yaw checkout. Total power loss going through 32,614m (107,000ft).Engine burn short of planned 01:27 duration. One APU restarted with emergency landing at Mud Lake.
3,693	5.44	84,300	144.7	Adams/Krier/Davey	Cold wall heat transfer check, Martin ablative panels test.
3,368	4.94	91,000	157.0	Cuthill/Evenson/Manke/ Evans	Full ablative coating and dummy scramjet installed for total flow test and ramjet separation tests. Ramjet ejected too close to the ground. Forward quarter of right window fogged by ablator.
3,115	4.63	84,400	147.3	Gentry/Jackson/Knight	Engine ignited on second try, 16 seconds after launch. Boost guidance test, cold wall heat transfer data, tip pod accelerometer data and boundary layer noise data. Inertial platform and ball nose failed just before touchdown.

PILOT	DATE	FLIGHT NO.	X-15	B-52	FLIGHT DETAILS			FLIGHT DETAILS (contd.)	
					Launch Time	Drop Lake	Burn Time	Landing Lake	Flight Time
Knight	03/10/67	188	-2	008	14:31:50.9	Mud	02:20.7	Rogers	08:17.0
Dana	04/10/67	189	-3	003	10:16:54.0	Smith Ranch	01:24.7	Rogers	10:46.0
Knight	17/10/67	190	-3	008	09:40:23.0	Smith Ranch	01:24.2	Rogers	10:06.3
Adams	31/10/67		-3		Malfunction to XLR-99 engine idler.				
Adams	15/11/67	191	-3	008	10:30:07.4	Delamar	01:22.3	Crashed	04:51.4
Dana	06/02/68		-1		Planned captive checkout flight after electrical fire on flight 184.				
Dana	07/02/68		-1		Failure to cabin pressurisation and SAS yaw check failed.				
Dana	27/02/68		-1		SAS failed.				
Dana	01/03/68	192	-1	008	11:28:11.0	Hidden Hills	01:05.6	Rogers	07:35.1
Dana	28/03/68		-1		Radio malfunction.				
Dana	03/04/68		-1		Bad weather.				
Knight	26/04/68	194	-1	008	11:51:49.8	Delamar	01:21.5	Rogers	09:17.1
Dana	23/05/68		-1		Bad weather.				
Dana	12/06/68	195	-1	008	08:31:01.0	Smith Ranch	01:23.4	Rogers	11:32.4
Knight	15/07/68		-1		BCS malfunction.				
Knight	16/07/68	196	-1	003	15:23:06.7	Railroad	01:20.5	Rogers	09:42.3
Dana	21/08/68	197	-1	003	-09:04:48.0	Railroad	01:22.9	Rogers	09:23.0
Knight	13/09/68	198	-1	003	11:19:23.2	Smith Ranch	01:24.3	Rogers	10:55.5
Dana	24/10/68	199	-1	003	10:02:47.3	Smith Ranch	01:23.2	Rogers	11:28.3
Knight	12/12/68		-1		Inertial system failure.				

Speed	Mach No.	Max. Altitude	Distance	Chase	Notes
4,520	6.70	102,100	213.7	Cuthill/Twinting/Krier/Adams	Full ablative coating test, stability and control data with dummy scramjet with flow control test, external tank separation data and wing tip accelerometer data. Longest burn time of XLR-99 and highest Mach number of the programme but shock waves burned through lower ventral causing small fire in engine bay. Heat ignited scramjet separation charges ejected over Edwards at Mach 1. Control gas conduit destroyed with loss of helium. Last flight of X-15A-2.
3,897	5.53	251,100	299.8	Cuthill/Krier/Gentry/Manke	Science and atmosphere measurements. Tip pod camera. Micrometeorite collector failed to fully retract for re-entry.
3,856	5.53	280,500	296.5	Cuthill/Twinting/Gentry/Adams	Science experiments. Tip pod camera. Third skid failed to deploy.
3,570	5.20	266,000	185.8	Cuthill/Jackson/Dana/Twinting	Science measurements. Tip pod camera. Disorientation caused by saturation of MH-96 resulted in X-15-3 crashing incurring the only fatality of the programme.
2,878	4.36	104,500	141.0	Twinting/Krier/Knight/Jackson	Checkout flight also for yaw ASAS. Pressure suited inflated on approach.
3,545	5.05	209,600	237.2	Manke/Krier/Livingston/Gentry/Fulton	Saturn rocket insulation tests. Horizon scanner evaluation.
3,563	5.15	220,100	294.4	Gentry/Manke/Jackson/Hoag/Fulton	Saturn rocket insulation tests. Horizon scanner evaluation. Fixed ball nose. Altitude build-up flight.
3,382	4.79	221,500	239.8	Gentry/Manke/Cuthill/Davey/Krier	First from Railroad Valley, with horizon scanner, sky brightness measurements and fixed alpha ball. Alternate profile selected when hydraulic gauge malfunctioned during boost.
3,443	5.01	267,500	234.1	Cuthill/Krier/Hoag/Gentry/Shawler	Measurements and tasks as per previous flight.
3,723	5.37	254,100	299.8	Twinting/Manke/Shawler/Gentry/Krier	Generally the same experiments as previous two flights.
3,716	5.38	255,000	297.4	Cuthill/Krier/Evenson/Hoag/Manke/Enevoldson	Fixed alpha cover, fluidic probe. No 2 BCS failed to turn on. Last flight in the programme.

Glossary

A24ST	An aluminium alloy of aluminium, copper and manganese
A-4/V2	German ballistic missile developed during World War Two
AACB	Aeronautics and Astronautics Coordinating Board
AAF	Army Air Forces
ACA	Advisory Committee for Aeronautics (British)
AERL	Aircraft Engine Research Laboratory
AFB	Air Force Base
AFCS	Adaptive Flight Control System
AISI	American Iron and Steel Institute
AM	Amplitude Modulated
AMAL	Aviation Medical Acceleration Laboratory
AMC	Air Materiel Command
APU	Auxiliary Power Unit
ARDC	Air Research and Development Command
ARS	American Rocket Society
ASAS	Alternate Stability Augmentation System
ASP	Aerospace Plane
BCS	Ballistic Control System
BoMi	Bomber Missile
Bps	Bits per second
BuAer	Bureau of Aeronautics, US Navy
C	Centigrade
Camber	Curvature relative to a fixed plane
CEU	Coupler Electronics Unit
Chord	Width of a wing from leading edge to training edge
CRD	Compressibility Research Division (CRD), Langley
CRT	Cathode Ray Tube
C-Stoff	A mixture of methanol, hydrazine hydrate, water and a catalyst as a reactant when mixed with T-Stoff as a hypergolic propellant
DDA	Digital Differential Analyser
DFRC	Dryden Flight Research Center, NASA
DoD	Department of Defense
ERTS	Earth Resource Technology Satellite, NASA
F	Fahrenheit
F-1	Rocket motor developed by Rocketdyne for the Saturn V
FAA	Federal Aviation Authority
FAI	Fédération Aéronautique Internationale
FICON	Fighter Conveyor
FM	Fidelity Modulated
FRC	Flight Research Center
FRT	Flight Rating Test
FST	Full Scale Tunnel (Langley)
FTC	Flight Test Center
FTS	Flight Test Station
GALCIT	Guggenheim Aeronautical Laboratory of the California Institute of Technology
GEDA	Goodyear Electronic Digital Analyzer
GNS	Guidance and Navigation System, Apollo
GP	General Purpose (part of a computer)
GSFC	Goddard Space Flight Center
HACTR	High Altitude Continuous Tracking Range
HADPPS	Hypersonic Airflow Direction & Pitot-Pressure Sensor
HIRES	Hypersonic In-Flight Refuelling System
HRE	Hypersonic Research Engine
HSFS	High Speed Flight Station
HST	High Speed Tunnel, Langley
Hyper-golic	Propellants which combust spontaneously when mixed
Hyper-sonic	Mach 5 plus
Hz	Hertz (cycles per second)
IBM	International Business Machines
ICBM	Intercontinental Ballistic Missile
IFDS	Inertial Flight Data System
ILC	International Latex Corporation
IMU	Instrument Measurement Unit
JATO	Jet Assisted Take-Off
JPL	Jet Propulsion Laboratory
K	Kilowatt
Kbps	Kilobits per second
Kc	Kilocycle
kN	Kilonewton
KPa	Kilopascals
Kph	Kilometres per hour
Laminar flow	Air particles travelling in smooth non-undulating paths
Lit	Litre
LOX	Liquid oxygen
MA-25S	External thermal insulation applied to X-15A-2
Mach number	Multiples of the speed of sound
Mano-meter	A device to measure low pressure
Max-q	Maximum dynamic pressure
Mbps	Megabits per second
MHz	Megahertz
MISS	Man In Space Soonest
MIT	Massachusetts Institute of Technology
Mono-coque	A structure in which tensile and compression forces are carried by the skin
Mph	miles per hour
MTBF	Mean Time Between Failure
N	Newton
N_2O_4	Nitrogen Tetroxide
NAA	North American Aviation
NACA	National Advisory Committee for Aeronautics
NAF	Naval Aircraft Factory
NAMC	Naval Air Materiel Center
NASA	National Aeronautics & Space Administration
NDRC	National Defense Research Committee
NOTS	Naval Ordnance Test Station
ONR	Office of Naval Research, US
ORI	Office of Research and Inventions, US Navy
PARD	Pilotless Aircraft Research Division, Langley
PCM	Pulse Code Modulation
PFRT	Preliminary Flight Rating Test
PIO	Pilot Induced Oscillation
Pitot tube	A tube for measuring the flow of a fluid
PSTS	Propulsion System Test Stand (Edwards AFB)
PRT	Propeller Research Tunnel
Q-ball	Nose sensor for measuring air flow, velocity and direction
RAS	Reaction Augmentation System
Reynolds number	Dimensionless value relating inertial forces to viscous forces
RFNA	Red Fuming Nitric Acid (propellant)
RFP	Request for Proposals
RMD	Rocket Motors Division. Thiokol
RMI	Reaction Motors Incorporated
RoBo	Rocket/reconnaissance Bomber
RTV	Research Test Vehicle
RTV	Room Temperature Vulcaniser (as a thermal coating)
SAB	Scientific Advisory Board, Air Force
SAC	Strategic Air Command
SADS	Shuttle Air Data System
SAG	Scientific Advisory Group, AAF
SAS	Stability Augmentation System
Semi-mono-coque	A structure in which some of the stress forces are alleviated by internal bracing or support
Spanwise	Alluding to the full span of the wing from tip to tip
SST	Supersonic Transport (airliner)
Super-sonic	Mach 1.3-5
T/c	Thickness/chord ratio (of a wing)
TD	Thoria-Dispersion
Transonic	Mach 0.8-1.2
T-Stoff	A high test peroxide (80-85 per cent) with water and stabilisers
UDMH	Unsymmetrical Dimethyl Hydrazine
USAF	United States Air Force
UV	Ultraviolet
VDT	Variable Density Tunnel (Langley)
Velocity	Speed defined by magnitude and direction
V-J Day	Victory over Japan Day
Viscous	Possessing a high resistance to flow
WADC	Wright Air Development Center

Index

Aircraft, Ships and Companies

Civilian Agencies and Departments and Non-government Organisations

Commercial Companies, Organisations and Products

Engines and Rocket Motors

Geographic Places

Military Units, Departments and Bases

People

Rockets, Missiles and Space Launch Vehicles

Spacecraft

Systems and Equipment